The Speculative Turn:
Continental Materialism and Realism

Levi Bryant, Nick Srnicek and
Graham Harman, editors

...rne 2011

re.press

PO Box 40, Prahran, 3181, Melbourne, Australia
http://www.re-press.org

British Library Cataloguing-in-Publication Data
A catalogue record for this book is available from the British Library

National Library of Australia Cataloguing-in-Publication Data

Title: The speculative turn : continental materialism and realism
/ edited by Levi Bryant, Nick Srnicek and Graham Harman.

ISBN: 9780980668346 (pbk.)
ISBN: 9780980668353 (ebook)

Series: Anamnesis.

Notes: Includes bibliographical references and index.

Subjects: Continental philosophy.

Other Authors/Contributors:
Bryant, Levi.
Srnicek, Nick.
Harman, Graham, 1968-

Dewey Number: 190

Designed and Typeset by *A&R*
Typeset in *Baskerville*

Printed on-demand in Australia, the United Kingdom and the United States. This book is produced sustainably using plantation timber, and printed in the destination market on demand reducing wastage and excess transport.

The Speculative Turn

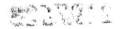

Anamnesis

Anamnesis means remembrance or reminiscence, the collection and re-collection of what has been lost, forgotten, or effaced. It is therefore a matter of the very old, of what has made us who we are. But *anamnesis* is also a work that transforms its subject, always producing something new. To recollect the old, to produce the new: that is the task of *Anamnesis*.

a re.press series

Contents

Towards a Speculative Philosophy

Levi Bryant, Nick Srnicek and Graham Harman

This anthology assembles more than two dozen essays by many of the key figures in present-day continental philosophy. They hail from thirteen countries, speak seven different native languages, and are separated from eldest to youngest by a range of more than forty years. (The collection would have been even more diverse, if not that several additional key authors were prevented by circumstance from contributing.) A number of well-established authors can be found in the pages that follow, joined by various emerging figures of the younger generation. These are exciting times in our field. No dominant hero now strides along the beach, as the phase of subservient commentary on the history of philosophy seems to have ended. Genuine attempts at full-blown systematic thought are no longer rare in our circles; increasingly, they are even expected. And whatever the possible drawbacks of globalization, the new global networks have worked very much in our favour: enhanced technologies have made the blogosphere and online booksellers major contributors to a new 'primordial soup' of continental philosophy. Though it is too early to know what strange life forms might evolve from this mixture, it seems clear enough that something important is happening. In our profession, there has never been a better time to be young.

The first wave of twentieth century continental thought in the Anglophone world was dominated by phenomenology, with Martin Heidegger generally the most influential figure of the group. By the late 1970s, the influence of Jacques Derrida and Michel Foucault had started to gain the upper hand, reaching its zenith a decade or so later. It was towards the mid-1990s that Gilles Deleuze entered the ascendant, shortly before his death in November 1995, and his star remains perfectly visible today. But since the beginning of the twenty-first century, a more chaotic and in some ways more promising situation has taken shape. Various intriguing philosophical trends, their bastions scattered across the globe, have gained adherents and started to produce a critical mass of emblematic works. While it is difficult to find a single adequate name to cover all of these trends, we propose 'The Speculative Turn', as a deliberate counterpoint to the now tiresome 'Linguistic Turn'. The words 'materialism' and 'realism' in our subtitle clarify further the nature of the new trends, but also preserve a possible *distinction* between the material and the real.

Following the death of Derrida in October 2004, Slavoj Žižek became perhaps the most visible celebrity in our midst, eased into this role by his numerous publications in English and his enjoyable public persona. To an increasing degree, Žižek became closely linked in the public mind with his confederate Alain Badiou, whose major works were increasingly available in English during the first decade of the century, with a key assist from Peter Hallward's encyclopaedic survey, *Badiou: A Subject to Truth.*[1] It is probable that Badiou and Žižek are the most widely read living thinkers in Anglophone continental philosophy today. But others of their approximate age group have entered the mix as well, championed initially by smaller groups of readers. Bruno Latour, already a giant in anthropology, sociology, and science studies, was smuggled into continental philosophy by way of the 'object-oriented ontology' of Ian Bogost, Levi Bryant, and Graham Harman. Somewhat ironically, Latour's longtime intellectual friend Isabelle Stengers followed a rather different path into the Anglophone debate, by impressing the younger Deleuzians with her work on Deleuze and Whitehead, and with her own series of books known as *Cosmopolitiques.*[2] The 'non-philosophy' of François Laruelle has captured the imagination of many younger readers, despite relatively little of his work being available in English so far. This rising generation of Laruellians has also tended to show great interest in cognitive science and the various practitioners of 'neurophilosophy'. Another important year was 2002, when Manuel DeLanda in *Intensive Science and Virtual Philosophy*[3] and Graham Harman in *Tool-Being*[4] both openly proclaimed their *realism*, perhaps the first time this had been done with a straight face in the recent continental tradition.[5] A half-decade later, this explicit call for realism was reinforced by what is so far the best-organized movement of the next generation. Inspired by the publication of Quentin Meillassoux's *Après la finitude*[6] (*After Finitude*) in early 2006, the first Speculative Realism event was held in April 2007 at Goldsmiths College, London. The original group included Ray Brassier, Iain Hamilton Grant, Harman, and Meillassoux; Alberto Toscano was moderator in 2007 and Meillassoux's replacement at the follow-up event at Bristol in 2009. But while the group has already begun to break into various fragments, it remains a key rallying point for the rising generation of graduate students. Thanks to the recent importance of the blogosphere, and the aggressive acquisitions policies of new publishers such as zerO Books, many of these students are already surprisingly well known. The editors of this volume are pleased to have Nick Srnicek on board as a fitting representative of this group.

AN INTRODUCTION TO CONTINENTAL MATERIALISM & REALISM

It has long been commonplace within continental philosophy to focus on discourse, text, culture, consciousness, power, or ideas as what constitutes reality. But despite

---

1. Peter Hallward, *Badiou: A Subject to Truth*, Minneapolis, University of Minnesota Press, 2003.

2. Isabelle Stengers, *Cosmopolitiques*, 2 vols., Paris, La Découverte, 2003.

3. Manuel DeLanda, *Intensive Science and Virtual Philosophy*, London, Continuum, 2002.

4. Graham Harman, *Tool-Being: Heidegger and the Metaphysics of Objects*, Chicago, Open Court, 2002.

5. Latour had already called himself a 'realist' in *Pandora's Hope*, but in an exotic and somewhat ironic sense having little to do with the independent existence of reality outside the perceiving of it. See Bruno Latour, *Pandora's Hope: Essays on the Reality of Science Studies*, trans. Catherine Porter, Cambridge, Harvard University Press, 1999.

6. Quentin Meillassoux, *Après la finitude: Essai sur la nécessité de la contingence*, Paris, Seuil, 2006.

the vaunted anti-humanism of many of the thinkers identified with these trends, what they give us is less a critique of humanity's place in the world, than a less sweeping critique of the self-enclosed Cartesian subject. Humanity remains at the centre of these works, and reality appears in philosophy only as the correlate of human thought. In this respect phenomenology, structuralism, post-structuralism, deconstruction, and postmodernism have all been perfect exemplars of the anti-realist trend in continental philosophy. Without deriding the significant contributions of these philosophies, something is clearly amiss in these trends. In the face of the looming ecological catastrophe, and the increasing infiltration of technology into the everyday world (including our own bodies), it is not clear that the anti-realist position is equipped to face up to these developments. The danger is that the dominant anti-realist strain of continental philosophy has not only reached a point of decreasing returns, but that it now actively limits the capacities of philosophy in our time.

Yet in the works of what we describe as 'The Speculative Turn', one can detect the hints of something new. By contrast with the repetitive continental focus on texts, discourse, social practices, and human finitude, the new breed of thinker is turning once more toward reality itself. While it is difficult to find explicit positions common to all the thinkers collected in this volume, all have certainly rejected the traditional focus on textual critique. Some have proposed notions of noumenal objects and causality-in-itself; others have turned towards neuroscience. A few have constructed mathematical absolutes, while others have attempted to sharpen the uncanny implications of psychoanalysis or scientific rationality. But all of them, in one way or another, have begun speculating once more about the nature of reality independently of thought and of humanity more generally.

This activity of 'speculation' may be cause for concern amongst some readers, for it might suggest a return to pre-critical philosophy, with its dogmatic belief in the powers of pure reason. The speculative turn, however, is not an outright rejection of these critical advances; instead, it comes from a recognition of their inherent limitations. Speculation in this sense aims at something 'beyond' the critical and linguistic turns. As such, it recuperates the pre-critical sense of 'speculation' as a concern with the Absolute, while also taking into account the undeniable progress that is due to the labour of critique. The works collected here are a speculative wager on the possible returns from a renewed attention to reality itself. In the face of the ecological crisis, the forward march of neuroscience, the increasingly splintered interpretations of basic physics, and the ongoing breach of the divide between human and machine, there is a growing sense that previous philosophies are incapable of confronting these events.

The Origins of Continental Anti-Realism

The new turn towards realism and materialism within continental philosophy comes in the wake of a long period of something resembling ethereal idealism. Even while disdaining the traditional idealist position that all that exists is some variation of mind or spirit, continental philosophy has fallen into an equally anti-realist stance in the form of what Meillassoux terms 'correlationism'. Stated simply, this is 'the idea according to which we only ever have access to the correlation between thinking and being, and never to either term considered apart from the other'.[7] This position tacitly holds

---

7. Quentin Meillassoux, *After Finitude: An Essay on the Necessity of Contingency*, trans. Ray Brassier, New York, Continuum, 2008, p. 5.

that we can aim our thoughts at being, exist as beings-in-the-world, or have phenomenal experience of the world, yet we can never consistently speak about a realm independent of thought or language. Such a doctrine, in its countless variations, maintains that knowledge of a reality independent of thought is untenable. From this correlationist stance, there results a subtle form of idealism that is nonetheless almost ubiquitous.

The origins of this correlationist turn lie in Immanuel Kant's critical philosophy, which famously abjured the possibility of ever knowing a noumenal realm beyond human access. In Kant's famous Copernican revolution, it is no longer the mind that conforms to objects, but rather objects that conform to the mind. Experience is structured by *a priori* categories and forms of intuition that comprise the necessary and universal basis for all knowledge. Yet the price to be paid for securing this basis is the renunciation of any knowledge beyond how things appear to us. Reality-in-itself is cordoned off, at least in its cognitive aspects.

Lee Braver's fine book recently showed that this Kantian prohibition, with its anti-realist implications, has wound its way through the continental tradition, taking hold of nearly every major figure from Hegel to Heidegger to Derrida.[8] While for Kant there remains the possibility of thinking the noumenal (if not knowing it), Hegel absolutizes the correlate to encompass all that exists: his critique of the noumenal renders it merely a phenomenal illusion, thus 'completing' the critical philosophy by producing an absolute idealism. This effacement of the noumenal continues with phenomenology, as ontology becomes explicitly linked with a reduction to the phenomenal realm. As Braver outlines, Heidegger furthers the anti-realist project by rejecting the possibility of Absolute Knowledge as the singular and total self-understanding of the Absolute Subject. Finally, with Derrida the mediation of language becomes all-encompassing, as the phenomenal realm of subjectivity becomes infested with linguistic marks. Throughout this process, any possibility of a world independent of the human-world correlate is increasingly rejected (as is nicely symbolized by Heidegger' famous crossing-out of the word 'Being').

This general anti-realist trend has manifested itself in continental philosophy in a number of ways, but especially through preoccupation with such issues as death and finitude, an aversion to science, a focus on language, culture, and subjectivity to the detriment of material factors, an anthropocentric stance towards nature, a relinquishing of the search for absolutes, and an acquiescence to the specific conditions of our historical thrownness. We might also point to the lack of genuine and effective political action in continental philosophy—arguably a result of the 'cultural' turn taken by Marxism, and the increased focus on textual and ideological critique at the expense of the economic realm.

The Speculative Turn

Against this reduction of philosophy to an analysis of texts or of the structure of consciousness, there has been a recent surge of interest in properly ontological questions. Deleuze was a pioneer in this field, including in his co-authored works with Félix Guattari. In these seminal texts of the 1970s and 1980s, Deleuze and Guattari set forth an ontological vision of an asubjective realm of becoming, with the subject and thought being only a final, residual product of these primary ontological movements. Rather than circling around the negative limitations of conceptual systems, Deleuze and

---

8. Lee Braver, *A Thing of This World: A History of Continental Anti-Realism*, Evanston, Northwestern University Press, 2007.

Guattari constructed a positive ontological vision from the ruins of traditional ontologies. While there are still significant questions about whether Deleuze managed to escape correlationism fully,[9] there can be little doubt that his project was aimed at moving beyond the traditional Kantian limitations of continental thought.[10] More recently, a number of other leading thinkers in the continental tradition have articulated philosophies that avoid its standard (and oft-ridiculed) tropes.

Žižek is one of the foremost exemplars of this new trend, drawing on the naturephilosophy of Schelling, the ontological vastness of Hegel, and the insights into the Real of Jacques Lacan.[11] In his recent major work *The Parallax View*, Žižek has denounced what he sees as the naïve materialist postulate that includes the subject as just another positive, physical thing within the objective world. He calls it naïve because it assumes the position of an external observer from which the entire world can be grasped—a position that presumes in principle to encompass all of reality by reducing its own perspective to a thing in the world. For Žižek, by contrast, 'Materialism means that the reality I see is never "whole"—not because a large part of it eludes me, but because it contains a stain, a blind spot, which indicates my inclusion in it'.[12] Reality, he repeatedly states, is non-All; there is a gap, a stain, an irresolvable hole within reality itself. The very difference between the for-itself and the in-itself is encompassed within the Absolute. Only by attending to this gap can we become truly materialist. But while Žižek has signalled a 'transcendental materialist' turn within recent continental thinking, it is perhaps Badiou who has raised the anti-phenomenological flag most explicitly, attempting thereby to clarify the ontological stakes of contemporary continental philosophy. This rejuvenation of ontology is particularly clear in his now famous declaration that 'mathematics = ontology'.[13] Taking mathematics to be the discourse of being—that which speaks of being as devoid of any predication (including unity), remaining only as a pure multiple—Badiou has constructed an elaborate ontology on the basis of set theory. In addition, Badiou has nobly resuscitated the question of *truth*, which was formerly a term of derision in much continental philosophy.

While still read more widely in the social sciences than in philosophy, Latour has nonetheless been an important figure in the recent Speculative Turn. Against all forms of reduction to physical objects, cultural structures, systems of power, texts, discourses, or phenomena in consciousness, Latour argues for an 'irreductionism' in which all entities are equally real (though not equally strong) insofar as they act on other entities. While nonhuman actors such as germs, weather patterns, atoms, and mountains obviously relate to the world around them, the same is true of Harry Potter, the Virgin Mary, democracies, and hallucinations. The incorporeal and corporeal realms are equally capable of having effects on the world. Moreover, the effort to reduce one level of reality to another invariably leaves residues of the reduced entity that are not ful-

---

9. For a few representative examples of such doubts, see, Alain Badiou, *Deleuze: The Clamor of Being*, trans. Louise Burchill, Minneapolis, University of Minnesota Press, 2000; and Ray Brassier, *Nihil Unbound: Enlightenment and Extinction*, New York, Palgrave Macmillan, 2007.

10. This attempt is arguably most evident in his magnum opus, *Difference and Repetition*, where Deleuze uses transcendental philosophy's own methods to uncover systems of intensities irrecoverable within any sort of subjectivist framework.

11. For by far the best exposition of Žižek's philosophical project and his use of these three figures, see Adrian Johnston, *Žižek's Ontology: A Transcendental Materialist Theory of Subjectivity*, Evanston, Northwestern University Press, 2008.

12. Slavoj Žižek, *The Parallax View*, Cambridge, The MIT Press, 2006, p. 17.

13. Alain Badiou, *Being and Event*, trans. Oliver Feltham, New York, Continuum, 2005, p. 6.

ly translatable by the reduction: no interpretation of a dream or a historical event ever gets it *quite* right, nor would it even be possible to do so.

Beyond the institutionalized sphere of philosophy, continental materialist and realist currents have had some of their deepest effects through a series of emerging online communities. This began in the late 1990s with the creation of the Cybernetic Culture Research Unit (CCRU)—a diverse group of thinkers who experimented in conceptual production by welding together a wide variety of sources: futurism, technoscience, philosophy, mysticism, numerology, complexity theory, and science fiction, among others. The creativity and productivity of this collective was due in no small part to their construction of a space outside the constrictions of traditional academia. It is notable, then, that many of the contributors to CCRU have continued to be involved in the online community and have continued to push philosophy ahead.

One of the most notable of these projects has been the journal *Collapse*, which along with the Warwick-based journal *Pli* has acted as one of the vanguard publications of recent continental realism and materialism. First issued in September 2006, *Collapse* has attempted to mobilize a cross-section of innovative thinkers from a wide range of disciplines. Combining philosophy, science, literature and aesthetics in a way that refuses to draw divisions between disciplines, *Collapse* has exemplified the spirit of assemblage—letting a heterogeneous set of elements mutually resonate to become something entirely unpredictable. As its opening salvo proclaims, 'the optimum circumstance would be if each reader picked up *Collapse* on the strength of only one of the articles therein, the others being involuntarily absorbed as a kind of side-effect that would propagate the eccentric conjuncture by stealth, and spawn yet others'.[14] In its third volume *Collapse* also reproduced the text of the first conference devoted to the speculative realist movement, a galvanizing event that did much to focus attention on the wider trends contained in this volume.

Along with *Collapse*, another non-institutional forum for conceptual production has been the online community. Initially operating in the 1990s through email listserves, online discussion has shifted to the blogosphere as this medium emerged in the opening decade of the century. Indeed, each of the editors of *The Speculative Turn* authors one or more philosophy blogs,[15] and in a further wondrous sign of the times, we have never met in person. As any of the blogosphere's participants can attest, it can be a tremendously productive forum for debate and experimentation.[16] The less formal nature of the medium facilitates immediate reactions to research, with authors presenting ideas in their initial stages of development, ideally providing a demystifying sort of transparency. The markedly egalitarian nature of blogs (open to non-Ph.Ds in a way that faculty positions are not) opens a space for collaboration amongst a diverse group of readers, helping to shape ideas along unforeseen paths. The rapid rhythm of online existence also makes a stark contrast with the long waiting-periods typical of refereed journals and mainstream publishers. Instant reaction to current events, reading

---

14. Robin Mackay, 'Editorial Introduction', *Collapse: Philosophical Research and Development*, vol. 1, p. 5.

15. Respectively, these are: Bryant (*Larval Subjects*), Srnicek (*The Accursed Share* and *Speculative Heresy*), and Harman (*Object-Oriented Philosophy*).

16. A small and incomplete list of some of the original and most consistently creative blogs would include: *Another Heidegger Blog, Eliminative Culinarism, Immanence, Infinite Thought, Jon Cogburn's Blog, K-Punk, Naught Thought, The Pinocchio Theory, Planomenology, Poetix, Rough Theory*, and *Splintering Bone Ashes*. Even during the editing phase of the present anthology, the internet saw further rapid proliferation of blogs discussing and producing Speculative Realism.

groups quickly mobilizing around newly published works, and cross-blog dialogues on specific issues, are common events in the online world. While some of the authors included in the present collection have been well-known for many years, it is difficult to believe that some of the others would already be so prominent if they had needed to wait for their places on a course syllabus. The online world has rapidly shifted the intellectual terrain, and it seems a fair bet that the experimentation has barely begun.

Lastly, another significant non-institutional space for the creation of these works has been the rise of open-access publishing. The natural and social sciences are already deeply committed to the open-access model, with arXiv and the Social Science Research Network (SSRN) among the best-known online archives of cutting-edge research (with key works often appearing here before they appear in more official publications). So far, philosophy has lagged behind these fields in constructing a forum for the dissemination of new research. But the tide seems to have turned, as a number of open-access philosophy publishers and journals have arisen in the past few years, in some cases having secured backing from major names in the field.[17] Open-access journals and books alike are becoming more prevalent, and it is perhaps only a matter of time before philosophy finds its homegrown equivalent of arXiv or SSRN.[18]

VARIETIES OF CONTINENTAL MATERIALISM AND REALISM

Continental Materialism and Realism

As should be clear from the earlier discussion of Deleuze, Žižek, Badiou, and Latour, the various strands of continental materialism and realism are all entirely at odds with so-called 'naïve realism'. One of the key features of the Speculative Turn is precisely that the move toward realism is not a move toward the stuffy limitations of common sense, but quite often a turn toward the downright bizarre. This can be seen quite clearly in the works of the four original members of the speculative realism group, perhaps the most visible group among those now reaching maturity.

Ray Brassier's work combines a militant enthusiasm for the Enlightenment with a theoretical position that drastically limits the presumptions of thought in its ability to grasp the nature of reality. Cutting across a number of closely-held human conceits—including our usual self-esteem as a species and our aspiration towards harmony with nature—Brassier's work aims at eliminating anything that might falsely make us feel at home in the world. The result is a position that might be called an eliminativist nihilism that takes the destruction of meaning as a positive result of the Enlightenment project: something to be pushed to its ultimate end, despite all protests to the contrary.

A stark contrast is provided by Iain Hamilton Grant's return to the naturephilosophy of Schelling, which aims to construct a transcendental naturalism capable of providing an ontological foundation for science. Grappling fully with the implications of Kant's critical turn even while constructively opposing it, Grant tries to move the transcendental project beyond its idealist tendencies so as to connect it with a dark and rumbling field of pure 'productivity' lying beneath all phenomenal products. It is from these very depths that nature, mind, society, and culture are all produced. Grant also aims to provide a consistent metaphysical foundation for contemporary science.

---

17. The publisher of the present collection—re.press in Melbourne, Australia—is a major example of this trend. See also the celebrity-laden editorial board of the open-access venture Open Humanities Press.

18. PhilPapers is currently the most likely candidate for this philosophical equivalent, though it remains to be seen whether philosophy will provide the same prestige to open-access publishing as other disciplines have.

A different approach to the non-human world is found in the object-oriented philosophy of Graham Harman. Like many of the Austrian philosophers of the late nineteenth century, Harman pursues a general theory of objects ranging from quarks to solar systems to dragons to insurgencies, but he also adds several weird twists to the theory. From one side he treats objects according to the Heideggerian insight that objects withdraw into depths inaccessible to all access. And from another side he follows Whitehead's model, in which the relation between human and world is merely a special case of any relation at all: when fire burns cotton, this is different only *by degree* from the human perception of cotton. Whereas the phenomenological method bracketed the natural world out of consideration, Harman treats the phenomenological and the natural, or the perceptual and the causal, as neighbours in a drama in which objects can only make *indirect* contact with one another.

Quentin Meillassoux, whose 2006 debut book might be called the trigger for the Speculative Realist movement, argues for a mathematical absolute capable of making sense of scientific claims to have knowledge of a time prior to humanity. These 'ancestral' statements pose a problem for philosophies that refuse any knowledge of a realm independent of empirical access to it. If we are to understand these ancestral statements literally, however, it must be shown that we already have knowledge of the absolute. Meillassoux's uniqueness lies in showing how correlationism (the idea that being and thought are only accessible in their co-relation) is self-refuting—that if we take it seriously, it already presupposes a knowledge of the absolute. Yet unlike the other Speculative Realists, Meillassoux is not dismissive of correlationism, but seeks to radicalize it from within. From the facticity of our particular correlation, Meillassoux derives the necessity of contingency or 'hyperchaos': the apparently counterintuitive result that anything is possible from one moment to the next.

OVERVIEW OF INCLUDED ESSAYS

The collection opens with Ben Woodard's interview with Alain Badiou, who discusses the importance of the emerging speculative trends. Situating his own work with respect to speculative realism, Badiou recognizes many shared principles, but notes the absence in the younger thinkers of anything resembling Badiou's own theory of the 'event'. Such a theory, Badiou insists, is both a political and metaphysical imperative for philosophy. This is immediately followed by the first section, which collects recent pieces by the original Speculative Realists; several of these were presented at the movement's second workshop, held in Bristol in April 2009. The second section compiles a series of critical responses to Meillassoux's *After Finitude*, a signature work of speculative realism. The third section assembles some of the emerging political work being done under the umbrella of continental materialism and realism. The fourth section mobilizes a range of metaphysical essays, showcasing the diversity and rigor of the new philosophical trends. The fifth and final section tackles the question of how continental materialism relates to science, offering a diverse set of perspectives on just what this entails.

Speculative Realism Revisited

In his essay 'On the Undermining of Objects', Graham Harman mounts a full-fledged defence of the importance of objects for present-day philosophy. He examines the work of his Speculative Realist colleague Iain Hamilton Grant by way of a reading of

Giordano Bruno, arguing that shared difficulties are found in the positions of Bruno and Grant. But while Grant's position functions as the prime topic of discussion, he is said to represent just one of the two unjust ways in which objects are obliterated by philosophy. Grant's transcendental naturalism follows a long philosophical tradition in its attempt to 'undermine' objects by explaining their existence in terms of a deeper material basis: whether it be God, physical elements, drives, or the preindividual. The equally bad alternative to this undermining strategy is what Harman calls 'overmining'—the attempt to disable individual objects by letting them exist only in their appearances, relations, qualities, or effects. These critiques lead Harman to what he provocatively terms a 'realism without materialism'.

In 'Mining Conditions', his response to Harman's critique, Iain Hamilton Grant argues that the genesis of objects necessarily occurs somewhere *outside* them, in a realm of productivity irreducible to fully constituted objects. By returning to early discussions on the philosophy of nature and geology, Grant tries to show that an actualist position like Harman's is incapable of grasping the anteriority upon which both ideation and objects depend. This anteriority is not just a different sort of substance, as Giordano Bruno would have it, but rather a power of pure productivity seen in the natural and inorganic world.

Ray Brassier's 'Concepts and Objects' begins with an emphatic argument for the significance of epistemological questions and the return to a notion of 'representation'—an idea often maligned within continental philosophy. Brassier's position, in which the question of what a representation *represents* plays a prominent role, is distinguished from those univocal ontologies that stake out an ontological equivalence between concepts and objects. Taking Latour as emblematic of this tendency, Brassier insists that Latour's univocal ontology must ultimately collapse upon itself. Against this collapse of concepts into objects and objects into concepts, Brassier argues that the only non-dogmatic position is able to recognize the extra-conceptual difference between objects and concepts—a distinction that operates within scientific representation while also providing the foundation for it.

In 'Does Nature Stay What It Is?', Iain Hamilton Grant returns to the fray with a lengthier contribution of his own. His primary concern is whether the principle of sufficient reason exhausts the nature of Ground. He describes this issue as central to such pressing topics in contemporary philosophy as Meillassoux's denial of the principle of sufficient reason, the resurgence of 'powers' metaphysics in recent analytic philosophy,[19] and the ambiguous status of matter *qua* ground in recent eliminativist philosophies. Grant is critical of recent claims to 'materialism' by contemporary thinkers such as Badiou (and by implication, Žižek). He draws instead on the dynamist concept of matter found intermittently from Plato up through the nineteenth century science of Oersted and Faraday, and extensively considers the recent claims by Gunnar Hindrichs (University of Pennsylvania) that Ground is more a formal problem than a material one. The background of this essay is Grant's more general view that present-day continental though is contaminated by neo-Fichteanism—a worry that nicely illustrates the contrast between Grant and such pro-Fichteans as Meillassoux and Žižek.

Alberto Toscano's paper, 'Against Speculation, Or, A Critique of the Critique of Critique', raises the question of whether materialism and speculation are possible, by way of a careful analysis of Meillassoux's *After Finitude* and the work of the Italian anti-

---

19. George Molnar, *Powers: A Study in Metaphysics*, Oxford, Oxford University Press, 2003.

Hegelian Marxist Lucio Colletti. Focusing on the role that pure mathematics plays in Meillassoux's metaphysics, Toscano argues that he covertly reintroduces idealism into the heart of ontology through the identification of mathematics with being. Toscano concludes that, in arguing that ontological truths can be deduced from logico-mathematico intuitions, Meillassoux banishes the material and effective causality that is necessary for a position to qualify as materialist.

After Finitude

The next part of our collection consists of reactions to Quentin Meillassoux's breakthrough work *After Finitude*. We begin with Adrian Johnston's critical chapter, 'Hume's Revenge: À *Dieu*, Meillassoux?' Johnston endorses Meillassoux's apparent atheist materialism, but openly doubts whether Meillassoux adheres to this position consistently enough. He is puzzled by the young French thinker's flirtation with a 'virtual' God that does not exist but may exist in the future, as found in Meillassoux's article 'Deuil à venir, dieu à venir'[20] and his still unpublished major work *L'inexistence divine*.[21] As Johnston sees it, this theological residue in Meillassoux's work is not just a dazzling high-wire act unrelated to his general position, but arises directly from his mistaken ontologization of Hume's epistemology. Hence it is Hume who must immunize us against any regrettable turn toward God, however virtual this God may be. In closing, Johnston also expresses a degree of scepticism toward the speculative realism movement, concerned that its dispute with idealism may be a 'tempest in a teacup' unless it turns from abstract argument toward more positive empirical projects.

Martin Hägglund, in his 'Radical Atheist Materialism', attempts to show how Meillassoux's argument for the necessity of contingency entails the necessity of a logic of succession or becoming that is antithetical to Meillassoux's own stated conclusions. In order to account for this logic of succession and flesh out the notion of 'absolute time', Hägglund argues that Meillassoux needs to take into account Derrida's notion of the 'trace'—a logical structure that undermines Meillassoux's proposed solution to the emergence of life, as well as his reliance on a non-contradictory entity. In place of Meillassoux's *ex nihilo* reading of emergence, Hägglund proposes a speculative distinction between animate and inanimate entities—one that follows from the logic of the trace and the findings of naturalist materialism, while simultaneously avoiding a collapse into vitalism. On the basis of this notion of the trace, Hägglund argues further for a more rigorously atheistic materialism that would refuse even the redeeming power of the virtual God that Meillassoux proposes. The logic of the trace refuses any redemption, based as it is upon the fundamental negation and destruction of the past. In light of these reflections, Hägglund offers some reflections on death and mourning, showing that we cannot truly desire immortality, but instead must recognize our own finitude as an intrinsic condition for any care.

Peter Hallward's article 'Anything is Possible' begins with a reconstruction of the chain of reasoning that leads Quentin Meillassoux to argue that modern philosophy not only can but *must* reject the critical limitations on thought and recuperate the 'great outdoors' of the absolute. This chain culminates in the destruction of the principle of sufficient reason, and the affirmation of a purely intelligible Chaos as the logical outcome of correlationism's own internal principles. For Hallward, however, Meil-

---

20. Quentin Meillassoux, '*Deuil à venir, dieu à venir*', *Critique*, nos. 704-5, 2006, pp. 105-15.

21. Quentin Meillassoux, *L'inexistence divine*, unpublished manuscript.

lassoux's project remains burdened by a number of crucial problems. In the first place, Hallward argues that Meillassoux's use of 'ancestral statements' fails to do what it declares—namely, provide an irresolvable aporia for correlationist philosophies. Likewise, Hallward argues that Meillassoux relies on a confusion between metaphysical and natural necessity, leading him to an unjustifiable derivation of pure Chaos. From this confusion, Meillasoux ends up incapable of thinking the nature of change, beyond arguing for it being a sequence of entirely unrelated instants. Finally, Hallward argues that Meillassoux neglects the distinction between pure and applied mathematics: while reasoning on the basis of pure mathematics, he applies the conclusions to statements that go well beyond these formalities. In conclusion, Hallward sees Meillassoux as overlooking the need for a philosophy of *relationality* as a means of understanding concrete change.

Nathan Brown's piece, 'The Speculative and the Specific', begins with a direct rejoinder to Hallward's critique of Meillassoux. Setting out the four dimensions along which Hallward reproaches Meillassoux, Brown argues the Hallward consistently takes Meillassoux's own arguments beyond their proper purview. In arguing against these criticisms, Brown highlights the ways in which he believes Meillassoux's project makes a number of fundamental contributions. From this basis Brown goes on to examine how Meillassoux's project relates to Hallward's own project, setting up the distinction as one between the speculative and the specific. As Brown portrays it, it is a question on one level of whether there are any structural invariants to the world (relationality for Hallward) or not (Meillassoux). It is from the perspective of the latter that Hallward's reference to a fundamental transcendental structure of relationality is shown to be historically and temporally contingent. Yet while Meillassoux's work provides a necessary corrective to Hallward's political project, the same holds true for the opposite relation: Meillassoux's work on the absolute nature of contingency requires specification through the relational medium of Hallward's thought. It is thus a question of the relation between speculative materialism and dialectical materialism. In this vein, Brown refracts the relation between the two through the sophisticated dialectical materialism of Louis Althusser, attempting to show how Meillassoux's work can contribute to Marxist philosophy. For Althusser, philosophy's political task is to defend materialism in the sciences against its idealist counterpart. In this light, Meillassoux has taken the current philosophical conjuncture of correlationism and shown how it is incapable of upholding the materialist primacy of being over thought. This materialist criticism allows Meillassoux to draw out the logical consequences of the necessity of contingency and the absolutization of hyperchaos. Nonetheless, Brown argues, a truly transformative materialism requires both of the variant forms of dialectical materialism found in Meillassoux and Hallward.

Politics

Nick Srnicek's 'Capitalism and the Non-Philosophical Subject' aims at a provisional realist model of a complex socio-political phenomenon. The essay begins with an exposition of Laruelle's unique reading of subjectivity as a formalistic procedure irreducible to any phenomenological or psychological basis. On the basis of this reading, Srnicek mobilizes the resources of Laruellian non-philosophy to highlight and resolve some of the limitations of autonomous Marxism and its understanding of real subsumption within the capitalist system. As critics have observed, Antonio Negri and Michael

Hardt are ultimately unable to produce a plausible vision of the multitude constitutive of and exceeding capitalism. Yet the non-philosophical subject provides the conceptual resources to understand (and undermine) the appearance of an all-encompassing capitalism. But while non-philosophy is ultimately capable of overcoming some of the impasses of contemporary leftism, Srnicek argues that it is nonetheless the case that any realist ontology must be devoid of grounds for ethical or political action. The suspension of capitalism's authority merely opens the space for political action without providing any guidelines or imperatives. Facing this new deadlock, Srnicek concludes the essay by exploring some of the possibilities for mobilizing a new world from a space foreclosed to the present one.

In his article 'Drafting the Inhuman', Reza Negarestani sets out to uncover the limits and potentials of a politics oriented by speculative thought. Negarestani takes aim at the linking of capitalism's dissolutory tendencies with the inhuman emancipation it purportedly provokes. Nick Land's work is taken as emblematic of this capitalist conception, where it is shown that the image of capital *qua* totalizing and inevitable force merely acts as a pragmatic support for capitalism's efforts to attain this image. Reading Ray Brassier's work against Nick Land's conception of capitalism, Negarestani demonstrates that though Brassier refuses the vitalistic horizon crucial to Land's thought, he remains incapable of justifying any stance against capitalism's colonizing trends. What both Land and Brassier miss is a third aspect of Freud's death drive, which argues that the dissipative tendency towards death must necessarily be channelled through the available affordances of the organism. It is this system of affordances that Negarestani labels the 'necrocracy' and it is the organism's local necrocracy which determines the possibilities and limits of any emancipatory image. Capitalism, as a necrocratic regime, is therefore a restrictive and utterly human system which binds the excess of extinction to a conservative framework grounded upon the human's means of channelling the death drive. As such, it remains incapable of any truly emancipatory potential, even in its accelerationist variants.

In a rich and elaborate piece, Slavoj Žižek asks the question, 'Is it Still Possible to be a Hegelian Today?' Against those narratives of German idealism that patch over the Hegelian rupture with reductive portraits of the philosopher, Žižek aims to show the truly historical Event produced by Hegel. Defending him against his Nietzschean and Marxist critics, Žižek portrays a Hegel whose system grounds the materialist struggles privileged by Marx, as well as elaborating a dialectical history whose necessity only emerges contingently and retroactively. Opposing the incremental development of evolutionist historicism, and any totalizing image of Hegel, Žižek shows that dialectical historicity is premised on an open Whole irremediably ruptured by absolute negativity. In this endeavour, Žižek uses the distinction drawn by Meillassoux between 'potentiality' and 'virtuality' (see Meillassoux's essay, next in order in this volume), in order to show how dialectical progression is 'the becoming of necessity itself'. The result is a system that explains the impossibility of ultimate social harmony, and thus the impossibility of banishing war from the political world.

Metaphysics

In 'Potentiality and Virtuality', Quentin Meillassoux returns to the classic Humean problem of grounding causal connections. Against its progressive abandonment as an ontological problem, Meillassoux asserts the possibility of taking Hume's problem as an ontological question amenable to resolution. Meillassoux begins by reformulating Hume's problem in a more general manner: 'can a decisive conclusion be made as to the necessity or lack of necessity of observed constants? ' A lack of necessity would not entail that constants change, but rather that it is entirely contingent whether they stay the same or not. Once such a lack of necessity has been accepted, the question of whether phenomenal laws will remain the same or not falls to the side. A different question rises in its place: if there are no necessary relations between observable instants, then why do phenomenal constants not change at every moment? Meillassoux argues that this apparent paradox is contingent upon the acceptance of a probabilistic reasoning about the universe as a whole. This probabilistic reasoning is based upon the totalization of the world of possibilities: the range of potentials which can then be assigned a probability of occurring. Yet if this totalization is impossible, as Cantor's discovery of multiple infinities suggests, then there is no basis for ascribing probabilities to any phenomenal event on the level of the universe. It is on the basis of this Cantorian advance that Meillassoux sets forth a fundamental distinction between potentiality and virtuality. Whereas the former is premised upon a totalization of the world, with a determinate set of possibilities inscribed within it, the latter rejects this totalization and asserts the fundamental novelty that is able to emerge beyond any pre-constituted totality.

François Laruelle undertakes an investigation into the generic in his contribution, entitled 'The Generic as Predicate and Constant (Non-Philosophy and Materialism)'. Setting 'genericity' apart from philosophical universality, Laruelle produces genericity as a means through which disciplines and epistemologies can be equalized in light of the generic's power of unilateral intervention. Genericity forms an a priori constant of knowledges, being axiomatically posited as the real immanence of Man-without-subjectivity. On this axiomatic basis, Laruelle undertakes a symptomology of its operations within philosophy, revealing the characteristics of the generic that make it irrecoverable within a philosophical or conceptual system. Through this investigation it is shown that genericity is what forms the 'sterile additive' base for philosophies and positive disciplines, only appearing as a subtractive instance from within these fields. Mirroring Badiou's own distinction between knowledge and truth, Laruelle argues that it is the generic as the 'True-without-truth' that forces knowledge, without in turn being affected, thereby acting as a 'weak force' that transforms philosophy.

In 'The Ontic Principle: Outline of an Object-Oriented Philosophy', Levi Bryant proposes a thought experiment in the spirit of Freud's *Beyond the Pleasure Principle*. Noting philosophy's epistemological obsession with the questions of where to begin, Bryant argues that the project of critique has become sterile, and invites the reader to imagine instead a new ontological beginning with what he calls 'the ontic principle'. The ontic principle proposes that prior even to questions of epistemology, all questions of ontology presuppose difference and, more specifically, the production of difference. From the thesis that to be is to make a difference, Bryant develops a critique of correlationist philosophy, along with a host of theses about the being of objects, by way of proposing an object-oriented ontology he refers to as 'onticology'. Objects or substances, in Bryant's view, are difference generators consisting of endo-relational structures defined by their affects or their capacity to act and be acted upon. In this wide-ranging essay, Bryant develops a critique of both relationism and anti-realism, and develops a realist ontology that strives to straddle the nature/culture divide typical of contemporary debates between naturalist/materialist orientations and humanistic/hermeneutic orientations of thought.

Steven Shaviro's contribution to this volume is entitled 'The Actual Volcano: Whitehead, Harman, and the Problem of Relations'. Shaviro notes that of all the Speculative Realist philosophies, Harman's is the one most closely allied with the thought of Alfred North Whitehead. Yet Shaviro is sceptical of Harman's non-relational ontology, which he sees as doing insufficient justice to change or process; by contrast, Whitehead and Deleuze are joined through their allegiance to becoming. But ultimately, Shaviro concludes that Harman and Whitehead differ largely in *aesthetic* terms. And here too, he finds Whitehead's position superior. While Harman's theory of 'allure' links him to the 'sublime' and hence to a now long-familiar tradition of aesthetic modernism, Whitehead's attention to 'beauty' (defined as 'the emergence of patterned contrasts') puts him in closer proximity to the reality of twenty-first century life.

Harman, in his 'Response to Shaviro', disputes these criticisms. When Shaviro critiques Harman's model of withdrawn objects, he effectively rejects the Heideggerian flavour of Harman's reading of Whitehead, and thereby pays a heavy philosophical price. Shaviro's proposed alliance of Deleuze and Whitehead on the issue of 'becoming' is rejected by Harman as a mere surface similarity: more important is the difference that Whitehead (like Latour) has an ontology of individual entities while Deleuze (like Bergson, Simondon, and Iain Hamilton Grant) do not view individuals as the basic personae of the world. Shaviro is accused of not proving the supposed link between relations and becoming, and Whitehead is described as a philosopher of *static instants* rather than flux and becoming. Harman also objects to the aesthetic portion of Shaviro's critique, stating that the link between modern aesthetics and the sublime remains unclear, and that Shaviro overidentifies the sublime with Harman's 'allure' in at least two different ways.

Bruno Latour's contribution to the volume, 'Reflections on Étienne Souriau's *Les différents modes d'existence*', gives us a foretaste of Latour's own coming major book. While the early Latour of *Irréductions*[22] followed the principle that all physical, mental, animal, and fictional actors are on the same philosophical footing, the later Latour (following the largely forgotten Souriau) insists on drawing distinctions between the many *different* modes of being. For Latour these modes emerge historically and internally to specific cultures, rather than being *a priori* categories of the mind or the world. While this new project dates from as early as 1987, it was not revealed to Latour's readership until two decades later, at the Cerisy conference on his work in June 2007. Drawing on the ideas of William James, Gilbert Simondon, and Alfred North Whitehead, Latour gives a brief tour of *five* modes of being from Souriau's own list: phenomenon, thing, soul, fiction, God. (At last count, Latour's own list contains *fourteen* modes.)

Science

In 'Outland Empire', Gabriel Catren proposes to weave together four strands of modern philosophy: the absolute, the system, phenomenology, and knowledge. Taking these together, Catren aims to show that a thoroughly critical philosophy is the only way forward for speculative philosophy. What emerges from this effort is not a reinscription of the subject's centrality to the absolute, but a properly Copernican revolution wherein the correlationist problematic falls to the side. This 'absolutely modern' philosophy is both conditioned by and desutured from modern science, taking

---

22. Latour, Bruno, 'Irreductions', trans. John Law, in *The Pasteurization of France*, trans. Alan Sheridan and John Law, Cambridge, Harvard University Press, 1988.

into account the rational insights of physics while maintaining the relative autonomy of philosophy. In order to uphold this thesis of an absolutely modern philosophy, Catren argues that science must incrementally fold the transcendental apparatus of philosophy back into science, thereby negating the limits philosophy seeks to place upon it. Philosophy, unburdened from its task of providing knowledge of the real, becomes a matter of the global compossibilization of different local thought procedures. Building upon this fundamental definition of philosophy's task, Catren sets out some of the procedures philosophical thought uses to compose different strands of thought into a single, atonal composition. From this, Catren elaborates the systemic lineaments of the modern absolute stemming from contemporary science and the philosophical compossibilization.

In her essay 'Wondering about Materialism', Isabelle Stengers takes issue with the eliminativist understanding of nature, in which all knowledge except that of physics must ultimately be eliminated. This eliminativist materialism acts to lay the groundwork not just for an understanding of human reality, but for a transformation of it. It is a question of power and control. Against this reductive naturalism, Stengers proposes a messier and more complex materialism, one based on struggle among multiple entities and levels and not upon reducing the diversity of the world to a single plane. Stengers asks us not to reduce the world immediately to a mathematico-physical framework, but to 'wonder' about it—to let it upset our established categories and shift our own theories. Wonder, Stengers writes, is not about mysticism, but rather about the true scientific spirit that refuses the tendency towards ordering and reduction in favour of an openness that leads science astray from established knowledge. Science, unlike judicial proceedings, is not guided by a firm and unwavering set of rules and procedures, but is the production of rare events that provide new insight into reality. The risk is that with the rise of a knowledge economy, science may indeed turn into a rigid practice unwilling to undermine the status quo due to political and economic interests. The issue then is to re-invoke a sense of wonder in order to counter these stratifying tendencies.

In 'Emergence, Causality, and Realism', Manuel DeLanda wades into debates surrounding emergence, proposing a non-mystical account of emergent systems based on singularities, attractors, and the virtual. Contesting the classical causal thesis that 'one cause implies one effect, always', DeLanda shows how sensitivity to initial conditions, coupled with interrelations between singularities, generate a host of non-linear phenomena and emergent properties. As a consequence of this analysis, DeLanda proposes an account of being that seeks to investigate the virtual dimension of phenomena or the powers locked within objects.

In his paper 'Ontology, Biology, and History of Affect', John Protevi explores Deleuze's concept of affect and its implications for social and political theory. Taking the affect of rage as a case study, Protevi develops a bio-cultural theory of affect that seeks to account for the genesis or production of affects as capacities to act and be acted upon. Drawing heavily on research in developmental systems theory as well as neurology and cognitive psychology, Protevi argues against gene-centrist accounts of affectivity, as well as purely sociological accounts of the genesis of bodies. Rather, Protevi shows how affects are produced through a developmental process involving both culture and biology, where individual bodies are not necessarily the only units of selection. In addition to selection on the level of individual bodies, selection also takes place at the level of what Protevi refers to as the 'body politic' pertaining to groups and institutions, where forms of subjectivity and experience are actively molded in conjunction with biology and neurology by way of social relations.

Conclusion

The collection concludes with Ben Woodard's interview with Slavoj Žižek, in which Žižek articulates his own materialist position by contrasting it with a series of other materialisms—naturalist, democratic, discursive, and speculative. For Žižek, contrary to all these positions, only the assertion of the nature of reality as 'non-All' can sustain a truly materialist position. Responding to various criticisms of his materialism, Žižek tries to show how Hegel's dialectical movement can resolve some of the paradoxes involved in causal determinism, evolutionary reformism and Meillassoux's hyperchaos. The standard Hegelian reading that sees contingency as merely mediating notional necessity must be supplemented with its opposite, in which necessity itself becomes contingent. Such a reading rejects the typical understanding of Hegel, which subsumes all contingencies as mere moments in the necessity of the Whole. While finding numerous such Hegelian resonances within Meillassoux's work, Žižek regards speculative realism as having faltered in not yet developing a sufficient account of subjectivity, or of being's appearing to itself.

THE FUTURE OF SPECULATIVE REALISM

Unresolved Issues

Given the relatively recent emergence of continental materialism and realism, the future of these trends is still unclear, and debates in a number of areas remain less than fully formed. Without presuming to provide an exhaustive account of these debates, we can note at least four of them: politics/ethics, temporality, subjectivity/consciousness, and science/truth.

It has become almost a matter of dogma within continental philosophy that 'politics is ontology, and ontology is politics', as if the basic determination of 'what is' were itself a contentious political matter. While not denying the importance of politics, several of the materialisms and realisms proposed in this book tacitly reject the strong version of this claim. If the basic claim of realism is that a world exists independent of ourselves, this becomes impossible to reconcile with the idea that all of ontology is simultaneously political. There needs to be an aspect of ontology that is independent of its enmeshment in human concerns. Our *knowledge* may be irreducibly tied to politics, yet to suggest that reality is also thus tied is to project an epistemological problem into the ontological realm.

A more serious issue for the new realisms and materialisms is the question of whether they can provide any grounds or guidelines for ethical and political action. Can they justify normative ideals? Or do they not rather evacuate the ground for all intentional action, thereby proposing a sort of political quietism? What new forms of political organization can be constructed on the basis of the ideas emerging from this movement? Several of the authors included in this work have developed explicit and sophisticated arguments for how materialism and realism shift our conceptions of politics, and analytic philosophy has a long history of analysing the relations between materialism and values, yet much work remains to be done in this field.

Temporality is another important issue for the new materialisms and realism, as yet not fully developed. The speculations of twentieth-century physics about time have captured widespread attention. The same was true of twentieth-century continental philosophy, with thinkers as diverse as Husserl, Heidegger, Bergson, Sartre, Derrida and Deleuze all making temporality quasi-foundational in their work. This tension between what physics, philosophy, and everyday experience say about time is something that needs to be addressed. The issue is particularly significant in light of Brassier's critiques of temporal syntheses as irreducibly idealist,[23] Metzinger's explanations of the emergence of linear time from neurological processes,[24] and Julian Barbour's arguments for the denial of ontological temporality.[25]

Closely related to these temporal issues is the place of subjectivity and phenomenal experience after the speculative turn. What ontological status should be granted to our everyday experience? Is there such a thing as a 'subject' to whom phenomena appear? Do the objects that populate phenomenal experience have an ontological role or are they merely epiphenomenal products of our particular neural circuitry? This also raises the question of the extent to which phenomenology and psychoanalysis can provide legitimate intuitions for the nature of reality. Are we inescapably deluded by conscious experience because of the way consciousness is produced? Does our familiar way of explaining behaviour have any grounding in reality, or is it a wildly inaccurate portrayal of what determines our actions? Finally, with the progress of neuroscience, artificial intelligence, and cognitive science, what are the potentials for and ramifications of virtual and artificial subjectivities?

This leads us to the next issue of concern—the relation of scientific discourse to the new realisms and materialisms. While some critics have already denounced the speculative turn as a return to 'positivism', this is far from the case. The relation between each thinker in this collection to science is a complex affair and in each case is ripe for further development. What is undeniably true, however, is that after a long period of mostly ignoring scientific results (whether this be cause or consequence of continental philosophy's forced passage into university literature departments) many of the thinkers involved in this new movement respect scientific discourse without making philosophy a mere handmaiden to the sciences. The result is that the new realisms have to grapple with all the issues that science raises: what is the status of scientific theories? Are they pragmatic constructions aimed at prediction, or do the entities they postulate really exist in 'realist' fashion? What do neuroscientific findings about consciousness, free will, and certainty say about our philosophical conceptions of the world and ourselves? What does modern fundamental physics say about the nature of reality, and can this be made consistent with what these new realisms and materialisms say?

Debates over science invariably become debates over truth as well, and this is another major issue for the new continental trends. One of the most important questions for these trends is how they can justify their own theories against Kant's critical reflections on our own ability to know? What does the emerging neuroscience of truth[26] say about our epistemological biases, and how is this reflected within our own theories?

23. Ray Brassier, *Nihil Unbound: Enlightenment and Extinction*, New York, Palgrave Macmillan, 2007.

24. Thomas Metzinger, *Being No-One: The Self-Model Theory of Subjectivity*, Cambridge, The MIT Press, 2004.

25. Julian Barbour, *The End of Time: The Next Revolution in Physics*, New York, Oxford University Press, 1999.

26. See, for example: Jean-Pierre Changeaux, *The Physiology of Truth: Neuroscience and Human Knowledge*, Cambridge, Harvard University Press, 2009; and Gerald Edelman, *Second Nature: Brain Science and Human Knowledge*, New Haven, Yale University Press, 2006.

Finally, as John Mullarkey has asked,[27] can theories of immanence (a common theme amongst the emerging realisms and materialisms) account for error? That is to say, from what non-transcendent perspective could any particular phenomenon be considered an error? More generally, is error an ontological property at all?

Concluding Remarks

We are hopeful that this collection will prove to be a landmark in the emergence of the new continental philosophy. It has been a pleasure working together on *The Speculative Turn*, despite (or perhaps because of) the fact that none of the three editors have ever met in person—a situation we hope to remedy soon. The editors wish to express special thanks to Ben Woodard for his invaluable assistance in preparing the volume.

---

27. John Mullarkey, *Post-Continental Philosophy: An Outline*, New York, Continuum, 2006.

2

Interview

Alain Badiou and Ben Woodard

Ben Woodard: The other day you positively mentioned what you called the new Speculative Philosophy. How do you see your work in relation to the work of the Speculative Realists (Quentin Meillassoux, Ray Brassier, Iain Hamilton Grant and Graham Harman). Meillassoux sees himself as a materialist and not a realist, is this distinction pivotal for the future of metaphysics and affirmation as you see it?

Alain Badiou: The work of Speculative Realists, from the beginning is very interesting for me, and they refer to me sometimes too. The rupture with the idealist tradition in the field of philosophic study is of great necessity today. We return to the question of realism and materialism later. It's a very complex question. The Speculative Realist position is the position where the point of departure of philosophy is not the relationship between the subject and object or the subject and the world and so on or what Quentin Meillassoux names correlationism. I have known Quentin Meillassoux for a long time—I was in his doctoral dissertation and so on—and from the very beginning I've thought this description of correlationism and the critique of correlationism is a very important point. It's not the classical distinction between realism and materialism, like in the Marxist tradition with Althusser and so on. It was something else. It is very interesting to see that the point of departure of Meillassoux is finally the relationship between Hume and Kant. The idea of Quentin Meillassoux is practically that all philosophical tradition is in the space of Kant, the sense that correlationism is the only clear answer to the question of Hume. The idea of Quentin Meillassoux is that there is another possibility. We are not committed to the choice between Kant and Hume.

My project is different in that it investigates different forms of knowing and action outside empirical and transcendental norms. My vision, however, is also that we must escape two correlationisms and it is a question of the destiny of philosophy itself. In the last century we had two ends of philosophy: the analytic (focusing on logic, sense and science) as a kind of new positivism. The other end was phenomenological with Heidegger. There is a strange alliance between the two in France particularly in terms of religious phenomenology (Marion, Ricour, Henry) and cognitivist analytics. They join together against French Philosophy since, as they say, the enemy of my enemy is my friend.

Against this, the fundamental affirmation of Speculative Realism is an ambitious point of view, a new possibility for philosophy. A new vision. Philosophy can continue. In this sense I am happy that it is not merely a continuation of classical metaphysics nor an end of it. In this sense I am in agreement with the word realism. We are beyond the end of metaphysics and classical metaphysics with the term realism. The question of realism as opposed to materialism is not a crucial question today. What is important is that it is not correlationist or idealist. It is a new space for philosophy, one with many internal differences but this is a positive symptom.

BW: You also spoke of time and the importance of a present that is not solely determined by the future. Does the speculative dimension of Speculative Realism not act on a certain futurity, does speculative thinking somehow negate or at least avoid the present, the possibility of a present of a real present, a true life?

AB: This is an important question. My answer will be an improvisation and not a meditation. There is a detachment from the present in SR, a kind of stoicism of the present. There is no clear presentation or vision of the present. This is very different from me. There is no theory of the event in SR. They need a vision of the becoming of the world which is lacking but it can be realist in a sense but as of yet they do not say what we need to do. For Meillassoux the future decides, the future and perhaps the dead will make the final judgment. This is a political weakness. The question is how is the Real of the present deployed for the future?

BW: Do you see any use in Laruelle's project of non-philosophy? Does his concept of the Real (as undecidable) not have some worth?

AB: I have difficulty in understanding Laruelle [laughs] especially regarding the question of the Real. The strength of philosophy is its decisions in regards to the Real. In a sense Laruelle is too much like Heidegger, in critiquing a kind great forgetting, of what is lost in the grasp of decision, what Heidegger called thinking. Beyond this, and not to judge a thinker only by his earliest work, his most recent work has a religious dimension. When you say something is purely in the historical existence of philosophy the proposition is a failure. It becomes religious. There is a logical constraint when you say we most go beyond philosophy. This is why, in the end, Heidegger said only a god can save us.

Ultimately, I do not see an opposition between being *qua* being (as multiplicity) and the Real, not at all. The Real can be decided except for the event which is always in relation to a particular world.

3

On the Undermining of Objects:
Grant, Bruno, and Radical Philosophy

Graham Harman

The phrase 'speculative realism' is no longer beloved by everyone it describes, and may be used less often in the future. I still find it to be an effective term, one that draws wide attention to a fairly diverse set of philosophical programmes by pointing accurately to key similarities among them. Though it is always a badge of honour for intellectuals to refuse being stamped with any sort of label, other fields of human innovation have a much stronger sense for the value of a brand name. The brand is not merely a degenerate practice of brainwashing consumerism, but a universally recognized method of conveying information while cutting through information *clutter*. Coining specific names for philosophical positions helps orient the intellectual public on the various available options while also encouraging untested permutations. If the decision were mine alone, not only would the name 'speculative realism' be retained, but a logo would be designed for projection on PowerPoint screens, accompanied by a few signature bars of smoky dubstep music. It is true that such practices would invite snide commentary about 'philosophy reduced to marketing gimmicks'. But it would hardly matter, since attention would thereby be drawn to the works of speculative realism, and its reputation would stand or fall based on the inherent quality of these works, of which I am confident.

As is already known, the phrase 'speculative realism' was coined in 2007 for our first event at Goldsmiths College in London. It was a lucky accident born from the spirit of compromise needed to place four loosely related authors under a single yoke. 'Realism' is already a fairly shocking word in European philosophy circles, and it still gives a fairly good sense of what all of us are doing. Usually, the main problem with the term realism is that it suggests a dull, unimaginative appeal to stuffy common sense. But this connotation is exploded in advance by the 'speculative' part of the phrase, which hints at starry landscapes haunted by poets and mad scientists. While in many ways I mourn the loss of the umbrella term 'speculative realism', there is also an immediate reward for this loss. No longer reduced to alliance under a single banner, the speculative realists now have a chance to wage friendly and futuristic warfare against one another. Intellectual fault lines have been present from the start. At the

Goldsmiths event two years ago,[1] I played openly with scenarios in which each of us might be isolated against a gang attack by the other three on specific wedge issues. In my new capacity as a blogger,[2] I have turned this into a scenario of outright science fiction, in which the continental landscape of 2050 is made up solely of warring clans descended from the various branches of 2007-era speculative realism. With the umbrella term now abandoned due to mounting defections, we can get down to work and move slowly toward the epic battles of four decades hence, to be carried on posthumously by our deviant intellectual heirs.

The faction of the former speculative realism to which I belong is already known by an accurate general name—'object-oriented metaphysics'. It is a fairly small faction at the moment, though the same is equally true of its rival splinter groups. Levi Bryant has partially embraced this term for his own approach to philosophy, as has the prominent videogame writer Ian Bogost and the prominent ecologist Timothy Morton. The phrase 'object-oriented' might even be used to refer to Bruno Latour, though perhaps he would reject this description for various reasons. Like 'speculative realism' itself, 'object-oriented metaphysics' conveys a good deal of information in just a few words. Above all, it is a *metaphysics*: a word even more out of fashion among continentals than 'realism' is. But more importantly, the 'object-oriented' part of the phrase is enough to distinguish it from the other variants of speculative realism. By 'objects' I mean unified entities with specific qualities that are autonomous from us and from each other. At first this might sound like a residue of common sense, whose presence in philosophy I otherwise condemn. It might sound like 'naive realism' to believe in independent things that exist even when we sleep or die, and which unleash forces against one another whether we like it or not. Some critics even hold that the object-oriented model is a superstition drawn from everyday life, bewitched by the 'manifest image' found in consciousness, and insufficiently rigorous to play any role in ontology. Yet as I will explain here, appeals to everyday first-person experience are by no means the key evidence in favor of objects in philosophy. And it is fascinating to note that almost every available 'radical' option in philosophy has targeted *objects* as what most need to be eliminated. There is already a long list of *anti*-object-oriented standpoints from which one can choose, which suggest that objects have a certain potency as philosophical personae that provokes reactive operations:

1. For correlationism[3] as well as idealism, the object is not a mysterious residue lying behind its manifestation to humans. If I claim to think of an object beyond thought, then I am *thinking* it, and thereby turn it into a correlate of thought in spite of myself. Hence the object is *nothing more than* its accessibility to humans.

2. We can also speak of *relationism*. Though Latour and especially Whitehead do not seem to reduce objects to their relations with humans, they still leave no room to speak of objects outside their relations or prehensions more generally. In Whitehead's words, to speak of an object outside its prehensions of other objects is to posit a 'vacuous actuality', a phrase meant in a spirit of contempt. And for Latour an object is nothing more than whatever it modifies, trans-

---

1. Brassier, Ray, Iain Hamilton Grant, Graham Harman, and Quentin Meillassoux, 'Speculative Realism', *Collapse: Philosophical Research and Development*, vol. III, Falmouth, UK, Urbanomic, 2007.

2. My 'Object-Oriented Philosophy' blog can be found at http://doctorzamalek2.wordpress.com/

3. The term 'correlationism' was first coined by Quentin Meillassoux in *After Finitude*, trans. R. Brassier, London, Continuum, 2008, p. 5.

forms, perturbs, or creates.[4] An object (or 'actor', as Latour calls it) is not an autonomous substance, but a 'score list' of victories and defeats in struggles with various other objects.[5] Here, the object is held to be *nothing more than* its effects on other things.

3. Even outright monism can sometimes be found in our midst, and in surprising places. For monism the individual object is nothing more than a specific event erupting from some deeper holistic unity. Anaxagoras is a good ancient example, with his boundless *apeiron* that shatters into specific things only when it is rotated quickly by mind (*nous*). In recent French philosophy we have the early Levinas,[6] for whom insomnia reveals the formless *il y a* (or 'there is') that only human consciousness can hypostatize into individual objects. In some of the more wildly speculative articles of Jean-Luc Nancy,[7] we find a shapeless 'whatever' that takes the form of definite objects only through relations. Here, the object is *nothing more than* a byproduct of a deeper primordial reality.

4. For other recent thinkers, such as Gilbert Simondon and Manuel DeLanda, the world is surely not a fully homogeneous lump. Yet it still consists of something not yet fully individual, even if somehow diversified into distinct zones. For these more nuanced heirs of the monist position, the object is still *nothing more than* the derivative actualization of a deeper reality—one that is more diverse than a lump, but also more continuous than specific horses, rocks, armies, and trees.

5. For others such as Bergson, it is flux or becoming that is primary, such that any theory of the object defined as a specific individual in a specific instant would be a fool's errand. Here the object is treated as *nothing more than* the fleeting crystallization of some impulse or trajectory that can never be confined to a single moment.

6. For scientific naturalism, millions of objects are eliminated in favor of more basic underlying objects that exhaustively explain them. 'Meinong's jungle' of real and unreal objects is cut down to make way for a series of laboratories devoted to particle physics and neuroscience. In this case the object is regarded as *nothing more than* either final microphysical facts, or as an empty figment reducible to such facts.

7. For Hume there are no objects, only 'bundles of qualities'. Here, the object is *nothing more than* a nickname for our habitual linking of red, sweet, cold, hard, and juicy under the single term 'apple'.

8. For the so-called 'genealogical' approach to reality, objects have no discernible identity apart from the history through which they emerged, which must be reconstructed to know what the thing really is. Here the object is taken to be *nothing more than* its history.

9. For philosophies of difference (and there may be some debate over who fits this mold) the object differs even from itself, and has no fixed identity. Supposedly the law of non-contradiction is violated, so that we can no longer speak of de-

---

4. Bruno Latour, *Pandora's Hope: Essays on the Reality of Science Studies*, Cambridge, Harvard University Press, 1999.

5. Bruno Latour, *Science in Action: How to Follow Scientists and Engineers Through Society*, Cambridge, Harvard University Press, 1987.

6. Emmanuel Levinas, *Existence and Existents*, trans. A. Lingis, The Hague, Martinus Nijhoff, 1988.

7. Jean-Luc Nancy, 'Corpus', trans. C. Sartiliot, in Jean-Luc Nancy, *The Birth to Presence*, trans. B. Holmes, et. al., Stanford, Stanford University Press, 1993.

terminate objects as playing any role in philosophy. Here the object is treated as *nothing more than* the grammatical superstition of traditionalist dupes, drugged by the opiate of noun/verb Western grammar.

There are other possible ways of discrediting objects in philosophy, some of them not yet invented. My purpose in this article is to emphasize that a counter-movement is both possible and necessary. Reviewing the list of strategies above, there seems to be a general assumption in our time that individual objects are the very embodiment of anti-philosophy, relics belonging to the age of muskets and powdered wigs. But all of these anti-object standpoints try to reduce reality to a single *radix*, with everything else reduced to dust. For this reason I propose that the phrase 'radical philosophy' now become a pejorative term rather than a slogan of pride. As an alternative to radicalism, I propose a philosophy with no *radix*, no ultimate root or ultimate surface of the world, but a *polarized* philosophy in which the object is torn asunder from its traits in two different directions. We should oppose radicalism not in the name of sober moderation (for in that case other career choices would be wiser than philosophy) but in the name of *weirdness*. Radical philosophy is never weird enough, never sufficiently attentive to the basic ambiguity built into substance from Aristotle onward. Radical philosophies are all reductionist in character. Whether they reduce upward to human access or downward to more fundamental layers, all say that a full half of reality is *nothing more than* an illusion generated by the other half. Objects by contrast are the site of polarization, ambiguity, or weirdness. On the one hand objects are autonomous from all the features and relations that typify them, but on the other they are not *completely* autonomous, for then we would have a multiverse of utterly disconnected zones that even an occasionalist God could not put back together again. In other words, we need to account for the difference between objects and their qualities, accidents, relations, and moments, without oversimplifying our work by reducing objects to any of these. For all of these terms make sense only in their strife with the unified objects to which they belong.

Whatever their differences, all of the nine or more complaints about objects employ one of two basic strategies. One option is to claim that objects are unreal because they are derivative of something deeper—objects are too superficial to be the truth. This is the more cutting-edge version of those recent European philosophies that have a certain realist flavor. The other and more familiar option, anti-realist in character, is to say that objects are unreal because they are useless fictions compared with what is truly evident in them—whether this be qualities, events, actions, effects, or givenness to human access. Here objects are declared too falsely deep to be the truth. In this way objects receive a torrent of abuse from two separate directions. This should be taken as a good omen, since being attacked simultaneously for opposite reasons is always the best sign of a genuine insight. While the first approach 'undermines' objects by trying to go deeper, we can coin a term and say that the second strategy 'overmines' objects by calling them too deep. Although undermining is obviously a more familiar English word, overmining is a far more common philosophical strategy for dissolving objects. To some extent it might even be called the central dogma of continental philosophy. This can be seen in correlationism and in full-blown idealism, which grant no autonomy to the object apart from how it is thought—no horse-in-itself apart from the horse accessed by the human subject. It is seen in relationism, which finds it nonsensical that things could be real apart from their system of relations. And it is seen even more clearly in Hume's widely accepted 'bundle of qualities' theory, in which the object is a mere bulk pseudonym for a series of genuine impressions and ideas. These positions are some of the 'overminers' of objects. Among the original speculative realists, it is Meillassoux who flirts most openly with overmining. Unlike his three associates, Meillassoux finds the correlationist standpoint worthy of great respect.[8] Indeed, he finds correlationism to be such an unsurpassable horizon that it can only be radicalized from within: as an 'inside job'. From the outside, the fortress strikes him as impregnable.

So far I have had little to say in print about the *undermining* of objects, largely because I have more sympathy for it than for the alternative. The descent into pre-objective, pre-individual depths is at least a laudable move away from the dogma of human access that I detest. Undermining occurs if we say that 'at bottom, all is one' and that individual objects are derivative of this deeper primal whole. It happens if we say that the process of individuation matters more than the autonomy of fully formed individuals. It also happens when we say that the nature of reality is 'becoming' rather than being, with individuals just a transient consolidation of wilder energies that have already moved elsewhere as soon as we focus on specific entities. There is undermining if we appeal to a pre-objective topology deeper than actuality, or if we insist that the object is reducible to a long history that must be reconstructed from masses of archival documents.

Among the original speculative realists, it is Iain Hamilton Grant who tends most clearly toward the undermining of objects. I am thereby left as the only full-blown defender of objects in the original speculative realist group. But this is not meant as some pathetically mournful cry of solitude. At the first Speculative Realism event two years ago, I already observed that each of the original members of the group could be seen as intellectually lonely when viewed from one specific angle. According to various criteria the four of us could be pitted against each other in any combination of two versus two, any cruel persecution of one by three, and also in my proposed four-way warfare of the year 2050: a scenario best described with Werner Herzog's famous phrase 'everyone for himself, and God against all'. In this article I will focus on Grant's position as developed in his Schelling book,[9] finally available in paperback. By looking at the specific way in which Grant sidesteps individual objects, and by placing his position side-by-side with the views of neighboring thinkers, the features of my object-oriented model will be clarified.

1. IAIN GRANT'S POSITION

Of all the positions described as 'speculative realist', Iain Grant's and my own are probably the closest match. This has not gone unnoticed by certain readers who have sometimes referred to both of us as 'panpsychists', 'vitalists', or even 'Schellingians'. In certain respects these terms are mistaken, but there is a good reason why the mistakes are made here and not elsewhere. What Grant and I obviously have in common is a tendency to treat the inanimate world as a philosophical protagonist, but not in any form that would be remotely acceptable to mainstream natural science. Perhaps a Schellingian attitude can be found in our shared enjoyment at the thought that electrical and geological facts are permeated by deeper metaphysical vibrations. Some have also noticed a similar upbeat irreverence in our writings. But we also agree on a number of more specific philosophical points.

---

8. Above all, see Meillassoux's words on this point in Brassier et al., 'Speculative Realism', p. 409.

9. Iain Hamilton Grant, *Philosophies of Nature After Schelling*, London, Continuum, 2006.

The first such point is an uncompromising realism. The world is not the world as manifest to humans; to think a reality beyond our thinking is not nonsense, but obligatory. In Grant's own words: 'while it is true that everything visible is becoming, it is not true that all becoming is visible [...]'[10] Or 'what phenomena are cannot be reduced to how they appear for any given apparatus of reception, [whether] technological or biological. This is why empiricism can never exhaust the phenomena [...]' [11] Hence Grant's well-known turn to Schelling:

> [...] Kant's is a 'merely relative idealism': an idealism conditioned, precisely, by the elimi-
> nation of nature, and therefore ideal relative to nature [...] [Yet] regardless of nature being
> thought, nature insofar as it is not thought, i.e., any nature independent of our thinking of
> it, necessarily exceeds and grounds all possible ideation. As the System of Transcendental
> Idealism puts it, reversing rather than extending the Kantian procedure, 'Anything whose
> conditions simply cannot be given in nature, must be absolutely impossible'.[12]

Grant therefore agrees with Badiou (as do I) that the endless reversals of Platonism in philosophy have grown tedious and fruitless. Given the alarming fact 'that postkantianism marks the horizon of contemporary philosophy exactly as it did in the early nineteenth century'[13] (!) our energies would be better invested in counteracting Kant, not Plato. Yet Grant also shares my skepticism toward Badiou's program of a return to classical philosophy by way of mathematics.[14]

Let's turn to another point of agreement. The word 'eliminative' usually refers to a parsimony that moves downward, cutting away various ghosts, dragons, saints, and qualia until nothing is left but some sort of respectable physical substrate. But Grant rightly notes that elimination often occurs upward as well: 'Because the expanded realism of Platonic physics manifestly exceeds speculative egoism both on the side of nature and the Idea, Schelling designated his a "real" or "objective idealism", and thus contested merely conditioned idealisms as thereby eliminative'.[15] Whether elimination occurs in the direction of microphysical agents or towards the surface of human access, in both cases the middle zone of reality is exterminated. The only thing Schelling favors eliminating is the supposed gulf between organic and anorganic nature. And 'this elimination does not merely entail a transcendental or ideal organicism applied all the way down to so-called inanimate matter, as the cliché regarding Romantic naturephilosophy would have it; it also entails an uninterrupted physicalism leading [upward] from "the real to the ideal"'.[16] In other words, the sphere of human access is not an ultimate reality to which all reality would be reduced, but a phenomenal product of such reality. But only rarely has continental philosophy pursued this global physics embracing all sectors of philosophy and ending the artificial gulf between human and world. Instead, one has adopted the tepid remedy of adding 'life' as a new term to complicate the picture of the human/world divide. As Grant delightfully puts it: 'Life acts as a kind of Orphic guardian for philosophy's descent into the physical. This is because life provides an effective alibi against philosophy's tendency to "antiphysics", while cen-

---

10. Grant, *Philosophies of Nature After Schelling*, p. 44.
11. Grant, *Philosophies of Nature After Schelling*, p. 145.
12. Grant, *Philosophies of Nature After Schelling*, pp. 65-66.
13. Grant, *Philosophies of Nature After Schelling*, p. 8, my emphasis.
14. Grant, *Philosophies of Nature After Schelling*, p. 199.
15. Grant, *Philosophies of Nature After Schelling*, p. 59.
16. Grant, *Philosophies of Nature After Schelling*, p. 11.

tralizing ethico-political or existential problematics as philosophy's true domain'.[17] And 'despite the naturephilosophy disputing this onesidedness, the metaphysical dissymmetry that retains biology as a philosophical science while rejecting geology or chemistry from its remit has haunted the philosophy of nature ever since [...]'[18] This resonates further with his complaint that 'ethicism is [generally purchased] at the cost of the elimination of nature',[19] and Grant, almost never a harsh personality, is always at his harshest whenever referring to those who call Schelling's philosophy an ethical project. Endorsing Schelling's own claim that philosophy is nothing other than speculative physics,[20] Grant asks neither philosophy nor physics to become the servant of the other. As he puts it, 'if Schelling does not cede philosophical authority to the sciences [...this does not] mean that the naturephilosophy takes up the office of critical judge presiding over [the sciences]'.[21] Philosophy will not be the handmaiden of the sciences any more than the reverse. And here too we are in agreement.

In fact, we really have just one point of disagreement, but it is decisive. Consider the phrase 'philosophy of nature' itself. While this would be a reasonably accurate description of what Grant does, it would not be even remotely accurate if applied to my own position, which considers all kinds of objects and not just natural ones. But the difference goes further than this. The main point is not that I like armies and plastic cups as much as natural objects, with Grant confining himself to sunsets and fields of daisies. Instead, Grant's problem is with objects *per se*, which obviously make up the very core of my position. Namely, he objects to what he calls 'somatism' (or a philosophy of bodies) in favor of a pre-somatic *dynamism*. To identify the latter with the philosophy of nature would be insufficiently precise. After all, a figure such as Whitehead must be described as a somatic philosopher of nature, given that he concedes a decisive role to individual entities that is absent from Grant's position. And furthermore, Grant tends to identify somatism with idealism, implying that bodies or objects exist only as phenomena, and that what exists in its own right is a dynamic nature never fully articulated into units. As we will see in a moment, this leads him to an unorthodox view of the history of philosophy in which Aristotle sides *with* Kant and *against* realism, since Aristotle's focus on individual substances supposedly turns him into an idealist. My own admittedly more mainstream view takes Aristotle to be the permanent ally of all brands of realism; whatever the flaws of Aristotelian substance may be, lack of reality outside the human mind is not one of them. Grant's relative hostility to Aristotle, as well as his general philosophical position, brings him very close to Giordano Bruno—less a philosopher of nature than a philosopher of matter, and of the infinite One that embraces both matter and form.

But let's stay with Grant for now. Citing Carl Friedrich Kielmeyer, Grant notes approvingly that 'nature is conceived not as a body, a collation of bodies, nor [even] a megabody or substrate, but rather in accordance with what is 'probably the first' concept of nature to have arisen, as «including within it emergence, becoming, birth»'.[22] Schelling, along with Plato, Bruno, and Grant himself

17. Grant, *Philosophies of Nature After Schelling*, p. 10.
18. Grant, *Philosophies of Nature After Schelling*, p. 10.
19. Grant, *Philosophies of Nature After Schelling*, p. ix.
20. Grant, *Philosophies of Nature After Schelling*, p. 188.
21. Grant, *Philosophies of Nature After Schelling*, p. 159.
22. Grant, *Philosophies of Nature After Schelling*, p. 126.

clearly opposes the Aristotelian and Kantian accounts of physics as the 'physics of all things' or 'bodies' (somatism), since [he] proposes that 'things', beings or entities, are consequent upon nature's activity, rather than this latter being inexplicably grounded in the properties or accidents of bodies. The philosophy of nature itself, in other words, is no longer grounded in somatism, but in the dynamics from which all ground, and all bodies, issue [....][23]

In short, 'physics is not restricted to somatics, as Aristotle and Kant maintain, but must treat also of the generation of bodies, relegating the latter to regionality within the former'.[24] Kant is said to be '[demonstrate] his Aristotelian inheritance'[25] through his phenomenalism, somatism, and formalism, which for Grant turn out to be practically interchangeable terms. To be a body means to be a form, and to be a form means to be phenomenal. In a surprising and refreshing citation, Grant summons Michael Faraday to give scientific weight to his own metaphysics, when he says that '"the material" is not conceived somatically, i.e. neither as substrate nor corpuscle, in accordance with the Aristotelian dichotomy; rather, it is dynamically conceived as consisting only in actions: "the substance is composed of its powers", as Faraday put it'.[26] The reference to 'powers' means that we are not speaking of a total set of current actions, as for an author like Latour, but of a turbulent dynamism from which all of a substance's possible actions emerge.

Kant, we read, joins Aristotle in rejecting the darkness of matter.[27] Grant is dismayed by what he calls a 'startling' removal of matter from Aristotle's metaphysics, which extracts matter from substantial existence and reduces it to something having a merely logical existence, just as Bruno complains.[28] This leads Grant to the daring conclusion that 'Aristotelian metaphysics is that science concerned with substance not insofar as this is particular, sensible or material, but insofar as it is a predicable essence, i.e., only insofar as it is the subject or hypokeimenon supporting a logos'.[29] Nor is it only the metaphysical theory that is affected, since even Aristotelian physics is described as a phenomenology.[30] Grant's assault on the mainstream reading of Aristotle continues on the following page, when Aristotelian primary substance (usually interpreted as concrete individual things) is placed on the side of logos and formal ontology, and thereby denied independence from the phenomenal realm.[31] Grant is not just reading by fiat here; he does cite numerous passages from Aristotle to establish his case. But the force of his argument lies less in these citations than in his general intuition (shared with Bruno) that form cannot belong autonomously to the things, and must be provided instead by the logos or by some sort of phenomenal character. Despite Grant's adoration for Leibniz, which I share, there is little trace of the Leibnizian substantial forms in the metaphysics that Grant draws from Schelling. The difference between matter and form is presented as though it were identical with that between real dynamism and the phenomenal realm. For although in Grant's eyes the phenom-

23. Grant, *Philosophies of Nature After Schelling*, p. 8.

24. Grant, *Philosophies of Nature After Schelling*, p. 28.

25. Grant, *Philosophies of Nature After Schelling*, p. 37.

26. Grant, *Philosophies of Nature After Schelling*, p. 39.

27. Grant, *Philosophies of Nature After Schelling*, p. 67.

28. Grant, *Philosophies of Nature After Schelling*, p. 34.

29. Grant, *Philosophies of Nature After Schelling*, p. 34.

30. Grant, *Philosophies of Nature After Schelling*, p. 34.

31. Grant, *Philosophies of Nature After Schelling*, p. 35.

enal emerges from a global physics as the highest product of that physics, it turns out that individual horses, centaurs, trees, and coins are forced to take a back seat to the dynamics of global nature.

Instead of the simple realist claim that reality always exceeds its appearances, which I also endorse, Grant appeals to a dynamic production that transcends its products: 'the 'nature that produces' cannot therefore be reduced to sensible nature because it is the production of sensible nature that is itself not sensible'.[32] Products are not even allowed the inertial right to remain just as they are, for 'productivity does not cease in the production of the product, but produces serially, reproduces it over and again'.[33] This reminds us of the separation of moments of time found in occasionalist philosophy, as seen all the more when Grant writes that 'between products [...] there is neither phenomenal nor temporal continuity, so that while becoming is infinite, it is not 'continuous', but generates a dynamic succession of stages in 'leaps', where each stage is the product of a power'.[34] The relation of productivity to product concerns 'the operations of a nature transcendental with respect to its products, but immanent with respect to its forces, or nature-as-subject'.[35] As we have seen, Grant's immanence has the happy effect that the phenomenal sphere is not something separate from nature, but belongs to nature as its product. For Schelling unlike for Kant, 'phenomenality is itself a natural production, having its a prioris not in mind, but in nature. As a result, naturephilosophy in no way proposes the elimination of empirical researches from the investigation of nature, but rather integrates such research at the phenomenal, or derivative level'.[36] The fact that this happens at the derivative level means, for example, that Schelling takes no stand on the 'merely empirical' question of whether light is a wave or a particle[37]—in contrast with Simondon's more provocative claim[38] that the depth of the pre-individual compared with all actualization might serve to explain this famous physical duality.

But there is a separate appearance of quanta or discrete chunks in the model Grant draws from Schelling. The appearance of products concerns what he calls the retardation of nature, which ensures that nature evolves at a finite speed through various stages or epochs rather than unfolding in a flash. Why is the whole course of evolution not instantaneous? Why are there ages of the world at all? In a moment strangely reminiscent of Paul Virilio, Grant speaks of a 'primary diversifying antithesis' in forces between infinite speed on the one hand and retardation on the other.[39] As Grant lucidly puts it: 'while the first, productive force would result in nothing were it not for the second, retarding force, no product, as the retardation of productivity, can recover or absorb productivity as such, or all of nature would result in a single product [...]'[40] Or in Schelling's words, 'every product is a point of inhibition, but in every such point there is again the infinite'.[41] Schelling's *Scheinprodukte*, or phenomenal products of na-

---

32. Grant, *Philosophies of Nature After Schelling*, p. 43.

33. Grant, *Philosophies of Nature After Schelling*, p. 169.

34. Grant, *Philosophies of Nature After Schelling*, p. 169.

35. Grant, *Philosophies of Nature After Schelling*, p. 139.

36. Grant, *Philosophies of Nature After Schelling*, p. 142.

37. Grant, *Philosophies of Nature After Schelling*, p. 142.

38. Gilbert Simondon, *L'indivduation à la lumière des notions de forme et d'information*, Grenoble, Millon, 2005, p. 27.

39. Grant, *Philosophies of Nature After Schelling*, p. 148.

40. Grant, *Philosophies of Nature After Schelling*, p. 173.

41. Grant, *Philosophies of Nature After Schelling*, p. 175.

ture, 'are phenomenal precisely insofar as they are not simply "remainders", but rather the repeated channels by which productivity is "retarded" into particular forms'.[42] And here again comes Grant's most crucial metaphysical decision, so different from my own, in which he identifies all specific entities with the phenomenal sphere: 'since productivity would be finite if it were restricted within a particular form (man, cosmic animal, minerality), phenomenality is not the appearing of a thing, but rather productivity appearing as things'.[43] Thus, no distinction remains for Grant between real and phenomenal things. To be phenomenal means to be retarded, and hence to be a specific thing means to be both phenomenal and retarded. Individual horses and minerals cannot exist in any mode other than the phenomenal one. This does have the benefit of ending the dreary double world of images and realities, but only at the cost of stripping all power from horses and minerals, which are allowed reality only insofar as they are phenomenal products. The supposed compensation is that since phenomena are products of nature, they are not 'mere' phenomena; yet there is still something very much 'mere' about them, since they are deprived of all productive force in their own right. *Qua* horse, it is hard to see how a horse could be dazzled by sunlight or stumble over a mineral. Grant has numerous allies in making such claims, which are so foreign to my own philosophical position. Let's turn briefly to one of the allies that he openly cites: Giordano Bruno, who surely ranks as one of the giants in the philosophy of the pre-individual. This comparison will give added historical depth to my differences with Grant.

2. GIORDANO BRUNO ON MATTER

Bruno was born in Nola near Naples in 1548. His colorful series of adventures and humiliations included an important stay in England. There he did his best philosophical work, while offending his hosts with diatribes on the crude behaviour of the English populace. Captured by the Inquisition after a foolish journey to Venice in 1592, he was burned at the stake in Rome after nearly eight years of interrogation and torture. As the Catholic Encyclopedia puts it: 'Bruno was not condemned for his defence of the Copernican system of astronomy, nor for his doctrine of the plurality of inhabited worlds, but for his theological errors, among which were the following: that Christ was not God but merely an unusually skilful magician, that the Holy Ghost is the soul of the world', and my personal favorite, 'that the Devil will be saved, etc'.[44] (Note the strategic silence on these issues by Iain Grant himself; in our times one must be cautious.) Bruno's philosophical writings are noteworthy for their literary and comedic genius, with unparalleled assaults on 'pedant' characters who make pompous Latin interruptions of worthwhile conversations held in Italian. Today Bruno is more a hero to natural scientists than to philosophers, due to his bold defence of the Copernican system, an infinite universe, and possible extraterrestrial life. But his philosophical spirit is alive and well, if not always acknowledged by name, and I was delighted by Grant's favorable remarks about him.

    Let's look at Bruno's *Cause, Principle, and Unity*, a work seldom discussed in present-day continental circles, even though it can easily be had in a fine English paperback

---

42. Grant, *Philosophies of Nature After Schelling*, p. 176.
43. Grant, *Philosophies of Nature After Schelling*, p. 176.
44. http://www.newadvent.org/cathen/03016a.htm

from Cambridge University Press.[45] One of my favorite exercises when looking at the history of philosophy is to rewrite the titles of famous books using synonyms. For instance, Heidegger's title *Being and Time* might be rewritten as *Withdrawal and Clearing*, *The Veiled and the Unveiled*, *Unity and Triplicity*, or in my own still controversial proposal: *Ready-to-Hand and Present-at-Hand*. In the case of Bruno's miniature masterpiece, *Cause, Principle, and Unity* is perhaps best rewritten as *Form, Matter, and Infinity*. Despite the repeated claims in these dialogues that there is no matter without form and vice versa, this supposed symmetry is misleading: no reader will finish the book believing that Bruno truly gives equal status to matter and form. Form in Bruno's thought is entirely subordinate to a global matter laced with all possible forms; forms are merely surfaces, drawn back into the bosom of matter from time to time like sap returning from the branches of a tree to its trunk. Form is derivative, and given that specific bodies are specific only through their forms, bodies are derivative too. But whereas Grant is simply no great fan of Aristotle, Bruno's contempt for 'the master of those that know' is proverbial. Here is a mild sample of Bruno's invective: 'Why do you claim, O prince of the Peripatetics, that matter is nothing, from the fact of its having no act, rather than saying that it is all, from the fact that it possesses all acts, or possesses them confusedly, as you prefer?'[46] This gentle sarcasm elsewhere gives way to much worse: 'with his harmful explanations and his irresponsible arguments, this arid sophist [Aristotle] perverted the sense of the ancients and hampered the sense of the truth, less, perhaps, out of intellectual weakness, than out of jealousy and ambition'.[47] But this shared distaste for Aristotle is merely the symptom of a deeper agreement between Bruno and Grant. Though both are committed to a robust reality deeper than all accidents and phenomenal appearance, both also seem to hold that specific forms or bodies are nothing but accidents and phenomenal appearance. It will come as no surprise that I agree on the first count and disagree on the second.

Although Bruno accounts for all four of the traditional Aristotelian causes, he groups them differently and explains them in a totally different manner. This difference is crucial to my topic in this article. In the Scholastic tradition, Aristotle's four causes are split into pairs as 'intrinsic' and 'extrinsic' causes. See for instance the beginning of *Metaphysical Disputations* 17 of the great Jesuit thinker Francisco Suárez, who (somewhat bizarrely) was born in the same year as Bruno himself. As Suárez puts it: 'now that we have considered the material cause and the formal cause, which are intrinsic causes, we have to follow this up with a discussion of the extrinsic causes: namely, the final and the efficient cause'.[48] For Bruno, by contrast, only matter is an intrinsic cause, which (simplifying Aristotle's less consistent use of the term) he calls a principle. The other three—formal, efficient, and final—are all called causes by Bruno. And he interprets them in a less than orthodox manner, to say the least. As Teofilo puts it: 'I say that the universal physical efficient cause is the universal intellect, which is the first and principal faculty of the world soul, which, in turn, is the form of it'.[49] Bruno's specific use of these neo-Platonic concepts has a huge impact, since it undermines the status of specific beings. When he says that the intellect and world soul are the 'univer-

45. Giordano Bruno, *Cause, Principle, and Unity*, trans. R. deLucca, Cambridge, Cambridge University Press, 1998.

46. Bruno, *Cause, Principle, and Unity*, p. 82.

47. Bruno, *Cause, Principle, and Unity*, p. 91.

48. Francisco Suárez, *On Efficient Causality: Metaphysical Disputations 17, 18, and 19*, trans. A. Freddoso, New Haven: Yale University Press, 1994, p. 3.

49. Bruno, *Cause, Principle, and Unity*, p. 37, my emphasis.

sal' efficient and formal causes, it is not as though he were still leaving plenty of room for particular causes. It will turn out that the efficient and formal causes of a hammer, dog, or tree are merely transient and accidental for Bruno. The universal intellect is really the sole efficient cause of all that occurs, and the world soul is the only genuine formal cause. Everything that happens will happen only in the deepest depths. The same holds for the final cause, which is not found in numerous different forms for numerous different entities, each with its own purpose. It is found instead only in a single, universal form—in the global aim of the universal intellect. As Dicsono puts it in the Second Dialogue: 'The aim, the final cause which is sought by the efficient, is the perfection of the universe, which consists of all forms having actual material existence: the intellect delights and takes such pleasure in pursuing this goal, that it never tires of calling forth from matter all sorts of forms, as Empedocles himself seems to maintain'.[50] Underneath all of this is matter. I will discuss this topic shortly, but it is designed to undermine Aristotle's substantial forms (which exist in drastically revised form in my own position under the name of 'objects'). Bruno is one of the great anti-object-oriented philosophers of all time, at least among those who could be called realists.

Given that the formal cause of the world is the world soul, everything that exists has soul. It would be easy to call this 'panpsychism', but 'pan-' implies a multiplicity of souls that simply does not exist in Bruno's standpoint. A better name might be 'henpsychism', or the doctrine of a single soul without parts. The pedant character Poliinnio switches into the vernacular tongue long enough to ask: 'Then a dead body has a soul? So, my clogs, my slippers, my boots... as well as my ring and my gauntlets are supposedly animated? My robe and [cloak] are animated?'[51] Teofilo responds that 'the table is not animated as table, nor are the clothes as clothes, nor leather as leather, nor the glass as glass [...]'[52] In other words, there is no soul of glass or soul of leather, not because these are inanimate objects, but because they are specific objects. If we follow the implications of this (as the Inquisition certainly must have done) then there is also no soul of monkey, dog, or human. There is only a single world soul, and by contrast individual souls seem even more transient and illusory for Bruno than for Plotinus. Teofilo continues: 'if life is found in all things, the soul is necessarily the form of all things, that form presides everywhere over matter [...] That is why it seems that such form is no less enduring than matter. [But] I conceive this form in such a way that there is only one for all things'.[53] And even though he later says that no part of matter exists without form,[54] all he means by this is that no part of matter exists in disconnection from the world soul. In short, Bruno consigns individual things to the slums of philosophy. Teofilo again: 'So only the external forms are changed, and even annihilated, because they are not things, but of things, and because they are not substances, but accidents and particularities of substance'.[55] But saying that external forms are 'not things, but of things' is quite misleading—there are simply no individual things at all for Bruno. Multiplicity is a mere surface effect. As Dicsono says in the Fifth Dialogue: 'what creates multiplicity in things is not being, is not the thing, but what appears, what is offered

---

50. Bruno, *Cause, Principle, and Unity*, p. 40.

51. Bruno, *Cause, Principle, and Unity*, p. 43

52. Bruno, *Cause, Principle, and Unity*, p. 44.

53. Bruno, *Cause, Principle, and Unity*, p. 45.

54. Bruno, *Cause, Principle, and Unity*, p. 47.

55. Bruno, *Cause, Principle, and Unity*, p. 45.

to the senses and lies on the surface of things'.[56] Using a term borrowed from the magnificent Nicholas of Cusa, Bruno says that only if we 'contract the genus to a particular species, [is] the essence of a man [...] incompatible with that of a lion'.[57] Before such contraction, 'because [matter] has them all, it has none of them, since what is so many different things is necessarily none of them in particular. What is everything must exclude all particular being'.[58] If we consider uncontracted matter, 'we cannot think in any way that the earth is a part of being, nor that the sun is part of substance, since the latter is indivisible'.[59] And as the clown character Gervasio puts it, 'it is nature's will, which orders the universe, that all forms yield to other forms'.[60] In other words, 'contraction' plays a role in Cusa and Bruno similar to that of retardation in Grant's book.

According to these positions there is no genuine form in the world other than the world soul. All other forms, for Bruno at least, are accidental forms. The only genuine substance turns out to be matter. 'Do you not see that what was seed becomes stalk, what was stalk becomes an ear of wheat, what was an ear becomes bread, what was bread turns to chyle, from chyle to blood, from blood to seed, from seed to embryo, and then to man, corpse, earth, stone or something else, in succession, involving all natural forms?'[61] Only matter is permanent, and therefore only matter can be substance. I regard this as a regrettable backslide from Aristotle, who was the first philosopher in ancient Greece to realize that substances need not be permanent in order to count as substances. But Descartes, Spinoza, and Leibniz all more or less follow Bruno in the archaic assumption that substantial means 'indestructible', a view that I see no reason to accept.

Lest it seem that I am criticizing everything and approving nothing in Bruno's position, he deserves praise for his insight that reality must never be relational. Teofilo criticizes the Peripatetics as follows: 'If they say [soul] is a principle of life, sense, vegetation and intellect, remark that, although that principle is a substance if one considers it fundamentally, as we do, they present it only as an accident. For the fact of being a principle of such and such a thing does not express an absolute and substantial nature, but a nature that is accidental and relative to that which is principled [...]'[62] More realist words than these were never spoken. We can only salute this awareness that substance must not be defined by its relation to anything else, but only in itself. The same holds for Dicsono's statement in the Fourth Dialogue that 'the expressed, sensible and unfolded being does not constitute the fundamental essence of actuality, but is a consequence and effect of it'.[63] This sort of non-relational vision of essence already sounds a lot like that of Xavier Zubíri[64] in the 1960's. Unfortunately, Bruno ruins it by claiming not only that the expressed is not the essence of reality, but also that individual things exist only insofar as they are expressed. This is why he loves universal matter so much, since by withholding itself from expression it also avoids degenerating into any set of relations. Dicsono continues: 'the principle being of wood and the essence of its actuality do not consist in its being a bed, but in its being a substance so constituted that it

---

56. Bruno, *Cause, Principle, and Unity*, p. 93.

57. Bruno, *Cause, Principle, and Unity*, p. 78, my emphasis.

58. Bruno, *Cause, Principle, and Unity*, p. 79.

59. Bruno, *Cause, Principle, and Unity*, p. 92, my emphasis.

60. Bruno, *Cause, Principle, and Unity*, p. 74.

61. Bruno, *Cause, Principle, and Unity*, p. 57.

62. Bruno, *Cause, Principle, and Unity*, p. 60, my emphasis.

63. Bruno, *Cause, Principle, and Unity*, p. 83.

64. Xavier Zubíri, *On Essence*, trans. A.R. Caponigri, Washington, Catholic University Press, 1980.

can be a bad, a bench, a beam, an idol, and anything else formed out of wood'.[65] And for Bruno, even this highly general 'wood' is still imprisoned in overly specific form, and can easily be transmuted into smoke, ash, worms, fish, human blood, and the like.

Bruno cites Averroës[66] and even Aristotle[67] as saying that matter does not receive its forms from outside. He admits that he used to agree with Avicebron, the Cyrenaics, the Cynics, and the Stoics that 'forms are nothing but certain accidental dispositions of matter'.[68] But later he found that 'we must recognize two kinds of substance in nature: namely, form and matter'.[69] This would be plausible enough if he meant only that matter was laced with world soul. But having first dismissed specific forms or entities as accidents that pass away so that only universal substance endures, he now tries to say that these specific forms are located in matter from the start. He says for instance that 'things come from matter by separation, and not by means of addition and reception. Therefore, rather than saying that matter is empty and excludes forms, we should say that it contains forms and includes them'.[70] The plural word 'forms' strikes me as unearned, since only the single form of the world soul has been affirmed while specific forms have been denigrated as accidental. Of matter, Teofilo says that

> just as wood does not possess, by itself, any artificial form, but may have them all as a result of the carpenter's activity, in a similar way the matter of which we speak, because of its nature, has no natural form by itself, but may take on all forms through the operation of the active agent which is the principle of nature. This natural matter is not perceptible, as is artificial matter, because nature's matter has absolutely no form [...][71]

In other words, the status of specific forms, and thus of specific entities *tout court*, has become rather opaque in Bruno's standpoint. In one sense specific forms such as apple, lymph, or blood are banished from philosophy as accidental insofar as they can be destroyed. Another reason they are unreal is that they are defined solely in relation to other things, and Bruno's realism leads him to champion the one thing—or rather, two—that he knows exist in their own right: matter and the world soul. But now we hear that all the specific forms are enfolded in matter from the start. And yet they are not specific forms, since it has all of them and therefore has none, since they all coincide and are not yet contracted into individual forms. Furthermore, it is never really explained how or why they contract, except that the universal final cause makes the universal intelligence desire to actualize as many of them as possible. Insofar as the specific forms are contained in matter, they are also invisible, since matter does not really have them; given that it has them all, it also has none. We will return to this point shortly.

From all of this Teofilo infers that 'nothing is ever annihilated and loses its being, except for the external and material accidental form'.[72] But this refers to all specific objects, since it is only 'the matter and the substantial form of any natural thing whatever (that is, its soul) [that] can be neither destroyed nor annihilated, losing their being completely'.[73] But recall that the phrase 'its soul' is a contradiction in terms, since dia-

---

65. Bruno, *Cause, Principle, and Unity*, p. 83.
66. Bruno, *Cause, Principle, and Unity*, pp. 80-81.
67. Bruno, *Cause, Principle, and Unity*, p. 82.
68. Bruno, *Cause, Principle, and Unity*, p. 55.
69. Bruno, *Cause, Principle, and Unity*, p. 55.
70. Bruno, *Cause, Principle, and Unity*, p. 83.
71. Bruno, *Cause, Principle, and Unity*, p. 86.
72. Bruno, *Cause, Principle, and Unity*, p. 59.
73. Bruno, *Cause, Principle, and Unity*, p. 59.

monds do not have souls *qua* diamonds, or clothing *qua* clothing; everything shares the same spark of life from the same unified world soul. Now, throughout the history of philosophy, 'substantial form' has usually referred not to what Bruno uses it for (namely, a universal world soul) but to the non-accidental forms of individual things. Bruno's use of 'substantial form' to refer to the world soul is more than a bit quirky, and he knows it. For this reason he makes sure to attack 'the substantial forms of the Peripatetics and others like them, which consist of nothing but accident, complexion, disposition of qualities, a principle of definition, quiddity'.[74] From there Bruno moves to a sample of outright ridicule that is worth quoting in full:

> Hence, some cowled and subtle metaphysicians among them, wishing to excuse rather than accuse their idol Aristotle, have come up with humanity, bovinity, oliveness, as specific substantial forms. This humanity—for example, Socrateity—this bovinity, this horseness, are individual substances. [...] They have never derived any gain from this, for if you ask them, point by point, 'In what does the substantial being of Socrates consist?', they will answer 'In Socrateity'; if you then ask, 'What do you mean by Socrateity?', they will answer, 'The substantial and proper matter of Socrates.[75]

This is all good clean fun at the expense of the Scholastics, and ought to be enjoyed for what it is. But notice that Bruno is trying to shift our attention away from a major problem with his own position. For if we asked Bruno himself 'In what does the substantial being of Socrates consist?', his own answer would be even less helpful than the Scholastic response. His first reply would be that Socrates has no substantial being, but is a mere accident; only matter and the world soul have substantial being. But he would then insinuate that the form of Socrates is already present in matter, simply enfolded and uncontracted in such a way that matter both has and does not have Socrates in it before Socrates is born. In short, Bruno ridicules individual substantial forms, but then adopts them anyway—merely transposing them from the supposedly accidental realm of individual things to an undermining realm of matter where they are both present and not present at the same time. The technical term for this maneuver is 'highway robbery', since Bruno is trying to preserve individual forms without paying for them. He cannot just say that the individual forms are potentially in matter, because he spews so much venom against Aristotle for saying that matter is merely potential; everywhere, he insists that matter is both potency and act. In a strange metaphor, Bruno says that matter 'is deprived of forms and without them, not in the way ice lacks warmth or the abyss is without light, but as a pregnant woman lacks the offspring which she produces and expels forth from herself [...]'[76] The problem with this analogy is that, from Bruno's standpoint, as soon as the child is 'expelled' it has entered the realm of the transient and accidental.

To conclude these remarks on Bruno, we should add that even this universal matter and form are both subordinated to the One. 'The universe', Teofilo says, 'is one, infinite, immobile'. This universe 'is not matter, because it is not configured or configurable, nor is it limited or limitable. It is not form, because it neither informs nor figures anything else, given that it is all, that it is maximum, that it is one, that it is universal'.[77] And in Bruno's infinite One, individual beings fare worse than ever: 'you come no nearer to [...] the infinite by being a man than by being an ant, or by being a star than

---

74. Bruno, *Cause, Principle, and Unity*, p. 59.
75. Bruno, *Cause, Principle, and Unity*, pp. 59-60.
76. Bruno, *Cause, Principle, and Unity*, p. 81.
77. Bruno, *Cause, Principle, and Unity*, p. 87.

by being a man, for you get no nearer to that infinite being by being the sun or the moon than by being a man, or an ant.[78] With even greater candor, Teofilo concludes that since 'unity is stable in its oneness and so remains forever [...] every other thing is vanity and nothingness'.[79] Individual forms are merely 'extrinsic', and escape the status of accidents only insofar as they are compressed in advance within the infinite bosom of matter. Bruno goes so far as to praise this matter with feminist tropes—not contesting the traditional identification of woman with matter, but retaining this traditional model while praising matter and woman as superior to form and man.

The reason I have spent so much time on Bruno is that he is very much with us today: not only in Iain Grant's model of nature retarded to yield specific things, but in a more widely popular trend that we might call 'pre-individualism'. Bruno's influence on Spinoza is sufficiently well known that some have gone so far as to accuse Spinoza of piracy, and of course the difference between Spinoza and Leibniz (that great reviver of individual substantial forms) is roughly analogous to the difference between pre-individualism and object-oriented metaphysics. Grant has already shown the extent to which Schelling builds on this tradition, and in more recent times there are many other representatives of it. My goal in the pages that remain is to urge that individual objects not be expelled from ontology in the manner that various radical philosophies have attempted.

3. ON BEHALF OF OBJECTS

Whatever the differences in the two positions just described, it would not be misleading to speak jointly of a Bruno/Grant option in metaphysics (though we should hope that the judicial system views the two authors differently). It is a refreshing option on which to reflect, after the long cold winter of human-world correlationism from which continental philosophy has barely begun to emerge. By invoking a reality deeper than any expression by the *logos*, indeed deeper than relations of any kind, this philosophy of matter strikes a crucial blow on behalf of realism. It is also a realism that we could safely call 'speculative' rather than commonsensical. My sole point of disagreement with this option lies in my view that *form* should not be viewed as purely *extrinsic*. According to that mistaken but popular view, things take on definite shape only when obstructed or when in some sort of relation, whether to the humans who like to observe and describe them or to non-human entities. Much as with neo-Platonism, things happen only *vertically* by retardation, contraction, or emanation from some more primal layer of the world. There is little room for *horizontal* interactions, as when fire burns cotton or rock shatters window. To use Bruno's own terminology, in a certain sense there is no cause from without, but all is principle from within. Matter already contains the seeds of all that it might become. Nothing important will ever come from the outside.

If primordial matter is something deeper than its articulation into specific pieces, then it is unclear why it should be laced in advance with pre-articulate seeds capable of generating specific trees and horses later on. In this way we run the risk of extreme monism, of a single rumbling *apeiron* without parts. More than this, individual entities are stripped of causal power here no less than in the occasionalist philosophies, even though pre-individual matter replaces God as the medium where things are tacitly linked. This is somewhat reminiscent of what DeLanda (following Bergson) calls the

---

78. Bruno, *Cause, Principle, and Unity*, p. 88.

79. Bruno, *Cause, Principle, and Unity*, p. 90.

'heterogeneous yet continuous' character of reality. Matter is allowed to be both one and many, profiting from the virtues of both unity and plurality without suffering from the vices of either. Since we pay a heavy price when we strip individual things of all causal power and turn them into a petrified forest at the surface of reality, it might be asked where the profit of this maneuver lies. What these positions hope to gain, I believe, is a worthy advance into a new spirit of realism. The position that I have called the Bruno/Grant option is well aware that when things are too highly specific they have little room to change. Therefore things are granted a depth beneath any specific form—deeper than all flowers, coins, and wood. This position is superior to many others in its awareness that things as encountered in relation are always a kind of distortion. We heard Bruno's own words to the effect that 'the fact of being a principle of [something] does not express an absolute and substantial nature, but a nature that is accidental and relative to that which is principled [...]'[80] What is offered instead is a subterranean kingdom that exists in its own right rather than for something else, and which is capable of becoming all things since it is all of them and none.

One problem with this model is that it solves the problem of communication between things only by fiat. I have often claimed that the forgotten problem of occasionalism still haunts contemporary philosophy in two different forms, and indeed this problem lies at the heart of both the undermining and overmining of objects. Occasionalism, in brief, means one or both of the following two related doctrines: first, no two things can relate to one another without God serving as the mediator; second, God must recreate the universe in every instant with no moment of time flowing smoothly into the next. In both forms occasionalism is a sort of quantized philosophy, with the world broken up into chunks of time or space that cannot easily be linked together again, so that only God can save us. This occasionalism has its origins in the theology of early medieval Iraq. For some students of the *Qur'an*, it was blasphemy not only to allow other creators besides God, but to allow any other causal agents at all. No entity affects any other; their proximity merely provides the occasion for God to intervene and make things happen directly. After a long delay, this notion finally enters Europe in the seventeenth century and runs rampant, with a number of prominent metaphysical systems allowing God alone to serve as a causal medium. In all of these philosophies except Berkeley's, the existence of individual substances is never denied; God is invoked only to explain their mutual interaction.

Now, this occasionalist position might seem like the opposite of the Bruno/Grant option, in which individual substances play little independent role, and where God is seemingly never invoked as the solution to any problem. But if we look a bit closer, the two positions (occasionalism and Bruno/Grant) begin to show similarities. It is noteworthy that both positions agree that relations are extrinsic, that nothing boils down to its relations. The sole and towering difference, of course, is that occasionalism holds that individual things have forms in their own right, while for Bruno/Grant any contracted or retarded form is already purely extrinsic. Even as concerns the narrower question of God, it is easy to find outright pantheism in Bruno, as when he refers in the Fifth Dialogue to the One as the 'supreme being' in which act does not differ from potency.[81] I will not speculate on Grant's theological views here, but even if he were to reject the 'pantheist' label, I very much doubt that he would feel repulsed or insulted by

---

80. Bruno, *Cause, Principle, and Unity*, p. 60, my emphasis.
81. Bruno, *Cause, Principle, and Unity*, p. 93.

it. In any case all of these can safely be called undermining positions, since they undercut individual objects with a global principle that underlies them all, whether matter
or God. Such positions hold surprising appeal even now, at least in beatnik-bohemi-
an circles like our own that make little effort to appeal to today's analytic mainstream.
The 'occasionalist God' version of this position can still be found in Whitehead, for
whom the eternal objects found in God are the medium for all relations between actual entities. But the 'turbulent pre-individual' version of the position is perhaps even
more appealing to readers today, and has other variants aside from those found in
Grant, DeLanda, and Simondon.

But the more popular option today is still the type that I have called 'overmining'. Here the individual object is not something too specific or too frozen into a determinate shape that needs some deeper principle of dynamism. Instead, the object is
treated as a useless fiction—a mere nickname for a set of relations, qualities, or parts
that are all tangibly accessible, not in the least bit spooky or mysterious. Such a position need not be correlationism. For instance, neither Latour nor Whitehead should
be called correlationists, since a human being does not need to be one of the two terms
in any relation. Nonetheless, both Latour and Whitehead must count as overminers
of objects. For as Latour puts it so clearly, an object is nothing more than whatever
it transforms, modifies, perturbs, or creates. And however one might read Latour on
the question of realism (the controversy continues), Whitehead is undeniably a realist. Why is this important? Because it suggests that *the distinction between realism and anti-
realism may not be the key question in metaphysics after all.* The reason is that any realist who
thinks that reality can be modeled in terms of tangibly accessible traits is in some ways
a nearer cousin of idealism than of other realist positions such as Bruno's, Grant's, or
my own, in which the work of the *logos* is always extrinsic and reality always exceeds
any attempt to grasp it.

Let me first recall briefly why I think the mainstream Hume- and Kant-inspired
philosophy of our time is really just an upside-down version of occasionalism. Remember first the biographical anecdote that the freethinker David Hume was a great ad-
mirer of the arch-Catholic occasionalist Nicolas Malebranche, viewed as his forerun-
ner in the assertion that there is no necessary connection between two things that seem
to happen together. Admittedly, while the solution of Malebranche is that only God
can relate two things together, it would be madness to claim that Hume says as much.
But notice that Hume merely draws the opposite lesson from precisely the same problem. For in a sense, there is no problem of relations for Hume at all. Things are *already*
linked in human experience or habit; what remains in doubt is whether they are independent things *outside* these relations, hidden entities laden with causal power. The
same holds *mutatis mutandis* for Kant, still the paragon of academically respectable philosophy in our time. In today's epistemological deadlock of mainstream philosophy we
start from the relations between things in experience, and maintain an agnostic distance from their autonomous power outside such experience. Even among those positions that pass for 'realism', there are many that earn this name only by thinking that
things are real outside the human mind, while assuming that these things themselves
would be nothing more than a bundle of objective qualities. For the undermining position, reality precedes relations—whether reality be individual substances linked by
God, or a pre-individual realm that serves many of the same functions as that God.
For the more socially acceptable overmining position, the things are already in rela-

tion to each other or to us, and what is called into question is simply their independence from all such relations.

Kant is often credited with rewriting the history of philosophy by distinguishing between rationalists and empiricists and mixing the best of both. With each passing year, this claim increasingly strikes me as false. Note that 'rationalism' and 'empiricism' are merely epistemological terms that refer to two ways of *knowing* the world. The deeper metaphysical distinction is the one I have just described between occasionalism and upside-down occasionalism. Only recently did I realize that scientific naturalism is not an undermining position at all, but an overmining one. Yes, naturalism generally holds that dreams, fables, societies, and unicorns can be undercut in favor of tiny physical particles, but this is merely a decision about what *kinds* of objects exist. More interesting is what they think happens when we finally reach the ultimate realities. And here we find that naturalism sees no great difficulty in replacing things with *models* of things—with a specific set of palpable qualities. Whether or not quarks turn out to be the final constituent of all hadrons, naturalism sees no problem with defining a quark in terms of a set of traits. Whereas the Bruno/Grant model sees Aristotle's substantial forms as too specific to be helpful, the naturalist model tends to view them the other way, as vague and useless compared with hardheaded evidence. In a metaphysical sense, it is true that naturalism is a form of realism. But insofar as it overmines rather than undermines the object by calling it a useless hypothesis and replacing it with a knowable set of features, it actually belongs on the same side of the fence as idealism, relationism, and correlationism—not on the side of the occasionalist or pre-individualist models where objects are a surface-effect rather than a useless hypothesis. And if this is true then the entire question of 'realism' may be misleading, given that such a diverse group as Berkeley, Meillassoux, Latour, Whitehead, Brassier, and the natural sciences would all fall on the same side of the fence, with Bruno, Grant, DeLanda, Bergson, and Simondon on the other. Note that in this model we have realists on both sides of this divide, and therefore 'realism' would not be a suitable mark of difference between two schools. Instead of distinguishing between realists and idealists, we might distinguish instead between the underminers and overminers of objects, who might be described respectively as the heirs of occasionalism and empiricism. But while the empiricist side would still be recognizable to its ancestors, what I have called the 'occasionalist' side abandons individual substances, and hence in our time looks a lot more like Bruno than Malebranche.

Admittedly, this view of the various philosophical positions is biased, since it makes sense only from the object-oriented perspective that I recommend. But there is no neutral history of philosophy; all such histories are guided by the view of the author as to what is more and less important, and by no means will we settle that issue here. What I have opposed are all the various 'radical' attempts to eliminate the object from philosophy, whether in the name of relations, qualities, shapeless matter, or anything else. The object is what is autonomous but not *entirely* autonomous, since it exists in permanent tension with all those realities that are meant to replace it completely—its qualities, its parts, its moments, its relations, its accidents, or its accessibility to humans.

I will close with a final thought about materialism. In this article I have criticized two opposite 'radical' strategies: undermining objects with a deeper principle, or overmining them with a series of visible relations or traits. There is another name besides 'radical philosophy' that applies to large portions of both sides of this divide, and that name is 'materialism'. For materialism can either mean the scientific materialism in which larger entities are explained by tinier physical entities whose qualities certainly do not withdraw from all access or measurement (overmining). Or, it can mean the Bruno/Grant option of a rumbling *materia* laced with all things, and flouting the good sense of the empirical sciences as we know them (undermining). In this respect, my own position amounts to *realism without materialism*. Or, turning from Werner Herzog to the style of Orwell's *Animal Farm*: 'Realism good! Materialism bad! Realism good! Materialism bad!'

4

Mining Conditions: A Response to Harman

Iain Hamilton Grant

First of all, let me reiterate the substantive lines of agreement Harman notes between us, and specifically the first of these lines, from which all the others stem—that the 'inanimate world' is a crucial orientation for any realist metaphysics. We both disagree, then, with Hegel's stupefying judgment in the *Encyclopaedia* (§ 339) that there is nothing philosophically pertinent in geology. And we agree on the *necessity*, as Harman pithily puts it, that metaphysics *think a reality beyond our thinking*, because if thinking is not thinking reality, there is not thinking at all.

Secondly, before I rush into a reply so brief as to be ungracious, let me express my profound thanks to Graham for transposing the problems addressed in my Schelling book into the richer philosophical world his thinking inhabits; and for risking ridicule by nominating me alongside Giordano Bruno as the co-authors of an option in metaphysics. Although it will appear churlish to scruple at such fine company, yet I must, since Bruno in the end proves too attached to the Aristotelian concepts of the ultimacy of substance onto which, as Harman delightedly catalogues, he nevertheless pours such scorn. Yet in so doing, Bruno identifies precisely the nature of the problem—is there a relation of anteriority between substance and potency in the nature of matter?

Accordingly, while I agree with Harman's assessment of our agreements, I disagree with him as regards our disagreement. I do not think, that is, that the difference between our realisms can be mapped onto the undermining One, as against a self-subsisting Many, substance problem as he does here. Rather, the difference lies between two conceptions of actuality, one of which I will call the depth model, and which consists either of objects all the way down or of a single ground from which all emerge; and the other, the genetic model, which makes depth regional with respect to anteriority. Moreover, although Harman identifies his disagreement with me as lying in the advocacy of a philosophy of nature in general, which he does not share, and in a dynamic or powers-ontological philosophy of nature in particular, since this has the effect of rendering form extrinsic or derived, a major element of his criticism of the undermining position is that it 'strip[s] all power from horses and minerals'. In other words, it is clear that it is a requirement of Harman's metaphysics that objects possess 'productive force in their own right'.[1] My question to him is therefore exactly the one he poses to me: how are such powers-possessing objects to be conceived on the object-oriented model?

To clarify both my reasons for scrupling at Bruno and disagreeing with Harman's disagreement with me, I will first outline the manner in which Bruno *equivocates over anteriority* with respect to substance and power, and the reason for it. I will then briefly explore the problem of anteriority before situating the problem of the extrinsic determination of objects from which our disagreement, on Harman's account, radiates, not in terms of the One-or-Many-substances problem as Harman presents it here, but rather in terms of the problem of the *possibility of powers* on the object-oriented model. My argument is that actuality must be "virtually" expanded if the objects whose metaphysical status Harman gloriously defends, are not to be rendered as impotent as he fears.

As Harman notes, Bruno does not so much abandon substance as maintain that it is one. It is precisely in order to maintain a single substance from which everything derives that Bruno's metaphysics is 'ambivalent', as Werner Beierwaltes has argued,[2] between substance and powers. In Cause, Principle and Unity, Teofilo stipulates that 'matter ... can be considered in two ways: first, as potency; second, as substratum',[3] and in fact maintains both. If the substratum is eliminated in the interests of potencies, and objects therefore undermined, the substantial unity of the universe is eliminated by the same token. Hence Teofilo's assertion that the 'one indivisible being ... is the matter in which so many forms are united'.[4] If, conversely, potencies are eliminated in the interests of the substrate, then no differentiation, no formation or information, of this unique substantial continuum may arise. Hence Bruno's conclusion that both substance and potency must be integrally maintained to form the One, Great, self-differentiating Object: it is only 'in the absolute potency and absolute act' that matter is 'all it can be',[5] and only 'as a substance' that 'the whole is one'.[6]

The problem is, however, that Bruno does not resolve this substance-potency bipolarity of matter, but resorts to making substance and potency coeval; more exactly, he denies the anteriority of potency with respect to substance: 'the power to be accompanies the being in act and does not come before it'.[7] This is, however, an asymmetrical denial of anteriority: none such is issued with respect to substance. In the end, Bruno is simply not anti-Aristotelian enough, because he maintains that there must be a ground to mine in the first place.

MINING AS SUCH

Now I do not dispute that ground is so mineable, nor indeed do I dispute the actuality of grounds. What I dispute is their metaphysical sufficiency. What happens when this ground *is* mined? Take any object whatsoever, on the Schellingian condition that it is

1. Graham Harman, 'On the Undermining of Objects', in Levi Bryant, Nick Srnicek and Graham Harman (eds.), *The Speculative Turn: Continental Materialism and Realism*, re.press, Melbourne, 2010, pp. 21-40, p. 33, my emphasis.

2. Werner Beierwaltes, *Identität und Differenz*, Frankfurt am Main, Klostermann, 1980, 188.

3. Giordano Bruno, *Cause, Principle and Unity*, trans. R. de Lucca, Cambridge, Cambridge University Press, 1998, p. 65.

4. Bruno, *Cause, Principle and Unity*, p. 77.

5. Bruno, *Cause, Principle and Unity*, p. 79.

6. Bruno, *Cause, Principle and Unity*, p. 69.

7. Bruno, *Cause, Principle and Unity*, p. 66.

not impossible in nature—a mountain, a phone, an idea, an animal, a hallucination—and ask what is involved in its existence. The conditions on which its existence depends do not belong to that object—they are not "its" conditions, but conditions that possibilize it. Since conditions exceed the object, they are equally the conditions involved in other existing objects, and that cannot therefore be specified as belonging to that object alone, nor as terminating in it. That is, the causes of mountain-formation are also causes of geogony, of ideation, of animals, of fever-dreams and of telecommunications. Were this not the case, then each set of objects would envelope its own, wholly separate universe. Either backtracking the causal sequence terminates—even if ideally—in a ground prior to all grounds, i.e., in *substance* or the 'ultimate subject [*hypokeimenon eschaton*]' (*Metaphysics* 1017b24), or it does not. If the former, we have the source of Bruno's problem in refusing to abandon Aristotelian substance in the philosophy of matter and the consequent yet insufficiently determining asymmetrical denial of anteriority to powers; and if the latter, then either substantial existence is self-limiting and inherently particular ('objects'), or it involves sequences that exceed it in principle and in fact. The problem is, I take it, that self-limiting particular substances involve the hypothesis of an irreducible object-actualism that rejects any prospect of the 'becoming of being', in the interests of a universe the actuality of which is eternally what and as it is. This is because if it does not involve such a hypothesis, then the question of what is involved in particular substances opens up onto their genesis. If the actual involves genesis, then at no point do presently actual objects exhaust the universe.

The denial that actuality involves genesis, and the question of the extrinsicality of form, is not confined to speculative metaphysics. A similar actualism formed the background to the epigenetic critique of preformationism in the late eighteenth century life sciences, in which proponents of the latter view argue for an 'emboîtement infini' of organism by organism, with no upper or lower limit, with the result that 'organisms are and remain through the centuries what they always have been [so that] the forms of animals are unalterable'.[8] Although Kant disparages preformationism as 'deny[ing] the formative force of nature to all individuals, so as to have [it] come directly from the hand of the creator' (Ak. V: 423)—that is, as asserting form as extrinsic to the individuals that possess it—Leibniz, similarly noting that here lies the problem of the 'origin of forms', argues exactly the converse: 'exact inquiries … have shown us that organic bodies in nature are never produced from chaos …, but always through seeds in which there is, no doubt, some preformation' (Monadology § 74). The origin of form problem thus encounters the problems of genesis not extrinsically, but intrinsically, since either substantial forms—the 'non-accidental forms of individual things', as Harman puts it—are always what they are, or they become what they are.

The same problem is echoed in Hegel's resolution of the neo-Platonist problem of the Eternity of the World, which Proclus advocated and Philoponus disputed. 'Eternity', says the *Encyclopaedia*, is the 'absolute present, the Now, without before and after'. Rather than denying, with Kant, the possibility of a solution to the problem of whether the world has a beginning in time, Hegel eliminates its actuality. That is, where preformationism denies actuality to genesis, Hegel expels the 'before and after' from an actualized eternity: 'the world is created, is now being created, and has eternally been created' (*Enc.* § 247). Anteriority becomes an ideal differentiation within an actual eter-

---

8. Etienne Geoffroy Saint-Hilaire, 'Divers mémoires sur des grands sauriens', *Mémoires de l'Academie Royale des Sciences de l'Institut de France*, no. 12, 1833, p. 89.

nity, so that it is only within this ideality that 'the planet is the veritable *prius*' (*Enc.* §
280). Geology isn't simply philosophically irrelevant to Hegel, but fatal to the eternity of the world, precisely because it *necessarily* posits an anteriority even to the becoming *of* the planetary object.

Putting both problems together, we can see how preformationist arguments for the
homunculus-in-the-egg having a homunculus in its egg[9] involve the incorporation of
anteriority and posteriority into just such an eternal present. The differences between
all these antagonists lie not only in their assumptions concerning a One or a Many of
substance, but in the means by which anteriority is eliminated by it. That is to say, anteriority does not remain extrinsic to substance, but is incorporated within it, suggesting a topological asymmetry between container and contained, with the former always
in excess of the latter, or the product in excess of its production, from the ground up.

THE GEOLOGY LESSON

So we begin to recover geology's philosophical significance from Hegel's dismissal of
it. We should not, however, hold Hegel alone responsible for this, since although he
doesn't draw directly on them, his theses echo James Hutton's famous declaration, in
his 'Theory of the Earth' that, in investigating the formation of the planet, 'we find no
vestige of a beginning,—no prospect of an end'.[10] Hutton is not, like Hegel, joining the
arguments concerning the eternity of the world, but pursuing the consequences of reasoning about its formation on the basis of observable causes. Despite its antipathy towards cosmogony, and to 'questions as to the origin of things',[11] the precise difference
between the Huttonian and Hegelian actualisms lies in the assertion of the former
that 'the oldest rocks' are 'the last of an antecedent series',[12] an antecedence that Hegel eliminates because it attests to anteriority as non-recoverable exteriority. Because
the geological series cannot complete the real-time recovery of its origins, and because
neither can it avoid opening onto cosmogonic questions, geology makes the depth of
the earth's crust into a relative measure of an antecedence exterior to it, sculpting it.

Thus the earth is not an object containing its ground within itself, like the prefor-
mationists' animal series; but rather a series or process of grounding with respect to its
consequents. If geology, or the 'mining process', opens onto an ungroundedness at the
core of any object, this is precisely because there is no 'primal layer of the world', no
'ultimate substrate' or substance on which everything ultimately rests. The lines of se-
rial dependency, stratum upon stratum, that geology uncovers do not rest on anything
at all, but are the records of *actions* antecedent in the production of consequents. Were
this not the case, how could inorganic nature be the philosophical protagonist that
Harman and I both argue it is?

Moreover, the antecedents in question are necessary if geology, mining, are to be
possible at all. In other words, geology *retrospects* a production antecedent to its beginning, but does so as a new production dependent on that same beginning. "No planet, no geology" is not just a truism with regard to the definition of that science; it

---

9. According to Gould, this as a 'caricature' of preformationism which he sets out to correct. Stephen Jay
Gould, *Ontogeny and Phylogeny*, Cambridge, Harvard University Press, 1977, p. 19.

10. James Hutton, 'Theory of the Earth; or an Investigation of the Laws Observable in the Composition, Dissolution and Restoration of Land upon the Globe', *Transactions of the Royal Society of Edinburgh*, no.
1, 1788, p. 304.

11. Charles Lyell, *Principles of Geology*, James Secord (ed.), Harmondsworth, Penguin, 1997, p. 8.

12. Lyell, *Principles of Geology*, p. 16.

also stipulates the physical conditions of ideation—meteorological metastasis, chemical complexification, speciation, neurogony, informed inquiry, and so forth—and that they have taken place. The geology lesson therefore teaches that objects or substantial forms depend on an anteriority always more extensive than them, and that such anteriority is always the domain of production.

THE BRUNO PROBLEM

This brings us back to the Bruno Problem, which consists of the asymmetrical denial of anteriority to powers in respect of substance. Positively construed, it amounts to the assertion of a substantial anteriority, of Aristotle's ultimate hypokeimenon, a ground as the base of each or of all things, and is the source, therefore, of Bruno's equivocation. The problem is, such a ground cannot be mined, as it is only on the basis of this ground that depth, the medium of mining, becomes possible. Undermining, in other words, becomes impossible on the basis of substantial anteriority. Since it is not substantiality as such that Harman seeks to defend against under- and over-miners, but substantial forms, the defence of objects 'all the way down' entails the abandonment of anteriority, not depth. Mining, for Harman, must always encounter objects (amongst which, he notes,[13] relations are to be included) without end. His assertion is therefore that there are always substances in the plural, which is how he resolves the Bruno problem.

The other way to resolve the Bruno problem is not to make the denial of anteriority symmetrical, which simply displaces the issue along an infinite chain, or brings it to an arbitrary halt, but to replace it with the assertion of anteriority as such. In this way, however, the endless displacement of the symmetrical denial already entails the necessity of at least relative anteriority, as we saw with Hutton's geological series: anteriority in no way negates the existence or possibility of substantial being, but is its *necessarily* ongoing production. At the very least, powers are entailed by the very possibility of an anterior and a posterior, if these are not merely relative; but these powers are the articulation of what is in particular and *contingent* ways. Otherwise, we have the inert being that Fichte, for instance, makes into a categorical imperative of the science of knowledge, and that Schelling's *Ideas for a Philosophy of Nature* struggles against in his diagnosis of the dualisms entailed by the passivist theories of matter common both to Fichtean subjectivist idealism and Newtonian mechanical materialism. Accordingly, mining is not undermining, but uncovering the necessary anteriority for any and all objects. This is the route that Kielmeyer's theories of natural history took, and that drove Schelling's investigations in the philosophy of nature. The philosophical pertinence of natural history consists therefore in the demonstration of the constancy of production, of powers *always at work*, always *intrinsic* to the formative process.

As in Bruno, so in contemporary philosophy of nature, powers are more often than not considered to be the properties or dispositions of *objects*, and to be grounded therein. The suspicion is that, were powers 'ungrounded' in such objects, all prospect of individuation would be lost. What this illustrates is the dualism that lies at the root of Bruno's post-Aristotelian substance-power problem and its modern proponents: powers, conceived in abstraction from substance, 'never travel', that is, they do nothing. Accordingly, substance, conceived in abstraction from powers, must somehow re-

---

13. Graham Harman, *Guerrilla Metaphysics: Phenomenology and the Carpentry of Things*, Chicago, Open Court, 2005, p. 90.

ceive articulation from a non-substantial exteriority in order to compose a powers on-tology that can account for discrete dispositional particularities.

Clearly, then, the problem stems from the mutual abstraction of becoming and thing, a problem whose solution Plato already foreshadowed in coining the principle of immanence in the form of 'the becoming of being [*genesis eis ousian*]' (*Philebus* 26d8): it cannot be other-than-being that becomes, or becoming would *not be* at all. In the present context, this means: 'the mark of all being is power'. Powers are inseparable from their products; if no products, then there were no powers, but not the reverse. It is neither the case that things ground powers, nor the converse; rather, powers *unground* the ultimacy attributed to substantial being and necessitate, therefore, rather than eliminate, the becomings of objects. Powers accordingly *are* natural history, in the precise sense that powers are not simply formally or logically inseparable from what they do, but *are* what they do, and compose being in its becoming. The thoroughgoing contingency of natural production undermines, I would claim, any account of permanently actual substantial forms precisely because such contingents entail the actuality not simply of abstractly separable forms, but of the powers that sculpt them. This is where Harman's retooling of vicarious causation will become the focus for discussion, but which must take place elsewhere.

Nonseparability or immanence is not therefore fatal to objects, but only to their actuality being reducible to their objectality. It is for this reason that I think the problem on the different sides of which Harman and I find ourselves needs to be played out at the level of the limits of the actual and the actuality of antecedence. What nonseparability is fatal to is any metaphysics of the ultimacy of impotent substance, whether of the One or the Many. If we are genuinely to take the 'inanimate world as a philosophical protagonist', as Harman and I both do, then its actions must involve powers that refuse reduction to the inert substratum that made matter into 'almost nothing' for Aristotle and Augustine.

5

Concepts and Objects

Ray Brassier

1. The question 'What is real?' stands at the crossroads of metaphysics and epistemology. More exactly, it marks the juncture of metaphysics and epistemology with the seal of conceptual representation.

2. Metaphysics understood as the investigation into *what* there is intersects with epistemology understood as the enquiry into how we *know* what there is. This intersection of knowing and being is articulated through a theory of conception that explains how thought gains traction on being.

3. That the articulation of thought and being is necessarily conceptual follows from the Critical injunction which rules out any recourse to the doctrine of a pre-established harmony between reality and ideality. Thought is not guaranteed access to being; being is not inherently thinkable. There is no cognitive ingress to the real save through the concept. Yet the real itself is not to be confused with the concepts through which we know it. The fundamental problem of philosophy is to understand how to reconcile these two claims.

4. We gain access to the structure of reality via a machinery of conception which extracts intelligible indices from a world that is not designed to be intelligible and is not originarily infused with meaning. Meaning is a function of conception and conception involves representation—though this is *not* to say that conceptual representation can be construed in terms of word-world mappings. It falls to conceptual rationality to forge the explanatory bridge from thought to being.

5. Thus the metaphysical exploration of the structure of being can only be carried out in tandem with an epistemological investigation into the nature of conception. For we cannot understand *what* is real unless we understand what 'what' *means*, and we cannot understand what 'what' means without understanding what 'means' *is*, but we cannot hope to understand what 'means' is without understanding what 'is' *means*.

6. This much Heidegger knew.[1] Unlike Heidegger however, we will not conjure a virtuous circle of ontological interpretation from the necessary circularity of our pre-

---

[1]. cf. Martin Heidegger, *Being and Time*, trans. J. Macquarrie and E. Robinson, Oxford, Blackwell, 1962, 'Introduction'.

ontological understanding of how things can be said to be. The metaphysical investigation of being cannot be collapsed into a hermeneutical interpretation of the being of the investigator and the different ways in which the latter understands things to be. Although metaphysical investigation cannot be divorced from enquiry into what meaning is, the point of the latter is to achieve a metaphysical circumscription of the domain of sense which avoids the phenomenological equivocation between meaning and being.

7. If we are to avoid collapsing the investigation of being into the interpretation of meaning we must attain a proper understanding of what it is for something to *be* independently of our conceiving, understanding and interpreting its being. But this will only be achieved once we possess a firm grip on the origins, scope, and limits of our ability to conceive, understand, and interpret *what* things are.

8. The metaphysical desideratum does not consist in attaining a clearer understanding of what we mean by being or what being means for us (as the entities we happen to be because of our natural and cultural history), but to break out of the circle wherein the meaning of being remains correlated with our being as enquirers about meaning into a properly theoretical understanding of what *is* real regardless of our allegedly pre-ontological understanding of it—but not, please note, irrespective of our ways of conceiving it. Such a non-hermeneutical understanding of metaphysical investigation imposes an epistemological constraint on the latter, necessitating an account that explains how sapient creatures gain cognitive access to reality through conception.

9. Some might be tempted to think that this arduous epistemological detour through the analysis of the conceptual infrastructure underlying our understanding of terms such as 'what', 'is', and 'real' can be obviated by a doctrine of ontological univocity which dissolves representation and with it the tri-partite distinction between representing, represented, and reality. Proponents of a univocal conception of being as difference, in which conception is just another difference in being, would effectively supplant the metaphysical question 'What differences are real?' with an affirmation of the reality of differences: differentiation becomes the sole and sufficient index of reality. If being is difference, and only differences are real, then the traditional metaphysical task of 'carving nature at the joints' via an adequate conception of being can be supplanted by re-injecting thought directly into being so as to obtain the non-representational intuition of being as real difference. This would be the Deleuzean option. However, the celebrated 'immanence' of Deleuzean univocity is won at the cost of a pre-Critical fusion of thinking, meaning, and being, and the result is a panpsychism that simply ignores rather than obviates the epistemological difficulties signaled above. The claim that 'everything is real' is egregiously uninformative—and its uninformativeness is hardly palliated by the addendum that everything is real precisely insofar as it thinks since, for panpsychism, to think is to differ.[2]

10. Meaning cannot be invoked either as originary constituent of reality (as it is for Aristotelian essentialism) or as originary condition of access to the world (as it is for Heidegger's hermeneutic ontology): it must be recognized to be a conditioned phenomenon generated through meaningless yet tractable mechanisms operative at the sub-personal (neurocomputational) as well as supra-personal (sociocultural) level. This

---

2. For a critical account of the role of panpsychism in Deleuze's ontology see my article 'The Expression of Meaning in Deleuze's Ontological Proposition', *Pli: The Warwick Journal of Philosophy*, no. 19, 2008, pp. 1-36.

is a naturalistic imperative. But it is important to distinguish naturalism as a metaphysical doctrine engaging in an ontological hypostasis of entities and processes postulated by current science, from naturalism as an epistemological constraint stipulating that accounts of conception, representation, and meaning refrain from invoking entities or processes which are in principle refractory to any possible explanation by current or future science. It is the latter that should be embraced. Methodological naturalism simply stipulates that meaning (i.e. conceptual understanding) may be drawn upon as an epistemological *explanans* only so long as the concomitant gain in explanatory purchase can be safely discharged at a more fundamental metaphysical level where the function and origin of linguistic representation can be accounted for without resorting to transcendental skyhooks (such as originary sense-bestowing acts of consciousness, being-in-the-world, or the *Lebenswelt*). The Critical acknowledgement that reality is neither innately meaningful nor inherently intelligible entails that the capacities for linguistic signification and conceptual understanding be accounted for as processes within the world—processes through which sapient creatures gain access to the structure of a reality whose order does not depend upon the conceptual resources through which they come to know it.

11. The junction of metaphysics and epistemology is marked by the intersection of two threads: the epistemological thread that divides sapience from sentience and the metaphysical thread that distinguishes the reality of the concept from the reality of the object. Kant taught us to discern the first thread. But his correlationist heirs subsequently underscored its significance at the expense of the metaphysical thread. The occultation of the latter, following the liquidation of the in-itself, marks correlationism's slide from epistemological sobriety into ontological incontinence.[3] The challenge now is to hold to the metaphysical thread while learning how to reconnect it to the epistemological thread. For just as epistemology without metaphysics is empty, metaphysics without epistemology is blind.

12. Kant underscored the difference between knowing, understood as the taking of something *as* something, classifying an object under a concept, and sensing, the registration of a somatic stimulus. Conception is answerable to normative standards of truth and falsity, correctness and incorrectness, which develop from but cannot be collapsed into the responsive dispositions through which one part of the world—whether parrot or thermostat—transduces information from another part of the world—sound waves or molecular kinetic energy. Knowledge is not information: to know is to endorse a claim answerable to the norm of truth *simpliciter*, irrespective of ends. By way of contrast, the transmission and transduction of information requires no endorsement; it may be adequate or inadequate relative to certain ends, but never 'true' or 'false'. The epistemological distinctiveness of the former is the obverse of the metaphysical ubiquity of the latter.

13. Critique eviscerates the object, voiding it of substance and rendering metaphysics weightless. Tipping the scale towards conception, it paves the way for conceptual idealism by depriving epistemology of its metaphysical counterweight. Conceptual idealism emphasizes the normative valence of knowing at the cost of eliding the metaphysical autonomy of the in-itself. It is in the work of Wilfrid Sellars that the delicate equilibrium between a critical epistemology and a rationalist metaphysics is re-

---

3. For an account of correlationism, see Quentin Meillassoux's *After Finitude: An Essay on the Necessity of Contingency*, trans. Ray Brassier, London and New York, Continuum, 2008.

stored.[4] Re-inscribing Kant's transcendental difference between noesis and aisthesis within nature, Sellars develops an inferentialist account of the normative structure of conception that allows him to prosecute a scientific realism unencumbered by the epistemological strictures of empiricism.[5] In doing so, Sellars augurs a new alliance between post-Kantian rationalism and post-Darwinian naturalism. His naturalistic rationalism[6] purges the latter of those residues of Cartesian dogmatism liable to be seized upon by irrationalists eager to denounce the superstition of 'pure' reason. Where the prejudices of metaphysical rationalism hinder reason in its struggle against the Cerberus of a resurgent irrationalism—phenomenological, vitalist, panpsychist—Sellars' account of the normative strictures of conceptual rationality licenses the scientific realism that necessitates rather than obviates the critical revision of the folk-metaphysical categories which irrationalism would consecrate.[7]

14. Ultimately, reason itself enjoins us to abjure supernatural (i.e. metaphysical) conceptions of rationality. An eliminative materialism that elides the distinction between sapience and sentience on pragmatist grounds undercuts the normative constraint that provides the cognitive rationale for elimination. The norm of truth not only

---

4. See in particular Sellars' demanding but profoundly rewarding *Science and Metaphysics: Variations on Kantian Themes*, London Routledge & Kegan Paul, 1968. Contrary to widespread opinion, Sellars is a philosophical writer of exceptional distinction and elegance. His prose—obdurate, lapidary, elliptical—exerts greater philosophical power and communicates more of genuine substance through obliquity than the unctuous blandishments of allegedly superior (i.e. more easily digestible) stylists. Vacuous suavity remains the abiding deficiency of self-consciously 'good' writing in the American pragmatist vein—a congruence of stylistic and philosophical facility particularly exemplified by James and Rorty—this is too often the specific context in which Sellars is chastised for not being a 'good' writer.

5. Sellars' inferentialist account of rationality has been developed and expanded by Robert Brandom, the contemporary philosopher who has probably done most to draw attention to the significance of Sellars' philosophical achievement. See Brandom's *Making it Explicit: Reasoning Representing and Discursive Commitment*, Cambridge, Harvard University Press, 1994 and *Articulating Reasons: An Introduction to Inferentialism*, Cambridge, Harvard University Press, 2000.

6. Or 'rationalistic naturalism': straddling as it does the divide between post- Kantian rationalism and post-Darwinian naturalism, Sellars' philosophical project is susceptible to very different interpretations depending on whether one emphasizes its rationalistic or naturalistic aspect. The rationalist component of Sellars' legacy has been developed by Robert Brandom. By way of contrast, its naturalistic aspect has influenced such uncompromising philosophical materialists as Paul Churchland, Ruth Garrett Millikan, and Daniel Dennett. Although Brandom's 'neo-Hegelian' interpretation of Sellars has dominated recent discussion of the latter's legacy—arguably to the detriment of his naturalism, and particularly his commitment to scientific realism—the importance accorded to the scientific image in Sellars' 'synoptic vision' has been emphasized by James O'Shea in his important recent study *Wilfrid Sellars: Naturalism with a Normative Turn*, Cambridge, Polity, 2007. O'Shea's work provides a much-needed corrective to the dominant neo-Hegelian appropriation of Sellars' legacy.

7. cf. Sellars, *Science and Metaphysics*, p. 173. The concept of 'folk metaphysics', understood as the set of default conceptual categories in terms of which humans make sense of the world prior to any sort of theoretical reflection, is beginning to play an increasingly important role in cognitive science. Faces, persons, bodies, solid objects, voluntary motion, cause-effect, are all examples of folk-metaphysical categories in this sense. One obvious implication of this research is that phenomenological ontology is simply folk metaphysics writ large. cf. Pascal Boyer 'Natural Epistemology or Evolved Metaphysics? Developmental Evidence for Early-Developed, Intuitive, Category-Specific, Incomplete and Stubborn Metaphysical Presumptions', *Philosophical Psychology*, no. 13, 2000, pp. 277 -297; Pascal Boyer and H. Clark Barrett 'Evolved Intuitive Ontology: Integrating Neural, Behavioral and Developmental Aspects of Domain-Specificity', in David Buss (ed.), *Handbook of Evolutionary Psychology*, New York, Wiley, 2005. Scott Atran provides a particularly suggestive account of the extent to which Aristotelian metaphysics systematizes pre-philosophical intuitions in his *Cognitive Foundations of Natural History: Towards an Anthropology Science*, Cambridge, Cambridge University Press, 1993. For a critical discussion of some of Atran's claims, see Michael T. Ghiselin, 'Folk Metaphysics and the Anthropology of Science', *Behavioural and Brain Sciences*, no. 21, 1998, pp. 573-574.

provides the most intransigent bulwark against the supernatural conception of norma-
tivity; it also provides the necessary rationale for the elimination of folk metaphysics.

15. Unless reason itself carries out the de-mystification of rationality, irrationalism
triumphs by adopting the mantle of a scepticism that allows it to denounce reason as
a kind of faith. The result is the post-modern scenario, in which the rationalist imperative to explain phenomena by penetrating to the reality beyond appearances is di-
agnosed as the symptom of an implicitly theological metaphysical reductionism. The
metaphysical injunction to know the noumenal is relinquished by a post-modern 'irreductionism' which abjures the epistemological distinction between appearance and reality the better to salvage the reality of every appearance, from sunsets to Santa Claus.[8]

16. Bruno Latour is undoubtedly among the foremost proponents of this irreductionist creed. His *Irreductions*[9] pithily distils familiar Nietzschean homilies, minus the
anxious bombast of Nietzsche's intemperate Sturm und Drang. With his suave and
unctuous prose, Latour presents the urbane face of post-modern irrationalism. How
does he proceed? First, he reduces reason to discrimination: "'Reason' is applied to the
work of allocating agreement and disagreement between words. It is a matter of taste
and feeling, know-how and connoisseurship, class and status. We insult, frown, pout,
clench our fists, enthuse, spit, sigh and dream. Who reasons?' (2.1.8.4) Second, he reduces science to force: 'Belief in the existence of science is the effect of exaggeration,
injustice, asymmetry, ignorance, credulity, and denial. If 'science' is distinct from the
rest, then it is the end result of a long line of coups de force'. (4.2.6.) Third, he reduces
scientific knowledge ('knowing-that') to practical know-how: 'There is no such thing
as knowledge—what would it be? There is only know-how. In other words, there are
crafts and trades. Despite all claims to the contrary, crafts hold the key to all knowledge. They make it possible to 'return' science to the networks from which it came'.
(4.3.2.) Last but not least, he reduces truth to power: 'The word 'true' is a supplement
added to certain trials of strength to dazzle those who might still question them'. (4.5.8.)

17. It is instructive to note how many reductions must be carried out in order for
irreductionism to get off the ground: reason, science, knowledge, truth—all must be
eliminated. Of course, Latour has no qualms about reducing reason to arbitration, science to custom, knowledge to manipulation, or truth to force: the veritable object of
his irreductionist afflatus is not reduction per se, in which he wantonly indulges, but
explanation, and the cognitive privilege accorded to scientific explanation in particular.
Once relieved of the constraints of cognitive rationality and the obligation to truth,
metaphysics can forego the need for explanation and supplant the latter with a series of
allusive metaphors whose cognitive import becomes a function of semantic resonance:
'actor', 'ally', 'force', 'power', 'strength', 'resistance', 'network': these are the master-met-
aphors of Latour's irreductionist metaphysics, the ultimate 'actants' encapsulating the
operations of every other actor. And as with any metaphysics built on metaphor, equivocation is always a boon, never a handicap: 'Because there is no literal or figurative

---

8. It is not enough to evoke a *metaphysical* distinction between appearance and reality, in the manner for instance of 'object-oriented philosophies', since the absence of any reliable cognitive criteria by which to measure and specify the precise extent of the gap between seeming and being or discriminate between the extrinsic and intrinsic properties of objects licenses entirely arbitrary claims about the in-itself. For an example
of 'object-oriented' philosophizing see Graham Harman, *Guerrilla Metaphysics: Phenomenology and the Carpentry
of Things*, Chicago, Open Court, 2005.

9. Included as Part Two of Latour's *The Pasteurization of France*, trans. A. Sheridan and J. Law, Cambridge,
Harvard University Press, 1993.

meaning, no single use of metaphor can dominate the other uses. Without propriety there is no impropriety [...]. Since no word reigns over the others, we are free to use all metaphors. We do not have to fear that one meaning is "true" and another "metaphorical". (2.6.3)

18. However, in the absence of any understanding of the relationship between 'meanings' and things meant—the issue at the heart of the epistemological problematic which Latour dismisses but which has preoccupied an entire philosophical tradition from Frege through Sellars and up to their contemporary heirs—the claim that nothing is metaphorical is ultimately indistinguishable from the claim that everything is metaphorical.[10] The metaphysical difference between words and things, concepts and objects, vanishes along with the distinction between representation and reality: 'It is not possible to distinguish for long between those actants that are going to play the role of "words" and those that will play the role of "things"'. (2.4.5). In dismissing the epistemological obligation to explain what meaning is and how it relates to things that are not meanings, Latour, like all postmodernists—his own protestations to the contrary notwithstanding—reduces everything to meaning, since the difference between 'words' and 'things' turns out to be no more than a functional difference subsumed by the concept of 'actant'—that is to say, it is a merely nominal difference encompassed by the metaphysical function now ascribed to the metaphor 'actant'. Since for Latour the latter encompasses everything from hydroelectric powerplants to toothfairies, it follows that every possible difference between powerplants and fairies—i.e. differences in the mechanisms through which they affect and are affected by other entities, whether those mechanisms are currently conceivable or not—is supposed to be unproblematically accounted for by this single conceptual metaphor.

19. This is reductionism with a vengeance; but because it occludes rather than illuminates differences in the ways in which different parts of the world interact, its very lack of explanatory purchase can be brandished as a symptom of its irreductive prowess by those who are not interested in understanding the difference between wishing and engineering. Latour writes to reassure those who do not really want to know. If the concern with representation which lies at the heart of the unfolding epistemological problematic from Descartes to Sellars was inspired by the desire not just to understand but to assist science in its effort to explain the world, then the recent wave of attempts to liquidate epistemology by dissolving representation can be seen as symptomatic of that cognophobia which, from Nietzsche through Heidegger and up to Latour, has fuelled a concerted effort on the part of some philosophers to contain if not neutralize the disquieting implications of scientific understanding.[11]

20. While irreductionists prate about the 'impoverishment' attendant upon the epistemological privileging of conceptual rationality, all they have to offer by way of

---

10. Much as the claim that everything is real turns out to be indistinguishable from the claim that nothing is real: with the dissolution of the distinction between appearance and reality, the predicate 'real' is subjected to an inflation that effectively renders it worthless.

11. For a succinct but extremely efficacious demolition of the various arguments (Latour's included) alleged to undermine the authority of scientific rationality, see Paul Boghossian's *Fear of Knowledge: Against Relativism and Constructivism*, Oxford, Oxford University Press, 2007. For a critique of Latour's claims specifically, see James Robert Brown, 'Critique of Social Constructivism' in *Scientific Enquiry: Readings in the Philosophy of Science*, R. Klee (ed.), Oxford, Oxford University Press, 1999, pp. 260-64. In *The Advancement of Science: Science without Legend, Objectivity without Illusions*, Oxford, Oxford University Press, 1993, Philip Kitcher mounts a magisterial defence of the rationality of science against its postmodern detractors, dispatching Latour in passing.

alternative is a paltry metaphorics that occludes every real distinction through which representation yields explanatory understanding.

21. *Pace* Latour, there is a non-negligible difference between conceptual categories and the objects to which they can be properly applied. But because he is as oblivious to it as the post-structuralists he castigates, Latour's attempt to contrast his 'realism' to postmodern 'irrealism' rings hollow: he is invoking a difference which he cannot make good on. By collapsing the reality of the difference between concepts and objects into differences in force between generically construed 'actants', Latour merely erases from the side of 'things' ('forces') a distinction which textualists deny from the side of 'words' ('signifiers').

22. Mortgaged to the cognitive valence of metaphor but lacking the resources to explain let alone legitimate it, Latour's irreductionism cannot be understood as a theory, where the latter is broadly construed as a series of systematically interlinked propositions held together by valid argumentative chains. Rather, Latour's texts consciously rehearse the metaphorical operations they describe: they are 'networks' trafficking in 'word-things' of varying 'power', nexuses of 'translation' between 'actants' of differing 'force', etc. In this regard, they are exercises in the practical know-how which Latour exalts, as opposed to demonstrative propositional structures governed by cognitive norms of epistemic veracity and logical validity. But this is just to say that the ultimate import of Latour's work is prescriptive rather than descriptive—indeed, given that issues of epistemic veracity and validity are irrelevant to Latour, there is nothing to prevent the cynic from concluding that Latour's politics (neo-liberal) and his religion (Roman Catholic) provide the most telling indices of those forces ultimately motivating his antipathy towards rationality, critique, and revolution.

23. In other words, Latour's texts are designed to do things: they have been engineered in order to produce an effect rather than establish a demonstration. Far from trying to prove anything, Latour is explicitly engaged in persuading the susceptible into embracing his irreductionist worldview through a particularly adroit deployment of rhetoric. This is the traditional modus operandi of the sophist. But only the most brazen of sophists denies the rhetorical character of his own assertions: 'Rhetoric cannot account for the force of a sequence of sentences because if it is called 'rhetoric' then it is weak and has already lost'. (2.4.1) This resort to an already metaphorized concept of 'force' to mark the extra-rhetorical and thereby allegedly 'real' force of Latour's own 'sequence of sentences' marks the nec plus ultra of sophistry.[12]

24. Irreductionism is a species of correlationism: the philosopheme according to which the human and the non-human, society and nature, mind and world, can only be understood as reciprocally correlated, mutually interdependent poles of a fundamental relation. Correlationists are wont to dismiss the traditional questions which have preoccupied metaphysicians and epistemologists—questions such as 'What is X?' and 'How do we know X?'—as false questions, born of the unfortunate tendency to abstract one or other pole of the correlation and consider it in isolation from its correlate. For the correlationist, since it is impossible to separate the subjective from the

---

12. Interestingly, Latour's own dissolution of the distinction between logic and rhetoric effectively undermines any attempt to segregate the conceptual content of his work from its rhetorical armature. To try to insulate 'actor network theory' from Latour's politics (or his religion) is to invoke a distinction between public theory and private practice which Latour's thought openly repudiates. I intend to carry out a more systematic dissection of Latour's claims, as well as of those philosophers who have taken up the banner of his irreductionism, in a future article.

objective, or the human from the non-human, it makes no sense to ask what anything is in itself, independently of our relating to it. By the same token, once knowledge has been reduced to technical manipulation, it is neither possible nor desirable to try to understand scientific cognition independently of the nexus of social practices in which it is invariably implicated. Accordingly, correlationism sanctions all those variants of pragmatic instrumentalism which endorse the primacy of practical 'know-how' over theoretical 'knowing-that'. Sapience becomes just another kind of sentience—and by no means a privileged kind either.

25. Ultimately, correlationism is not so much a specific philosophical doctrine as a general and highly versatile strategy for deflating traditional metaphysical and episte-mological concerns by reducing both questions of 'being' and of 'knowing' to concat-enations of cultural form, political contestation, and social practice. By licensing the wholesale conversion of philosophical problems into symptoms of non-philosophical factors (political, sociocultural, psychological, etc.), correlationism provides the (often unstated) philosophical premise for the spate of twentieth century attempts to dissolve the problems of philosophy into questions of politics, sociology, anthropology, and psy-chology. To reject correlationism and reassert the primacy of the epistemology-meta-physics nexus is not to revert to a reactionary philosophical purism, insisting that phi-losophy remain uncontaminated by politics and history. It is simply to point out that, while they are certainly socially and politically *nested*, the problems of metaphysics and epistemology nonetheless possess a relative autonomy and remain conceptually irre-ducible—just as the problems of mathematics and physics retain their relative auton-omy despite always being implicated within a given socio-historical conjuncture. The fact that philosophical discourse is non-mathematical and largely (but by no means en-tirely) unformalized (but certainly not unformalizable), does not provide a legitimate warrant for disregarding its conceptual specificity and reducing it to a set of ideologi-cal symptoms. Again, this is not to assert (absurdly) that the problems of metaphysics or epistemology have no social determinants or political ramifications, but simply to point out that they can no more be understood exclusively in those terms than can the problems of mathematics or physics.

26. To refuse correlationism's collapsing of epistemology into ontology, and of ontology into politics, is not to retreat into reactionary quietism but to acknowledge the need to forge new conditions of articulation between politics, epistemology, and metaphysics. The politicization of ontology marks a regression to anthropomorphic myopia; the ontologization of politics falters the moment it tries to infer political prescriptions from metaphysical description. Philosophy and politics cannot be met-aphysically conjoined; philosophy intersects with politics at the point where critical epistemology transects ideology critique. An emancipatory politics oblivious to epis-temology quickly degenerates into metaphysical fantasy, which is to say, a religious substitute.[13] The failure to change the world may not be unrelated to the failure to un-derstand it.

27. The assertion of the primacy of correlation is the condition for the post-mod-ern dissolution of the epistemology-metaphysics nexus and the two fundamental dis-tinctions concomitant with it: the sapience-sentience distinction and the concept-

---

13. In this regard, the notable preponderance of theological motifs in those variants of critical theory that have abandoned epistemology provides a telling symptom of the slide from ideological critique to metaphys-ical edification: 'redemption', 'reconciliation', 'Utopia', 'Messianism', 'grace', 'fidelity', 'faith', etc.

object distinction. In eliding the former, correlationism eliminates epistemology by reducing knowledge to discrimination. In eliding the latter, correlationism simultaneously reduces things to concepts and concepts to things. Each reduction facilitates the other: the erasure of the epistemological difference between sapience and sentience makes it easier to collapse the distinction between concept and object; the elision of the metaphysical difference between concept and object makes it easier to conflate sentience with sapience. Thus Latour's reduction of things to concepts (objects to 'actants') is of a piece with his reduction of concepts to things ('truth' to force).

28. The rejection of correlationism entails the reinstatement of the critical nexus between epistemology and metaphysics and its attendant distinctions: sapience/sentience; concept/object. We need to know what things are in order to measure the gap between their phenomenal and noumenal aspects as well as the difference between their extrinsic and intrinsic properties. To know (in the strong scientific sense) what something is is to conceptualize it. This is not to say that things are identical with their concepts. The gap between conceptual identity and non-conceptual difference—between what our concept of the object is and what the object is in itself—is not an ineffable hiatus or mark of irrecuperable alterity; it can be conceptually converted into an identity that is not of the concept even though the concept is of it. Pace Adorno, there is an alternative to the negation of identity concomitant with the concept's failure to coincide with what it aims at: a negation of the concept determined by the object's non-conceptual identity, rather than its lack in the concept. Pace Deleuze, there is an alternative to the affirmation of difference as non-representational concept (Idea) of the thing itself: an affirmation of identity in the object as ultimately determining the adequacy of its own conceptual representation. The difference between the conceptual and the extra-conceptual need not be characterized as lack or negation, or converted into a positive concept of being as Ideal difference-in-itself: it can be presupposed as already-given in the act of knowing or conception. But it is presupposed without being posited. This is what distinguishes scientific representation and governs its stance towards the object.[14]

29. What is real in the scientific representation of the object does not coincide with the object's quiddity as conceptually circumscribed—the latter is what the concept *means* and what the object *is*; its metaphysical quiddity or essence—but the scientific posture is one which there is an immanent yet transcendental hiatus between the reality of the object and its being as conceptually circumscribed: the posture of scientific representation is one in which it is the former that determines the latter and forces its perpetual revision. Scientific representation operates on the basis of a stance in which something in the object itself determines the discrepancy between its material reality—the fact *that* it is, its existence—and its being, construed as quiddity, or *what* it is. The scientific stance is one in which the reality of the object determines the meaning of its conception, and allows the discrepancy between that reality and the way in which it is conceptually circumscribed to be measured. This should be understood in contrast to the classic correlationist model according to which it is conceptual meaning that determines the 'reality' of the object, understood as the relation between representing and represented.

---

14. This is one of the most valuable insights in the mid-period work of François Laruelle (which he refers to as *Philosophie II*): see *En tant qu'un: la non-philosophie expliqué au philosophes*, Paris, Aubier, 1991. Unfortunately, its importance seems to diminish in Laruelle's subsequent work.

30. The distinction between the object's conceptual reality and its metaphysical reality has an analogue in the scholastic distinction between objective and formal reality. Yet it is not a dogmatic or pre-critical residue; rather, it follows from the epistemological constraint that prohibits the transcendentalization of meaning. The corollary of this critical constraint is the acknowledgement of the transcendental difference between meaning and being, or concept and object. Contrary to what correlationists proclaim, the presupposition of this difference is not a dogmatic prejudice in need of critical legitimation. Quite the reverse: it is the assumption that the difference between concept and object is always internal to the concept—that every difference is ultimately conceptual—that needs to be defended. For to assume that the difference between concept and object can only be internal to the concept is to assume that concepts furnish self-evident indexes of their own reality and internal structure—that we know what concepts are and can reliably track their internal differentiation—an assumption that then seems to license the claim that every difference in reality is a conceptual difference. The latter of course provides the premise for conceptual idealism, understood as the claim that reality is composed of concepts—precisely the sort of metaphysical claim which correlationism is supposed to abjure. Yet short of resorting to the phenomenological myth of an originary, self-constituting consciousness (one of the many variants of the myth of the given, denounced by Sellars[15]), the same critical considerations that undermine dogmatism about the essence and existence of objects also vitiate dogmatism about the essence and existence of concepts (whether indexed by signifiers, discursive practices, conscious experiences, etc). Thus it is not clear why our access to the structure of concepts should be considered any less in need of critical legitimation than our access to the structure of objects.[16] To assume privileged access to the structure of conception is to assume intellectual intuition. But this is to make a metaphysical claim about the essential nature of conception; an assumption every bit as dogmatic as any allegedly metaphysical assertion about the essential nature of objects. Thus, correlationism is perpetually tottering on the cusp of the slippery slope to conceptual idealism. The latter begins by assuming that knowledge of identity and difference in the concept is the precondition for knowledge of identity and difference in the object, before going on to conclude that every first-order difference between concept and object must be subsumed by a second-order conceptual difference, which must also in turn be conceptually subsumed at a higher level, and so on all the way up to the Absolute Notion. But unless it can be justified by the anticipation of a conceptual Absolute retrospectively enveloping every past difference, the subordination of every difference to the identity of our current concepts is more not less dogmatic than the transcendental presupposition of an extra-conceptual difference between concept and object.

31. More often than not, this idealist premise that every difference must be a difference in the concept underwrites the argument most frequently adduced by correlationists against metaphysical (or transcendental) realism. This argument revolves around a peculiar fallacy, which David Stove has christened 'the Gem'.[17] Its locus clas-

---

15. See Wilfrid Sellars, *Empiricism and the Philosophy of Mind*, Cambridge, Harvard University Press, 1997.

16. The signal merit of Paul Churchland's work, following Sellars', is to challenge the myth that the nature of concepts is given. See Paul Churchland, *A Neurocomputational Perspective: The Nature of Mind and the Structure of Science*, Cambridge, MIT, 1989.

17. See David Stove, 'Idealism: A Victorian Horror Story (Part Two)' in *The Plato Cult and Other Philosophical Follies*, Oxford, Blackwell, 1991, pp. 135-178. Stove is a curious figure: a philosophical writer of outstanding analytical acumen and scathing wit, he is too acerbic to be respectable but too brilliant to be dismissed

sicus can be found in paragraph 23 of Berkeley's Treatise Concerning the Principles of Human Knowledge, where Berkeley challenges the assumption that it is possible to conceive of something existing independently of our conception of it (we will disregard for present purposes the distinction between conception and perception, just as Berkeley does):

> But, say you, surely there is nothing easier than for me to imagine trees, for instance, in a park, or books existing in a closet, and nobody by to perceive them. I answer, you may so, there is no difficulty in it; but what is all this, I beseech you, more than framing in your mind certain ideas which you call books and trees, and the same time omitting to frame the idea of any one that may perceive them? But do not you yourself perceive or think of them all the while? This therefore is nothing to the purpose; it only shews you have the power of imagining or forming ideas in your mind: but it does not shew that you can conceive it possible the objects of your thought may exist without the mind. To make out this, it is necessary that you conceive them existing unconceived or unthought of, which is a manifest repugnancy. When we do our utmost to conceive the existence of external bodies, we are all the while only contemplating our own ideas. But the mind taking no notice of itself, is deluded to think it can and does conceive bodies existing unthought of or without the mind, though at the same time they are apprehended by or exist in itself. A little attention will discover to any one the truth and evidence of what is here said, and make it unnecessary to insist on any other proofs against the existence of material substance.[18]

32. Berkeley's reasoning here is instructive, for it reveals the hidden logic of every correlationist argument. From the indubitable premise that 'One cannot think or perceive something without thinking or perceiving it', Berkeley goes on to draw the dubious conclusion that 'Things cannot exist without being thought or perceived'. Berkeley's premise is a tautology, since the claim that one cannot think of something without thinking of it is one that no rational being would want to deny. But from this tautological premise Berkeley draws a non-tautological conclusion, viz., that things *depend* for their existence on being thought or perceived and are *nothing apart from* our thinking or perceiving of them. Yet Berkeley's argument is clearly formally fallacious, since one cannot derive a non-tautological conclusion from a tautological premise. How then does it manage to exude its modicum of plausibility? As Stove points out, it does so by equivocating between two senses of the word 'things': things as conceived or perceived (i.e. *ideata*), and things *simpliciter* (i.e. physical objects). This is of course the very distinction Berkeley seeks to undermine; but he cannot deny it from the outset without begging the question—the negation of this distinction and the metaphysical claim that only minds and their *ideata* exist is supposed to be the consequence of Berkeley's argument, not its presupposition. Yet it is only by substituting 'things' in the first and tautological sense of *ideata* for 'things' in the second and non-tautological sense of physical objects that Berkeley is able to dismiss as a 'manifest absurdity' the realist claim that it is possible to conceive of (physical) things existing unperceived or unthought. For it would indeed be a manifest absurdity to assert that we can conceive of physical things without conceiving of them. But it would be difficult to find any metaphysical realist who has ever endorsed such an absurdity. Rather, the realist claims that her concep-

---

as a crank. No doubt Stove's noxious political views (fanatical anti-communism coupled with not so thinly veiled racism and sexism) prevented him from gaining the recognition his work might have won had he been of a more benign temper. Some will cite his reactionary opinions as reason enough to dismiss him; correlationists in particular are liable to conclude from the fact that Stove, who defended realism, was a racist and a sexist, that realism entails racism and sexism.

18. http://www.uoregon.edu/~rbear/berkeley.html

tion of a physical thing and the physical thing which she conceives are two different things, and though the difference is perfectly conceivable, its conceivability does not render it mind-dependent—unless of course one is prepared to go the whole Hegelian hog and insist that it is conceptual differences all the way down (or rather, up). But then it will take more than the Gem to establish the absolute idealist claim that reality consists entirely of concepts; indeed, once the fallacious character of the Gem has been exposed, the absolute idealist claim that everything is conceptual (there are no things, only concepts) has little more to recommend it than the vulgar materialist claim that nothing is conceptual (there are no concepts, only things).

33. The difficulty facing the proponent of the Gem is the following: since the assumption that things are only *ideata* is every bit as metaphysical ('dogmatic') as the assumption that *ideata* are not the only things (that physical things are not ideas), the only way for the idealist to trump the realist is by invoking the self-authenticating nature of her experience as a thinking thing (or mind) and repository of ideas. But this she cannot do without invoking some idealist version of the myth of the given (which I take Sellars to have convincingly refuted). So in this regard, the alleged 'givenness' of the difference between concept and object would be no worse off than that of the identity of the concept (*qua* self-authenticating mental episode). Obviously, this does not suffice to vindicate metaphysical realism; what it does reveal however is that the Gem fails to disqualify it. It is undoubtedly true that we cannot conceive of concept-independent things without conceiving of them; but it by no means follows from this that we cannot conceive of things existing independently of concepts, since there is no logical transitivity from the mind-dependence of concepts to that of conceivable objects. Only someone who is confusing mind-independence with concept-independence would invoke the conceivability of the difference between concept and object in order to assert the mind-dependence of objects.

34. The paradigmatic or Berkeleyian version of the Gem assumes the following form:

> 'You cannot conceive of a mind-independent reality without conceiving of it. Therefore, you cannot conceive of a mind-independent reality'.

Note that the Gem does not assert that there is no mind-independent reality; it merely says that it must remain inconceivable. This is of course the classic correlationist claim. But as we have seen, it is predicated on a fundamental confusion between mind-independence and concept-independence. To claim that Cygnus X-3 exists independently of our minds is not to claim that Cygnus X-3 exists beyond the reach of our minds. Independence is not inaccessibility. The claim that something exists mind-independently does not commit one to the claim that it is conceptually inaccessible. By implying that mind-independence requires conceptual inaccessibility, the Gem saddles transcendental realism with an exorbitant burden. But it is a burden which there is no good reason to accept.

35. That one cannot conceive of something without conceiving it is uncontroversial. But the tautological premise in a Gem argument need not be so obvious. All that is necessary is that it exhibit the following form:

> 'You cannot do X unless Y, some necessary condition for doing X, is met'.
> Thus a Gem is any argument that assumes the following general form:
> 'You cannot X unless Y, a necessary condition for Xing things, is met.
> Therefore, you cannot X things-in-themselves'.

One gets a Gem by substituting for X and Y:

'You cannot experience/perceive/conceive/represent/refer to things unless the necessary conditions of experience/perception/conception/ representation/reference obtain.

Therefore, you cannot experience/perceive/conceive/represent/refer to things-in-themselves'.

Of course, having distinguished Xed things from things-in-themselves and relegated the latter to the wastes of the inconceivable, the pressure soon mounts to dispense with the in-itself altogether and to shrink all reality down to the confines of the 'for us' (the phenomenal). Thus, although it is only supposed to secure correlationist agnosticism about the in-itself, rather than full-blown conceptual idealism, the Gem invariably heralds the slide towards the latter. In this regard, Stove catalogues, in an amusing and often acerbic manner, the various Gems mobilized in the service of post-Kantian idealism. But the Gem is better viewed as an argument for correlationism rather than for full blown conceptual idealism. For there are any number of human activities besides thinking or conceiving that can be substituted for X, thereby yielding an equally wide assortment of non-idealist anti-realisms: pragmatism, social constructivism, deconstruction, etc. Thus, it comes as no surprise that the Gem should have proved the trusty adjutant for almost every variety of late 20th Century correlationism, from Goodman and Rorty at one end to Latour and Foucault at the other. But unfortunately for correlationism, no amount of inventiveness in substituting for X and Y can suffice to palliate the fallaciousness of the Gem, which Stove understandably dismissed as 'an argument so bad it is hard to imagine anyone ever being swayed by it'.[19]

36. Yet ironically, and notwithstanding Stove's incredulity, correlationism's status as the regnant intellectual orthodoxy throughout the humanities and social sciences would seem to indicate the triumph of the Gem. There is little doubt that correlationism's appeal can be attributed to factors that have little or nothing to do with its logical probity—factors that are at once emotional (the defence of value through the subversion of fact); psychological (cutting the inhuman world down to human size); and political (the ontological investiture of politics compensating for its replacement by management in the public sphere). Argumentative stringency has never been the litmus test for the success of any philosopheme. Nevertheless, given the striking discrepancy between the cogency of correlationism's principal argumentative gambit and its academic popularity, one might be forgiven for asking (paraphrasing Stove): 'Can it be by this contemptible argument that the West was won for correlationism?'[20]

37. In light of this argumentative paucity, it is somewhat perplexing to see Quentin Meillassoux, the philosopher who has done more than anyone to challenge the hegemony of correlationism, declare his admiration for 'the exceptional strength of this [correlationist] argumentation, apparently and desperately implacable [.... It is] an argument as simple as it is powerful: No X without a givenness of X, no theory about

---

19. Stove, 'Idealism: A Victorian Horror Story', p. 147. As Stove himself remarks, the Gem's ubiquity in some philosophical quarters is such as to discourage attempts to catalogue individual instances of its occurrence. Stove discusses the Gem primarily in the context of nineteenth and early twentieth Century idealism, but any account of it now also has to consider its role in the vast literature comprised under the heading 'continental philosophy'. Here again, the sheer number and variety of Gems threatens to overwhelm the investigator, reducing her to numbed catatonia. Nevertheless, Alan Musgrave and James Franklin have both helped expand Stove's catalogue of Gems beyond the corpus of idealism by recording instances of the Gem in contemporary varieties of anti-realism. See Alan Musgrave 'Realism and Antirealism' in R. Klee (ed.), *Scientific Enquiry: Readings in the Philosophy of Science*, Oxford, Oxford University Press, 1999, pp. 344-352; James Franklin 'Stove's Discovery of the Worst Argument in the World' *Philosophy*, no. 77, 2002, pp. 615-24.

20. Stove, 'Idealism: A Victorian Horror Story', p. 147.

X without a positing of X'.[21] What Meillassoux is entreating us to admire here is the high transcendentalist variant of the Gem, where 'givenness' and 'positing' stand for the conditions of reception and reflection respectively, and X is the object whose necessary conditions they provide. In order for X to be given, the necessary conditions of givenness must obtain (transcendental affection). In order for there to be a theory of X, the necessary conditions of positing must obtain (transcendental reflection). Meillassoux has Fichte rather than Kant in mind here.[22] For as he points out, it is not Kant but Fichte who is the veritable architect of the correlationist circle, understood as the abolition of the Kantian dualism of concept and intuition. Fichte overcomes the Kantian duality of active conception and passive affection through his notion of the Tathandlung, which is at once the positing of the given and the giving of the posited. By construing the correlation as a self-positing and thereby self-grounding act, Fichte seals the circle of correlation against any incursion of dogmatically posited exteriority—in other words, he eliminates the thing-in-itself. For Fichte, the non-I through which the I is affected is merely the posited residue of the absolute I's free and spontaneous act of self-positing. Thus, it is Fichte who uncovers the full idealist potency of transcendental reflection by tracking the power of positing back to its source in the unobjectifiable activity of the absolute ego.

38. Meillassoux underlines the extent to which Fichte's radicalization of transcendental reflection seems to preclude any possibility of metaphysical realism. Reflection as condition of objectification (representation) is precisely what cannot be objectified (represented); thus, Meillassoux argues, one cannot defeat correlationism merely by positing an unobjectifiable real as the allegedly mind-independent condition of objectification, for in doing so one is effectively contradicting oneself, since the non-posited status of the reality that is the content of one's thought is effectively contradicted by the act of thinking through which one posits it. Thus, transcendental realism understood as the positing of what is allegedly non-posited becomes self-refuting. According to Meillassoux, one is merely dogmatically *seceding* from rather than rationally *refuting* Fichtean correlationism if one thinks that positing an un-posited reality suffices to exempt one from the circle of transcendental reflection. By emphasizing what he takes to be the exceptional rigour of Fichtean correlationism, Meillassoux reasserts his conviction that correlationism can only be overcome from within: since Fichte has disqualified the possibility of positing the absolute as an object, the only non-dogmatic alternative to Fichte's transcendentalization of reflection consists in absolutizing the contingency of the correlation; i.e. the inability of positing to ground its own necessity, which Meillassoux sees exemplified by Fichte's characterization of the *Tathandlung* as a *free* act—in other words, something that is contingent rather than necessary:

> We choose whether or not to posit our own subjective reflection, and this choice is not grounded on any necessary cause, since our freedom is radical. But to say this is just to recognize, after Descartes, that our subjectivity cannot reach an absolute necessity but only a conditional one. Even if Fichte speaks abundantly of absolute and uncondition-

---

21. Quentin Meillassoux, 'Speculative Realism', *Collapse*, vol. 3, 2007, p. 409.

22. Interestingly, a good case can be made for the claim that Kant's work is far less indebted to the Gem than that of many Kantians. This is a point made by James Franklin (Franklin, 'Stove's Discovery of the Worst Argument in the World'). Among the many merits of the Sellarsian reconstruction of Kant is that it gives us a Gem free Kant: Sellars shows that transcendental philosophy can and should be dissociated from transcendental idealism, and that Kant's transcendental distinction between concepts and intuitions can and should be dissociated from his arguments for the ideality of space and time.

al necessity, his necessity is no longer a dogmatic and substantial necessity, but a necessity grounded in a freedom that is itself ungrounded. There can be no dogmatic proof that the correlation exists rather than not.[23]

39. Meillassoux is surely right to identify Fichte as the veritable founder of strong correlationism (as opposed to weak or Kantian correlationism). But transcendental realists may be forgiven for remaining unmoved by the claim that the free act of positing reflection disqualifies every invocation of a non-posited reality. Fichte's characterizations of freedom and reflection cannot but strike one as instances of gratuitous idealist dogmatism. Reflection is supposed to disqualify the in-itself because it is the unobjectifiable condition of representation and as such renders all objects, even and precisely those objects represented as existing in-themselves, into objects that are merely *for us*. Yet even if we grant the assertion (which seems to be based on little besides an appeal to the phenomenology of conscious experience) that reflection as condition of cognitive representation cannot be objectively known, how does this license the claim that reflection, which is supposedly only accessible through a conscious experience of subjective spontaneity (here automatically equated with indetermination) indexes a genuinely transcendental freedom? Meillassoux is overly indulgent towards Fichte's reckless equations between reflection and activity, spontaneity and freedom; he is too quick to license Fichte's hypertrophic inflation of terms like 'reflection', 'act', and 'freedom'.

40. Moreover, the Fichtean distinction between objectification and reflection hardly ameliorates correlationism's rational credibility once we realize that the attempt to indict realism of performative contradiction is simply an elaborately camouflaged version of the Gem. Consider:

> 'One cannot posit Saturn unless the conditions of positing (the free and unobjectifiable activity of the absolute ego) obtain.
>
> Therefore, one cannot posit Saturn as non-posited (existing independently of the free and unobjectifiable activity of the absolute ego)'.

Here once again, the sleight of hand consists in the equivocation between what should be two distinct functions of the word 'Saturn'. (We will use 'Saturn' when mentioning the word and **Saturn** when designating the concept for which the word stands). In order for the premise to be safely tautological (rather than an outrageously metaphysical begging of the question), the word 'Saturn' must be understood to mean *sense* (or 'mode of presentation') of the concept **Saturn**. But in order for the conclusion to be interesting (as opposed to blandly tautological), the word 'Saturn' must be understood to mean the *referent* of the concept **Saturn**. Once this is understood, it becomes clear that the considerations that make it true to say that **Saturn** cannot be posited independently of the conditions of its positing (i.e. the conditions for the proper use of the concept), do not make it true to say that Saturn cannot be posited as non-posited (i.e. that Saturn cannot exist unless there are conditions for the proper use of **Saturn**).

41. When I say that Saturn does not need to be posited in order to exist, I am not saying that the meaning of the concept **Saturn** does not need to be posited by us in order to exist—quite obviously, the concept **Saturn** means what it does because of us, and in this sense it is perfectly acceptable to say that it has been 'posited' through human activity. But when I say that Saturn exists un-posited, I am not making a claim about a word or a concept; my claim is rather that the planet which is the referent of

---

23. Meillassoux, 'Speculative Realism', p. 430.

the word 'Saturn' existed before we named it and will probably still exist after the beings who named it have ceased to exist, since it is something quite distinct both from
the word 'Saturn' and the concept **Saturn** for which the word stands. Thus the 'Saturn' that is synonymous with 'correlate of the act of positing' (i.e. **Saturn** as the sense
of the word 'Saturn') is not synonymous with the Saturn probed by Cassini-Huygens.
To say that Saturn exists un-posited is simply to say that Cassini-Huygens did not
probe the sense of a word and is not in orbit around a concept.

42. It might be objected that we need **Saturn** to say *what* Saturn is; that we cannot refer to Saturn or assert that it is without **Saturn**. But this is false: the first humans
who pointed to Saturn did not need to know and were doubtless mistaken about what
it is: but they did not need to know in order to point to it. To deny this is to imply that
Saturn's existence—that it is—is a function of what it is—that Saturn is indissociable
from **Saturn** (or whatever else people have believed Saturn to be). But this is already
to be a conceptual idealist. Even were the latter to demonstrate that the conditions of
sense determine the conditions of reference, this would still not be enough to show that
the existence of the referent depends upon the conditions of reference. To do that, one
would have to show that 'to be' means 'to be referred to'; an equation tantamount to
Berkeley's equation of 'to be' with 'to be perceived'; yet it would require more than
another Gem to dissolve such a fundamentally normative distinction in meaning. Of
course, this distinction can be challenged by questioning the nature of the relation between sense and reference and interrogating the relation between words and things.[24]
The more sophisticated varieties of anti-realism have done so in interesting and instructive ways. But the claim that the difference between what things are and that they
are is not ultimately conceptual cannot be challenged by willfully conflating the sense
of a word with the referent of its concept, as the Fichtean argument above does. Fichte
notwithstanding, there would seem to be good cognitive grounds for distinguishing
words from things and meanings from objects. One can of course contest this cognitive
conviction by alleging that it is a rationally indefensible dogma; but confusing **Saturn**
with Saturn is not the way to do it. It is tautologically true to say that one cannot posit something without positing it; but it no more follows from this that the posited X is
nothing apart from its positing than that **Saturn** is the same thing as Saturn.

43. Since Fichte's purported disqualification of transcendental realism relies entirely on this trivial confusion, there is no reason for us to lend it any more credence
than we accord to Berkeley's 'proof' of the impossibility of conceiving independently
existing material objects. But Berkeley has more than one version of the Gem. His argument can also be reformulated as follows:

All our knowledge of physical objects begins in experience.

1. But the only things we directly experience are ideas.
2. Therefore all the properties by which we know physical objects, whether
   these are sensory properties (as in the case of secondary qualities like smell,
   colour, touch, taste), or conceptual properties (as in the case of primary qualities like figure, motion, extension, mass, velocity), are ideas, i.e. experiences.

---

24. Sellars for one does not believe that meaning can be understood as a set of relations between words
and things (whether mental or physical); his 'conceptual role' account of meaning is one in which reference
can no longer be construed as a relation between words and extra-linguistic items. Sellars' account is far too
intricate to be addressed here; but suffice it to say that Sellars remained committed to a naturalistic (scientific) realism and that his philosophy of language provides no warrant for the sort of anti-realism we have
been considering here.

3. Consequently, when we say we know a physical object, what we really mean is that we are experiencing a collection of properties (whether primary or secondary).

4. But experiences cannot exist unless they are experienced.

5. Therefore physical objects cannot exist apart from our experiences of them.

The fallaciousness of this version of the argument becomes apparent when we notice that Berkeley has already smuggled in his conclusion in step 3, where he simply identifies ideas with experiences. Having done so, it follows that the idea of something existing independently of thought becomes self-contradictory because it is equivalent to an *experiencing* of something that is *un-experienced*. This is obviously contradictory; but it is contradictory only because Berkeley has illegitimately identified the *act* of thinking (the experiencing) with the *object* of thinking (the experienced). Thus to identify physical objects with experiences is already to assume that they do not exist independently of experience. This is why Berkeley is able to maintain that to try to think of something that exists outside thought is contradictory because it is tantamount to thinking a thought that is not a thought. But to say that I can think of something existing independently of my thought need not be flagrantly contradictory once I distinguish the claim that my thoughts cannot exist independently of my mind, which is trivially true, from the claim that *what* my thoughts are about cannot exist independently of my mind, which simply does not follow from such a trivial truth. Thus, to take one of Berkeley's own favoured examples, the fact that I cannot think of an uninhabited landscape without thinking of it does not mean that this landscape becomes inhabited merely by virtue of my thinking about it. It is certainly true that I cannot think about the Empty Quarter without thinking about it; but it does not follow from this that the Empty Quarter is populated by my thinking about it. To insist that it does would be like claiming that it is impossible to paint an uninhabited landscape because the act of painting it renders it inhabited. But this would be to confuse the act of painting with *what* is painted, or the act of thinking with *what* is thought. As with Berkeley, Fichte's putative refutation of transcendental realism rests on precisely this equivocation between the necessary or *formal* conditions for the being of the act and the *real* conditions for the being of its correlate. The correlationist conceit is to suppose that formal conditions of 'experience' (however broadly construed) suffice to determine material conditions of reality. But that the latter cannot be uncovered independently of the former does not mean that they can be circumscribed by them.

44. Meillassoux insists that transcendental realism remains a secession from rather than a refutation of Fichtean correlationism. But there is no need to secede from something whose cogency evaporates upon critical scrutiny. Once one realizes that Fichte's intimidating Teutonicisms mask flimsy Berkeleyian Gems, it becomes no more impossible to refute Fichtean correlationism than it was to refute Berkeleyian immaterialism. Fichte's *Tathandlung* is merely the most rarefied species of Gem as that form of argumentation that slides from the true claim that we need a concept of mind-independent reality in order to make claims about the latter to the false claim that the very concept of mind-independent reality suffices to convert the latter into a concept, which is by definition mind-dependent. This is the fatal non-sequitur at the root of every variant of correlationism; one rendered all the more egregious by its reliance on a naive folk-psychological theory of the nature of conception. But a thesis as dubious as subjective idealism does not become miraculously more cogent once bedecked in transcendental

fancy-dress and subjectivism is not rendered any more plausible once festooned with the mysterious activities of the absolute ego's 'positing' and 'reflecting'. The word 'transcendental' has for too long been invested with magical powers, immunizing any term to which it is affixed against the critical scrutiny to which it is susceptible in its ordinary or 'empirical' use. *Pace* Meillassoux, the burden of proof lies squarely with correlationism, not with transcendental realism.

45. The problem of objective synthesis (or what Laruelle calls 'philosophical decision') is basically that of how to adjudicate the relationship between conceptual thought and non-conceptual reality. But that we have a concept of the difference between **Saturn** and Saturn does not entail that the difference is a difference in the concept: concept of difference ≠ conceptual difference. The acknowledgement of this non-equivalence is the basic premise of transcendental realism, which cannot be subverted simply by equivocating, in the manner of strong or Fichtean correlationism, between the conditions of positing and the being of the posited. For as Laruelle points out, even this equivocation cannot but invoke the absolute reality of the Tathandlung or act of self-positing: the Fichtean cannot help but be a realist about her own positing activity.[25] Realism is uncircumventable, even for the most stubborn anti-realist. The problem is to identify the salient epistemological considerations so that the question of what to be a realist about may be rationally adjudicated. In this regard, the sorts of phenomenological intuition about conscious activity resorted to by Fichteans and other idealists remain a dubious source of authority. More fundamentally, the question is why those who are so keen to attribute absolute or unconditional reality to the activities of self-consciousness (or of minded creatures) seem so loath to confer equal existential rights upon the un-conscious, mindless processes through which consciousness and mindedness first emerged and will eventually be destroyed.

46. Kantians rightly charge dogmatic metaphysicians with ignoring the problem of cognitive access: this is the Critical problem of the relation between representation and reality. Yet far from resolving the access problem, strong correlationism simply dissolves it by abolishing the in-itself. Acknowledging the autonomy of the in-itself, transcendental realism faces the problem of determining what is real. This cannot be addressed independently of scientific representation. For those of us who take scientific representation to be the most reliable form of cognitive access to reality, the problem is one of granting maximal (but not, please note, incorrigible) authority to the scientific representation of the world while acknowledging that science changes its mind about *what* it says there is. Accordingly, the key question becomes: How can we acknowledge that scientific conception tracks the in-itself without resorting to the problematic metaphysical assumption that to 150do so is to conceptually circumscribe the 'essence' (or formal reality) of the latter? For we want to be able to claim that science knows reality without resorting to the Aristotelian equation of reality with substantial form. This

---

25. Ironically enough, although Meillassoux invokes Fichte in order to refute what he sees as Laruelle's dogmatic realism, Laruelle has cited Fichte as a decisive early inspiration (See François Laruelle, *Le déclin de l'écriture*, Paris, Aubier-Flammarion, 1977). The irony is that when Meillassoux indicts Laruelle of a performative (or 'pragmatic') contradiction between the act of positing and the non-posited reality posited through that act, he is making the same Fichtean allegation against Laruelle as the latter makes against philosophers when he charges them of a performative contradiction between the non-thetic reality of the act of philosophical decision and the thetic reality that is synthesized (i.e. decided) through that act. Once one strips away the extraneous post-Heideggerian rhetoric about its supposedly 'non-philosophical' status, it becomes possible to discern in Laruelle's radically immanent 'One' or 'Real' an updated (Michel Henry influenced) version of Fichte's absolute ego.

is to say that the structure of reality includes but is not exhausted by the structure of discretely individuated objects. Indeed, it is the nature of the epistemological correlation between individuated concepts and individual objects that is currently being investigated by cognitive science. Here again, Sellars' work provides an invaluable starting point, since his critique of the given shows that we require a theory of concepts as much as a theory of objects; indeed, folk psychology is itself a proto-scientific theory of mind which can be improved upon. The science of objects must be prosecuted in tandem with a science of concepts, of the sort currently prefigured by Sellarsian naturalists such as Paul Churchland, although we cannot follow the latter in maintaining that pragmatic-instrumentalist constraints provide a secure epistemological footing for the connection between concepts and objects.

47. Of course, recognizing this does not resolve or answer any of the profound epistemological and metaphysical difficulties which confront us in the wake of science's remarkable cognitive achievements. But it may help us realize that these difficulties cannot be circumvented, as both correlationists and dogmatic metaphysicians seek to do, by dispensing with those hard-won dualisms that have helped clarify what distinguishes scientific representation from metaphysical fantasy. Dualisms such as those of meaning and being, and of knowing and feeling, are not relics of an outmoded metaphysics; they are makeshift but indispensable instruments through which reason begins to be apprized both of its continuity and its discontinuity with regard to what it is still expedient to call 'nature'.

6

Does Nature Stay What-it-is?:
Dynamics and the Antecendence Criterion

Iain Hamilton Grant

> No analysis whatsoever ... is possible without synthesis, and
> thus it is easily possible, in fact, to derive the original force of
> attraction from the mere concept of matter, once the concept
> has first been synthetically produced. One should not, howev-
> er, believe it is possible to derive this force from a merely logi-
> cal concept of matter ... according to the principle of non-con-
> tradiction alone. For the concept of matter is itself, by origin,
> synthetic; a purely logical concept of matter is meaningless,
> and the real concept of matter itself first proceeds from the syn-
> thesis of those forces by the imagination.
>
> —Friedrich Schelling[1]

The following essay[2] erupts from the middle of a problem: whether the nature of Ground can be exhaustively satisfied by the Principle of Sufficient Reason (hereafter 'PSR'). In one sense, the problem concerns the relation between logical and real grounds, and assuming the two not to be completely reversible in the Hegelian manner ('the real is the rational and the rational is the real'), what exactly this distinction consists in. If, for instance, this distinction maintains that there is a difference between logical and real grounds, then in what sense can the former be regarded as 'grounding' at all? If, by contrast, the distinction is made at the level of the extension of logical and real grounds, then although what Spinoza's *Treatise on the Emendation of the Intellect*[3]

---

1. Friedrich Schelling, *Ideas for a Philosophy of Nature*, trans. Errol E. Harris and Peter Heath, Cambridge, Cambridge University Press, 1988, pp. 187-188; and Friedrich Schelling, *Schellings sämmtliche Werke*. XIV vols, vol. II, Stuttgart and Augsburg, J.G. Cotta, 1856-61, p. 235.

2. This is a much revised and augmented version of the paper I read at the Bristol Speculative Realism workshop, held at the University of West England on 24 April 2009.

3. 'It is in the nature of a thinking being ... to form true and adequate thoughts'. Baruch Spinoza, *Ethics, Treatise on the Emendation of the Intellect and Selected Letters*, trans. Samuel Shirley, Indianapolis, Hackett, 1992, p. 252.

identifies as the 'natural' contact of thinking with being is maintained, logical need not exhaust real grounds, nor the latter the former. In other words, ground could exceed the satisfaction of reason, or reason exceed its grounding in the real.

A second dimension of the problem emerges when material grounds are added to the mix, insofar as the problem is then affected by an additional possible non-equivalence, this time between the real and the material. If the extensions of the real and the material are non-equivalent, then either there is more to the real than the material, or more to the material than the real. The former case holds matter to be non-fundamental in some manner, due either to some dualist imperative, or to some field-theoretical naturalism that holds matter to be a regional state of the physical. To argue in the other direction that there is more to the material than the real makes the real identical in extension to the actual, while making the material into the possible, and the possible into the material, so that the 'boundless sea of diversity' inflects ground with ceaseless mobility.

Amongst the various reasons why this problem is a problem for contemporary philosophy, I will mention three as the immediate contexts for this intervention. Firstly, there is Quentin Meillassoux's thesis that contingency is the only necessity, according to which there is no single reason for what exists and how it exists. Apparently a denial of the PSR, Meillassoux's claim is in fact expressly designed to satisfy it, albeit paradoxically.[4] Yet the character of the question is irrevocably altered if it is asked what grounds any particular satisfaction of the principle; or again, as Meillassoux notes,[5] what necessitates contingency in nature. Now this recursivity or regress might be held to afflict any putative satisfaction of the PSR; but it indicates that although the PSR is logically satisfied, it is not, nor can it be, really or materially satisfied by reason alone.

The second reason concerns the dispute regarding groundedness that has arisen in the contemporary philosophy of nature. This has arisen due to the majority habit amongst contributors to that field of considering the powers they theorize as dispositional properties. The problem is, if powers are grounded as the properties of substances of whatever nature, the ontology becomes dualistic, comprising powers irreducible to substances and substances without powers as inert substrata for them, but with no account of a *vinculum* to bond them. Accordingly, some have argued for the ungroundedness of powers, leaving a one-tier ontology with powers all the way down. This is a spectacular replay of Schelling's theory of *Potenzen* on the one hand, but also of a speculative tradition derived from John Locke's powers metaphysics, on the other, and best exemplified by Whitehead's reworking of the Lockean theory of powers in *Process and Reality*.

The third reason concerns the philosophy of matter. Rather than wasting time complaining about those contemporary philosophers who call their models 'materialist' on the wholly spurious grounds of the experiential ubiquity of the elements so christened, I maintain that this is a problem that organizes the core tasks of the philosophy of nature. The dualism of atoms and force that lay at the core of Newtonian mechanistic materialism, and which is evident in the 'grounded' powers theorists in the philosophy of nature noted above, attests to an unresolved problem as regards the metaphys-

4. See Quentin Meillassoux, *After Finitude*, trans. Ray Brassier, London, Continuum, 2008. For his exchange with me on the subject of the principle of sufficient reason, see the transcript of the London *Speculative Realism* workshop, in Ray Brassier, et al., 'Speculative Realism', *Collapse*, vol. 3, 2007, pp. 443-444.

5. Brassier, Ray, Iain Hamilton Grant, Graham Harman, and Quentin Meillassoux, 'Speculative Realism', *Collapse*, vol. 3, 2007, 2007, p. 444.

ics of matter, namely, the conception of an inert, underlying substance. This remains unresolved because of the difficulty of conceiving of matter as anything other than the ground on which all things rest; in other words, because of the insistence on thinking matter in terms of the concepts by which Aristotle theorizes substance. Matter, that is, is the ultimate ground supporting each stratum of being. It is on this basis, for example, that it is possible to argue that existents and their supposed properties may be edited from our ontologies on the basis of whether or not they are material or not. The paradoxical dualism inherent in the ontology of the eliminative materialist that I noted at the 2007 Speculative Realism workshop, stems precisely from this conception; ultimately, however, all eliminativisms, whether materialist or idealist, derive from either the concept of substrate or superstratum, depending on which way round dependency is conceived. Only if materialism is regarded as an ontological thesis, rather than a place-holder within the epistemological concerns of the philosophy of science,[6] or as a precursor for an ethico-political project,[7] do the true dimensions of the problem emerge: if materialism is true, nothing is not material. It is this thesis that has led Galen Strawson to advocate a 'real materialism' that, for example, entails panpsychism[8] but also, unfortunately, to deny materiality to abstracta such as numbers and concepts. Yet there is a problem with this claim, not least because this is precisely what Leibniz designed the PSR to do: to enable the 'ascent' from the contingent physical world to the eternal order of reasons, and thus to include each in the other. Should materiality be withdrawn from one region of being then materialism, as defined above, is not true. Hence, for instance, Plotinus' assertion that in the Intelligible World, 'there is matter there too',[9] namely, 'the substance of the Ideas in general'.[10]

Conceived as an ontological problem, the role of matter would be equivalent to that of ground. The philosophical position for which matter grounds beings is a naturalistic materialism. Yet any appeal to self-evidence the equivalence of matter and ground may have enjoyed is shattered by the problems of the primordiality of matter with respect to energy which, although overt in Plato, were only introduced into physics in the mid-nineteenth century, and much amplified in the twentieth. If, for example, 'material states' are regional turbulences in flows and counterflows of energy, then 'matter' can no longer maintain its ontological role as ground—the basis of beings—while 'ground', by contrast, has nothing substance-like about it, but consists instead of powers. An anti-naturalistic materialism may then maintain that 'matter as

---

6. Galen Strawson, in *Real Materialism and Other Essays*, Oxford, Oxford University Press, 2008, p.19, is prompted to an 'agnosticism' as regards basing our accounts of the nature of matter on the best available physics by the insuperable contingency of any scientific model thereof, and so rejects this epistemic constraint on the nature of matter.

7. Alain Badiou's *Logics of Worlds*, trans. Alberto Toscano, London, Continuum, 2009 provides exactly this analysis of the virtues of materialism, specifically conceived as a 'materialist dialectic' to make good the shortcomings of the 'democratic materialism' of bodies and languages as the most ubiquitous elements of experience. Noting that the elements of speech and animality are derived from Aristotle's analysis of the essence of the human being from the *Nichomachean Ethics* as present to its democratic variety, it is no surprise that the aim of the 'materialist dialectic' is to develop these 'material' elements of our being in order to answer the question 'What is it to live?'. As such, this sophisticated species of neo-Fichteanism amounts in fact to an ethics.

8. Strawson repeatedly notes a plausible non-distinguishability of his account of materialism from certain (although perhaps not German) idealisms (*Real Materialism and Other Essays*, pp. 23, 41). For his account of the panpsychist implications of 'real materialism', see pp. 53-74 of the same work.

9. Plotinus, *The Enneads*, trans. Stephen MacKenna, vol. 2, New York, Larson Publications, 1992, p. 4.

10. Plotinus, *The Enneads*, vol. VI, p. 6.

such' is characterized not by the ground-function, but rather by precisely its regionality, its finitude, with the consequence that there is no dualism inherent in superadding immaterials of whatever nature to an ontology that nevertheless accommodates matter. Materialism thereafter becomes the philosophy of finitude, or of macroreality,[11] and has nothing to do, therefore, with subatomic or relativity physics—or with physics at all—on the one hand, nor with the metaphysics of ground, on the other. Neither physical nor grounding, then, in what sense does such a materialism rely on 'matter' at all, rather than, for instance, on experience? Postponing for the present the problem of substance-or-power aspect-duality which, as Bruno noted in the late fifteenth century, characterizes the metaphysics of matter, it is rather the concept of ground that is too rapidly given up here. That ground may not be substantial does not mean that it cedes priority with respect to the grounded, which is henceforth the totality of the actual. To reject this latter view is to assert what we might call the antecedence criterion that attaches to ground.

Of course, antecedence can be maintained without reference to physicalism or naturalism, and 'ground' therefore considered as a formal rather than a material problem. This is the approach taken recently by Gunnar Hindrichs,[12] and which we will examine in what follows. Hindrichs provides a functionalist model of the operation of grounding, which amounts to asserting the equivalence of ground, act and form. Yet there is no reason why act is form only, rather than matter, unless matter is conceived as inherently inert, i.e. as non-act or nonactual in the manner common to Aristotle, St Augustine and Fichte, on the one hand, but also to the entire tradition stemming from the Newtonian duality of matter and force known as mechanistic materialism, and those contemporary philosophers who assert that if powers play any role in the metaphysics of nature, it can only be as the properties of some unnamed substance.

Prior to the substance model, there is also the dynamist conception of matter, as introduced into physics by Hans Christian Oersted in 1820,[13] but into philosophy by Plato. A dynamical conception of matter as ground therefore entails an extended reexamination of the potentiality-actuality couple in Aristotelian metaphysics, and in consequence, an extension of the somewhat limited scope of the modern concept of modality.

While, through Badiou and others, 'materialisms' enjoy a considerable and widespread contemporary press, unexamined at their core remains the nature of matter. Many materialisms are in consequence dependent, as we shall see, on a meontology, that is, on an eliminativism that transforms 'crude matter' into 'the essence of nonessence'. With regard to such 'materialisms', we agree with Heidegger's diagnosis that

---

11. d'Espagnat, Bernard, *Physics and Philosophy*, Princeton, Princeton University Press, 2006, pp. 274 ff.

12. See Gunnar Hindrichs, *Das Absolute und das Subjekt: Untersuchungen zur Verhältnis von Metaphysik und Nachmetaphysik*, Frankfurt, Vittorio Klostermann, 2008.

13. Oersted's experimental demonstration of electromagnetism was published in 1820 as 'Experimenta circa effectum conflictus electrici in acum magneticam'. Seventeen years earlier, however, in *Materialen zu einer Chemie des Neunzehnten Jahrhunderts* (Regensburg, Montag- und Weißische Buchhandlung, 1803), Oersted was already speculating about the unity of the forces of nature: 'The constituent principles of heat which play their role in the alkalis and acids, in electricity, and in light are also the principles of magnetism, and thus we have the unity of all forces which, working on each other, govern the whole cosmic system, and the former physical sciences thus combine into one united physics [...]. Our physics would thus be no longer a collection of fragments on motion, on heat, on air, on light on electricity, on magnetism, and who knows what else, but we would include the whole universe in one system'. See Robert Stauffer, 'Speculation and experiment in the background of Oersted's discovery of electromagnetism', *Isis*, no. 48, 1957, pp. 33-50.

'materialism itself is simply not something material. It is itself a shape of mind',[14] which brings such materialisms into far closer proximity with even German Idealisms than Strawson[15] fears.

For such philosophies, materialism is that position which denies the possibility of any being-in-itself of matter. To the extent that what motivates such 'materialism' is the rejection of any preintentional or non-actuous existent, it is equivalent to a subjective idealism of a Berkeleyan stamp. What differentiates materialism from Berkeleyan immaterialism, therefore, is not matter as such, but matter only insofar as it is formed by activity. Matter not so formed is, 'almost nothing', as Augustine has it,[16] so act-materialism entails a meontology and a practical eliminativism with respect to matter as such, which procedure I have elsewhere called the ethical process. Accordingly, the antithetical relation of materialism to matter opens up the ontological problem of the relative primacy of matter (as 'mere' possibility) and activity in the determination of actuality, the struggle given form by Fichte's eliminativist calculus of activity's triumph over being. Because such an idealist gambit continues to underwrite materialist philosophies, it will be important for us to consider it in this paper from the naturalist perspective initially opened up by Fichte's own contemporaries in the natural sciences.

Yet there is a further, metaphysical objection to any ontological inquiry that takes 'matter' as its focus. This view suggests that 'matter', as contingent rather than necessary, can only belong to metaphysics, but has no place in ontology, now recast as the science of what necessarily is. An overt Cartesianism[17] opens up at this juncture, since the reason of being—the ground—need not, and therefore cannot, be supplied by matter.

The problem of what matter is involves two main paths of metaphysical inquiry. Firstly, the problem of substance and force, exemplified philosophically by Bruno's 'ambiguous' account of matter conceived as substance or as force; and physically by Michael Faraday's definition, 'the substance is ... its powers'. The second path arises directly from this physical dimension, and concerns the problem of ground. The logical dimension of the problem concerns ground as 'reason-supplying' for being, or the satisfaction of the PSR. Yet the PSR, as Leibniz formulates it, embraces both physics and metaphysics. Asking after the ground of being in this sense entails asking both that the Principle be logically satisfied and that ground itself be explicated both in terms of the reason for being and its physical basis. Thus the problem of ground turns towards ontology, from which it turns back to matter. The inquiry into ground is therefore the metaphysical problem of matter, understood ontologically and physically; or, in other words, in terms of a philosophy of nature.

Yet naturalism, or some version of it, are not the only possible routes for the ontological explication of matter or of ground. (1) Field-theoretic physics and metaphysics supplant both the material and the naturalistic conception of ground. We shall

---

14. Martin Heidegger, *The Principle of Reason*, trans. Reginald Lilly, Bloomington, Indiana University Press, 1991, p. 199. Lilly's translation gives 'mind-set' for Heidegger's *Gestalt des Geistes* (p.122), thus obscuring its echo of Hegel's *Phenomenology of Spirit*.

15. Strawson, *Real Materialism and Other Essays*, p. 41.

16. Augustine, *Confessions*, trans. Henry Chadwick, Oxford, Oxford University Press, 1998, XII.8.

17. And Aristotelianism, from which the ascription of relative not-being to matter stems. cf. *Metaphysics* IV,4, 1007b27-9 (Aristotle, *Metaphysics*, trans. Hugh Tredennick, Cambridge, Harvard University Press, 1961-62) where, speaking of Anaxagoras' 'panchrematism', he writes, 'they are speaking of the indeterminate; and while they think they are speaking of what exists, they are really speaking of what does not; for the Indeterminate is that which exists potentially but not actually'.

see this in Fichte's attempt, following Kant's self-confessed failure, pursuing a force-theoretical physics, to ground the basic forces of a dynamic nature, to ground them not in being at all, but in a 'meontology' of acting. (2) anti-naturalistic conceptions of ground have found their way again into recent speculative philosophy, in Meillassoux (despite appearances), and in Gunnar Hindrichs, whose *Das Absolute und das Subjekt* involves a highly developed account of a denatured, logical conception of ground that in many ways follows from Kant's reconception of ground as 'ground of possibility', yet leaves the nature of possibility—of potency or power—unexamined. As we shall see, Hindrichs' account attempts to make good on this Kantian deficit by replacing *dunamis* in logical space alone, an approach he shares with much contemporary modal metaphysics.

Common to both these approaches is the wresting of dynamics from nature, and the consequent ontological demotion of physis to a metaphysical option. In many ways, this is prepared for by Aristotle's accounting of physis as only one mode of being ('nature is only a genus of being'[18]). Dynamics becomes an activity henceforth considered antithetical to a dead nature, or inhering only in logical space. Both, then, involve the progressive abstraction of the PSR from its naturalistic beginnings: it is by means of this 'great principle', writes Leibniz, that 'we rise from physics to metaphysics'.[19] Now since beginnings are precisely what ground is supposed to furnish, such accounts of ground are in fact ungroundings of it. The dilemma for a naturephilosophical ontology arises precisely here: for ungrounding is exactly what a field-theoretic meta-physics entails, so any protest against the ungroundedness of anti-naturalistic accounts of ground would stand *ipso facto* against naturalistic field-theoretic accounts in turn. The alternative, therefore, with its intuitively comforting advantages, is to return the problem of matter to a substance-metaphysical basis. It is the near inconceivability of matter without substantial being that prompts Bruno's ambivalent (and Aristotelian, all his ascerbic protestations to the contrary) oscillation between matter and force.

The Platonic alternative of conceiving being as power (*Sophist* 247e4), ungrounds the primacy of substance with respect to powers, whether at the level of possessing subjects, as in contemporary philosophies of nature, or at the level of mechanical materialism in general. What this does to the substance-basis of the problem of matter is what remains uninvestigated. As a prologue to a fuller investigation of the problem as a whole, therefore, I propose in what follows to investigate the relations between dynamics, matter and nature, on the one hand, and between the dynamics of reason and the operation of grounding, on the other. I treat of Fichte in the first part, since on the face of things, while self-presenting as the antithete to naturalism, Fichte's own adoption of dynamics has fascinating consequences as regards the naturalisms stemming from it. In the second part, I examine the recent attempt, by Gunnar Hindrichs, to reopen the problem of ground from the perspective of a dynamics inhering in reason alone, and inflecting only therefore logical space. Both, as we shall see, regionalize dynamics with respect to being as a means to eliminate dimensions of the problem of ground. The essay will conclude with an attempt to outline the antecedence that powers introduce across every dimension of the problem of ground.

---

18. Aristotle, *Metaphysics*, 1005a35.

19. G.W. Leibniz, *Principles of Nature and Grace, Based on Reason*, in *Philosophical Essays*, trans. R. Ariew and D. Garber, Indianapolis, Hackett, 1989, §7.

DYNAMICS AND THE INACTUALITY OF MATTER IN FICHTE

> It is certainly not true that the pure I is a product of the not-I .... The assertion that the pure I is a product of the not-I expresses a transcendental materialism which is completely contrary to reason. —Fichte[20]

It is not easy to see why reason would be contradicted—why the law of non-contradiction would be violated—by the physical production and determination of apperception. Yet in keeping with the grounding of the *Wissenschaftslehre* in dynamics, Fichte's point is not merely that an I *is not* generated in this way, it is that *it cannot be so generated.* Nor is the point simply that an I cannot arise from what is not-I; it is rather that were it to be so considered, the result would be the contradiction, $I=(\neg I)$.

Yet the contradiction has not only a formal but also, as it were, a 'material' element. Fichte's contemporary Andreas Hülsen explains in the context of an essay on the *Bildungstrieb*, the 'formative force':

> It is necessary in itself that as certainly as we are generally active, we must in general also have an end for our activity. For a freely acting being, however, this end cannot lie outside self-determination [...]. But if ... we consider the phenomena of active life, then we must allow that contingency has a power over us, so indeed that our freedom cannot sustain the determination of this end [...]. We confront this contradiction in the explanation of free activity in accordance with the facts of experience .... [21]

Here the material element consists in *experience.* In explaining this, Hülsen adds further information to our account of Fichte's rejection of transcendental materialism. The contradiction $I=\neg I$ expresses the encounter of the necessity of activity on the part of the I and the 'power of contingency' on the part of nature, which counters it. 'Experience' then consists in the encounter between the contingent and the necessary; that this necessity *can* be countered by contingency, however, further informs us that its nature is hypothetical: that is, for end *x*, action *p* is necessary. And the 'ground' therefore of this explanation can be afforded only by 'free activity' or '*selfactivity*'.[22]

Hülsen provides the formal contradiction of transcendental materialism and the I with material conditions. Yet Fichte's statement of the contradiction further develops the theme of 'material conditions'. The argument runs:

> $I \neq I$; therefore, the I is not *generated* from a not-I.

Fichte calls this error 'transcendental materialism' because the conditions under which it claims to supply the *generative* conditions of the I are material, physical, so that we may conclude: $(\neg I)$ = matter, goal-vitiating contingency. We may further conclude that it is not only the case that $I \neq$ matter, but *also that this applies all the way down*: the ground of the I is the I; that of matter, matter. Thus Fichte's claim of contradiction is not founded only on the formal difference $I/\neg I$, but also on the material difference between purposive activity and contingent vitiation *and* on the difference in the conditions of generation: transcendental materialism is an error—a contradiction—because in it, the causes of *being* are exchanged for the causes of *activity*.

---

20. J. G. Fichte, *Some Lectures Concerning the Scholar's Vocation* (1794) in J. G. Fichte, *Fichtes sämmtliche Werke*, ed. I. H. Fichte, XI vols., Berlin, de Gruyter, 1971, VI, pp. 294-295, and J. G. Fichte, *Fichte. Early Philosophical Writings*, trans. Daniel Breazeale, Ithaca, Cornell University Press, 1988, p. 147.

21. August Ludwig Hülsen, 'Über den Bildungstrieb', in *Philosophisches Journal einer Gesellschaft Teutscher Gelehrten* vol.7 (1798). 'Cited from Martin Oesch, *Aus den Frühzeit des deutschen Idealismus. Texte zur Wissenschaftslehre Fichtes 1794-1804*, Würzburg, Königshausen und Neumann, 1987, pp. 99-101.

22. Hülsen, 'Über den Bildungstrieb', cited in Oesch, *Aus den Frühzeit des deutschen Idealismus*, pp. 102-103.

Ultimately, it is the difference of being from activity (a distinction Hülsen denies it is possible to make) that drives Fichte's programme:

> the concept of being [*Seyns*] is by no means regarded as a primary and original [*erster und unsprünglicher*] concept, but merely as derivative, as a concept derived... through counterposition [*Gegensatz*] to activity, and hence as a merely negative concept.[23]

This is the ontological problem that grounds the contradiction of I and ¬I: whatever *is*, does not *act*; what *acts*, *is not*. The *Foundations of Natural Right* provides the next step in this division:

> on its own, nature... cannot really bring about change in itself. All change is contrary to the concept of nature[24]

Meanwhile, the final step is already overt in the 1794 *Wissenschaftslehre*: 'everything reproduces itself';[25] 'every thing is what it is'.[26] Fichte moves from material to formal, and then from formal to generative grounds, ceding generative power only to activity, not to being: production *is not*, but *acts*.

Of the many points of interest here, we single out four: firstly, Fichte provides an account of sufficient reason or ground that has hypothetical (dependent or conditional) necessity competing with contingency to determine the *nature* or *character* of actuality; secondly, that this ground is considered not only as a 'space of reasons' but also as a causal ground; thirdly, that this posits an epigenetic-inductive genetic procedure involving the self-reproduction of the same (I from I, not-I from not-I) generating what may be called the *order of eternals*: if everything is what it is = reproduces itself, no thing has never come to be (contrary to the hypothesis of transcendental materialism), nor can it even cease to be—a 'thing' has such limited *potentia* that it *cannot even not be*, while its actuality consists in its always being what it is. Fourthly, there is here, contrary to appearances, a direct engagement with the problems of materialism; specifically, transcendental materialism is demonstrated necessarily false to clear the way for a formally generated, rationally grounded materialist concept of causation whose necessity is hypothetical only. Transcendental materialism is so-called because according to it, all of nature, including mind, is generated by and as a matter that self-transcends in becoming *other than it is*, and thus contradicting the order of eternals by which Fichte defines a nature to which change is contrary.

This was already explicit in *Concerning the Concept of the Wissenschaftslehre* (1794):

> The *Wissenschaftslehre* furnishes us with nature [1ᵉ: 'with a not-I'] as something necessary—with nature as something which, both in its being and its specific determinations, has to be viewed as independent of us. It also furnishes ... the laws according to which nature should and must be observed. But the power of judgment still retains its complete freedom to apply these laws or not ...'.[27]

We discover here that nature is 'necessary in its being and in its specific determinations', or rather, that the *Wissenschaftslehre* or 'theory of science' *furnishes* us with such

23. Fichte, *Fichtes sämmtliche Werke*, I, p. 499, and J. G. Fichte, *The Science of Knowledge*, trans. Peter Heath and John Lachs, Cambridge, UK: Cambridge University Press, 1982.

24. Fichte, *Fichtes sämmtliche Werke*, Vol. III, p. 115, and J. G. Fichte, *Foundations of Natural Right*, trans. Frederick Neuhouser, Cambridge, UK: Cambridge University Press, 2000, p. 105.

25. Fichte, *Fichtes sämmtliche Werke*, Vol. I, pp. 170-171, and Fichte, *The Science of Knowledge*, pp. 158-159.

26. Fichte, *Fichtes sämmtliche Werke*, Vol. I, p. 154, and Fichte, *The Science of Knowledge*, p. 154.

27. Fichte, *Fichtes sämmtliche Werke*, Vol. I, pp. 64-65, and Fichte. *Early Philosophical Writings*, p. 121.

a nature, which *must be viewed as* 'independent of us'. This sounds like a contradiction: the necessary being of nature and its specific determinations, is 'our' product that we must consider *not* to be 'our' product. but it is not a contradiction. Rather, the theory of science *supplies the formal ground* for the determination of the material: the determination of the power of judgment by a rule furnished by a necessity that *must be considered* as proper to nature.

The clarity of Fichte's completion of Kant is evident by contrast with the following passage concerning nature from the *Jäsche Logic*:

> Everything in nature, in the lifeless as well as in the living world, happens in accordance with rules, even if we will never know these rules [...]. All of nature in general is simply nothing but a continuum of appearances in accordance with rules, and there is simply no rulelessness.[28]

Fichte asks us not simply to consider how nature (or the not-I) is (i.e., in its necessity), but rather how it 'should and must be observed' (in its multiple determinability), in which act of observation it becomes subject to final determination by the *free* power of judgment.[29] Necessity is, according to the *Theory of Science*, subject to determination because the power of judgment lies not in being but in acting (the material contradiction), in the positing that sets off myriad possible determinations of unlimited space: The theory of science furnishes us with space as something necessary and with the point as absolute limit. But it grants to the imagination complete freedom to place this point wherever it likes.[30]

The task of Fichte's *Science* is not simply to declare the priority of ethics over ontology, but rather to provide a method or a proceedure by means of which this is to be achieved. Hülsen's *material* contradiction becomes the formal ground for its solution: Considered as a reciprocal determination of the not-I by the I, acting strives to reduce being to zero, to the free point which is the permanently recoverable origin of free activity. Fichte's formalism designs and implements an operation that, in the free activity of the reduction of being, reacts on itself, recursively increasing the quantity of free activity in a determinable field consisting of quanta of being and activity. Hülsen summarizes:

> our activity stands in a necessary and immediate relation to nature. It is real contact. We are active in nature through our own free determination, and nature acts on us in turn, determining through our representations of its forces and ends our effectiveness in it .... The ends of nature must therefore correspond to our own, and its forces have their ground in one and the same principle as do ours.[31]

The theory of science, then, supplies formal *and* material grounds on the basis of which transcendental materialism is necessarily false, and supplants that transcendental materialism that would, paradoxically, determine the being of activity, with an ideal materialism, that will determine being *by* activity.

---

28. Immanuel Kant, *Kants gesammelte Schriften*, Königlich Preussische Akademie der Wissenschaften, vols. XXIX, vol. IX, Berlin, Walter de Gruyter, 1902, p. 11.

29. Schelling was appalled: '[W]hat is, in the end, the essence of his entire understanding of nature? It is that nature must be employed, used, and that it exists no further than it is thus employed; the principle in accordance with which he views nature is economic-teleological: 'It must be thus', he says (that is, we must appropriate nature), so that human life gains freedom through its own freedom. Now for this it is necessary that one subjugate natural forces to human ends'. Schelling, *Schellings sämmtliche Werke*, vol. VI, p. 370.

30. Fichte, *Fichtes sämmtliche Werke*, vol. I, p. 64, and Fichte, *Early Philosophical Writings*, p. 121.

31. Hülsen, 'Über den Bildungstrieb', pp. 110-111.

It is precisely in this ideal materialism that Fichte's formalism acquires in turn a material ground, one moreover that unites the ideal and the physical:

1. Being, thought as Aristotelian substance, is supplanted by dynamics;[32] inert matter becomes 'the matter of reciprocity [*die Materie des Wechsels*]'[33] because 'the truth is that we cannot separate being from activity'.[34] This brought Fichte the support of medical researchers such as Andreas Röschlaub, Schelling's co-editor on the *Annals of Scientific Medicine* (1806-7), and erstwhile Brunonian;

2. Bodies in empty space become an abstraction, ultimately ethically determined, to be replaced by a field ontology. Both consequences together satisfy Faraday's formula towards field theories in physics: 'the substance is composed of its powers'. [35]

It is in this regard that Fichte's theory of science raises the question concerning the adequacy of a merely formal account of the problem of ground, and its separation from the material context of the problems of generation (causality), real contradiction (contrary pressures), hypothetical and natural necessity (the possibility or actuality of unconditioned necessity) and physicalism (the nature of substance).

While Fichte does indeed engage the problem of ground across these areas, the theory of science ultimately filters them through the lens of judgment, so that, with some modifications, 'the theory of judgment (apophantics) and the theory of being (ontology) coincide'.[36]

THE COINCIDENCE OF JUDGMENT AND BEING: OPERATIONAL LOGICAL SPACE

Hindrichs' excellent work, *Das Absolute und das Subjekt*, provides an innovative account of ground and grounding. As in Fichte, Hindrichs finds a formalism to accommodate the problem of genesis and ontology, and a concept of ground independent therefore of the elements of this formalism, although the latter is not expressly exclusive of a nature outside it. Unlike Fichte, Hindrichs is entirely unconcerned with any problem of materialism, so that the dynamics it involves has not even the faintest analogical relation to nature. As Hegel said of Kant, in Hindrichs, 'concepts remain contingent with respect to nature just as nature does with respect to the concepts'.[37] That his account of the *logical space* of the operation of grounding succeeds Fichte's will make clear the deficiencies of a formalism with respect to the problem of ground.

Hindrichs' starting point for the thinking of ground is a reassessment of Kant's refutation of the ontological argument as a positive account of the nature of the absolute. 'The concept of the absolute receives its true determination in Kant's critique of the ontological proof', and it is only now, he writes, that

---

32. 'The *Science of Knowledge* replaces Aristotelian metaphysics. The latter was the science of being as being. The science of knowledge is to be 'the pragmatic history of the human mind' [*IWI*, p. 222; 1982, pp. 198-199]. This new conception of 'history', which is to be an 'experimental perceiving' [*IWI*, p. 222; 1982, p. 199], is directed towards the grounding experiment with a new—unknown until then—dynamism'. Nelly Tsouyopoulos, 'Die neue Auffassung der klinischen Medizin als Wissenschaft unter dem Einfluß der Philosophie im frühen 19. Jahrhundert', *Berichte zur Wissenschaftsgeschichte* 1 (1978), p. 91.

33. Fichte, *Fichtes sämmtliche Werke*, vol. I, pp. 170-171 and Fichte, *The Science of Knowledge*, p. 159.

34. Hülsen, 'Über den Bildungstrieb', pp. 118.

35. Michael Faraday, *Experimental researches in Electricity*, vols. 3, vol. 1, London, Taylor, 1839, p. 362.

36. Hindrichs, *Das Absolute und das Subjekt*, pp. 174-175.

37. G. W. F. Hegel, *The Difference Between Fichte's and Schelling's System of Philosophy*, trans. Walter Cerf and H. S. Harris, New York, SUNY Press, 1977, p. 164.

the ontological argument can be understood, now that it has been crushed. But the ontological argument was that argument that was to have led to the absolute. [… I]t therefore
follows that only now can we understand the concept of the absolute. In Kant's critique it
reached the end of its legitimate application and at the same time its ground.[38]

Whether for Hindrichs or the Classical German Idealists, the task for all post-Kantian
philosophers is no longer to supply an answer to the question: 'why are there beings rather
than nothing?', that is, to satisfy the PSR; it is rather to argue from the conditioned to the
totality of all conditions. Kant shatters ground into grounds, making the absolute into their
totality (*omnitudo realitatis*), a totality that it is not possible for finite thinking to think unless
it is able to recover its own conditions and thus present itself *as* absolute or unconditioned.

As a post-Kantian, Hindrichs' own solution is to seek the ground of the absolute in
a logical space incorporating a functional account of reference, and it is this move, its
mechanism and its significance, that demonstrates the extent of Hindrichs' neo-Fichteanism. For what is it, exactly, that is or can be grounded *exclusively* in logical space?
Rather, than seeking 'the ground' or 'the reason' as such, Hindrichs' investigates the
space of reasons for the operation of grounding:

> Every thing that the principle of reason [*Satz vom Grund*] governs, it governs in such a way
> that this thing is either a ground or a grounded. But a ground and a grounded are in turn
> a ground of some thing, and a grounded by some thing.[39]

Hindrichs' account of this operation effectively makes grounding into a function of
reasons, so that grounding is achieved when a state of affairs satisfies or saturates the
ground given by that operation. What thus satisfies the grounding function is the reference of one well-ordered element in a system to another such element. 'Order' is here
conceived in the following manner:

> Every singular that is possible stands in a possible order of singulars. This possible order
> itself stands in an order of possible orders. All these orders are determined by the princi-
> ple of reason. Something ordered is in consequence grounded.[40]

To be grounded, meanwhile, is to ground another singular and to be grounded by
another—that is, to stand in an order. Grounding and ground, each ordered singular, form a network of relations. 'Relatedness' means 'on the one hand its relatedness
as grounded to its ground, and on the other hand, its relatedness as ground to what
it grounds';[41] any singular that is *not* related is not saturated; that is, it is *defunctionalized*
to the extent it does not relate.[42] This analysis of ground therefore produces the shat-
tering of ground as the preparation for the absolute. That there is a reason for beings
turns out not to be grounded in singulars, but rather in the analysis of being: singulars
do not possess being except in their relatedness to others—*esse in alio*. A being is nothing other therefore than a 'vertex' in the grounding network, or 'an occasional conduit
for the process of ground and consequent'.[43]

The proximity *at this point* of Hindrichs' scheme to Graham Harman's metaphysics is as striking as their differences—for while Hindrichs follows Fichte's dis-

---

38. Hindrichs, *Das Absolute und das Subjekt*, p. 123.

39. Hindrichs, *Das Absolute und das Subjekt*, p. 199.

40. Hindrichs, *Das Absolute und das Subjekt*, pp. 206-207.

41. Hindrichs, *Das Absolute und das Subjekt*, p. 210.

42. Interestingly, Hindrichs here provides a solution to the necessity (albeit hypothetical) of connected-
ness that troubles Humeans.

43. Hindrichs, *Das Absolute und das Subjekt*, p. 210.

solution of being, replacing it not with activity, but with function, for Harman it is *things* that have their being in another. The question may best perhaps be answered by him, therefore, as to whether this logical order satisfies things, while of course things, as referents of propositions, satisfy those propositions simply by obtaining-or-not. The question this raises is, simply put, whether Hindrichs' ontology extends beyond judgments at all, or whether it consists solely and exclusively in judgments and their satisfactions.

Having pursued the analysis to the point where singulars have disappeared into other-relating relations, Hindrichs proceeds to the—necessary, he says—synthesis. This synthesis is not, as for the crass formalisation of which Hegelianism has been caricatured, the union of opposites (the absolute and the subject—although it *is in fact*), but rather reverts to the order of the possibles referred to earlier, and pursues this by means of the order of 'conduits', or of grounds and groundeds. If singulars are ordered by relations, then that order,

> as the grounding continuum of singulars—presents itself in turn as a synthesis of singulars into a closed unity. Thus the analysis of the orderly leads to the synthesis that refers to the order of beings.[44]

The hinge articulating the operations of analysis and synthesis is *reflexion*, which Hindrichs describes as 'not the simple application of thought to itself', but rather that application 'after thought has gone out of itself to things; it is the being-with-itself of thought and, in this, being in another'.[45] Reflexion is not what Hegel condemned, but rather the process he followed; what is reflected is not a supposed content of thought, but rather its structure is reflected in all its operations.

While following Kant's simultaneous hypothetical totalisation of conditions and their actual exponentiation, Hindrichs' account of the way to the absolute turns away from conditions of possibility or of hypothetical necessity, and towards the totality of possible orders that form 'logical space'.[46] The order so presented by the grounding continuum of singulars has no being unless it is related to another order—this time an order of orders: 'the order of the continuum of grounds therefore constitutes itself the ground of a second order order'.[47] Pursued to its synthetic ends, Hindrichs thus satisfies the Kantian programme, precisely where he argues that Hegel and the postkantians failed, grounding an absolute:

> The principle of reason operates in the order of orders: in logical space.[48]

At this point, we have a functional account of the absolute that rules everything out except insofar as it satisfies those functions, i.e., the principle of sufficient reason. It is important to note, however, that it is not beings *per se* that satisfy propositions concerning singulars, but rather relations between singulars as conduits for grounding in a continuum of orders. Thus, while Hindrichs' speculative audacity aims, like all metaphysics, at 'the conceptual structure of a total continuum',[49] no qualitative difference is made to the 'order of being' by the inclusion, amongst the order of orders, of possible orders, even of *all possible* orders.

---

44. Hindrichs, *Das Absolute und das Subjekt*, pp. 213-214.
45. Hindrichs, *Das Absolute und das Subjekt*, p. 149.
46. Hindrichs, *Das Absolute und das Subjekt*, p. 203.
47. Hindrichs, *Das Absolute und das Subjekt*, p. 214.
48. Hindrichs, *Das Absolute und das Subjekt*, p. 203.
49. Hindrichs, *Das Absolute und das Subjekt*, p. 224.

Accordingly, the mooted identity of judgment and being is true if and only if the *act* or *operation* of judgment has its content (being) in itself; in other words, either the ground of being is any judgment whatever, or 'being' is only that content immanent to the operation of judgment. Is the contention that the description of relations in logical terms allows being to be deduced from it? Is this not simply the ontological proof in turn, albeit limited to the genesis of additional elements to form a logical (meta)order? Ironically, this 'working Hegel' turns out to reproduce, in the Absolute ground, the unrelatedness of reason to nature that was for Hegel the hallmark of Kant's philosophy of nature. The absolute, as the totality of conditions, contains only one set of conditioneds: thoughts having as their content the identity of judgment and being.

*   *   *

A thought that is unconditioned—now *that* is a contradiction. By what is it conditioned? This takes us back to the investigation of the dimensions of the problem of ground with which we began.

For all the operativity in Hindrichs' orders, logical space remains timeless and ungenerated. The order of orders invites an obvious Platonic parallel: just as the operators, the conduits and relations, satisfactions and movements of thought form the permanent furniture of the intelligible, of the 'space of reasons', for Hindrichs, so for Plato the Ideas are the higher attractors of the lower, marking out the possible motions of the thinkable. Yet Plato's attractor-Ideas also orient all the motions of material becomings, of the processes in nature. While the Ideas are the Intelligibles against which natural production invariably falls short (so runs the story), they are invariably embroiled in the turbulences of becoming, since without this latter, Plato would not have advanced one step beyond the Parmenidean One.

Hindrichs attempts to counter something of this order of objections when he considers a criticism he attributes to Jacobi: that the order of reasons has been confused with the order of causation:

> Conceptions that think the world from the principle of reason confuse timeless ground and temporal causation. Although they speak about the world and therefore about temporal causal relations, they leap immediately into the atemporal relations of grounding that is logic, which is of course to be distinguished from what is.[50]

Hindrichs' counterobjections are twofold; firstly, epistemological: without the timeless relations of logical relations of grounding, *we simply could not comprehend* temporal causal relations. The second counter is that, the objection misunderstands the nature of the conceptual series which is, *ex hypothesi*, a timeless series of 'grounds and consequents'. Again, this reinforces Hegel's judgment that 'time [...] has no philosophical significance whatever'.[51] But the Jacobian objection has more to it than that: it is neither an epistemological nor a conceptual objection but rather, as is the constant theme of his *Spinoza* book, a *material* objection. If we apply, that is, the timeless order of grounding relations to the world, we generate the following problem:

> Since no part of the manifest cosmos is everything that it can be [since it could be otherwise than it is], how could the existing whole, composed of many such parts, express the completeness of nature which is everything that it can be, and cannot be what it is not?[52]

---

50. Hindrichs, *Das Absolute und das Subjekt*, p. 215. Compare Friedrich Heinrich Jacobi, *Über die Lehre des Spinoza*, Hamburg, Felix Meiner Verlag, 2000, p. 282.

51. Hegel, *Philosophy of Nature*, Oxford, Oxford University Press, 1997, § 339. See also § 249: 'Chronological difference has no interest whatsoever for thought'.

52. Jacobi, *Über die Lehre des Spinoza*, pp. 207-8.

Even if the order of orders includes by definition all possible orders, there is a differ-ence between the kinds of order that obtain and those that do not. Given the obtain-ing order (the 'manifest cosmos'), there are clearly possibilities for its change, and con-ditions of its change, that are such that could never exhaust the totality of possibilities. Jacobi here in effect conceives temporal causal relations as grounded in a specifical-ly determinate nature and as selecting from its possibilities. It is not, in other words, the simple timelessness of grounding-relations, but rather their absolute insusceptibil-ity to the possibilities of physical nature that are themselves temporal (earlier condi-tioning later) and causal (operations on determinate selections of possibilia that are in principle inexhaustible). The existing whole of the manifest cosmos not only could be otherwise, but has the inexhaustible possibility of being other than it is—or even of not being at all.

Although Jacobi's is an objection to the principle of (sufficient) reason itself, the confusion it accuses rationalist accounts of—and against which Hindrichs defends the order of orders—is in fact core to an understanding of the problem of ground, which can neither be thought without nature and causal powers, nor without rational struc-tures. In consequence, we shall pick up the problem of material possibility in the con-cept of ground in the light of the dynamic-formalist and functional-formalist accounts of that concept we have so far examined.

BEING ALL THAT IT IS: THE DIMENSIONS OF THE PROBLEM OF GROUND

Wavering between 'being all that it is' and the inexhaustible possibility of being other than it is, nature, whether manifest or not, seems to repudiate the PSR, whether satis-fiable or not, as an artifice of reason. On what grounds, however, can the assumption be made that reason is thus separable from remaining nature, rather than that being amongst its potentia? Assuming that it is so begs the question of the PSR, rather than satisfying or refuting it, which is why Jacobi's problem has bite: if the PSR is to be sat-isfied, it cannot not include the order of necessary reasons and the order of contingent nature. That this cannot be done is, as we have seen, precisely the claim made by Fich-te, made concrete in the 'First Introduction' to the *Wissenschaftslehre*:

> Intellect and thing are thus exactly counter-posited [*entgegengesetzt*]: they inhabit two worlds between which there is no bridge.[53]

The satisfaction of the space of reasons, however, is only one dimension of the PSR, and one that cannot be met independently of establishing the ground of a nature that cannot be assumed to have exhausted its potentials in its current state.

It is precisely this relation that Leibniz considers the 'great principle' to furnish. Section 7 of *Principles of Nature and Grace* (1714) asserts that its employment provides the means whereby we 'rise' from physics to metaphysics, and thus connecting nature and reason, contingency and necessity. Accordingly, the PSR states that

> *nothing takes place without sufficient reason*; that is to say, that nothing happens with its being possible for one who should know things sufficiently, to give a reason which is sufficient to determine why things are so and not otherwise.[54]

At this stage, the problem of ground is formulated in event-terms, not in entity terms. This is instructive, insofar as it asserts that (a) things *take place* or happen, rather than

---

53. Fichte, *Fichtes sämmtliche Werke*, vol. I, p. 436, & Fichte, *The Science of Knowledge*, 1982, p. 17, trans. modified.

54. G.W. Leibniz, *Philosophical Essays*, trans. Roger Ariew and Daniel Garber, Indianapolis, Hackett, 1989, pp. 209-10.

straightforwardly 'are'; and (b) that the giving of reasons follows *after* these takings-place, or are themselves takings-place. The event-register brings reason-giving into proximity to the causal relations articulated in nature, suggesting that they are not different in kind. Hence the equivalence between the orders of reason and nature, as asserted, for example, in the *Primary Truths* (1686): '*nothing is without reason, or there is no effect without a cause*'.[55] Behind the assertion, however, lies a claim concerning the dimensions of the PSR, or the Leibnizian account of grounding as dependent on an *equivalence* in the temporal sequencing entailed *both* in causal relations and in reason-giving. The same sequencing is even an element in the account of predication Leibniz gives in *Primary Truths*:

> a predicate, or consequent, is always present in a subject, or antecedent; and in this fact constists the universal nature of truth, or the connection between the terms of the assertion, as Aristotle has also observed. [...] Moreover, this is true for every affirmative truth, universal or particular, necessary or contingent.[56]

We might consider the consequent's presence in the antecedent to deny the antecedence of the antecedent and the consequence of the consequent. Yet the 'always present'—the register of 'being' in which, in contrast to the later *Principles of Nature and Grace*, the PSR is couched—only cancels the antecedent-consequent relation in the course of time, that is, in the producing of that truth, and in the contingent conditions about and from which that truth is produced. It is to this that the substitutability of 'subject' and 'antecedent' draws attention. The universal nature of truths, that is, entails that the 'always present' of the antecedent-consequent is true of all truths; thus it is not the *contingency* of the contingent that is here being qualified, but rather its *universal* nature. Thus the PSR is misunderstood to the extent that the 'wondrous secret', as Leibniz notes, of the differentiation between the time of antecedence and consequence and the time of the satisfaction of reason

> goes unnoticed, this secret that reveals the nature of contingency, or the essential distinction between necessary and contingent truths.[57]

This is why Leibniz is the German Plato: because all truths are of the same nature, the order of eternity is *what* satisfies reason; but reason's satisfaction *takes place* in the connection of antecedence and consequents, so that reason as a whole consists in the 're-versibility' of the connection. Contingent truths can therefore 'suffice', and indeed, do so necessarily insofar as they are truths. But, *qua* contingent, it is impossible that there will not always be more such truths. *It is because this is true of all truths that the time of antecedence and consequence is real*, and that there is an *equivalence* between the giving of reasons and the actions of causes.

Accordingly the PSR rejoins physics from metaphysics. For it is this equivalence that holds sway in the use of PSR in the mechanical physics that long outlasted Leibniz. The principle's use in that context is efficiently summarized by Isabelle Stengers: 'the full cause is *equivalent* to the entire effect'.[58] In the physical context, equivalence means that the efficacy—the *power*—of the cause is given as and by the *extent* of the effect. For example, this is the 'best of all possible worlds', argues Leibniz, because the

---

55. Leibniz, *Philosophical Essays*, p. 31.

56. Leibniz, *Philosophical Essays*, p. 31.

57. Leibniz, *Philosophical Essays*, p. 31.

58. Isabelle Stengers, *Power and Invention*, trans. Paul Bains, Minneapolis, University of Minnesota Press, 1997, p.25.

actual (and *therefore* the best) world is the extent of the effect, so that its cause must have sufficient 'fullness' or perfection to actualize it.

It is here that we see the force of Jacobi's objection to Leibniz on the question of powers and actuality: it is impossible that nature, if composed of powers rather than particular bodies, could exhaust or have exhausted these powers *in any particular state*. Yet this too is countered in the *Principles of Nature and Grace*. With regard to the problem of contingent states and their grounding by the PSR, section 8 of the *Principles* states that 'the sufficient reason for the existence of the universe cannot be found in the series of contingent things, that is, in the series of bodies and their representations in souls'.[59] This is because, applied to particulars, the PSR would seek 'the explanation of everything by something else', which clearly must result in an infinite regress.[60] Leibniz illustrates precisely this point in relation to material particulars:

> since matter is in itself indifferent to motion and to rest and to one or another particular motion, we cannot find in it the reason of motion and still less the reason of one particular motion. And although the motion which is at present in matter comes from the preceding motion, and that again from another preceding motion, we are no farther forward, however far we go; for the same question always remains.[61]

Leibniz finally gives God as the 'ultimate ground' of things, and so on the face of things reintroduces the problem of ungrounded contingency that the 'great principle' is designed to resolve. It is this solution against which Jacobi's criticism is in fact directed, since Leibniz's God, as 'a necessary being, bearing in itself the reason of its own existence', must, if considered the 'substance which is the cause of this sequence', be equivalent, by the PSR, to the actual Cosmos that is its effect and which, in turn, must therefore be 'all it can be'.

If this conclusion, however, is contrasted with the question that precedes it, as cited above, as to whether matter is capable of supplying the ground of motion, a different conclusion follows. *That* it cannot entails that no halt can be brought to the sequencing of motion, since motion *by its nature* must always rely on a preceding motion for its velocity and trajectory, and that motion on its antecedent in turn. However, that matter *might* be considered a candidate ground constitutes a problem for two reasons. Firstly, it constitutes a critique of the passivist concept of matter that informs the dualism of matter and force in mechanical materialism, insofar as the idea that matter could thus ground motion depends on conceiving matter as inert in the first place. The second reason, however, maintains that material grounds cannot satisfy the PSR since, if the above concept of matter is rejected in the interests of the 'living force' argument with regard to material nature, and of which Leibniz was a proponent, then motion cannot be self-grounding, since it relies on antecendent and coincident motions. Although therefore neither matter nor motion satisfy the PSR, it *maintains the necessity of the contingency of material grounds*, rather than denying that any grounding whatever takes place in the order of nature. Moreover, we note that the problem of irrevers-

---

59. Leibniz, *Philosophical Essays*, p. 210.

60. Exactly as Bernard Bosanquet notes, in *Logic, or the Morphology of Knowledge*, 2nd edition, Oxford, Oxford University Press, 1911, p. 215: 'The Law of Sufficient Reason represents the demand of intelligence for the explanation of everything by something else. And it is plain that in the case of anything but the absolute whole this demand must go on to infinity. [...] It rests on the relations of parts in abstraction from the whole, or in other words, without the element of totality'.

61. Leibniz, *Philosophical Essays*, p. 210.

ible antecendence becomes, for Leibniz, the mark of material grounds. God, in other words, cannot be separated from the ungrounded series of material grounds of which he is the substantial cause and reason.

What emerges from this brief survey of Leibniz's formulation of the 'great principle' is the following: Grounds are neither reducibly logical, i.e., applying only to the space of reasons; nor reducibly material, i.e. applying only to physical particulars; the reason of being necessarily comprises the sequencing of reasons and causes.

UNGROUND AND ANTECEDENCE

We are now in a position to see how it is that Fichte's and Hindrichs' accounts of grounding *regionalize* dynamics with respect to being as a means to eliminate dimensions of the problem of ground. Fichte resolves the materialism problem in the interests of activity, but, in keeping with the refutation of transcendental materialism as the thesis that nature produces the I, eliminates powers from nature and makes activity into the source and product of reason alone. Accordingly, although perfectly susceptible to accomodation by physicalists and ethico-materialists, grounding is achieved not by virtue of the resolution of the problem of matter, but by its elimination.

Similarly, Hindrichs' grounding operation, while it satisfies the logical dimension of grounding, posits being as following from it. Grounding therefore consists in the antecendence of logic with respect to a nature whose contingency is merely the exteriority of the latter with respect to the former, as it was for Hegel. Dynamics therefore belongs, as for Fichte, not to nature or to being, but solely to reason, so that Hindrichs' Absolute becomes a version of the ontological proof if not of the existence of a divine being, then of being at all, insofar as being is equivalent to judgment.

What both struggle to eliminate is the antecendence that make material grounds nonrecoverable by reason. Yet antecendence is required in order that there be thought at all, unless thought is to be considered something different in kind to material being. If this is not the case, the causes of thinking are the same as those of that object antecedent to thinking which thinking thinks. Consider a mountain: the thinking of this mountain entails (a) that there is already a mountain to be thought, whatever its nature; and (b) that the causes of the existence of the mountain must also be involved in the thinking of the mountain. When thinking attempts to recover the causes of its thinking of the mountain, it reaches two nonfinite series that vitiate this project: firstly, the thinking about the mountain is always antecedent to any thinking about the thinking of the mountain, so that the object-thinking is always the product of an actual thinking with which the causal sequence keeps pace in fact, but cannot be recovered in thought in principle. Secondly, in retrospecting the causes of mountain formation, let alone the formation of thought thereupon, or of geology, the track taken by those causes invariably fails to reduce specifically to the object from which the thinking started: the causes of mountain formation are also, that is, involved in speciation, meteorological metastasis, and so on. Accordingly, being is antecedent to thinking precisely because if it were not, not only would there be nothing to think, but neither could there be any thinking.

Thus the attempted recovery of antecedence ungrounds physical particulars for the thinking about them; but physical particulars are themselves ungrounded, specifically because each particular physical determination rests in turn upon antecedent physical determinations. Viewed thus in reverse, all is ungrounded because there is no ultimate ground of things, no substance in which all these causes inhere, or of which all these powers are accidents or properties. But precisely because nature is never all it can be, nor simply and reducibly what it is, that what is ungrounded in reverse runs forward as the operations of powers, of *potentia* or productivity. Here we have a dynamics that precisely cannot be regionalized with respect to being, and that therefore fully satisfies the PSR: it is a necessary truth about nature reasoning about itself that antecedence is non-recoverable. This is why, then, even the concept of matter is synthetic; what the PSR demonstrates is that this synthesis necessarily embraces the entire cosmos.

7

Against Speculation,
or, A Critique of the Critique of Critique:
A Remark on Quentin Meillassoux's *After Finitude*
(After Colletti)

Alberto Toscano

This paper seeks to explore a stark and deceptively simple question elicited by Quentin Meillassoux's *After Finitude*: are materialism and speculation compatible? In order to outline a response I will take what might initially seem a somewhat arbitrary detour through a seemingly unrelated line of thought, namely that of the Italian anti-Hegelian Marxist Lucio Colletti, focussing in particular on his 1969 *Marxism and Hegel*—a book which in its time had a remarkable impact on the discussion of historical and dialectical materialism. By means of this theoretical contrast, I will try to elucidate what appear to me as some of the stakes of Meillassoux's powerful book. In this regard my guiding question will open onto some subsidiary ones, two of them being of particular significance: 'Is non-metaphysical speculation possible?' and 'What is the difference between realism and materialism (and indeed between these two and naturalism)?' In the background of these questions lies the issue of demarcation—especially the three-way demarcation between science, philosophy and ideology. This contrast with a line of inquiry within twentieth-century Marxism, which bears a number of affinities with Meillassoux's proposal is also useful to the extent that it allows us to address one of the strong rhetorical gestures that lends *After Finitude*—inasmuch as we can speak of a politics immanent to philosophy as a *Kampfplatz* or battlefield—a Kantian image dear to Althusser. Meillassoux's gesture involves enlisting a speculative materialism against the pernicious extra-philosophical effects of correlationism, encapsulated by the notion of *fideism*. When it comes to these arguments, principally rehearsed in Chapter 2 of *After Finitude*, I think it is fair to say, in terms of the aforementioned issue of demarcation, that Meillassoux is engaging in an ideological struggle founded on the specific demarcation between philosophy and science, as the two impinge on questions of necessity and belief. Speculative materialism is here also an *ideological operation*, aimed at terminating correlationism's collusion with irrationalism ('Dialectical Materialism and Irrationalism', incidentally, was the subtitle of Colletti's book).

Meillassoux brings his investigation into explicit contact with the issue of ideology when he characterizes speculative materialism as an approach that does away with any 'dogmatic metaphysics', as a rejection of real necessity and sufficient reason grounded in the following operation: 'to reject dogmatic metaphysics means to reject all real necessity, and a fortiori to reject the principle of sufficient reason, as well as the ontological argument, which is the keystone that allows the system of real necessity to close in upon itself'. He goes on to declare that 'such a refusal of dogmatism furnishes the minimal condition for every critique of ideology, insofar as an ideology cannot be identified with just any variety of deceptive representation, but is rather any form of pseudo-rationality whose aim is to establish that what exists as a matter of fact exists necessarily'.[1] At bottom, Meillassoux wishes to combine and revitalise two aspects of the Enlightenment critique of metaphysics and religion. On the one hand, a speculative materialism is aimed at undermining the doctrine of necessary entities, the dogmatism of classical metaphysics, rationalism included. On the other, speculative materialism is targeted against the way in which correlationism makes any belief equally legitimate by rejecting the absoluteness of reality (i.e. by making the arche-fossil unthinkable). But this entails that the critique of metaphysics not be a deflationary, relativist or conventionalist critique, in other words that it not be a correlationist critique.

The brilliance (but as I will suggest also the problematic character) of Meillassoux's enterprise stems from the manner in which he articulates the two seemingly antinomic requirements of anti-dogmatism and speculation. Accordingly, as he writes 'we must uncover an absolute necessity that does not reinstate any form of absolute necessary entity', thus demarcating absolutizing from absolutist thought, and speculation from metaphysics. This requires resisting what Meillassoux calls the 'de-absolutizing implication', which posits that 'if metaphysics is obsolete, so is the absolute'.[2] Kantianism, or, in Meillassoux's vocabulary 'weak correlationism', is partially responsible for this, though the fact that it maintains an uncorrelated non-contradictory real as thinkable entails that it does not harbour the same irrationalist consequences as strong correlationism, especially in the latter's Heideggerian or Wittgensteinian varieties. It is in discussing strong correlationism that Meillassoux's attempt to infuse speculative materialism with the polemical spirit of the radical Enlightenment is particularly in evidence, leading to the formulation of what we could call an absolute Enlightenment.

Meillassoux's indictment of strong correlationism as a new obscurantism, as a *carte blanche* for any and all superstitions, centres on the category of facticity. The latter designates those structural invariants or transcendental parameters that govern a given world or domain of correlation without themselves being open to rational explanation, deduction or derivation. In this respect, facticity is a form of reflexive ignorance. In Meillassoux's words, it 'consists in not knowing why the correlational structure has to be thus'.[3] Facticity is here synonymous with finitude and with a form of anti-foundationalism whose converse, as Meillassoux writes, 'is that nothing can be said to be absolutely impossible, not even the unthinkable'. Strong correlationism generates a form of philosophically vouchsafed permissiveness, which makes it impossible to establish the very criteria that might make it possible to 'disqualify' irrational discourses.

---

1. Quentin Meillassoux, *After Finitude: An Essay on the Necessity of Contingency*, trans. Ray Brassier, London, Continuum, 2008, pp. 33-4.

2. Meillassoux, *After Finitude*, p, 34.

3. Meillassoux, *After Finitude*, p. 39.

As Meillassoux notes, while weak correlationism had done away with naïve realism, strong correlationism further undoes a notion of the absolute by pitting the facticity of the correlation against any speculative idealism.

It is the complicity of strong correlationism with a return of religiosity that lends Meillassoux's speculative denunciation its ideological urgency. Its 'contemporary predominance', he writes, is 'intimately connected to the immunity from the constraints of conceptual rationality which religious belief currently seems to enjoy'.[4] According to *After Finitude*, we live in a time where the ideological hegemony of strong correlationist philosophies, with their assertion of a facticity beyond explanation, their dumb wonderment at things as they are, has revoked any of the rational instruments available for refuting or dismissing irrational beliefs. Intriguingly, and I'll return to this when I move to Colletti, for Meillassoux correlationist irrationalism is founded on its termination of the Parmenidean identity of being and thought; the consequence that correlationism draws from facticity that 'being and thinking must be thought as capable of being wholly other'.[5] From such a vantage point, is impossible to rule out the radical incommensurability between the in-itself and thought. What follows from this? That thought's claim to think the absolute is drastically withdrawn but irrational absolutes remain, nay proliferate. Hence the basically unchallenged contemporary sway of a sceptically permissive and pluralistic 'fideism of any belief whatsoever'.

It is not clear whether Meillassoux actually thinks that correlationism has played a causal part in abetting current returns of the religious, but he does draw out very neatly the manner in which it implies it. In his own words:

> The end of metaphysics, understood as the 'de-absolutization of thought', is thereby seen to consist in the rational legitimation of any and every variety of religious (or 'poetico-religious') belief in the absolute, so long as the latter invokes no authority beside itself. To put it in other words: by forbidding reason any claim to the absolute, the end of metaphysics has taken the form of an exacerbated return to the religious.[6]

On the basis of this argument, Meillassoux frames his own project in the classical terms of the French *lumières*, especially of Voltaire, as a struggle against fanaticism (characteristically, Meillassoux does not use the Kantian definition of fanaticism, or *Schwärmerei*, which for Kant involves the hyper-rationalist delusion of 'seeing the infinite', against which the critical philosophy erects its iconoclastic proscriptions). The relation between fideism and fanaticism is somewhat fuzzy, but it is intriguing, and one might argue somewhat worrying, that Meillassoux flirts with the conservative thesis that a relativistic proliferation of beliefs, beyond any horizon of legitimacy, is a form of de-Christianization, the obverse of his equally questionable conviction that critical Western rationality is a 'progressive rationalization of Judeo-Christianity under the influence of Greek philosophy'.[7]

In pure Enlightenment style, Meillassoux wants to argue that strong correlationism, in colluding with the religionization of reason, has left us powerless to argue rationally—rather than on *ad hoc* moral grounds—against all varieties of *fanaticism*, including, in an odd allusion, those which may deal out 'the worst forms of violence', and whose claim to access an irrational absolute correlationist fideism cannot allow itself to

---

4. Meillassoux, *After Finitude*, p. 43.

5. Meillassoux, *After Finitude*, p. 44.

6. Meillassoux, *After Finitude*, p. 45.

7. Meillassoux, *After Finitude*, p. 47.

disqualify. At the end of Chapter 2 of *After Finitude*, Meillassoux even goes so far as to claim that contemporary 'fanaticism' is the *effect* of critical rationality, a by-product of the latter's *effectively emancipatory* attack on dogmatism, which has in removed any fetter on the claims of 'blind faith'. Without dwelling on the under-determined and exceedingly allusive references to contemporary fanaticism that lend Meillassoux's claims their charge of urgency, as well as on the rather dubious claims made about the relation between Christianity and Western reason, in the remainder of this article I want to challenge the plausibility of Meillassoux's Enlightenment reloaded, as I mentioned by a detour through Lucio Colletti's *Marxism and Hegel*.

I want to put forward two inter-related arguments. First, that attending to the distinction between Kant and Hegel as formulated by Colletti, allows us to cast doubt on the very possibility of a *speculative* materialism, and provides a qualified Marxian defence for weak Kantian correlationism as a component of a genuine materialist thinking. Second, and much more briefly, that Colletti's related discussion of hypostasis and 'real abstraction' demonstrates the weakness of Meillassoux's attempt to revitalise the Enlightenment attack on fanaticism. Behind these two claims lies the conviction that, despite its undeniable subtlety, Meillassoux's attack on the idealist parameters of correlationism is ultimately idealist in form, a problem that also affects its attempt to ideologically intervene, through a recasting of the Enlightenment fight against fanaticism, in the contemporary 'return to the religious'.

The reasons that govern the juxtaposition with Colletti are several. To begin with, I want to use this contrastive and disjunctive exercise to begin to think through the relationship between Meillassoux's speculative materialism and the kinds of materialisms of practice or history that refer back to Marx. The choice of Colletti is dictated by the very nature of his intervention in Marxism and Hegel and related writings: it was designed to counter the obfuscatory idealism and rejection of science which he saw as the Hegelian legacy within Western Marxism. In this respect its spirit, if not its specific targets, is not so distant from Meillassoux. What's more, Colletti bears a more specific affinity with Meillassoux.[8] Both regard scientific thought as inseparable from an affirmation of the principle of non-contradiction. Meillassoux argues, towards the end of chapter 3 of *After Finitude* that: 'Dialectics and paraconsistent logics would be shown to be studies of the ways in which the contradictions of thought produce effects in thought, rather than studies of the supposedly ontological contradictions which thought discovers in the surrounding world'.[9] The distinction between contradictions in thought and in reality is so central to Colletti's work that it eventually led to his abandonment of Marxism, guilty in his eyes of maintaining the possibility of contradictions in the real. But the different ways of arguing against contradictions in reality in Colletti and Meillassoux are already indicative of the broader differences in their

---

8. There is a further convergence in these two attempts to recast materialism. As their discussions of non-contradiction suggest, both rely on a preliminary 'atomization' of things, objects and laws. In the case of Meillassoux one could perhaps critically refer to Anton Pannekoek's critique of *Materialism and Empirio-Criticism*, according to which 'for Lenin "nature" consists not only in matter but also in natural laws directing its behaviour, floating somehow in the world as commanders who must be obeyed by the things'. Anton Pannekoek, *Lenin as Philosopher*, ed. Lance Byron Richey, Milwaukee, Marquette University Press, 2003 [1938], p. 129. In order for Meillassoux's reasoning to operate, is there not a need to pre-emptively reduce the real to a domain of entities rather than relations, such that arguments based on the principle of non-contradiction can have their purchase? And is there not a parallel weakness in Colletti's refusal to consider the position according to which a materialist ontology may be concerned with processes, not things?

9. Meillassoux, *After Finitude*, p. 79.

philosophical defences of science against idealism. Colletti turns to Kant's 1763 essay on negative magnitudes to argue that:

> The fundamental principle of materialism and of science ... is the principle of non-con-
> tradiction. Reality cannot contain dialectical contradictions but only real oppositions,
> conflicts between forces, relations of contrariety. The latter are *ohne Widerspruch*, i.e. non-
> contradictory oppositions, and not dialectical contradictions. These assertions must be
> sustained, because they constitute the principle of science itself. Now science is the only
> means of apprehending reality, the only means of gaining knowledge of the world. There
> cannot be two (qualitatively different) forms of knowledge. A philosophy which claims a
> status for itself superior to that of science, is an edifying philosophy—that is, a scarcely
> disguised religion.[10]

Rather than relying on a notion of material reality to argue against dialectical contradiction, Meillassoux's discussion of non-contradiction is wholly intra-speculative. Non-
contradiction must be respected to ward off the metaphysical spectre of an absolutely
necessary entity that forfeiting this principle would involve. Thus, contrary to the customary link between dialectical contradiction and an ontology of flux or process, for
Meillassoux a contradictory entity 'could never become other than it is because there
would be no alterity for it in which to become'.[11] In other words, as I'll try to show,
while Colletti takes a materialist critique of the dialectic to imply the extra-logical
character of reality, the fact that deriving the dynamics of the real from the logical is
illegitimate and idealist, for Meillassoux the denial of real contradiction takes place on
intra-logical grounds. To pursue this point further, it is worth delving deeper into the
rationale behind Colletti's anti-Hegelian revision of Marxism.

Let's begin where the contrast appears greatest: Colletti's plea for a pro-scientific
materialism takes the form of a defence of the finite. At the very start of his book, he
isolates the crux of idealism in Hegel's statement from the *Science of Logic* according to
which: 'The idealism of philosophy consists in nothing else than in recognizing that
the finite has no veritable being'.[12] Consequently, 'the finite is ideal', in two senses: it
is a mere abstraction, a fleeting isolation from the concrete universality of the Whole,
and, conversely, it is only granted its true being when comprised as a moment of the
ideal. In Hegel's formulation, from the Encyclopaedia: 'The truth of the finite is ... its
ideality.... This ideality of the finite is the chief maxim of philosophy'.[13] The labour of
speculative reason (*Vernunft*), as opposed to the intellect or understanding (*Verstand*), is
to traverse the various configurations of the finite and to undo its separateness. Colletti will diagnose this contempt towards the isolated thing and the thought that thinks it
(mere intellect as opposed to reason) as a constant within idealist philosophy, including
that of dialectical materialism—the polemical target of his book. For Colletti, sympathy towards the Hegelian critique of the intellect and of the Kantian restrictions placed
on reason—which he encounters in a motley host of thinkers, from Rickert to Mar-
cuse, from Bergson to Lukács—is a sign of an abdication of materialism and of a position towards science which, in according philosophy the sovereign right to legislate
about reality, turns the former it into a 'scarcely disguised religion'. What's more, to the
extent that science is seen to isolate entities and treat them as both finite and external
to the mind is paradigmatically a product of the intellect, and is consequently viewed

---

10. Lucio Colletti, 'Marxism and the Dialectic', *New Left Review*, no. 1/93, 1975, pp. 28-9.

11. Meillassoux, *After Finitude*, p. 69.

12. Lucio Colletti, *Marxism and Hegel*, trans. Lawrence Garner, London, New Left Books, 1973, p. 7.

13. Colletti, *Marxism and Hegel*, p. 14.

as a merely abstract and incomplete form of thinking—a feature most evident in Bergsonism, but present, as Colletti demonstrates, in a broad range of nineteenth and twentieth-century philosophy. For Colletti, speculation, conceived as the pretension of philosophical thought to logically encompass being, is fundamentally incompatible with materialism. Indeed, he insists on Hegel's conviction that he was returning to rationalism, but stripping it of its reliance on a materialist, or scientific form of argument. In passing, we could note that Meillassoux's return to rationalism, and to Descartes in particular, takes the inverse approach: maintaining the materialist form of rationalism, and stripping it of its idealist or theological content.

Thus, it is the repudiation of the finite as separate and self-standing, and the attempt to overcome finitude, understood as the inability for thought or logic to determine being, which for Colletti marks idealism's hostility to scientific materialism. In other words, it is because of a denial of finitude, and not because of its assertion, that for idealism 'an independent material world no longer exists'.[14] The idea of real opposition, Kant's *Realrepugnanz*, is significant because it is only by upholding the principle of non-contradiction and the idea of real exteriority in the material world that materialism can avert being enveloped by an idealism for which the material world is merely an incarnation of a fundamentally inclusive and unlimited reason. As Colletti remarks, 'since Hegel transforms the logical inclusion of opposites that is reason into the very principle of idealism (reason is the sole reality, there is nothing outside it), he excludes precisely that exclusion of opposites (the externality of being in relation to thought) that is the very principle of materialism)'.[15]

In Marxism and Hegel, idealism *qua* speculation is identified with 'the negation of any extralogical existence'.[16] This is also why materialism is always to some extent an Unphilosophie, an anti-philosophy, based on the idea of an externality of thought to being, and on a related irreducibility of scientific epistemology to speculative logic. While, in Colletti's formulation, 'Kant constantly remarks that if one wants to have knowledge, one must refer thought back to that which is other than itself',[17] Meillassoux's attempt to break out of a correlationist circle of Kantian provenance into what he calls 'the great outdoors' involves generating a new figure, under the aegis of a necessary and radical contingency, of thought's Parmenidean identity with being, or, as he very lucidly outlines, inventing a novel type of non-metaphysical speculation.

Let's sum up the results of this contrast. In Meillassoux's work, a speculative materialism counters correlationism by undermining the thesis of finitude (or rather, via the passage from facticity to factuality, by turning correlationist finitude against itself), and by engaging in a non-metaphysical deployment of a '*logos* of contingency' relying on the intra-logical principle of non-contradiction and the ultimate identity of being and thought. In Colletti, on the contrary, a critical materialism depends on asserting the *extra-logical* character of reality, and the related and irreducible distinction between logical contradiction and real opposition. What's more, for Colletti it is precisely by turning the finite into an ideality, which is in turn encompassed by logical thinking, that speculation—which for him can *only* be idealist—transforms the world into an 'ephemeral' entity, something that Meillassoux's *logos* of contingen-

---

14. Colletti, *Marxism and Hegel*, p. 19.
15. Colletti, *Marxism and Hegel*, p. 34.
16. Colletti, *Marxism and Hegel*, p. 49.
17. Colletti, *Marxism and Hegel*, p. 202.

cy would seem to do as well. It is worth quoting here at length from Colletti's exposition of his critical materialism:

> Dogmatism is metaphysics; critical thought is materialism. The antithesis, with respect to Hegel, could not be more pronounced. Metaphysics is the identity of thought and being; its contents are 'already' within thought, they are independent of experience, i.e. supersensible. Ergo, form and content are forever united, knowledge is already formed, and it is impossible to pose the problem of the origin of the knowledge that we possess. Critical thought, contrariwise, identifies itself with the position that presupposes the heterogeneity, i.e. a real and not formal (or purely 'logical') difference, between being and thought. Thereby one can pose the 'critical' problem of the origin of our knowledge, inasmuch as knowledge itself is not already given. Which in turn presupposes, in a word, that the sources of knowledge are two: the spontaneity of the mind and whatever data are given to the receptivity of our senses.[18]

In Colletti, the scientific content of Kantian finitude—severed from its moral dimension—is to prohibit the self-sufficient of thought, i.e. speculation. In his words: 'If one denies that there exist premises in reality for thought, then one is forced to take up knowledge itself as a presupposed and given reality'.[19] Accordingly, it is imperative that epistemology, understood as the study of thought's relation to being as relates to the scientific enterprise, not be reduced to logic, the theory of thought's coherent relation to itself.

Among the issues at stake in this contrast is the standing of the absolute. Colletti and Meillassoux appear to converge on the notion of the absolute as something that is separate from what the latter would refer to as a correlationist circle. As is stated at the beginning of Chapter 2 of *After Finitude*, the task of speculative materialism 'consists in trying to understand how thought is able to access the uncorrelated, which is to say, a world capable of subsisting without being given. But to say this is just to say that we must grasp how thought is able to access an absolute, i.e. a being whose severance (the original meaning of *absolutus*) and whose separateness from thought is such that it presents itself to us as non-relative to us, and hence as capable of existing whether we exist or not'.[20] In Colletti's account it is precisely this absoluteness of extra-logical reality that is the nemesis of idealism. As he notes: 'For Hegel, the '"intellect" is dogmatic because it makes the finite absolute. The meaning of this term is the same as its etymology: *solutus ab...*, freed from limitations, existing on its own, and therefore unrestricted and independent'.[21] But, and this is the important point, Meillassoux does not limit himself to the severance of extra-logical reality, precisely because his refutation of correlationism is a logical, or speculative one.

Looking through the prism of Colletti's critique of Hegelianism, we can recognise two senses of the absolute in *After Finitude*: on the one hand, the absoluteness of the arche-fossil, an absoluteness that fits quite well with Colletti's defence of the finite against its idealist sublations; on the other, the absoluteness of a reason or logic that is assumed to be congruent with being, and that can legislate about modality and change with no reference to anything extrinsic to it, be it experience or matter. The uniqueness of Meillassoux's account lies of course in the dexterous and fascinating manner in which he seems to need the second absolute, the absolute of speculation (or what we might call the absolute absolute) to shore up the second (the relative or negative abso-

---

18. Colletti, *Marxism and Hegel*, pp. 90-1.

19. Colletti, *Marxism and Hegel*, p. 89.

20. Meillassoux, *After Finitude*, p. 28.

21. Colletti, *Marxism and Hegel*, p. 82.

lute, the absolute *from thought*) and vanquish correlationism. Viewed from the vantage point of Colletti's argument, Meillassoux poses the ontological presuppositions of correlationist epistemology, but resolves it by logical means, thus ultimately undermining his own materialist aims, and creating something like a detotalized and contingent 'logical mysticism', to employ Marx's characterisation of Hegel's system. We could thus articulate this contrast in terms of the distinction between a *materialism of the intellect* and a *materialism of reason*, or a *realism of the intellect* and a *realism of reason*. From the vantage point of Colletti's defence of intellect against reason, *After Finitude*'s attempt at defending the expansive and speculative uses of a 'totally a-subjective' reason by getting rid of fideism jettisons along with correlationism with it the criticism, revision and scientificity that marks the extra-logical character of reality in a Kant-inspired materialist epistemology.

But is a restatement of Kantian epistemology as a materialist precursor all that there is to Colletti's position? No. Crucial to Marxism and Hegel is the highlighting of Marx's theory of real abstraction, to wit the idea that the excesses of speculation and the hypostases of idealism are not merely cognitive problems, but are deeply entangled with abstract categories and entities that have a real existence in what, following Hegel, Marx was wont to call an upside-down world. Thus the State, and its philosophical expression in Hegel, and Capital, and its theoretical capture in the political economy of Smith and Ricardo, are not simply thought-forms that could be dispelled by some enlightened emendation of the intellect, or a valiant combat against superstitions. As Colletti writes: 'For Marx, in fact, metaphysics is the realism of universals; it is a logical totality which posits itself as self-subsisting, transforms itself into the subject, and which (since it must be self-subsisting) identifies and confuses itself acritically with the particular, turning the latter—i.e. the actual subject of reality—into its own predicate or manifestation'.[22] Again, this is not a merely logical but a real process. To return to the earlier remarks on Meillassoux's attempt to revive the Enlightenment war on fanaticism within his broader critique of correlationist fideism, what Marx's notion of real abstraction permits us to think—and the reason why it is an important advance with respect to the idea of ideology as a merely cognitive matter—is that ideologies, including those of correlationism, fideism and fanaticism, are social facts and objects of practical struggles.

In trying to maintain the speculative sovereignty of philosophical reason, albeit advocating a principle of unreason and breaking correlationist self-sufficiency, Meillassoux can be seen to reintroduce idealism at the level of form at the same time as he valiantly seeks to defeat it at the level of content. This is so in two senses. First, by presuming the possibility of drawing ontological conclusions from logical intuitions—a problem that can be registered in the inconsistent use of the notion of the absolute: as the absolute absolute of the *logos* of contingency, and as the relative absolute of the entity severed from correlation. The former, logical absolute leads to a variant of Hegel's transubstantiation of material or effective causality into a moment within ideal causality—though of course in Meillassoux this is explicitly an *acausality*, stripped of teleology. Second, by presuming that a speculative philosophy in conjunction with a mathematized science can struggle against abstractions that are perceived as mere errors of the intellect, and not as abstractions that have any basis in a social, material and extra-logical reality. Logical form undermines materialist content, the struggle against finitude reproduces the ideality of the finite, the intellectualist defence of the Enlightenment conceals the reality of abstractions. The antidote to a post-Kantian catastrophe threatens to turn into a neo-Hegelian reverie.

---

22. Colletti, *Marxism and Hegel*, p. 198.

8

Hume's Revenge: À Dieu, Meillassoux?[1]

Adrian Johnston

Materialism certainly is enjoying a renaissance today. One of the defining features of contemporary theoretical work situated in the shadows of the traditions constituting 'Continental philosophy' undeniably is a concern with once again overcoming idealism, however varyingly construed. Perhaps the sole lowest common denominator amongst these multiple manifestations of materialism, apart from the shared use of the label 'materialism', is an agreement with Engels and Lenin that the main fault line of struggle (or, as Mao would put it, the 'principal contradiction'[2]) within the field of philosophy and its history is the irreconcilable split between idealist and materialist orientations.[3] Borrowing additional concept-terms from the lexicon of Mao's political thought, perhaps the time has come for the bouquet of the thousand blooming flowers of different recent currents of materialism to be sifted through with a nose to discerning which differences between these currents are non-antagonistic and which are actually antagonistic.[4]

Alain Badiou, in his early Maoist period, rightly depicts materialism as 'a philosophy of assault'.[5] Of course, one of the main targets repeatedly attacked by this combative philosophical trajectory is nebulous spiritualism in its many varied forms and (dis)guises. Religiosity, insofar as part of its essence consists in positing that a being other than physical materiality lies at the base and/or pinnacle of reality, obviously is a pri-

1. I would like to thank the participants in my 2009 Spring Semester seminar on Alain Badiou in the Department of Philosophy at the University of New Mexico, including my colleague Paul Livingston, for helping to inspire several of the ideas and arguments contained in this essay. I also owe gratitude to those who generously furnished me with critical feedback on this piece: Martin Hägglund, Aaron Hodges, Paul Livingston, Knox Peden, and Kathryn Wichelns.

2. Mao Tse-Tung, *Selected Readings from the Works of Mao Tse-Tung*, Peking, Foreign Languages Press, 1971, pp. 102, 109-113, 116-117.

3. Frederick Engels, *Ludwig Feuerbach and the Outcome of Classical German Philosophy*, C.P. Dutt (ed.), New York, International Publishers Co., Inc., 1941, pp. 20-21, and V.I. Lenin, *Materialism and Empirio-Criticism*, Peking, Foreign Languages Press, 1972, pp. 1, 22-23, 33-34, 106, 410, 431, 434.

4. Mao Tse-Tung, *Selected Readings from the Works of Mao Tse-Tung*, pp. 125-127, 433-435, 441-444, 462-463.

5. Alain Badiou, *Théorie du sujet*, Paris, Éditions du Seuil, 1982, p. 202.

mary natural enemy of anti-idealist materialism.[6] But, nowadays, something weird is happening: the materialist camp within domains intersecting with European and European-inspired theory has come to harbour individuals wishing to reassert, supposedly from inside the strict confines of materialism proper, the enduring validity and indispensability of theological frameworks. Marx and Engels must be rolling around in their graves. Despite the virulent theoretical and practical campaigns against religion carried out under the guidance of Marxist historical and dialectical materialisms, Marx's ostensible heirs in Continental philosophy generally seem to be tolerantly treating the theologically inclined mingling amongst them as non-antagonistic rather than antagonistic others (sometimes even as sympathetic fellow travelers sincerely committed to the materialist cause). As this author has asserted elsewhere, Badiou himself, in his later work starting in the mid-1980s, arguably has come to defend a specious sort of 'materialism' suffused with metaphysical realism, hostility to the empirical sciences of nature, and barely concealed fragments of Christianity appropriated with little to no significant modification.[7]

Badiou's student, Quentin Meillassoux, certainly would appear, at first glance, to be a thoroughly atheistic materialist. He even voices worries apropos his teacher's 'troubling' religious leanings.[8] Meillassoux's 2006 debut book, *Après la finitude: Essai sur la nécessité de la contingence*, puts itself forward as an overcoming of the most potent and sophisticated strains of modern idealism (i.e. Kantian transcendental idealism and its offshoots, especially phenomenology beginning with Husserl). This overcoming ostensibly enables the affirmation of a realist 'speculative materialism' in accord with, to paraphrase Louis Althusser, the spontaneous philosophy of the experimental physical sciences.[9] Additionally, in his first and only book to date, Meillassoux also bemoans today's 'exacerbated return of the religious'.[10] More precisely, he maintains that the purported 'end of metaphysics' ushered in at the close of the eighteenth century with Kant's critical philosophy has permitted, thanks to prohibiting self-assured atheism as a subspecies of a banished ontological absolutism, the flourishing of 'fideism' defined as the faith of a hazy, diluted religiosity believing in an enigmatic Other transcendent in relation to that which can be grasped by secular reason. Fideism flourishes under the protection of a post-absolutist relativism, a tepid agnosticism obsessed with respecting purported epistemological (and ethical) limits associated with human subjective finitude.[11]

And yet, in an article entitled 'Deuil à venir, dieu à venir' published in the journal *Critique* at the same time as the release by Éditions du Seuil of *After Finitude*, Meil-

---

6. Adrian Johnston, 'Conflicted Matter: Jacques Lacan and the Challenge of Secularizing Materialism', *Pli: The Warwick Journal of Philosophy*, vol. 19, Spring 2008, pp. 166-167.

7. Adrian Johnston, 'What Matter(s) in Ontology: Alain Badiou, the Hebb-Event, and Materialism Split From Within', *Angelaki: Journal of the Theoretical Humanities*, vol. 13, no. 1, April 2008, pp. 27-49; Adrian Johnston, 'Phantom of Consistency: Alain Badiou and Kantian Transcendental Idealism', *Continental Philosophy Review*, vol. 41, no. 3, September 2008, pp. 345-366; Adrian Johnston, 'The World Before Worlds: Quentin Meillassoux and Alain Badiou's Anti-Kantian Transcendentalism', *Contemporary French Civilization*, vol. 33, no. 1, Winter/Spring 2008, pp. 73-99; Adrian Johnston, *Badiou, Žižek, and Political Transformations: The Cadence of Change*, Evanston, Northwestern University Press, 2009.

8. Quentin Meillassoux, 'Histoire et événement chez Alain Badiou: Intervention au séminaire «Marx au XXIe siècle: l'esprit et la letter—Paris: 2 février 2008»', http://semimarx.free.fr/IMG/pdf/Meillassoux_Paris-fev08.pdf

9. Quentin Meillassoux, *After Finitude: An Essay on the Necessity of Contingency*, trans. Ray Brassier, London, Continuum, 2008, pp. 13, 26-27, 36-38, 113, 121.

10. Meillassoux, *After Finitude*, p. 45.

11. Meillassoux, *After Finitude*, pp. 44-49.

lassoux strangely speculates that a God resembling the divinities of monotheistic religions, although he admits that such a deity has been and continues to be non-existent, could come to exist at any moment in the future. Meillassoux's 'thesis of divine inexistence' states that, 'God doesn't yet exist'.[12] A component of the background to this is a particular distinction between 'metaphysics' and 'speculation'[13]: Metaphysics is defined as a philosophical position combining an epistemology of access to the asubjective absolute with an ontology in which some being thereby accessed is necessary in the sense of necessarily existent (early modern Continental rationalism, with its substance metaphysics, exemplifies this position). Non-metaphysical speculation—for Meillassoux, every metaphysics is speculative, but not all speculation is metaphysical—is defined as a philosophical position accepting the epistemological part of (pre-Kantian) rationalist metaphysics while rejecting its ontological part (i.e., for Meillassouxian speculation, with its denial of the principle of sufficient reason, absolute being in and of itself involves no necessity, resting on the baseless base of the ultimate fact of a brute contingency).[14] Traditional theologies are metaphysical,[15] whereas Meillassoux wants to advance what could be described as a speculative *qua* non-metaphysical theology (which he calls a 'divinology'[16]). Playing with the phrase 'divine inexistence', he has it signify not only 'the inexistence of the religious God' (i.e., the deity of metaphysical monotheistic theologies), but also, at the same time, the ostensibly irrefutable 'possibility of a God still yet to come'[17] (Meillassoux's justifications for why this possibility is irrefutable will be addressed soon). What's more, this *Dieu à venir* might be willing and able to perform such miraculous gestures as resurrecting the dead and righting the wrongs piled up over the course of a brutal, unjust human history.[18] How could the author of *After Finitude*, with its polemics against the new fideism of 'post-secular' thought sheltering under the cover of post-Kantian epistemological skepticism regarding claims about the objective nature of being an sich—ironically, the motif of the à venir is, as is common knowledge, dear to partisans of the post-secular turn in Continental philosophy—simultaneously indulge himself in musings about a virtual, spectral *peut-être* interminably holding out the promise, however uncertain or unlikely, of the *ex nihilo* genesis of a divinity fulfilling the expectations of the most fanatical of the faithful?

Essential ingredients of this odd non-metaphysical theology actually can be found within the pages of *After Finitude* itself. This flirting with religion isn't dismissible as an extraneous article-length afterthought tacked onto an entirely separate and more substantial book-length manifesto for what otherwise would be a solidly materialist and atheist philosophical edifice. Without getting bogged down in exegetically unpacking this book in its entirety (solid summaries of it already have been written[19]), the focus in what follows partly will be on the role of Hume in Meillassoux's arguments for both

---

12. Quentin Meillassoux, 'Deuil à venir, dieu à venir', *Critique*, no. 704/705, January/February 2006, p. 110.

13. Meillassoux, 'Deuil à venir, dieu à venir', p. 115.

14. Meillassoux, 'Deuil à venir, dieu à venir', p. 110; Meillassoux, *After Finitude*, pp. 33-34, 60, 71, 124-125; Quentin Meillassoux, 'Potentiality and Virtuality', trans. Robin Mackay, *Collapse* 2, March 2007, pp. 59-61.

15. Meillassoux, 'Deuil à venir, dieu à venir', pp. 110-112.

16. Meillassoux, 'Deuil à venir, dieu à venir', p. 115.

17. Meillassoux, 'Deuil à venir, dieu à venir', p. 110.

18. Meillassoux, 'Deuil à venir, dieu à venir', pp. 105-109.

19. Ray Brassier, *Nihil Unbound: Enlightenment and Extinction*, Basingstoke, Palgrave Macmillan, 2007, pp. 49-94; Graham Harman, 'Quentin Meillassoux: A New French Philosopher', *Philosophy Today*, vol. 51, no. 1, Spring 2007, pp. 104-117; Peter Hallward, 'Anything is possible', *Radical Philosophy*, no. 152, November/December 2008, pp. 51-57; Johnston, 'The World Before Worlds', pp. 73-99.

his speculative materialism and its parallel peculiar divinology. The core maneuver lying at the very heart of Meillassoux's project is an ontologization of Hume's epistemology[20] (Meillassoux does with respect to Hume what Slavoj Žižek's Hegel does with respect to the epistemology of Kant[21]). Through complicating the reading of Hume upon
which Meillassoux relies, the former's empiricist philosophy can and should be turned
against Meillassouxian speculative materialism, with its accompanying theology (however non-metaphysical), and wielded as a weapon on behalf of a real(ist) and atheist
materialism worthy of the name. This non-Meillassouxian materialism is truly attuned
to praxis, both in terms of the practices of the empirical sciences (it will be alleged below, in connection with the figure of Hume, that Meillassoux's appeals to science don't
constitute a deep and defensible materialist philosophical engagement with properly
scientific handlings of physical reality) as well as the ideological and institutional stakes
of the practices of politics (speculative materialism/realism seems, at least thus far, unconcerned with these sorts of practical dimensions[22]). In fidelity to the materialist tradition inaugurated with Marx's 1845 'Theses on Feuerbach', this intervention insists
upon keeping simultaneously in view the different praxes of the really existing natural
sciences and those of the surrounding political circumstances of the times.

Apart from its denunciation of fideism, *After Finitude*, apparently irreligious but
concealing kernels of religiosity which explode into plain view in 'Deuil à venir, dieu à
venir', employs a tactic repeatedly used by Lenin in *Materialism and Empirio-Criticism*: a
reduction of all idealisms (including Kantian transcendental idealism) and fence-strad-
dling agnostic stances between idealism and materialism, no matter how elaborate and
intricate, to the absurdity of a Berkeley-style solipsism[23] (Lenin's philosophically crude
simplifications of Hume and Kant vis-à-vis Berkeley at least are arguably justified on
the basis of 'a concrete analysis of a concrete situation' in relation to his practical and
theoretical conjunctures situated around the turn of the century[24]). This absurd anti-
materialist, anti-realist dead-end (i.e. Berkeleyian philosophy) is compared by Meillassoux to some of the more extreme and ridiculous characteristics of certain versions of
Christianity.[25] Incidentally, to make an observation whose import quickly will become
increasingly apparent, neither Lenin nor Meillassoux possesses open-and-shut, iron-
clad debunking refutations of a strictly logical-rational sort of Berkeley and his solip-
sistic ilk (as Hume would predict, radical idealism is dismissed by Lenin and Meillassoux as obviously preposterous, rather than rationally disproven for good through the
proofs of philosophical logic). Along related lines, several authors have noted the striking similarities between Lenin's 1908 book and Meillassoux's debut text.[26] Žižek even

20. Meillassoux, *After Finitude*, pp. 53, 91-92; Meillassoux, '*Deuil à venir, dieu à venir*', pp. 112-115; Quentin
Meillassoux, 'Speculative Realism: Presentation by Quentin Meillassoux', *Collapse* 3, November 2007, pp.
433-434, 441-442; Harman, 'Quentin Meillassoux', p. 109; Graham Harman, 'Speculative Realism: Presentation by Graham Harman', *Collapse*, vol. 3, p. 385.

21. Adrian Johnston, *Žižek's Ontology: A Transcendental Materialist Theory of Subjectivity*, Northwestern University Press, 2008, pp. 12-13, 15, 128-133, 165-166, 172, 240-241.

22. Hallward, 'Anything is possible', pp. 55, 57.

23. Lenin, *Materialism and Empirio-Criticism*, pp. 18-19, 38, 45-46, 68-69, 95, 139, 142-145, 152-153, 177-178,
195, 203, 205, 216, 305, 310-314, 420, 426.

24. Louis Althusser, 'Lenin and Philosophy', *Lenin and Philosophy and other essays*, trans. Ben Brewster, New
York, Monthly Review Press, 2001, pp. 16-18, 31-34, 37-38, 40-42.

25. Meillassoux, *After Finitude*, pp. 17-18; Johnston, 'The World Before Worlds', pp. 78-79.

26. Brassier, *Nihil Unbound*, pp. 246-247; Johnston, 'The World Before Worlds', p. 78; Slavoj Žižek, 'An Answer to Two Questions', in Johnston, *Badiou, Žižek, and Political Transformations*.

claims that, '*After Finitude* effectively can be read as '*Materialism and Empirio-Criticism* rewritten for the twenty-first century'.'[27]

As an aside appropriate at this juncture, Žižek's comments on Leninist theoretical (as distinct from practical-political) materialism frequently evince a marked ambivalence, the negative side of which is expressed in the objection that Lenin's naïve materialist philosophy fails to include and account for the place and role of the mental observer of the non-mental objective facts and realities revealed by scientific siftings of cognitive representations of states of affairs in the world.[28] According to the Žižekian indictment, with which this author agrees, one cannot be an authentic materialist if one presupposes the being of a mind distinct from matter without delineating the material production of this very distinction itself. So, it might be the case that Žižek's comparison of Meillassoux with Lenin amounts to a backhanded compliment. In fact, as does the materialism of *Materialism and Empirio-Criticism* critiqued by Žižek, the speculative materialism of *After Finitude* simply assumes the existence of minds both sentient and sapient, consciousnesses through which mind-independent realities are registered (at least at the Galilean-Cartesian level of 'primary qualities' *qua* mathematizable-quantifiable features of objects and occurrences[29]), without offering anything by way of an explanation, essential to any really materialist materialism, of what Anglo-American analytic philosophers of mind, following David Chalmers, correctly identify as the thorny 'hard problem': an account of the relationship between mind and matter not just in terms of the former's epistemological access to the absolute being of the latter in itself, but in terms of whether or not mind can be explained as emergent from and/or immanent to matter (and, if so, what such an explanation requires epistemologically, ontologically, and scientifically). Ray Brassier, the translator of *After Finitude* and a thinker profoundly sympathetic to Meillassoux, concedes that 'Meillassoux's own brand of speculative materialism' remains haunted by the ghost of 'the Cartesian dualism of thought and extension'[30] (however, Brassier's nihilism-prompted turn to the eliminative neuro-materialism of Paul and Patricia Churchland creates its own swarm of difficulties[31]). Similarly, it remains to be seen whether speculative materialism effectively can engage with non-reductive theories of subjects and, as per Žižek and related to such theories, the Hegelian-Marxian-Lacanian phenomena of 'real abstractions'.

As will be commented upon subsequently, Meillassoux, in an essay entitled 'Potentiality and Virtuality', attempts to account for the vexing mind-body problem (and the equally challenging related mystery of the surfacing of sentient life) on the basis of his

27. Žižek, 'An Answer to Two Questions'.

28. Slavoj Žižek, 'Postface: Georg Lukács as the Philosopher of Leninism', in Georg Lukács, *A Defence of History and Class Consciousness: Tailism and the Dialectic*, trans. Esther Leslie, London, Verso, 2000, pp. 179-180, and Slavoj Žižek, 'Afterword: Lenin's Choice', in V.I. Lenin, *Revolution at the Gates: Selected Writings of Lenin from 1917*, Slavoj Žižek (ed.), London, Verso, 2002, pp. 178-181, and Slavoj Žižek and Glyn Daly, *Conversations with Žižek*, Cambridge, Polity Press, 2004, pp. 96-97, and Slavoj Žižek, *The Parallax View*, Cambridge, MIT Press, 2006, p. 168, and Slavoj Žižek, 'The Fear of Four Words: A Modest Plea for the Hegelian Reading of Christianity', in Creston DavisSlavoj Žižek and John Milbank (eds.), *The Monstrosity of Christ: Paradox or Dialectic?*, Cambridge, MIT Press, 2009, p. 97, 100.

29. Galileo Galilei, 'The Assayer', *Discoveries and Opinions of Galileo*, trans. Stillman Drake, New York, Anchor Books, 1957, pp. 274-278, and Meillassoux, *After Finitude*, pp. 1-3, 8, 13.

30. Brassier, *Nihil Unbound*, pp. 88-89.

31. Brassier, *Nihil Unbound*, pp. 3-31, 245; Adrian Johnston, 'The Emergence of Speculative Realism: A Review of Ray Brassier's *Nihil Unbound: Enlightenment and Extinction*', *Journal of the British Society of Phenomenology*, 2009; Johnston, *Žižek's Ontology*, pp. 203-209, 241, 269-287; Adrian Johnston, 'Slavoj Žižek's Hegelian Reformation: Giving a Hearing to *The Parallax View*', *Diacritics*, vol. 37, no. 1, Spring 2007, pp. 3-20.

speculative position. But, as will be argued in response, this solution, as Martin Häg-glund contends, is entirely out of step with the life sciences themselves.[32] One might be tempted to go so far as to charge that Meillassoux's explanation (or, rather, non-expla-nation) of the 'hard problem' amounts to an anti-scientific sophistical sleight-of-hand that places Meillassoux in undeniable proximity to the same Christian creationists he mocks in *After Finitude*. Considering this in conjunction with Žižekian denunciations of the 'hidden idealism' of Leninist theoretical materialism,[33] *After Finitude* suffers from the same major defect as *Materialism and Empirio-Criticism* without retaining one of the principle redeeming values of Lenin's text, namely, its merciless combative assault on any and every form of idealist religiosity or spiritualism. The door Lenin bravely tries so hard to slam shut, for practical as well as theoretical reasons, is thrown wide open by *After Finitude*. And, like Jehovah's Witnesses at the threshold of one's doorstep, who, with happily smiling aggression, will take a conversational mile if offered the inch of a cracked answered door, those faithful to theologies (especially advocates of so-called 'theological materialism') likely will take heart from several characteristics of Meillas-souxian speculation, including its rendering of their beliefs seemingly un-falsifiable and apparently not entirely irrational.

Within the pages of *After Finitude*, the key kernel forming the germinal seed of Meillassoux's new 'rational' speculative religion (i.e., his divinology) is his concept of 'hyper-Chaos'.[34] Through responding to Hume's empiricist version of the problem of induction via a non-Humean ontological move[35]—Meillassoux transforms the episte-mological problem of induction into the ontological solution of a radical contingency unbound by the principle of sufficient reason—reason's inability to prove that observed cause-and-effect patterns are expressive of underlying 'necessary connections' inhering within material reality apart from the mind of the observer shifts from being a priva-tion of knowledge to becoming a direct positive insight into the real absence of any ne-cessity in absolute objective being an sich.[36] Unlike the ontologies of the pre-Kantian rationalists, the ontology envisioned in *After Finitude* forbids positing any necessities at all to what and how being is in and of itself (for Meillassoux, the one and only aspect of Kant's critical turn which should be affirmed as impossible to regress back behind is its rejection of the various versions of metaphysical necessity hypothesized by, in par-ticular, early modern Continental rationalism à la Descartes, Spinoza, and Leibniz[37]). This leads him to assert the existence of a specific ultimate real as underlying mate-rial reality: a time of discontinuous points of instantaneity which, at any point, could, in a gratuitous, lawless, and reasonless manner ungoverned by anything (save for the purely logical principle of non-contradiction), scramble and reorder *ex nihilo* the cause-and-effect patters of the physical universe in any way whatsoever and entirely without constraints imposed by past states of affairs both actual and possible/potential. This temporal absolute of ground-zero contingency, as a necessarily contingent, non-facti-cally factical groundless ground, is Meillassouxian hyper-Chaos.[38]

---

32. Martin Hägglund, 'Radical Atheist Materialism: A Critique of Meillassoux', in this volume.

33. Žižek and Daly, *Conversations with Žižek*, pp. 96-97.

34. Meillassoux, *After Finitude*, p. 64, and Brassier, *Nihil Unbound*, pp. 67-68, and Hägglund, 'Radical Athe-ist Materialism'.

35. Meillassoux, 'Potentiality and Virtuality', p. 58.

36. Meillassoux, *After Finitude*, pp. 52-53, 62, 91-92.

37. Meillassoux, *After Finitude*, pp. 32-34, 49.

38. Meillassoux, *After Finitude*, pp. 53, 57-60, 63-64, 73-75, 79-80, 82-83; Meillassoux, 'Potentiality and Virtu-

As regards Hume, whose treatment of the topic of causality with respect to the problem of induction is of paramount importance for Meillassoux's arguments leading to the ontological vision of a hyper-chaotic being, one should begin by considering the link conjoining his recasting of the idea of cause-and-effect relations with the distinction between the rational and the reasonable implicitly operative in the twelfth and final section (entitled 'Of the Academical or Sceptical Philosophy') of his 1748 *An Enquiry Concerning Human Understanding*. This distinction between the rational and the reasonable also is discernible already in Pascal's wager. Contra Descartes and those like him—this would apply to Spinoza and Leibniz too—Pascal maintains that the arguments, concepts, ideas, and proofs of philosophical reason (and of the human intellect more generally) cannot truly touch the infinitely transcendent super-reality that is God. Obviously, this includes a ban on attempts to prove the existence of God. On the basis of faith rather than reason, one must take the leap of wagering on God's existence without prior rational guarantees vouching for the validity of one's decision to bet/gamble one way rather than another. However, through the presentation of the wager, Pascal tries to persuade one that wagering on the existence of God is reasonable given the permutations of possible consequences in terms of the outcomes of the different ways of wagering, although this wager on faith admittedly is not rational insofar as neither empirical/inductive nor logical/deductive reasoning is able decisively to determine the choice[39] (the matter of risk, associated with wagers, will resurface here in several significant incarnations).

Likewise, in the last section of *An Enquiry Concerning Human Understanding*, Hume, apropos the perennial philosophical difficulties posed by skepticism, pleads for a reasonable attenuated skepticism (such as he sees following from his analysis of causality) and against a rational hyperbolic/extreme skepticism (such as the denial of any possibility of knowing the world as it really is). In Hume's eyes, it's impossible rationally to refute, for instance, outright solipsism (a radical idealism) once and for all on the logical terrain of pure philosophical reason. In fact, if anything, the solipsist, as a figure of hyperbolic/extreme skepticism (i.e., 'Pyrrhonism'), can put forward irrefutable arguments of a purely logical-rational sort in favor of his/her position against realist adversaries who cannot logically-rationally prove the superiority of their contrary stance. According to Hume, the sole refutation, a refutation of enormous forcefulness despite being deprived of the intellectual-philosophical strength of strict logic and reason, resides in practice, in the irresistible default inertia of practical doings beyond the artificial cocoon of the armchair of contrived speculative game playing.[40] It's worth remarking here in passing that, in *After Finitude*, Meillassoux has counter-arguments against non-absolutist correlationisms but not against an 'absolutization of the correlate',[41] solipsism being subsumable under the heading of the absolute idealism of the latter. He merely tries to force non-absolutist correlationists (such as Kantian transcendental idealists and various stripes of phenomenologists) to choose between realism (such as that of anti-correlational speculative materialism) and absolute idealism (which, as Meillassoux's reference to Berkeley reveals, is presumed without argument to be prima facie untenable in its ridiculous absurdity). Similarly, in 'Potentiality and Virtuality', a sheer preference, perhaps guided

ality', pp. 59-60, 72, 75; Meillassoux, 'Speculative Realism', pp. 428-429, 432; Brassier, *Nihil Unbound*, pp. 70-71.

39. Blaise Pascal, *Pensées*, trans. A.J. Krailsheimer, London, Penguin Books, 1966, pp. 83-87, 149-155.

40. David Hume, *An Enquiry Concerning Human Understanding*, Eric Steinberg (ed.), Indianapolis, Hackett, 1993 [second edition], pp. 103-107, 109-113.

41. Meillassoux, *After Finitude*, pp. 10-11, 35, 37-38, 48; Brassier, *Nihil Unbound*, pp. 64-65.

by the aesthetics of a certain philosophical taste, for a 'strong' (i.e., ontological) response to Hume's problem of induction (as per *After Finitude*) over a 'weak' (i.e., critical-episte-mological) response seems to license Meillassoux's opting for the former resolution[42]; no logical-rational justifications are offered for choosing thus in this context (presuma-bly, one would have to return to the arguments in *After Finitude* against transcendental idealism to find the support for this favoring of the 'strong' over the 'weak' resolution).

For Hume, his empiricist reflections on epistemology, especially those concern-ing causality in light of the problem of induction, lead to a confrontation with the ei-ther/or choice between: one, a rational but unreasonable hyperbolic/extreme skepti-cism (including solipsism *qua* absolute idealism, with its irrefutable refutations of 'naïve realism'); or, two, an irrational (as not decisively demonstrable by pure philosophical logic-reason alone) but reasonable realist faith (i.e., a 'belief' in Hume's precise sense[43]) that, as Hume himself insists,[44] the mind is (naturally and instinctively) attuned to the world—albeit attuned in modes such that an attenuated skepticism equivalent to a non-dogmatic openness to the perpetual possibility of needing to revise one's ideation-ally mediated knowledge of extra-ideational reality (in the form of conceptual struc-tures of cause-and-effect patterns) ought to be embraced as eminently reasonable and realistic. From this vantage point, Meillassoux's alternate rational solution to Hume's problem (via his 'speculative turn') would be, to both Hume and most (if not all) prac-ticing scientists, utterly unreasonable. Why is this so? And, what are the consequences for Meillassouxian materialism?

Hume devotes the tenth section of *An Enquiry Concerning Human Understanding* to the issue of (supposed) miracles. Therein, departing from the standard definition of a mir-acle as 'a violation of the laws of nature',[45] he offers arguments against the plausibili-ty and/or existence of 'miraculous' happenings. As regards the majority of ostensible instances, in which a miracle is attested to not by direct first-person experience but, instead, by the testimony of second-hand oral or written reports, Hume persuasively observes, on the basis of a number of reasons, that the weight of past first-person expe-rience should outweigh second-hand testimony when the latter contradicts the former (in this case, when a purported miracle is reported that violates one's customary under-standing of what can and cannot happen in the natural world with which one is em-pirically acquainted). As regards such instances, Hume's analysis raises the question of which is more likely: that a violation of what one takes to be the laws of nature, attest-ed to by the weighty bulk of a mass of innumerable prior direct experiences, actually transpired as maintained by the source bearing witness, or that this source is distort-ing or lying about the evidence? For Hume, the second possibility is undoubtedly the more likely.[46] Meillassoux's deployment of the distinction between 'chance' and 'contin-gency' against such Humean considerations will be disputed shortly. For the moment, the upshot being driven home in this context is that Meillassoux's idiosyncratic ration-alism is utterly unreasonable.

But, what about an instance in which one experiences oneself as witnessing first-hand the occurrence of a miracle as an event that violates the laws of nature? Draw-

42. Meillassoux, 'Potentiality and Virtuality', pp. 67-68.

43. Hume, *An Enquiry Concerning Human Understanding*, pp. 30-32.

44. Hume, *An Enquiry Concerning Human Understanding*, pp. 35-37, 70-72.

45. Hume, *An Enquiry Concerning Human Understanding*, p. 76.

46. Hume, *An Enquiry Concerning Human Understanding*, pp. 75, 77-79, 81, 87-88.

ing on his recasting of causality as decoupled from the assumption that observed and cognized cause-and-effect patterns immediately manifest the 'necessary connections' of inviolable laws inherent to material being an sich, Hume is able to gesture at a stunningly simple but powerful argument against the very existence of miracles as violations of the (presumed) laws of nature: there is no such thing as a miracle because, if one experiences what is taken to be a violation of a law of nature, this means not that a real law of nature (as a necessary connection inhering within the natural world in and of itself apart from the minds of observers) actually has been violated, but that one was wrong about what one previously took to be an established law of nature.[47] Like a registered anomaly in relation to the practices of the sciences, a 'miracle' ought to be construed as nothing more than a catalyst prompting the revision of features of the established picture of the world at the epistemological level of knowledge.

In 'Potentiality and Virtuality', Meillassoux even employs the word 'miracle' (albeit qualified in a fashion to be addressed here later) to characterize the instantaneous intervention of an omnipotent hyper-chaotic temporal power of contingent change-without-reason.[48] And, what Hume says about miracles would apply equally to Meillassoux's transubstantiation of the epistemological problem of induction into the ontological solution of absolute contingency. How so? Hyper-Chaos either appears as miraculous in the sense critically scrutinized by Hume, in which case it succumbs to Hume's objections, or it cannot appear at all. Why the latter? And, what does this mean?

A couple of additional questions warrant consideration at this juncture: how would one recognize an instance of the intervention of hyper-chaotic temporal contingency? On the basis of what criteria would one distinguish between an anomalous observation as indicative of an epistemological error versus as indicative of being's ontological chaos/contingency? With these queries in mind, the example of the revolution in physics during the early part of the twentieth century—other examples of (to resort to Thomas Kuhn's [in]famous notion-phrase) 'paradigm shifts' in the history of the sciences easily could be employed to make the same point just as effectively—calls for pause for thought. On the basis of Meillassoux's philosophy, what would prevent someone from claiming that this revolution wasn't a result of past physics having been wrong about the mind-independent material universe, but, instead, a consequence of a contingent change in the real patterns of the physical universe such that the universe itself underwent a hyper-chaotic process of lawless transformation sometime early in the twentieth century in which it went from being Newtonian to becoming post-Newtonian? On this illustrative hypothetical account, which it isn't evident Meillassouxian speculative materialism as a philosophical system is able to disqualify a priori in a way flowing consistently from its core tenets, the post-Galilean mathematically parsed world up through the beginnings of the twentieth century actually would have been Newtonian in and of itself, really becoming post-Newtonian an sich at some arbitrary instant of time at the start of the twentieth century. Incidentally, this example also highlights a serious problem with excessively and unreservedly privileging, with insufficient sensitivity to the history of science generally and the history of scientific and mathematical techniques/technologies of applied quantification specifically, Galilean-Cartesian primary qualities, *qua* quantifiable properties of perceived/observed objects, as directly revelatory

---

47. Hume, *An Enquiry Concerning Human Understanding*, p. 77.
48. Meillassoux, 'Potentiality and Virtuality', p. 75.

of objects' objectivity as knowable things-in-themselves.[49] If, as Meillassoux wants to maintain through his resuscitation of the distinction between primary and secondary qualities, mathematics immediately manifests real material beings as they are in and of themselves,[50] then one is obliged to explain, which Meillassoux doesn't, why Galileo and Newton, among others, weren't already and automatically in firm possession centuries ago of the unvarnished truth about objective physical reality (reasonably assuming, from a post-Newtonian perspective, that they weren't). The hyper-chaotic early-twentieth-century becoming-post-Newtonian of the material universe in itself should strike one as an absurdity at least as absurd as the conceptual contortions Meillassoux claims correlationists and Christian creationists would resort to when faced with his argumentative mobilization of the 'arche-fossil' in *After Finitude*.[51]

For reasonable scientific practitioners, Ockham's razor always would slice away from Meillassoux's hyper-Chaos and in a direction favoring the presumption that observed anomalies deviating from prior anticipations/expectations regarding cause-and-effect patterns appear as anomalous due to a deficit of past knowledge and not a surplus of anarchic being. In fact, just as miracles cannot appear as such in the domains of science—any miracle, traditionally defined as a violation of the laws of nature, merely signifies, as Hume indicates, that one was wrong before about what one previously took to be the laws of nature supposedly violated by the speciously miraculous—so too for hyper-Chaos. In terms of scientific practice, Meillassoux's speculative materialism, centered on the omnipotent sovereign capriciousness of an absolute time of ultimate contingency, either makes no difference whatsoever (i.e., self-respecting scientists ignore it for a number of very good theoretical and practical reasons) or licenses past scientific mistakes and/or present bad science being sophistically conjured away by cheap-and-easy appeals to hyper-Chaos. As regards the second prong of this discomforting fork, one should try imagining a particle physicist whose experimental results fail to be replicated by other particle physicists protesting that, in the intervening time between his/her experiments and their subsequent re-enactment by others, an instantaneous contingent shift in the causal mechanisms of nature in itself intervened. Why should this physicist correct him/her-self when he/she conveniently can blame his/her epistemological errors on the speculated ontological reality of hyper-Chaos? Insofar as Meillassoux's claims allow for (to the extent that they don't rule out) such highly dubious interpretive maneuvers, these maneuvers threaten speculative materialism with a reductio ad absurdum rebuttal. Moreover, they are an awkward embarrassment to a philosophy that proudly presents itself, especially by contrast with idealist correlationism (as both anti-materialist and anti-realist) from Kant to Husserl and company, as rigorously in line with the actual, factual physical sciences.[52]

As regards the first prong of the above-wielded fork (i.e. speculative materialism makes no difference to the actual practice of science), Meillassoux confesses that this is how he sees the relation between his theories and others' practices—'our claim is that it is possible to sincerely maintain that objects could actually and for no reason whatsoever behave in the most erratic fashion, without having to modify our usual everyday re-

49. Johnston, 'The World Before Worlds', pp. 89-95.

50. Meillassoux, *After Finitude*, pp. 1-3, 12-13.

51. Meillassoux, *After Finitude*, pp. 10, 14, 16-18, 20-23, 26-27, 34.

52. Meillassoux, *After Finitude*, pp. 12, 26-27, 113, 115-116, 118, 120.

lation to things'[53] (one safely can surmise here that he would acknowledge scientists' presumptions apropos the stability of familiar patterns of causal sequences to be part of the outlook of quotidian non-scientific and non-philosophical individuals too). As asserted previously (and as will be rearticulated below), this should signal again to any materialist influenced by the materialism of the Marxist tradition as developed specifically by Engels, Lenin, and Mao—recalling 'Thesis XI' alone suffices—that Meillassoux relies on a strict separation between levels (i.e. the metaphysical-pure-logical-ontological versus the physical-applied-empirical-ontic) closer to the structures essential to idealism and anathema to authentic materialism. Related to this, Nathan Brown's defence of Meillassoux contra Peter Hallward's criticisms of *After Finitude* ends up confirming that a Meillassouxian, when faced with the empirical evidence of scientific practice (not to mention everyday experience), quickly has to retreat to the irrefutable safety of a seemingly pure theoretical dimension unaffected by what are dismissed hastily as matters beneath the dignity of philosophy proper.[54] This author sides squarely with Hallward.

It must be observed that Hume's problem of induction arises in connection with the limited nature of finite human experience. Hence, Meillassoux's anti-phenomenological rationalism of logic alone isn't really based on pure reason only. It departs from an experience-based problem as its push-off point. Therefore, experience, the preponderance of which speaks in one loud voice against the truth of hyper-Chaos, is not without its relevance in evaluating Meillassoux's ideas. To be more precise, Meillassoux cherry-picks from the empirical realms of the experiential (seizing upon Hume's problem of induction) and the experimental (extracting the arche-fossil from certain physical sciences and also dabbling in speculations superimposed upon biology). Debates presently emerging around *After Finitude* seem to indicate that Meillassouxians, if they can be said to exist, believe it legitimate, after the fact of this cherry-picking, to seal off speculative materialism as an incontestable rationalism of the metaphysical-pure-logical-ontological when confronted with reasonable reservations grounded in the physical-applied-empirical-ontic. But, this belief is mistaken and this move intellectually dishonest: Meillassoux's arbitrary borrowings from and engagements with things empirical block such a path of all-too-convenient retreat. Advocates of a Meillassouxian rationalism want to pluck select bits from the experimental physical sciences without these same sciences' reasonable empirical and experiential criteria and considerations clinging to the bits thus grabbed.

Of course, Meillassoux would attempt to respond to the scientists for whom Ockham's razor invariably cuts against hyper-Chaos when they face anomalous data (i.e., data deviating from previous cause-and-effect patterns concerning similar objects and occurrences) with his arguments against the presuppositions underpinning the scientists' assumption regarding the constancy of causal configurations in material reality. These arguments hinge on a distinction between 'chance' (*hasard*) and 'contingency' (*contingence*) and involve recourse to Cantor's revolutionary alteration of the mathematical conception of the infinite as per his trans-finite set theory (as well as recourse to Badiou's 'meta-ontological' reading of post-Cantorian pure mathematics). To be brief, Meillassoux's rationalist ontologization of Hume's empiricist epistemology of causality saddles him with the necessity of surmounting the problem of 'frequentialism'[55]:

53. Meillassoux, *After Finitude*, p. 85.

54. .Nathan Brown, 'On *After Finitude*: A Response to Peter Hallward', in this volume.

55. Meillassoux, *After Finitude*, pp. 91-92; Harman, 'Quentin Meillassoux', pp. 112-113.

If material being an sich is contingent *qua* containing within itself no law-like neces-sary connections, then why isn't reality and the experience of it a violently anarchic and frenetic flux? Asked differently, how come there are apparently stable causal or-ders and structures if absolute being actually is hyper-chaotic? Neither Brassier nor Graham Harman, another 'speculative realist' sympathetic to Meillassoux, are satis-fied with Meillassoux's answers (or lack thereof) to this question, particularly as word-ed in the second fashion.[56] Meillassoux flatly denies that 'the constancy of the phenom-enal world' amounts to a 'refutation of the contingency of physical laws'.[57] But, what buttresses this denial and its complementary affirmation that stable constancy, just because it's an epistemological pre-condition for the formation of empirical scientific knowledge, isn't necessarily also an ontological condition of reality thereby known?[58]

Although Meillassoux states that he is far from being simply a disciple of his teach-er Badiou[59]—this statement isn't accompanied by any details about what he perceives as the crucial differences between his own philosophy and Badiou's—the Badiouian appropriation of Cantorian mathematics, as per *Being and Event*, is integral to Meillas-soux's deployment of the chance-contingency distinction in response to the difficulty of frequentialism created by the introduction of hyper-Chaos as the consequence of on-tologizing the Humean problem of induction. Without the time to do justice to Badiou in the constrained context of a critical evaluation of Meillassoux, suffice it to say a few things about the Badiouian philosophical framework circa 1988 so crucial to this fea-ture of the project delineated in *After Finitude*. In 'Part III' of *Being and Event* ('Being: Na-ture and Infinity. Heidegger/Galileo'), Badiou slides from pure to applied mathemat-ics, displaying disregard for this distinction. He asserts that Cantor's infinitization of infinity itself—in the nineteenth century, the infinite goes from having been conceived of as the single grand totality of a unique One-All to being shattered into an infinite variety of incommensurable, non-totalizable infinities proliferating without end—not only kills (the theosophical idea of) God and renders invalid the entire enterprise of ra-tional theology, but also, at the level of the applied mathematics indispensible to post-Galilean modern science, dissolves and destroys Nature-with-a-capital-N as the mas-sive-but-unified totality of an all-encompassing cosmos, a singularly infinite material universe as a gargantuan sole whole.[60]

Meillassoux adopts this direct transposition of trans-finite set theory onto the mathematized physical reality of the Galileo-inaugurated natural sciences of moder-nity. Badiou and Meillassoux both reason that if the advent of modern science in the early seventeenth century marks a transition 'from the closed world to the infinite uni-verse' (as per the title-phrase of the book by French historian and philosopher of sci-ence Alexandre Koyré upon whom Badiou and Meillassoux each lean), then Can-tor's subsequent radical reworking of the rational-mathematical concept of infinity also must apply retroactively to the infinite universe of the experimental sciences opened up by the Galilean gesture of mathematizing the empirical study of nature. Foreshad-owing an objection to be formulated at greater length shortly, this teacher-student duo

56. Brassier, *Nihil Unbound*, p. 82; Harman, 'Quentin Meillassoux', p. 114.

57. Meillassoux, *After Finitude*, p. 93.

58. Meillassoux, *After Finitude*, pp. 93-94; Brassier, *Nihil Unbound*, pp. 78-79.

59. Meillassoux, '*Histoire et événement chez Alain Badiou*'; Johnston, 'The World Before Worlds', p. 76.

60. Alain Badiou, *Being and Event*, trans. Oliver Feltham, London, Continuum, 2005, pp. 140-141, 273, 277; Alain Badiou, *Briefings on Existence: A Short Treatise on Transitory Ontology*, trans. Norman Madarasz, Albany, State University of New York Press, 2006, pp. 29-31.

violates its own level-distinction between the ontological and the ontic, leaping without sufficient explanatory justification from pure mathematics as purportedly indicative of being *qua* being (*l'être en tant qu'être*) to applied mathematics as reflective of material entities. When Meillassoux, in *After Finitude*, explicitly appeals to Badiou in conjunction with his utilization of the difference between chance and contingency, he clearly assumes that Badiou's Cantor-inspired meta-ontological de-totalization of ontological being *qua* being applies equally and immediately to the ontic spheres of the physical universe(s) too.[61]

So, how does Meillassoux distinguish between chance and contingency? And, what does this distinction have to do with frequentialism? Meillassoux maintains that the probabilistic 'aleatory reasoning'[62] employed by those who would recoil with horror at the idea of hyper-Chaos, being convinced that this idea leads inevitably and without delay to a hyperactively fluctuating anarchic abyss or vortex of a maximally volatile material real lacking any causal constancy whatsoever (i.e., a frequently changing unstable world manifestly at odds with the stable world encountered by experiment and experience), erroneously assumes the universe of possibilities for permutations of causal structures to be a totalized One-All. Such disbelievers in hyper-Chaos are said to cling to calculations of the likely frequency of change based on a mathematically outdated and disproven pre-Cantorian conception of infinity. They think in terms of chance, hypothesizing (whether implicitly or explicitly) the existence of an immensely large but nonetheless totalizable number of possible outcomes. Contingency, by contrast, is thought by Meillassoux in conformity with the post-Cantorian conception of infinity (or, more precisely, infinities) of trans-finite set theory. This unbounded infinite of multiplicities-without-limits rationally bars that upon which the probabilistic aleatory reasoning of chance allegedly depends, namely, the presumed existence of a totality of possible outcomes.[63]

But, even if one concedes the validity of Meillassoux's (and Badiou's) questionable abrupt move from pure to applied mathematics and the ontic domains covered by the latter, an obvious question begs to be posed here: Why should the de-totalization of the totality posited in connection with chance, a de-totalization supposedly requiring the replacement of chance with contingency, make the flux of inconstancy less rather than more likely? How does this solve the problem of frequentialism raised against the speculative materialist thesis of hyper-Chaos? As Meillassoux notes, probabilistic reckonings tied to the notion of chance often rest upon metaphorical picture-thinking, imagining a die with however many sides repeatedly being cast. With this image of the die in hand, those who resist accepting the doctrine of being's absolute contingency ask: If the same face keeps turning up roll after roll (i.e. given the apparent constancy and stability of cause-and-effect patterns in the physical universe), isn't it reasonable to conclude that the die is loaded (i.e. that something other and more than a random string of lawless and discrete isolated temporal instants, whether sufficient reason[s] and/or really existing laws of nature as necessary connections, is continually operative in material reality)? Meillassoux appears to believe that subverting the picture-thinking metaphor of the die is sufficient to solve the problem posed to the concept of hyper-Chaos by frequentialism. However, simply because one cannot probabilistical-

61. Meillassoux, *After Finitude*, pp. 103-107.

62. Meillassoux, *After Finitude*, p. 103.

63. Meillassoux, *After Finitude*, pp. 100-107.

ly calculate chances in this mode doesn't mean that the glaringly and undeniably visible stable constancy of the world has been explained in anything close to a satisfactory manner. If contingency involves an incalculably and immeasurably vaster number of infinite possibilities than chance, isn't it even more probable (although by exactly how much more cannot be determined with numerical exactitude due to the mathematics involved) that an ontology of hyper-chaotic contingency would entail frequently fluctuating worlds as a Heraclitian flux of ceaseless, restless becoming? Just because transfinite contingency is less readily calculable than pre-Cantorian chance doesn't mean that it's less chancy. If anything, it seems more reasonable to wager that it would be even chancier (as a chanciness beyond chance [*hasard*] in Meillassoux's sense), thus further inflating the entire problem of frequentialism facing speculative materialist hyper-Chaos. Even if there are an infinite number of possible universes in which what human knowledge here, in this actual universe, takes to be stable laws of physics are the same, why wouldn't it be the case that the cardinality of this infinity, as the measured size of this set of possible universes, is dwarfed in size by the cardinality of the infinity measuring the set of possible universes in which one or more of these laws of physics differ in any mind-boggling number of possible ways (and each at perhaps an even more mind-boggling number of discrete temporal instants)? If it is the case, then it's certainly plausible that, relative to the cardinality of the latter infinity, the former infinity would be incredibly small such that the likelihood of stable constancy in an ontology of hyper-chaotic being is itself incredibly small. In this case, the problem of frequentialism is just as, if not more, problematic after the replacement of pre-Cantorian chance with post-Cantorian contingency.

Meillassoux, in 'Potentiality and Virtuality', contends that, 'Hume's problem becomes the problem of the difference between chance and contingency'.[64] Of course, Hume wouldn't see it this way. For him, belief in the future enduring constancy of any cause-and-effect pattern is proportional to the past frequency with which this pattern regularly has unfolded for the mental observer—the greater the number of anomaly-free past instances of an observed causal sequence (i.e., 'constant conjunction', in Hume's parlance[65]), the greater the strength of accustomed/habituated belief in the accuracy and validity of the idea of this causal association between spatially and temporally proximate entities and events.[66] Hence, in the Humean account of causality, there is no recourse, not even tacitly, to probabilistic aleatory reasoning as the vain effort imaginarily to catalog all of the possible variations on causal patterns in order to estimate the likelihood of a given idea of a particular cause-and-effect relation continuing to hold true. In his discussions of the belief in causality, Hume proportionally indexes the strength of belief (itself an un-analyzable elementary phenomenon) to the number of past experiences, free of the admixture of anomalous instances, of a given sequence of events involving given types of observed objects—and that's it.

This aside and returning to Meillassoux's philosophy, some additional remarks about the role and status of mathematics in the systems of both Badiou and Meillassoux merit mention. To be more precise, four points should be made here (the first three won't be delved into at any length since they have been elaborated upon extensively elsewhere). First, as both this author and Brassier propose in other contexts,

64. Meillassoux, 'Potentiality and Virtuality', p. 64.

65. Hume, *An Enquiry Concerning Human Understanding*, pp. 46, 49-50, 52.

66. Hume, *An Enquiry Concerning Human Understanding*, p. 39.

Badiou and Meillassoux excessively fetishize mathematics, thereby regrettably skewing and narrowing the picture of the empirical sciences.[67] Second, as Hallward succinctly and forcefully argues in his compact and effective review of *After Finitude*, speculative materialism sometimes conflates, without accompanying explicit justifications, the metaphysical-pure-logical-ontological and the physical-applied-empirical-ontic—at other times, speculative materialism insists upon the utter incommensurability of these dimensions—failing to explain and defend this conflation (one significant version of which is the juxtaposition of post-Cantorian trans-finite set theory, as pure mathematics, and the physical space-time mapped by the application of mathematical frameworks other than set theory).[68] As claimed above, this criticism is readily applicable to Badiou too.

Third—the third and fourth points are closely connected—Meillassoux, in a brilliant essay critically analyzing the engagement with mathematics in *Being and Event*, describes how Badiou's distinction between being and event rests on a gamble betting that no unforeseeable future events in the formal science of mathematics will happen that overturn (if indeed any branch or sub-branch of mathematics can be said to be 'overturned') the set theoretic basis for this distinction (something Badiou himself cannot entirely discount given his theory of events in philosophy's four 'conditions' of art, love, politics, and science).[69] Although he doesn't acknowledge this, the same historical instability holds for the early modern Galilean-Cartesian distinction between primary (i.e., quantitative) and secondary (i.e., qualitative) qualities, a distinction Meillassoux attempts to reactivate starting in the opening pages of *After Finitude*.[70] Fourth, finally, and in relation to this previous point, the wager Meillassoux accurately identifies as lying at the very heart of Badiou's system as per *Being and Event* is symptomatic of what is one of the great virtues of Badiouian philosophical thought: its combination of a Pascalian-existentialist sensibility with rigorous systematicity. Summarizing too much too quickly, in delegating ontology to mathematics, Badiou makes a series of preliminary choices leading to his novel meta-ontology: a choice between all the different branches of pure mathematics; a choice between all the different branches of pure mathematics that vie for the title of being the 'foundational' branch of all other branches of mathematics (here, Badiou chooses set theory, despite its claim to foundational status, and even what such a claim by any branch or sub-branch of mathematics might mean, having become increasingly questionable during the past several decades); a choice between all the different axiomatizations of set theory (here, Badiou chooses Zermelo-Fraenkel plus the axiom of choice [ZFC], even though there are other axiomatized versions of set theory, including versions allowing for the recognized existence of the Badiou-banished 'One' of a set of all sets). And, in the background motivating this chain of concatenated choices lurks Badiou's fundamental 'decision' that, as he puts it in the first meditation of *Being and Event*, 'the One is not'.[71]

---

67. Johnston, 'What Matter(s) in Ontology', pp. 27-49; Johnston, 'The World Before Worlds', pp. 73-99; Ray Brassier, 'Speculative Realism: Presentation by Ray Brassier', *Collapse*, vol. 3, pp. 331-333.

68. Hallward, 'Anything is possible', pp. 55-56; Meillassoux, 'Potentiality and Virtuality', pp. 65-67.

69. Quentin Meillassoux, '*Nouveauté et événement*', *Alain Badiou: Penser le multiple—Actes du Colloque de Bordeaux, 21-23 octobre 1999*, Charles Ramond (ed.), Paris, L'Harmattan, 2002, pp. 39-41, 50-54; Brassier, *Nihil Unbound*, p. 109; Johnston, 'The World Before Worlds', pp. 90-94.

70. Johnston, 'The World Before Worlds', pp. 93-94.

71. Badiou, *Being and Event*, p. 23.

For Badiou, there are philosophically unavoidable ontological questions—even Kant, whose transcendental idealist approach can be understood as limiting philosophy to epistemology and correlatively prohibiting the pursuit of an ontology, arguably cannot avoid tacitly reintroducing an implicit ontology into his critical system, an ontology consisting of answers to questions always-already posed—which can and must be answered with a pure decision. In other words, they can and must be answered without even the minimal assistance of (absent/lacking) guiding gut-level intuitions apparently favoring the decision to arrive at one answer rather than others. Badiou's choice of ZFC, itself one sub-branch of one branch amongst a large number of branches and sub-branches of mathematics, is comprehensible and defensible exclusively in light of this prime Ur-decision on the One's non-existence in response to the inescapable Parmenidean-Platonic query 'Being, One or Many?' In an interview with Bruno Bosteels, Badiou, reminiscing about his intellectual youth, confesses that, 'I remember very clearly having raised the question, having formed the project of one day constructing something like a Sartrean thought of mathematics, or of science in general, which Sartre had left aside for the most part'.[72] *Being and Event* fulfills this planned project of the young Badiou insofar as the mathematical ontology and parallel meta-ontology forming the basis of this magnum opus serving as the nucleus of his mature system initially stems from the first cause of the groundless ground of the freedom of a pure decision in response to one of several unavoidable questions of/about being, questions into which everyone is always-already thrown, whether they know and acknowledge it or not. The implications for Meillassoux's thought of Badiou's innovative combination of the non-foundational foundation of the existentialist wager (as per Pascal and Sartre, among others) with the form of mathematical rationality à la philosophically systematic structures will be explored in what ensues very soon.

Returning one last time to the topic of Meillassoux's problematic relationship to the empirical sciences (before turning attention back to his startling proximity to strains of idealist religiosity despite his self-presentation as an irreligious materialist), 'Potentiality and Virtuality' contains a brief effort to apply the speculative materialist concept of hyper-Chaos to the field of biology, specifically, the enigma of the emergence of sentient life out of non-sentient physical matter. As Meillassoux makes clear here, hyper-Chaos permits reviving the originally religious notion of creation *ex nihilo* (although, like Badiou with respect to the loaded idea-word 'grace',[73] he protests that this is a non-religious version of the *ex nihilo*, a secular 'miracle'—this protest will be addressed momentarily).[74] It permits this insofar as, at each discretely isolated and contingent temporal instant ungoverned by sufficient reason or causal necessity, anything could emerge for no reason whatsoever and out of no prior precedent as a preceding potential (i.e., out of nothing). With these theses in place, Meillassoux then has the luxury of being able effortlessly to dispatch with a riddle that has bedeviled the very best minds in the life sciences and those philosophers seriously contending with these

---

72. Alain Badiou, 'Can Change Be Thought?: A Dialogue with Alain Badiou [with Bruno Bosteels]', *Alain Badiou: Philosophy and Its Conditions*, Gabriel Riera (ed.), Albany, State University of New York Press, 2005, p. 242.

73. Alain Badiou, *Saint Paul: The Foundation of Universalism*, trans. Ray Brassier, Stanford, Stanford University Press, 2003, p. 71; Alain Badiou, 'Politics and Philosophy: An Interview with Alain Badiou [with Peter Hallward]," in *Ethics: An Essay on the Understanding of Evil*, trans. Peter Hallward, London, Verso, 2001, p. 123; Alain Badiou, *Logiques des mondes: L'être et l'événement, 2*, Paris, Éditions du Seuil, 2006, pp. 534, 536.

74. Meillassoux, 'Potentiality and Virtuality', pp. 72, 75.

sciences: The 'hard problem' of how sentient life, as consciousness, arises out of non-conscious matter isn't a problem at all—this genesis is simply an instance of the *ex nihilo* made possible by the time of hyper-chaotic absolute contingency.[75] Abracadabra!

Hägglund quite appropriately submits Meillassoux's treatment of the problem of conscious life to pointed criticism as scientifically suspect.[76] This author fully, albeit selectively, endorses Hägglund's employment specifically of his Derridean dynamic of 'the becoming space of time' (as distinct from its flip side, 'the becoming time of space') to complicate (in the name of, among other things, the life sciences) the speculative materialist mystifying obfuscation of this mystery of the emergence of sentience through appeals to a sovereign temporal power utterly independent of spatial materiality. In addition to Hägglund's objections, it ought to be underscored that not only does this application of hyper-Chaos to biology contradict Meillassoux's (and Brown's) insistence elsewhere (as remarked on above) that absolute contingency is postulated on a rational level separate and unrelated to the domains of the reasonable empirical sciences of nature—it illustrates a contention advanced earlier here, namely, that the hyper-Chaos of Meillassouxian speculative materialism is stuck stranded between the Scylla and Charybdis of two undesirable options: either, one, it cannot or should not be applied to real scientific practices concerned with actual entities and events (in which case, from the standpoint of this intervention's materialism, it's inconsequential and uninteresting); or, two, in being applied to the sciences, it licenses, without consistent intra-systemic means of preventing, the intellectual laziness of the cheap trick of transubstantiating ignorance into insight (i.e., the lack of a solid scientific solution to the 'hard problem' of the emergence of sentient life is itself already a direct insight into a momentous moment of lawless, reasonless genesis out of thin air). Finally and in short, if emergence *ex nihilo* sparked by an omnipotent power isn't a religious idea, then what is?

The time has come to circle from science back to religion as regards Meillassoux's speculative materialism. Hallward perceptively draws readers' attention to the similarities between Meillassouxian hyper-Chaos, as per *After Finitude*, and the divinities of monotheistic religions.[77] Meillassoux furnishes Hallward with plenty of evidence for this comparison.[78] However, both Meillassoux and Brassier struggle to refute such a resemblance. The former, in, for example, 'Deuil à venir, dieu à venir', contrasts his 'contingent' and 'unmasterable' God-to-come with the traditional God of pre-Kantian rationalist metaphysics (i.e., a necessary and rational supreme being eternally existent).[79] For Meillassoux, hyper-Chaos testifies to 'the inexistence of the divine' to the extent that positing this absolute contingency correlatively entails denying the existence of the divinity of metaphysical theosophy (as though the signifier 'God' can and does refer exclusively to this sort of divine as its invariant, one-and-only signified). Brassier adds that, because of the disturbing Otherness of its anarchic capriciousness, this omnipotent hyper-Chaos cannot be the object of fideistic adoration, respect, reverence, worship, etc.; in its unpredictable lawlessness, the alterity of this transcendent time of unlimited creative powers is unsuited to be the addressee of the aspirations, desires, and

---

75. Meillassoux, 'Potentiality and Virtuality', pp. 73, 79-80.

76. Hägglund, 'Radical Atheist Materialism'.

77. Hallward, 'Anything is possible', pp. 55-56.

78. Meillassoux, *After Finitude*, pp. 61-62, 64-66, & Meillassoux, 'Potentiality and Virtuality', pp. 59, 72, 75.

79. Meillassoux, *'Deuil à venir, dieu à venir'*, p. 112.

dreams of the religiously and spiritually inclined.[80] Of course, as the article 'Deuil à venir, dieu à venir' shows, this doesn't stop Meillassoux himself from pinning his hopes
on it for the incalculably improbable springing to life of a God closely resembling that
of the most established Christianity in every respect save for his speculated non-necessity (analogous to how perhaps the sole thing saving Kant from being Berkeley is the
hypothesized noumenal *Ding an sich*).

When undergraduate students first are exposed to Leibniz's depiction of God in
his rationalist ontology, many of them invariably express some version of a predictable reaction according to which this depiction illegitimately limits God's freedom to do
as he pleases by restrictively compelling him, through the principle of sufficient reason, to actualize, out of the infinity of possible worlds of which he's omnisciently cog-
nizant, the single 'best of all possible worlds' (disarming this objection obviously begins with explaining how, in the history of Western philosophy going back to Plato's
Socrates, acting under the commanding governance of reason, on the one hand, and
authentic autonomy, on the other hand, aren't opposed as mutually exclusive—doing
what one wants isn't, for most philosophers, being truly free). Although Meillassoux's
hyper-Chaos differs from Leibniz's God in that the former, unlike the latter, is liberated from the supposedly tyrannical yoke of the principle of sufficient reason—one additionally might mention here hyper-Chaos' lack of intentional agency/will, although
the God-to-come of speculative divinology made possible by hyper-Chaos looks to
be endowed with these same subjective features and faculties exhibited by the Leibnizian God—this absolute contingency is very much like the God undergraduates invoke against Leibniz's divinity metaphysically constrained by his perfect moral and rational nature. Succinctly stated, Meillassoux's hyper-Chaos resembles the God of 'the
spontaneous theosophy of non/not-yet-philosophers' (with reference to Althusser but
not to François Laruelle). While not a pre-Kantian metaphysical God, Meillassoux's
speculative hyper-Chaos, with its *Dieu à venir*, nonetheless is disturbingly similar to this
God of (post-)modern non/not-yet-philosophers. In fact, Meillassoux splits up and dis-
tributes the bundle of features attributed by pre-Kantian rationalist metaphysicians
to God alone across these two entities (i.e., hyper-Chaos and divinology's *Dieu à venir*).

What's more, Meillassoux's style of philosophizing is, in many ways, Leibnizian,
discounting the empirical, experiential, and experimental in favor of the logical-rational and leading to the formulation of an entirely unreasonable worldview that is
both incontestable and yet counter-intuitive, utterly at odds with what empirically informed reasoning tells investigators about the reality of the world. Sticking stubbornly
to the logic and rationality of the mathematics of his day alone, Leibniz is led to deny
the substantial real being not only of physical atoms, but of matter in general; the result is a metaphysical monism of divinely harmonized and orchestrated monads, as immaterial 'formal atoms', that couldn't be further from any and every materialism. As
intellectually entertaining as it might be to follow along with Leibniz's incredibly clever conceptual acrobatics and contortions, does one really want to go back to philosophizing in this pre-Kantian style, even if the philosophical content is post-Kantian?
Moreover, on the basis of pure reason alone, why should one prefer Meillassouxian
speculation over Leibnizian metaphysics? On this basis, there is no reason. As Kant
convincingly proves in 'The Dialectic of Pure Reason', the quarrels amongst the pri-
or rationalist philosophers about being *an sich* are no more worth taking philosophical-

---

80. Brassier, *Nihil Unbound*, p. 71.

ly seriously than silly squabbles between sci-fi writers about whose concocted fantasy-world is truer or somehow more 'superior' than the others; such quarrels are nothing more than vain comparisons between equally hallucinatory apples and oranges, again resembling the sad spectacle of a bunch of pulp fiction novelists bickering over the cor-rectness-without-criteria of each others' fabricated imaginings and illusions. Discard-ing everything in Kant apart from his critical destruction of metaphysical absolutes, as does Meillassouxian speculative materialism, is tantamount to lifting the lid contain-ing the swirling maelstrom of the specters of all other logically possible philosophies of pure reason (i.e., other than Meillassouxian speculative materialism). Only if one takes into account reasonable empirical considerations rooted in an experiential and/or experimental ground (as per, for example, Hume and his problem of induction) does Meillassoux's system appear relatively more preferable, if at all, to the innumerable other rationalisms licensed by mere logical possibility. But, as stated previously, as soon as reasonable empirical considerations are (re-)admitted, hyper-Chaos is immediately in trouble again. Such considerations are a bind for Meillassoux as conditions both for (as necessary for the Humean problem motivating the project of *After Finitude* as well as for the scientific arche-fossil hurled at correlationism) and simultaneously against (as unanimously testifying on behalf of alternate explanations different from those offered in *After Finitude*) his speculative philosophy with its absolute contingency.

Referring again to Žižekian philosophy is requisite at this stage. Speaking in a po-litical register, Žižek insists that 'true materialism' is inextricably intertwined with the matter of the chancy contingency of risk.[81] The same should be asserted apropos the-oretical (in addition to practical-political) materialism. But, what would this entail for Meillassoux and his speculative materialism? To begin with, and once more invoking Hallward, Meillassoux's 'materialism' privileges 'maybe' over 'be', *peut-être* over *être*.[82] That is to say, speculative materialism, as the concluding pages of *After Finitude* cor-roborates, relies upon a presumed strict separation between, on the one hand, the physical-applied-empirical-ontic, and, on the other hand, the metaphysical-pure-logi-cal-ontological[83] (and, as maintained previously here, Brown's responses to Hallward's objections to the arguments of *After Finitude* seem to reinforce that this is indeed the case). Both Badiou and Meillassoux suffer from a Heideggerian hangover, specifical-ly, an acceptance unacceptable for (dialectical) materialism of the veracity of ontologi-cal difference, of a clear-cut distinction between the ontological and the ontic.[84] In this regard, one of the imperatives of a contemporary scientifically well-grounded materi-alism, a dialectical materialism, is the injunction 'Forget Heidegger!' Genuine materi-alism, including theoretical materialist philosophy, is risky, messy business (something Brassier, for one, appreciates[85]). It doesn't grant anyone the low-effort luxury of flee-ing into the uncluttered, fact-free ether of a 'fundamental ontology' serenely separate from the historically shifting stakes of ontic disciplines. Although a materialist philos-ophy cannot be literally falsifiable as are Popperian sciences, it should be contestable *qua* receptive, responsive, and responsible vis-à-vis the sciences.

---

81. Slavoj Žižek, 'Foreword to the Second Edition: Enjoyment within the Limits of Reason Alone', *For they know not what they do: Enjoyment as a political factor*, 2nd ed., London, Verso, 2002, p. lii; Johnston, *Badiou, Žižek, and Political Transformations*.

82. Hallward, 'Anything is possible', p. 51.

83. Meillassoux, *After Finitude*, pp. 127-128.

84. Johnston, 'What Matter(s) in Ontology', pp. 27-29, 44.

85. Brassier, *Nihil Unbound*, p. 63.

Recalling the earlier discussion of the Pascalian-Sartrean wager of Badiou's equation of ontology with the ZFC axiomatization of set theory, this wager illustrates Badiou's conception of philosophy as a betting on the unforeseeable fortunes of the amorous, artistic, political, and scientific truths of its time—in this precise case, a wager on post-Cantorian trans-finite set theory as a scientific condition of Badiouian philosophy (as noted above, Meillassoux himself emphasizes that this is a gamble by Badiou, the leap into historical uncertainty of an existential choice/decision). This conception of philosophy, to be endorsed by a materialism of chancy contingency indebted to the dialectical materialist tradition, directly links philosophizing with the taking of risks with respect to its amorous, artistic, political, and scientific conditions.

Insofar as the arche-fossil he arbitrarily and selectively borrows from the physical sciences is merely a disposable propaedeutic on the way to the overcoming of correlationism, with this overcoming then resulting in a speculative materialist doctrine of hyper-Chaos (pretending to be) thereafter immune to science-based contestation, Meillassoux, unlike his teacher Badiou, avoids taking any real risks at the level of his philosophy's rapport with science. He clings to an unreasonable rationalism that appears reasonable solely when one disregards, on the questionable basis of an anti-immanentist appeal to a (too) neat-and-clean distinction between the physical-applied-empirical-ontic and the metaphysical-pure-logical-ontological, the actual practices of today's really existing sciences of material beings. This, combined with his related desire for absolute certainty, puts him in the company not only of pre-Kantian theosophical idealists—just as the one thing that saves Kant from being Berkeley is the thing-in-itself, the one thing that saves Meillassoux from being an early modern rationalist (i.e., a theosophical idealist) is his 'intellectual intuition'[86] of the all-powerful (in)existent divine as capricious—but also of any number of outlandish and politically backward religious fideists and fanatics. Like solipsism, Pyrrhonic extreme/hyperbolic skepticism, religious dogmatism, and/or Berkeley's philosophy—if, as per Lenin and Meillassoux, one becomes prima facie absurd through being brought into uncomfortably close company with Berkeley, then Meillassoux should be worried given his desire for absolutely certain irrefutability—Meillassouxian speculative materialism poses as incontestable, as an easily defended (but empty) fortress. After relying on the realm of the reasonable, it tries to evade further critical evaluation at the level of the reasonable by attempting to escape into the confined enclosure of the strictly rational. It risks nothing, which is perhaps why, scientifically speaking, it says nothing (or, at least, nothing that should be taken seriously in empirical-material practice, unless one wishes to throw the door of the sciences wide open to transubstantiations of ignorance into insight, including *ex nihilo* creationist confabulations). Erroneously pointing out that this rational yet supposedly materialist philosophy is impervious to being delivered any scientifically backed death blows is already to deliver the coup de grâce.

The critique of Meillassoux laid out in the preceding actually is twofold. On the one hand, it's charged that the vaguely Heideggerian version of ontological difference operative in Meillassoux's (and Badiou's) philosophy is inadmissible and invalid for a properly materialist philosophy. On the other hand, the additional indictment is issued that Meillassoux nonetheless doesn't invariably heed this stratified level-distinction between rational ontology and the reason(ableness) of ontic regions. At times

---

86. Meillassoux, *After Finitude*, p. 82.

and in an inconsistent fashion, he transgresses the line of ontological difference which his philosophy claims to maintain and respect.

Given Meillassoux's rationalist absolutism-without-an-absolute,[87] he's profoundly averse to skepticism. But, this phobic aversion lulls him into overlooking a Badiouian manner of recuperating Humean attenuated skepticism so as riskily to wager on aspects of the contemporary sciences: just as there is no guarantee of future continued confirmation of any given scientific claim, so too is there no guarantee of future disconfirmation either (as Meillassoux would have to grant, considering both his glosses on Badiou's appropriation of mathematics as well as his explanations for why the concept of hyper-Chaos doesn't entail a Heraclitian flux doctrine[88]). Along these lines, Hume's skepticism is far from encouraging one to be hand-wringingly non-committal vis-à-vis empirical scientific claims (all of which, according to Hume, are based on the ideational relation of cause-and-effect). Rather, Humean attenuated skepticism means one is aware that philosophically drawing upon the sciences is indeed far from being a 'sure thing', amounting instead to risks, to bets or gambles that lack any promises or guarantees of final correctness in a future that can and will retroactively pass judgments on these present wagers. But, as with Pascal's wager, there's no honest and true way to avoid these risks.

Moreover, a subtle but significant link connects Hume and historical/dialectical materialism à la Marx, Engels, Lenin, and Mao—and this despite Engels and Lenin associating Humean ontological agnosticism with idealism[89] (for Pascal, agnostically not choosing to believe in God is choosing not to believe in God, namely, choosing atheism; similarly, for Lenin, agnostically not choosing to be a committed materialist is choosing not to be a materialist, namely, choosing idealism, however overt or covert). Both Hume and historical/dialectical materialism in certain Marxist veins propose a non-absolutist (*qua* fallible) realism of revisable knowledge of the real world with the courage of conviction to wager on its own correctness in the absence of any absolute a priori assurances—and, in the process, also to risk being wrong in exposure both to theoretical contestation as well as to the danger of the falsification of the scientific materials upon which its wagers are placed. Incidentally, as regards the entire 'speculative realism' movement largely inspired by Meillassoux's work, a warning is in order against the danger of getting stuck in endless philosophical tempests-in-teacups pitting realist materialism against idealist anti-materialism: even if the content of one's position is realist and/or materialist, conceding the form of an interminable and unwinnable epistemological debate is itself idealist. As others in the history of philosophy have observed, some problems are more effectively solved by being justly ignored, by not being dignified with any further engagement. There is a big difference between arguing for materialism/realism versus actually pursuing the positive construction of materialist/realist projects dirtying their hands with real empirical data.

Circumnavigating back to one of the initial points of reference for this intervention, a short, direct bridge connects Meillassoux's *After Finitude* with his 'Deuil à venir, dieu à venir'.[90] It's terribly tempting to indulge in a Dawkins-style move and joke about a 'flying spaghetti monster *à venir*'. Of all the incalculable contingent (im)possibilities

---

87. Meillassoux, *After Finitude*, pp. 33-34.

88. Meillassoux, 'Potentiality and Virtuality', pp. 58-59.

89. Engels, *Ludwig Feuerbach and the Outcome of Classical German Philosophy*, pp. 22-23; Lenin, *Materialism and Empirio-Criticism*, pp. 1, 22-23, 61, 65, 109-111, 127-129, 142, 152-153, 177-178, 188-189, 191, 241, 284, 312-313.

90. Meillassoux, *After Finitude*, pp. 64-66.

permitted by Meillassoux's hyper-Chaos, he ends up speculating, in his article on a God-to-come, about the infinitely much less than one-in-a-trillion possibility of the arrival of a divinity resembling that mused about by the most traditional monotheistic religions and their old prophecies. This is telling. Shouldn't the de-totalizing of probabilistic chance in favor of trans-finite contingency make this even less worth pondering, forcing its likelihood asymptotically but rapidly to approach zero?

Additionally, from this perspective, Meillassoux can be viewed as an inversion of Žižek, as an anti-Žižek: whereas Žižek tries to smuggle atheism into Christianity via the immanent critique of a Hegelian dialectical interpretation of Christianity for the sake of a progressive radical leftist politics of Communism, Meillassoux, whether knowingly or unknowingly, smuggles idealist religiosity back into materialist atheism via a non-dialectical 'materialism'. Meillassoux's divinology and emergent life *ex nihilo* are rigorously consequent extensions of the speculative materialism (with its central concept of hyper-Chaos) of *After Finitude*. These very extensions arguably bear damning witness against the project of this book—*After Finitude* has many striking virtues, especially in terms of its crystalline clarity and ingenious creativeness, and deserves credit for having played a role in inspiring some much-needed discussions in contemporary Continental philosophy—at least for any atheist materialism concerned with various modes of scientific and political *praxis*. Alert, sober vigilance is called for against the danger of dozing off into a speculative, but no less dogmatic, slumber.

9

Radical Atheist Materialism:
A Critique of Meillassoux

Martin Hägglund

The difficulty of distinguishing the genuine philosopher from the eloquent sophist is never more pressing than when someone comes forth and lays claim to a new paradigm for thinking. The uncertainty concerning the merit and depth of the discourse typically precipitates two types of responses, both aimed at settling the question of legitimacy once and for all. On the one hand, the enthusiasm of those who join 'the movement', convinced that they have found the genuine new philosopher. On the other hand, the cynicism of those who dismiss the emerging paradigm as a design to dazzle the young, convinced that the supposedly groundbreaking thinker is a sophist in disguise.

The work of Quentin Meillassoux seems destined to provoke these types of responses. Meillassoux himself is adamant that his work goes to the heart of classical metaphysical questions in order to answer them anew, and his former teacher Alain Badiou even holds that 'Meillassoux has opened a new path in the history of philosophy'.[1] Judging from the rapidly growing interest in Meillassoux after the English translation of his first book *After Finitude*, and the announcement of the movement of 'speculative realism' in its wake, there are many who seem willing to subscribe to the truth of Badiou's statement. Conversely, the apparently fashionable character of Meillassoux's philosophy cannot but provoke suspicion among the already established, especially since Meillassoux situates himself polemically vis-à-vis all forms of transcendental philosophy and phenomenology.

Nevertheless, it would be a mistake to endorse either of these two attitudes to Meillassoux's thinking. The considerable merit of his work is that it invites philosophical *argumentation* rather than reverence or dismissal. Hence, I will confront the logic of Meillassoux's arguments with the logic I articulate in my book *Radical Atheism*. Parallels between *After Finitude* and *Radical Atheism* have already been noted. In a recent

---

1. Alain Badiou, 'Preface', in Quentin Meillassoux, *After Finitude: An Essay on the Necessity of Contingency*, trans. R. Brassier, London, Continuum, 2008, p. vii.

essay, Aaron F. Hodges stages a confrontation between the two works in terms of the question of materialism, which is an instructive focal point for our respective trajectories.[2] Both books criticize the prevalent 'turn to religion', in the course of reactivating fundamental questions of contingency and necessity, time and space, life and death. Returning to these questions here, I will not only seek to critically assess Meillassoux's work and press home the stakes of radical atheism, but also to delineate the consequences of the debate for the notion of materialism.

Meillassoux targets nothing less than the basic argument of Kant's transcendental philosophy, which holds that we cannot have knowledge of the absolute. Against all forms of dogmatic metaphysics which lay claim to prove the existence of the absolute, Kant argues that there can be no cognition without the forms of time and space that undercut any possible knowledge of the absolute. The absolute would have to be exempt from time and space, whereas all we can know is given through time and space as forms of intuition. As is well known, however, Kant delimits the possibility of knowledge in order to 'make room for faith'. By making it impossible to prove the existence of the absolute Kant also makes it impossible to refute it and thus rehabilitates the absolute as an object of faith rather than knowledge.

In contrast, Meillassoux seeks to formulate a notion of the absolute that does not entail a return to the metaphysical and pre-critical idea of a necessary being. He endorses Kant's critique of dogmatic metaphysics, but argues that we can develop a 'speculative' thinking of the absolute that does not succumb to positing a necessary being. According to Meillassoux, 'it is absolutely necessary that every entity might not exist. This is indeed a speculative thesis, since we are thinking an absolute, but it is not metaphysical, since we are not thinking any *thing* (any entity) that would *be* absolute. The absolute is the absolute impossibility of a necessary being'.[3] The absolute in question is the power of *time*. Time makes it impossible for any entity to be necessary, since the condition of temporality entails that every entity can be destroyed. It is precisely this destructibility that Meillassoux holds to be absolute: 'only the time that harbours the capacity to destroy every determinate reality, while obeying no determinate law—the time capable of destroying, without reason or law, both words and things— can be thought as an absolute' (62). Armed with this notion of the absolute, Meillassoux takes contemporary philosophers to task for their concessions to religion. By renouncing knowledge of the absolute, thinkers of the 'wholly other' renounce the power to refute religion and give the latter free reign as long as it restricts itself to the realm of faith rather than knowledge. As Meillassoux puts it with an emphatic formulation: '*by forbidding reason any claim to the absolute, the end of metaphysics has taken the form of an exacerbated return of the religious*' (45).

Although Meillassoux rarely mentions him by name, Derrida is clearly one of the intended targets for his attack on the idea of a 'wholly other' beyond the grasp of reason. As I demonstrate in *Radical Atheism*, however, Derrida's thinking of alterity cannot be aligned with any religious conception of the absolute.[4] For Derrida, alterity is indis-

---

2. See Aaron F. Hodges, 'Martin Hägglund's Speculative Materialism', *CR: The New Centennial Review*, vol. 9, no. 1, 2009, special issue *Living On: Of Martin Hägglund*. Some of my arguments concerning Meillassoux were first articulated in my response essay for the same issue of *CR*; see Martin Hägglund, 'The Challenge of Radical Atheism: A Response'.

3. Meillassoux, *After Finitude*, p. 60. Subsequent page-references given in the text.

4. See Martin Hägglund, *Radical Atheism: Derrida and the Time of Life*, Stanford, Stanford University Press, 2008, in particular chapter 3 and 4.

sociable from the condition of temporality that exposes every instance to destruction. Consequently, Derrida's notion of the 'absolutely' or 'wholly' other (*tout autre*) does not refer to the positive infinity of the divine but to the radical finitude of every other. Every finite other is absolutely other, not because it is absolutely in itself but, on the contrary, because it can never overcome the alterity of time and never be in itself. As long as it exists, every entity is always becoming other than itself and cannot have any integrity as such. Far from consolidating a religious instance that would be exempt from the destruction of time, Derrida's conception of absolute alterity spells out that the subjection to the violent passage of time is absolutely irreducible.

Nevertheless, there are central and decisive differences between the conception of time proposed by Meillassoux and Derrida respectively. For Meillassoux, the absolute contingency of time (the fact that anything can happen) has an ontological status which entails that the advent of the divine is possible. Despite his critique of religion, Meillassoux advocates a *divinology* according to which *God is possible*, not because it is possible that God may currently exist but because it is possible that he may come to exist in the future.[5] While this may seem to be Meillassoux's weakest and most extravagant proposal, I will argue that it follows from fundamental problems in his theorization of time. For Meillassoux, absolute time is a 'virtual power' that only entails the possibility—and not the necessity—of destruction. Furthermore, the destructive effects of temporality that do take place can supposedly be reverted by the virtual power of contingency, which according to Meillassoux even allows for the possible resurrection of the dead. I will show that these arguments are untenable, since there can be no contingency without the succession of time, which entails irreversible destruction and rules out the possibility of resurrection a priori.

My argument has two steps. First, I demonstrate that the conception of time as dependent on the structure of 'the trace' provides a better model for thinking temporality and contingency than the one proposed by Meillassoux. Derrida defines the structure of the trace as the becoming-space of time and the becoming-time of space. I proceed by demonstrating how the structure of the trace can be deduced from the philosophical problem of succession. The structure of the trace entails what I call the 'arche-materiality' of time, which is crucial for thinking the relation between the animate and the inanimate, while undermining Meillassoux's notion of the virtual power of time. Contrary to what Meillassoux holds, time cannot be a virtual power to make anything happen, since it is irreversible and dependent on a spatial, material support that restricts its possibilities. Second, I confront Meillassoux's divinology with the logic of radical atheism. Radical atheism targets an axiom shared by both religion and traditional atheism, namely, that we *desire* the state of immortality. The radical atheist counter-argument is not only that immortality is impossible but also that it is *not* desirable in the first place. Through Meillassoux's own examples, we will see that the purported desire for immortality in fact is motivated by a desire for mortal *survival* that precedes it and contradicts it from within. In clarifying the status of this desire for survival, I conclude by showing how it is crucial for radical atheist materialism.

Meillassoux's point of departure is the empirical phenomenon of what he calls *arche-fossils*, namely, objects that are older than life on Earth and whose duration it is possible to measure: 'for example an isotope whose rate of radioactive decay we know, or the luminous emission of a star that informs us as to the date of its formation' (10).

---

5. See Quentin Meillassoux, 'Spectral Dilemma', *Collapse*, no. 4, 2008, p. 269.

Such arche-fossils enable scientists to date the origin of the universe to approximate-ly 13.5 billion years ago and the origin of life on Earth to 3.5 billion years ago. Accord-ing to Meillassoux, these 'ancestral' statements are incompatible with the basic presup-position of transcendental philosophy, which holds that the world cannot be described apart from how it is given to a thinking and/or living being. The ancestral statements of science describe a world in which *nothing was given* to a thinking or living being, since the physical conditions of the universe did not allow for the emergence of a life or con-sciousness to which the world could be given. The ensuing challenge to transcenden-tal philosophy 'is not the empirical problem of the birth of living organisms, but the ontological problem of the coming into being of givennness as such' (21). Rather than being able to restrict time to a form of givenness for consciousness, we are confront-ed with an absolute time 'wherein *consciousness* as well as *conscious time* have *themselves emerged in time*' (21).

Meillassoux is well aware that he could here be accused of conflating the empiri-cal with the transcendental. Empirical bodies emerge and perish in time, but the same cannot be said of transcendental conditions. The transcendental subject is not an em-pirical body existing in time and space, but a set of conditions through which knowl-edge of bodies in time and space is possible. Thus, a scientific discourse about em-pirical objects or the empirical universe cannot have purchase on the transcendental subject, since the latter provides the condition of possibility for scientific knowledge.

In response to such an objection, Meillassoux grants that the transcendental sub-ject does not exist in the way an object exists, but insists that the notion of a transcen-dental subject nevertheless entails that it must *take place*, since it 'remains indissocia-ble from the notion of a *point of view*' (25). The transcendental subject—as both Kant and Husserl maintain—is essentially *finite*, since it never has access to the world as a to-tality but is dependent on receptivity, horizon, perceptual adumbration, and so on. It follows that although transcendental subjectivity is not reducible to an objectively ex-isting body, it must be incarnated in a body in order to be what it is. Without the in-carnation in a body there would be no receptivity, no limited perspective on the world, and hence no point of view. As Meillassoux puts it: 'that the transcendental subject has *this* or that body is an empirical matter, but that *it has* a body is a non-empirical condi-tion of its taking place' (25). Consequently, when scientific discourse 'temporalizes and spatializes the emergence of living bodies' it also temporalizes and spatializes the ba-sic condition for the taking place of the transcendental (25). Thus, Meillassoux argues that the problem of the ancestral 'cannot be thought from the transcendental view-point because it concerns the space-time in which transcendental subjects went from not-taking-place to taking-place—and hence concerns the space-time anterior to spa-tiotemporal forms of representation' (26). Far from confirming the transcendental re-lation between thinking and being as primordial, the ancestral discloses 'a temporality within which this relation is just one event among others, inscribed in an order of suc-cession in which it is merely a stage, rather than an origin' (10).

Despite highlighting the problem of succession, however, Meillassoux fails to think through its logical implications. Meillassoux argues that the principle of non-contra-diction must be 'an absolute ontological truth' (71) for temporal becoming to be pos-sible. If a contradictory entity existed, it could never become other than itself, since it would already contain its other within itself. If it *is* contradictory, it could never cease to be but would rather continue to be even in not-being. Consequently, the existence of a contradictory entity is incompatible with temporal becoming; it would eliminate 'the dimension of alterity required for the deployment of any process whatsoever, liquidating it in the formless being which must always already be what it is not' (70). This argument is correct as far as it goes, but it does not consider that the same problem arises if we posit the existence of a non-contradictory entity. A non-contradictory entity would be indivisibly present *in itself*. Thus, it would remove precisely the 'dimension of alterity' that is required for becoming. Contrary to what Meillassoux holds, the movement of becoming cannot consist in the movement from one discreet entity to another, so that 'things must be this, *then* other than this; they are, *then* they are not' (70). For one moment to be succeeded by another—which is the minimal condition for any becoming whatsoever—it cannot *first* be present in itself and *then* be affected by its own disappearance. A self-present, indivisible moment could never even begin to give way to another moment, since what is indivisible cannot be altered. The succession of time requires not only that each moment be superseded by another moment, but also that this alteration be at work from the beginning. Every moment must negate itself and pass away *in its very event*. If the moment did not immediately negate itself there would be no time, only a presence forever remaining the same.

This argument—which I develop at length in *Radical Atheism*—does not entail that there *is* a contradictory entity that is able to contain its own non-being within itself. On the contrary, I argue that the constitution of time entails that there cannot be any entity (whether contradictory or non-contradictory) that contains itself within itself. The succession of time requires that nothing ever is *in itself*, but is always already subjected to the alteration and destruction that is involved in ceasing-to-be.

It follows that a temporal entity cannot be indivisible but depends on the structure of the trace. The trace is not itself an ontological entity but a *logical structure* that explains the becoming-space of time and the becoming-time of space. A compelling account of the trace therefore requires that we demonstrate the logical co-implication of space and time. The classical distinction between space and time is the distinction between simultaneity and succession. The spatial can remain the same, since the simultaneity of space allows one point to coexist with another. In contrast, the temporal can never remain the same, since the succession of time entails that every moment ceases to be as soon as it comes to be and thus negates itself. By the same token, however, it is clear that time is impossible without space. Time is nothing but negation, so in order to be anything it has to be spatialized. There is no 'flow' of time that is independent of spatialization, since time has to be spatialized in order to flow in the first place. Thus, everything we say about time (that it is 'passing', 'flowing', 'in motion' and so on) is a spatial metaphor. This is not a failure of language to capture pure time but follows from an originary *becoming-space of time*. The very concept of duration presupposes that something remains across an interval of time and only that which is spatial can remain. Inversely, without temporalization it would be impossible for a point to *remain* the same as itself or to exist *at the same time* as another point. The simultaneity of space is itself a temporal notion. Accordingly, for one point to be simultaneous with another point there must be an originary *becoming-time of space* that relates them to one another.[6] The structure of the trace—as the co-implication of time and space—is therefore

---

6. See Derrida's argument that 'simultaneity can appear *as such*, can be simultaneity, that is a *relating* of two points, only in a synthesis, a *complicity*: temporally. One cannot say that a point is *with* another point, there cannot be an *other* point with which, etc., without a temporalization'. Jacques Derrida, 'Ousia and Grammè', in *Margins of Philosophy*, trans. A. Bass, Chicago, University of Chicago Press, 1984, p. 55.

the condition for everything that is temporal. Everything that is subjected to succession is subjected to the trace, whether it is alive or not.

It is important to underline, however, that Derrida does not generalize the trace structure by way of an assertion about the nature of being as such. The trace is not an ontological stipulation but a logical structure that makes explicit what is implicit in the concept of succession. To insist on the logical status of the trace is not to oppose it to ontology, epistemology, or phenomenology, but to insist that the trace is a metatheoretical notion that elucidates what is entailed by a commitment to succession in either of these registers. The logical structure of the trace is expressive of *any* concept of succession—regardless of whether succession is understood in terms of an ontological, epistemological, or phenomenological account of time.

By the same token, one can make explicit that the structure of the trace is implicit in scientific accounts of how time is recorded in biological processes and material structures. For reasons that I will specify, the structure of the trace is implicit not only in the temporality of the living but also in the disintegration of inanimate matter (e.g. the 'half-life' of isotopes). The logic of the trace can thereby serve to elucidate philosophical stakes in the understanding of the relation between the living and the nonliving that has been handed down to us by modern science.[7] I will here seek to develop this line of inquiry by demonstrating how the logic of the trace allows one to take into account the insights of Darwinism. Specifically, I will argue in favor of a conceptual distinction between life and nonliving matter that nevertheless asserts a continuity between the two in terms of what I call the 'arche-materiality' of time.[8]

The arche-materiality of time follows from the structure of the trace. Given that every temporal moment ceases to be as soon as it comes to be, it must be inscribed as a trace in order to be at all. The trace is necessarily spatial, since spatiality is characterized by the ability to persist in spite of temporal succession. Every temporal moment therefore depends on the material support of spatial inscription. Indeed, the material support of the trace is the condition for the synthesis of time, since it enables the past to be retained for the future. The material support of the trace, however, is itself temporal. Without temporalization a trace could not persist across time and relate the past to the future. Accordingly, the persistence of the trace cannot be the persistence of something that is exempt from the negativity of time. Rather, the trace is always left for an unpredictable future that gives it both the chance to live on and to be effaced.

The logical implications of the succession of time are directly relevant for the main argument in *After Finitude*, which seeks to establish the necessity of contingen-

---

7. I am grateful to Joshua Andresen, Ray Brassier, and Henry Staten for a set of incisive questions that forced me to clarify the status of 'the trace' in my argument. My understanding of the logical, rather than ontological, status of the trace is also indebted to conversations with Rocio Zambrana and to her work on Hegel's *Logic*. See Rocio Zambrana, 'Hegel's Hyperbolic Formalism', forthcoming in *Bulletin of the Hegel Society of Great Britain*, nos. 60/61.

8. Several respondents to *Radical Atheism* have pointed out that I equivocate between describing the structure of the trace as a general condition for everything that is temporal, and as a general condition for *the living*. The precise relation between the temporality of the living and the temporality of nonliving matter is thus left unclear in *Radical Atheism*. See Nathan Brown, 'To Live Without an Idea', *Radical Philosophy*, no. 154, pp. 51-53; William Egginton, 'On Radical Atheism, Chronolibidinal Reading, and Impossible Desires', *CR: The New Centennial Review*, vol. 9, no. 1, pp. 191-208; Samir Haddad, 'Language Remains', *CR: The New Centennial Review*, vol. 9, no. 1, pp. 127-146; and Aaron Hodges, 'Martin Hägglund's Speculative Materialism', *CR: The New Centennial Review*, vol. 9, no. 1, pp. 87-106. I am grateful for these responses to my work, which have led me to elaborate how the relation between life and nonliving matter should be understood in terms of the logic of the trace.

cy. As Meillassoux formulates his guiding thesis: 'Everything is possible, anything can happen—except something that is necessary, because it is the contingency of the entity that is necessary, not the entity' (65). This notion of contingency presupposes succession, since there can be no contingency without the unpredictable passage from one moment to another. To establish the necessity of contingency, as Meillassoux seeks to do, is thus also to establish the necessity of succession.

Meillassoux himself, however, does not theorize the implications of succession, and this comes at a significant cost for his argument. In a recent essay, Aaron F. Hodges has suggested that Meillassoux's critique of the principle of sufficient reason is potentially damaging for my notion of radical destructibility, which holds that everything that comes into being must pass away.[9] In fact, however, it is rather my notion of radical destructibility that allows us to locate an inconsistency in Meillassoux's argument. Let me quote in full the passage from Meillassoux to which Hodges calls attention:

> To assert ... that everything must necessarily perish, would be to assert a proposition that is *still* metaphysical. Granted, this thesis of the precariousness of everything would no longer claim that a determinate entity is necessary, but it would continue to maintain that a determinate situation is necessary, viz., the destruction of this or that. But this is still to obey the injunction of the principle of reason, according to which there is a necessary reason why this is the case (the eventual destruction of X), rather than otherwise (the endless persistence of X). But we do not see by virtue of what there would be a reason necessitating the possibility of destruction as opposed to the possibility of persistence. The unequivocal relinquishment of the principle of reason requires us to insist that both the destruction and the perpetual preservation of a determinate entity must equally be able to occur for no reason. Contingency is such that anything might happen, even nothing at all, so that what is, remains as it is. (62-63)

While emphasizing that a necessary entity is impossible, Meillassoux maintains that it is possible for nothing to happen, so that the entity remains as it is. As soon as we take into account the intrinsic link between contingency and succession, however, we can see that the latter argument is untenable. If nothing happened and the entity remained as it is, there would be no succession, but by the same token there would be no contingency. An entity to which nothing happens is inseparable from a necessary entity. In order to be subjected to succession—which is to say: in order to be contingent—the entity must begin to pass away as soon as it comes to be and can never remain as it is. Consequently, there *is* a reason that necessitates destruction, but it does not re-import the metaphysical principle of reason. On the contrary, it only makes explicit what is implicit in the principle of unreason that Meillassoux calls the necessity of contingency. Contingency presupposes succession and there is no succession without destruction. If the moment were not destroyed in being succeeded by another moment, their relation would not be one of succession but of co-existence. Thus, to assert the necessity of contingency is to assert the necessity of destruction.

For the same reason, Meillassoux's opposition between destruction and persistence is misleading. Persistence itself presupposes an interval of time, which means that nothing can persist unscathed by succession. The destruction that is involved in succession makes any persistence dependent on the *spacing* of time, which inscribes what happens as a spatial trace that remains, while exposing it to erasure in an unpredictable future. The erasure of the spatial trace is indeed a *possibility* that is not immediate-

---

9. See Hodges, 'Martin Hägglund's Speculative Materialism', pp. 102-03.

ly actualized, but it already presupposes the *necessity* of destruction that is operative in succession. Given that nothing can persist without succession, destruction is therefore at work in persistence itself.

Meillassoux's response would presumably be that his notion of time does not depend on succession, but designates a 'virtual power' that may leave everything as it is *or* subject it to succession. To posit such a virtual power, however, is not to think the implications of time but to posit an instance that has power *over* time, since it may stop and start succession at will. In contrast, I argue that *time is nothing in itself*; it is nothing but the negativity that is intrinsic to succession. Time cannot, therefore, be a virtual power. Given that time is nothing but negativity, it does not have the power to *be* anything or *do* anything on its own. More precisely, according to my arche-materialist account, time cannot be anything or do anything without a spatialization that constrains the power of the virtual in making it dependent on material conditions.

We can clarify the stakes of this argument by considering the example of the emergence of life, which for Meillassoux is a 'paradigmatic example' of the virtual power of time.[10] His way of formulating the problem, however, already reveals an anti-materialist bias. According to Meillassoux, 'the same argumentative strategies are reproduced time and time again in philosophical polemics on the possibility of life emerging from inanimate matter':

> Since life manifestly supposes, at least at a certain degree of its evolution, the existence of a set of affective and perceptive contents, either one decides that matter already contained such subjectivity in some manner, in too weak a degree for it to be detected, or that these affections of the living being did not pre-exist in any way within matter, thus finding oneself constrained to admit their irruption *ex nihilo* from that matter—which seems to lead to the acceptance of an intervention transcending the power of nature. Either a 'continuism', a philosophy of immanence—a variant of hylozoism—which would have it that *all* matter is alive to some degree; or the belief in a transcendence exceeding the rational comprehension of natural processes.[11]

It is striking that a philosopher with Meillassoux's considerable knowledge of science would present such an inadequate description of the actual debates about the emergence of life. A materialist account of the emergence of life is by no means obliged to hold that all matter is alive to some degree. On the contrary, such vitalism has been thoroughly debunked by Darwinism and its most prominent philosophical proponents. For example, what Daniel Dennett analyzes as Darwin's dangerous idea is precisely the account of how life evolved out of nonliving matter and of how even the most advanced intentionality or sensibility originates in mindless repetition.[12] Rather than vitalizing matter, philosophical Darwinism devitalizes life. For Meillassoux, however, life as subjective existence is something so special and unique that it requires an explanation that is refractory to materialist analysis.[13] In Dennett's language, Meillassoux thus refuses the 'cranes' of physical and biological explanation in favour of the 'skyhook' of a virtual power that would allow for the emergence of life *ex nihilo*.

---

10. Quentin Meillassoux, 'Potentiality and Virtuality', in this volume.

11. Meillassoux, 'Potentiality and Virtuality', p. 235.

12. See Daniel Dennett, *Darwin's Dangerous Idea: Evolution and the Meaning of Life*, New York, Simon and Schuster, 1995.

13. See Meillassoux's lecture 'Temps et surgissement ex nihilo', where he explicitly rejects Dennett's materialist analysis of the emergence of life. The lecture is available online at http://www.diffusion.ens.fr/index.php?res=conf&idconf=701

To be sure, Meillassoux tries to distinguish his notion of irruption *ex nihilo* from the theological notion of creation *ex nihilo*, by maintaining that the former does not invoke any transcendence that would exceed rational comprehension but rather proceeds from the virtual power of contingency that Meillassoux seeks to formulate in rational terms. In both cases, however, there is the appeal to a power that is not limited by material constraints. Symptomatically, Meillassoux holds that 'life furnished with sensibility' emerges '*directly* from a matter within which one cannot, short of sheer fantasy, foresee the germs of this sensibility'.[14] As Meillassoux should know, this is nonsense from a scientific point of view. Life furnished with sensibility does not emerge directly from inanimate matter but evolves according to complex processes that are described in detail by evolutionary biology. If Meillassoux here disregards the evidence of science it is because he univocally privileges logical over material possibility.[15] Contingency is for him the virtual power to make anything happen at any time, so that life furnished with sensibility can emerge without preceding material conditions that would make it possible. This idea of an irruption *ex nihilo* does not have any explanatory purchase on the temporality of evolution, however, since it eliminates time in favour of a punctual instant. Even if we limit the notion of irruption *ex nihilo* to a more modest claim, namely, that the beginning of the evolutionary process that led to sentient life was a contingent event that could not have been foreseen or predicted, there is still no need for Meillassoux's concept of contingency as an unlimited virtual power to explain this event. Consider, for example, Dennett's Darwinian argument concerning the origin of life:

> We know as a matter of logic that there was at least one start that has us as its continuation, but there were probably many false starts that differed *in no interesting way at all* from the one that initiated the winning series. The title of Adam is, once again, a retrospective honour, and we make a fundamental mistake of reasoning if we ask, *In virtue of what essential difference* is this the beginning of life? There need be no difference at all between Adam and Badam, an atom-for-atom duplicate of Adam who just happened not to have founded anything of note.[16]

The beginning of life is here described as a contingent event, but notice that the contingency does not depend on a punctual event of irruption but on what happens successively. There is no virtual power that can determine an event to be the origin of life. On the contrary, which event will have been the origin of life is an effect of the succession of time that can never be reduced to an instant. Consequently, there is no need for Meillassoux's skyhook of irruption *ex nihilo* to explain the emergence of life. The emergence of life is certainly a contingent event, but this contingency cannot be equated with a power to make anything happen at any time. Rather, the emergence is dependent both on preceding material conditions that restrict what is possible and on succeeding events that determine whether it will have been the emergence of anything at all.

Thus, I want to argue that the notion of time as *survival*—rather than as virtual power—is consistent with the insights of Darwinism. The logic of survival that I develop in *Radical Atheism* allows us to pursue the consequences of the arche-materiality of time, as well as the general co-implication of persistence and destruction. If some-

---

14. Meillassoux, 'Potentiality and Virtuality', p. 232, my italics.

15. See also Peter Hallward's astute observation that Meillassoux tends to treat 'the logical and material domains as if they were effectively interchangeable'. Peter Hallward, 'Anything is Possible', in this volume.

16. Dennet, *Darwin's Dangerous Idea*, p. 201.

thing survives it is never present in itself; it is already marked by the destruction of a past that is no longer while persisting for a future that is not yet. In its most elementary form, this movement of survival does not hinge on the emergence of life. For example, the isotope that has a rate of radioactive decay across billions of years is *surviving*—since it remains and disintegrates over time—but it is not alive.

Consequently, one can make explicit a continuity between the nonliving and the living in terms of the structure of the trace. The latter is implicit not only in our understanding of the temporality of living processes but also in our understanding of the disintegration of inanimate matter. On the one hand, the disintegration of matter answers to the *becoming-time of space*. The simultaneity of space in itself could never allow for the successive stages of a process of disintegration. For there to be successive disintegration, the negativity of time must be intrinsic to the positive existence of spatial matter. On the other hand, the disintegration of matter answers to the *becoming-space of time*. The succession of time could not even take place without material support, since it is nothing in itself and must be spatialized in order to *be* negative—that is, to negate anything—at all. The notion of arche-materiality thereby allows us to account for the minimal synthesis of time—namely, the minimal recording of temporal passage—without presupposing the advent or existence of life. The disintegration of matter records the passage of time without any animating principle, consciousness, or soul.

Accordingly, there is an asymmetry between the animate and the inanimate in the arche-materiality of the trace. As soon as there is life there is death, so there can be no animation without the inanimate, but the inverse argument does not hold. If there were animation as soon as there is inanimate matter, we would be advocating a vitalist conception of the universe, where life is the potential force or the teleological goal of existence. The conception of life that follows from the arche-materiality of the trace is as far as one can get from such vitalism, since it accounts for the utter contingency and destructibility of life. As Henry Staten formulates it in a recent essay: 'the strong naturalist view, from which Derrida does not deviate, holds that matter organized in the right way brings forth life, but denies that life is somehow hidden in matter and just waiting to manifest itself .... Life is a possibility of materiality, not as a potential that it is 'normal' for materiality to bring forth, but as a vastly improbable possibility, by far the exception rather than the rule'.[17]

What difference is at stake, then, in the difference between the living and the nonliving? The radioactive isotope is indeed surviving, since it decays across billions of years, but it is indifferent to its own survival, since it is not alive. A living being, on the other hand, cannot be indifferent to its own survival. Survival is an unconditional condition for everything that is temporal, but only for a living being is the *care* for survival unconditional, since only a living being cares about maintaining itself across an interval of time The care in question has nothing to do with a vital force that would be exempt from material conditions. Rather, the care for survival is implicit in the scientific definition of life as a form of organization that of necessity is both open and closed. On the one hand, the survival of life requires an *open* system, since the life of a given entity must be able to take in new material and replenish itself to make up for the breakdown of its own macromolecular structures. On the other hand, the survival of life requires a certain *closure* of the system, since a given entity must draw a boundary between it-

17. Henry Staten, 'Derrida, Dennett, and the Ethico-Political Project of Naturalism', *Derrida Today*, no. 1, 2008, pp. 34-35.

self and others in order to sustain its own life. It follows that the care for survival is inextricable from the organization of life. Neither the openness to replenishment nor the closure of a boundary would have a function without the care to prevent a given life or reproductive line from being terminated.

The distinction between matter and life that I propose, however, is not meant to settle the empirical question of where to draw the line between the living and the nonliving. Rather, it is meant to clarify a *conceptual* distinction between matter and life that speaks to the philosophical stakes of the distinction. This conceptual distinction allows us to take into account the Darwinian explanation of how the living evolved out of the nonliving, while asserting a distinguishing characteristic of life that does not make any concessions to vitalism. The care for survival that on my account is coextensive with life does not have any power to finally transcend material constraints but is itself a contingent and destructible fact. Without care everything would be a matter of indifference *and that is a possibility*—there is nothing that necessitates the existence of living beings that care. The fact that every object of care—as well as care itself—is destructible does not make it insignificant but is, on the contrary, what makes it significant in the first place. It is *because* things are destructible, because they have not always been and will not always be, that anyone or anything cares about them. Far from depriving us of the source of vitality, it is precisely the radical destructibility of life that makes it a matter of care.

In Meillassoux, the problem of care emerges most clearly in his divinology, where he transitions from a speculative exposition of the conditions for being in general to an engagement with questions of death and resurrection, which by definition only matter to a being that cares about its own survival. By examining this transition, I will seek to press home the stakes of my argument and its consequences for a materialist thinking. Indeed, we will see how Meillassoux's divinology allows us to assess both the ontological consequences of his attempt to separate the necessity of contingency from the necessity of destruction and the theological consequences of his conception of desire.

The point of departure for Meillassoux's divinology is what he calls *the spectral dilemma*, which arises in response to 'terrible deaths' that one cannot accept. The victims of these deaths return as 'spectres' that haunt the living and preclude the achievement of an 'essential mourning' that would enable one to come to terms with what has happened. For Meillassoux, the main obstacle to achieving essential mourning is the forced alternative between a religious position that affirms the existence of God and an atheist position that denies the existence of God. According to Meillassoux, both of these positions are 'paths to despair when confronted with spectres'.[18]

Meillassoux draws his conclusion by staging a dialogue between the two positions, recounting what he regards as the strongest responses to mourning by the religious apologist and the atheist respectively. For the religious apologist, 'the idea that all justice is impossible for the innumerable massed spectres of the past corrodes my very core, so that I can no longer bear with the living .... I must hope for something *for* the dead also, or else life is vain. This something is another life, another chance to live— to live something other than that death which was theirs' (264). The atheist in turn responds that this promise of justice in fact is a threat of the worst injustice, since 'it would be done under the auspices of a God who had himself allowed the worst acts to be committed ... who has let men, women and children die in the worst circumstances, when he could have saved them without any difficulty whatsoever ... I prefer for them, as for

---

18. Meillassoux, 'Spectral Dilemma', p. 263. Subsequent page-references given in the text.

myself, nothingness, which will leave them in peace and conserve their dignity, rather than putting them at the mercy of the omnipotence of your pitiless Demiurge' (264-65). This is, according to Meillassoux, the spectral dilemma: 'either to despair of another life for the dead, or to despair of a God who has let such deaths take place' (265).

While Meillassoux subscribes to neither of these positions, he retains an essential premise from each of them. On the one hand, Meillassoux retains the religious premise that the hope for justice requires the hope for a life beyond death. On the other hand, Meillassoux retains the atheist premise that the existence of God is an obstacle to the existence of justice, since the existence of God would mean that He has allowed terrible deaths. The key to resolving the spectral dilemma is thus, for Meillassoux, to find a third option that combines '*the possible resurrection of the dead*—the religious condition of the resolution—*and the inexistence of God*—the atheistic condition of the resolution' (268). This third option hinges on what Meillassoux calls *divine inexistence*, which has two meanings. On the one hand, divine inexistence means that there is no God, no metaphysical Principle or Creator of the world. On the other hand, divine inexistence means that 'what remains still in a virtual state in present reality harbors *the possibility* of a God still to come, become innocent of the disasters of the world, and in which one might anticipate the power to accord to spectres something other than their death' (268, emphasis added). Accordingly, it is possible to hope for a God who does not yet exist—and hence is innocent of the atrocities of history—but who may come to exist in the future and resurrect the dead.

In proposing this resolution to the spectral dilemma, Meillassoux appeals to his argument that the laws of nature can change at any moment for no reason whatsoever. I will here not examine the details of this argument, which involves a lengthy treatment of Hume's problem of causal necessity.[19] Rather, my point is that, even if we grant Meillassoux's argument about the contingency of the laws of nature, it cannot support his divinological thesis. As we have seen, the latter holds that a transformation of the laws of nature may allow a God to emerge and resurrect the dead. The contingency of the laws of nature would thus allow for the possibility of reversing the destructive effects of time. In fact, however, Meillassoux's own account of time shows why such redemption of the past is not even possible in principle. As he emphasizes in *After Finitude*, the contingency of the laws of nature hinges on 'the idea of a *time* that would be capable of bringing forth or abolishing everything':

> This is a time that cannot be conceived as having emerged or as being abolished except in time, which is to say, in itself. No doubt, this is a banal argument on the face of it: 'it is impossible to think the disappearance of time unless this disappearance occurs in time; consequently, the latter must be conceived to be eternal'. But what people fail to notice is that this banal argument can only work by presupposing a time that is not banal—not just a time whose capacity for destroying everything is a function of laws, but a time which is capable of the *lawless destruction of every physical law*. It is perfectly possible to conceive of a time determined by the governance of fixed laws disappearing in something other than itself—it would disappear in another time governed by *alternative* laws. But only the time that harbors the capacity to destroy every determinate reality, while obeying no determinate law—the time capable of destroying, without reason or law, both worlds and things—can be thought as an absolute. (61-62)

It follows from this argument—even though Meillassoux does not acknowledge it—that the succession of time would not be abolished even if a set of natural laws were

---

19. See, in particular, chapter 3 of Meillassoux's *After Finitude*, and his essay 'Potentiality and Virtuality'.

abolished, since the former is the condition of possibility for any change or disappearance of natural laws. Contingency—no matter how absolute it may be—cannot redeem the destructive effects of time. Given that contingency presupposes succession, and that succession hinges on the destructive passage from one moment to another, there is only ever contingency at the price of destruction. The destruction in question is *irreversible*—and hence irredeemable—since what distinguishes temporal succession from spatial change is precisely that the former is irreversible.

My radical atheist argument, however, is not limited to a logical refutation of the possibility of redeeming temporal being; it is also directed at the assumption that such redemption is *desirable*. We can thereby approach the motivation for Meillassoux's divinology, and read it against itself from within.

Recall that the spectral dilemma is essentially a problem of *mourning*, since it arises because one is unable to accept a terrible death. Now, if one did not care that a mortal being live on, one would have no trouble letting go and accepting death. The spectral dilemma that Meillassoux locates in the struggle for justice thus presupposes the care for survival. If one did not care for the survival of someone or something, there would be nothing that compelled one to fight for the memory of the past or for a better future. Indeed, without the care for survival one would never be haunted by the fate of the dead, since one would not care about anything that has happened or anything that may happen.

The constitutive care for survival allows us to read the so-called desire for immortality against itself. The desire to *live on* after death is not a desire for immortality, since to live on is to survive as a temporal being. The desire for survival cannot aim at transcending time, since temporality is intrinsic to the state of being that is desired. There is thus an internal contradiction in the purported desire for immortality. If one did not care for mortal life, one would not fear death and desire to live on. But for the same reason, the prospect of immortality cannot even hypothetically appease the fear of death or satisfy the desire to live on. Rather than redeeming death, the state of immortality would *bring about* death, since it would put an end to mortal life.

The distinction between survival and immortality is directly relevant for Meillassoux's proposed solution to the spectral dilemma, according to which a god can emerge and resurrect the victims of terrible deaths. Meillassoux does not make clear whether the resurrection of the dead would entail immortality in the strict sense or whether it would allow the dead to simply live on as mortals. But even if we grant the latter alternative, we can see that it offers no solution to the spectral dilemma of mourning terrible deaths. If the dead are resurrected as they were at the time of death, they will come back as victims of severe trauma and still face the problem of how to mourn what happened to them. Alternatively, if the idea is to resurrect the dead without the memory of their terrible death, the problem of mourning is still not resolved but only cancelled out. The resurrected would not have to mourn *that* particular death, but in living on they could be subject to another terrible death, in which case a new inexistent god would have to emerge and erase the memory of what happened.

These speculations may seem absurd, but they reveal that Meillassoux's solution to the spectral dilemma would require the advent of immortality. If the world continues to be populated by mortal beings after the emergence of the inexistent god, then nothing can prevent terrible deaths from occurring again and the new god will soon be guilty of having allowed them to happen. The only way to avoid this problem would be to install a state of immortality that would not allow any terrible deaths to take place. As we have seen, however, the state of immortality cannot answer to the survival that is cared for and that motivates the struggle against the injustice of terrible deaths. On the contrary, the state of immortality would eliminate the 'capacity-not-to-be' and the 'dimension of alterity' that according to Meillassoux himself is necessary for the existence of any given being (see 58, 70). It follows that the state of immortality cannot satisfy the hope that is at the root of the spectral dilemma, namely, the hope that singular mortal beings will be given another chance to live. Far from providing another chance to live, the state of immortality would terminate life.

Following this logic of radical atheism, we can undermine the conception of desire that informs Meillassoux's articulation of the spectral dilemma. According to Meillassoux, 'the atheist is atheist because religion promises a fearful God; the believer anchors his faith in the refusal of a life devastated by the despair of terrible deaths'.[20] Both the positions would thus be dictated by despair before the absence of divine justice and immortality. But in fact, we can see that both the atheist and the believer proceed from a radical atheist desire for survival, since their despair does not stem from the absence of God or immortality but from their care for the fate of mortal beings. Without such care there would be no struggle for justice in the first place. The mortality of life is not only an unavoidable necessity but also the reason why we care about anyone's life at all and seek to combat the injustice of terrible deaths. Inversely, the state of immortality cannot satisfy the hope for 'another life' for the mortal beings that have passed away. Rather than allowing mortal beings to live on, the state of immortality would eliminate the possibility of life.

Both the hope for another life and the despair over terrible deaths are thus dictated by a desire for mortal survival, which entails that the problem of mourning cannot even in principle be resolved. Meillassoux's mistake is to treat death and spectrality as something that can be removed without removing life itself. In contrast, the radical atheist argument is that spectrality is an indispensable feature of life in general. When I live on from one moment to another, I am already becoming a spectre for myself, haunted by who I was and who I will become. Of course, the loss that is inherent in this experience of survival is made much more palpable in the actual mourning of someone's death, but it is operative on a minimal level in everything I experience, since it is inextricable from the mortal being that I am. If I survived wholly intact, I would not be surviving; I would be reposing in absolute presence. Thus, in living on as a mortal being there is always an experience of irrevocable loss, since the movement of survival necessarily entails the eradication of what does *not* survive.

The loss in question is not necessarily tragic. Depending on the content and the situation, one may want to welcome or resist, embrace or lament, the loss of the past. The point, however, is that one always has to *reckon* with it. Whatever one does, one is haunted by a past that is repressed or commemorated, and indeed often repressed precisely by being commemorated or vice versa. That is why there is always a process of mourning at work, as Derrida maintains in *Spectres of Marx*, and why one must always respond to the past by 'burying' the dead, either in the sense of forgetting or remembering.

The comparison with Derrida is instructive here, since he also treats the interconnection between spectrality and mourning, but in a radically different way than Meillassoux. For Derrida, the spectrality of mourning is not an affliction that ought to be

---

20. Meillassoux, 'Spectral Dilemma', p. 265.

redeemed by divine intervention, but a constitutive double bind. On the one hand, mourning is an act of fidelity, since it stems from the attachment to a mortal other and from the desire to hold on to this mortal other. On the other hand, mourning is an act of infidelity, since one can only mourn if one has decided to live on without the other and thus leave him or her or it behind. This betrayal is certainly unavoidable—the only alternative to surviving the other is to kill oneself and thereby kill the memory of the other as well—but the violence of living on is nonetheless real. To live on, I cannot be absolutely faithful to the other, since I have to mobilize my ability to do without the other and in the process 'kill' my previous attachment to a greater or lesser degree. Thus, the survival of life necessarily engenders ghosts, since it must demarcate itself against a past that cannot be comprehended and a future that cannot be anticipated.

For Meillassoux, however, the spectrality of mourning is not a structural feature of life and can potentially be overcome by a miraculous event of redemption. This is a profoundly depoliticizing move, since it removes attention from the ways in which the problem of mourning is mediated historically, in favour of a general 'resolution' of the problem by divine intervention. The deconstructive notion of an irreducible spectrality is, on the contrary, a notion that politicizes the question of mourning all the way down. Such politicization does not consist in deriving a prescription for mourning from the deconstructive analysis. If a prescription were possible to derive from the deconstructive analysis, the question of mourning would once again be depoliticized, since there would be a criterion for addressing it that is exempt from political contestation and struggle. The hyperpolitical move of deconstruction is, on the contrary, to account for the irreducible necessity of politics as a historical and material praxis. Precisely because the work of mourning cannot operate without exclusion, and cannot justify these exclusions a priori, it will always be necessary to evaluate their effects on a historical and material level.

Accordingly, Derrida's 'hauntological' analysis does not seek to resolve the problem of mourning, but to account for why the work of mourning will always have to reckon with discrimination. As Derrida argues in *Spectres of Marx*, any act of mourning, any watch over the dead that seeks to remember what has been excluded, 'will fatally exclude in its turn':

> It will even annihilate, by watching (over) its ancestors rather than (over) certain others. At this moment rather than at some other moment. By forgetfulness (guilty or not, it matters little here), by foreclosure or murder, this watch itself will engender new ghosts. It will do so by choosing already among the ghosts, its own from among its own, thus by killing the dead: law of finitude, law of decision and responsibility for finite existences, the only living-mortals for whom a decision, a choice, a responsibility has meaning and a meaning that will have to pass through the ordeal of the undecidable.[21]

What Derrida here calls the 'law of finitude' is not something that one can accept or refuse, since it precedes every decision and exceeds all mastery. There can be no taking of responsibility and no making of decisions without the temporal finitude of survival, which always entails a violent discrimination. The experience of survival—here figured as the burial of the dead—is thus what raises the concern for justice in the first place. If life were fully present to itself, if it were not haunted by what has been lost in the past and what may be lost in the future, there would be nothing that could cause

---

21. Jacques Derrida, *Spectres of Marx: The State of the Debt, the Work of Mourning, and the New International*, trans. P. Kamuf, London, Routledge, 1994, p. 87.

the concern for justice. Indeed, justice can only be brought about by 'living-mortals' who will exclude and annihilate by maintaining the memory and life of certain others at the expense of other others.

For Meillassoux, however, the desired state of being is a community that would prevail beyond violence. Following a pious logic, he ends his essay on the spectral dilemma with the hope for a god that would be 'desirable, lovable, worthy of imitation' and who would make us participate in 'a becalmed community of living, of dead, and of reborn' (275). The radical atheist argument is not simply that such a peaceful state of being is impossible to actualize, as if it were a desirable, albeit unattainable end. Rather, the logic of radical atheism challenges the very idea that it is desirable to overcome violence and spectrality. A completely reconciled life—which would not be haunted by any ghosts—would be nothing but complete death, since it would eliminate every trace of survival. In pursuing this argument, radical atheism does not seek to repudiate but to *re-describe* the hope that animates the struggle against the injustice of terrible deaths. The struggle for justice and the hope for another life have never been driven by a desire to transcend temporal finitude but by a desire for mortal survival.

Schematically, then, radical atheist materialism can be said to have two major consequences. First, it establishes the arche-materiality of time, in distinction from all idealist or speculative attempts to privilege temporality over spatiality. The constitutive negativity of time immediately requires a spatial, material support that retains the past for the future. The virtual possibilities of temporality are therefore always already restricted by the very constitution of time, since the material support necessarily places conditions on what is possible. Contrary to what Meillassoux holds, the contingency of time cannot be a pure virtuality that has the power to make anything happen. The spatiality of material support is the condition for there to be temporality—and hence the possibility of unpredictable events through the negation of the present—but it also closes off certain possibilities in favour of others. Second, the necessity of discrimination and material support allows for a hyperpolitical logic. Given that the contingency of time cannot be a pure virtuality, but is itself dependent on material support, there can be no line of flight from the exigencies of the actual world and its particular demands. Furthermore, the conception of desire that informs radical atheism is in fact indispensable for a materialist analysis of social struggle. If we argue that social struggles are not in fact concerned with the religious end they profess but rather with material injustice—that is, if we politicize social struggles—we presuppose the radical atheist conception of desire, according to which struggles for justice are not concerned with transcending the world but rather with survival. Rather than a priori dismissing struggles that are fought in the name of religious ideals as deluded, the logic of radical atheism allows us to see that these struggles, too, are a matter of survival and thus essentially material in their aims.

Whether a given struggle for survival should be supported or resisted is a different question, and one that only can be settled through an actual engagement with the world rather than through an analysis of its hauntological condition. Everything thus remains to be done, and what should be done cannot be settled on the basis of radical atheism. Rather, the logic of radical atheism seeks to articulate *why* everything remains to be done, by refuting the untenable hope of redemption and recalling us to the material base of time, desire, and politics.

10

Anything is Possible: A Reading of Quentin Meillassoux's *After Finitude*[1]

Peter Hallward

Philosophical speculation can regain determinate knowledge of absolute reality. We can think the nature of things as they are in themselves, independently of the way they appear to us. We can demonstrate that the modality of this nature is radically contingent—that there is no reason for things or 'laws' to be or remain as they are. Nothing is necessary, apart from the necessity that nothing be necessary. Anything can happen, any place and at any time, without reason or cause.

Such is the ringing message affirmed by the remarkable French philosopher Quentin Meillassoux in his first book, *After Finitude*, originally published by Seuil in 2006. Against the grain of self-critical and self-reflexive post-Kantian philosophy, Meillassoux announces that we can recover 'the great outdoors, the absolute outside of pre-critical thinkers', the utterly 'foreign territory' that subsists in itself, independently of our relation to it.[2] And when we begin to explore this foreign land that is reality in itself, what we learn is that

> there is no reason for anything to be or to remain thus and so rather than otherwise [...]. Everything could actually collapse: from trees to stars, from stars to laws, from physical laws to logical laws; and this not by virtue of some superior law whereby everything is destined to perish, but by virtue of the absence of any superior law capable of preserving anything, no matter what, from perishing.[3]

Neither events or laws are governed, in the end, by any necessity other than that of a purely 'chaotic becoming—that is to say, a becoming governed by no necessity whatsoever'.[4]

For Meillassoux, as for Plato or Hegel, philosophy's chief concern is with the nature of absolute reality, but as Meillassoux conceives it the nature of this reality demands that philosophy should think not 'about what is but only about what can be'.

---

1. A shorter version of this essay first appeared as a review in *Radical Philosophy*, no. 152, 2008, pp. 51-7.

2. Quentin Meillassoux, *After Finitude: An Essay on the Necessity of Contingency*, trans. Ray Brassier, London, Continuum, 2008, pp. 27, 7.

3. Meillassoux, *After Finitude*, p. 53.

4. Quentin Meillassoux, 'Potentiality and Virtuality', in this volume, p. 226.

The proper concern of a contemporary (post-metaphysical, post-dogmatic but also post-critical) philosophy is not with being but with may-being, not with *être* but with *peut-être*.[5] If Meillassoux can be described as a 'realist', then, the reality that concerns him does not involve the way things are so much as the possibility that they might always be otherwise.

It is the trenchant force of this affirmation, no doubt, that accounts for the enthusiasm with which Meillassoux's work has been taken up by a small but growing group of researchers exasperated with the generally uninspiring state of contemporary 'continental' philosophy. It's easy to see why Meillassoux's *After Finitude* has so quickly acquired something close to cult status among some readers who share his lack of reverence for 'the way things are'. The book is exceptionally clear and concise, entirely devoted to a single chain of reasoning. It combines a confident insistence on the self-sufficiency of rational demonstration with an equally rationalist suspicion of mere experience and consensus. The argument implies, in tantalizing outline, an alternative history of the whole of modern European philosophy from Galileo and Descartes through Hume and Kant to Heidegger and Deleuze. It is also open to a number of critical objections. In what follows I reconstruct the basic sequence of the argument (also drawing, on occasion, on articles published by Meillassoux in the last few years), and then sketch three or four of the difficulties it seems to confront.

I

The simplest way to introduce Meillassoux's general project is as a reformulation and radicalization of what he on several occasions describes as 'Hume's problem'. As everyone knows, Hume argued that pure reasoning a priori cannot suffice to prove that a given effect must always and necessarily follow from a given cause. There is no reason why one and the same cause should not give rise to a 'hundred different events'.[6] Meillassoux accepts Hume's argument as unanswerable, as 'blindingly obvious': 'we cannot rationally discover any reason why laws should be so rather than otherwise, that is to say why they should remain in their current state rather than being arbitrarily modified from one moment to the next'.[7]

Hume himself, however, (along with both Kant and the main thrust of the analytical tradition) retreats from the full implications of his demonstration. Rather than ditch the concept of causal necessity altogether, he affirms it as simply beyond demonstration, and thus invulnerable to scepticism: Hume accepts as a matter of 'blind faith' that every natural sequence of events is indeed governed by 'ultimate causes', which themselves remain 'totally shut up from human curiosity and enquiry'.[8] Whether this belief is then a matter of mere habit (Hume) or an irreducible component of transcendental logic (Kant) is, as far as Meillassoux is concerned, a secondary quarrel. Ever since, analytical philosophers have tended to assume that we should abandon ontological specula-

---

5. Quentin Meillassoux, 'Speculative Realism', *Collapse: Philosophical Research and Development*, vol. 3, 2007, p. 393; Quentin Meillassoux, 'Time without Becoming', talk presented at Middlesex University, 8 May 2008.

6. David Hume, *Enquiry Concerning Human Understanding*, C. W. Hendel (ed.), New York, The Liberal Arts Press, 1957, p. 44, cited in Meillassoux, *After Finitude*, p. 88; see also Quentin Meillassoux, 'Matérialisme et surgissement ex nihilo', *MIR: Revue d'anticipation*, no. 1, June 2007, pp. 9-11 (of 12 page typescript).

7. Meillassoux, *After Finitude*, pp. 90-91, translation modified; Meillassoux, 'Spectral Dilemma', *Collapse: Philosophical Research and Development*, vol. 4, 2008, p. 274.

8. Hume, *Enquiry*, p. 45, cited in Meillassoux, *After Finitude*, p. 90. Hume thus 'believes blindly in the world that metaphysicians thought they could prove' (Meillassoux, *After Finitude*, p. 91).

tion and retreat instead to reflection upon the way we draw inductive inferences from ordinary experience, or from ordinary ways of talking about our experience.

In keeping with a tactic he deploys elsewhere in his work, Meillassoux himself quickly turns Hume's old problem into an opportunity. Our inability rationally to determine an absolute necessity or sufficient reason underlying things, properly understood, can be affirmed as a demonstration that there in fact is no such necessity or reason. Rather than try to salvage a dubious faith in the apparent stability of our experience, we should affirm the prospect that Hume refused to accept: there is no reason why what we experience as constant laws should not break down or change at any point, for the simple reason there is no such thing as reason or cause. The truth is not just that a given cause might give rise to a hundred different effects, but that an infinite variety of 'effects' might emerge on the basis of no cause at all, in a pure eruption of novelty *ex nihilo*. After Hume, 'we must seriously maintain that the laws of nature could change, not in accordance with some superior hidden law—the law of the modification of laws, which we could once more construe as the mysterious and immutable constant governing all subordinate transformations—but for no cause or reason whatsoever'.[9]

In other words, Hume liberated the world from the necessity imposed on it by the old metaphysical principle of sufficient reason, i.e. the idea that there is some higher power—fate, divine providence, intelligent design, modern progress, the iron laws of historical development...—which causes worldly phenomena to be what they are. Hume discovers a world freed from

> ...that principle according to which everything must have a reason to be as it is rather than otherwise [...]. The unequivocal relinquishment of the principle of reason requires us to insist that both the destruction and the perpetual preservation of a determinate entity must equally be able to occur for no reason. Contingency is such that anything might happen, even nothing at all, so that what is, remains as it is. [...]. There is nothing beneath or beyond the manifest gratuitousness of the given—nothing but the limitless and lawless power of its destruction, emergence, or persistence.[10]

The vision of the acausal and an-archic universe that results from the affirmation of such contingency is fully worthy of Deleuze and Guattari's appreciation for those artists and writers who tear apart the comfortable normality of ordinary experience so as to let 'a bit of free and windy chaos'[11] remind us of the tumultuous intensity of things:

> If we look through the aperture which we have opened up onto the absolute, what we see there is a rather menacing power—something insensible, and capable of destroying both things and worlds, of bringing forth monstrous absurdities, yet also of never doing anything, of realizing every dream, but also every nightmare, of engendering random and frenetic transformations, or conversely, of producing a universe that remains motionless down to its ultimate recesses, like a cloud bearing the fiercest storms, then the eeriest bright spells, if only for an interval of disquieting calm [...]. We see something akin to Time, but a Time that is inconceivable for physics, since it is capable of destroying, without cause or reason, every physical law, just as it is inconceivable for metaphysics, since it is capable of destroying every determinate entity, even a god, even God.[12]

---

9. Meillassoux, *After Finitude*, p. 83.

10. Meillassoux, 'Potentiality and Virtuality', pp. 226; Meillassoux, *After Finitude*, p. 63.

11. Gilles Deleuze and Félix Guattari, *What is Philosophy?*, trans. Hugh Tomlinson and Graham Burchell, New York, Columbia University Press, 1994, p. 203, referring to D.H. Lawrence, 'Chaos in Poetry'.

12. Meillassoux, *After Finitude*, p. 64.

Without flinching from the implications, Meillassoux attributes to such 'time without development [devenir]' the potential to generate life *ex nihilo*, to draw spirit from matter or creativity from stasis—or even to resurrect an immortal mind from a lifeless body.[13]

Rational reflection encourages us to posit the absence of sufficient reason and to speculate about the potentialities of this absolute time: it is only our experience, precisely, that holds us back. Our ordinary sensory experience discourages us from abandoning a superstitious belief in causality. Conversion of Hume's problem into Meillassoux's opportunity requires, then, a neo-Platonic deflation of experience and the senses. It requires not a reversed but an 'inverted' Platonism, 'a Platonism which would maintain that thought must free itself from the fascination for the phenomenal fixity of laws, so as to accede to a purely intelligible Chaos capable of destroying and of producing, without reason, things and the laws which they obey'.[14] Drawing on an analogy with the development of non-Euclidean geometries, Meillassoux suggests that such quasi-Platonic insight into the acausal nature of things might account in a more rigorous way for both our ordinary cause- and sense-bound experience and also for infinitely larger super-sensible, super-empirical domains.[15]

The plain fact remains, however, that the world we experience does not seem chaotic but stable. Meillassoux does not deny it, and he knows that such stability is a necessary presupposition of any experimental science. He accepts the fact that our experience is framed by fixed and constant forms, while insisting that their constancy is simply a matter of fact rather than necessity, a facticity that 'can only be described, not founded'.[16] Since nothing is necessary, it is not necessary that things change any more than that remain the same. But how exactly are we to explain the fact of everyday empirical consistency on the basis of radical contingency and the total absence of causal necessity? If physical laws could actually change for no reason, would it not be 'extraordinarily improbable if they did not change frequently, not to say frenetically'?[17]

This question frames a second stage in Meillassoux's argument. Since the earth so regularly rotates around the sun, since gravity so consistently holds us to the ground, so then we infer that there must be some underlying cause which accounts for the consistency of such effects. Meillassoux claims to refute such reasoning by casting doubt on the 'probalistic' assumption that underlies it. An ordinary calculation of probabilities—say, the anticipation of an even spread of results from a repeated dice-throw—assumes that there is a finite range of possible outcomes and a finite range of determining factors, a range that sets the criteria whereby a given outcome is more or less likely in relation to others. At this point, following Badiou's example, Meillassoux plays his Cantorian trump card. 'It is precisely this totalization of the thinkable which can no longer be guaranteed a priori. For we now know—indeed, we have known it at least since Cantor's revolutionary set-theory—that we have no grounds for maintaining that the conceivable is necessarily totalizable'. Cantor showed that there can be no all-inclusive set of all sets, leaving probabilistic reason with no purchase on an open or 'detotalized' set of possibilities. '[L]*aws which are contingent, but stable beyond all probability, there-*

---

13. See in particular, Meillassoux, 'Spectral Dilemma', pp. 267-269; Meillassoux, 'Matérialisme et surgissement ex nihilo', pp. 5-9 (of 12 page typescript).

14. Meillassoux, 'Spectral Dilemma', p. 274.

15. Meillassoux, *After Finitude*, p. 92.

16. Meillassoux, *After Finitude*, p. 39.

17. Meillassoux, *After Finitude*, p. 98.

by become conceivable.[18] Taken together, Hume and Cantor allow us to envisage 'a time capable of bringing forth, outside all necessity and all probability, situations which are not at all pre-contained in their precedents'.[19]

On this basis, Meillassoux aims to restore the rights of a purely 'intelligible' insight, i.e. to reinstate the validity of pre- or non-critical 'intellectual intuition' and thereby challenge the allegedly stifling strictures of Kant's transcendental turn.[20] Rather than propose a merely 'negative ontology', he seeks to elaborate 'an ever more determinate, ever richer concept of contingency', on the assumption that these determinations can then be 'construed as so many absolute properties of what is', or as so many constraints to which a given 'entity must submit in order to exercise its capacity-not-to-be and its capacity-to-be-other'.[21]

A first constraint required by this capacity entails rejection of contradiction. The only law that survives the elimination of causal or sufficient reason is the law of non-contradiction. Why? Because a contradictory entity would be utterly indeterminate, and could thus be both contingent *and* necessary. In order to affirm the thesis that any given thing can be *anything*, it is necessary that this thing both actually be what it is here and now, and also forever capable of being determined as something else. In other words, where Kant simply posited that things-in-themselves existed and existed as non-contradictory, Meillassoux claims to deduce the latter property directly from the modality of their existence.

What does it mean, however, to say that such things exist? Meillassoux's approach to this question circumscribes a second, more far-reaching determination of contingency: absolute and contingent entities or things-in-themselves must first observe the logical principle of non-contradiction, and they must also submit to rigorous mathematical measurement. Here again, Meillassoux's strategy involves the renewal of perfectly classical concerns. In addition to an affirmation of the ontological implications of the scientific revolution, it involves the absolutization of what Descartes and then Locke established as a thing's primary qualities—those qualities like its dimensions or weight, which can be mathematically measured independently of the way an observer experiences and perceives them, i.e. independently of secondary qualities like texture, colour, taste, and so on. But whereas Descartes conceived of such qualities in geometric terms, as aspects of an extended substance, Meillassoux takes a further step, and isolates the mathematizable from extension itself,[22] so as then 'to derive from a contingency which is absolute, the conditions that would allow me to deduce the absolutization of mathematical discourse' and thus 'ground the possibility of the sciences to speak about an absolute reality [...], a reality independent of thought'.[23]

Meillassoux admits that he has not worked out a full version of this deduction, but the closing pages of *After Finitude* imply that his approach will depend on the presumption that 'what is mathematically conceivable is absolutely possible'.[24] It will involve a demonstration that mathematized empirical science not only applies to mind-independent facts of our actually existing world, but also (as a result of Cantor's de-totali-

18. Meillassoux, *After Finitude*, p. 103; Meillassoux, 'Potentiality and Virtuality', p. 230.

19. Meillassoux, 'Potentiality and Virtuality', p. 232.

20. Meillassoux, *After Finitude*, pp. 82-83.

21. Meillassoux, *After Finitude*, p. 101, 66.

22. Meillassoux, *After Finitude*, p. 3.

23. Meillassoux, 'Speculative Realism', p. 440.

24. Meillassoux, *After Finitude*, p. 126.

zation of number) 'states something about the structure of the possible as such, rather than about this or that possible reality. It is a matter of asserting that the possible as such, rather than this or that possible entity, must necessarily be un-totalizable'.[25] In a recent lecture, Meillassoux gave a further clue to the future development of this argument by insisting on the absolutely arbitrary, meaningless and contingent nature of mathematical signs *qua* signs (e.g. signs produced through pure replication or reiteration, indifferent to any sort of pattern or 'rhythm'). Perhaps an absolutely arbitrary discourse will be adequate to the absolutely contingent nature of things.[26]

II

The main obstacle standing in the way of this anti-phenomenological return 'to the things themselves', naturally, is the widely held (if not tautological) assumption that we cannot, by definition, think any reality independently of thought itself. Meillassoux dubs the modern currents of thought that accept this assumption 'correlationist'. A correlationist humbly accepts that 'we only ever have access to the correlation between thinking and being, and never to either term considered apart from the other', such that 'anything that is totally a-subjective cannot be'.[27] Nothing can be independently of thought, since here 'to be is to be a correlate'.[28] Paradigmatically, to be is to be the correlate of either consciousness (for phenomenology) or language (for analytical philosophy).

Kant is the founding figure of correlationist philosophy, of course, but the label applies equally well, according to Meillassoux, to most strands of post-Kantian philosophy, from Fichte and Hegel to Heidegger or Adorno. All these philosophies posit some sort of fundamental mediation between the subject and object of thought, such that it is the clarity and integrity of this relation (whether it be clarified through logical judgment, phenomenological reduction, historical reflection, linguistic articulation, pragmatic experimentation or intersubjective communication) that serves as the only legitimate means of accessing reality. The overall effect has been to consolidate the criteria of 'lawful' legitimacy as such. Correlationism figures here as a sort of counter-revolution that emerged in philosophy as it tried, with and after Kant, to come to terms with the uncomfortably disruptive implications of Galileo, Descartes and the scientific revolution. Post-Copernican science had opened the door to the 'great outdoors': Kant's own so-called 'Copernican turn' should be best understood as a Ptolemaic attempt to slam this door shut.[29]

How then to re-open the door? Since a correlationist will assume as a matter of course that the referent of any statement 'cannot possibly exist' or 'take place [... as] non-correlated with a consciousness',[30] Meillassoux claims to find the Achilles heel of correlationism in its inability to cope with what he calls 'ancestral' statements. Such statements refer to events or entities older than any consciousness, events like the emergence of life, the formation of Earth, the origin of the universe, and so on. 'The ancestral does not designate an absence in the given, and for givenness, but rather an absence of givenness as such'. Ancestrality refers to a world 'prior to givenness in its en-

25. Meillassoux, *After Finitude*, p. 127.

26. Meillassoux, 'Time without Becoming'.

27. Meillassoux, *After Finitude*, p. 5, 38.

28. Meillassoux, *After Finitude*, p. 28.

29. Meillassoux, *After Finitude*, p. 121.

30. Meillassoux, *After Finitude*, pp. 16-17.

tirety. It is not the world such as givenness deploys its lacunary presentation, but the world as it deploys itself when nothing is given, whether fully or lacunarily'.[31] Insofar as correlation can only conceive of an object that is given to a subject, how can it cope with an object that pre-dates givenness itself?

Now Meillassoux realizes that it order to overcome the Ptolemaic-correlationist counter-revolution it is impossible simply to retreat from Kant back to the 'dogmatic' metaphysics of Descartes, let alone to the necessity- and cause-bound metaphysics of Spinoza or Leibniz. He also accepts that you cannot refute correlationism simply by positing, as Laruelle does, a mind-independent reality.[32] In order to overcome the correlational obstacle to his acausal ontology, in order to know mind-independent reality as non-contradictory and non-necessary, Meillassoux thus needs to show that the correlationist critique of metaphysical necessity itself enables if not requires the speculative affirmation of non-necessity.

This demonstration occupies the central and most subtle sections of *After Finitude*. The basic strategy again draws on Kantian and post-Kantian precedents. Post-Kantian metaphysicians like Fichte and Hegel tried to overcome Kant's foreclosure of absolute reality by converting correlation itself, the very 'instrument of empirico-critical de-absolutization', into the model for a new type of absolute'.[33] This idealist alternative to correlationist humility, however, cannot respond in turn to the 'most profound' correlational decision—the decision which ensures, in order to preserve the ban on every sort of absolute knowledge, that correlation too is just another contingent fact, rather than a necessity. As with his approach to Hume's problem, Meillassoux's crucial move here is to turn an apparent weakness into an opportunity. The correlationist, in order to guard against idealist claims to knowledge of absolute reality, readily accepts not only the reduction of knowledge to knowledge of facts: the correlationist also accepts that this reduction too is just another fact, just another non-necessary contingency. But if such correlating reduction is not necessary then it is of course possible to envisage its suspension: the only way the correlationists can defend themselves against idealist absolutization requires them to admit 'the impossibility of giving an ultimate ground to the existence of any being', including the impossibility of giving a ground for this impossibility.[34]

All that Meillassoux now has to do is absolutize, in turn, this apparent failure. We simply need to understand 'why it is not the correlation but the facticity of the correlation that constitutes the absolute. We must show why thought, far from experiencing its intrinsic limits through facticity, experiences rather its knowledge of the absolute through facticity. We must grasp in facticity not the inaccessibility of the absolute but the unveiling of the in-itself and the eternal property of what is, as opposed to the mark of the perennial deficiency in the thought of what is'.[35] In knowing that we know only contingent facts, we also know that it is necessary that there be only contingent facts. We know that facticity itself, and only facticity itself, is not contingent but necessary. Recognition of the absolute nature or absolute necessity of facticity then allows Meillassoux to go on to complete his deduction 'from the absoluteness of this facticity

31. Meillassoux, *After Finitude*, p. 21.
32. Meillassoux, 'Speculative Realism', pp. 418-419.
33. Meillassoux, *After Finitude*, p. 52.
34. Meillassoux, 'Speculative Realism', p. 428.
35. Meillassoux, *After Finitude*, p. 52.

those properties of the in-itself which Kant for his part took to be self-evident', i.e. that it exists (as radically contingent), and that it exists as non-contradictory.[36] By affirming this necessity of contingency or 'principle of factuality', Meillassoux triumphantly concludes, 'I think an X independent of any thinking, and I know it for sure, thanks to the correlationist himself and his fight against the absolute, the idealist absolute'.[37]

III

Unlike Meillassoux, I believe that the main problem with recent French philosophy has been not an excess but a deficit of genuinely relational thought.[38] From this perspective, despite its compelling originality and undeniable ingenuity, Meillassoux's resolutely absolutizing project raises a number of questions and objections.

First, the critique of correlation seems to depend on an equivocation regarding the relation of thinking and being, of epistemology and ontology. On balance, Meillassoux insists on the modern 'ontological requisite' which stipulates that 'to be is to be a correlate' of thought.[39] From within the correlational circle, 'all we ever engage with is what is given-to-thought, never an entity subsisting by itself'.[40] If a being only is as the correlate of the thought that thinks it, then from a correlationist perspective it must seem that a being older than thought can only be 'unthinkable'. A consistent correlationist, Meillassoux says, must 'insist that the physical universe could not really have preceded the existence of man, or at least of living creatures'.

As far as I know, however, almost no-one actually thinks or insists on this, apart perhaps from a few fossilized idealists. Even an idealist like Husserl only conceives of natural objects in terms of 'concatenations of consciousness' to the degree that he brackets (rather than addresses or answers) questions about the existence or reality of such objects. Almost no-one actually balks at ancestral statements because correlationism as Meillassoux defines it is in reality an epistemological theory, one that is perfectly compatible with the insights of Darwin, Marx or Einstein. There's nothing to prevent a correlationist from thinking ancestral objects or worlds that are older than the thought that thinks them, or indeed older than thought itself. Even from an orthodox Kantian perspective there is little difference in principle between my thinking an event that took place yesterday from an event that took place six billion years ago. It's not clear that Kant should have any more trouble in accepting an ancestral statement about the accretion of the earth than he would in accepting a new scientific demonstration of the existence of previously unperceived 'magnetic matter', or the discovery of hitherto undetected men on the moon (to cite two of his own examples).[41] As Meillassoux knows perfectly well, all that the correlationist demands is an acknowledgement that when you think of an ancestral event, or any event, you are indeed thinking

---

36. Meillassoux, *After Finitude*, p. 76.

37. Meillassoux, 'Speculative Realism', p. 432; cf. Quentin Meillassoux, 'Spéculation et contingence', in Emmanuel Cattin et Franck Fischbach (eds.), *L'Héritage de la raison: Hommage à Bernard Bourgeois*, Paris, Ellipses, 2007.

38. cf. Peter Hallward, 'The One or the Other? French Philosophy Today', *Angelaki*, vol. 8, no. 2, 2003, pp. 1-32.

39. Meillassoux, *After Finitude*, p. 28; my emphasis.

40. Meillassoux, *After Finitude*, p. 36.

41. On Kantian grounds, cognition of an event doesn't require that a witness be present at the event itself. All that is required is an ability to grasp the event in terms of the relation basic to the 'cognition of any possible experience', i.e. in terms of the relation between what (a) sensible intuition can perceive of it or its traces, and (b) the conceptual conditions that order our perception of temporal events 'according to a rule', i.e. as a causal succession.

of it. I can think of this lump of ancient rock as ancient if and only if science currently provides me with reliable means of thinking it so.[42]

Genuine conquest of the correlationist fortress would require not a reference to objects older than thought but to processes of thinking that proceed without thinking, or objects that are somehow presentable in the absence of any objective presence or evidence—in other words, processes and objects proscribed by Meillassoux's own insistence on the principle of non-contradiction. This is the problem with using a correlationist strategy (the principle of factuality) to break out of the correlationist circle: until Meillassoux can show that we know things exist not only independently of our thought but independently of our thinking them so, the correlationist has little to worry about. Anyone can agree with Meillassoux that 'to think ancestrality is to think a world without thought—a world without the givenness of the world'.[43] What's less obvious is how we might think such a world without thinking it, or how we might arrive at scientific knowledge of such pre-given objects if nothing is given of them.

Along the same lines, Meillassoux's rationalist critique of causality and necessity seems to depend on an equivocation between metaphysical and physical or natural necessity. The actual target of Meillassoux's critique of metaphysics is the Leibnizian principle of sufficient reason. He dispatches it, as we've seen, with a version of Hume's argument: we cannot rationally demonstrate an ultimate reason for the being of being; there is no primordial power or divine providence that determines being or the meaning of being to be a certain way. What Meillassoux infers from this critique of metaphysical necessity, however, is the rather more grandiose assertion that there is no cause or reason for anything to be the way it is. He affirms 'the effective ability of every determined entity—event, thing, or law of subjectivity—to appear and disappear with no reason for its being or non-being'.[44] This inference relies on a contentious understanding of the terms reason, cause and law. It's been a long time since scientists confused 'natural laws' with logical or metaphysical necessities. There is nothing to stop a biologist from reconstructing the locally effective reasons and causes that have shaped, for instance, the evolution of aerobic vertebrate organisms; there was nothing necessary or predictable about this evolution, but why should we doubt that it conformed to familiar 'laws' of cause and effect? What does it mean to say that the ongoing consequences of this long process might be transformed in an instant—that we might suddenly cease to breathe oxygen or suffer the effects of gravity? Although Meillassoux insists that contingency applies to every event and every process, it may well be that the

---

42. Althusser's basic affirmation of materialism proceeds on the same basis. A materialist presumes a fundamental 'distinction between matter and thought, the real and knowledge of the real—or, to put it differently and more precisely, the distinction between the *real process* and the *process of knowledge*', and then insists 'on the primacy of the real process over the process of knowledge; on the knowledge-effect produced by the process of knowledge in the process of correlating *[dans le procès de mise en correspondance]* the process of knowledge with the real process' (Louis Althusser, *The Humanist Controversy*, trans. G. M. Goshgarian, London, Verso, 2003, pp. 265-266). But of course only knowledge allow us to *know* that the real process is primary in relation to the knowledge process. 'For us', Althusser insists, 'the 'real' is not a *theoretical slogan*; the real is the real object that exists independently of its knowledge—but which can only be defined by its knowledge. In this second, theoretical, relation, the real is identical to the means of knowing it, the real is its known or to-be-known structure, it is the very object of Marxist theory, the object marked out by the great theoretical discoveries of Marx and Lenin: the immense, living, constantly developing field, in which the events of human history can from now on be mastered by men's practice, because they will be within their conceptual grasp, their knowledge' (Louis Althusser, *For Marx*, trans. Ben Brewster, London, Allen Lane, 1969, p. 246).

43. Meillassoux, *After Finitude*, p. 28.

44. Meillassoux, 'Speculative Realism', p. 431.

only event that might qualify as contingent and without reason in his absolute sense of the term is the emergence of the universe itself.

Meillassoux's acausal ontology, in other words, includes no account of an actual process of transformation or development. There is no account here of any positive ontological or historical force, no substitute for what other thinkers have conceived as substance, or spirit, or power, or labour. His insistence that anything might happen can only amount to an insistence on the bare possibility of radical change. So far, at least, Meillassoux's affirmation of 'the *effective ability* of every determined entity' to persist, change or disappear without reason figures as an empty and indeterminate postulate. Once Meillassoux has purged his speculative materialism of any sort of causality he deprives it of any worldly-historical purchase as well. The abstract logical possibility of change (given the absence of any ultimately sufficient reason) has little to do with any concrete process of actual change. Rather like his mentor Badiou, to the degree that Meillassoux insists on the *absolute* disjunction of an event from existing situations he deprives himself of any concretely mediated means of thinking, with and after Marx, the possible ways of changing such situations.

The notion of 'absolute time' that accompanies Meillassoux's acausal ontology is a time that seems endowed with only one essential dimension—the instant. It may well be that 'only the time that harbours the capacity to destroy every determinate reality, while obeying no determinate law—the time capable of destroying, without reason or law, both worlds and things—can be thought as an absolute'.[45] The sense in which such an absolute can be thought as distinctively temporal, however, is less obvious. Rather than any sort of articulation of past, present and future, Meillassoux's time is a matter of spontaneous and immediate irruption *ex nihilo*. Time is reduced, here, to a succession of 'gratuitous sequences'.[46] The paradigm for such gratuitous irruption, obviously, is the miracle. Meillassoux argues that every absolute or 'miraculous' discontinuity testifies only to the 'inexistence of God', i.e. to the lack of any metaphysical necessity, progress or providence.[47] It may be, however, that an argument regarding the existence or inexistence of God is secondary in relation to arguments for or against belief in this quintessentially 'divine' power—a super-natural power to interrupt the laws of nature and abruptly re-orient the pattern of worldly affairs.

The argument that allows Meillassoux to posit a radically open miraculous time depends on reference to Cantor's 'de-totalization' of every attempt to close or limit a denumerable set of possibilities. A still more absolute lack of mediation, however, seems to characterize Meillassoux's appeal to mathematics as the royal road to the in-itself. Cantor's transfinite set theory concerns the domain of pure number alone. The demonstration that there is an a open, unending series of ever larger infinite numbers clearly has decisive implications for the foundations of mathematics, but Meillassoux needs to demonstrate more exactly how these implications apply to the time and space of our actually existing universe. In what sense is our material universe itself infinite? In what sense has the evolution of life, for instance, confronted an actually infinite (rather than immensely large) number of actual possibilities? It is striking that Meillassoux pays little or no attention to such questions, and sometimes treats the logical and material domains as if they were effectively interchangeable.

---

45. Meillassoux, *After Finitude*, p. 62.

46. Meillassoux, 'Matérialisme et surgissement ex nihilo', p. 12 (of 12 page typescript).

47. Meillassoux, 'Potentiality and Virtuality', p. 233n.7.

Admittedly, you can make a case for the equation of mathematics and ontology in the strict sense, as Badiou does, such that post-Cantorian theory serves to articulate what can be thought of pure being-*qua*-being (once being is identified with abstract and absolute multiplicity, i.e. a multiplicity that does not depend on any preliminary notion of unit or unity). Such an equation requires, however, that ontological questions be strictly preserved from merely 'ontic' ones: as a matter of course, a mathematical conception of being has nothing to say about the material, historical, or social attributes of specific beings. A similar 'ontological reduction' must apply to Meillassoux's reliance on Cantorian mathematics. Here again he seems to equivocate, as if the abstract implications of Cantorian detotalization might concern the concrete set of possibilities at issue in a specific situation, e.g. in an ecosystem, or in a political conflict. He implies that the Cantorian transfinite—a theory that has nothing to do with any physical or material reality—might underwrite speculation regarding the 'unreason' whereby any actually existing thing might suddenly be transformed, destroyed or preserved.

In short, Meillassoux seems to confuse the domains of pure and applied mathematics. In the spirit of Galileo's 'mathematization of nature', he relies on pure mathematics in order to demonstrate the integrity of an objective reality that exists independently of us—a domain of primary (mathematically measurable) qualities purged of any merely sensory, subject-dependent secondary qualities. Pure mathematics, however, is arguably the supreme example of absolutely subject-dependent thought, i.e. a thought that proceeds without reference to any sort of objective reality 'outside' it.[48] No-one denies that every mathematical measurement is 'indifferent' to the thing it measures. But leaving aside the question of why an abstract, mathematized description of an object should be any less mind-dependent or anthropocentric than a sensual or experiential description, there is no eliding the fundamental difference between pure number and an applied measurement. The idea that the meaning of the statement 'the universe was formed 13.5 billion years ago' might be independent of the mind that thinks it only makes sense if you disregard the quaintly parochial unit of measurement involved (along with the meaning of words like 'ago', to say nothing of the meaning of meaning *tout court*). As a matter of course, every unit of measurement, from the length of a meter to the time required for a planet to orbit around a star, exists at a fundamental distance from the domain of number as such. If Meillassoux was to carry through the argument of 'ancestrality' to its logical conclusion, he would have to acknowledge that it would eliminate not only all reference to secondary qualities like colour and texture but also all conventional primary qualities like length or mass or date as well. What might then be known of an 'arche-fossil' (i.e. a thing considered independently of whatever is given of it, including its material extension) would presumably have to be expressed in terms of pure numbers alone, rather than dates or measurements. Whatever else such (neo-Pythagorean?) knowledge amounts to, it has no obvious relation with the sorts of realities that empirical science tries to describe, including realities older than the evolution of life.

After Finitude is a beautifully written and seductively argued book. It offers a welcome critique of the ambient 'necessitarian' worldview, that pensée unique which tells us 'there is no alternative', and which underlies both the listless political apathy and the deflating humility of so much contemporary philosophy and critical theory. In the ra-

---

48. Badiou himself, for instance, emphasizes precisely this, at several key moments in the elaboration of his ontology.

tionalist tradition of the Enlightenment and of ideology-critique, Meillassoux launches a principled assault on every 'superstitious' presumption that existing social situations should be accepted as natural or inevitable.[49] His suggestion that such situations are actually a matter of uncaused contingency, however, offers us little grip on the means of their material transformation. The current fascination with his work, in some quarters, may be a symptom of impatience with a more modest but also more robust conception of social and political change—not that we might abruptly be other than we are, but that we might engage with the processes whereby we have become what we are, and thus begin to become otherwise. A critique of metaphysical necessity and an appeal to transfinite mathematics will not provide, on their own, the basis upon which we might renew a transformative materialism.

---

49. Meillassoux, *After Finitude*, p. 34.

11

The Speculative and the Specific:
On Hallward and Meillassoux

Nathan Brown

THE SPECULATIVE AND THE EMPIRICAL

In his review of Quentin Meillassoux's *After Finitude*,[1] Peter Hallward charges Meillassoux's work with four major flaws:

1. An equivocation regarding the relation of thinking and being, or epistemology and ontology.
2. An equivocation between metaphysical and physical or natural necessity.
3. A confusion of pure and applied mathematics.
4. An incapacity to think concrete processes of social and political change.

Although Hallward expresses a certain admiration for Meillassoux's book, these are serious objections. My initial goal is to indicate, as briefly as possible, the false premises upon which I believe each of Hallward's accusations to rest. I then turn toward a broader consideration of the relationship between their respective projects, before attempting to articulate, via Althusser, the sense in which Meillassoux's speculative materialism could be understood as a contribution to dialectical materialism. But let me attend, first of all, to the four critical points made by Hallward in his review.

1. Hallward asserts that Meillassoux holds the correlationist responsible for an ontological argument regarding ancestral phenomena, despite the fact that 'correlationism as Meillassoux defines it is in reality an epistemological theory'. Considered as an epistemological problem, Hallward argues, the problem of ancestrality posed by Meillassoux is no problem at all, since 'there's nothing to prevent a correlationist from thinking ancestral objects or worlds that are older than the thought that thinks them, or indeed older than thought itself'.[2]

Hallward's statement fails, however, to account for the logic of succession inherent in such a thought, which constitutes the crux of Meillassoux's analysis of correlationism's approach to the problem of ancestrality. When the correlationist thinks the ancestral object *qua* correlate of thought, she effects a temporal retrojection of the past

---

1. Peter Hallward, 'Anything is Possible', *Radical Philosophy*, no. 152, 2008, pp. 51-57.
2. Hallward, 'Anything is Possible', p. 55.

from the present, such that 'it is necessary to proceed from the present to the past, following a logical order, rather than from the past to the present, following a chronological order'. For the correlationist, Meillassoux argues, 'the deeper sense of ancestrality resides in the logical retrojection imposed upon its superficially chronological sense'.[3]

Thus, stricto sensu, the correlationist cannot think ancestral objects as prior to the thought that thinks them. Meillassoux's argument is simply that if we accept the priority of logical over chronological succession (the 'transmutation of the dia-chronic past into a retrojective correlation')[4] we will be unable to assess scientific statements regarding ancestral phenomena without destroying the veritable meaning of those statements, which concern the chronological priority of that which came before thought, regardless of any temporal retrojection performed by thinking. What is at stake here apropos of 'thinking and being' is a disagreement regarding the priority of the logical correlation between thinking and being over the chronological disjunction of thinking and being. Meillassoux's point is that the correlationist's insistence upon the priority of the former eviscerates the proper import of the latter. The remit of *After Finitude* is not to solve this problem, but merely to formulate it as a problem. Hallward does not engage the problem as it is formulated insofar as he ignores Meillassoux's critique of logical retrojection altogether.

2. Hallward contends that Meillassoux's critique of causality and necessity—his critique of the principle of sufficient reason—blurs the distinction between metaphysical and physical or natural necessity. 'It's been a long time', writes Hallward, 'since scientists confused 'natural laws' with logical or metaphysical necessities'.[5] My own exposure to the rhetoric of contemporary science assures me that, on the contrary, scientists either perform or are afflicted by precisely that confusion fairly regularly. It might be more to the point, however, to ask why Meillassoux continues to rely upon the concept of 'law' at all, as he seems to do despite his argument that 'the laws' may be subject to change without reason. But this is not what Hallward does.

The problem with Hallward's own formulations in this section of his review is that they are both question-begging and irrelevant to the purview of Meillassoux's arguments. Hallward posits that it is 'perfectly possible, of course, to reconstruct the locally effective reasons and causes that have shaped, for instance, the evolution of aerobic vertebrate organisms'.[6] Regardless of whether or not we agree with this contention, it has strictly nothing to do with Meillassoux's book, since it is an assertion about the operation of evolution as we know it, whereas Meillassoux's arguments concern the possibility that precisely such processes may become entirely otherwise without reason. Hallward continues, 'there was nothing necessary or predictable about this evolution, but why should we doubt that it conformed to familiar 'laws' of cause and effect?'[7] Here he simply begs Hume's question (a question at the core of Meillassoux's project) regarding the putative 'familiarity' of such laws. And when Hallward suggests that 'the only event that might qualify as contingent and without reason in [Meillassoux's] absolute sense of the term is the emergence of the universe itself' he again addresses a speculative question concerning the possible contingency of the laws from within an em-

3. Meillassoux, Quentin. *After Finitude: An Essay on the Necessity of Contingency*, trans. Ray Brassier, London, Continuum, 2008, p. 16.

4. Meillassoux, *After Finitude*, p. 123.

5. Hallward, 'Anything is Possible', p. 55.

6. Hallward, 'Anything is Possible', p. 55.

7. Hallward, 'Anything is Possible', p. 55.

pirical framework pertaining only to the laws as they currently are or have been. Any effort to undermine arguments concerning the absolute contingency of physical law *tout court* on the basis of any given regime or local case of physical law will obviously be unsuccessful. It is not the case that Meillassoux equivocates between metaphysical and natural necessity, but rather that Hallward arrives at this judgment through his own conflation of speculative and empirical registers.

3. Perhaps Hallward's most serious accusation is that Meillassoux flatly confuses pure and applied mathematics. First, he takes issue with Meillassoux's use of transfinite set theory to undermine 'every attempt to close or limit a denumerable set of possibilities'. Conceding that Cantor's 'demonstration that there is an open, unending series of ever larger infinite numbers clearly has decisive implications for the foundations of mathematics', Hallward argues that 'Meillassoux needs to demonstrate more exactly how these implications apply to the time and space of our actually existing universe'.[8]

Again, Hallward collapses the speculative register of Meillassoux's argument into the empirical. Meillassoux deploys Cantorian detotalization in order to counter resolutions of Hume's problem that rely upon a probabalistic logic dependent upon a totality of cases. As Meillassoux makes clear, it is these arguments that operate by 'applying the calculus of probability to our world as a whole, rather than to any phenomenon given within the world' and which thus rely upon 'an a priori totalization of the possible'.[9] Meillassoux's argument from transfinite mathematics strikes at this mathematical model itself, thereby attempting to undermine the validity of the probabilistic consequences that are drawn from it. When Hallward writes that Meillassoux 'seems to equivocate, as if the abstract implications of Cantorian detotalisation might concern the concrete set of possibilities at issue in a specific situation, eg. in an ecosystem, or in a political conflict'[10] he misunderstands or misrepresents the structure of Meillassoux's argument, which aims solely at the mathematical grounds of his opponent's logic. If Meillassoux seems to hold, as Hallward writes, that 'the Cantorian transfinite … might underwrite speculation regarding the 'unreason' whereby any actually existing thing might suddenly be transformed, destroyed or preserved',[11] he does not do so directly. He (1) deploys transfinite mathematics to counter an objection to the validity of such speculation; he then (2) proceeds to speculate that the reason we have been unable to resolve Hume's problem is that it indexes a positive ontological fact (absence of any sufficient reason for the manifest regularity of physical law) rather than an epistemological lacuna. The first argument does not directly entail the other; it merely opens a path to its plausible articulation by refuting an obvious counter-argument.

Second, Hallward charges that Meillassoux 'elides the fundamental difference between pure number and an applied measurement'. Hallward wonders 'why an abstract, mathematized description of an object should be any less mind-dependent or anthropocentric than a sensual or experiential description'. He then goes on to argue, 'the idea that the meaning of the statement 'the universe was formed 13.5 billion years ago' might be independent of the mind that thinks it only makes sense if you disregard the quaintly parochial unit of measurement involved'.[12] Again, this point has force only

---

8. Hallward, 'Anything is Possible', p. 56.
9. Meillassoux, *After Finitude*, pp. 106-107.
10. Hallward, 'Anything is Possible', p. 56.
11. Hallward, 'Anything is Possible', p. 56.
12. Hallward, 'Anything is Possible', p. 56.

insofar as it stretches Meillassoux's arguments beyond the proper domain of their application—to which Meillassoux himself is careful to restrict them. Meillassoux does not argue that units of measurement or mathematical descriptions of objects 'might be independent of the mind'. He argues that 'what is mathematizable cannot be reduced to a correlate of thought'.[13] For Meillassoux (after Descartes) the mathematical descriptions of physics or cosmology index primary qualities. What interests Meillassoux about the science of dating is that it is capable of establishing standards of measure that specify an order of chronological succession. He does not defend the thesis that any such measure is absolute or mind independent. On the contrary, what matters about these measurements is precisely their relative relations. However, Meillassoux holds that those relative relations amount to revisable hypotheses that concern an absolute reality (which is not reducible to a correlate of thought): simply that, for example, the accretion of the earth occurred prior to my thought of that event. That the correlationist purportedly acknowledges this obvious fact while interpreting it in a manner that undermines its straightforward sense is what Meillassoux finds problematic. The science of dating indexes, through relative units of measure, an order of chronological succession that is absolute (i.e. it does not itself depend upon any unit or experience of measure relative to us). While I concur with Hallward that the question of measure, considered more generally, may well constitute a problem for Meillassoux, Hallward would have to properly engage the structure of Meillassoux's argument in order to undermine the latter's efforts to resuscitate the theory of primary and secondary qualities. Moreover, he would have to do so not simply by reasserting the dictates of transcendental idealism on this point, but while accounting for Meillassoux's intra-systemic critique of transcendental idealism—a critique that does not rely upon the problem of ancestrality, but rather attempts to undermine transcendental idealism through the logical exigencies of its own defence against absolute idealism.

4. Hallward feels that Meillassoux's speculative affirmation of absolute contingency compromises his capacity to think concrete political situations. 'Rather like his mentor Badiou', Hallward writes, 'to the degree that Meillassoux insists on the absolute disjunction of an event from existing situations he deprives himself of any concretely mediated means of thinking, with and after Marx, the possible ways of changing such situations'. That is because, for Hallward, 'the abstract logical possibility of change (given the absence of any ultimately sufficient reason) has strictly nothing to do with any concrete process of actual change'.[14]

With this last point, I could not agree more: Meillassoux's book has nothing whatsoever to do with an empirical analysis of political or social situations or possible ways of transforming them. Unlike Badiou, Meillassoux does not forward a theory of political change, nor does he forward a theory of the subject. But the arguments put forward in *After Finitude* concerning the absolute contingency of the factic structure of situations do not 'deprive' Meillassoux of the means to think concrete processes of actual change within those situations, or, more broadly, within the order of physical law as we presently know it. (The latter is precisely the task that Meillassoux accords to science, whose empirical operations his work leaves unscathed). Hallward speculates that 'the current fascination with [Meillassoux's] work, in some quarters, may be a symptom of impatience with a more traditional conception of social and political change—not that

---

13. Meillassoux, *After Finitude*, p. 117.
14. Hallward, 'Anything is Possible', p. 55.

we might abruptly be other than we are, but that we might engage with the processes whereby we have become what we are, and might now begin to become otherwise'.[15] Here Hallward writes as though those of us who have taken an especial interest in Meillassoux's book have done so because we think that a 'hyper-chaos', 'an absolute time able to destroy and create any determined entity—event, thing, or law' might eventually perform just those miraculous alterations of the universe that we would deem most desirable—as though the wayward youth of the contemporary continental philosophy scene had put their faith in an obscure cosmological power that might terminate the predations of neoliberalism, grant rights of citizenship to the sans-papiers, or deliver a new constitution to Bolivia without anyone anywhere lifting a finger.

The obvious fact that *After Finitude* does not address possible ways of changing social and political situations does not imply that Meillassoux's philosophy impedes or compromises our capacity to do so. A speculative demonstration that whatever-situation is contingent rather than necessary (despite its manifest stability) does not undermine the political urgency of working toward the contingent stability of *another* situation—toward just and equitable ways of structuring or distributing relations among the given. An insistence upon—or a rational demonstration of—the contingency of *any* stable situation that we might imagine or construct, and which we might care to preserve, would seem to encourage rather than disable the active task of such preservation, however fragile that task may be. Precisely *because* any given or constructed situation is absolutely contingent rather than necessary, it has to be upheld by conviction and by force, even if we cannot assure its protection against the perpetual threat of disintegration. Contingency means that stability amounts to a perpetual process of holding-stable, and the fact than 'an absolute time' may abolish all 'concrete' human projects without reason hardly vitiates the rationale for engaging in them.

***

Throughout Hallward's criticisms of *After Finitude*, the basic move is to extend the book's arguments beyond the proper domain of their application and then to hold Meillassoux accountable for the resulting difficulties. If many of us have found Meillassoux's volume invigorating, that is because it opens the promise of a new relation between rationalism and empiricism—between apparently opposed traditions stemming from Descartes and Hume that are most powerfully and discrepantly represented, today, by the work of Badiou and Deleuze. If *After Finitude* might thus be taken to indicate one possible way out of a certain deadlock confronting contemporary philosophy, it only does so insofar as we grasp the subtlety with which Meillassoux's speculative approach sustains a rigorous disjunction between the rational and the empirical precisely in order to articulate the possibility of a new way of thinking their relation. Insofar as Hallward's evaluation of Meillassoux's work fails to respect that subtlety, it misses the point.

THE SPECULATIVE AND THE SPECIFIC

Let me return to the last of the Hallward's critical points by shifting the terms of this debate toward an Althusserian criteria for evaluating the 'correctness' [justesse] of Meillassoux's philosophical theses and Hallward's critique thereof: an assessment not only of argumentative technicalities, but of their effects, their practical adjustment

---

15. Hallward, 'Anything is Possible', p. 57.

[ajustement] of existing ideas, their inflection of the balance of forces constitutive of the conjuncture.[16] Since Hallward is one of the foremost political thinkers and commentators on French philosophy of his generation, his own work constitutes an important part of that conjuncture. In what follows I want to take his intervention as an opportunity to consider just what is at stake in the relationship of his own positions to those of *After Finitude*.[17]

The impetus at the core of Hallward's work is his commitment to sustaining a focus upon the dimension of the specific, against its absorption into either the 'specified' or the 'singular'.[18] What Hallward terms the specified 'extends only to the realm of the passive or the objectified;' it 'can only define the realm of the essence or the essentialist, where the demarcation of an individual (subject, object or culture) follows from its accordance with recognized classifications'.[19] Insofar as it is externally reduced to an identity, the specified is absolutely determined. The singular, on the other hand, 'is constituent of itself, expressive of itself, immediate to itself;' the fact that it 'creates the medium of its existence means it is not specific to external criteria or frames of reference'.[20] The singular might thus be thought as at once absolutely determinate (insofar as it constitutes itself as One) and absolutely undetermined (as a force of immanent Creativity).[21] The dimension of the specific—the proper domain of Hallward's thought—displaces the non-relation of the specified and the singular: it is 'the space of interests in relation to other interests, the space of the historical as such, forever ongoing, forever incomplete'.[22] The specific is the relational mediation of determination and indetermination, the medium of both contextual coherence and of universal principle. It is contextually coherent insofar as it 'implies a situation, a past, an intelligibility constrained by inherited conditions'. But it is also the domain of universal principle insofar as such a principle is 'imposed in a specific situation through a specific intervention'. 'A principle is universal', writes Hallward, 'if it is universalisable, i.e. if it holds as valid for all relations within that situation'. Thus, the dialectical mediation of the historical and the universal constitutive of the specific is such that 'universals are posited so as to enable relational consistency'.[23] If the opposition of the specified and the singular opposes absolute inertia to absolute creation, the specific is the medium of 'constrained free-

---

16. cf. Althusser, Louis. 'Philosophy and the Spontaneous Philosophy of the Scientists', trans. Warren Montag, in *Philosophy and the Spontaneous Ideology of the Scientists*, London, Verso, 1990, pp. 102-105.

17. See Peter Hallward, *Absolutely Postcolonial: Writing Between the Singular and the Specific*, Manchester, Manchester University Press, 2001; Peter Hallward, *Badiou: A Subject To Truth*, Minneapolis, University of Minnesota Press, 2003; Peter Hallward, *Out of This World: Deleuze and the Philosophy of Creation*, London, Verso, 2006; Peter Hallward, *Damming the Flood: Haiti, Aristide, and the Politics of Containment*, London, Verso, 2007; Peter Hallward (ed.), *The One or the Other: French Philosophy Today*, Special Issue of *Angelaki*, vol. 8, no. 2, 2003. Hallward's most incisive interventions in political philosophy are 'The Politics of Prescription', *South Atlantic Quarterly*, 104:4, 2005, pp. 769-789 and 'The Will of the People: Notes Towards a Dialectical Voluntarism', *Radical Philosophy*, no. 155, 2009, pp. 17-29. See also his review essay on Alain Badiou's *Logiques des Mondes*, 'Order and Event', *New Left Review*, no. 58, 2008, pp. 97-122, as well as his assessment of Jacques Rancière's work, 'Staging Equality: On Rancière's Theocracy', *New Left Review*, no. 37, 2006, pp. 109-129.

18. I will cite in what follows from Hallward's expansive treatment of this problematic in *Absolutely Postcolonial: Writing Between the Singular and the Specific*, but for a condensed treatment see his article 'The Singular and the Specific: Recent French Philosophy', *Radical Philosophy*, no. 99, 2000, pp., 6-18.

19. Hallward, *Absolutely Postcolonial*, p. 40.

20. Hallward, *Absolutely Postcolonial*, p. 3.

21. Hallward, *Absolutely Postcolonial*, p. 50.

22. Hallward, *Absolutely Postcolonial*, p. 4.

23. Hallward, *Absolutely Postcolonial*, p. 5.

dom'[24] wherein 'we make our own history but not in circumstances of our choosing'.[25] We are 'specific to but not specified by our situation',[26] and insofar as we become specific, 'we become subjects as opposed to objects, we learn to think rather than merely recognize or represent, to the degree that we actively transcend the specified or the objectified'. For Hallward, 'the subject is nothing other than the conversion of determination into relational indetermination—without appeal to a realm of absolute indetermination or pure Creativity'.[27] Thus, 'to move from the specified to the specific, without yielding to the temptation of the singular ... is perhaps the only general goal that can be ascribed to critical theory as such'.[28]

We can see, then, exactly what is at stake when Hallward opens the critical section of his review by drawing the following line of demarcation:

> Unlike Meillassoux, I believe that the main problem with recent French philosophy has been not an excess but a deficit of genuinely relational thought.[29] From this perspective, despite its compelling originality and undeniable ingenuity, Meillassoux's resolutely absolutizing project raises a number of questions and objections.[30]

Hallward draws a line between the relational and the non-relational, between 'concretely mediated ways of thinking'[31] and 'Meillassoux's resolutely absolutizing project'. What is at stake, for Hallward, is precisely the problem of moving from the specified (principle of sufficient reason) to the specific (history), without yielding to the temptation of the singular (absolute contingency). Between the concretely mediated and the absolute, the specific and the singular, what would seem to be at stake is the difference between *dialectical materialism* and *speculative materialism*. If we seek to discern whether this line of demarcation is correctly inscribed—and thus if the stakes for thinking 'with and after Marx' are as Hallward says they are—then our question will be twofold:

What is the relation of the speculative to the specific?

1. What is the relation of speculative materialism to dialectical materialism?

2. At the crux of Meillassoux's refutation of the principle of sufficient reason and his articulation of absolute contingency is the principle of factiality (*le principe de factualité*), which states that 'to be is necessarily to be a fact'. According to Meillassoux, this is 'the only absolute necessity available to non-dogmatic speculation—the necessity for everything that is to be a fact'.[32] The principle of factiality is set against the specified, since 'to be a fact', in the lexicon of *After Finitude*, is first and foremost to be subtracted from the purview of the principle of sufficient reason. If the principle of sufficient reason demands that we not only 'account for the facts of the world by invoking this or that worldly law' but also that we 'account for why these laws are thus and not otherwise,

---

24. Hallward, *Absolutely Postcolonial*, p. 49.

25. Hallward, *Absolutely Postcolonial*, p. 5.

26. Hallward, *Absolutely Postcolonial*, p. 49.

27. Hallward, *Absolutely Postcolonial*, p. 50.

28. Hallward, *Absolutely Postcolonial*, p. 48.

29. cf. Peter Hallward, 'The One or the Other: French Philosophy Today', *Angelaki*, vol. 8, no. 2, 2003, p. 23: 'Today's French philosophers have developed a conception of singular or non-relational thought as varied and ingenious as any in the history of philosophy. The task of tomorrow's generation of thinkers may be to develop an equally resilient relational alternative'.

30. Hallward, 'Anything is Possible', p. 54.

31. Hallward, 'Anything is Possible', p. 55.

32. Meillassoux, *After Finitude*, p. 79.

and therefore account for why the world is thus and not otherwise',[33] then to be a 'fact', is to exist within a world that may be submitted to certain structural constraints ('this or that worldly law'), yet a world in which these structural constraints themselves are not *necessary*. To affirm the condition of being a fact is thus to affirm the minimal degree of contingency required to move from the specified to the specific.

But the principle of factiality does not only state that 'to be is to be a fact'; it states that 'to be is *necessarily* to be a fact'. This is evidently where Hallward and Meillassoux part ways, given the radical consequences the latter draws from this apparently modest onto-logical kernel: the necessity of contingency, hyper-chaos, absolute time. From Hallward's perspective, it would seem, the conditions of the specific are no sooner distinguished from the specified in *After Finitude* than they are dissolved into the singular. But what exactly is the relation between the singular and the specific here? As I have already argued, the necessity of contingency—'the absolute necessity of everything's non-necessity'[34]—in no way elides or evacuates the local stability of particular situations and the concretely mediated processes of relational transformation that are possible therein through the constrained freedom of rational subjects or what Hallward calls the 'dialectical voluntarism' of collective self-determination.[35] On the contrary, Chapter 4 of *After Finitude* is concerned to establish that the intelligibility of the historical—'a situation, a past, an intelligibility constrained by inherited conditions'[36]— is not dissolved by the principle of factiality.[37] The necessity of contingency in no way obviates the relational specificity of the specific. What it *does* challenge, however, is any claim that relational specificity should itself be conceived as an absolute necessity. For what is asserted by the principle of factiality is that 'those structural invariants that govern our world'[38]—such as relation per se—are necessarily exposed to the possibility of contingent alteration. That is: *the principle of factiality requires that we think relation as a fact, rather than an absolute*. It does so because it holds that structural invariants are facts—and that this is not a fact, but a necessity. So if it is relationality that constitutes the *différend* between Hallward and Meillassoux, what is at issue is not so much the relative predominance of relational or non-relational thinking in recent French philosophy but, rather, clearly demarcated questions: Can we think the structural invariants of our experience, such as relationality, as an absolute? Yes or no? Is it the case that these structural invariants are facts, or are they necessities? Is it possible to sustain the first option against absolute idealism without having to affirm that the facticity of such invariants is not itself a fact, but a necessity, and thereby having to affirm the principle of factiality?

From a position established by positing relationality as a first principle, Hallward asks how Meillassoux's principle of factiality could possibly inform any concrete process of actual change; but we might also consider the consequences of the questions

---

33. Meillassoux, *After Finitude*, p. 33. Translation modified: I have substituted 'worldly law' ('loi du monde') for Brassier's 'global law', the latter of which might be taken to imply the totalizing purview of a law. But such a totality is only demanded by the second condition of the principle of sufficient reason enumerated above, not the first.

34. Meillassoux, *After Finitude*, p. 62.

35. cf. Hallward, 'The Will of the People'.

36. Hallward, *Absolutely Postcolonial*, p. 5.

37. cf. Meillassoux, *After Finitude*, p. 92, 106.

38. Meillassoux, *After Finitude*, p. 39.

posed above for the position from which Hallward levels his critique. For although Hallward twice mentions Meillassoux's 'insistence' upon absolute contingency,[39] the argument for absolute contingency in fact follows from the demonstration of the principle of factiality that occupies Chapter 3 of *After Finitude*, and this demonstration is not a matter of insistence. Rather, it is a matter of establishing an anhypothetical principle through an indirect argument[40]—an argument that Hallward summarizes, but which he does not directly confront. For a moment, then, let's turn the tables: rather than considering Meillassoux's position from Hallward's perspective, let's consider Hallward's position from the vantage point of the principle of factiality.

It is in *Absolutely Postcolonial* that Hallward articulates a position on relationality that, in my view, continues to undergird his important essays on 'The Politics of Prescription' and 'Dialectical Voluntarism'.[41] 'It is the unconditional status of relationality itself', Hallward argues, 'that allows us to anticipate and disarm an eventual deconstruction of the specific'.[42] According to Hallward, 'there can be no question of deconstructing relation as such: the related terms only have the degree of self-identity that they have *because* they are differed and deferred through the medium of the relation itself'.[43] 'Relation', he claims, 'is not made up of anything more primitive than itself, and has no substance other than the individuals it relates;' it is 'the unchanging medium and transcendental condition of our existence'.[44] For Hallward, then, relationality qualifies as one among several 'genuine *species requirements*' which he describes in the following terms:

> certain properly basic degrees of agency, subjectivity, relationality, sexuality, identification, and so on, must all be posited as transcendental processes in this strict sense. They are transcendental to any particular human experience because no such experience would be conceivable without them (including the effort to deny them their transcendental status). And they are purely formal, contentless, for the same reason: because fully transcendental to any experience, there is nothing 'in' them to fill, orient or determine that experience in a particular way. The experience must conform to their formal requirements, but how it does so is indeed invariably specific to the situation of that experience.[45]

These species requirements are thus accorded the role of the *a priori* conditions of all possible experience described by Kant or, more broadly, of those correlational 'structural invariants' described by Meillassoux:

> invariants which may differ from one variant of correlationism to another, but whose function in every case is to provide the minimal organization of representation: principle of causality, forms of perception, logical laws, etc. These structures are fixed—I never experience their variation, and in the case of logical laws, I cannot even represent to myself their modification (thus, for example, I cannot represent to myself a being that is contradictory or non self-identical). But although these forms are fixed, they constitute a fact,

39. Hallward, 'Anything is Possible', p. 55, 57.

40. Meillassoux, *After Finitude*, p. 61: 'This proof, which could be called 'indirect' or 'refutational', proceeds not by deducing the principle from some other proposition—in which case it would no longer count as a principle—but by pointing out the inevitable inconsistency into which anyone contesting the truth of the principle is bound to fall. One establishes the principle without deducing it, by demonstrating that anyone who contests it can do so only in by pre-supposing it to be true, thereby refuting him or herself'.

41. See note 17, above.

42. Hallward, *Absolutely Postcolonial*, p. 4.

43. Hallward, *Absolutely Postcolonial*, p. 250.

44. Hallward, *Absolutely Postcolonial*, p. 252.

45. Hallward, *Absolutely Postcolonial*, p. 180.

rather than an absolute, since I cannot ground their necessity—their facticity reveals itself with the realization that they can only be described, not founded.[46]

It is this facticity of the correlation—the position maintained by Kant—that Meillassoux will absolutize in the principle of factiality,[47] against the absolutization of the correlation itself by the speculative idealist and against the fideist's limitation of reason to make room for faith. What is the situation of Hallward's 'species requirements' with regard to these positions?

According to Meillassoux, the structural invariants of correlationist philosophy cannot be founded, but only described. But Hallward does not only describe the species requirements to which he refers; he refers the question of their foundation to the empirical findings of evolutionary psychology and sociobiology. 'The nature of these transcendental requirements', he states, 'is not properly a philosophical so much as a scientific problem'. And again: 'the term 'transcendental', then, relates more to our peculiar biological history than to philosophy'.[48] The difficulty I would isolate here is not at all due to an appeal to empirical science for data concerning the development of cognitive structures and capacities; rather it arises from the effort to secure through such an appeal the 'unconditional', 'unchanging', and indeed 'ahistorical, non-contextual'[49] status of transcendental requirements 'in the strict sense', as Hallward says. The difficulty, that is to say, is precisely the sort of equivocation between levels of reflection of which Hallward accuses Meillassoux. For how are we to understand the ahistorical status of transcendental structural invariants that develop through evolutionary history? This is a question that Meillassoux directly addresses in the opening chapter of *After Finitude*, but before turning to his response we need to unpack Hallward's account in more detail.[50]

Citing the sociobiologist Robin Fox on genetically inherited structures of cultural competence, Hallward writes:

> it's not merely that the potential for culture lies in the unique biology of *homo sapiens*, any more than the general potential to learn, reason, or speak; as Fox suggests, this very biology, beginning with our unusual brain development, is itself partly the result of our 'cultural' inventions. By using tools, acting collectively, developing ever more complex forms of communication, and so on, 'man took the cultural way before he was clearly distinguishable from the [other] animals, and in consequence found himself stuck with this mode of adaptation'.[51]

While such an empirical theory might feasibly be deployed in order to account for transcultural structures of 'cultural competence'—as it is by Hallward—it cannot ground

46. Meillassoux, *After Finitude*, p. 39.

47. Meillassoux, *After Finitude*, p. 76: 'Non-metaphysical speculation', writes Meillassoux, 'proceeds in the first instance by stating that the thing-in-itself is nothing other than the facticity of the transcendental forms of representation'.

48. Hallward, *Absolutely Postcolonial*, p. 180.

49. Hallward, *Absolutely Postcolonial*, p. 253.

50. cf. Meillassoux, *After Finitude*, pp. 22-26. Meillassoux's response to the objection that his treatment of ancestrality confuses the empirical and transcendental is an addition to the English translation of *Après la Finitude*, and is not included in the original French edition. Meillassoux also adds to the English text an account of the relation of spatially and temporally distant (unperceived) phenomena to the problem of ancestrality. Compare the English text, *After Finitude* pp. 18-26 with *Après la Finitude: Essai sur la nécessité de la contingence*, Paris, Seuil, 2006, pp. 36-37.

51. Hallward, *Absolutely* Postcolonial, p. 81. Hallward cites Fox, Robin. *The Search for Society: Quest for a Biosocial Science and Morality*, New Brunswick, Rutgers University Press, 1989, p. 30.

the ahistorical, non-contextual status of those structures. It cannot do so because, as Fox argues, those structures develop in and through historical and cultural contexts of collective action. Hallward's account would require that, through such contexts, these structures became transcendental: no longer historical, no longer contextual. We develop 'ever-more complex forms of communication' prior to the clear distinction of our species, but at some point—evidently instantaneous—this development is frozen into ahistorical 'species requirements' that transcendentally ground our human capacities. 'We must depoliticize (and dehistoricize) the conditions of possibility for politics', writes Hallward in 'The Politics of Prescription'.[52] The 'species requirements' that constitute conditions of possibility for politics are not, for Hallward, historical, yet they are to be located in evolutionary history.

The contradictory nature of this argument is of a piece with the vicious circularity of the sociobiological account upon which Hallward relies—a circularity that is, in my view, symptomatic of the idealist, teleological concept of 'man' upon which that account relies. For Fox, it is already 'man' who 'took the cultural way before he was clearly distinguishable from the animals', yet it is this cultural way that results in his distinction. 'It is scarcely surprising', Fox writes in a passage cited by Hallward, 'that man continually reproduces that which produced him. He was selected to do precisely this'.[53] Man implicitly precedes his own production, in Fox's account, because 'he was selected' to reproduce his own production. Rather than critically confronting the teleological circularity of this account, Hallward attempts to evade it by subtracting species requirements absolutely from any process of development. If Hallward's account of the specific can in fact be deconstructed, it is because the unconditional status of relationality upon which it relies ('there is nothing more primitive of which it is made up'; it is 'the unchanging medium and transcendental condition of our existence') is grounded upon the ahistorical extraction of the transcendental from the empirical: that is, quite precisely, upon the non-relationality of relation as a transcendental condition. But since the development of human animals as a distinctive species is indeed specific—contextual and historical—the critical point is that the evolutionary processes through which this development occurs are incompatible with both the circularity of Fox's account and the exemption of transcendental structures from history and from context upon which Hallward relies.

Thus it is not so simple to claim, as Hallward does in his review of *After Finitude*, that 'correlationism as Meillassoux defines it is in reality an epistemological theory, one that is perfectly compatible with the insights of Darwin, Marx or Einstein'.[54] It is not simple because Kant and Husserl subtract transcendental conditions from history and from evolutionary time. Despite his appeal to evolutionary psychology and sociobiology, Hallward must do the same because it is, in fact, impossible to square the strictly ahistorical status of the transcendental with evolutionary time—unless one claims that our capacity to think the latter must be grounded upon the former, and not the other way around. But if Husserl fully assumes the consequences of this position by positing the transcendental ego as 'eternal', Hallward's effort to evade those consequences through an appeal to empirical science renders his own account contradictory, for if our 'species requirements' developed in evolutionary time then they are, precisely

---

52. Hallward, 'The Politics of Prescription', p. 783.
53. Quoted in Hallward, *Absolutely Postcolonial*, p. 81.
54. Hallward, 'Anything is Possible', p. 55.

in evolutionary time. To admit as much is to concede that they are neither ahistorical nor non-contextual, and therefore to concede that they are not properly transcendental. From a Kantian perspective such an admission is incoherent, since it would itself presuppose the very forms of intuition and categories of the understanding whose transcendental status it would depose. And indeed, Hallward resorts to such a perspective when he argues that species requirements are 'transcendental to any particular human experience because no such experience would be conceivable without them (including the effort to deny them their transcendental status)'.[55] In other words, despite his claim that the nature of transcendental requirements is not so much a philosophical problem as a scientific one, Hallward's own argument subjects the scientific theories he cites to a transcendental a priori: for Hallward any empirical account of the development of species requirements already presupposes their transcendental operation. Hence we enter into the correlationist circle. As Hallward's own account makes evident, however, that circle contains a well-known circle of its own: the problem of the genesis of transcendental conditions.

This is why, in order to break the correlationist circle into a spiral, Meillassoux opens *After Finitude* with the heuristic of the arche-fossil. And this is why he seeks to exit that spiral by establishing the non-correlational autonomy of absolute time through an intra-systemic critique of Kant, rather than exposing himself to an external critique from the latter's position. Between these tactical manoeuvres, Meillassoux directly confronts the contradiction into which I have claimed Hallward's account of the transcendental falls. Responding to the anticipated correlationist objection that his argument from the arche-fossil betrays an amphibolous conception of the relation between the empirical and the transcendental by conflating 'the objective being of bodies, which do in fact emerge and perish in time, with the conditions for the objective knowledge of the objective being of bodies, which have nothing to do with any sort of time',[56] Meillassoux argues that the consistency of transcendental idealism requires us to think the body as a "retro-transcendental' condition for the subject of knowledge'.[57] Since the subject of transcendental idealism (as opposed to that of absolute idealism) is 'indissociable from the notion of a point of view' (the localization of that subject within a world by the piecemeal process of perceptual adumbration, the horizonal limitation of perspective, etc.), that subject 'remains indissociable from its incarnation in a body'.[58] Thus the transcendental subject is 'instantiated', if not 'exemplified', by a thinking body, and the problem of ancestrality raises the question of 'the temporality of the conditions of instantiation'.[59] What Meillassoux calls 'the time of science' poses this question to philosophy; but it is indeed a philosophical, rather than a scientific question. Meillassoux's approach to this question differs from Hallward's precisely insofar as it recognizes it as a question posed to philosophy by science, and not the other way around. On this point he is in accord with Kant. But unlike Kant, Meillassoux also recognizes that 'this problem simply cannot be thought from the transcendental viewpoint because it concerns the space-time in which transcendental subjects went from not-taking-place to taking-place—and hence concerns the space-time anterior to

55. Hallward, *Absolutely Postcolonial*, p. 180.
56. Meillassoux, *After Finitude*, p. 23.
57. Meillassoux, *After Finitude*, p. 25.
58. Meillassoux, *After Finitude*, p. 25.
59. Meillassoux, *After Finitude*, p. 25.

the spatio-temporal forms of representation'.[60] In other words, what Meillassoux terms 'the paradox of manifestation' must be registered as a paradox if we are to think our way out of the contradictions entailed by both Kant's unilateral subjection of the time of science to the time of the subject and the vicious circularity of Hallward's subjection of the transcendental to the empirical under the condition of the transcendental.

We can now return to the principle of factiality. Again: Meillassoux knows perfectly well that to expose the ancestral circle within the correlationist circle only fractures these two circles in order to fuse them into a spiral, and that is why his central demonstration proceeds not through the argument from the arche-fossil, nor through mere 'insistence', but by establishing an anhypothetical principle through indirect argument. 'We must demonstrate', writes Meillassoux, 'how the facticity of the correlation, which provides the basis for the correlationist's disqualification of dogmatic idealism as well as dogmatic realism, is only conceivable on condition that one admits the absoluteness of the contingency of the given in general'.[61] The question concerns the 'invariants' of our thought and experience: of how their facticity can be defended against absolute idealism and of whether that defence requires us to think their facticity as an absolute.

So then, are the 'species requirements' upon which Hallward's account of the specific relies a fact, or a necessity? If they are a necessity, then we either concede the specific to the singular by falling into absolute idealism or we concede the specific to the specified by falling into naturalist determinism. But if they are a fact, how are we to think the possibility upon which their facticity rests: the possibility of their alteration? As Meillassoux argues, and as Hallward himself points out, we cannot do so within the confines of the correlation.[62] When Hallward asks 'what it means' to say 'that we might suddenly cease to breath oxygen or suffer the effects of gravity', the force of his question rests upon this prior impossibility—the impossibility of affirming the rational coherence of such a possibility from within the structural invariants of our experience. But this is precisely why the only way to properly think the facticity of the correlation—the fact that these invariants could themselves change—is by thinking it as an absolute: as a datum which can be affirmed by reason, but which is beyond the purview of the correlation. When Meillassoux makes this 'resolutely absolutizing'[63] move, his resolution stems from a desire to defend facticity against its absorption into absolute idealism—the philosophy of the singular par excellence—and also to prevent facticity from buttressing the fideist's abdication of reason. Thus, to absolutize facticity does not merely entail logical possibilities, but logical consequences. Meillassoux does not simply argue that we 'can' think absolutely contingency, but that we must. So if one rejects Meillassoux's articulation of the logical necessities stemming from the relation between transcendental idealism, absolute idealism, and dogmatic realism, it is necessary to indicate precisely where Meillassoux's argument in Chapter 3 of *After Finitude* goes astray and precisely how it is possible to defend the facticity of the correlation without appealing to an absolute.

---

60. Meillassoux, *After Finitude*, p. 26.

61. Meillassoux, *After Finitude*, p. 54.

62. Again, Hallward states that 'no [human] experience would be conceivable' without transcendental requirements (Hallward, *Absolutely Postcolonial*, p. 180). And from this perspective, we cannot even think the factical status of such requirements by acknowledging that they—and therefore 'human experience'—could have *not* evolved in the first place, since we cannot coherently think the *evolution* of the transcendental (as 'ahistorical, non-contextual') at all, neither as necessary nor contingent.

63. Hallward, 'Anything is Possible', p. 54.

Hallward and Meillassoux share the same philosophical enemy—a metaphysics 'invariably characterized by the fact that it hypostatizes some mental, sentient, or vital term'. Meillassoux succinctly lists the representatives of such a singularizing metaphysics as follows: 'the Leibnizian monad; Schelling's Nature, or the objective subject-object; Hegelian Mind; Schopenhauer's Will; the Will (or Wills) to Power in Nietzsche; perception loaded with memory in Bergson; Deleuze's Life, etc'.[64] As we have seen, however, Hallward's own account also has to hypostatize relation as an 'unchanging medium'. Attempting to guard against its becoming-singular, Hallward holds that 'the condition of relation is itself transcendental with all specificity and indifferent to any attempt at singularization (it is impossible to 'become-transcendental')'.[65] But that impossibility is exactly what must have taken place at some point in evolutionary history according to Hallward's account, which, by hypostatizing a developmental process into a transcendental unconditional, implicitly relies upon its singularization (by his own criteria). It also implicitly relies upon an absolute time, in which species requirements developed. If, according to Meillassoux, the necessary facticity of the correlation requires us to think that absolute time may not obey the relational structure of the given, such a time is no more 'singular' in that sense than the non-relational ('non-contextual') status of relationality itself in Hallward's account of the ahistorical conditions of possibility for the specific. Where Meillassoux installs the singular at the level of absolute contingency and absolute time, Hallward installs the singular in the emergence of the very capacity (a human capacity) to move from the specified to the specific.[66] This is why it is illuminating to consider the consequences of Meillassoux's argumentative tactics for Hallward's own position. In my view, the contradictions inherent to Hallward's account of species requirements indicate the futility of attempting to ground the subjective capacity to move from the specified to the specific upon the transcendental status of correlational structures rather than upon the facticity of those structures. The central argument of *After Finitude* is that in order to be thought at all, such facticity must be thought as an absolute. The very possibility of the specific, then—the factical non-necessity of that which is the case—requires us to think the necessary contingency of the structural invariants of our experience.

As I have hoped to make clear, there is an insuperable conflict within Hallward's account, in Absolutely Postcolonial, of the conditions of possibility for the specific—a conflict due to the fundamental incompatibility of that account with the Kantian epistemology it both relies upon and oversteps. But if it is correct to argue that the absolute status of facticity (the necessity of contingency) does not undermine the dimension of political practice theorized by Hallward in his work on prescription and the will, then what we require is an articulation of the singular and the specific that does not dissolve either one into the other. According to Meillassoux's speculative materialism, the specific is necessarily exposed to some singularity. But exposure to the possibility of a singular instance does not foreclose or absorb the domain of the specific. This is what distinguishes speculative materialism from any form of subjective idealism. What Meillassoux calls 'speculation' is concerned with 'the non-factual essence of fact as such', which Meillassoux designates as the domain of his investigation.[67] By def-

---

64. Meillassoux, *After Finitude*, p. 37.

65. Hallward, *Absolutely Postcolonial*, p. 330.

66. 'The point is not that the human being is a political animal', states Hallward in 'The Politics of Prescription', 'but that the human is capable of doing more than any sort of being' (p. 783).

67. Meillassoux, *After Finitude*, p. 79.

inition such an investigation has nothing to say about the domain of what Hallward calls the specific. But that is precisely why it is not necessary to disjoin the speculative and the specific: they already designate distinct domains of investigation. What is necessary is to accord them their distinction, to acknowledge that there is no real conflict between them, and then to think them both according to their differential exigencies.

We can therefore grant the last sentence of Hallward's review without according it much polemical force: 'A critique of metaphysical necessity and an appeal to transfinite mathematics will not provide, on their own, the basis upon which we might renew a transformative materialism'.[68] Though this is by no means all that *After Finitude* has to offer, that is not to say that everything it does have to offer is 'enough' to think the speculative and the specific together. That is a task for which we need both Meillassoux and Hallward—and for which we need to think the relationship between their discrepant domains of investigation. And that is also why, in order to think the contribution of speculative materialism to the renewal of a transformative materialism, we need to consider the part it plays in a battle that—for Engels, for Lenin, for Althusser—defines the philosophical field per se: the struggle of materialism against idealism. Having thus attempted to elucidate the stakes of our first question, concerning the relationship of the speculative and the specific, we are now in a position to address our second: what is the relationship of speculative materialism to dialectical materialism?

MATERIALISM AND EMPIRIO-CRITICISM

As Ray Brassier has pointed out, *After Finitude* revisits and recasts Lenin's attack on the 'correlativist' and 'fideist' orientation of post-Kantian philosophy in *Materialism and Empirio-Criticism*.[69] And indeed, there is no better text than Lenin's for reminding oneself of the degree to which Marxism should be incompatible with correlationism (despite the impostures of historicism). But to properly account for the precise relationship between politics and philosophy that links Meillassoux's and Lenin's texts, we need to consider the mediation of that link by Althusser's reformulation of dialectical materialism in 'Lenin and Philosophy' (1968) and the 'Philosophy Course for Scientists' (1967)[70]: a reformulation that drew extensively upon Lenin's intervention in materialist philosophy and which to my mind remains fundamental.

Before turning to Althusser, I should say that there will be no space here to offer a critical assessment of his work—to either defend or take issue with it on particular points. My goal is descriptive: to articulate the sense in which Meillassoux's project is consistent with the reformulation of dialectical materialism that we find in Althusser and thereby with a strain of 'Marxist philosophy' for which Lenin's intervention in philosophical materialism is a key text (however unsatisfactory one might find its local arguments). The point of this manoeuvre is thus to convert a question about Meillassoux into a question about Althusser: about the manner in which his theory of dialectical materialism allows us to think, 'with and after Marx', the concretely mediated manner in which philosophy relates to politics. Although shifting the question in this way is a limited gesture—insofar as I cannot fully unpack my own position on Althusser's controversial theory—it is intended to transform the frame of Hallward's critique

---

68. Hallward, 'Anything is Possible', p. 57.

69. See Ray Brassier, *Nihil Unbound: Enlightenment and Extinction*, London, Palgrave, 2007, pp. 246-247.

70. Louis Althusser, 'Lenin and Philosophy', trans. Ben Brewster, in *Philosophy and the Spontaneous Ideology of the Scientists*, London, Verso, 1990, pp. 167-202; Althusser, 'Philosophy and the Spontaneous Philosophy of the Scientists'.

by situating his question about *After Finitude*, a question concerning the relation of philosophy and politics, *inside* the Marxist tradition. My goal is certainly not to argue that Meillassoux is a 'Marxist philosopher', since it is not his own motives or commitments that are at issue here. Rather, my goal is to offer a brief account of how *After Finitude* could be understood to contribute to a certain tradition—indeed, a canonical tradition—of what Althusser called 'Marxist philosophy'.

Let's quickly review Althusser's theses in 'Lenin and Philosophy' (1968) and his 'Philosophy Course for Scientists' (1967): philosophy has no history and it has no object, insofar as the philosophical field is defined by a perpetual struggle between materialism and idealism. Philosophical practice consists in formulating theses that draw lines of demarcation between positions within this field. Awareness of the immersion of this practical operation within a theoretico-political conjuncture is the minimal condition of dialectical materialism. Whereas historical materialism intervenes scientifically in politics (through the economic analysis of class relations within the mode of production), dialectical materialism intervenes politically in the sciences. Scientific practice is conditioned by ideology, and political practice in philosophy consists in the partisan defence of the materialist 'spontaneous ideology of the scientists' (SPS1) against its idealist counterpart (SPS2), by which SPS1 is 'massively dominated'.[71] Philosophy intervenes politically—it practices politics—only by intervening in the relation of science to ideology.[72] Thus Marxism entails 'not a (new) philosophy of praxis, but a (new) practice of philosophy':

> This new practice of philosophy can transform philosophy, and in addition it can to some extent *assist* in the transformation of the world. Assist only, for it is not theoreticians, scientists or philosophers, nor is it 'men', who make history—but the 'masses', i.e. the classes allied in a single class struggle.[73]

For Althusser, it is not dialectical materialism but rather historical materialism which informs us of this last point. That is to say, the discourse which investigates the conditions under which the world might be transformed by the masses is not Marxist philosophy but Marxist science: Marxian political economy, 'the science of history'. The role accorded to dialectical materialism, or Marxist philosophy, is a defence of the materialism of science per se against its 'exploitation' by idealism.[74] The upshot of this theory is that to the degree one demands a directly political vocation for philosophy, one both undervalues the role of political economy and fails to think the relation between philosophy and politics dialectically.

Althusser offers his most precise definition of dialectical materialism in a 1965 essay, 'Theory, Theoretical Practice and Theoretical Formation: Ideology and Ideological Struggle':

In dialectical materialism, it can very schematically be said that it is *materialism* which represents the aspect of *theory*, and *dialectics* which represents the aspect of method. But each of these terms includes the other. *Materialism* expresses the effective conditions of the practice that produces knowledge—specifically: (1) the *distinction between*

---

71. Althusser, 'Philosophy and the Spontaneous Philosophy of the Scientists', p. 134.

72. Nor does philosophy evade the problem of its own distinction from ideology: on the contrary, it perpetually practices and produces that distinction within (rather than from) the conjunctural field. For a clear example of how such practice *works*, see the first lecture of Althusser's Course for Scientists, 'Philosophy and the Spontaneous Philosophy of the Scientists', pp. 73-100.

73. Althusser, 'Lenin and Philosophy', p. 201.

74. Althusser, 'Lenin and Philosophy', p. 197.

the real and its knowledge (distinction of reality), correlative of a correspondence (adequacy) between knowledge and its object (correspondence of knowledge); and (2) *the primacy of the real over its knowledge, or the primacy of being over thought*. Nonetheless, these principles themselves are not 'eternal' principles, but the principles of the *historical nature of the process in which knowledge is produced*. That is why materialism is called *dialectical*: dialectics, which expresses the relation that theory maintains with its object, expresses this relation not as a relation of two simply distinct terms but as a relation within a process of transformation, thus of real production.[75]

It would be no exaggeration to say that both the structural articulation and the argumentative method of *After Finitude* adhere directly to these determinations—or better, that they emerge from the exigencies of these codeterminations.

Note that the first of Althusser's materialist criteria—itself double—in no way challenges the program of transcendental idealism: distinction between the real and its knowledge (noumena/phenomena); correspondence of knowledge and its object (synthesis of the manifold by forms of intuition and categories of the understanding). The materialist problematic, however, is how to meet that double epistemological exigency while rigorously meeting the ontological demand of Althusser's criteria: '*the primacy of the real over its knowledge, or the primacy of being over thought*'. Meillassoux's strategy is thus to begin with this crux in Chapter 1 of *After Finitude*, by showing how the problem of the arche-fossil exposes the impossibility of properly affirming the primacy of being over thought from within the correlationist dispensation (that is, of properly affirming the *chronological anteriority* of being over the *logical anteriority* of thought). The difficulty for the materialist then becomes how to meet the ontological criterion of *primacy* while meeting the double epistemological criteria of *distinction* and *adequacy*. Doing so involves moving from the heuristic of the arche-fossil to a refutation of the correlationist, who either rejects the order of primacy (absolute idealism) or covertly undermines its proper sense (transcendental idealism). The effect of this refutation is to produce a line of demarcation between materialism and idealism.

The method by which Meillassoux performs this refutation over the course of Chapters 2 and 3 is 'dialectical' in precisely the sense articulated by Althusser. He first 'accounts for the historical nature of the process in which knowledge is produced' by diagnosing the complicity of fideist correlationism with the 'postmodern' return of the religious. He thereby establishes the most pertinent historical condition of his philosophical practice through an analysis of the theoretical-ideological conjuncture (a conjuncture, for example, in which so-called 'constructivist' epistemologies of science are routinely deployed by the religious right against evidence of global warming or in favour of creationist 'alternatives' to Darwin's theory evolution). Meillassoux then takes up his philosophy's relation to that conjuncture as a 'process of transformation' by working within the positions of his opponents, gauging the implications of those positions for each other until he locates the weakest link in the system of their relationships and then demarcating the stake inherent to that weakness. Having done so, he draws the consequences of taking any one of several possible sides on two precise questions: Is the correlation itself contingent or not? Is its contingency itself contingent, or is it necessary? The consequences that follow from a taking of sides vis-à-vis these questions

---

75. Louis Althusser, 'Theory, Theoretical Practice and Theoretical Formation: Ideology and Ideological Struggle', trans. James H. Kavanagh, in *Philosophy and the Spontaneous Philosophy of the Scientists*, London, Verso, 1990, p. 9.

are thus consequences inherent to the conjuncture, drawn through an assessment of the relational field of forces therein. The import of Meillassoux's 'anhypothetical' argumentative procedure is that it does not simply posit philosophical principles in an axiomatic fashion and then draw the consequences[76]; on the contrary, it marks an acknowledgement that any and all philosophical hypotheses are already immersed in the historicity of their development and the conjunctural field within which one has to take a position. Indeed, it would be difficult to imagine a more exact demonstration of philosophical practice as it is defined by Althusser, on the model of Lenin's attack on his correlationist contemporaries, than Meillassoux's anhypothetical demonstration of the principle of factiality in Chapter 3 of *After Finitude*.

Meillassoux then returns—in Chapters 4 and 5—to the materialist upshot of this dialectical procedure: having produced a line of demarcation between materialism and idealism through the relation between correlationist positions (and through their ideological entailments). How can we now affirm, from the side of materialism, both the distinction of the real from knowledge and the adequacy of knowledge to its object while properly recognizing the primacy of being over thought? This question formulates the conditions for the absolutization of mathematical discourse outlined in the final two chapters of Meillassoux's book: 'what is mathematizable'—such as the arche-fossil's evidence of the primacy of being over thought—'cannot be reduced to a correlate of thought'[77] (distinction) and thus mathematical physics manifests 'thought's capacity to think what there is whether thought exists or not'[78] (adequacy). In other words, the mathematization of experimental science enables the adequation of our thought to the distinction of the real. And, most pertinently for the materialist criteria outlined by Althusser, it enables us to adequately think what there was before thought: for Meillassoux, it is the mathematical formalization of empirical science that enables the adequation of thought to the distinction of a real which is prior to thought.

What Meillassoux thus offers in *After Finitude* is not only a speculative materialism but a rigorous effort to fulfil the conditions of a properly dialectical materialism. Where the text is at its most argumentatively 'abstract'—in its demonstration of the principle of factiality—it is at its most dialectical. And where it claims allegiance to 'an in-itself that is Cartesian, and no longer just Kantian'[79]—one articulated by mathematical formalism—it does so in the name of a materialism whose requirements, outlined by Althusser, are more difficult to hold together than one might like to imagine. Should it seem counterintuitive that Meillassoux finds it necessary to enlist such weapons as absolute contingency in the dialectical defence of such a materialism, we might concede that our intuition is an unreliable guide in such matters—especially when it comes to the results and operations of science.

It is through their discrepant approaches to the results and operations of science that we have to think the complex relation of *After Finitude* to Lenin's *Materialism and Empirio-Criticism*. Meillassoux's project is closest to Lenin's in its unabashed defence of the literalism of scientific statements, or what Althusser would call the spontaneous materialism of the scientist: a 'belief in the real, external and material existence of the object of scientific knowledge' and a 'belief in the existence and objectivity of the scientific

---

76. This marks one significant divergence in Meillassoux's philosophical method from that of his mentor, Alain Badiou.

77. Meillassoux, *After Finitude*, p. 117.

78. Meillassoux, *After Finitude*, p. 116.

79. Meillassoux, *After Finitude*, p. 111.

knowledges that permit knowledge of this object'.[80] Lenin's target in the section of *Materialism and Empirio-Criticism* titled 'Did Nature Exist Prior to Man?' is precisely that of Meillassoux's chapter on ancestrality: the post-Kantian presumption that we can intelligibly extend a 'chain of experience' of possible objects of perception through a time-series prior to the evolution of perception per se.[81] This 'idealist sophistry' is glossed by Lenin as follows: 'only if I make the admission (that man could be the observer of an epoch at which he did not exist), one absurd and contradictory to natural science, can I make the ends of my philosophy meet'.[82] Like Lenin, whose goal in *Materialism and Empirio-Criticism* was to 'liberate the realm of objects from the yoke of the subject',[83] Meillassoux seeks to defend the realist sense of scientific statements against the juridical ideology of critical idealism, which 'subjects the sciences and scientific practice to a preliminary question that already contains the answer which it innocently claims to be seeking'.[84] It is thus the 'literal' significance of science's ancestral statements that the first chapter of *After Finitude* defends against their inversion by correlationists. 'An ancestral statement', Meillassoux declares, 'only has sense if its literal sense is also its ultimate sense',[85] and this literal sense amounts to both an 'irremediable realism' (which maintains against transcendental idealism that 'either this statement has a realist sense, and only a realist sense, or it has no sense at all')[86] and a 'materialism of matter' (which maintains against subjective idealism that 'there is nothing living or willing in the inorganic realm').[87]

Unlike Lenin, however, Meillassoux does not endorse the literal sense of scientific statements as a 'direct connection of the mind with the external world',[88] but rather as a discourse enabled by mathematical formalization. That is, Meillassoux accepts Bachelard's dictate that 'the world in which we think is not the world in which we live'.[89] Meillassoux endorses the 'literal sense' of scientific statements only on the condition that we attend to the powerful counter-intuitions that they harbor, attending to the paradox of manifestation with which the scientific enunciation of ancestral statements confronts anyone who thinks through their consequences. For his part, Lenin has little to say about an absolute contingency inherent to absolute time, stigmatized by Hallward as 'a quintessentially 'divine' power'.[90] How are we to consider the relation of this aspect of Meillassoux's argument to his defence of scientific materialism?

If we are to take this problem seriously we have to consider it dialectically, by thinking through a methodological practice of philosophy. For Meillassoux, the argument for absolute contingency is not a matter of 'belief'[91]; nor does it follow, as Hall-

---

80. Althusser, 'Philosophy and the Spontaneous Philosophy of the Scientists', p. 133.

81. cf. Section Six of the Antinomy of Pure Reason, 'Transcendental idealism as the key to solving the cosmological dialectic', Immanuel Kant, *Critique of Pure Reason*, trans. Paul Guyer and Allen W. Wood, Cambridge, Cambridge University Press, 1998, A491/B519—A497/B525, esp. A495/B523.

82. V.I. Lenin, *Materialism and Empirio-Criticism*, Vol. XIII, *Collected Works of V.I. Lenin*, New York, International Publishers, 1927, p. 67.

83. Lenin, *Materialism and Empirio-Criticism*, p. 61.

84. Althusser, 'Philosophy and the Spontaneous Philosophy of the Scientists', p. 128.

85. Meillassoux, *After Finitude*, p. 17 (original italics).

86. Meillassoux, *After Finitude*, p. 17.

87. Meillassoux, *After Finitude*, p. 38.

88. Lenin, *Materialism and Empirio-Criticism*, p. 31.

89. Gaston Bachelard, *The Philosophy of No*, trans. G.C. Waterston, New York, Orion Press, 1968, p. 95.

90. Hallward, 'Anything is Possible', p. 56.

91. Hallward, 'Anything is Possible', p. 56.

ward asserts, from the ontological radicalization of Hume's problem of induction found in Chapter 4 of *After Finitude*.[92] As I have argued, it follows from the logical consequences of the absolutization of facticity arrived at in Chapter 3, which itself follows from an indirect demonstration based on the competing claims of discrepant correlationist positions.[93] In other words, according to Meillassoux's argument, the affirmation of a hyper-Chaos 'for which nothing would seem to be impossible'[94] is the sole absolute which it is possible to salvage from correlationism—and therefore the sole means of refuting the latter's limitation of reason to make room for faith. The rationalist delineation of absolute contingency's structural position within a balance of philosophical forces follows from the dialectical recognition that the effects of philosophical arguments—and of their mutual interpellations—are irreversible. It follows from a commitment, in Althusserian terms, to the fact that 'there is a history in philosophy rather than a history of philosophy: a history of the displacement of the indefinite repetition of a null trace whose effects are real'.[95] The principle of factiality registers a displacement of the 'null trace' dividing materialism and idealism, and the necessity of thinking an absolute contingency inherent to absolute time registers the fact that the displacement of this trace has real effects in philosophy. This displacement and these effects result from nothing other than an immersion in the restrictive dialectical exigencies of correctly reinscribing the line of demarcation between materialism and idealism drawn by Lenin. For Lenin, the exact placement of this line is subject to conjunctural shifts, even as the philosophical stakes of its delineation are absolutely determinate:

> the sole 'property' of matter—with the recognition of which materialism is vitally connected—is the property of being objective reality, of existing outside of our cognition …the electron is as inexhaustible as the atom, nature is infinite, but it exists infinitely; and only this categorical, unconditional recognition of its existence beyond the consciousness and sensation of man distinguishes dialectical materialism from relativist agnosticism and idealism.[96]

It is this *generic* principle of materialism—the existence of matter 'beyond the consciousness and sensation of man'—that the principle of factiality seeks to buttress by novel means, through a counter-intuitive argumentative strategy responsive to the effects of null traces whose displacements are refractory to common sense. The *absolute* character of time and contingency for which *After Finitude* argues should thus be understood as fully consistent with its *dialectical* method.

---

92. Hallward, 'Anything is Possible', p. 55: 'The actual target of Meillassoux's critique of metaphysics is the Leibnizian principle of sufficient reason. He dispatches it, as we've seen, with a version of Hume's argument: we cannot rationally demonstrate an ultimate reason for the being of being; there is no primordial power or divine providence that determines being or the meaning of being to be a certain way. What Meillassoux infers from this critique of metaphysical necessity, however, is the rather more grandiose assertion that there is no cause or reason for *anything* to be the way it is'. Hallward's take on the structural articulation of Meillassoux's argument is perhaps influenced by Meillassoux's article, 'Potentiality and Virtuality', in which Meillassoux offers a compressed version of *After Finitude*'s fourth chapter in isolation from the larger argument of the book. In considering the stakes of Meillassoux's arguments however, it seems crucial to recognize that these *follow from their structure*—and it is therefore crucial to attend strictly to the order of reasons as it unfolds in *After Finitude*. See also Meillassoux, Quentin. 'Potentiality and Virtuality', in this volume.

93. cf. Meillassoux, *After Finitude*, p. 62: 'Only unreason can be thought as eternal, because only unreason can be thought as at once anhypothetical *and* absolute. Accordingly, we can say that it is possible to *demonstrate the absolute necessity of everything's non-necessity*. In other words, it is possible to establish, through indirect demonstration, the absolute necessity of the contingency of everything'.

94. Meillassoux, *After Finitude*, p. 64.

95. Althusser, 'Lenin and Philosophy', p. 197.

96. Lenin, *Materialism and Empirio-Criticism*, p. 220.

Similarly, the defence of scientific materialism inherent to this philosophical strategy inheres precisely where we might least expect to find it: in its rejection of the principle of the uniformity of nature. Ray Brassier helps to clarify the relation, on this point, between Meillassoux's position and Karl Popper's anti-inductivist epistemology of science.[97] Popper defends the invariance of natural laws as a methodological rule, but rejects the principle of the uniformity of nature as a metaphysical interpretation of that rule. According to this position, any absolute affirmation of the invariance of physical law falls afoul of the problem of induction, and thus threatens the conceptual validity of the empirical operations of science. Thus Popper 'abstain[s] from arguing for or against faith in the existence of regularities'.[98] For Meillassoux, however, this abstention would itself constitute a threat to science, insofar as the limitation upon thought that it imposes would concede that which lies beyond reason to piety, and thus tolerate a 'seesawing between metaphysics and fideism'.[99] Even if science must remain indifferent to philosophical legislation concerning the invariance of physical law, any effort to guard such questions against rational inquiry remains deleterious insofar as such abdications of reason only serve to 'resuscitate religiosity'.[100] Since philosophy cannot absolutely secure the uniformity of nature for science—and since science has no need of such security—the role of philosophy is thus to foreclose the metaphysical/theological appropriation of the question by refuting the basis of that appropriation: by showing, through rational argument, that we cannot secure the absolute uniformity of nature because it is necessary that such uniformity is contingent. A speculative demonstration of the absolute contingency of uniformity in nature would thus function as a bulwark, in philosophy, against idealism and spiritualism: against the (Kantian) pretence of philosophy to rationally ground the rules of scientific practice, against the (Cartesian/Leibnizian) assertion of a metaphysical guarantee of natural uniformity, and against the fideist abdication of the question of uniformity to 'faith'. Science does not need philosophy in order to dispose of its rules or to inform us of their ground; but philosophy can aid the operations of science by defending it 'epistemological obstacles'[101]: against its subtle exploitation by idealism and against the predations of religion.

If there is no contradiction, then, but rather a relation of positive reinforcement between Meillassoux's defence of absolute contingency and the fundamental role that Althusser accords to dialectical materialism—the defence of the materialist tendency of scientific practice against its domination by idealism and spiritualism—one can hardly deny that this defence is more complex, more counter-intuitive, and ultimately more persuasive in *After Finitude* than in *Materialism and Empirio-Criticism*. Whereas Meillassoux, for example, reinscribes the distinction between primary and secondary qualities, Lenin holds that there is no 'inherent incompatibility between the outer world and our sense perceptions of it',[102] that 'perceptions give us correct impressions of things' by which 'we directly know objects themselves'.[103] Again, however, Meillassoux's tactics on

97. See Brassier, *Nihil Unbound*, pp. 247-248. cf. Karl Popper, *The Logic of Scientific Discovery*, London, Routledge, 2002, pp. 250-251. As Brassier points out, Meillassoux's own interpretation of Popper's position on this matter is contentious. cf. Meillassoux, *After Finitude*, pp. 133-134, n. 2.

98. Popper, *The Logic of Scientific Discovery*, p. 250.

99. Meillassoux, *After Finitude*, p. 82.

100. cf. Meillassoux, *After Finitude*, p. 82.

101. cf. Gaston Bachelard, *The Formation of the Scientific Mind*, Manchester, Clinamen, 2002.

102. Lenin, *Materialism and Empirio-Criticism*, p. 83.

103. Lenin, *Materialism and Empirio-Criticism*, p. 81.

this point affirm the self-evidence of science—rather than of common sense—by allowing for discrepancies between the scientific image and the manifest image, and thus asserting that it is mathematical physics which provides us with the knowledge of the real that Lenin accords to the senses. Lenin's goal is the same as Meillassoux's: to defend both the 'distinction of reality' and what Althusser terms the 'correspondence of knowledge' while rigorously maintaining the primacy of being over thought. But while Lenin fails to adequately grasp the formidable difficulties that these exigencies impose upon anyone who would meet them after Kant, it is a sober assessment of these difficulties to which the counter-intuitions of *After Finitude* attest.

It is on these grounds that we can align *After Finitude* with Althusser's 'philosophical "dream"' of a text that could complete and correct the program of Marxist philosophy undertaken by Lenin:

> If it is true, as so many signs indicate, that today the lag of Marxist philosophy can in part be overcome, doing so will not only cast light on the past, but also perhaps transform the future. In this transformed future, justice will be done equitably to all those who had to live in the contradiction of political urgency and philosophical lag. Justice will be done to one of the greatest: to Lenin. Justice: his philosophical work will then be perfected. Perfected, i.e. completed and corrected. We surely owe this service and this homage to the man who was lucky enough to be born in time for politics, but unfortunate enough to be born too early for philosophy. After all, who chooses his own birthdate?[104]

In order to grasp the extent to which *After Finitude* fulfils this Althusserian prophecy we can review, in tandem, Lenin's and Meillassoux's treatments of the problem of ancestrality.[105] But in order to understand why this dream is nonetheless just a dream, as Althusser immediately acknowledges, one has only to read Hallward's account of the recent political history of Haiti.[106] There will never be a time at which we do not live in the contradiction of political urgency and philosophical lag, and this contradiction is itself the urgency from which Hallward's defence of the dimension of the specific stems.

One might situate the work of Hallward and Meillassoux with respect to this contradiction—that is, with respect to Marxist philosophy, to 'thinking with and after Marx'—by aligning their projects with two broadly Leninist legacies: the task of aligning revolutionary theory and revolutionary praxis, and the task of defending scientific materialism against idealism and spiritualism. Part of the task of a properly transformative materialism, I would argue, is to think the compossibility of those projects, rather than exacerbating their severance. If Meillassoux transforms Lenin's early philosophical work on behalf of dialectical materialism, and if Hallward orients contemporary thought toward Lenin's political urgency, then it is only insofar as their projects 'correct' one another—adjust one another without cancellation—that they can orient us within the lived contradiction of the present tense.

---

104. Althusser, 'Lenin and Philosophy', p. 185.
105. cf. Lenin, *Materialism and Empirio-Criticism*, pp. 52-62 and Meillassoux, *After Finitude*, pp. 1-27.
106. Hallward, *Damming the Flood*.

12

Capitalism and the Non-Philosophical Subject[1]

Nick Srnicek

'The real problem is not how to intervene in the world of philosophy, such as it supposedly subsists in-itself, or how to transform it from within. The problem is how to use philosophy so as to effect a real transformation of the subject in such a way as to allow it to break the spell of its bewitchment by the world and enable it to constitute itself through a struggle with the latter'.[2]
—François Laruelle

After being stuck within the self-imposed limits of discourse, subjectivity, and culture for far too long, through this collection it is clear that continental philosophy is at last making a push away from the artificial constraints of correlationism[3]—the presupposition that being and thought must necessarily be reciprocally related. One of the main themes running throughout all of these diverse thinkers is a fierce desire to break through the finitude of anthropomorphism and finally move away from the myopic and narcissistic tendencies of much recent philosophy. In particular, the non-philosophical movement assembled within the work of François Laruelle and Ray Brassier has examined the way in which the form of philosophy has continually idealized the immanence of the Real by making it reciprocally dependent upon the philosophical system which purports to, at last, grasp it. In contrast to philosophies which aim at the Real, non-philosophy provides the most intriguing conceptual tools to begin thinking 'in accordance with' the Real.[4] However, while the undeniably useful, in-

1. My sincere thanks goes out to Kieran Aarons, Taylor Adkins, Ray Brassier, and Ben Woodard for providing invaluable assistance and criticism during the formulation of this paper. An earlier, slightly different, version of this essay was published in *Pli: The Warwick Journal of Philosophy*, no. 20, 2009.

2. François Laruelle, 'What Can Non-Philosophy Do?', *Angelaki*, vol. 8, no. 2, 2003, p. 179.

3. For a concise and excellent outlining of 'correlationism', see: Quentin Meillassoux, *After Finitude: An Essay on the Necessity of Contingency*, trans. Ray Brassier, New York, Continuum, 2008.

4. It should be made explicit here that we will not be entering into a discussion of alternative readings of Laruelle. For our purposes, it is Brassier who has made clear the realist implications of Laruelle and so this essay will focus solely on Brassier's reading of Laruelle. There are two main differences between Laruelle's and Brassier's work. The first is that Brassier refuses the universal scope that Laruelle attributes to philosophical Decision. The second can be seen in their respective identifications of radical immanence—whereas Laruelle will end up privileging the subject Man, Brassier will instead argue that real immanence is of the object *qua* being-nothing. See: Ray Brassier, *Nihil Unbound: Enlightenment and Extinction*, New York,

teresting, and important philosophical work that has been done by non-philosophical thinkers is significant in itself, there is nonetheless a notable absence so far when it comes to issues of subjectivity and politics. Laruelle's own works on Marxism have been largely formalistic and unconcerned with practical or ontic politics. Brassier, on the other hand, has acknowledged the importance of politics in a number of essays, but has not yet developed a systematic account of how non-philosophy changes our relation to everyday politics. The risk in the meantime, however, is that the multi-faceted work of these thinkers appears to outsiders as simply an interesting, but ultimately useless theoretical venture. This is especially pertinent considering the radically nihilistic project of Brassier—one which could easily be taken to eliminate the very possibility of politics through its welding together of the implications of cosmological annihilation, eliminative materialism, non-philosophy, and the nihilistic drive of the Enlightenment project.[5] So the question becomes, what sort of insights can non-philosophy offer that have not already been given by deconstruction, psychoanalysis, feminism, or Marxism? It is the aim of this paper to begin to answer these types of questions, beginning by first examining non-philosophy and its particular type of subject in more depth.[6] We will then see how the self-sufficiency of Deleuze and Guattari's capitalist socius can be opened up through a non-Decisional approach, and finally we will develop some preliminary thoughts on what non-philosophy can provide for a political project.

Prior to beginning this project, it will undoubtedly be of use to first examine the rudiments of non-philosophy as articulated by Brassier and Laruelle. The near-complete absence of Laruelle's work in English makes it a widely overlooked—although increasingly less so—position in the English-speaking world. To add to this linguistic divide is the sheer difficulty of Laruelle's writing and the intricacy of his project. In this regards, Brassier and John Mullarkey[7] have provided an admirable service in their exporting of this French thinker to the English-speaking world. In addition, Brassier has also made his idiosyncratic reconstruction of Laruelle available online.[8] With that easily attainable and comprehensive resource available, we feel justified in limiting our discussion of Laruelle here to only the most pertinent points.

NON-PHILOSOPHY

Non-philosophy, in its most basic sense, is an attempt to limit philosophy's pretensions in the name of the Real of radical immanence. It is an attempt to shear immanence of any constitutive relation with the transcendences of thought, language, or any other form of ideality, thereby revealing the Real's absolute determining power—independently-of and indifferently-to any reciprocal relation with ideality. It is true that numerous philosophies have proclaimed their intentions to achieve immanence, with a number of them going to great lengths to eschew all ideality and reach a properly immanent and real-

---

Palgrave Macmillan, 2007, pp. 127-38.

5. Brassier has elsewhere suggested that his defence of nihilism is in part a response to the theologization of politics that has become popular in continental circles (Emmanuel Levinas and Jacques Derrida being two exemplars of this trend). Also see: Dominique Janicaud, et. al., *Phenomenology and The 'Theological Turn': The French Debate*, trans. Bernard Prusak, New York, Fordham University Press, 2000.

6. Laruelle has described this subject as 'the Stranger', while Brassier has preferred to describe it as an 'Alien-subject' evoking the radical alterity which science fiction has attempted to attain.

7. John Mullarkey, *Post-Continental Philosophy: An Outline*, New York, Continuum, 2007.

8. Ray Brassier, 'Alien Theory: The Decline of Materialism in the Name of Matter', unpublished doctoral thesis, University of Warwick, 2001. A copy of this dissertation can be found here: <http://www.cinestatic.com/trans-mat/>.

ist beginning. What Laruelle reveals, however, is that all these previous attempts have been hindered—not by their content, which is overtly materialist, but rather by their very form of philosophizing. It is this form which Laruelle gives the name of Decision.[9] Even materialist philosophies are turned into idealisms by Decision making them reliant on a synthesis constituted by and through thought. Put simply, through Decision, philosophy has continually objectified the Real within its own self-justified terms.

Decision is the constitutive self-positing and self-giving gesture of philosophy, and one which invariably (and problematically) makes philosophy circular and reciprocally constitutive of the Real. In its simplest form, Decision consists of three elements: (1) a presupposed empirical datum—the conditioned; (2) a posited a priori faktum—the specific conditions; and (3) their posited as given synthetic unity.[10] What is important to note, to avoid confusion, is that the datum and the faktum here are structural positions capable of being filled in with a wide variety of content (such as phenomena/phenomenality, known/knower, ekstasis/enstasis, conditioned/condition, actual/virtual, presence/archi-text, etc.). As such, Laruelle can plausibly argue that philosophy has invariably made use of this structure, despite the obvious historical diversity of philosophies.[11] In any particular philosophy, these terms are established through the method of transcendental deduction that comprises philosophical Decision.[12] Faced with an always-already given, indivisible immanence, philosophy proceeds by first drawing a distinction between an empirical faktum and its a priori categorial conditions. From this presupposed empirical data, its specific a priori categorial conditions are derived. Secondly, these derived categories are unified into a single transcendental Unity acting as their universally necessary condition—the original synthetic unity that makes all other syntheses possible. On this basis, we can now move in the opposite direction to the third step, whereby the transcendental Unity is used to derive the way in which the categories provide the conditions for the empirical, i.e. the way in which they are all synthesized (and systematized) together. With this three-step process in mind, we can see why Laruelle claims that Decision finds its essential moment in the Unity of the transcendental deduction. This Unity (which is a unity by virtue of synthesizing the datum and faktum into a hybrid of both, not because it need be objectified or subjectified— hence even Derrida's differánce and Deleuze's intensive difference[13] can be included as examples) acts both as the immanent presupposition of the transcendental method and the transcendent result/generator of the presupposed empirical and posited a priori. In other words, this dyad of faktum and datum is presupposed as immanently given in ex-

---

9. As should become apparent, Decision constitutes the essence of philosophy for Laruelle, so that when he speaks of 'non-philosophy' this should be taken as a synonym for non-Decisional philosophy. In this regards, Laruelle's own work is a non-Decisional *form* of philosophy, rather than the simple renunciation of philosophy. We will follow Laruelle's use of 'philosophy', however its specificity should be kept in mind when we move to the more explicit political sections of this paper. There we will see that capitalism itself operates as a philosophy.

10. There is a more complicated version of Decision that Brassier outlines, but for our purposes this version will suffice. The interested reader, however, can find more here: Brassier, 'Alien Theory', p. 155.

11. While the universalist claims of this philosophical structure are debatable, much like Meillassoux's correlationist structure, it does appear to be common to nearly all post-Kantian philosophies.

12. We borrow this step-by-step methodology from Brassier, who himself models it after Laruelle's discussion in the essay 'The Transcendental Method'. See: Brassier, *Nihil Unbound*, pp. 123-4.

13. To be clear, while it is true that Deleuze's intensive difference in fact indexes a *splitting*, it does so only by simultaneously joining together what it splits. This is precisely the synthetic mixture that Brassier will denounce as inevitably idealist.

perience and derived as the transcendental conditions for this experience. Unsurprisingly then, philosophy's inaugural distinction between a datum and a faktum finds only the synthesis of this distinction as the end result of the transcendental method, a synthesis which then circles back to validate philosophy's initial distinction. Thus, the gesture of Decision effectively determines not only the synthetic unity/hybrid, but also the nature of the empirical and the a priori as the moments of this synthetic unity. As a result, Decision makes philosophy ubiquitous—everything becomes material for philosophy to think, and philosophy becomes co-extensive with (and co-determining of) reality.

Against this imperial form of philosophy, non-philosophy will resolutely refrain from attempting to think immanence or to establish any relation between philosophy and the Real (even as its absolute Other). What is called for, through a suspension of Decision, is a non-reflexive non-philosophy; one which would not be inaugurated by a reflexive decision determining the nature of the Real in advance. Non-philosophy will not be a thought of the Real, but rather a thought according to the Real. With this in mind, it 'suffices to postulate—not a thought adequate to it—a type of experience of the Real which escapes from self-position, which is not a circle of thought and the Real, a One which does not unify but remains in-One, a Real which is immanent (to) itself rather than to a form of thought, to a 'logic', etc'.[14] It is this Real as the radically immanent One,[15] which provides the means for non-philosophy to break free of and explain philosophy's vicious circle. It is this radical immanence which we mentioned before was always already given prior to philosophy's Decision.[16] This indivisible One is radically indifferent to thought and to the determinations involved within the philosophical Decision. Thus, speaking of it involves axioms—entirely immanent descriptions posited by the Real itself—rather than referential statements.[17] On the basis of its indivisibility, we must also uphold that prior to any philosophical positing of a 'Decisional transcendence/non-Decisional immanence' dualism, this separation is always already given. Moreover, as outside of philosophical positing, the One can be given without the philosophical requirement of a transcendental mode of givenness. In other words, the Real *qua* One can be described as the (admittedly unwieldy) always-already-given-without-givenness. All of this does not, however, entail that it is radically isolated from language, thought, etc.—which would return it to an external transcendence—instead it is simply not involved in a reciprocal relation with these transcendences of philosophical Decisions. It is indifferent to philosophical determinations (such as predication or definition, whether through the mediums of thought or language), not external to them.

14. François Laruelle, *Principes de la Non-Philosophie*, Paris, Presse Universitaires de France, 1996, p. 6. Translation graciously provided by Taylor Adkins.

15. We will see in the section on unilateral duality that one reason for describing the Real as 'One' is because it is devoid of all differentiating relations. Relations fall solely within the ambit of philosophy. To be clear, however, the One does not entail a unity in any sense, and the Real itself is ontologically inconsistent. The One is indifferent to any philosophical characterization in terms of unity/multiplicity.

16. In some sense, Laruelle's project can be seen as a radical continuation of Husserl's project to begin with ultimate immanence. But whereas Husserl and every phenomenologist afterwards have characterized immanence in relation to some other basic term, Laruelle is suspending the self-sufficiency of *all* these determinations.

17. As Brassier helpfully notes, it is not that the Real is ineffable (which would be again to separate it from philosophy), but rather that it is 'inexhaustively effable as what determines its own effability'. (Personal communication, 1/26/09) Or in other words, it is not a matter of concepts determining the Real, but of the Real determining the concepts appropriate to it.

But the skeptical critic will immediately ask—does not the distinction between the One and the Decisional dyad re-introduce precisely the dualism of Decision? To counter this claim, Laruelle will answer that instead of the difference being presupposed and posited by a philosophical Decision, it is instead posited as already given. From philosophy's perspective, the difference must be constituted by philosophy's gestures of separation; but from the non-philosophical perspective, what is given(-without-givenness) is its already achieved separation. Furthermore, what this separation separates is the realm of separability itself (i.e. philosophy and its systems of relations) from the Inseparable as that which is indifferent to philosophical distinctions.[18] This Inseparable does not oppose philosophy, nor does it negate it—rather it simply suspends its self-sufficient autonomy in order to open it up to determination by the radically immanent Real. We will later on have a chance to more fully examine these claims in light of the concept of 'unilateral duality'.

With all this in mind, we must now broach the more pertinent question: what does non-philosophy do? We have outlined some of the basis axioms of non-philosophy and set out its understanding of philosophy, but when we put it into action what does this theory achieve? First and foremost, we must realize that non-philosophy is not a discourse about radical immanence, but rather a means to explain philosophy.[19] Radical immanence is simply the invariant X that is posited as always-already-given-without-givenness. The Real is unproblematic—by virtue of being always-already-given, the interesting question becomes how to proceed from the immanent Real to the transcendence of philosophy. As Brassier puts it, 'it is the consequences of thinking philosophy immanently that are interesting, not thinking immanence philosophically'.[20] Philosophy—with its Decisional auto-positional structure—is constitutively unable to account for itself, which leaves non-philosophy as the sole means to do so.[21] What this entails is that philosophy is not merely an extraneous, impotent and ultimate useless endeavour. Rather, from the perspective of non-philosophy, philosophy itself must be taken as the material without which non-philosophy would be inoperative (while, for its part, the Real would remain indifferent regardless). The operation performed here, as we will now see, is given the name of 'cloning' by Laruelle. It is this approach which will suspend the self-sufficiency of philosophical thought and remove the limits imposed by a particular philosophy in order to attain a thinking in accordance with the Real. In other words, we are entering onto the terrain of the non-philosophical subject.

THE NON-PHILOSOPHICAL SUBJECT

Cloning, in a general sense, refers to the way in which philosophy can be acted upon by the Real through non-philosophical thinking. Given a philosophical system, the initial step of cloning is to locate the specific dyad constitutive of its Decision. The 'real'

---

18. 'Not only is the difference between unobjectifiable immanence and objectifying transcendence only operative on the side of the latter; more importantly, the duality between this difference and the real's indifference to it becomes operative if, and only if, thinking *effectuates* the real's foreclosure to objectification by determining the latter in-the-last-instance'. Brassier, *Nihil Unbound*, p. 142.

19. Brassier, 'Alien Theory', p. 128.

20. Ray Brassier, 'Axiomatic Heresy: The Non-Philosophy of François Laruelle', *Radical Philosophy*, no. 121, 2003, p. 33.

21. As a pre-emptive retort to scientistic critics, we would add that even science has its own forms of Decision, as Brassier outlines with respect to W.V.O. Quine and Paul Churchland. As a result, even science and the study of neurology and cognitive psychology cannot ultimately provide a full account of philosophy. See: Brassier, 'Alien Theory', pp. 165-215.

term is then isolated, broken apart from its constitutive relation to the other 'ideal' term. For instance, the virtual would be isolated from the actual in Deleuze's system as the term designating its pretension to grasp Being. Lastly, this real term 'is identified as the Real, an 'as if' identification that performs rather than represents the Real'.[22] In this subtle shift, non-philosophy effectively instantiates its experimental approach: it operates through the hypothetical question of 'what if this philosophy was not about the Real, but rather determined by the Real?' Cloning, in other words, suspends the auto-sufficiency of philosophical Decision in order to open it onto determination-in-the-last-instance by radical immanence.

Considering the significance of this notion of determination-in-the-last-instance, it is important to provide some clarification about its nature. The most recent use of this concept comes from Louis Althusser who used it to explain how the Marxist base and superstructure operated together. Contrary to standard Marxism, Althusser accorded the superstructure some measure of relative autonomy, while nevertheless arguing that the economy was determining-in-the-last-instance. This entailed that while the superstructure had some effective power within social formations, it was the economy which ultimately determined how much power it had. The determination-in-the-last-instance determined the effective framework for the relative autonomy of the superstructure. What Laruelle criticizes in this account, however, is the ultimately relative nature of the determination-in-the-last-instance—the fact that it finds its last instance in the economy rather than Real immanence. As he will argue, 'The Real is not, properly speaking, an 'instance' or a 'sphere', or eventually a 'region', to the degree that, by definition, it does not belong to the thought-world or to the World—this is the meaning of the 'last instance'.[23] Whereas Althusser relativizes the last-instance to the economy, thereby incorporating it within a philosophical Decision as to the nature of materialism, Laruelle will argue for the last-instance to stem from the properly non-philosophical understanding of matter. The last-instance, for Laruelle, must escape any sort of relative and regional determination—as an empirically given base, or as a relative structuralist position. Only the Real as radical immanence can provide a sufficient base, otherwise one invariably makes the last-instance relative to its philosophical definition.

Similarly, 'determination' also undergoes a non-philosophical reinvention. As Laruelle says, "Determination' is not an auto-positional act, a Kantian-critical operation of the primacy of the determination over the determined. Here the reverse primacy is already announced without a return to dogmatism, yet still under an ambiguous form. It is the determined, the real as matter-without-determination, that makes the determination'.[24] The determined here is the real as last-instance—that presupposition of philosophy which itself escapes from all philosophical determination as the always-already determined in-itself. It determines, in turn, the philosophical world, acting as the last-instance which determines the framework for the relative autonomy of philosophy. The nature of this determination, however, must also escape from all metaphysical concepts of causation: 'It is not an ontic and regional concept with a physico-chemical or linguistic-structuralist model: nor ontological (formal, final, efficient, and … material, which Marx forgets to exclude with the other forms of metaphysical

22. Mullarkey, *Post-Continental Philosophy*, p. 146.

23. François Laruelle, *Introduction au non-Marxism*, Paris, PUF, 2000, pp. 43. Trans. provided by Taylor Adkins.

24. Laruelle, *Introduction au non-Marxism*, 45.

causality)'.[25] As such, it is a type of determination which is itself indifferent to what it determines, while maintaining its radical immanence to what it determines. This entails that the real as last-instance must take up two simultaneous readings: 'in order not to render immanence relative to that which it transcendentally determines, Laruelle will carefully distinguish immanence as a necessary but negative condition, as sine *qua* non for the relation of determination, from its effectuation as transcendentally determining condition insofar as this is contingently occasioned by the empirical[26] instance that it necessarily determines'.[27]

It is cloning which effectuates the second aspect, by suspending the auto-sufficiency of the intra-philosophical conditions (which comprise a vicious circle), and opening them onto the transcendental conditions for the particular empirical instance determined-in-the-last-instance by radical immanence. What is cloned, however? The real foreclosure of the Real to Decision is cloned *as* a non-philosophical transcendental thought foreclosed to Decision. These two foreclosures are themselves Identical-in-the-last-instance, yet the Real itself is foreclosed to the clone (i.e. non-philosophical thought). We must be careful to distinguish then, between (1) the Real foreclosure of radical immanence and (2) the transcendental foreclosure of non-philosophical thought. This non-philosophical thinking, in the end, simply is the 'unilateral duality' established between the Real *qua* determining force and Decision *qua* determinable material. It is the 'force-(of)-thought' or the 'organon' as the determining instance through which the philosophical material has its pretensions to absolute autonomy suspended by being taken as material determined-in-the-last-instance by the Real. Or, to put it in other words, non-philosophical thought doubles the separation 'between' immanence and philosophy with a transcendental unilateral duality 'between' the force-(of)-thought and the specific philosophical material in question. Importantly, the philosophical instance which provides the material from which the Real's foreclosure can be cloned is itself *non-determining*—i.e. there is no subtle reintegration of a bilateral relation between thought and the Real here. Rather the unilateral duality—as the non-relation between the clone and Decision—guarantees their non-reciprocity.

This unilateral duality must be carefully distinguished from the more common notion of a unilateral relation. Whereas philosophy has typically taken the unilateral relation to be one where 'X distinguishes itself from Y without Y distinguishing itself from X in return',[28] it has also inevitably reintroduced a reciprocal relation at a higher level—that of the philosopher overlooking the relation from a transcendent position. In non-philosophy, this transcendence is clearly untenable. Instead, what unilateral duality refers to is the way in which philosophy distinguishes itself from the force-(of)-thought, but with an additional unilateralizing of the initial unilateral duality. Thus, the distinction between the force-(of)-thought and philosophy is operative only on the side of philosophy. Only within philosophy can one presume to take a transcendent perspective on its (non-)separation from philosophy (this, again, points to the illusory self-sufficiency of the philosophical Decision). In the end, and despite some loose use of words earlier to ease the reader into non-philosophy, it must always be remembered

25. Laruelle, *Introduction au non-Marxism*, 45.

26. 'Empirical' here refers to philosophy as the occasional cause suitable as material for non-philosophy. From the perspective of non-philosophy, all philosophical Decisions are equal and open to being used as 'empirical' material.

27. Brassier, 'Alien Theory', 180.

28. Brassier, 'Axiomatic Heresy', p. 27.

that only philosophy institutes relations. Non-philosophy and the Real itself are Identical in-One in-the-last-instance; or to put it a bit more paradoxically: non-philosophy only has one term—philosophy *qua* material.

Once we have been given the occasioning instance of philosophical material and given the process of non-philosophical cloning, the question to be asked is who or what carries out this transformation? To whom—if that can even be properly asked—is this non-Decisional thinking occurring to? Here we enter into the subjectivity of non-Philosophy—what Laruelle has called 'the Stranger' and Brassier the 'Alien-subject'. In fact, we have already been grasping towards the non-philosophical subject in our preceding discussion of the force-(of)-thought and the transcendental clone—all of these terms ultimately point towards the non-Decisional subject as that which acts in accordance with Real immanence to determine-in-the-last-instance particular philosophical Decisions.

Following upon these initial reflections, and recalling its foreclosure to the Decisional circle, it should be clear that the non-philosophical subject must—much like Badiou's subject—be radically non-intuitable, non-phenomenological, non-empirical, non-reflexive and non-conceptual. As with non-philosophy, the 'non-' here refers not to a simple negation, but rather a radical foreclosure of the subject to philosophical dyads like intuition/concept, phenomena/phenomenality, materialism/idealism, etc. The subject is simply indifferent to these philosophical characterizations, being always already given prior to any Decisional dyad. As Brassier will claim, the non-philosophical subject is instead 'simply a function …, an axiomatizing organon, a transcendental computer'.[29] Or in other words, the subject is performative: it simply is what it does.[30]

What is it that the subject does? It carries out the operation involved in unilateral duality. This is the key point—the non-philosophical subject simply is the unilateral duality through which the Real as determining power determines a philosophical Decision as determinable instance, without itself being reciprocally determined by philosophy. This encompasses the basic structure of non-philosophical theory. The act of cloning, therefore, takes the empirico-transcendental hybrid of philosophical Decision and uncovers the non-philosophical subject as the transcendental condition which has (always-already) unilateralized this reciprocal relation by suspending the auto-sufficiency of the philosophical Dyad. From the separate-without-separation between immanence and Decision, we are shifted to the unilateral duality carried out by the non-philosophical subject. In this way, the subject, as the force-(of)-thought, is both the cause and the object of its own knowledge—it determines its own knowledge of itself.[31]

The subject then, as the act of unilateralizing, requires two distinct causes—a necessary, but necessarily insufficient Real cause (determination-in-the-last-instance) and a sufficient, but necessarily contingent occasional cause (philosophy as contingently given). On the one hand, the former necessarily determines the unilateral duality through which the subject effectuates the Real's foreclosure to Decision. Yet, in itself it

---

29. Brassier, 'Axiomatic Heresy', pp. 30-1.

30. This also entails the counter-intuitive claim, again like Badiou's own subject, that there is no necessary relation between the subject of non-philosophy and what has typically been labeled subjectivity in philosophy (i.e. self-reflective consciousness as the property solely of humans). As an ontological function, the non-philosophical subject could also be manifested as something utterly inhuman and machinic.

31. 'This identity of cause and known object is essential, since one of the characteristics that distinguishes materialism from non-philosophy is materialism's tendency to divide the material cause and the philosophical theory of this cause'. Laruelle, *Introduction au non-Marxism*, pp. 48-49.

is not sufficient; the Real is indifferent to thought and to philosophy. As a result, non-philosophy requires the latter cause as the occasional instance from which it can transform philosophical material from self-sufficiency to relative autonomy by effectuating a thought in accordance with the Real (achieved through the process of cloning). This latter cause makes the subject always a Stranger for the philosophical 'world'[32] whose Decisional structure it suspends. In this sense, we can draw a loose form of logical time, wherein (1) we proceed from the Real as always-already-given to (2) the instance of philosophy as given through its own mode of givenness (its self-sufficiency) to, finally, (3) non-philosophy as the transformation of philosophy and a cloning of a thought in accordance with the Real.

Through this transformation, we can clearly see that the non-philosophical subject must (of necessity if it is to act alongside the Real) be foreclosed to the world as the realm opened by philosophical Decision. As such, this subject functions as a locus equally irreducible to its socio-historical context, the constituting power of language, power, or culture, and any relational system philosophy might generate. It functions, in other words, as an always-already-given (in-the-last-instance) non-space from which it becomes possible to suspend and criticize the dominant horizon of phenomena. 'Consequently, the distinction is not so much between the world and another realm of practice in-itself, or between the world and a transcendent realm of practice, but between two ways of relating to the world, one governed by the world, the other determined-according-to the Real'.[33] We thus have two conceptions of the subject—on the one hand, the more traditional subject as that entity (or function or position) occupying a world, supported by the illusion of philosophy's self-sufficiency, and determined by the phenomenological coordinates it sets out. On the other hand, the non-philosophical subject which is engendered from philosophy as occasional cause and which takes philosophy as material to be thought in accordance with the Real or as determined-in-the-last-instance. Thus, we can see why Laruelle will claim that, 'the problem is how to use philosophy so as to effect a real transformation of the subject in such a way as to allow it to break the spell of its bewitchment by the world and enable it to constitute itself through a struggle with the latter'.[34]

As we will see in our discussion in the next section, however, the question of the non-philosophical subject's intervention in the world must negotiate around the pitfalls involved in the philosophical elaboration of 'intervention'.[35] The immediate consequence of the philosophical concept of intervention is that since philosophy is itself responsible for the determination of what 'reality' is, any intervention into that reality will already be circumscribed within the idealist structure of Decision. It takes as given its own conditions for practice and validates them by measuring all practice against that philosophically established standard. Philosophical practice, therefore, remains formally encompassed within its constitutive horizon, even when that horizon is given as a field of multiplicity or difference that nominally privileges becoming and transformation. The constitutive horizon of these philosophies of difference nevertheless limits practice and limits thought to the phenomenological parameters provided by the philosophical Decision, while simultaneously prohibiting any transformation of

---

32. 'World' here refers to the space opened by philosophical Decision as that which is philosophizable (which, from its own perspective is everything).

33. Laruelle, 'What Can Non-Philosophy Do?', p. 181.

34. Laruelle, 'What Can Non-Philosophy Do?', p. 179.

35. Laruelle, 'What Can Non-Philosophy Do?', pp. 183-4.

that horizon itself.[36] Moreover, the very act of intervention, by relying upon the philosophical Decision which makes it intelligible, ultimately reinstates and reproduces the world despite any attempts at intra-worldly transformation. In this specific sense, philosophical intervention can be seen as self-defeating. Contrary to philosophical intervention which aims to intervene in the world, the non-philosophical subject will take the world (i.e. the empirico-transcendental doublet auto-generated by Decision) as its object to transform.

THE CAPITALIST SOCIUS

With this discussion of the non-philosophical subject we have seen how it is possible to take up the perspective of the Real radically foreclosed to philosophy. In this way, the self-sufficiency of the philosophical Decision is suspended and made only relatively autonomous with respect to the determination-in-the-last-instance of the Real itself. While the non-philosophical subject provides this possibility, it relies on the empirical given of a philosophical or ideological system with which it can use as material for its cloning. In this regards, it is not simply an abstract movement of thought, but is rather intimately intertwined with the particular philosophical systems providing our contemporary phenomenological coordinates, using them as occasional causes for thinking in accordance with the Real.

Katerina Kolozova has provided an exemplary instance of this in analyzing present-day gender theory from the non-philosophical perspective.[37] Her own ruminations have shown the capacity for individual resistance to the constituting forces of power and knowledge, evoking a unitary subject irreducible to the field of socio-historical constructions. However, while her work is a great addition as a counterweight to the unending discussions of discourse and culture, it is our contention that the most pertinent Decisional field in our present situation is not gender theory.

Our aim here, on the contrary, will be to tackle the currently hegemonic Decision providing the matrix within which nearly every contemporary phenomenon appears. In our own age, there is little doubt that it is capitalism which provides this dominant—and arguably all-encompassing—horizon through which various objects, subjectivities, desires, beliefs and appearances are constituted. Capitalism, in other words, is the philosophical structure presently given to us as material for the non-philosophical subject to operate with.[38]

Before proceeding, however, let us make clear that we are not suggesting that the capitalist Decisional structure was the result of some philosophical act of thought, as though it's mere positing in thought were sufficient to bring about its effective reality. Rather, the Decisional structure has been the unintentional product of the numerous and varied social practices which led to capitalism. In good Marxist fashion, we are suggesting that society acted in a manner that constructed its own self-sufficient circle—a manner which only later became replicated in thought. With the rise of commodity production, free labour, and sufficient stores of money, capitalism

---

36. As Brassier will note, one of the main consequences of the self-sufficiency of Decision is that since each Decision takes itself to be absolute, each is forced to regard alternative Decisions as mutually exclusive. It is a war of philosophy against philosophy (Brassier, 'Alien Theory', p. 126).

37. Katerina Kolozova, *The Real and 'I': On the Limit and the Self*, Skopje, Euro-Balkan Press, 2006.

38. Brassier also speaks of capitalism and non-philosophy in the conclusion of *Alien Theory*, but despite the undeniable brilliance of the rest of the dissertation and *Nihil Unbound*, his concluding proposals come across as overly optimistic.

began to unmoor itself from its material grounding and bring about an ontological inversion whereby it progressively recreated the world in the image of the abstract value-form.[39] Instead of everything being material for philosophy, everything became material for capitalist valorization. We will all too briefly return to these ideas in the conclusion.

With this in mind, it is easy to see that it is Deleuze and Guattari who have provided us with the most explicit model of how capitalism installs itself as a self-sufficient structure—specifically, through their concept of the capitalist socius. In their analysis, capital (as with all the modes of social-production) has the property of appearing as its own cause: 'It falls back on all production constituting a surface over which the forces and agents of production are distributed, thereby appropriating for itself all surplus production and arrogating to itself both the whole and the parts of the process, which now seem to emanate from it as a quasi cause'.[40] This socius (whether capitalist or not) acts as an effect produced by society and its multiplicity of relations and forces of production; yet once produced it functions to unify the disparate social practices into a coherent whole. While achieving this unification through the regulation of social relations in accordance with its image of the whole, the socius simultaneously comes to organize the productive and cooperative practices it originally emerged from. For example, capital deterritorializes archaic social formations in order to reterritorialize the released material flows in a temporary, but exploitative relation—conjoining heterogeneous flows of labour and capital in order to convert them into quantities from which surplus-value can be extracted. Furthermore, capital becomes an all-encompassing productive force in that it ends up producing even subjectivity itself—hence the mobile, flexible worker of contemporary neoliberalism is a product of the deterritorialization carried out by capital,[41] being produced as a residue of the process (a similar process occurs with the consumer). In a very real sense, therefore, the socius both causes the mode of production[42] to emerge and is produced as an effect of it. This is a paradoxical claim, and one worth looking at again in more detail in order to clearly understand the logic. On one hand, it is clear that there is a historical process involved in producing the particular mode of production—i.e. the socius is an effect of the inventive and constituent power of the multitude; it is produced by their labour power, prior to any appropriation by capital. But on the other hand, with the emergence of capitalism, capital itself begins to quasi cause production by coercing it and employing constituent power within its functioning. What occurs then, is a sort of asymptotical approach towards the particular mode of production on the level of the historical processes; and then—in a moment of auto-positioning— the socius itself emerges simultaneously as both cause and effect, as both presupposing its empirical reality (through the productive power of the multitude) and positing its a priori horizon (the full body of capital), while positing as presupposed their syn-

---

39. See Christopher Arthur's work, *The New Dialectic and Marx's Capital*, Boston, Brill Publishing, 2004 for a detailed explanation of the rise of the value-form and its consequent ontological inversion.

40. Gilles Deleuze and Felix Guattari, *Anti-Oedipus*, Minneapolis, University of Minnesota Press, 1983, p. 10.

41. Even in its briefly liberating phase, the flexible subject was a reaction against (and hence relied upon) the Fordist mode of production. See: Paolo Virno, *A Grammar of the Multitude*, Los Angeles, Semiotext(e), 2004, pp. 98-9 .

42. Following Jason Read, we will use 'modes of production' in an expanded sense to include the production of subjectivity, desires, beliefs, along with the more common material basis. See: Jason Read, *The Micro-Politics of Capital: Marx and the Prehistory of the Present*, Albany, State University of New York Press, 2003.

thesis in a transcendental unity (the Body without Organs, or BwO, as the absolute condition, or the plane of absolutely deterritorialized flows). While counterintuitive, this claim should nevertheless be familiar from our reading of the structure of philosophical Decision. As a ubiquitous structure, we should not be surprised to discern it operating in a variety of fields. Thus we can clearly see that the 'philosophical' Decision is as much a 'political' Decision as an 'economic' Decision.[43] In this regards, Steven Shaviro has recently provided a particularly illuminating description of this capitalist Decisional structure:

> The socius, or 'full body of capital', is entirely composed of material processes in the phenomenal world; and yet, as the limit and the summation of all these processes, it has a quasi-transcendental status. That is to say, the body of capital is not a particular phenomenon that we encounter at a specific time and place; it is rather the already-given presupposition of whatever phenomenon we *do* encounter. We cannot experience this capital-body directly, and for itself; yet all our experiences are lodged within it, and can properly be regarded as its effects. The monstrous flesh of capital is the horizon, or the matrix, or the underlying location and container of our experience, as producers or as consumers. In this sense, it can indeed be regarded as something like what Kant would call a transcendental condition of experience. Or better—since it is a process, rather than a structure or an entity—it can be understood as what Deleuze and Guattari call a basic 'synthesis' that generates and organizes our experience.[44]

It is this complex structure—which includes the 'material processes in the phenomenal world', the 'capital-body' as the socius organizing the practices, and the BwO as the immanent synthesis of these two terms—which we will subject to the non-Decisional method.

By making the self-sufficiency of capitalism explicit, we are in a position that allows us to begin to explain a number of important contemporary phenomena—most notably, the real subsumption carried out by capitalism. With this notion, it has been declared that capitalism constitutively has no outside—all of society, including everyday innocuous socializing processes, becomes productive for capital as it shifts to immaterial labour. As such, resistance cannot place itself in an external relation to capitalism, and tends to instead work solely with immanent tendencies—tendencies that are unfortunately all too easily reincorporated within capitalism. However, the recognition of capitalism as an instance of the auto-positing structure of Decision already gives us a non-philosophical—or rather, a non-capitalist—perspective on this situation. We can see that the reason for our present inability to escape the world of capitalist Decision is because it constitutes the Real in its own inescapable terms. In the same way that philosophy makes everything material for philosophy, so too does capitalism make everything material for productive valorization. Moreover, as our earlier discussion of philosophical intervention pointed out, practice based within the world opened by a Decision is necessarily incapable of affecting the horizon of that world; at best, it can reconfigure aspects given in the world without being able to transform the mode of givenness of the world. So political action based within the world will inevitably fail at revolution (as the radical transformation from one Decision to another). What is re-

---

43. Or more specifically, Decision is not intrinsically philosophical at all—just as Brassier argues that philosophy is not intrinsically Decisional. Rather, Decision constitutes an important mechanism which subsumes everything within its purview; one which is operative in a variety of domains.

44. Steven Shaviro, 'The Body of Capital', *The Pinocchio Theory*, 2008 <http://www.shaviro.com/Blog/?p=641> [accessed 26 June 2008]

quired is a transformation of this capitalist structure and a concomitant transformation of the corresponding subject.[45]

In this project, Antonio Negri and Michael Hardt's work—despite its flaws—is indispensable. Heavily borrowing from Deleuze and Guattari, Negri and Hardt have re-fashioned the 'productive forces/capitalist socius' dyad in terms of the 'multitude/capital' and the 'constituent/constituted power' dyads. In their works, the multitude is a political body both produced from common cooperation and productive of the common, as the residual product of the multitude's cooperation. So, for example, everyday interactions involving social and affective knowledge are both the source of cooperation and the production of community. The problem is that with the hegemony[46] of immaterial labour (e.g. service and knowledge-based industries), capitalism has taken these immediately creative and productive capacities of the multitude and integrated them within its operations. The reliance of the capitalist socius on the social and affective knowledge of the multitude, moreover, is reciprocated by capital's production of subjectivity. Capital and surplus-value are, in other words, produced by the labour of the multitude, yet at the same time responsible for inciting, incorporating, organizing and creating the multitude (even its 'free time')—effectively establishing a self-sufficient circle.

To suspend capitalism's pretension at self-sufficiency, we will therefore initially take the capitalist dyad of multitude/capital or constituent/constitutive power and separate the real term—multitude—from its reliance on the opposing term.[47] We must now suspend any philosophical or capitalist constitution of the multitude and instead take it as an axiom determined-in-the-last-instance by the Real itself. Thus, whereas Antonio Negri and Michael Hardt will submit the multitude to a dyadic relation with capital, and philosophically determine the nature of real immanence, non-philosophy forecloses this possibility by positing the multitude as always already given-without-givenness—prior to any enmeshment in Marxist discourse or systems of social relations. The non-philosophical multitude[48] is cloned as the transcendental conditions foreclosed to the operations of the capitalist socius. Which is also to say that the multitude performs the Real, acts in accordance with it, prior to any incorporation within the capitalist or philosophical Decision. Moreover, it is this non-capitalist multitude

45. 'It [i.e. non-philosophy] transforms the subject by transforming instances of philosophy'. François Laruelle, 'A New Presentation of Non-Philosophy' <http://www.onphi.net/texte-a-new-presentation-of-non-philosophy-32.html> [accessed 15 July 2008].

46. To be clear, hegemony does not mean quantitative majority—rather the hegemony of immaterial labour points to the way in which it shifts *all* forms of labour according to its precepts. For example, even industrial labour has begun to incorporate and rely upon immaterial labour in its production process.

47. Multitude is clearly the real term of the dyad because Negri and Hardt assert that a constituent power has no need for constituted power—i.e. it is ontologically sufficient in-itself, with capital being merely a secondary parasitic body. The problem, as with all Decisions, is that despite its materialist pretensions, the very form of philosophizing involved surreptitiously makes the immanence of the multitude dependent upon the constituted powers it struggles against. In a very real way, this Decisional enmeshing of the two reveals why Negri and Hardt come across as overly optimistic in their claims that the multitude can surpass and extricate itself from capital—as though the real world made clear their Decisional synthesis, despite Negri and Hardt's claims to the contrary.

48. An important caveat: the non-capitalist multitude, as foreclosed to capitalist determination, must necessarily be left unqualified by determining predicates like 'class' and 'proletariat'. 'Multitude' is instead an axiomatic here; a name of the Real posited by the Real itself as always-already foreclosed to capitalism. We can't, in other words, say 'what' this multitude is—merely that it is and that it is determining-in-the-last-instance. The difficulty, as we will cover in the conclusion, is how to incorporate this instance of the already-determined-without-determination into politics.

which effectively acts as the Identity (without-unity) underlying its various, heterogeneous worldly appearances. Kolozova's work points the way towards this, by re-conceiving Identity in non-philosophical terms as that invariant = X irreducible to any sort of linguistic, conceptual, or relational determination.[49] In her work these socio-historical determinations are carried out by structures of power and language, as explicated by constructivist gender theory. The (non-)multitude, on the other hand, takes capitalism as the determining world which it remains irreducible or foreclosed to. In either case, however, the Real invariant always already retains the potential to resist and refuse the determinations imposed upon it. Unlike the singularities constitutive of Negri and Hardt's multitude, the non-capitalist subject, the force-(of)-thought specific to capitalism, is determined-in-the-last-instance by a Real radically indifferent to its capitalist enmeshment. Instead of Negri and Hardt's singularity, Laruelle will speak of a radical solitude proper to the non-philosophical subject, to mark its irreducibility to any worldly determination, even class, gender, race and ethnicity.[50] It is the implicitly presupposed, yet non-posited immanence of capitalism.

Therefore, what the non-philosophical take has to offer over and above the philosophical conception of the multitude is an always already given locus of resistance to any form of control by capitalism. As Shaviro has pointed out,[51] what is ultimately naively utopian about Negri and Hardt's concept of the multitude is its valorization of the multitude's creativity without the simultaneous recognition that it is capitalism that incites, organizes and appropriates this creativity. Despite Negri and Hardt's optimism, their conception of the multitude therefore remains irreducibly intertwined with capital. In these regards, the multitude offers no exit from capitalism, but is instead simply a creative power for capitalism's self-perpetuation.[52] Non-philosophy, on the other hand, separates (in the non-philosophical sense) the multitude as Real force-(of)-thought from its immersion in the capitalist world. It indexes a territory incapable of being colonized by capital's imperialist ambitions—one where capitalism's tendency to reduce all of being to commodities and tools for capitalism is always already suspended and where the Real itself determines the nature of the capitalist world. In doing so, both thought and practice remove the limits imposed upon them by capitalism, framed as they were by the horizon of the capital-body. New options, unimaginable for capitalism, become available to thought and practice. The new options cannot be intentionally accessed, of course, but the non-philosophical subject (the multitude, in our non-capitalism) becomes capable of acting in accordance with the Real in such a way that is not bound by the strictures of phenomenological legitimation, thereby opening the space for an event incommensurable with the dominant Decision.[53]

---

49. Kolozova, *The Real and 'I'*, pp. 4-30.

50. We can see Negri and Hardt's reintroduction of singularity into the world through their description of the multitude as a class concept, even if it is distinguished from traditional class concepts. See: Antonio Negri, 'Towards an Ontological Definition of Multitude' trans. Arriana Bove <http://multitudes.samizdat.net/spip.php? article269> [accessed 15 July 2008].

51. Steven Shaviro, 'Monstrous Flesh', *The Pinocchio Theory*, 2008 <http://www.shaviro.com/Blog/?p=639> [accessed 26 June 2008].

52. This also has parallels to Žižek's critique of Deleuze and Guattari as the archetypal philosophers of capitalism—espousing endless creativity, and novel products and modes of jouissance that are all perfectly compatible with capitalism.

53. Despite some overt similarities, this idea of deregulating philosophical limits goes beyond even the absolute deterritorialization espoused by Deleuze and Guattari. Whereas the latter remains a hybrid synthetic unity of the terms it separates, the 'beyond' of non-philosophy is foreclosed to any such dyad. In this

Yet, what are we left with after all this theoretical elaboration? We have tried to show that non-philosophy opens a space beyond any philosophical or capitalist Decision, thereby offering an always-already-given locus of resistance. This space also makes possible the advent of a radically new determination (from the perspective of the world). But we have no way in which to effectively use this space for resisting capitalism. The use of this space requires a project to work towards, which in turn appears to necessarily entail some philosophical world provided by a Decision. In some ways, we have reached the limit of Laruelle's non-philosophy—at least in terms of developing a political project based on it. As Brassier will say, 'there can be no 'ethics of radical immanence' and consequently no ethics of non-philosophy. The very notion of an 'ethics of immanence' is another instance of the way in which philosophical decision invariably subordinates immanence to a transcendental teleological horizon'.[54] Non-philosophy thus appears as a significant and important rejoinder to philosophical (or political, as we saw) pretensions, limiting philosophy in much the same way that Kant limited metaphysics. But beyond this it can make no positive pronouncements in itself. This is perhaps unsurprising, since as we mentioned earlier, non-philosophy is largely an explanatory framework, seeking to heteronomously explain philosophy's relative autonomy, or in this case, capitalism's purported self-sufficiency.

CONCLUSION

In our conclusion, we will try and move beyond this dead-end by turning towards some more speculative propositions concerning how non-philosophy must change our conceptions of politics. Brassier hints at these options when he criticizes Laruelle's universal claims about Decisions (i.e. that all philosophy is constituted by a Decisional structure).[55] Rather than reducing philosophy to a simple invariant and content-less structure, non-philosophy must realize its claims about Decision are localizable within only a portion of philosophy's history. With this de-universalization of Laruelle's claims, the door is now open for methods of non-philosophy other than the ones Laruelle outlines. A careful thinker could both escape the Decisional structure of auto-positing and escape the limited methods used by Laruelle (such as cloning).[56] These new methods, therefore, can be used to develop philosophical themes in a non-philosophical manner alongside the Real. Meillassoux's project seems to us to be an example of this possibility, operating not through some delineation of transcendental and empirical structures, but rather through an argument aimed at undermining the limits of a typical philosophical position (correlationism). With a specific focus on the political aspects we are concerned with here, it can be seen that a non-Decisional form of philosophy need not be reduced to the solely negative restrictions placed on politics by Laruelle's own version of non-Decisional philosophy. Instead, a more fully developed (non-)politics could be constructed that recognizes the political potential of the transcendental locus of resistance offered by non-philosophy, while also integrating it into the capitalist world through a productive political subject and project.

---

way it remains radically immanent and radically foreclosed to any decisional determination or limitation. For more on Deleuze and Guattari's plane of immanence as a hybrid, see: Brassier, 'Alien Theory', p. 54-84.

54. Brassier, 'Axiomatic Heresy', p. 33.

55. Brassier, *Nihil Unbound*, pp. 131-4.

56. Laruelle himself admits this possibility when he claims 'non-philosophy [may] not yet represent the most widely agreed upon mutation of foundation … *others are still obviously possible* and will be, in any event, sought by generations which will not, like ours, let themselves be enclosed in their history' Laruelle, 'A New Presentation of Non-Philosophy', emphasis added.

Before embarking on this project, though, it is important to clarify that a realist system such as the present one offers *no* positive vision for politics. As the previous sections have hopefully made clear, the non-philosophical Real is neither conceptualizable nor recoverable within a political system of thought. As we aim to show in the conclusion here, what non-philosophy can instead offer to politics is the immanent space to suspend the pretensions of any totalizing system, as well as an elaboration of how non-philosophical revolution might appear within the world. It cannot, however, offer any positive prescriptions for action, or values for motivation, or grounds for certainties. As radically indifferent to any conceptual system, the Real provides no comfort to political or ethical ventures.

Despite the non-prescriptive nature of non-philosophy, it is still possible to undertake an analysis of the appearance *within* the world of a new Decisional space, i.e. a new world. This line of thought stems from two pieces of evidence. The first is our earlier claim that capitalism was the result of a *historical* process that emerged from the concerted effort of innumerable workers and individuals interacting with their natural environment. Historically, it is clear that capitalism, despite being a self-sufficient structure, had relations in some sense with the pre-capitalist world. This suggests the possibility of constructing new Decisions within the given world. But this claim must rest upon our second piece of evidence: Laruelle's argument for the 'non-sufficiency' of the Real. In his words,

> the One ... in no way produces philosophy or the World ...—there is no real genesis of philosophy. This is the *non-sufficiency* of the One as necessary but non-sufficient condition. ... A givenness of philosophy is thus *additionally* necessary if the vision-in-One is to give philosophy according to its own mode of being-given. ... The vision-in-One gives philosophy *if* a philosophy presents itself. But philosophy gives itself according to the mode of its own self-positing/givenness/reflection/naming, or according to that of a widened self-consciousness or universal *cogito*.[57]

The Real itself does not give philosophy (or rather, Decision), but must instead rely upon the contingent occasion of a philosophy giving itself 'according to the mode of its own self-positing/givenness/reflection/naming'. The reason for this is because the unilateral relation permits only philosophy to distinguish itself from immanence. The Real itself does not distinguish itself from philosophy, remaining indifferent to its transcendence, and so the occasioning cause necessary for non-philosophical thought (i.e. philosophy as material) requires that philosophy give itself according to its own mode of givenness. Without the latter operation, there would never be any transcendence from which non-philosophy could operate. The question that is immediately raised here is where does this givenness of philosophy come from? A purely *ex nihilo* incarnation would seem to suggest a space irreducible to both immanence and philosophy— something which would seem a priori impossible in a system premised on determination-in-the-last-instance by the Real. The more plausible answer is that the givenness of novel philosophical Decisions is produced in a non-reductive manner through the material of previous philosophical worlds. Using our example of capitalism, the shift from a pre-capitalist formation to a properly capitalist formation can be seen as an unintentional and contingent result of the shifting relations between forces and relations of production (including the subjectivities produced). Which means that while the Real may be the determination-in-the-last-instance, the phenomenological world

---

57. François Laruelle, 'A Summary of Non-Philosophy', *Pli: The Warwick Journal of Philosophy*, no. 8, 1999, p. 142.

within which we *qua* individuals operate appears to in some sense overdetermine the Real. As mentioned previously, unlike Althusser, the overdetermination here would not be determined-in-the-last-instance by some fundamental contradiction, but instead by the radically foreclosed Real.[58] Moreover, overdetermination would also remain foreclosed to determining the Real, instead sufficing to determine the contingent progression of philosophical Decisions through intra-worldly transformations. Such a proposition would remain within the ambits of non-philosophy by refusing to establish a philosophical dyad, instead merely taking non-philosophy's requirement for material at its word—even the novel worldly formations determined-in-the-last-instance by the Real require some material to be always-already given.

Most importantly, this notion of intra-worldly transformation simultaneously proposes the distinct possibility of a collective subject operating within the Decisional space. Acting in accordance with the Real, such a collective group would entail both an identity-in-the-last-instance with the Real (by virtue of being determined by it) and a duality-without-synthesis effectuated by the unilateral relation carried out from philosophy's reflective perspective.[59] Such a subject would of necessity be foreclosed to any definite identifying predicates such as class, race, gender, or even minority status. The corollary to this requirement would be the counter-intuitive claim that any sociological group could have the possibility to act in accordance with radical immanence, simply by taking up this simultaneous identity and duality involved there.[60] In relation to our earlier discussion of the non-philosophical subject, this intra-worldly subject would act as the phenomenal manifestation of that non-philosophical subject. We must be careful here, however—this 'manifestation' would be an event, but a non-philosophical form of event that occurs without regard for any philosophical conception of the event, hindered as they are by a Decision which makes their concept the result of reducing temporal continuities in the name of the philosophical 'real' shining through.[61] In contrast to the intra-worldly events which occupy philosophy's attention, this non-philosophical event is properly an Advent of the philosophical world itself.[62] The collective subject would be the manifestation of a new world acting in accordance with a Real indifferent to the limitations of the present world. In what way then, does this Advent manifest itself phenomenally? It is worth quoting in full Laruelle's description:

> 'The Advent, we now know, does not lie at the world's horizon and is not the other side of that horizon (Heidegger). But neither can it be said to constitute an infinite of reverse verticality, of reverse transcendence which would pierce or puncture the horizon (Levinas). The Advent comes neither from afar nor from on high. It emerges as a radical solitude that it is impossible to manipulate, to dominate, to reduce, like the solitude of the great works of art .... It no longer announces anything, it is neither absence nor presence

---

58. Louis Althusser, 'Overdetermination and Contradiction' in *For Marx*, trans. by Ben Brewster, New York, Verso, 2005, pp. 106-7.

59. To be clear, it is an identity, by virtue of being identical with radical immanence (which does not distinguish itself from anything), and a duality by virtue of effectuating a unilateral duality from the internal perspective of philosophy.

60. Although this claim should be less counter-intuitive when it is recalled that Marx saw in the bourgeoisie a revolutionary group, relative to its feudal origins. A revolutionary group need not be a progressive group, nor must it remain revolutionary.

61. 'The event focuses within its apparently ineffable simplicity the entire structure of that which I call the philosophical Decision'. François Laruelle, 'Identity and Event', *Pli: The Warwick Journal of Philosophy*, no. 9, 2000, pp. 177-8.

62. Laruelle, 'Identity and Event' p. 184.

nor even an 'other presence', but rather unique solitude given-in-One in-the-last-instance. It emerges as the identity of a unique face without a 'face to face'.[63]

It is in this manner that the Advent presents itself, with a portion being given in solitude (its immanent cause as determination-in-the-last-instance) and another portion relative to the world (from which it draws its material and occasional cause for its 'unique face').[64] In this way it can both escape any determining constraints imposed upon the Real by the world, and use the world as a sufficient but non-necessary source of material. In other words, while we are always already determined in accordance with the Real, we are only phenomenalized as potential political actors in the world, through the material provided by our contemporary Decisional structures. The intra-worldly subject, therefore, is merely the phenomenal face of the non-philosophical subject—the radical locus of resistance clothed in an arbitrary, yet non-determining, philosophical material. It is with this material clothing that we can function to effect transformations—not in, but of—the phenomenological world we inhabit.

Returning to our example of the pre-capitalist situation, we can perceive in its historical advent, the slow but persistent accumulation of philosophical material that eventually functioned as the occasional cause for a non-philosophical Advent. While the potential for determination-in-the-last-instance to be effectuated in non-philosophical thought is always already there, it is perhaps only in certain worldly moments that the self-sufficiency constitutive of the world becomes less than certain, thereby opening the space for the Advent of a non-philosophical subject capable of radically transforming the very horizon of Being.

What still remains to be thought, however, is the manner in which the solitude of the Advent can be transformed, or perhaps simply extended, into the type of full-fledged world in which we are normally given. What is required, in other words, is some functional equivalent to Badiou's concept of forcing, whereby the event is investigated and its findings integrated into a new situation.[65] With that project incomplete, the suspension of Decision and the advent of a non-philosophical subject can only constitute the necessary, but not yet sufficient, conditions for constructing new empirico-transcendental spaces incommensurable with the capitalist socius.

---

63. Laruelle, 'Identity and Event', p. 186.

64. We earlier referred to this structure as its simultaneous identity (without-unity) and duality (without-synthesis).

65. Alain Badiou, *Being & Event*, trans. Oliver Feltham, New York, Continuum 2007, pp. 410-30.

13

Drafting the Inhuman: Conjectures on Capitalism and Organic Necrocracy

Reza Negarestani

'And beyond all this we have yet to disturb the peace of this
world in still another way...'[1]

Quod exitus sectabor iter?

With the burgeoning popularity of speculative thought, it is becoming more evident
that what is labelled as 'speculative' is more an epiphenomenon of the inquisitive re-
negotiation of human faculties, their limits and vulnerabilities rather, than a counter-
intuitive foray into the abyssal vistas unlocked by contemporary science. Accordingly,
in the more extreme forms of speculative thought, political intervention and political
analysis have been curtailed or at least have been temporarily suspended. This is because the horizon of agency (of emancipation or intervention), ontological privileges
and conditions of experience are precisely those ingredients of political thought which
are under the process of critical interrogation. Yet strangely, it seems that speculative
thought has not given up remarking on capitalism—this hypothetical mathesis uni-
versalis of politico-economic problems—even in some of its most apolitical moments.[2]
For the purpose of understanding some of the disjunctive impasses between speculative thought and politics as well as possibilities for mobilizing a politics capable of using the resources of speculative thought, this essay will concentrate its energy on the
most recurring politico-economic figure of speculative thought: Capitalism. To do so,
we shall, in proceeding steps, dissect the uncanny affinities between contemporary
capitalism's insinuations of an inhuman politics and speculative thought's assault on
the human's 'empirically overdetermined set of cognitive faculties impose[d] upon the
speculative imagination'.[3] We shall subsequently investigate the lines of correspond-

1. Sigmund Freud, *Introductory Lectures on Psychoanalysis*, New York, W. W. Norton & Company, 1977, p. 353.

2. Capitalism is a hypothetical universal platform of problem-solving and information processing which
for every problem and desire determines a solution—a market—by recourse to an immanent death which
exteriorizes it as a liquidating form of animation (production?) which intensifies and becomes more intricate as it encompasses more problems (potential resources).

3. Ray Brassier, *Alien Theory: The Decline of Materialism in the Name of Matter*, Warwick University, PhD
Dissertation, 2001. Online available at: http://www.cinestatic.com/trans-mat/Brassier/ALIENTHEO-
RY.pdf, pg. 163.

ence between the inhumanist conception of capitalism and speculative thought's more extreme attempts for precluding all anthropomorphic predications so as to understand the limits of a politics nurtured by the outcomes of speculative thought. It is only by re-orienting the vectors of speculative thought in relation to these limits that various possibilities or obstacles of a politics capable of mirroring and mobilizing the vectors of speculative thought come to light.

I

Whereas numerous texts have been written on Freud's energetic model of the nervous system presented in *Beyond the Pleasure Principle*, few of them have continued developing Freud's energetic analysis in the same speculative spirit. Yet even among the handful of these works, nearly all the emphasis has been put on the most explicitly expressed lines of *Beyond the Pleasure Principle* in regard to the inevitability of regression toward inorganic exteriority *qua* death. What can be called thanatropic regression or the compulsion of the organic to return to the inorganic state of dissolution has been frequently accentuated at the cost of sacrificing the more speculative fronts of Freud's energetic model in regard to trauma and the economic order of the organism. Following Deleuze and Guattari's lead regarding the intimate relationship between Freud's account of the death-drive and capitalism, Freud's theory of thanatropic regression has become a recurrent speculative tool in building a double-faced and hence elusive image of capitalism which despite its adherence to the conservative interests of humans registers itself as a planetary singularity which is at once inevitable and disenchantingly emancipating.

> Freud himself indeed spoke of the link between his 'discovery' of the death instinct and World War I, which remains the model of capitalist war. More generally, the death instinct celebrates the wedding of psychoanalysis and capitalism; their engagement had been full of hesitation. What we have tried to show apropos of capitalism is how it inherited much from a transcendent death-carrying agency, the despotic signifier, but also how it brought about this agency's effusion in the full immanence of its own system: the full body, having become that of capital-money, suppresses the distinction between production and antiproduction: everywhere it mixes antiproduction with the productive forces in the immanent reproduction of its own always widened limits (the axiomatic). The death enterprise is one of the principal and specific forms of the absorption of surplus value in capitalism. It is this itinerary that psychoanalysis rediscovers and retraces with the death instinct [...][4]

According to this double-faced image of capitalism predicated upon the politico-economical insinuations of the death-drive, in gaining its own angular momentum capitalism brings forth an emancipation in terms other than those of the human. In this case, whilst capitalism is open to human interests, it also moves toward a planetary emancipation wherein the capitalist singularity departs from human purposiveness and privileges. This image of capitalism as something that can simultaneously be in the service of human interests and be an inhuman model of emancipation has become a common romantic trope among philosophers who advocate capitalism as that which is capable of wedding the concrete economy of human life to a cosmos where neither being nor thinking enjoy any privilege.

As Nick Land has elaborated in *The Thirst for Annihilation* as well as his essays, what brings about the possibility of this weird marriage between human praxis and

---

4. Gilles Deleuze and Felix Guattari, *Anti-Oedipus: Capitalism and Schizophrenia*, Minneapolis, University of Minnesota Press, 1983, p. 335, my emphasis.

inhuman emancipation is the tortuous economy of dissipation inherent to capital-ism as its partially repressed desire for meltdown.[5] Although the economy of dissipa-tion can be captured by humans through a libidinal materialist participation with the techno-capitalist singularity, it ultimately escapes the gravity of humans and entails their dissolution into the inorganic exteriority. Capitalism in this sense is not an at-tainable state but rather a dissipative (anti-essence) tendency or process which moves along the detours of organizational complexity, increasing commodification and con-voluted syntheses of techné and physis so as to ultimately deliver human's conserva-tive horizon into an unbound state of dissolution. Immunological impulses of capi-talism against its implicit desire for meltdown are doomed to fail as capitalism fully gains it angular momentum by reaping planetary resources and conceiving its irrep-arably schizophrenic image.

> Machinic desire can seem a little inhuman, as it rips up political cultures, deletes tradi-tions, dissolves subjectivities, and hacks through security apparatuses, tracking a soulless tropism to zero control. This is because what appears to humanity as the history of cap-italism is an invasion from the future by an artificial intelligent space that must assemble itself entirely from its enemy's resources.[6]

It is this singularized deliverance of the human to the state of dissolution—concomi-tant with its pulverizing impact on the correlation between thought and the self-love of man (*viz.* organic survivalism)—that assigns capitalism an inhuman emancipative role. This model of emancipation is comparable with H.P. Lovecraft's fantastic concept 'holocaust of freedom' which celebrates the consummation of human doom with hu-man emancipation. Thus through a politico-economic reappropriation of Freud's the-ory of the death-drive, Nick Land identifies capital as a planetary singularity toward utter dissipation whose dynamism becomes more complicated as it circuitously verg-es upon zero.

> Once the commodity system is established there is no longer a need for an autonomous cultural impetus into the order of the abstract object. Capital attains its own 'angular mo-mentum', perpetuating a run-away whirlwind of dissolution, whose hub is the virtual zero of impersonal metropolitan accumulation. At the peak of its productive prowess the hu-man animal is hurled into a new nakedness, as everything stable is progressively liquidat-ed in the storm.[7]

Now compare Land's trenchant veneration of Freud's account of the death-drive as a creativity that pushes life into its extravagances with the inhumanist model of capital-ism wherein the affirmation of and demand for *more* is but 'a river's search for the sea'.

> The death drive is not a desire for death, but rather a hydraulic tendency to the dissi-pation of intensities. In its primary dynamics it is utterly alien to everything human, not least the three great pettinesses of representation, egoism, and hatred. The death drive is Freud's beautiful account of how creativity occurs without the least effort, how life is pro-pelled into its extravagances by the blindest and simplest of tendencies, how desire is no more problematic than a river's search for the sea.[8]

---

5. Despite all approaching critical evidences, few of the conjectural lines in this essay could have been de-veloped without Nick Land's original contributions which have irreproachably left their distinctive marks on the larval body of speculative thought.

6. Nick Land, 'Machinic Desire', *Textual Practice*, vol. 7, no. 3, 1993, p. 479.

7. Nick Land, *The Thirst for Annihilation: Georges Bataille and Virulent Nihilism*, London, Routledge, 1992, p. 80.

8. Nick Land, 'Making It with Death: Remarks on Thanatos and Desiring Production', *British Journal of Phenomenology*, vol. 24, no. 1, 1993, pp. 74-75.

Land here presents a model or definition of capitalism which despite its collusive entanglements with human's desires and interests is a detoured and hence complex singularity toward the inorganic exteriority which ultimately enforces an all-inclusive liberation from the conservative nature of the organism and its confines for thought. Yet the question we must ask is whether the capitalist dissipative singularity is really emancipative or not? And even more crucially, does the capitalist model of accelerating planetary dissipation really effectuate an inhumanist model of emancipation that breaks away from the conservative ambits of the human? The ambition of this essay is, accordingly, to renegotiate the definition of the capitalist singularity through a closer and more extreme engagement with Freud's speculative thesis on thanatropic regression. Accordingly, we shall investigate if this emancipative conception of capitalism genuinely presents a radical model of the Inhuman or not.

The collusion between science and capitalism imparts an alarmingly critical significance to such inspections into the relation between capitalism and its image as an inevitable singularity that coheres with the compulsive regression of the organism toward the inorganic exteriority. The collusion of capitalism with science enables capitalism to incorporate contemporary science's continuous disenchantment of cosmos as the locus of absolute objectivity and inevitable extinction. In doing so, capitalism can establish a concurrently inevitable and emancipative image of itself: Capitalism is inevitable because it terrestrially coincides with and converges upon the cosmic 'truth of extinction' (Brassier); it is emancipative because it harbours the debacle of human and binds the enlightening disenchantment implicit in dissolution as an objectifying truth.[9] In other words, the complicity of science and capitalism provides capitalism with a speculative weapon capable of imposing capitalism as the universal horizon of politic-economic problems as well as the ultimate mode of departure from the restricting ambit of the terrestrial sphere. Whilst the former grants capitalism a vector of participation, the latter constitutes capitalism's crafty model of emancipation.

In a sense, probably nothing has been more profitable for capitalism than its clandestine alliance with science through whose support capitalism has become increasingly elusive, more difficult to resist, harder to escape and more seductive for those who await the imminent homecoming of scientific enlightenment or the advent of technological singularities. Antihumanism, in this regard, has ironically become the formidable assassin of capitalism in that it connects capitalism with an inhumanist model of emancipation or grants capitalism mythical powers against various manifests of humanist hubris. Therefore, this essay can also be read as a speculative reprisal against the supposedly antihumanist aspects of capitalism which contribute to its image as an irresistible singularity. This essay, consequently, shall attempt to wrest a radical conception of inhumanism from the Capital-nurturing hands of antihumanism in its various forms. In the wake of the complicity between science and capitalism, it is becoming more evident that the inhumanist resistance against capitalism should not dabble in preaching against humanism and its philosophical minions. Instead, it should dispose of the kind of antihumanist thought that romantically—whether willingly or not—contributes to the cult of Capital and occludes both thinking and praxis. One can recapitulate the above suspicions in regard to an antihumanist definition of capitalism in two questions:

---

9. See Ray Brassier, *Nihil Unbound: Enlightenment and Extinction*, Basingstoke, Palgrave Macmillan, 2007, pp. 205-239.

1. To what extent does the Freudian appropriation of Capital—tipped by Deleuze and Guattari and fully fashioned by Nick Land through the politico-economic unbinding of Freud's theory of thanatropic regression—as an antihumanist yet emancipative conception shatter the illusive sovereignty of the human and ally itself with the inhumanism that it claims to be the harbinger of?

2. Does the cosmological reinscription of Freud's account of the death-drive that extends the thanatropic regression from the organism to all other forms of embodiment (from organic life to the plant to stellar formations down to matter itself) repudiate the image of capitalism as an inexorable yet emancipative twister toward utter liquidation? Can the reinscription of Freud's theory of thanatropic regression on a cosmic level redeem antihumanism and rescue it from the clutches of capitalism? For it seems that in his recent work *Nihil Unbound*, Ray Brassier, following Land's novel approach to Freud in *The Thirst for Annihilation*, has resorted to the latter solution in order to wipe the stains of capitalism from the face of a cosmically eliminativist model of enlightenment (i.e. scientific nihilism as the daredevil of speculative thought)?

II

The identification of capitalism as a singularity at once participatory (hence open to praxis) and emancipative should not be oversimplified as an impotently phantasmic conception which passively awaits its actualization. It is rather a potent support and guarantor for the creative praxis of capitalism on all levels. It is the seamless integration of singularized inevitability and emancipative ubiquity that calls for a spontaneous praxis. And it is the emphasis on praxis that speeds the awakening of Capital's sweeping whirlwind. Therefore, such an identification of capitalism has become a programmatic form of apologetics for capitalism's ubiquity which in turn justifies the axiomatic assimilation of all planetary systems, forms of life and vectors of thought by the mimetic flow of Capital. The ubiquity of capitalism, to this extent, is affirmed precisely by its identification as a liquidating storm which is in the process of dethroning the human from its terrestrial ivory tower. And it is this undulating deluge toward dissipation of matter and energy that either deceitfully mimics or genuinely coincides with the cosmic extinction or the asymptotic disintegration of the universe on an elementary material level, that is to say, the ubiquitous and all-inclusive cosmic truth of extinction, the truth of extinction as such. For this reason, the supposedly inhumanist identification of capitalism serves as a programmatic—rather than merely theoretic—contribution to the pragmatic ethos and assimilating nature of capitalism. This programmatic contribution is conducted by means of drawing a line of correspondence and coincidence between the dissolving forces of capital on the one hand and the disintegrating cosmic forces vigorously heralded by contemporary science on the other. This is why the antihumanist definition of capitalism—especially as a singularity that miraculously weaves participation, cosmic disenchantment and emancipation together—has turned into an allure for various affinities of speculative philosophy and imaginative politics. Whilst the former has been disillusioned in regard to the restrictions of matter as well as subjective or inter-subjective conditions for experience, the latter has grown weary of the romantic bigotries of kitsch Marxism and ruinous follies of liberalism.

In *The Thirst for Annihilation* and later in his numerous essays, Land introduces an inhumanist model of capitalism through a reappropriation of Freud's energetic model of the nervous system. The reason for Land's emphatic recourse to Freud's energetic model is that the extremity and terrestrial generality of Freud's account of the death-drive are able to universally mobilize capitalism beyond its historic and particular conditions. In other words, it is the death-drive that transcendentally and from within universalizes capital as the all-encompassing capitalism. Furthermore, as Land points out, if death is already inherent to capital as a 'machine part', the 'death of capitalism' is a delusion either generated by anthropomorphic wishful thinking or neurotic indulgence in victimhood.[10] In short, Land assumes that the emancipative conception of capitalism requires a realist model capable of positing the reality of emancipation exterior to ontological and subjective privileges of human. And it is Freud's energetic model that as a prototypical model of speculative thought revokes the enchanted ontological privileges of life by presenting life as a temporal scission from its precursor exteriority *qua* inorganic. Both the life of thought and the life of the human body are externally objectified by the originary exteriority that pulls them back toward a dissolution which is posited in anterior posteriority to life. The external objectification of the human hardware—coincidental with the independent reality of dissolution—undermines the monopoly and hegemony of the human genetic lineage as the vehicle of social dynamics. On the other hand, the objectification of thought is traumatically bound as a vector of disillusionment in regard to radical deficiencies of life as the constitutive horizon of thought's topology and dynamism. Such disillusionment paves the road toward an abyssal realm where thought must be armed with a speculative drive. Accordingly for Land, Freud's energetic model is comprised of an emancipative yet implicitly antihumanist front in that it posits the anterior posteriority of dissolution as a radical truth determined to flush human faculties down the latrine of pure objectivity.

However, Freud's energetic model is constituted of another front which does not thoroughly exclude the human: The traumatic scission from the inorganic or any precursor exteriority brings about the possibility of life which consists of energetic opportunities. These energetic opportunities are conservatively enveloped and developed to support the survival (from basic perseverance to complexification) of the organism or the index of interiority. Correspondingly, the energetic opportunities occasioned by the traumatic scission from the precursor exteriority are posed as tortuous driveways toward the originary state of dissolution. The conservative nature of the organism or the emerged interiority utilizes these energetic opportunities—ensued by an originary differentiation from the precursor exteriority—for intensive and extensive activities of sustenance. For this reason, the complication and explication of these energetic opportunities which are in accordance with the conservative nature of the organism can be taken as lines of participation. These opportunities can be programmed to change the topology, economy and dynamism of the inevitable return to the precursor exteriority. In short, the traumatic scission of the organic from the inorganic provides the organism with energetic opportunities which are posited as sites and conditions for participation. The second front of Freud's energetic model of thanatropic regression, accordingly, brings about the possibility of participation without ceasing to be ultimately emancipative and crushingly disenchanting. These two fronts are respectively (a) the emancipative front where dissolution and the disenchanting truth conjoin, and (b) the

---

10. Land, *Making It with Death*, p. 68.

participative front where the energetic opportunities of the conservative organism can be utilized as accelerative and programmatic vectors in the direction of the aforementioned emancipation.

These two fronts of Freud's model are connected by a maze of material and energy dissipation, an intricately circuitous curve whose slant can become steeper and thereby be *accelerated* toward the ultimate emancipation. It is here that capitalism is identified with this curve or maze of dissipation that links the conservative nature of the system to an emancipation which knows nothing of the human. The intertwinement of a predisposition for accumulation and a passion for liquidation within capitalism resonates with Freud's energetic model in which the conservative nature of the organism is a dissipative twist toward the inorganic exteriority. Capitalism, in this sense, is a dissipative tendency that unfolds through the complicated paths of the conservative horizon, turning the conditions for complexification of life (i.e. resources, techniques, participations, etc.) into conditions for its acceleration and perpetuating its angular momentum. Capitalism's parasitic insistence on its survival is the expression of its constitutive dissipative tendency (desire for meltdown) that must effectuate its singularity *by all means and at all costs*—hence the machinic conception of capitalism as an open system that assimilates every antagonism or exception as its axioms and resources. This is why in order to present an antihumanist model of capitalism, Land uses the direct correspondence between the conservative-dissipative conception of capitalism and Freud's energetic model of thanatropic regression for the organic conservation. The topologic, economic and dynamic calculi of this definition or model of capitalism as a 'liquidating storm against everything solid' can be found in Freud's theory of thanatropic regression. According to this definition of capitalism, although capitalism is ultimately emancipative in terms other than those of human, it can be participated and accelerated by human and for this reason, it does not exclude an ethics or politics of praxis.

In his tour de force on nihilism and enlightenment, *Nihil Unbound*, Ray Brassier seems to be fully aware of the threats that the Landian definition of capitalism poses against the disenchanting potentials of Freud's account of the death-drive. In the wake of such a definition, the emancipative energy of the truth of extinction implicated in the theory of thanatropic regression is converted to an alien and thus impartial justification for capitalist indulgences which conflate anthropic interests with the ever more complicating paths of organic survivalism. In other words, the inevitable truth of extinction as the apotheosis of the enlightenment's project of disenchantment is exploited by the Freudian reformulation of capitalism. In this way, the 'anterior posteriority' of extinction as an ultimate disenchantment affirms and reenacts human not only as the participating and accelerating element but also as something which deviously reconciles vitalism with the disenchanting 'truth of extinction'.[11] In order to purge Freud's theory of thanatropic regression from such manipulations and draw an 'intimate link between the will to know and the will to nothingness', Ray Brassier presents a genuinely speculative solution.[12] Brassier proposes that Freud's theory of thanatropic regression must be reinscribed on a cosmic level so that not only the organic dissolves into the inorganic but also the inorganic gains a dissipative or loosening tendency to-

---

11. 'It [extinction] retroactively disables projection, just as it pre-emptively abolishes retention. In this regard, extinction unfolds in an 'anterior posteriority' which usurps the 'future anteriority' of human existence'. Brassier, *Nihil Unbound*, p. 230.

12. Brassier, *Nihil Unbound*, p. xii.

ward the precursor exteriority *qua* the anterior posteriority of extinction. The 'cosmological re-inscription of Freud's account of the death-drive' unshackles the disenchanting and hence emancipative truth of extinction from the capitalism-friendly horizon of vitalism.[13] Just as the organic interiority is deserted on behalf of the inorganic, the inorganic materials as conditions of embodiment are deserted on behalf of an unbound cosmic exteriority where even the elementary fabric of matter is an index of interiorization and must be undone. It is in loosening every index of interiority and deserting their domain of influence that the truth of extinction forces thought to be a speculative imagination for and of the cosmic abyss.

> Since cosmic extinction is just as much of an irrecusable factum for philosophy as biological death—although curiously, philosophers seem to assume that the latter is somehow more relevant than the former, as though familiarity were a criterion of philosophical relevance—every horizonal reserve upon which embodied thought draws to fuel its quest will be necessarily finite. Why then should thought continue investing in an account whose dwindling reserves are circumscribed by the temporary parameters of embodiment? Why keep playing for time? A change of body is just a way of postponing thought's inevitable encounter with the death that drives it in the form of the will to know. And a change of horizon is just a means of occluding the transcendental scope of extinction, precisely insofar as it levels the difference between life and death, time and space, revoking the ontological potency attributed to temporalizing thought in its alleged invulnerability to physical death.[14]

Brassier's cosmic reinscription of Freud's thanatropic regression is an attempt to enact eliminativism as an ultimate vector of enlightenment and emancipative disenchantment. Yet to cosmically enact eliminativism, one must have a model to divest all horizons of interiority (from organisms to stars to galaxies and even matter itself) of their ontological potencies and so-called vitalistic opportunities for carrying on the life of thought. The model capable of guaranteeing such a great purge is Freud's account of the death-drive. However, as Brassier knows, there are two obstacles for the appropriation of Freud's model: First, as we argued earlier, the allegedly inhumanist conception of capitalism and especially Nick Land's Freudian reformulation of Capital justifies capitalist indulgences of anthropic agencies as ethical and political vectors. Therefore, the inhumanist conception of capitalism strategically venerates vitalism and its affirmationist policies on behalf of Freud's theory of the death-drive. The second obstacle is that Freud's account of the death-drive merely includes a disintegrating transition from the organic to the inorganic, which is to say, the thanatropic regression is peculiar to organic life in general. For this reason, Brassier tweaks Freud's account of the death-drive by reinscribing and reenacting it on a cosmic level. This way the vector of eliminativism can abandon the horizon of every interiority—whether of the organic or the inorganic (base-matter as such)—and in doing so, ensures the cosmic unbinding of enlightenment's project of disenchantment. Concurrently, the cosmic reinscription of Freud's account of the death-drive can terminate the sufficiency of capitalist participation for accelerating the disenchanting emancipation harboured by the truth of extinction. As even matter is deserted in order to unbind the abyssal realms of speculative thought, human participation for accelerating capitalist singularity loses its momentum as the bilateral aspect of participation is usurped by the unilateralizing power of the ultimate cosmic extinction. Yet the cancellation of suffi-

---

13. Brassier, *Nihil Unbound*, p. 204.

14. Brassier, *Nihil Unbound*, p. 228-229.

ciency neither guarantees an immaculate future for enlightenment nor provides adequate reasons as to why *senseless* human participations in capitalism must be stopped. Brassier's cosmic reinscription of Freud's model only manages to successfully eliminate the vitalistic horizon implicit in the antihumanist definition of capitalism proposed by Land. Yet it leaves the aporetic truth of capitalism as an inevitable singularity for dissipation bound to the conservative order of the anthropic horizon unharmed. By leaving the fundamental body and the primary front of the Landian definition of capitalism unharmed, Brassier's own project of enlightenment ironically turns into a dormant ethico-political enterprise with an utopianistic twist. Brassier's account of eliminativist enlightenment, in this sense, basks in the comforts of an utopianistic trust in opportunities brought about by the neurocognitive plasticity whilst peacefully cohabiting with capitalism on the same earth.

In the next section, we shall see why Brassier's cosmic reinscription of Freud's energetic model fails to disturb the integrity of capitalism as a singularity for dissipation adopted by the economic order of the human organism in its accelerating pursuit for intensive preservation and extensive sustenance (complexification). In this regard, we shall elaborate how singling out certain aspects of Freud's theory of thanatropic regression enables Land to erroneously attribute antihumanist and hence disenchantingly emancipative aspects to capitalism. Also in the same vein, we shall argue that the persuasion of Land's discriminating reading of Freud's account of the death-drive ultimately renders Brassier's cosmic reinscription of the death-drive unobjectionable and oblivious to the aporetic truth of capitalism. The next section will also attempt to answer the two questions posed at the end of section I.

III

In what seems to be the apotheosis of *Beyond the Pleasure Principle*, Freud writes:

> In the last resort, what has left its mark on the development of organisms must be the history of the earth we live in and of its relation to the sun. [...] It would be in contradiction to the conservative nature of the instincts if the goal of life were a state of things which had never yet been attained. On the contrary, it must be an old state of things, an initial state from which the living entity has at one time or other departed and to which it is striving to return by the circuitous paths along which its development leads. If we are to take it as a truth that knows no exception that everything living dies for internal reasons—becomes inorganic once again—then we shall be compelled to say that 'the aim of life is death' and, looking backwards, that 'inanimate things existed before living ones'. [...] For a long time, perhaps, living substance was thus being constantly created afresh and easily dying, till decisive external influences altered in such a way as to oblige the still surviving substance to diverge ever more widely from its original course of life and to make ever more complicated détours before reaching its aim of death. These circuitous paths to death, faithfully kept to by the conservative instincts, would thus present us to-day with the picture of the phenomena of life.[15]

Freud then explicitly characterizes the nature of this thanatropic tendency as a monopolistic regime of death supported by economical limits and conservative conditions of the organism:

> They [self-preservative instincts] are component instincts whose function it is to assure that the organism shall follow its own path to death, and to ward off any possible ways of returning to inorganic existence other than those which are immanent in the organism it-

---

15. Sigmund Freud, *Beyond the Pleasure Principle*, New York, W. W. Norton & Company, 1961, p. 32.

self. We have no longer to reckon with the organism's puzzling determination (so hard to fit into any context) to maintain its own existence in the face of every obstacle. What we are left with is the fact that the organism wishes to die only in its own fashion.[16]

Freud's account of the death-drive or theory of thanatropic regression consists of three interconnected aspects, a speculative daemon with a tri-lobed head. Despite having their own lines of speculative thought with their respective consequences, these three aspects are intricately connected and cannot operate without each other. For the sake of analytical precision, we shall dissect these lobes or interconnected aspects as follows:

1. The first aspect (the disenchanting / objectifying truth of extinction): The organism (as an index of interiority) temporally extends from the inorganic state yet it is energetically driven—*by all means* and *at all costs*—to its precursor exteriority by flexing its contraction back to the inorganic (decontraction). The thanatropic regression aims toward a death whose reality can neither be indexed as a past state (hence not susceptible to retrogressive experience) nor a future point (hence independent of the reality of the organism). The reality of the originary death is exorbitantly exterior to conditions of life to which it traumatically gives rise to. *Thanatropic regression harbours the disenchanting truth of extinction as an anterior posteriority* whose actual yet independent objectivity and unilateral demand for objectification make it inassimilable for transcendental subjectivity. Since the actuality and independence of extinction concurrently precede and supersede existential temporality, extinction is thus irreducible to varieties of death-spiritualism.

2. The second aspect (the praxis of dissipation): Although the thanatropic regression toward the precursor exteriority is unilateralized by the precursor exteriority, its dynamic course and economy follows the conservative nature of the organism. The dissipative tendency, or more accurately, the course of decontraction toward the originary exorbitant death is shaped by the conservative nature of the organism. The energetic incongruity between the dysteleologic death and the organic conservative nature (i.e. the medium-course) causes the thanatropic regression to be topologically, dynamically and economically conceived as a twist or an inflective curve. Life, in this sense, is an inflection of death. Despite the inevitability of death, life's dynamic and economic twist opens up convoluted horizons for participation. *The umwege of life or the inflection of death is twistedly open to praxis (hence the possibility of political intervention and economic participation).*

3. The third aspect (the dictatorial tendency of affordance): Since the course and the medium of thanatropic regression are determined by the economic order and conservative conditions of the organism, the *modus operandi* of the organism's dissipative tendency is subjected to the quantitative and qualitative reductions dictated by the economical affordability of the organism. To put it differently, conservative conditions of the organism impose an economical restriction on the dissipative tendency of the organism so that the organism only dies in those ways which are immanent to, or more precisely, affordable for it. *The organism can only follow its own affordable and thus economically conservative path to death in order to decontract.* Accelerating the dissipative tendency through political and economic praxis, therefore, does not lead to divergence

16. Freud, *Beyond the Pleasure Principle*, p. 33.

from the conservative economy, but to the intensive re-enactment of such economy's dictatorial foundations in regard to death.

4. According to what we elaborated earlier in section II, Land's libidinal materialist conception of capitalism as an inhumanist praxis which is open to the liquidating process of emancipation accentuates the second aspect of Freud's model. Yet at the same time, it also relatively adopts the first aspect of Freud's account of the death-drive within the terrestrial or rather a non-ubiquitous scope. Consequently, in Land's account of capitalism the politico-economic praxis (conceived by the detours and anomalies of life) meets and coincides with the cosmic vector of emancipation. Yet, through the cosmic reinscription of the first aspect, Brassier elegantly shows that the emancipative truth of extinction ultimately annuls the vitalistic proclivities in the second aspect and widens the scope of emancipation from the terrestrial to the cosmic. And it is this cosmic unbinding that inflicts a decisive blow against the sufficiency of human interests and desires surreptitiously integrated within capitalism as propulsive elements. Brassier cosmically reinscribes the first aspect of Freud's theory of thanatropic regression in order to extend the eliminativist / disenchanting vector of enlightenment all the way to the cosmic exteriority as the unilateralizing truth for the mobilization of speculative thought. However, Brassier's cosmic reinscription of Freud's account of the death-drive also results in the cosmic unbinding of the second aspect (*viz.* the theory of *umwege*) which is inseparable from the first. Yet in this case the increasing convolutions of the dissipative tendency do not suggest new opportunities for prolonging the life of thought. Instead these mazy convolutions bespeak of a twisted chain of traumatically nested horizons of interiorities which must be deserted or betrayed, one in favour of another. Here *umwege* presents a graph for the external objectification of thought, a turning inside-out of thought whereby the commitment to thought is supplanted by the treachery of the object on behalf of extinction. This is why Brassier's cosmic reinscription of the first aspect ingeniously conjures a shadow of a non-vitalist ethics or a desertifying politics of eliminativism which aims at objectifying every horizon of interiority (including thought and embodiment) so as to expose them to the desertifying vector of eliminativism. However, both Land and Brassier seem to remain oblivious to the implications of the third aspect (*viz.* the dictatorial tendency of affordance) and exclude it from their calculations in regard to capitalism and enlightenment.

Life of the organism is determined by the way it must return to the inorganic state. Human life, correspondingly, is determined by the human's path to its precursor exteriority. The thanatropic regression which registers itself as a dissipative tendency for matter and energy is conducted through this path. Such a path for human is drawn by the conservative conditions of the human organism. We call this conservative regime of the open system or the organism which forces the dissipation or the thanatropic regression to be in conformity to the dynamic capacity of the organism or the organism's affordable economy of dissipation, *necrocracy*. In short, necrocracy suggests the strictures of the conservative economy not in regard to life but in regard to ways the organism dies; and it is the way of returning to the originary death that prescribes the course of life for the organism. Accordingly, necrocracy does not imply that every life brings with it the *de facto* reign of death from the beginning or that *living* is *submitting* to the rule of death. Instead necrocracy suggests that the organism must die or bind the precursor exteriority only in ways that its conservative conditions or economic order can afford. The principle of affordability in regard to the fashion of the thanatropic regression strictly conforms to the economic order of the organism, but it is primarily conditioned by the exorbitance and the inevitability of death postulated by the anterior posteriority of extinction. Hence, necrocracy is decided by conservative conditions of the living agency which cannot repel the inevitability of death, nor can it *unconditionally* return to the inorganic state.

As we shall later elaborate, the unconditionality of death or extinction must not be confused with the conditionality of returning to the originary death. The latter is imposed by the formation of the organism where capacities and conditions for conservation are inextricable from terms of decontraction posited by the unconditional death. For the living agency, the path to death is dictated by its dynamic capacity for conservation which can only afford to die or dissipate according to conditions posed by the intensive and extensive factors of affordability. Affordability, in this sense, is the correlation between the economy of sustenance and the excess of the outside which manifests in the economical correlation between the complicative introgression and the explicative progression of the organism or open system. For this reason, the emerging complexity of the living agency which corresponds with its ability to temporally postpone death and convert the acquired time to capitalizable 'interest' for the living organism bespeaks of nothing but the affordable way to die or dissipate. In its tendency for complexification, axiomatic assimilation of all resources and insistence upon an internal autonomy despite its accelerative movement toward meltdown, capitalism corresponds to the principles of an affordable path toward dissolution prescribed and conditioned by the conservative capacity of the anthropic system in regard to the inevitability of death.

Once the necrocratic regime of the organism—implicated in the third aspect of Freud's account of the death-drive—is exposed, capitalism is revealed as the last conservative front which the human organism is not willing to surrender. The implications of the necrocratic regime of the organism disarm Land's conception of emancipative 'capitalism as a whirlwind of dissolution' by emptying it from its seemingly inhumanist bravado. At the same time, such implications tarnish the disenchanting vector of speculative thought harboured by the truth of extinction which lies at the center of Brassier's project. Although human, its faculties and privileges are objectified and subsequently extinguished by the truth of extinction, for the human the implications of such truth can only register in conformity with the strictly conservative aspects of the human organism. Even though the human and its wherewithal are unilaterally objectified by the truth of extinction on a cosmic level, the course of their objectification *qua* dissolution stringently corresponds to the intrinsic conservative formation and interiorizing terms of the anthropic sphere. The speculative vectors mobilized by the cosmic truth of extinction, therefore, are forcefully trammeled by the necrocratic regime in which the human can only bind and inflect upon 'exorbitant death' (Brassier) *qua* extinction in terms conforming to its economical order and affordability.[17] This is to say that even though the cosmic truth of extinction points to a disenchanting moment, its locus of registration abides by the conservative economy and the restrictive affordabil-

---

17. Brassier, *Nihil Unbound*, p. 238.

ity of the human organism. Since the truth of extinction is exorbitant to the organism, its wealth is always energetically subjected to the affordability of the organism.[18] The 'speculative opportunities' (Brassier) of the truth of extinction, to this extent, obliquely affirm and reinforce the conservative and interiorizing truth of the human affordability.[19] The implications of the necrocratic regime of the organism, as we shall see, outline the limits of both an emancipative conception of capitalism and the speculative opportunities generated by the truth of extinction.

IV

The necrocratic regime of the organism has two economic ramifications: (a) the conservative nature of the organism asserts that the organism should only follow its own path to death and all other ways of inflecting upon the precursor exteriority which are not immanent to, or more accurately, not affordable for the organism must be averted; (b) any change or reformation aimed at the organism's course of life or its respective problems is ultimately in accordance with the organism's circumscribed path to death which is affordable by and exigently in conformity to the economical order of the organism. The path to death demarcates the modal range by which the organism must die because these are the ways or modes of dissipation which are intensively and extensively affordable by the economy of the organism. Thus the second necrocratic law can also be put differently: Variations in ways of living and pursuing one way over another for the better or worse of the organism remain within the confines of the organism's inherent economical and conservative nature which is demarcated by its restricted economy or exclusivist policy toward death. The capitalist production of lifestyles, in this sense, is nothing more than the consequence of capitalism's submission to the necrocratic regime whereby the organism must only perish or bind negativity in ways affordable for its conservative economy. The so-called openness of capitalism toward modes of life and its obsession with life-oriented models of emancipation attests to its progressive refusal in questioning the necrocratic regime. It suggests the intrinsic inability of capitalism in posing alternative ways of inflecting upon death and binding exteriority other than those afforded by the conservative horizon. Any model of emancipation aimed at the life of the organism is confined to the monopolistic horizon of necrocracy which is in complete accordance with the economic order of the organism. Life-oriented models of emancipation merely mark the various possibilities of the organism's life as the *modi vivendi* dictated by the necrocratic regime of the organism. In doing so, such models dissimulate their fundamentally restricted framework and mask their obedient nature toward the oppressive regime of necrocracy which restricts modes (*modi operandi*) of inflecting upon death or binding exteriority.[20]

---

18. Affordability should not be understood solely in terms of the organism but also as an economical correlation through which the continuity between the excess that gives rise to the organism and the exteriorizing excess of death can be maintained through and within the economic order of the organism or the open system.

19. Brassier, *Nihil Unbound*, p. xi.

20. Throughout the entire history of philosophy, a unanimously established law of binding has been held and maintained without interrogation. Parallel to the energetic model of organic dissipation or death, this law or axiomatic principle holds that death or cosmic exteriority can be bound in one and one way only. As a result, extinction or cosmic exteriorization always appears as a singular point of departure or pull-back (inflection) toward the precursor exteriority whose monistic path the organism cannot diverge. The establishment of this model of binding is due to the insufficiency of philosophical thought and imagination with regard to thinking extinction as contingently 'different or alternative' ways or courses of binding cosmic exteriority. The model of death or exteriorization as a singularity creates an impasse for thought that results

Counter-intuitively, associating inhumanism with Capital's singularity toward dissolution is faulty if not humanly myopic. This is because the accelerative vector of Capital for dissolution strictly remains in the confines of the necrocratic regime of the organism wherein the restrictive policy in regard to modes of dissolution fundamentally abides by the conservative economy and interiorizing conditions of the (human) organism. In other words, capitalism's dissipative tendency is deeply in thrall to the constitutional limit of the anthropic sphere in that the anthropic horizon is not fundamentally distinguished by its model(s) of life but its simultaneously restricted and restrictive attitude toward the exteriorizing death. Capitalism is, in fact, the very affordable and conservative path to death dictated by the human organism on an all-encompassing level. Capitalism does not repel the excess of the exorbitant truth of extinction as much as it economically affirms (i.e. mandates the affordability of) such an excess. The economical binding or affording of the excess of the truth of extinction is certainly an unsuccessful binding, but an essential 'unsuccessful binding' necessitated for underpinning the aporetic truth of capitalism without abolishing it. In fact, affording never implies a successful binding of an exorbitant truth; it is insistently an unsuccessful, or more precisely, economical binding tethered to the capacity of the conservative order. Under the economic aegis of an unsuccessfully bound truth of extinction, capitalism is able to utilize the inevitability and ubiquity of extinction to respectively feign its singularity and vindicate its assertive omnipresence. By presenting singularity and ubiquity as its undisputable verities, capitalism can craftily dissimulate its anthropic economic order as an all-inclusive and prevalent terrestrial way of binding exteriority which happens to be 'a little inhuman' (Land). Yet, in reality, it is the economic decision of the human organism in regard to the originary death which capitalism universalizes through politico-economic opportunities brought about by the 'unsuccessful binding' of the truth of extinction.

According to Freud, the organism shall only follow its own path to death. This thanatropic path consists of those modes of dissipation which are fundamentally affordable by the conservative nature of the organism. Alternative ways of returning to the originary state of dissolution are in contradiction with the conservative nature of the organism's own way of thanatropic regression and are excluded by the necrocratic regime. Therefore, if the ultimate conception of capitalism is an accelerative and inevitable singularity of dissolution which assimilates every planetary resource, then it cannot be a radically alternative way of dissolution to those already affordable by the (human) organism. Because if capitalism was indeed a vector of dissolution external to the conservative ambit of human, it would have already been excluded and ferociously warded off by the economic order of the human organism. This is because, as we stated, it is not alternative modes of living which are staved off by the organism but alternative ways of inflecting upon the originary death and binding exteriority. For this reason, capitalism is nothing but the very mode of dissipation and dissolution which

---

in a naturalized inability to think an alternative model of binding exteriority or cosmic extinction. Because such an alternative model of binding, dying or exteriorization is misconstrued either as another form of 'living' (vitalistically escaping the thought of extinction) or an impossible form of exteriorization and death that ironically must be warded off on both philosophical and political grounds. The restricted economy of death as a singularity can only afford the idea of extinction in accordance with the given 'possibility(-ies)' of the world and never according to the contingency inherent to exteriority—a contingency that is irreducible to both possibilities of the world and possible worlds. Therefore in order to embrace the thought of extinction as the unilateral expression of absolute contingency, we must first break away from the model of death-as-a-singularity which is but death according to the 'world of given possibilities'.

is exclusive to the anthropic horizon because it is in complete conformity with the capacity of human's interiorized formation in its various economic configurations. Since capitalism is the fundamentally affordable way of dissipation for the economic order of the anthropic horizon, it is inherently hostile toward other modes of 'binding exteriority' which cannot be afforded by the anthropic horizon. In other words, the truth of capitalism's global dominance lies in its monopolistic necrocracy: A feral vigilance against all alternative ways of binding exteriority or returning to the originary death other than those which are immanent to and affordable for the anthropic horizon. Only a vigilance beyond hate and enmity but blinded by the economic order of the organism and its pressing demands can describe capitalism's actively militant and intelligent alertness against all other modes of dissolution and negativity. This vigilance manifests in capitalism's restless assimilation of every form of negativity so as to reintegrate it as another mode or style of life. In doing so, capitalism can prevent the mobilization of that negativity as an alternative way for binding exteriority and therefore, maintains its dominantly prevalent position in regard to the human.

Conditioned by the conservative formation of the organism, the economic order of the organism determines the way by which the organism must return to the originary 'state of dissolution'. The criterion for such determination (dying in one way rather than another) is the affordability of the organism. Openness, correspondingly, is a dynamic economical correlation between the organism's intensive and extensive economic factors. The openness of the organism to the outside is conducted through an affordable path which consists of a range of activities corresponding to the economic conditions of the organism. This does not mean that the organism's economic order is oblivious to the inevitability of death or dissolution but on the contrary, it factors in the certainty of death in each and every calculation. In grasping the organic as an inflection-sequence of the inorganic, the terms of decontraction which have been unconditionally posited by the inorganic are inseparable from the conditions inherent to the contracted organic agency. Only by including the inevitability of dissolution, can the capacity simultaneously preserve the organism's conservative economy and engage in extensive / explicative activities which involve risks and hazardous expenditures. Thus more than postponing the time of death and escaping the truth of extinction, the conservative formation of the organism strives to make the unconditional death affordable and express the truth of extinction in its own economical terms. Affordability ensures that the unilaterality implied by the inevitability of extinction be economically and hence, *unsuccessfully* bilateralized. The aim of affordability is to make the discrepancy between the inherent desire for self-preservation and the inevitability of death consistent with the economic order of the organism. The vigilant stance against alternative paths to death infers the economic bilateralization of death's unilateral terms, because here bilaterlization attests to the binding of the truth of extinction in no other terms than those of the organism and its economic order. The disenchanting influences of extinction on thought, consequently, are dampened by the economic bilateralization of death. For the anthropic horizon, such bilateral *qua* affordable terms conform to the truth of schizophrenically unbound capitalism as the dominantly affordable mode of dissipation or thanatropic regression. If 'the truth of extinction' is unsuccessfully bound as a vector of dissipation whose terms are affordable for the organism and if for the anthropic horizon capitalism stands as the dominant set of such terms, then the economical binding of the truth of extinction inaugurates the truth of capitalism.

In the end, what capitalism's vigilance against non-dialectical forms of negativity suggests is that the exorbitant truth of extinction has been bound by the conservative terms of the anthropic horizon which are reflected in the dissipative tendency of Capital. Moreover, this axiomatic vigilance indicates that capitalism is not willing to share the truth of extinction outside of its own economically paved dissipative path. In this case, speculative opportunities brought about by the exorbitant truth of extinction contribute to the militant potency of capitalism in staving off alternative ways of binding exteriority and obstructing the remobilization of non-dialectical negativity in ways which do not conform to the economic order of the conservative horizon.

The reason for the vigilance against alternative paths of dissipation can be put in simple terms: The organism insists on binding death only in its own terms. These terms are the conditions inherent to the organism's capacity to conserve and respectively, its affordability to mobilize such conservation in any direction. Correspondingly, these terms are the economical premises which mark the boundaries of the organism and determine its conception. What primarily forces the organism to fashion its own path to death is the impossibility of bargaining the compulsory terms of an exorbitant death. In other words, it is the unilaterality of extinction—the traumatically exorbitant immensity of the truth of extinction—which inspires and contributes to the organism's exclusivist regime of dissipation. For the anthropic horizon, capitalism corresponds to such a necrocratic regime whereby inflecting upon the originary death and binding exteriority are conducted in terms which strictly conform to the conservative formation of the interiorized horizon. Consequently, it is the exorbitant immensity of the truth of extinction that inspires the emergence and acceleration of capitalism as the economically affordable tendency for dissipation and liquidation. When it comes to an exorbitant truth, whether it is of the sun or cosmic extinction, the speculative choices are limited to how the exorbitant wealth (speculative opportunities?) is to be squandered. This dictum lies at the heart of capitalism as the speculative consequence of an exorbitant truth for which the traumatic compulsion for squandering must intertwine and unite with the inherently conservative economy of affording more. Capitalism's incessant production of modi vivendi (courses of life) is the result of capturing the compulsory and exorbitant terms of extinction in bilateral and affordable terms. This is because the possibility of living is guaranteed by these bilateral terms according to which death can be exigently approached in terms of the organic capacity and its interiorizing affordability. Accordingly, contra Land's dismissal of the third aspect of Freud's energetic model as a 'security hallucination', the organic necrocracy does not make death subordinate to the organism, it is on the contrary the result of full subordination to death.[21]

The exclusivist stance of the organism in regard to its path to death is the very expression of the insurmountable truth of death within the organic horizon as a dissipative tendency which is supposed to mobilize the conservative conditions of the organism toward death. Unconditional submission to death—or a death whose path is not paved by the economic terms of the organism—bespeaks of the impossibility of the temporality of the organic life from the outset. A death that does not allow the organism to die in its own terms is a death that usurps all conditions required for the organ-

---

21. 'What Freud calls the organism's 'own path to death' is a security hallucination, screening out death's path through the organism. '[T]he organism wishes to die only in its own fashion', he writes, as if death were specifiable, privatizable, subordinate to a reproductive order [...]' Land, 'Machinic Desire', p. 481.

ic differentiation and temporary survival. Yet the contingent and undeniably scarce instances of organic life and transient survival imply that the thanatropic regression is merely unconditional in regard to the inevitable unilateralizing power of death, but in terms of its 'course of conduction' it is conditional. The inevitability of death does not point to its absolute unconditionality but rather to the compulsive attempt of the organism to bind its precursor exteriority by mustering all its own intensive and extensive economic conditions toward dissolution. The detours of life are drawn not because death should be unconditionally embraced but because the organism is itself the inflection of death, a slope-curve between the inevitability of death and conservative conditions of the organism. It is this very conception of organism as a differential ratio between the insurmountable truth of death and conservative organic conditions for binding such a truth that brings about the possibility of acceleration or hastening toward dissolution. Yet, as we argued, such hastening is not a radical embracing of the exorbitant truth of extinction, but rather an affordable and hence, a purely economical (unsuccessful) way of binding the excess of such a truth. It is the unbindable excess of the truth of extinction—as that which cannot be circumvented—that necessitates such an affordable way of binding within the economic order of the organism. And it is this affordable binding that can indeed be conceived in terms of acceleration.[22]

V

A simultaneously inhumanist and emancipative conception of capitalism as a runway for imaginative (speculative?) praxis is a hastily crafted chimera. This is not because capitalism is not really a partially repressed desire for meltdown but because the image of capitalism as a planetary singularity for dissipation testifies to its rigid conformity to the anthropic horizon which only follows an affordable path to death. In doing so, capitalism as a twisted dissipative tendency rigidly wards off all other ways of dissolution and binding exteriority which are not immanent to or affordable for the anthropic horizon. This is because the conservative obligation of the dominant dissipative tendency (*viz.* the organic path to dissolution) is to thwart any disturbance which might be directed at the bilateral or conservative approach of the organism to death. At the same time, the insistence on speculative opportunities begotten by the disenchanting truth of extinction *qua* 'anterior posteriority' is a bit more than a philosophical over-confidence in the enlightening consummation of nihilism and an underestimation of anthropomorphic trickeries. For as we argued, in the ambit of the organism the exorbitant truth of extinction registers as a conservative path to extinction, which is to say, it is bound as a mediocrely affordable truth. On the other hand, we argued that the exorbitant truth of extinction inspires and contributes to the dominantly necrocratic dissipative tendency of the organism which in the case of the anthropic horizon forms the truth of capitalism. For this reason, the truth of extinction is not sufficient to guarantee either the imaginative praxis of capitalism or speculative opportunities harboured by the nihilistic sublimation of the Enlightenment. The ostensibly inhumanist creativities of capitalism and the speculative implications of a cosmological eliminativism respectively become parts of an antihumanist convention or a nihilist lore which ultimately

---

22. Whilst for Land the possibility of accelerating capitalism rests on the economical binding of an exorbitant index of exteriority within the energetic scope of the organism, for Brassier the possibility of philosophical binding of extinction can only be anchored by an economical binding of the exorbitant truth of extinction. This economical binding can be understood in terms of a deepened Freudian account of trauma whose topology and energetic model are casually engaged and strategically affirmed by both Land and Brassier.

and ironically lack a cunning vision of doom. The blunt confidence of both in the truth of extinction as either that which mysteriously sorts everything out or the gate-opener of speculative vistas sterilized of human mess, voluntary or not, contributes to the truth of capitalism without bothering to disturb its comfort zones.

It is the registering of the exorbitant truth of extinction as an affordable dissipative tendency that enables the organism to actively but economically (*viz.* unsuccessfully) bind extinction. And it is the economical binding of extinction as a guarantor for active dissipation that forces the organism to take an exclusivist policy toward other possible ways of binding the originary death or loosening into exteriority *qua* non-conceptual negativity. Whereas the former impediment in regard to the truth of extinction complicates ventures of speculative thought, the latter obstacle imposed by the exclusive policy toward alternative ways of binding exteriority sets a major limit against the possibility of having a politico-economical counterpart for speculative thought. Yet as we stated in the beginning, once these limits come to light, philosophical thought and political praxis can either attempt to breach them or move in another direction where such impasses have less paralyzing influence. At this point, we shall briefly touch on some of the purely conjectural alternatives brought about by the unveiling of the aforementioned limits.

If we identify the life of the anthropic horizon—of both human material hardware and thought—as a set of dynamic yet affordable and exclusivist ways for the anthropic horizon to bind the precursor exteriority, then we can tentatively define the Inhuman by the possibility of *alternative* ways of binding exteriority *qua* concept-less negativity. The Inhuman, respectively, is outlined by those ways of binding exteriority or complicity with non-conceptual negativity which are not immanent to the anthropic horizon and betray the economical order of the anthropic horizon in regard to exteriority. Such alternatives do not simply suggest dying in ways other than those prescribed by the organism, but rather the mobilization of forms of non-dialectical negativity which can neither be excluded by the dominant dissipative tendency of the anthropic horizon nor can be fully sublated by its order. For this reason, these remobilized forms of non-dialectical negativity should not be completely unaffordable or external to the economical order, for such absolute resistance to conservative conditions or exteriority to the affordability of the horizon is indexed as an *exorbitant* negativity. As we showed earlier, this is precisely the un-affordability of the exorbitant negativity *qua* death—as that which is foreclosed to negotiation—that inspires the conservatively necrocratic approach of the organism toward exteriority. And it is the insistence on affording (*viz.* economically affirming) such an exorbitant and externalized negativity that turns into a compulsion for the organism to exclude other possible ways of binding exteriority. Such exclusion is conducted through the compulsive elimination of all traces of non-dialectical negativity other than those affordable by the economic order of the horizon. Consequently, it is the compulsive elimination of alternative traces of non-dialectical *qua* unilateralizing negativity that forestalls the unfolding of speculative thought and its praxis. However, just as these mobilized forms of non-dialectical negativity should not be posited as indexes of exorbitant externality, they should not succumb to a consistently positive status for affirming and re-enacting the conservative horizon either.

In order to charge and remobilize traces of non-dialectical negativity as alternative ways of binding exteriority, the negativity should neither affirm the conservative horizon nor posit itself as exorbitantly external to it. Such a remobilization of non-dialectical negativity, to this extent, brings to mind the treacherous pragmatics of the Insider—an interiorized yet inassimilable (unilateralized) negativity which uses the economical affordability of the conservative horizon as an alternative medium for the eruption of exteriority.[23] The remobilization of non-dialectical negativity as the so-called Insider, for this reason, requires an equivocal conception of the void as its principle of negativity. This is because an equivocal conception of the void does not celebrate its exteriority as an exorbitant externality which enforces negativity in the form of a conservative dissipative tendency to the outside (extensive subtraction). The equivocal conception of the void not only brings about the possibility of negativity but also makes such negativity infectious, for equivocality here means that the void as the principle of negativity is intensively and problematically open to interiorizing terms and conditions of the conservative horizon without ceasing to be exterior or losing its inassimilable negativity. Since the equivocal conception of the void can be interiorized but cannot be assimilated, it interiorizes non-dialectical negativity's 'power of incision' (Brassier) as the creativity of perforation which effectuates the inassimilability *qua* unilaterality of negativity as a nested exteriority that loosens itself within the interiorized horizon.[24] Only the acceleration of a world-capitalism perforated by such insider conceptions of non-dialectical negativity is tantamount to the metastatic propagation of an exteriorizing terror which is too close to the jugular vein of capital to be either left alone or treated.

In short, the equivocal conception of the void as the principle of negativity mobilizes a logic of negativity that does not require operating on an exorbitantly external level or turning into a positive salvation. Whilst the exorbitant conception of negativity as an *external* index of resistance feeds capitalism's conservative impetus for widening its limits (*affording more*), the positive stance of affirmation is an artless re-enactment of the conservative horizon. Therefore, the programmatic objective of an inhuman praxis is to remobilize non-dialectical negativity beyond such Capital-nurturing conceptions of negativity. Without such a programmatic sponsor, alternative ethics of openness or politics of exteriorization, the speculative vectors of thought are not only vulnerable to the manipulations of capitalism but also are seriously impeded.

One can reformulate the limits discussed in this essay in terms of the limits implicit in the terrestrial image of thought. If according to Freud, the development of the organism is molded by the extensive correlation between the earth and the sun, then what are the implications of this relation for the terrestrial thought? For it seems that the earth's conservative-dissipative correlation with the sun has entrenched its traces in thought as a dominant model for the economy, topology and dynamism of life. This is not just because a major part of formations on the planet (including all human endeavours) are directly contingent upon the sun, but also because the sun's exorbitant exteriority ingrains a conservative image of exteriority in thought. Such exorbitant exteriority can only be bound as an affordable dissipative tendency which rigidly limits the image of exteriority and in doing so, restricts all other possible ways for binding exteriority. The energetic sun-earth axis has become a burdening chain for the terrestrial image of thought insofar as it constitutes the exclusivist model of death and dissipation

23. For more details on an equivocal conception of the void, see: Reza Negarestani, 'Differential Cruelty: A Critique of Ontological Reason in Light of the Philosophy of Cruelty', *Angelaki*, vol. 14, no. 3, 2009, pp. 69-84.

24. Brassier, *Nihil Unbound*, p. 146.

which restricts the scope of thought in regard to its own death. The question, to this extent, is how to break the hegemonic model of the sun in regard to death and exteriority without submitting to another star, another horizon or even investing in the truth of extinction whose exorbitance leads to restrictions reminiscent of those imposed by solar excess. Does the speculative unbinding of terrestrial thought from the sun as an exclusivist mode of dissipation which must be afforded by all means require a different conception of terrestriality that binds exteriority in different modes other than those prescribed by the solar economy? Or does such a task require a vector of thought capable of circumventing the earth so as to evade the limits posed by the solar economy, the order of economical affordability and the restrictive image of exteriority immanent to it? But then what is the relation of such thought that has dispossessed itself of its immediate resources with 'extralimital idealism'?

14

Is it Still Possible to be a Hegelian Today?

Slavoj Žižek

The main feature of historical thought proper is not 'mobilism' (the motif of the flu-idification or historical relativization of all forms of life), but the full endorsement of a certain *impossibility*: after a true historical break, one simply cannot return to the past, one cannot go on as if nothing happened—if one does it, the same practice acquires a radically changed meaning. Adorno provided a nice example with Schoenberg's aton-al revolution: after it took place, one can, of course, (and one does) go on composing in the traditional tonal way, but the new tonal music has lost its innocence, since it is already 'mediated' by the atonal break and thus functions as its negation. This is why there is an irreducible element of *kitsch* in the twentieth century tonal composers like Rachmaninov—something of a nostalgic clinging to the past, of an artificial fake, like the adult who tries to keep alive the naïve child in him. And the same goes for all do-mains: after the emergence of philosophical analysis of notions with Plato, mythical thought lost its immediacy, all revival of it is a fake; after the emergence of Christian-ity, all revivals of paganism are a nostalgic fake.

Writing/thinking/composing as if a Rupture didn't occur is more ambiguous than it may appear and cannot be reduced to a non-historical denial. Badiou once famously wrote that what unites him with Deleuze is that they are both classic phi-losophers for whom Kant, the Kantian break, didn't happen—but is it so? Maybe this holds for Deleuze, but definitely not for Badiou.[1] Nowhere is this clearer than in their different handling of the Event. For Deleuze, an Event effectively is a pre-Kan-tian cosmological One which generates multitude, which is why Event is absolutely immanent to reality, while the Badiouian Event is a break in the order of being (tran-scendentally constituted phenomenal reality), an intrusion into it of a radically het-erogeneous ('noumenal') level, so that we are clearly in (post-)Kantian space. This is why one can even define Badiou's systematic philosophy (developed in his last mas-

---

1. Even with Deleuze, one can claim that his Spinoza is a post-Kantian Spinoza, a Spinoza impercepti-bly re-read through post-Kantian frame. Deleuze does something like Fellini in *Satyricon*, where he stages the Roman pagan universe the way it appears retrospectively, from the Christian standpoint—with the un-derlying idea that one can really grasp what paganism was only in this retrospective way.

terpiece *Logics Of Worlds*) as Kantianism reinvented for the epoch of radical contingency: instead of one transcendentally-constituted reality, we get the multiplicity of
worlds, each delineated by its transcendental matrix, a multiplicity which cannot be
mediated/unified into a single larger transcendental frame; instead of the moral Law,
we get fidelity to the Truth-Event which is always specific with regard to a particular situation of a World.

Is Hegel's speculative idealism not *the* exemplary case of such a properly historical
impossibility? Can one still be a Hegelian after the post-Hegelian break with traditional metaphysics which occurred more or less simultaneously in the works of Schopenhauer, Kierkegaard and Marx? After this break, is there not something inherently false
in advocating a Hegelian 'absolute Idealism'? Is, then, any re-affirmation of Hegel not
a victim of the same anti-historical illusion, by-passing the impossibility to be a Hegelian after the post-Hegelian break, writing as if the post-Hegelian break did not happen? Here, however, one should complicate things a little bit: in some specific conditions, one can and should write as if a break didn't happen—in what conditions? To
put it simply and directly: when the break we are referring to is not the true break but
a false break, the one which obliterates the true break, the true point of impossibility.
Our wager is that this, precisely, is what happened with the 'official' post-Hegelian an-
ti-philosophical break (Schopenhauer-Kierkegaard-Marx): although it presents itself
as a break with idealism as embodied in its Hegelian climax, it ignores the crucial dimension of Hegel's thought, i.e., it ultimately amounts to a desperate attempt to *go on
thinking as if Hegel did not happen*—the hole of this absence of Hegel is, of course, filled in
with the ridiculous caricature of Hegel the 'absolute idealist' who 'possessed absolute
Knowledge'. The re-assertion of Hegel's speculative thought is thus not what it may appear to be, the denial of the post-Hegelian break, but the bringing-forth of the dimension whose denial sustains the post-Hegelian break itself.

HEGEL VERSUS NIETZSCHE

Let us develop this point apropos Gerard Lebrun's posthumously published *L'envers de
la dialectique*[2], one of the most convincing and forceful attempts to demonstrate the impossibility of being Hegelian today—and, for Lebrun, 'today' stands under the sign of
Nietzsche.

Lebrun accepts that one cannot 'refute' Hegel: the machinery of Hegel's dialectics
is so all-encompassing that nothing is easier for Hegel than to demonstrate triumphantly how all such refutations are inconsistent, to turn them against themselves—'one cannot refute an eye disease', as Lebrun quotes approvingly Nietzsche. Most ridiculous
among such critical refutations is, of course, the standard Marxist-evolutionist idea
that there is a contradiction between Hegel's dialectical method which demonstrates
how every fixed determination is swiped away by the movement of negativity, how every determinate shape finds its truth in its annihilation, and Hegel's system: if the destiny of everything is to pass away in the eternal movement of self-sublation, doesn't the
same hold for the system itself? Isn't Hegel's own system a temporary, historically-rel-
ative, formation which will be overcome by the progress of knowledge? Anyone who
finds such refutation convincing is not to be taken seriously as a reader of Hegel.

---

2. See Gerard Lebrun, *L'envers de la dialectique. Hegel a la lumière de Nietzsche*, Paris, Editions du Seuil, 2004.
The irony is that, three decades earlier, Lebrun published one of the greatest books on Hegel, defending him
from his critics: *La patience du concept*, Paris, Gallimard, 1973.

How, then, can one move beyond Hegel? Lebrun's solution is Nietzschean historical philology: one should bring to light the 'eminently infra-rational' lexical choices,
takings of sides, which are grounded in how living beings are coping with threats to
their vital interests. Before Hegel set in motion his dialectical machinery which 'swallows' all content and elevates it to its truth by destroying it in its immediate being, im-
perceptibly a complex network of semantic decisions has already been taken. In this
way, one begins to 'unveil the obverse of the dialectics. Dialectics is also partial. It also
obfuscates its presuppositions. It is not the meta-discourse it pretends to be with regard
to the philosophies of 'Understanding".[3] Lebrun's Nietzsche is decidedly anti-Heideg-
gerian: for Lebrun, Heidegger re-philosophizes Nietzsche by way of interpreting the
Will to Power as a new ontological First Principle. More than Nietzschean, Lebrun's
approach may appear Foucauldian: what Lebrun tries to provide is the 'archaeology'
of the Hegelian knowledge', its genealogy in concrete life-practices.

But is Lebrun's 'philological' strategy radical enough in philosophical terms? Does
it not amount to a new version of historicist hermeneutics or, rather, of Foucauldian succession of epochal episteme? Does this not—if not legitimize, at least—make
understandable Heidegger's re-philosophication of Nietzsche? That is to say, one
should raise the question of the ontological status of the 'power' which sustains particular 'philological' configurations—for Nietzsche himself, it is the will to power; for
Heidegger, it is the abyssal game of 'there is' which 'sends' different epochal configurations of the disclosure of the world. In any case, one cannot avoid ontology: historicist hermeneutics cannot stand on its own. Heidegger's history of Being is an attempt
to elevate historical (not historicist) hermeneutics directly into transcendental ontology: there is for Heidegger nothing behind or beneath what Lebrun calls infra-rational
semantic choices, they are the ultimate fact/horizon of our being. Heidegger, however,
leaves open what one might call the ontic question: there are obscure hints all around
his work of 'reality' which persists out there prior to its ontological disclosure. That is to
say, Heidegger in no way equates the epochal disclosure of Being with any kind of 'creation'—he repeatedly concedes as an un-problematic fact that, even prior to their epochal disclosure or outside it, things somehow 'are' (persist) out there, although they do
not yet 'exist' in the full sense of being disclosed 'as such', as part of a historical world.
But what is the status of this ontic persistence outside ontological disclosure?[4]

From the Nietzschean standpoint, there is more in the 'infra-rational' semantic decisions than the fact that every approach to reality has to rely on a pre-existing set of
hermeneutic 'prejudices' or, as Heidegger would have put it, on a certain epochal disclosure of being: these decisions effectuate the pre-reflexive vital strategy of the Will to
Power. To such an approach, Hegel remains a profoundly Christian thinker, a nihilist thinker whose basic strategy is to revamp a profound defeat, a withdrawal from full
life in all its painful vitality, as the triumph of the absolute Subject. That is to say, from
the standpoint of the Will to Power, the effective content of the Hegelian process is one
long story of defeats and withdrawals, of the sacrifices of vital self-assertion: again and
again, one has to renounce vital engagement as still 'immediate' and 'particular'. Ex-

---

3. Lebrun, *L'envers de la dialectique*, p. 23.

4. And, incidentally, Lacan's *prima facie* weird decision to stick to the term 'subject' in spite of Heidegger's
well-known critique of subjectivity is grounded precisely in this obscure excess of the ontic over its ontological disclosure: 'subject' is for Lacan not the self-present autonomous agent reducing entire reality to its object, but a *pathetic* subject, that which suffers, which pays the price for being the site of the ontological disclosure in ontic flesh—the price whose Freudian name is, of course, 'castration'.

emplary is here Hegel's passage from the revolutionary Terror to the Kantian morality: the utilitarian subject of the civil society, the subject who wants to reduce the State
to the guardian of his private safety and well-being, has to be crushed by the Terror of
the revolutionary State which can annihilate him at any moment for no reason whatsoever (which means that the subject is not punished for something he did, for some
particular content or act, but for the very fact of being an independent individual opposed to the universal)—this Terror is his 'truth'. So how do we pass from revolutionary Terror to the autonomous and free Kantian moral subject? By what, in more contemporary language, one would have called full identification with the aggressor: the
subject should recognize in the external Terror, in this negativity which threatens all
the time to annihilate him, the very core of his (universal) subjectivity, i.e., he should
fully identify with it. Freedom is thus not freedom *from* Master, but a replacement of
one Master with another: the external Master is replaced with an internal one. The
price for this identification is, of course, the sacrifice of all 'pathological' particular
content—duty should be accomplished 'for the sake of duty'.

Lebrun demonstrates how this same logic holds also for language: 'State and language are two complementary figures of the Subject's accomplishment: here as well as
there, the sense that I am and the sense that I enounce are submitted to the same im-
perceptible sacrifice of what appeared to be our 'self' in the illusion of immediacy'.[5] Hegel was right to point out again and again that, when one talks, one always dwells in the
universal—which means that, with its entry into language, the subject loses its roots in
the concrete life-world. To put it in more pathetic terms, the moment I start to talk, I
am no longer the sensually-concrete I, since I am caught into an impersonal mechanism which always makes me say something different from what I wanted to say—as
the early Lacan liked to say, I am not speaking, I am being spoken by language. This
is one of the ways to understand what Lacan called 'symbolic castration': the price the
subject pays for its 'transubstantiation' from the agent of a direct animal vitality to the
speaking subject whose identity is kept apart from the direct vitality of passions.

A Nietzschean reading easily discerns in this reversal of Terror into autonomous
morality a desperate strategy of turning defeat into triumph: instead of heroically fighting for one's vital interests and stakes, one pre-emptively declares total surrender, gives
up all content. Lebrun is here well aware how unjustified is the standard critique of
Hegel according to which the dialectical reversal of the utter negativity into new higher positivity, of the catastrophe into triumph, functions as a kind of *deux ex machina*, precluding the possibility that the catastrophe remains the final outcome of the process—
the well-known common sense argument: 'But what if there is no reversal of negativity
into a new positive order?' This argument misses the point, which is that this, precisely, is what happens in the Hegelian reversal: there is no effective reversal of defeat into
triumph but only a purely formal shift, change of perspective, which tries to present
defeat itself as a triumph. Nietzsche's point is that this triumph is a fake, a cheap magician's trick, a consolation-prize for losing all that makes life worth living: the real loss
of vitality is supplemented by a lifeless spectre. To Lebrun's Nietzschean reading, Hegel
thus appears as a kind of atheist Christian philosopher: like Christianity, he locates the
'truth' of all terrestrial finite reality into its (self)annihilation i.e., all reality reaches its
truth only through/in its self-destruction; unlike Christianity, Hegel is well aware that
there is no Other World in which we would be repaid for our terrestrial losses: tran-

5. Lebrun, *L'envers de la dialectique*, p. 83.

scendence is absolutely immanent, *what is 'beyond' finite reality is nothing but the immanent process of its self-overcoming*. Hegel's name for this absolute immanence of transcendence is 'absolute negativity', as he makes it clear in an exemplary way in the dialectics of Master and Servant: the Servant's secured particular/finite identity is unsettled when, in experiencing the fear of death during his confrontation with the Master, he gets the whiff of the infinite power of negativity; through this experience, the Servant is forced to accept the worthlessness of his particular Self:

> For this consciousness was not in peril and fear for this element or that, nor for this or that moment of time, it was afraid for its entire being; it felt the fear of death, the sovereign master. It has been in that experience melted to its inmost soul, has trembled throughout its every fibre, and all that was fixed and steadfast has quaked within it. This complete perturbation of its entire substance, this absolute dissolution of all its stability into fluent continuity, is, however, the simple, ultimate nature of self-consciousness, absolute negativity, pure self-relating existence, which consequently is involved in this type of consciousness.[6]

What, then, does the Servant get in exchange for renouncing all the wealth of his particular Self? Nothing—in overcoming his particular terrestrial Self, the Servant does not reach a higher level of a spiritual Self; all he has to do is to shift his position and recognize in (what appears to him as) the overwhelming power of destruction which threatens to obliterate his particular identity the absolute negativity which forms the very core of his own Self. In short, the subject has to fully identify with the force that threatens to wipe him out: what he feared in fearing death was the negative power of his own Self. There is thus no reversal of negativity into positive greatness—the only 'greatness' there is is this negativity itself. Or, with regard to suffering: Hegel's point is not that the suffering brought about by alienating labour of renunciation is an intermediary moment to pass, so that we should just endure it and patiently wait for the reward at the end of the tunnel—there is no prize or profit to be gained at the end for our patient submission, suffering and renunciation are their own reward, all that is to be done is to change our subjective position, to renounce our desperate clinging to our finite Self with its 'pathological' desires, to purify our Self to universality. This is also how Hegel explains the overcoming of tyranny in the history of states: 'One says that tyranny is overturned by the people because it is undignified, shameful, etc. In reality, it disappears simply because it is superfluous'.[7] It becomes superfluous when people no longer need the external force of the tyrant to make them renounce their particular interests, but when they become 'universal citizens' by directly identifying the core of their being with this universality—in short, people no longer need the external master when they are educated into doing the job of discipline and subordination themselves.

The obverse of Hegel's 'nihilism' (all finite/determinate forms of life reach their 'truth' in their self-overcoming) is its apparent opposite: in continuity with the Platonic metaphysical tradition, he is not ready to give its full right to negativity, i.e., his dialectics is ultimately an effort to 'normalize' the excess of negativity. For late Plato already, the problem was how to relativize-contextualize non-being as a subordinate moment of being (non-being is always a particular/determinate lack of being measured by the fullness it fails to actualize, there is no non-being as such, there is always only 'green' which participates in non-being by not being 'red' or any other colour, etc.). In the

---

6. G.W.F. Hegel, *Phenomenology of Spirit*, trans. A.V. Miller, Oxford, Oxford University Press, 1977, p. 117.

7. G.W.F. Hegel, *Jenaer Realphilosophie*, Hamburg, Felix Meiner Verlag, 1969, pp. 247-8.

same vein, Hegelian 'negativity' serves to 'proscribe absolute difference' or 'non-being'[8]: negativity is constrained to the obliteration of all finite/immediate determinations. The process of negativity is thus not just a negative process of the self-destruction of the finite: it reaches its telos when finite/immediate determinations are mediated/maintained/elevated, posited in their 'truth' as ideal notional determinations. What remains after negativity has done its work is the eternal parousia of the ideal notional structure. What is missing here, from the Nietzschean standpoint, is the affirmative no: a no of the joyous and heroic confrontation with the adversary, a no of struggle which aims at self-assertion, not self-sublation.

STRUGGLE AND RECONCILIATION

This brings us to back to the incompatibility between Hegel's thought and any kind of evolutionary or historicist 'mobilism': Hegel's dialectics excludes all 'mobilism', it 'in no way involves the recognition of the irresistible force of becoming, the epopee of a flux which takes everything with it':

> The Hegelian dialectics was often—but superficially—assimilated to a mobilism. And it is undoubtedly true that the critique of the fixity of determinations can give rise to the conviction of an infinite dialectical process: the limited being has to disappear again and always, and its destruction extends to the very limit of our sight .... However, at this level, we are still dealing with a simple going-on (*Geschehen*) to which one cannot confer the inner unity of a history (*Geschichte*).[9]

To see this, to thoroughly reject the 'mobilist' topic of the eternal flux of Becoming which dissolves all fixed forms, is the first step towards dialectical reason in its radical incompatibility with the allegedly 'deep' insight into how everything comes out of the primordial Chaos and is again swallowed by it, the Wisdom which persists from ancient cosmologies up to the Stalinist dialectical materialism. The most popular form of 'mobilism' is the traditional view of Hegel as the philosopher of 'eternal struggle' popularized by Marxists from Engels to Stalin and Mao: the well-known 'dialectical' notion of life as an eternal conflict between reaction and progress, old and new, past and future. This belligerent view which advocates our engagement on the 'progressive' side is totally foreign to Hegel, for whom 'taking sides' is as such illusory (since it is by definition unilateral). Let us take social struggle at its most violent: war. What interests Hegel is not struggle as such, but the way the 'truth' of the engaged positions emerges through it, i.e., how the warring parties are 'reconciled' through their mutual destruction. The true (spiritual) meaning of war is not honour, victory, defence, etc., but the emergence of absolute negativity (death) as the absolute Master which reminds us of the false stability of our organized finite lives. War serves to elevate individuals to their 'truth' by making them obliterate their particular self-interests and identify with the State's universality. The true enemy is not the enemy we are fighting but our own finitude—recall Hegel's acerbic remark on how it is easy to preach the vanity of our finite terrestrial existence, but much more difficult to accept this lesson when it is enforced by a wild enemy soldier who breaks into our home and starts to cut members of our family with a sabre ....

In philosophical terms, Hegel's point is here the primacy of 'self-contradiction' over external obstacle (or enemy). We are not finite and self-inconsistent because our

---

8. Lebrun, *L'envers de la dialectique*, p. 218.

9. Lebrun, *L'envers de la dialectique*, p. 11.

activity is always thwarted by external obstacles; we are thwarted by external obstacles because we are finite and inconsistent. In other words, what the subject engaged in a struggle perceives as the enemy, the external obstacle he has to overcome, is the materialization of the subject's immanent inconsistency: the fighting subject needs the figure of the enemy to sustain the illusion of his own consistency, his very identity hinges on his opposing the enemy, so that his (eventual) victory over the enemy is his own defeat, disintegration. As Hegel likes to put it, fighting the external enemy, one (unknowingly) fights one's own essence. So, far from celebrating engaged fighting, Hegel's point is rather that every struggling position, every taking-sides, has to rely on a necessary illusion (the illusion that, once the enemy is annihilated, I will achieve the full realization of my being). This brings us to what would have been a properly Hegelian notion of ideology: the misapprehension of the condition of possibility (of what is an inherent constituent of your position) as the condition of impossibility (as an obstacle which prevents your full realization)—the ideological subject is unable to grasp how his entire identity hinges on what he perceives as the disturbing obstacle. This notion of ideology is not just an abstract mental exercise: it fits perfectly the Fascist anti-Semitism as the most elementary form of ideology, one is even tempted to say: ideology as such, *kat' exochen*. The anti-Semitic figure of the Jew, this foreign intruder who disturbs and corrupts the harmony of the social order, is ultimately a fetishist objectivization, a stand-in, for the 'inconsistency' of the social order, for the immanent antagonism ('class struggle') which generates the dynamic of the social system's instability.

Hegel's interest in the topic of struggle, of the 'conflict of the opposites', is thus that of the neutral dialectical observer who discerns the 'Cunning of Reason' at work in struggle: a subject engages in struggle, is defeated (as a rule in his very victory), *and this defeat brings him to his truth*. We can measure here clearly the distance that separates Hegel from Nietzsche: the innocence of exuberant heroism that Nietzsche wants to resuscitate, the passion of risk, of fully engaging in a struggle, of victory or defeat, they are all gone—the 'truth' of the struggle only emerges in and through defeat.

This is why the standard Marxist denunciation of the falsity of the Hegelian reconciliation (already made by Schelling) misses the point. According to this critique, the Hegelian reconciliation is false, it occurs only in the Idea, while real antagonisms persist—in the 'concrete' experience of the 'real life' of individuals who cling to their particular identity, state power remains an external compulsion. Therein resides the crux of the young Marx's critique of Hegel's political thought: Hegel presents the modern constitutional monarchy as a rational State in which antagonisms are reconciled, as an organic Whole in which every constituent (can) find(s) its proper place, but he thereby obfuscates the class antagonism which continues in modern societies, generating the working class as the 'non-reason of the existing Reason', as the part of modern society which has no proper part in it, as its 'part of no-part' (Rancière).

What Lebrun rejects in this critique is not its diagnosis (that the proposed reconciliation is dishonest, false, an 'enforced reconciliation' [*erpresste Versoehnung*—the title of one of Adorno's essay] which obfuscates the antagonisms' continuous persistence in social reality): 'what is so admirable in this portrait of the dialectician rendered dishonest by his blindness is the supposition that he could have been honest'[10]. In other words, instead of rejecting the Hegelian false reconciliation, one should reject as illusory the very notion of dialectical reconciliation, i.e., one should renounce the demand for a

---

10. Lebrun, *L'envers de la dialectique*, p. 115.

'true' reconciliation. Hegel was fully aware that reconciliation does not alleviate real suffering and antagonisms—his formulas of reconciliation from the foreword to his Philosophy of Right is that one should 'recognize the Rose in the Cross of the present', or, to put it in Marx's terms, in reconciliation, one does not change external reality to fit some Idea, one recognizes this Idea as the inner 'truth' of this miserable reality itself. The Marxist reproach that, instead of transforming reality, Hegel only proposes its new interpretation, thus in a way misses the point—it knocks on an open door, since, for Hegel, in order to pass from alienation to reconciliation, one does not have to change reality, but the way we perceive it and relate to it.

The same insight underlies Hegel's analysis of the passage from labour to thought in the subchapter on Master and Servant in his Phenomenology of Spirit. Lebrun is fully justified in emphasizing, against Kojève, that Hegel is far from celebrating (collective) labour as the site of the productive self-assertion of human subjectivity, as the process of forceful transformation and appropriation of natural objects, their subordination to human goals. All finite thought remains caught in the 'spurious infinity' of the never-ending process of the (trans)formation of objective reality which always resists the full subjective grasp, so that the subject's work is never done: 'As an aggressive activity deployed by a finite being, labour signals above all man's impotence to integrally take possession of nature'.[11] This finite thought is the horizon of Kant and Fichte: the endless practico-ethical struggle to overcome the external obstacles as well as the subject's own inner nature. Their philosophies are the philosophies of struggle, while in Hegel's philosophy, the fundamental stance of the subject towards objective reality is not the one of practical engagement, of confrontation with the inertia of objectivity, but the one of letting-it-be: purified of its pathological particularity, the universal subject is certain of itself, it knows that his thought already is the form of reality, so it can renounce enforcing its project on reality, it can let reality be the way it is.

This is why labour gets all the more close to its truth the less I work to satisfy my need, i.e., to produce an object I will consume. This is why industry which produces for the market is spiritually 'higher' than production for one's own needs: in market-production, I manufacture objects with no relation to my needs. The highest form of social production is therefore that of a merchant: 'the merchant is the only one who relates to the Good as a perfect universal subject, since the object in no way interests him on behalf of its aesthetic presence or its use value, but only insofar as it contains a desire of an other'.[12] And this is also why, in order to arrive at the 'truth' of labour, one should gradually abstract from the (external) goal it strives to realize. The parallel with war is appropriate here: in the same way that the 'truth' of the military struggle is not the destruction of the enemy, but the sacrifice of the 'pathological' content of the warrior's particular Self, its purification into the universal Self, the 'truth' of labour as the struggle with nature, its stuff, is also not victory over nature, it is not to compel nature to serve human goals, but the self-purification of the labourer itself. Labour is simultaneously the (trans)formation of external objects and the disciplinary self-formation/education (*Bildung*) of the subject itself. Hegel here celebrates precisely the alienated and alienating character of labour: far from being a direct expression of my creativity, labour forces me to submit to artificial discipline, to renounce my innermost immediate tendencies, to alienate myself from my natural Self:

11. Lebrun, *L'envers de la dialectique*, p. 207.
12. Lebrun, *L'envers de la dialectique*, p. 206.

> Desire has reserved to itself the pure negating of the object and thereby unalloyed feeling of self. This satisfaction, however, just for that reason is itself only a state of evanescence, for it lacks objectivity or subsistence. Labour, on the other hand, is desire restrained and checked, evanescence delayed and postponed; in other words, labour shapes and fashions the thing.[13]

As such, labour prefigures thought, it achieves its *telos* in thinking which no longer works on an external stuff, but is already its own stuff, or, which no longer imposes its subjective/finite form onto external reality, but is already in itself the infinite form of reality. For the finite thought, the concept of an object is a mere concept, the subjective goal one actualizes when, by way of labour, one imposes it onto reality. For the speculative thought, on the contrary, thought is not merely subjective, it is in itself already objective, i.e., it renders the objective conceptual form of the object. This is why the inner Spirit, certain of itself,

> ...no longer needs to form/shape nature and to render it spiritual in order to fixate the divine and to make its unity with nature externally visible: insofar as the free thought thinks externality, it can leave it the way it is *(kann er es lassen wie er ist)*.[14]

> This sudden retroactive reversal from not-yet to already-is (we never directly realize a goal—we directly pass from striving to realize a goal to a sudden recognition that the goal already is realized) is what distinguishes Hegel from all kinds of historicist topic, inclusive of the standard Marxist critical reproach that the Hegelian ideal reconciliation is not enough, since it leaves reality (the real pain and suffering) the way it is, so that what is needed is actual reconciliation through radical social transformation. For Hegel, the illusion is not that of the enforced 'false reconciliation' which ignores the persisting divisions; the true illusion resides in not seeing that, in what appear to us as the chaos of becoming, the infinite goal *is already realized*:

> Within the finite order, we cannot experience or see that the goal is truly achieved. The accomplishment of the infinite goal resides only in overcoming the illusion (*Taeuschung*— deception) that this goal is not yet achieved.[15]

In short, the ultimate deception is not to see that one already has what one is looking for—like Christ's disciples who were awaiting his 'real' reincarnation, blind for the fact that their collective already was the Holy Spirit, the return of the living Christ.

A STORY TO TELL

How are we to counter this diagnosis of the 'disease called Hegel' which centres on the dialectical reversal as the empty/formal gesture of presenting defeat as victory? The first observation that imposes itself is, of course, that reading the 'infra-rational' semantic choices as expressing a strategy of coping with obstacles to the assertion of life is in itself already an 'infra-rational' semantic choice. But more important is to note how such a reading subtly imposes a narrow version of Hegel which obliterates many key dimensions of his thought. Is it not possible to read Hegel's systematic 'sublation' of each and every shape of consciousness or social life-form as, precisely, the description of all possible life-forms, vital 'semantic choices', and of their inherent antagonisms ('contradictions')?[16] If there is a 'semantic choice' that underlies Hegel's thought, it is

---

13. Hegel, *Phenomenology of Spirit*, p. 118.

14. G.W.F. Hegel, *Philosophie der Geschichte (Werke, Vol. XI)*, Frankfurt, Suhrkamp Verlag, 1970, p. 323.

15. G.W.F. Hegel, *Philosophy of Mind*, Oxford, Clarendon Press, 1992, par. 442.

16. In this precise sense, the eight hypotheses in the part II of Plato's *Parmenides* form a Hegelian systematic exercise: they deploy the matrix of all possible 'semantic choices' in the relationship between the One and

not the desperate wager that, retroactively, one will be able to tell a consistent all-encompassing meaningful story within which each detail will be allotted its proper place, but, on the contrary, the weird certainty (comparable to the psychoanalyst's certainty that the repressed will always return, that a symptom will always spoil every figure of harmony) that, with every figure of consciousness or form of life, things will always somehow 'go wrong', that each position will generate an excess which will augur its self-destruction.

Does this mean that Hegel does not advocate any determinate 'semantic choice', since, for him, the only 'truth' is the very endless process of 'generation of corruption' of all determinate 'semantic choices'? Yes, but on condition that we do not conceive this process in the usual 'mobilist' sense.

How, then, does the truly historical thought break with such universalized 'mobilism'? In what precise sense is it historical and not simply the rejection of 'mobilism' on behalf of some eternal Principles exempted from the flow of generation and corruption? Here, one should again differentiate historicity proper from organic evolution. In the latter, a universal Principle is slowly and gradually differentiating itself; as such, it remains the calm underlying all-encompassing ground that unifies the bustling activity of struggling individuals, their endless process of generation and corruption that is the 'cycle of life'. In history proper, on the contrary, the universal Principle is caught into the 'infinite' struggle with itself, i.e., the struggle is each time the struggle for the fate of the universality itself. This is why the eminently 'historical' moments are those of great collisions when a whole form of life is threatened, when the reference to the established social and cultural norms no longer guarantees the minimum of stability and cohesion; in such open situations, a new form of life has to be invented, and it is at this point that Hegel locates the role of great heroes. They operate in a pre-legal, stateless, zone: their violence is not bound by the usual moral rules, they enforce a new order with the subterranean vitality which shatters all established forms. According to the usual doxa on Hegel, heroes follow their instinctual passions, their true motifs and goals are not clear to themselves, they are unconscious instruments of the deeper historical necessity of giving birth to a new spiritual life form—however, as Lebrun points out, one should not impute to Hegel the standard teleological notion of a hidden Reason which pulls the strings of the historical process, following a plan established in advance and using individuals' passions as the instruments of its implementation. First, since the meaning of one's acts is a priori inaccessible to individuals who accomplish them, heroes included, there is no 'science of politics' able to predict the course of events: 'nobody has ever the right to declare himself depositary of the Spirit's self-knowledge'[17], and this impossibility 'spares Hegel the fanaticism of 'objective responsibility''[18]—in other words, there is no place in Hegel for the Marxist-Stalinist figure of the Communist revolutionary who knows the historical necessity and posits himself as the instrument of its implementation. However, it is crucial to add a further twist here: if we merely assert this impossibility, we are still 'conceiving the Absolute as Substance, not as Subject'—we still surmise that there is some pre-existing Spirit imposing its substantial Necessity on history, we just accept that the insight into this Necessity is inaccessible to us. From a con-

---

Being, with the final 'nihilistic' outcome that there is no ultimate Ground guaranteeing the consistent unity of reality, i.e., that the ultimate reality is the Void itself.

17. Lebrun, *L'envers de la dialectique*, p. 40.

18. Lebrun, *L'envers de la dialectique*, p. 41.

sequent Hegelian standpoint, one should go a crucial step further and realize that no historical Necessity pre-exists the contingent process of its actualization, i.e., that the historical process is also in itself 'open', undecided—this confused mixture 'generates sense insofar as it unravels itself':

> It is people, and they only, who make history, while Spirit explicates itself through this making. [...] The point is not, as in a naïve theodicy, to find a justification for every event. In actual time, no heavenly harmony resonates in the sound and fury. It is only once this tumult recollects itself in the past, once what took place is conceived, that we can say, to put it briefly, that the 'course of History' is a little bit better outlined. History runs forward only for those who look at it backwards; it is linear progression only in retrospect. [...] The Hegelian 'providential necessity' has so little authority that it seems as if it learns from the run of things in the world which were its goals.[19]

This is how one should read Hegel's thesis that, in the course of the dialectical development, things 'become what they are': it is not that a temporal deployment merely actualizes some pre-existing atemporal conceptual structure—this atemporal conceptual structure itself is the result of contingent temporal decisions. Let us take the exemplary case of a contingent decision whose outcome defines the agent's entire life, Caesar's crossing of Rubicon:

> It is not enough to say that crossing Rubicon is part of the complete notion of Caesar. One should rather say that Caesar is defined by the fact that he crossed Rubicon. His life didn't follow a scenario written in the book of some goddess: there is no book which would already have contained the relations of Caesar's life, for the simple reason that his life itself is this book, and that, at every moment, an event is in itself its own narrative.[20]

But why shouldn't we then say that there is simply no atemporal conceptual structure, that all there is is the gradual temporal deployment? Here we encounter the properly dialectical paradox which defines true historicity as opposed to evolutionist historicism, and which was much later, in French structuralism, formulated as the 'primacy of synchrony over diachrony'. Usually, this primacy was taken to mean the ultimate denial of historicity in structuralism: a historical development can be reduced to the (imperfect) temporal deployment of a pre-existing atemporal matrix of all possible variations/combinations. This simplistic notion of the 'primacy of synchrony over diachrony' overlooks the (properly dialectical) point, made long ago by (among others) T.S. Eliot in his 'Tradition and Individual Talent', on how each truly new artistic phenomenon not only designates a break from the entire past, but retroactively changes this past itself. At every historical conjuncture, present is not only present, it also encompasses a perspective on the past immanent to it—say, after the disintegration of the Soviet Union in 1991, the October Revolution is no longer the same historical event, i.e., it is (for the triumphant liberal-capitalist view) no longer the beginning of a new progressive epoch in the history of humanity, but the beginning of a catastrophic mis-direction of history which reached its end in 1991. Or, back to Caesar, once he crossed Rubicon, his previous life appeared in a new way, as a preparation for his later world-historical role, i.e., it was transformed into the part of a totally different lifestory. This is what Hegel calls 'totality' or what structuralism calls 'synchronic structure': a historical moment which is not limited to the present but includes its own past and future, i.e., the way the past and the future appeared to and from this moment.

---

19. Lebrun, *L'envers de la dialectique*, pp. 41-44.
20. Lebrun, *L'envers de la dialectique*, p. 87.

It is, however, at this very point, after fully conceding Hegel's radical break with traditional metaphysical theodicy, that Lebrun's makes his critical move. The fundamental Nietzschean strategy of Lebrun is first to admit the radicality of Hegel's undermining of the traditional metaphysics, but then, in the crucial second step, to demonstrate how this very radical sacrifice of the metaphysical content saves the minimal form of metaphysics. The accusations which concern Hegel's theodicy, of course, fall too short: there is no substantial God who writes in advance the script of History and watches over its realization, the situation is open, truth emerges only through the very process of its deployment, etc., etc.—but what Hegel nonetheless maintains is the much deeper presupposition that, at the end, when the dusk falls over the events of the day, *the Owl of Minerva will take flight*, i.e., that there always is a story to be told at the end, the story which ('retroactively' and 'contingently' as much as one wants) reconstitutes the Sense of the preceding process. Or, with regard to domination, Hegel is of course against every form of despotic domination, so the critique of his thought as the divinization of the Prussian monarchy is ridiculous; however, his assertion of subjective freedom comes with a catch: it is the freedom of the subject who undergoes a violent 'transubstantiation' from the individual stuck onto his particularity to the universal subject who recognizes in the State the substance of his own being. The mirror-obverse of this mortification of individuality as the price to be paid for the rise of the 'truly' free universal subject is that the state's power retains its full authority—what only changes is that this authority (as in the entire tradition from Plato onwards) loses its tyrannical-contingent character and becomes a rationally-justified power.

The question is thus: is Hegel effectively enacting a desperate strategy of sacrificing everything, all the metaphysical content, in order to save the essential, the form itself (the form of a retrospective rational reconstruction, the form of authority which imposes onto the subject the sacrifice of all particular content, etc.)? Or is it that Lebrun himself, in making this type of reproach, enacts the fetishist strategy of *je sais bien, mais quand même …*—'I know very well that Hegel goes to the end in destroying metaphysical presuppositions, but nonetheless …'? The answer to this reproach should be a pure tautology which marks the passage from contingency to necessity: there is a story to be told *if* there is a story to be told. That is to say, *if* there is a story to be told (if, due to contingency, a story emerges at the end), *then* this story will appear as necessary. Yes, the story is necessary, but its necessity itself is contingent.

Is there nonetheless not a grain of truth in Lebrun's critical point—does Hegel effectively not presuppose that, contingent and open as the history may be, a consistent story can always be told afterwards? Or, to put it in Lacan's terms, is the entire edifice of the Hegelian historiography not based on the premise that, no matter how confused the events, a subject supposed to know will emerge at the end, magically converting nonsense into sense, chaos into new order? Recall just his philosophy of history with its narrative of world history as the story of the progress of freedom …. And is it not true that, if there is a lesson of the twentieth century, it is that all the extreme phenomena that took place in it cannot ever be unified in a single encompassing philosophical narrative? One simply cannot write a 'phenomenology of the twentieth century Spirit', uniting technological progress, the rise of democracy, the failed Communist attempt with its Stalinist catastrophe, the horrors of Fascism, the gradual end of colonialism …. But why not? Is it really so? What if, precisely, one can and should write a Hegelian history of the twentieth century, this 'age of extremes' (Eric Hobsbawm), as a global narrative delimited by two epochal constellation: the (relatively) long peaceful period of capitalist expansion from 1848 till 1914 as its substantial starting point whose subterranean antagonisms then exploded with the First World War, and the ongoing global-capitalist 'New World Order' emerging after 1990 as its conclusion, the return to a new all-encompassing system signaling to some a Hegelian 'end of history', but whose antagonisms already announce new explosions? Are the great reversals and unexpected explosions of the topsy-turvy twentieth century, its numerous 'coincidences of the opposites'—the reversal of liberal capitalism into Fascism, the even more weird reversal of the October Revolution into the Stalinist nightmare—not the very privileged stuff which seems to call for a Hegelian reading? What would Hegel have made of today's struggle of Liberalism against fundamentalist Faith? One thing is sure: he would not simply take side of liberalism, but would have insisted on the 'mediation' of the opposites.[21]

POTENTIALITY VERSUS VIRTUALITY

Convincing as it may appear, Lebrun's critical diagnosis of the Hegelian wager that there is always a story to tell nonetheless again falls short: Lebrun misses an additional twist which complicates his image of Hegel. Yes, Hegel sublates time in eternity—but this sublation itself has to appear as (hinges on) a contingent temporal event. Yes, Hegel sublates contingency in a universal rational order—but this order itself hinges on a contingent excess (say, State as a rational totality can only actualize itself through the 'irrational' figure of the King at its head). Yes, struggle is sublated in the peace of reconciliation (mutual annihilation) of the opposites, but this reconciliation itself has to appear as its opposite, as an act of extreme violence. So Lebrun is right in emphasizing that Hegel's topic of the dialectical struggle of the opposites is as far as possible from an engaged attitude of 'taking sides': for Hegel, the 'truth' of the struggle is always, with an inexorable necessity, the mutual destruction of the opposites—the 'truth' of a phenomenon always resides in its self-annihilation, in the destruction of its immediate being. Does, however, Lebrun here nonetheless not miss the proper paradox: not only did Hegel have no problem with taking sides (with an often very violent partiality) in the political debates of his time; his entire mode of thinking is deeply 'polemical', always intervening, attacking, taking sides, and, as such, as far as possible from a detached position of Wisdom which observes the ongoing struggles from a neutral distance, aware of their nullity *sub specie aeternitatis*. For Hegel, the true ('concrete') universality is accessible only from an engaged 'partial' standpoint.

The way one usually reads the Hegelian relationship between necessity and freedom is that they ultimately coincide: for Hegel, true freedom has nothing to do with capricious choices; it means the priority of self-relating to relating-to-other, i.e., an entity is free when it can deploy its immanent potentials without being impeded by any external obstacle. From here, it is easy to develop the standard argument against Hegel: his system is a fully 'saturated' set of categories, with no place for contingen-

---

21. And, let us not forget that, for Hegel himself, his philosophical reconstruction of history in no way pretends to 'cover everything', but consciously leaves blanks: the medieval time, for example, is for Hegel one big regression—no wonder that, in his lectures on the history of philosophy, he dismisses the entire medieval thought in a couple of pages, flatly denying any historical greatness to figures like Thomas Aquinas. Not even to mention the destructions of great civilizations like the Mongols' wiping out so much of the Muslim world (the destruction of Baghdad, etc.) in the 13th century—there is no 'meaning' in this destruction, the negativity unleashed here did not create the space for a new shape of historical life.

cy and indeterminacy, i.e., in Hegel's logic, each category follows with inexorable immanent-logical necessity from the preceding one, and the entire series of categories
forms a self-enclosed Whole... We can see now what this argument misses: the Hegelian dialectical process is not such a 'saturated' self-contained necessary Whole, but
the open-contingent process through which such a Whole forms itself. In other words,
the reproach confuses being with becoming: it perceives as a fixed order of Being (the
network of categories) what is for Hegel the process of Becoming which, retroactively, engenders its necessity.

The same point can also be made in the terms of the distinction between potentiality and virtuality. Quentin Meillassoux has outlined the contours of a post-metaphysical materialist ontology whose basic premise is the Cantorian multiplicity of infinities
which cannot be totalized into an all-encompassing One. Such an ontology of non-All
asserts radical contingency: not only are there no laws which hold with necessity, every law is in itself contingent, it can be overturned at any moment. What this amounts
to is the suspension of the Principle of Sufficient Reason: not only the epistemological suspension, but also the ontological one. That is to say, it is not only that we cannot ever get to know the entire network of causal determinations, this chain is in itself
'inconclusive', opening up the space for the immanent contingency of becoming—such
a chaos of becoming subjected to no pre-existing order is what defines radical materialism. Along these lines, Meillassoux proposes a precise distinction between *contingency*
and *chance*, linking it to the distinction between *virtuality* and *potentiality*:

> *Potentialities* are the non-actualized cases of an indexed set of possibilities under the condi-
> tion of a given law (whether aleatory or not). *Chance* is every actualization of a potentiali-
> ty for which there is no univocal instance of determination on the basis of the initial given
> conditions. Therefore I will call *contingency* the property of an indexed set of cases (not of a
> case belonging to an indexed set) of not itself being a case of a set of sets of cases; and *vir-*
> *tuality* the property of every set of cases of emerging within a becoming which is not dom-
> inated by any pre-constituted totality of possibles.[22]

A clear case of potentiality is the throw of a die through which what was already a possible case becomes a real case: it was determined by the pre-existing order of possibilities that there is a 1/6 chance for number 6 to turn up, so when number 6 does turn
up, a pre-existing possible is realized. Virtuality, on the contrary, designates a situation
in which one cannot totalize the set of possibles, so that something new emerges, a case
is realized for which there was no place in the pre-existing set of possibles: 'time creates the possible at the very moment it makes it come to pass, it brings forth the possible as it does the real, it inserts itself in the very throw of the die, to bring forth a seventh case, in principle unforeseeable, which breaks with the fixity of potentialities'.[23]
One should note here Meillassoux's precise formulation: the New arises when an X
emerges which does not merely actualize a pre-existing possibility, but whose actualization creates (retroactively opens up) its own possibility:

> If we maintain that becoming is not only capable of bringing forth cases on the basis of
> a pre-given universe of cases, we must then understand that it follows that such cases ir-
> rupt, properly speaking, *from nothing*, since no structure contains them as eternal potenti-
> alities before their emergence: *we thus make irruption* ex nihilo *the very concept of a temporality
> delivered to its pure immanence.*[24]

22. Quentin Meillassoux, 'Potentiality and Virtuality', in this volume, pp. 231-2
23. Meillassoux, 'Potentiality and Virtuality', p. 233.
24. Meillassoux, 'Potentiality and Virtuality', p. 232.

In this way, we obtain a precise definition of time in its irreducibility: time is not only the 'space' of future realization of possibilities, but the 'space' of the emergence of something radically new, outside the scope of the possibilities inscribed into any atemporal matrix. The emergence of a phenomenon *ex nihilo*, not fully covered by the sufficient chain of reasons, is thus no longer—as in traditional metaphysics—the sign of the direct intervention of some super-natural power (God) into nature, but, on the contrary, the sign of the *inexistence* of God, i.e., a proof that nature is not-All, not 'covered' by any transcendent Order or Power which regulates it. A 'miracle' (whose formal definition is the emergence of something not covered by the existing causal network) is thus converted into a *materialist* concept:

> Every 'miracle' thus becomes the manifestation of the inexistence of God, in so far as every radical rupture of the present in relation to the past becomes the manifestation of the absence of any order capable of overseeing the chaotic power of becoming.[25]

On the basis of these insights, Meillassoux brilliantly undermines the standard argument against the radical contingency of nature and its laws (in both senses: of the hold of laws and of the laws themselves): how come that nature is so permanent, that it (mostly) conforms to laws? Is this not highly improbable, the same improbability as that of the die always falling on 6 up? This argument relies on a possible totalization of possibilities/probabilities, *with regard to which* the uniformity is improbable: if there is no standard, nothing is more improbable than anything else. This is also why the 'astonishment' on which the Strong Anthropic Principle in cosmology counts is false: we start from human life, which could have evolved only within a set of very precise preconditions, and then, moving backwards, we cannot but be astonished at how our universe was furnished with precisely the right set of characteristics for the emergence of life—just a slightly different chemical composition, density, etc., would have made life impossible .... This 'astonishment' again relies on the probabilistic reasoning which presupposes a preexisting totality of possibilities.

This is how one should read Marx's well-known statement, from his introduction to the *Grundrisse* manuscripts, about the anatomy of man as a key to the anatomy of ape: it is profoundly materialist, i.e., it does not involve any teleology (man is 'in germ' already present in ape, ape immanently tends towards man). It is precisely because the passage from ape to man is radically contingent/*imprévisible*, because there is no inherent 'progress' in it, that one can only retroactively determine/discern the conditions (not 'sufficient reasons') for man in ape. And, again, it is crucial to bear in mind here that the non-All is ontological, not only epistemological: when we stumble upon 'indeterminacy' in nature, when the rise of the New cannot be fully accounted for by the set of its preexisting conditions, this does not mean that we encountered the limitation of our knowledge, our inability to understand the 'higher' reason at work here, but, on the contrary, that we demonstrated the ability of our mind to grasp the non-All of reality:

> The notion of virtuality permits us [...] to reverse the signs, making of every radical irruption the manifestation, not of a transcendent principle of becoming (a miracle, the sign of a Creator), but of a time that nothing subtends (an emergence, the sign of non-All). We can then grasp what is signified by the impossibility of tracing a genealogy of novelties directly to a time before their emergence: not the incapacity of reason to discern hidden potentialities, but, quite on the contrary, the capacity of reason to accede to the inef-

---

25. Meillassoux, 'Potentiality and Virtuality', p. 233 n7.

fectivity of an All of potentialities which would pre-exist their emergence. In every radical novelty, time makes manifest that it does not actualize a germ of the past, but that it brings forth a virtuality which did not pre-exist in any way, in any totality inaccessible to time, its own advent.[26]

For us Hegelians the crucial question here is: where is Hegel with regard to this distinction between potentiality and virtuality? In a first approach, there is massive evidence that Hegel is *the* philosopher of potentiality: is not the whole point of the dialectical development as the development from In-itself to For-itself that, in the process of becoming, things merely 'become what they already are' (or, rather, were from all eternity)? Is the dialectical process not the temporal deployment of an eternal set of potentialities, which is why the Hegelian System is a self-enclosed set of necessary passages? However, this mirage of overwhelming evidence dissipates the moment we fully take into account the radical *retroactivity* of the dialectical process: the process of becoming is not in itself necessary, but the *becoming* (the gradual contingent emergence) *of necessity itself*. This is (also, among other things) what 'to conceive substance as subject' means: subject as the Void, the Nothingness of self-relating negativity, is the very *nihil* out of which every new figure emerges, i.e., every dialectical passage/reversal is a passage in which the new figure emerges *ex nihilo* and retroactively posits/creates its necessity.

THE HEGELIAN CIRCLE OF CIRCLES

The stakes of this debate—is Hegel a thinker of potentiality or a thinker of virtuality?—are extremely high: they concern the (in)existence of the 'big Other' itself. That is to say, the atemporal matrix which contains the scope of the possibilities is one of the names of the 'big Other', and another name is the totalizing story we can tell after the fact, i.e., the certainty that such a story will always emerge. What Nietzsche reproaches to modern atheism is precisely that, in it, the 'big Other' survives—true, no longer as the substantial God, but as the totalizing symbolic frame of reference. This is why Lebrun emphasizes that Hegel is not an atheist conveniently presenting himself as Christian, but effectively the ultimate Christian philosopher. Hegel always insisted on the deep truth of the Protestant saying 'God is dead': in his own thought, the substantial-transcendent God dies, but is resurrected as the symbolic totality which guarantees the meaningful consistency of the universe—in a strict homology with the passage from God *qua* substance to the Holy Spirit as the community of believers in Christianity. When Nietzsche talks about the death of God, he does not have in mind the pagan living God, but precisely THIS God *qua* Holy Spirit, the community of believers. Although this community no longer relies on a transcendent Guarantee of a substantial big Other, the big Other (and thereby the theological dimension) is still here as the symbolic frame of reference (say, in Stalinism in the guise of the big Other of History which guarantees the meaningfulness of our acts). Did Lacan himself not point in this direction when, in 1956, he proposed a short and clear definition of the Holy Ghost: 'The Holy Ghost is the entry of the signifier into the world. This is certainly what Freud brought us under the title of death drive'.[27] What Lacan means, at this moment of his thought, is that the Holy Ghost stands for the symbolic order as that which cancels (or, rather, suspends) the entire domain of 'life'—lived experience, the libidinal flux, the wealth of emotions, or, to put it in Kant's terms, the 'pathological': when

26. Meillassoux, 'Potentiality and Virtuality', p. 235.

27. Jacques Lacan, *Le seminaire, livre IV: La relation d'objet*, Paris, Editions du Seuil, 1994, p. 48.

we locate ourselves within the Holy Ghost, we are transubstantiated, we enter another life beyond the biological one.

But is *this* shift from the living gods of the real to the dead God of the Law really what happens in Christianity? Is it not that this shift already takes place in Judaism, so that the death of Christ cannot stand for this shift, but for something much more radical—precisely for the death of the symbolic-'dead' big Other itself? The key question is thus: is the Holy Spirit still a figure of the big Other, or is it possible to conceive it outside this frame? If the dead God were to morph directly into the Holy Ghost, then we would still have the symbolic big Other. But the monstrosity of Christ, this contingent singularity interceding between God and man, is the proof that the Holy Ghost is not the big Other which survives as the spirit of the community after the death of the substantial God, but a collective link of love without any support in the big Other. Therein resides the properly Hegelian paradox of the death of God: if God dies directly, as God, he survives as the virtualized big Other; only if he dies in the guise of Christ, his earthly embodiment, he also disintegrates as the big Other.

When Christ was dying on the cross, earthquake and storm broke out, a sign that the heavenly order itself—the big Other—was disturbed: not only something horrible happened in the world, the very coordinates of the world were shaken. It was as if the *sinthom*, the knot tying the world together, was unravelled, and the audacity of the Christians was to take this is a good omen, or, as Mao put it much later: 'there is great disorder under heaven, the situation is excellent'. Therein resides what Hegel calls the 'monstrosity' of Christ: *the insertion of Christ between God and man is strictly equivalent to the fact that 'there is no big Other'—Christ is inserted as the singular contingency on which the universal necessity of the 'big Other' itself hinges.* In claiming that Hegel is the ultimate Christian philosopher, Lebrun is thus—to paraphrase T.S. Eliot—right for the wrong reason.

Only if we bear in mind this dimension, can we really see why the Darwinian (or other evolutionary) critics of Hegel miss the point when they ridicule Hegel's claim that there is no history in nature, that there is history only in human societies: Hegel does not imply that nature is always the same, that forms of vegetal and animal life are forever fixed, so that there is no evolution in nature—what he claims is that there is no history proper in nature: 'The living conserves itself, it is the beginning and the end; the product in itself is also the principle, it is always as such active'.[28] Life eternally repeats its cycle and returns to itself: substance is again and again reasserted, children become parents, etc. The circle is here perfect, at peace with itself. It is often perturbed—from without: in nature, we, of course, do have gradual transformations of one species into another, and we do get clashes and catastrophes which obliterate entire species; what one does not get in nature is the Universal appearing (posited) as such, in contrast to its own particular content, a Universal in conflict with itself. In other words, what is missing is nature is what Hegel called the 'monstrosity' of Christ: the direct embodiment of the *arkhe* of the entire universe (God) in a singular individual which walks around as one among the mortals. It is in this precise sense that, in order to distinguish natural from spiritual movement, Hegel uses the strange term 'insertion': in an organic process,

> ...nothing can insert itself between the Notion and its realization, between the nature of the genus determined in itself and the existence which is conformed to this nature; in the domain of the Spirit, things are wholly different.[29]

---

28. G.W.F. Hegel, *Philosophie der Religion (Werke, Vol. XVI)*, Frankfurt, Suhrkamp Verlag 1970, pp. 525-526.
29. Hegel, *Philosophie der Geschichte*, p. 90.

Christ is such a figure which 'inserts itself' between God and its creation. Natural development is dominated-regulated by a principle, *arkhe*, which remains the same through the movement of its actualization, be it the development of an organism from its conception to its maturity or the continuity of a species through generation and decay of its individual members—there is no tension here between the universal principle and its exemplification, the universal principle is the calm universal force which totalizes/encompasses the wealth of its particular content; however, 'life doesn't have history because it is totalising only externally'[30]—it is a universal genus which encompasses the multitude of individuals who struggle, but this unity is not posited in an individual. In spiritual history, on the contrary, this totalization occurs for itself, it is posited as such in the singular figures which embody universality against its own particular content.

Or, to put it in a different way, in organic life, substance (the universal Life) is the encompassing unity of the interplay of its subordinate moments, that which remains the same through the eternal process of generation and corruption, that which returns to itself through this movement; with subjectivity, however, *predicate passes into subject*: substance doesn't return to *itself*, it is re-totalized by what was at the beginning its predicate, its subordinated moment. This is how the key moment in a dialectical process is the 'transubstantiation' of its focal point: what was first just a predicate, a subordinate moment of the process (say, money in the development of capitalism), becomes its central moment, retroactively degrading its presuppositions, the elements out of which it emerged, into its subordinate moments, elements of its self-propelling circulation. And this is also how one should approach Hegel's outrageously 'speculative' formulations about Spirit as its own result, a product of itself: while 'Spirit has its beginnings in nature in general',

> the extreme to which spirit tends is its freedom, its infinity, its being in and for itself. These are the two aspects but if we ask what Spirit is, the immediate answer is that it is this motion, this process of proceeding from, of freeing itself from, nature; this is the being, the substance of spirit itself.[31]

Spirit is thus radically de-substantialized: Spirit is not a positive counter-force to nature, a different substance which gradually breaks and shines through the inert natural stuff, it is *nothing but* this process of freeing-itself-from. Hegel directly disowns the notion of Spirit as some kind of positive Agent which underlies the process:

> Spirit is usually spoken of as subject, as doing something, and apart from what it does, as this motion, this process, as still something particular, its activity being more or less contingent [...] it is of the very nature of spirit to be this absolute liveliness, this process, to proceed forth from naturality, immediacy, to sublate, to quit its naturality, and to come to itself, and to free itself, it being itself only as it comes to itself as such a product of itself; its actuality being merely that it has made itself into what it is.[32]

If, then, 'it is only as a result of itself that it is spirit',[33] this means that the standard talk about the Hegelian Spirit which alienates itself to itself and then recognizes itself in its otherness and thus reappropriates its content, is deeply misleading: the Self to which spirit returns is produced in the very movement of this return, or, that to which the

30. Lebrun, *L'envers de la dialectique*, p. 250.
31. G.W.F. Hegel, *Philosophie des subjektiven Geistes*, Dordrecht, Riedel 1978, pp. 6-7.
32. Hegel, *Philosophie des subjektiven Geistes*, pp 6-7.
33. Hegel, *Philosophie des subjektiven Geistes*, pp 6-7.

process of return is returning to is produced by the very process of returning. In a subjective process, there is no 'absolute subject', no permanent central agent which plays with itself the game of alienation and disalienation, losing/dispersing itself and then re-appropriating its alienated content: after a substantial totality is dispersed, it is another agent—previously its subordinated moment—which re-totalizes it. It is this shifting of the center of the process from one to another moment which distinguishes a dialectical process from the circular movement of alienation and its overcoming; it is because of this shift that the 'return to itself' coincides with accomplished alienation (when a subject re-totalizes the process, its substantial unity is fully lost). In this precise sense, substance returns to itself as subject, and this trans-substantiation is what substantial life cannot accomplish.

Perhaps what is missing in Lebrun is the proper image of a circle that would render the unique circularity of the dialectical process. For pages, he fights with different images to differentiate the Hegelian 'circle of circles' from the circularity of traditional (pre-modern) Wisdom, from the ancient topic of the 'cycle of life', its generation and corruption. How, then, are we to read Hegel's description which seems to evoke a full circle in which a thing merely becomes what it is? 'Necessity only shows itself at the end, but in such a way precisely that this end reveals how it was equally the First. Or, the end reveals this priority of itself by the fact that, in the change actualized by it, nothing emerges which was not already there'.[34] The problem with this full circle is that it is too perfect, that its self-enclosure is double—its very circularity is re-marked in yet another circular mark. In other words, the very repetition of the circle undermines its closure and surreptitiously introduces a gap into which radical contingency is inscribed: if the circular closure, in order to be fully actual, has to be re-asserted as closure, it means that, in itself, it is not yet truly a closure, i.e., that it is only the (contingent excess of) its repetition which makes it a closure. (Recall again the paradox of the Monarch in Hegel's theory of rational State: one needs this contingent excess to actualize the State as rational totality. This excess is, in Lacanese, the excess of the signifier without signified: it adds no new content, it just performatively enregisters something that is already there.) As such, this circle undermines itself: it only works if we supplement it with an additional inside-circle, so that we get the figure of the 'inside-inverted eight' (regularly referred to by Lacan, and also once invoked by Hegel). This is the true figure of the Hegelian dialectical process, a figure missing in Lebrun's book.

HEGEL AND REPETITION

Perhaps, however, we do encounter here the limit of Hegel, although not in the Nietzschean sense deployed by Lebrun. If life is a substantial universality, is then what inserts itself in the gap between its Notion and the Notion's actualization, and what thereby breaks the substantial circularity of life, not *death*? To put it bluntly: if Substance is Life, is Subject not Death? Insofar as, for Hegel, the basic feature of pre-subjective Life is the 'spurious infinity' of the eternal reproduction of the life-substance through the incessant movement of the generation and corruption of its elements, i.e., the 'spurious infinity' of a repetition with no progress, the ultimate irony we encounter here is that Freud, who called this excess of death over life 'death drive', conceived it precisely as repetition, as a compulsion-to-repeat. Can Hegel think this weird repetition which is not progress, but also not natural repetition through which substantial life reproduces

---

34. Hegel, *Phenomenology of Spirit*, p. 297.

itself? A repetition which, by its excessive insistence, precisely breaks the cycle of natural repetition?

As was indicated already by Deleuze, the true move 'beyond Hegel' is thus not to be sought in the post-Hegelian return to the positivity of 'real life', but in the strange affirmation of death in the guise of *pure repetition*—the affirmation which puts into the same line two strange bedfellows, Kierkegaard and Freud. In Hegel, repetition plays a crucial role, but within the economy of *Aufhebung*: through a mere repetition, an immediacy is elevated into universality, a contingency is transformed into necessity—after his death, Caesar repeats itself as 'caesar', i.e., no longer the designation of a particular individual, but the name of a universal title. Hegel was unable to think 'pure' repetition, a repetition not yet caught into the movement of *Aufhebung*.

A further paradox here is that this limitation of Hegel points not only towards Freud but also towards Marx. In a certain sense, the speculative movement of Capital can also be said to indicate a limit of the Hegelian dialectical process, something that eludes Hegel's grasp. It is in this sense that Lebrun mentions the 'fascinating image' of Capital presented by Marx (especially in his *Grundrisse*): 'a monstrous mixture of the good infinity and the bad infinity, the good infinity which creates its presuppositions and the conditions of its growth, the bad infinity which never ceases to surmount its crises, and which finds its limit in its own nature'[35]. Actually, it is in Capital itself that we find this Hegelian description of the circulation of capital:

> ...in the circulation M-C-M, both the money and the commodity represent only different modes of existence of value itself, the money its general mode, and the commodity its particular, or, so to say, disguised mode. It is constantly changing from one form to the other without thereby becoming lost, and thus assumes an automatically active character. If now we take in turn each of the two different forms which self-expanding value successively assumes in the course of its life, we then arrive at these two propositions: Capital is money: Capital is commodities. In truth, however, value is here the active factor in a process, in which, while constantly assuming the form in turn of money and commodities, it at the same time changes in magnitude, differentiates itself by throwing off surplus-value from itself; the original value, in other words, expands spontaneously. For the movement, in the course of which it adds surplus-value, is its own movement, its expansion, therefore, is automatic expansion. Because it is value, it has acquired the occult quality of being able to add value to itself. It brings forth living offspring, or, at the least, lays golden eggs.
>
> Value, therefore, being the active factor in such a process, and assuming at one time the form of money, at another that of commodities, but through all these changes preserving itself and expanding, it requires some independent form, by means of which its identity may at any time be established. And this form it possesses only in the shape of money. It is under the form of money that value begins and ends, and begins again, every act of its own spontaneous generation.[36]

Note how Hegelian references abound here: with capitalism, value is not a mere abstract 'mute' universality, a substantial link between the multiplicity of commodities; from the passive medium of exchange, it turns into the 'active factor' of the entire process. Instead of only passively assuming the two different forms of its actual existence (money—commodity), it appears as the subject 'endowed with a motion of its own, passing through a life-process of its own': it differentiates itself from itself, positing its otherness, and then again overcomes this difference—the entire movement is *its own*

---

35. Lebrun, *L'envers de la dialectique*, p. 311.

36. Quoted from http://www.marxists.org/archive/marx/works/1867-c1/ch04.htm.

movement. In this precise sense, 'instead of simply representing the relations of commodities, it enters […] into private relations with itself': the 'truth' of its relating to its otherness is its self-relating, i.e., in its self-movement, the capital retroactively 'sublates' its own material conditions, changing them into subordinate moments of its own 'spontaneous expansion'—in pure Hegelese, it posits its own presuppositions.

Crucial in the quoted passage is the expression 'an automatically active character', an inadequate translation of the German words used by Marx to characterize capital as 'automatischem Subjekt', an 'automatic subject', the oxymoron uniting living subjectivity and dead automatism. This is what capital is: a subject, but an automatic one, not a living one—and, again, can Hegel think this 'monstrous mixture', a process of subjective self-mediation and retroactive positing of presuppositions which as it were gets caught in a substantial 'spurious infinity', a subject which itself becomes an alienated substance? (This, perhaps, is also the reason why Marx's reference to Hegel's dialectics in his 'critique of political economy' is ambiguous, oscillating between taking it as the model for the revolutionary process of emancipation and taking it as the mystified expression of the logic of the Capital.)[37]

But there is a paradox which complicates this critique of Hegel: is the absolute negativity, this central notion of Hegel's thought, not precisely a philosophical figure of what Freud called 'death drive'? Is, then, insofar as—following Lacan—the core of Kant's thought can be defined as the 'critique of pure desire', the passage from Kant to Hegel not precisely the passage from desire to drive? Do the very concluding lines of Hegel's *Encyclopaedia* (on the Idea which enjoys to repeatedly transverse its circle) not point in this direction? Is the answer to the standard critical question addressed to Hegel—'But why does dialectical process always go on? Why does dialectical mediation always continue its work?'—not precisely the *eppur si muove* of pure drive? This structure of negativity also accounts for the quasi-'automatic' character of the dialectical process—one often reproaches Hegel the 'mechanical' character of dialectics: belying all the assurances that dialectics is open to the true life of reality, the dialectical process is like a processing machine which indifferently swallows and processes all possible contents, from nature to history, from politics to art, delivering them packed in the same triadic form ….

The underlying true problem is the following one: the standard 'Hegelian' scheme of death (negativity) as the subordinate/mediating moment of Life can only be sustained if we remain within the category of Life whose dialectic is that of the self-mediating Substance returning to itself from its otherness. The moment we effectively pass from Life(-principle) to Death(-principle), there is no encompassing 'synthesis', death in its 'abstract negativity' forever remains as a threat, an excess which cannot be economized. In social life, this means that Kant's universal peace is a vain hope, that *war* forever remains a threat of total disruption of organized state Life; in individual subjective life, that *madness* always lurks as a possibility.

Does this mean that we are back at the standard topos of the excess of negativity which cannot be 'sublated' in any reconciling 'synthesis', or even at the naïve Engelsian view of the alleged contradiction between the openness of Hegel's 'method' and

---

37. And, perhaps, this same limitation of Hegel also accounts for his inadequate understanding of mathematics, i.e., for his reduction of mathematics to the very model of the abstract 'spurious infinity'. What Hegel was unable to see is how, like the speculative movement of the capital in Marx, modern mathematics also displays the same 'monstrous mixture of the good infinity and the bad infinity': the 'bad infinity' of repetition gets combined with the 'good infinity' of self-relating paradoxes.

the enforced closure of his 'system'? There are indications which point in this direction: as was noted by many perspicuous commentators, Hegel's 'conservative' political writings of his last years (like his critique of the English Reform Bill) betray a fear of any further development which will assert the 'abstract' freedom of the civil society at the expense of the State's organic unity, and open up a way to new revolutionary violence.[38] Why did Hegel shirk back here, why did he not dare to follow his basic dialectical rule, courageously embracing 'abstract' negativity as the only path to a higher stage of freedom? Furthermore, do Hegel's clear indications of the historical limitations of his system (things to be discovered in natural sciences; the impossibility of grasping the spiritual essence of countries like North America and Russia which will deploy their potentials only in the next century) not point in the same direction?

Hegel may appear to celebrate the prosaic character of life in a well-organized modern state where the heroic disturbances are overcome in the tranquility of private rights and the security of the satisfaction of needs: private property is guaranteed, sexuality is restricted to marriage, the future is safe …. In this organic order, universality and particular interests appear reconciled: the 'infinite right' of subjective singularity is given its due, individuals no longer experience the objective state order as a foreign power intruding onto their rights, they recognize in it the substance and frame of their very freedom. Lebrun asks here the fateful question: 'Can the sentiment of the Universal be dissociated from this appeasement?'[39] Against Lebrun, our answer should be: yes, and this is why war is necessary—in war, universality reasserts its right against and over the concrete-organic appeasement in the prosaic social life. Is thus the necessity of war not the ultimate proof that, for Hegel, every social reconciliation is doomed to fail, that no organic social order can effectively contain the force of abstract-universal negativity? This is why social life is condemned to the 'spurious infinity' of the eternal oscillation between stable civic life and wartime perturbations.

---

38. Hegel died a year after the French revolution of 1830.
39. Lebrun, *L'envers de la dialectique*, p. 214.

15

Potentiality and Virtuality[1]

Quentin Meillassoux
translated by Robin Mackay

1. A DISSOLVED ONTOLOGICAL PROBLEM

'Hume's problem', that is to say, the problem of the grounding of causal connection, has known the fate of most ontological problems: a progressive abandonment, legitimated by the persistent failure that various attempts at resolving it have met with. Thus Nelson Goodman, in a famous article[2] can affirm without hesitation the 'dissolution of the old problem of induction'. This dissolution, as laid out by Goodman, concerns the ontological character of Hume's problem, which obliges whoever accepts its terms to accept the necessity of a principle of the uniformity of nature, a principle the proof of whose existence will then be attempted. The argument which, in Goodman, concludes with the dissolution of the 'old problem of induction' is as follows:

- The problem of induction as formulated by Hume consists fundamentally in asking how we can justify that the future should resemble the past.
- Goodman, following Hume, fully affirms that we simply cannot do so: this justification is impossible by rational means.
- We must therefore abandon this undecidable problem, in order to pose it under another form, in which it will once again become amenable to treatment, namely: which rule, or set of rules, do we apply when we—and above all, when scientists—make inductive inferences? The question therefore no longer consists in proving the resemblance of the future and the past, but in describing an existing practice (induction) so as to try to extract its implicit rules. The dissolution of the ontological problem is thus accompanied by its methodological and epistemological reformulation: instead of vainly trying to prove the necessity of observable constants, we must set ourselves the task of describing the precise rules which scientists apply, usually implicitly, when they present us with inductive inferences. Thus Goodman can consider Hume's solution of

1. Originally published as 'Potentialité et virtualité', *Failles* no. 2, Spring 2006. This translation first appeared in *Collapse II*, 2007, pp. 55-81.

2. Nelson Goodman, *Fact, Fiction and Forecast*, 4th ed., Cambridge, Harvard University Press, 1983, ch. 3.

his own problem—that our belief in induction derives from habit and not from consequent reasoning—correct in principle, however partial it might be: because in passing from the insoluble problem of the justification of an ontological principle to that of an effective genesis in the mind, Hume had already registered the intuition that the only adequate treatment of such a problem would consist in describing the effective process by which we draw inductions, not in seeking a metaphysical foundation for it. Consequently, Goodman proposes to follow such a path, forsaking however the psychological description of the spontaneous behaviour of individuals to which Hume confined himself (*viz.*, that we believe in our inductive inferences because of our faculty of believing more and more intensely in recurrent phenomena) in favour of a description of the practices and procedures of the scientific community.

In short, the dissolution of the problem of induction comprises two phases:

- A negative phase of abandonment of the supposedly insoluble problem.
- A phase of recomposition or reformulation of the problem, which consists in passing from an ontological question—is there something like a necessary connection between events?—to a question which evacuates all ontological problems, applying itself instead to the description of effective practices by which scientific inductions are carried out.

2. PRECIPITATION OF THE PROBLEM

My proposal is as follows: to contest the dissolution of Hume's problem, that is to say the abandonment of the ontological formulation of the problem, by maintaining that the latter can be resolved in a way which has, so it would seem, been hitherto neglected. I will intervene, then, only in the first stage of dissolutory reasoning—which is presupposed by the second (the recomposition of new problems): the proposition that the ontological problem of induction must be abandoned, since it is insoluble.

To open anew the ontological problem of the necessity of laws, we must distinguish this problem from that posed by Hume, which is in fact a *particular, already oriented*, formulation of this problem taken in its full generality.

Hume's formulation of the problem is as follows: Can we prove the effective necessity of the connections observed between successive events? The presupposition made both by Hume and by Goodman is that, if we cannot, then *any* ontological treatment of what is called real necessity (that is to say, of the necessity of laws, as opposed to so-called logical necessity) is consigned to failure, and consequently must be abandoned. I believe that it is possible at once to accept the Hume-Goodman verdict of failure, and yet to dispute that it follows that every ontological approach to the problem is thereby disqualified. For the ontological question of real necessity, formulated in its full generality, is not married to the Humean formulation, but rather can be formulated as follows: Can a conclusive argument be made for the necessity *or the absence of necessity* of observable constants? Or, once again: is there any way to justify either the claim that the future must resemble the past, *or* the claim that the future might *not* resemble the past? In the latter case, it is a question of establishing, not that the observable laws must change in the future, but that it is contingent that they should remain identical. This perspective must be distinguished from any thesis affirming the necessity of the changing of laws—for such a thesis would be a variant of the solution envisaged by Hume: this changing of laws, precisely in so far as it is necessary, would suppose yet another law, in a higher sense—a law, itself immutable, regulating the future changes of current constants. Thus it would lead straight back to the idea of a uniformity of nature, simply pushing it back one level.

On the contrary, the ontological approach I speak of would consist in affirming that it is possible rationally to envisage that the constants could effectively change *for no reason whatsoever*, and thus with no necessity whatsoever; which, as I will insist, leads us to envisage a contingency so radical that it would incorporate all conceivable futures of the present laws, *including that consisting in the absence of their modification*. It is thus a question of justifying the effective existence of a radical contingency not only of events submitted to laws, but of laws themselves, reduced to factical constants, themselves submitted to the eventuality of an ultimately chaotic becoming—that is to say, a becoming governed by no necessity whatsoever.

Let us be sure to grasp the significance of such a position, and what it involves. The problem of induction, as soon as it is formulated as the problem of the effective necessity of laws, issues in an avowal of the defeat of reason, because nothing contradictory can be detected in the contrary hypothesis of a changing of constants. For reason does not seem to be capable of prohibiting *a priori* that which goes against the purely logical necessity of non-contradiction. But in that case, a world governed by the imperatives of reason, would be governed only by such logical imperatives. Now, this would mean that anything non-contradictory *could* (but not *must*) come to pass, implying precisely the *refusal* of all causal necessity: for causality, on the contrary, asserts that amongst different, equally conceivable events certain of them must come to pass rather than others. This being so, we would indeed have to agree that *in a rational world everything would be devoid of any reason to be as it is*. A world which was entirely governed by logic, would in fact be governed *only* by logic, and consequently would be a world where nothing has a reason to be as it is rather than otherwise, since nothing contradictory can be perceived in the possibility of such a being-otherwise. Every determination in this world would therefore be susceptible to modification: but no ultimate reason could be given for such modifications, since in that case a prior cause would have to be supposed, which it would not be possible to legitimate in preference to another, equally thinkable. But what would such a world be? To speak in Leibnizian terms, it would be a world *emancipated from the Principle of Sufficient Reason*—a world discharged of that principle according to which everything must have a reason to be as it is rather than otherwise: a world in which the logical exigency of consistency would remain, but not the metaphysical exigency of persistence.

Hume's discovery, according to our account, is thus that *an entirely rational world would be by that very token entirely chaotic*: such a world is one from which the irrational belief in the necessity of laws has been extirpated, since the latter is opposed in its very content to what constitutes the essence of rationality. If, contrary to our hypothesis, one were to *supplement* logical necessity with real necessity, if one were to doubly limit the possible both by non-contradiction and by actual constants, one would then create an artificial riddle irresoluble by reason, since such an hypothesis would amount to the explicit, wholesale fabrication of a necessity foreign to all logic. *The Principle of Sufficient Reason is thus another name for the irrational*—and the refusal of this principle, far from being a way of doing away with reason, is in my opinion the very condition of its philosophical reactualization. The refusal of the Principle of Sufficient Reason is not the refusal of reason, but the discovery of the power of chaos harboured by its fundamental principle (non-contradiction), as soon as the latter is no longer supplemented by anything else—the very expression 'rational chaos' from that moment on becoming a pleonasm.

But such a point of view also provides us with a new understanding of the 'end of metaphysics'. If metaphysics is essentially linked to the postulation—whether explicit or not—of the Principle of Sufficient Reason, the former cannot be understood, in Heideggerian fashion, as the final accomplishment of reason, but as the final accomplishment of real necessity, or again of what I call the reification of rational necessity. From this point of view, I understand by metaphysics, any postulation of a real necessity: so that it would constitute a metaphysical postulation that all or certain given determinate situations in this world are necessary (a determination being definable as a trait capable of differentiating one situation from another, equally thinkable situation). A metaphysics would thus affirm that it is possible, and moreover that it is the very task of reason, to establish why things must be thus rather than otherwise (why some particular individuals, law(s), God(s), *etc.*, rather than other individuals, laws, etc.)

3. ONTOLOGICAL REFORMULATION

The question now is as follows: in accepting the possibility of a change in natural constants, have we not suppressed the problem of induction itself? In other words: once the idea of a necessary constancy of laws is refused, can Hume's question still be posed in the form of a *problem* to be resolved, and more precisely as an ontological problem? It certainly can.

I would affirm that, indeed, there is no reason for phenomenal constants to be constant. I maintain, then, that these laws could change. One thereby circumvents what, in induction, usually gives rise to the problem: the proof, on the basis of past experience, of the future constancy of laws. But one encounters another difficulty, which appears at least as redoubtable: if laws have no reason to be constant, *why do they not change at each and every instant?* If a law is what it is purely contingently, it could change at any moment. The persistence of the laws of the universe seems consequently to break all laws of probability: for if the laws are effectively contingent, it seems that they must frequently manifest such contingency. If the duration of laws does not rest upon any necessity, it must be a function of successive 'dice rolls', falling each time in favour of their continuation or their abolition. From this point of view, their manifest perenniality becomes a probabilistic aberration—and it is precisely because we never observe such modifications that such a hypothesis has seemed, to those who tackled the problem of induction, too absurd to be seriously envisaged.

Consequently, the strategy of the reactualization of the ontological problem of induction will be as follows:

1. We affirm that there exists an ontological path which has not been seriously explored: that consisting in establishing, not the uniformity of nature, but the contrary possibility of every constant being submitted to change in the same way as any factual event in this world—and this without any superior reason presiding over such changes.

2. We maintain that the refusal to envisage such an option for the resolution of the problem is based on an implicit probabilistic argument consisting in affirming that every contingency of laws must manifest itself in experience; which amounts to identifying the contingency of laws with their frequent modification.

3. Thereby, we have at our disposal the means to reformulate Hume's problem

without abandoning the ontological perspective in favour of the epistemic per-spective largely dominant today. Beginning to resolve the problem of induc-tion comes down to *delegitimating the probabilistic reasoning at the origin of the refus-al of the contingency of laws*. More precisely, it is a matter of showing what is falla-cious in the inference from the contingency of laws to the frequency (and thus the observability) of their changing. This amounts to refusing the application of probability to the contingency of laws, thereby producing *a valuable conceptu-al distinction* between contingency understood in this radical sense and the usu-al concept of contingency conceived as chance subject to the laws of probabili-ty. Given such a distinction, it is no longer legitimate to maintain that the phe-nomenal stability of laws compels us to suppose their necessity. This permits us to demonstrate that, without serious consequence, real necessity can be left be-hind, and with it the various supposedly insoluble enigmas it occasioned.

In short, Hume's problem becomes the problem of the difference between chance and contingency.

4. PRINCIPLE OF THE DISTINCTION CHANGE/CONTINGENCY

To demonstrate why laws, if they can change, have not done so frequently, thus comes down to disqualifying the legitimacy of probabilistic reasoning when the latter is ap-plied to the laws of nature themselves, rather than to events subject to those laws. Here is how such a distinction can, in my opinion, be effectively made: to apply a probabil-istic chain of reasoning to a particular phenomenon supposes as given the universe of possible cases in which the numerical calculation can take place. Such a set of cases, for example, is given to a supposedly symmetrical and homogeneous object, a die or a coin. If the die or the coin to which such a calculative procedure is applied always falls on the same face, one concludes by affirming that it has become highly improba-ble that this phenomenon is truly contingent: the coin or die is most likely loaded, that is to say, it obeys a law—for example the law of gravitation applied to the ball of lead hidden within. And an analogous chain of reasoning is applied in favour of the neces-sity of laws: identifying the laws with the different faces of a universal Die—faces repre-senting the set of possible worlds—it is said, as in the precedent case, that if these laws are contingent, we would have been present at the frequent changing of the 'face'; that is to say, the physical world would have changed frequently. Since the 'result' is, on the contrary, always the same, the result must be 'loaded' by the presence of some hidden necessity, at the origin of the constancy of observable laws. In short, we begin by giv-ing ourselves a set of possible cases, each one representing a conceivable world having as much chance as the others of being chosen in the end, and conclude from this that it is infinitely improbable that our own universe should constantly be drawn by chance from such a set, unless a hidden necessity presided secretly over the result.[3]

---

3. It was through reading Jean-René Vernes' *Critique de la raison aléatoire*, Paris, Aubier, 1981, that I first grasped the probabilistic nature of the belief in the necessity of laws. Vernes proposes to prove by such an argument the existence of a reality external to the representations of the Cogito, since it alone would be ca-pable of giving a reason for a continuity of experience which cannot be established through thought alone. As I have remarked elsewhere, I believe that an equally mathematical—more specifically, probabilistic—ar-gument underlies the Kantian transcendental deduction of the categories in the *Critique of Pure Reason*. Kant's argument—as elaborate as it might be in its detail—seems to me to be in perfect continuity with what we might call the argument of 'good sense' against the contingency of natural laws. I argue that Kant's deduc-tion consists simply in exacerbating the 'probabilistic sophism' critiqued in the present article, to the point where the following is argued: if laws were contingent, they would change so frequently, so frenetically, that

Now, if this reasoning cannot be justified, it is because there does not truly exist any means to construct a set of possible universes within which the notion of probability could still be employed. The only two means for determining a universe of cases are recourse to experience, or recourse to a mathematical construction capable of justifying unaided the cardinality (the 'size') of the set of possible worlds. Now, both of these paths are equally blocked here. As for the empirical approach, obviously no one—unless perhaps Leibniz's God—has ever been at leisure to survey the entire set of possible worlds. But the theoretical approach is equally impossible: for what would be attempted here would be to affirm that there is an infinity of possible worlds, that is to say of logically thinkable worlds, which could only reinforce the conviction that the constancy of just one of them is extraordinarily improbable. But it is precisely on this point that the unacceptable postulate of our 'probabilist sophism' hinges, for I ask then: of which infinity are we speaking here? We know, since Cantor, that infinities are multiple, that is to say, are of different cardinalities—more or less 'large', like the discrete and continuous infinities—and above all that these infinities constitute a multiplicity it is impossible to foreclose, since a set of all sets cannot be supposed without contradiction. The Cantorian revolution consists in having demonstrated that infinities can be differentiated, that is, that one can think the equality or inequality of two infinities: two infinite sets are equal when there exists between them a biunivocal correspondence, that is, a bijective function which makes each element of the first correspond with one, and only one, of the other. They are unequal if such a correspondence does not exist. Further still, it is possible to demonstrate that, whatever infinity is considered, an infinity of superior cardinality (a 'larger' infinity) necessarily exists. One need only construct (something that is always possible) the set of the parts of this infinity. From this perspective, it becomes impossible to think a last infinity that no other could exceed.[4]

But in that case, since there is no reason, whether empirical or theoretical, to choose one infinity rather than another, and since we can no longer rely on reason to constitute an absolute totality of all possible cases, and since we cannot give any particular reason upon which to ground the existence of such a universe of cases, we cannot legitimately construct any set within which the foregoing probabilistic reasoning could make sense. This then means that it is indeed incorrect to infer from the contingency of laws the necessary frequency of their changing. So it is not absurd to suppose that

---

we would never be able to grasp anything whatsoever, because none of the conditions for the stable representation of objects would ever obtain. In short, if causal connection were contingent, we would know it so well that we would no longer know anything. As can be seen, this argument can only pass from the notion of contingency to the notion of frequency given the presupposition that it is extraordinarily improbable that the laws should remain constant rather than being modified in every conceivable way at every moment. ('Temps et surgissement ex nihilo', presentation in the seminar series *Positions et arguments* at the École Normale Supérieure, April 2006. See http://www.diffusion.ens.fr/index.php? res=conf&idconf=701).

4. The set of parts of a set is the set of subsets of that set, that is to say the set of all possible regroupings of its elements. Take, for example, the finite set comprising three elements: (1, 2, 3). The set of its parts comprises (apart from the empty set, which is a part of every set): (1), (2) and (3) (the 'minimal' parts composed from its elements alone), (1,2), (1,3), (2,3), and (1,2,3)—this last part (1,2,3) being considered as the maximal part of the set, identical to it. It is clear that this second set is larger (possesses more elements) than the first. It can be proved that this is always the case, the case of an infinite set included. It is thus possible, for every infinite set, to construct a set of superior cardinality: the infinity which comprises the set of its parts. But this construction can equally be carried out on this new infinity, and so on indefinitely. For a clear introduction to axiomatic set theory, see Laurent Schwarz, *Analyse I*, Paris, Hermann, 1991. The reference work on the philosophical importance of set-theory remains for me Alain Badiou's *L'être et l'événement*, Paris, Seuil, 1988, translated by Oliver Feltham as *Being and Event*, London, Continuum, 2006.

the current constants might remain the same whilst being devoid of necessity, since the notion of possible change—and even chaotic change, change devoid of all reason— can be separated from that of frequent change: *laws which are contingent, but stable beyond all probability, thereby become conceivable.*

We must add, however, that there are two possible versions of such a strategy of resolution:

- A 'weak version'—a critical version, let us say—that would consist in limiting the application of aleatory reasoning to cases already submitted to laws (to observable events governed by the constants determining the universe where the calculation is carried out) but not to the laws themselves. Thereby, one would not be able to demonstrate positively the absence of real necessity, but only that its presupposition is of no use in giving an account of the stability of the world. One would content oneself with emphasizing the theoretical possibility of contingent but indefinitely stable laws, by disqualifying the probabilist reasoning which concludes that such an hypothesis is aberrant. The two terms of the alternative—real necessity, or the contingency of laws—being equally non-demonstrable, the heuristic advantage of choosing the second hypothesis is invoked, by showing that it would obviate certain classical speculative enigmas linked to the unchallenged belief in the uniformity of nature.
- A 'strong', that is to say, speculative, version of the response to Hume's problem, would consist in maintaining positively the contingency of laws. Such an approach would incorporate the assets of the argument from heuristics in the above approach to its profit, but would go further, claiming to effectuate the consequences of the Cantorian intotalization.

My overall project is to not limit myself to the critico-heuristic path, but to reactivate a speculative path (claiming to speak for the things themselves, despite the critical proscription), without ever reactivating metaphysics (that is to say, the absolutization of a real necessity). Since it is impossible to give the full details of such an approach here, I will content myself with isolating the principal aspects of the critico-heuristic path.[5]

5. ONTOLOGICAL CONSEQUENCES OF THE NON-ALL

We will adopt the following perspective: we suppose the ontological effectivity of the intotalization of cases, in order to draw the consequences of such a hypothesis upon the notion of becoming, and to envisage its speculative advantages over the inverse hypothesis of the pertinence of real necessity. In order to do this, let us reconsider the notion of the contingency of laws by restricting the notion of law to what constitutes its minimal condition, if not its complete definition: namely a determinate set, finite or infinite, of possible cases—a law, deterministic or aleatory, always comes down to a specific set of indexed cases.[6] We will try to determine the sense of a becoming within which laws

---

5. For further indications as to the exigency of this reactivation, see my *Après la Finitude: Essai sur la nécessité de la contingence*, Paris, Seuil, 2006. I lay out the possible principles of the speculative approach in a forthcoming paper to be published by Éditions Ellipses (proceedings of Francis Wolff's Nanterre 2001 seminar series Positions et arguments).

6. I obviously do not claim that a law can be reduced to a set of possible cases, but that a condition of every law consists in the supposition that a determinate set of possible 'reals' can be discriminated amongst mere logical possibilities. I am thus adopting an argument a minima: I challenge the idea that one can even consider that there exists a set such that it would permit make of laws themselves cases of a Universe of laws (of a set of possible worlds determined by different laws). Since even this minimal condition of every law which is the definition of a determinate set of cases is not respected, this disqualifies a fortiori every attempt

themselves would be contingent, by comparing such a conception with the traditional vision according to which becoming is only thinkable as governed by immutable laws.

Every postulation of a legality, whether determinist or aleatory, identifies the world with a universe of possible cases indexable in principle, that is to say, pre-existing their ultimate discovery, and thereby constituting the potentialities of that universe. Whether a supposed law is considered probabilistic or deterministic, it posits in any case a pre-given set of possible cases which no becoming is supposed to modify. The affirmation of a fundamental hazard governing becoming thus does not challenge, but on the contrary presupposes, the essential fixity of such a becoming, since chance can only operate on the presupposition of a universe of cases determined once and for all. Chance allows time the possibility of a 'caged freedom', that is to say the possibility of the advent without reason of one of those cases permitted by the initial universe; but not the freedom of extracting itself from such a universe to bring forth cases which do not belong to the set thus defined. One cannot, within the aleatory vision of the world, deduce in univocal fashion the succession of events permitted by the law, but one can in principle *index* these events in their totality—even if, in fact, their apparent infinity prohibits for all time the definitive foreclosure of their recollection. In our terminology, such a belief in the aleatory legality of the world would constitute a *metaphysics of chance*, in so far as chance supposes the postulation of a law which would prescribe the fixed set of events within which time finds itself free to oscillate without any determined order. The belief in chance is inevitably a metaphysical belief, since it incorporates the belief in the factual necessity of determinate probabilistic laws, which it is no longer possible to account for except via the necessity of supposed deterministic laws.

In the guise of a radical evolution, it seems that since the Greeks, one conception, and one only, of becoming, has always imposed itself upon us: time is only the actualization of an eternal set of possibles, the actualization of Ideal Cases, themselves inaccessible to becoming—this latter's only 'power' (or rather 'impotence') being that of distributing them in a disordered manner. If modernity is traditionally envisaged, as in Koyré's expression, as the passage from the closed world to the infinite universe, it remains no less true that modernity does not break with Greek metaphysics on one essential point: finite or infinite, the world remains governed by the law—that is, by the All, whose essential signification consists in the subordination of time to a set of possibles which it can only effectuate, but not modify.

Now, it is such a decision, common to the Greeks and to the moderns, from which we believe to have extracted ourselves, *by detotalizing the possible*, and as a result liberating time from all legal subordination. In supposing the ontological legitimacy of the Cantorian conception of the infinite, we distinguish the infinite from the All, since the infinity of the possible cannot be equated with its exhaustion (every infinite set has a determinate cardinality, which another infinity is capable of exceeding). From this decision results the possibility of clearly distinguishing between the notions of contingency and chance, and indeed between the notions of potentiality and virtuality. *Potentialities* are the non-actualized cases of an indexed set of possibilities under the condition of a given law (whether aleatory or not). *Chance* is every actualization of a potentiality for which there is no univocal instance of determination on the basis of the initial given

---

to think such laws in the same way as an event submitted to a law. To review the most important contemporary discussions of the notion of law, cf. A. Barberousse, P. Ludwig, M. Kistler, *La Philosophie des sciences au XXè siècle*, Paris, Flammarion, 2000, chs. 4 and 5.

conditions. Therefore I will call *contingency* the property of an indexed set of cases (not of a case belonging to an indexed set) of not itself being a case of a set of sets of cases; and *virtuality* the property of every set of cases of emerging within a becoming which is not dominated by any pre-constituted totality of possibles.

In short: I posit that the law can be related to a universe of determinate cases; I posit that there is no Universe of universes of cases; I posit that time can bring forth any non-contradictory set of possibilities. As a result, I accord to time the capacity to bring forth new laws which were not 'potentially' contained in some fixed set of possibles; I accord to time the capacity to bring forth situations *which were not at all contained in precedent situations* : of creating new cases, rather than merely actualizing potentialities that eternally pre-exist their fulguration. If we maintain that becoming is not only capable of bringing forth cases on the basis of a pre-given universe of cases, we must then understand that it follows that such cases irrupt, properly speaking, *from nothing*, since no structure contains them as eternal potentialities before their emergence: *we thus make irruption* ex nihilo *the very concept of a temporality delivered to its pure immanence.*

This merits further explanation. If one thinks becoming in the mode of a temporality which does not supervene upon any determinate law, that is to say, any fixed set of possibles, and if one makes of laws themselves temporal events, without subordinating the possible passage from one law to another to a higher-level law which would determine its modalities, time thus conceived is not governed by any non-temporal principle—it is delivered to the pure immanence of its chaos, its illegality. But this is just another way to emphasize—something Hume was the first to maintain—that from a determinate situation, one can never infer *a priori* the ensuing situation, an indefinite multiplicity of different futures being envisageable without contradiction. Grafting the Humean thesis onto that of Cantorian intotality, we see emerging a time capable of bringing forth, outside all necessity and all probability, situations which are not at all pre-contained in their precedents, since according to such a perspective, the present is never pregnant with the future. The paradigmatic example of such an emergence, to which we shall return, is obviously that of the appearance of a life furnished with sensibility directly from a matter within which one cannot, short of sheer fantasy, foresee the germs of this sensibility, an apparition which can only be thought as an supplement irreducible to the conditions of its advent.

As it emerges according to the model of intotality, time might either, for no reason, maintain a universe of cases, a configuration of natural laws, within which it is possible to index a determinate set of recurrent situations constituting its 'potentialities'—or might, equally without reason, cancel the old universe, or supplement it with a universe of cases which were not at all pre-contained in the precedents, nor in any other Substrate wherein the possibilities of being would be ranged for all eternity. We must thus grasp the fact that the inexistence of a pre-constituted All of possibles makes of the emergence of a possible anticipated by nothing in the preceding situation, the very manifestation of a time underwritten by no superior order: every emergence of a supplement irreducible to its premises, far from manifesting the intervention of a transcendent order in rational becoming, becomes the rigorous inverse: a manifestation of a becoming which nothing transcends.[7]

---

7. To be more precise, we must say that the distinction potentiality/virtuality is gnoseological rather than ontological, in so far as it designates essentially a difference in our cognitive relation with temporality. The perpetuation of a Universe of already-known cases (the constancy of laws) itself also escapes all consideration in terms of potentiality. For if one can determine potentialities within a determinate set of possibles, the

Thus, for 'potentialism' (the doctrine that sees in each possibility only a potentiality), time can only be the medium by which what was already a possible case, becomes a real case. Time, then, is the throw with which the die offers us one of its faces: but in order for the faces to be presented to us, it must be the case that they preexisted the throw. The throw manifests the faces, but does not engrave them. According to our perspective, on the contrary, time is not the putting-in-movement of possibles, as the throw is the putting-in-movement of the faces of the die: time creates the possible at the very moment it makes it come to pass, it brings forth the possible as it does the real, it inserts itself in the very throw of the die, to bring forth a seventh case, in principle unforeseeable, which breaks with the fixity of potentialities. Time throws the die, but only to shatter it, to multiply its faces, beyond any calculus of possibilities. Actual events cease to be doubled by phantomatic possibilities which prefigure them before they occur, to be conceived instead as pure emergences, which before being are nothing, or, once again, which do not pre-exist their existence.

In other words, the notion of virtuality, supported by the rationality of the Cantorian decision of intotalising the thinkable, makes of irruption *ex nihilo* the central concept of an immanent, non-metaphysical rationality. Immanent, in that irruption *ex nihilo* presupposes, against the usually religious vision of such a concept, that there is no principle (divine or otherwise) superior to the pure power of the chaos of becoming; non-metaphysical in that the radical rejection of all real necessity assures us of breaking with the inaugural decision of the Principle of Sufficient Reason.

The most effective way to grasp properly the sense of the thesis proposed here is perhaps, as mentioned, to subtract it from the heuristic interest. This separation can be carried out through a series of elucidations permitted by such a model—elucidations of problems generally held to be insoluble, and thus sterile.

Firstly, as we have already said, such a model permits us to dissociate the notion of the stability of the empirical world from that of real necessity. The reprise of the problem of induction sought to show that it is possible to abandon the idea of a necessary constancy of laws, without this abandonment leading to the opposite idea of a *necessarily* disordered world. For the disqualification of the probabilist reasoning which implicitly founds the refusal of a contingency of laws suffices to demonstrate that the possible changing of constants of this world does not indicate their necessary continual upheaval: by affirming that the world could really submit its laws to its own becoming, one posits the concept of a contingency superior to all necessity, *one whose actualization is therefore subject to no constraint*—and above all not that of a frequential law supposed to render more and more improbable the noneffectuation of certain possibilities. For to affirm that the changing of laws, if it *could* happen, *must* happen, is to subordinate anew the contingency of becoming to the necessity of a law, according to which every possible must eventually be actualized. An entirely chaotic world—submitting every law to the power of time—could thus in principle be phenomenally *indiscernible* from a world

maintenance across time of a determinate law itself cannot be evaluated in terms of potentiality (one possible case in a set of others). Even if the case which comes to pass is already indexed, it is only foreseen upon condition—an unforeseeable and improbabilizable condition—of the maintenance of the old set of possibles. Ultimately, the Universe can be identified with the factual re-emergence of the same Universe on the ground of non-totality. But the virtualizing power of time, its insubordination to any superior order, lets itself be known, or is phenomenalized, when there emerges a novelty that defeats all continuity between the past and the present. Every 'miracle' thus becomes the manifestation of the inexistence of God, in so far as every radical rupture of the present in relation to the past becomes the manifestation of the absence of any order capable of overseeing the chaotic power of becoming.

subject to necessary laws, since a world capable of everything must *also* be able *not* to effect all that it is capable of. Thus it becomes possible to justify the postulate of all natural science—namely the reproducibility of experimental procedures, supposing a general stability of phenomena—whilst assuming the effective absence of a principle of uniformity of nature, and by the same token abandoning the canonical enigmas linked to the hypothesis of a necessity of laws. But this abandonment does not proceed, as in Goodman, from a simple refusal to think the problem, a refusal justified by its supposed insolubility: it proceeds from the conviction that one can think the contingency of constants compatibly with their manifest stability.

The critique of the probabilistic sophism given above can also be extended to its application in various analogous arguments, which generally seek to restore a certain form of finalism. I will content myself here with mentioning one example of such an extension of the critical analysis, that of anthropism.

The thesis of anthropism—more precisely, of what is known as the Strong Anthropic Principle—rests fundamentally upon the following hypothesis:[8] one imagines oneself able to vary in an arbitrary fashion the initial givens of a universe in expansion, such as the numbers which specify the fundamental laws of contemporary physics (that is to say the relations and constants involved in these laws). One is then in a position to determine the evolution of these artificial universes, and one notes, in almost all cases, that these latter are incapable of evolving towards the production of the components indispensable for the emergence of life and, a fortiori, of intelligence. This result, which emphasizes the extreme rarity of universes capable of producing consciousness, is then presented as deserving of astonishment—astonishment before the remarkable coincidence of the contingent givens of our universe (contingent in so far as there is no means to deduce their determinations—they can only be observed within experience) with the extremely restrictive physical conditions presiding over the appearance of conscious life: how is it that our universe should be so precisely furnished with the necessary characteristics for our appearance, whereas these characteristics prove to be of such rarity on the level of possible universes? Such an astonishment thus rests upon reasoning that is clearly probabilistic, relating the number of possible universes to the number of universes capable of life. The anthropist begins by being surprised by a coincidence too strong to be imputed to chance alone, and then infers the idea of an enigmatic finality having predetermined our universe to comprise the initial constants and givens which render possible the emergence of man. Anthropism thus reactivates a classical topos of finalist thought: the remarking of the existence of a highly-ordered reality (inherent to the organized and thinking being) whose cause cannot reasonably be imputed to chance alone, and which consequently imposes the hypothesis of a hidden finality.

Now, we can see in what way the critique of the probabilist sophism permits us to challenge such a *topos* in a new way. For such reasoning is only legitimate if we suppose the existence of a determinate set (whether finite or infinite) of possible universes, obtained through the antecedent variation of the givens and constants of the observable universe. Now, it appears that there are no legitimate means of constituting the universe of possibles within which such reasoning could make sense, since this means, once more, could be neither experimental nor simply theoretically: as soon as one frees oneself from the imperatives of experience, in the name of what principle can one lim-

---

8. For a definition of the various versions of the Anthropic Principle, See J.D. Barrow and F.J. Tipler, *The Anthropic Cosmological Principle*, Oxford, Oxford University Press, 1986, Introduction and Section 1.2.

it, as the Anthropic Principle implicitly does, the set of possible worlds to those obtained solely by the linear variation of constants and variables found in the currently observable universe, and in whose name do we limit such a set of worlds to a determinate infinity? In truth, once the possible is envisaged in its generality, every totality becomes unthinkable, and with it the aleatory construction within which our astonishment finds its source. The rational attitude is not, in actual fact, to seek an explanation capable of responding to our astonishment, but to trace the inferential genealogy of the latter so as to show it to be the consequence of an application of probabilities outside the sole legitimate field of their application.

Finally, the abandonment of real necessity permits one last elucidation, this time concerning the emergence of new situations, whose qualitative content is such that it seems impossible to detect, without absurdity, its anticipated presence in anterior situations. So that the problem appears in all clarity, let us take the classical example of the emergence of life, understood here not merely as the fact of organization but as subjective existence. From Diderot's hylozoism, to Hans Jonas' neo-finalism,[9] the same argumentative strategies are reproduced time and time again in philosophical polemics on the possibility of life emerging from inanimate matter. Since life manifestly supposes, at least at a certain degree of its evolution, the existence of a set of affective and perceptive contents, either one decides that matter already contained such subjectivity in some manner, in too weak a degree for it to be detected, or that these affections of the living being did not pre-exist in any way within matter, thus finding oneself constrained to admit their irruption *ex nihilo* from that matter—which seems to lead to the acceptance of an intervention transcending the power of nature. Either a 'continuism', a philosophy of immanence—a variant of hylozoism—which would have it that all matter is alive to some degree; or the belief in a transcendence exceeding the rational comprehension of natural processes. But such a division of positions can once more be called into question once irruption *ex nihilo* becomes thinkable within the very framework of an immanent temporality. We can then challenge both the necessity of the preformation of life within matter itself, and the irrationalism that typically accompanies the affirmation of a novelty irreducible to the elements of the situation within which it occurs, since such an emergence becomes, on the contrary, the correlate of the rational unthinkability of the All. The notion of virtuality permits us, then, to reverse the signs, making of every radical irruption the manifestation, not of a transcendent principle of becoming (a miracle, the sign of a Creator), but of a time that nothing subtends (an emergence, the sign of the non-All). We can then grasp what is signified by the impossibility of tracing a genealogy of novelties directly to a time before their emergence: not the incapacity of reason to discern hidden potentialities, but, quite on the contrary, the capacity of reason to accede to the ineffectivity of an All of potentialities which would pre-exist their emergence. In every radical novelty, time makes manifest that it does not actualize a germ of the past, but that it brings forth a virtuality which did not pre-exist in any way, in any totality inaccessible to time, its own advent.[10]

---

9. See for example Hans Jonas, *The Imperative of Responsibility*, Chicago, University of Chicago, 1985, ch. 3, 4, 3b: 'The Monist Theory of Emergence'.

10. It might be objected that in the preceding arguments I tend to conflate potentialism—which makes of every possible a potentiality—and a continuism which claims to discern for every present novelty a past situation wherein all the elements of such a novelty already existed, if at a lesser degree. It will be objected that one might at once claim that the world is subject to immutable laws, and refuse the actualism of preformationism, which sees the world as a set of Russian dolls where everything is already effective before

We thus glimpse if all-too-briefly, the outlines of a philosophy emancipated from the Principle of Sufficient Reason, and endeavouring, in this very recommencement, to maintain the double exigency inherent to the classical form of rationalism: the ontology of that which is given to experience, and the critique of representation.

---

being manifest. I respond that I certainly do not conflate the two theses, but that potentialism and preformationism, having in common the refusal of virtuality, are equally incapable of thinking a pure novelty: potentialism, in particular, if it claims that sensation is a potentiality of matter which was not actualised by it before its emergence in the living, would accumulate disadvantages, since it would be constrained to combine the mystery of real necessity (matter is ruled by laws which give birth to sensitive contents under determinate conditions) and that of irruption *ex nihilo* (these contents are in no way contained in the conditions that make them emerge).

16

The Generic as Predicate and Constant: Non-Philosophy and Materialism[1]

François Laruelle
translated by Taylor Adkins

WHEN DO WE SPEAK OF THE 'GENERIC'?

What sort of fate is reserved for the montages which we receive from the tradition which distribute knowledge? One of these classical montages is called 'generic' but gains importance, if not in a confused way, in relation to the traditional epistemological distributions of knowledge, although it remains quite indeterminate despite its continuous ascent. The generic has two or three sources that we propose to unify from the inside in a science-thought. The first is philosophical and well known but worn out or dried up; the second is epistemological and sociological, full of promises but still not elucidated; the third that gives rise to a philosophy of the first order (Badiou) is mathematical but too narrow and technical to be usable for our project here.

The philosophical source is Feuerbach's 'generic man' which breaks with the 'philosophy' whose proper name is Hegel, symbol of the idealist absolute system. But Feuerbach more widely situates himself in a tradition which is not simply Hegelian or pre-Marxist. It begins at least (with and after Luther) with Hamann (against Kant), Jacobi (against Fichte), Eschenmayer (against Schelling), the young Hegelians properly speaking up to Stirner, and culminates with Kierkegaard (against Hegel). One specific trait common to these doctrines is *how to break with philosophy and its systematic aspect* in the name of passion, faith, and feeling? In the name of the existing and religious individual? In the name of a non-philosophy? Feuerbach's specific support is the 'generic' break as the humanist and naturalist reversal of Hegel. The generic also introduces a revolt—albeit of a religious essence—against the philosophy of the system and does not simply prepare the passage to Marx. Perhaps we forget too often that these 'religious thinkers', now effaced in the continuum of the 'history of philosophy', were accompanied by a tradition of revolt crushing the tradition of the philosophers of systematic Reason. As minoritarian or minor thinkers, they have opened a wound in the

---

1. Originally published in French in: Laruelle, François, *Introduction aux sciences generiques*, Editions Petra, Paris, 2008, ch. 2 and 5.

flank of 'grand rationalism' that refuses to close up (Michel Henry, cf. his *Marx*). When it is a question of breaking with philosophical sufficiency, of elaborating a new and more concrete universalism, the generic is the front upon which a certain experience of 'man' leads the struggle against philosophical capture. Although this struggle is still very 'humanist' and coordinated by Feuerbach with religion rather than science—as we shall do by borrowing from a part of this tradition—, it is inevitable that we shall at least adopt it as *symptom*, just as non-philosophy, as we conceive it, always does so as to better transform the sense of the latter and displace its revolutionary bearing from the 'essence of Christianity' to the essence of science. We intend to stitch up this wound opened by 'man' in the flank of philosophy but in such a way that the generic suture does not leave an indelible scar which would testify to a poorly practiced operation with crude, mechanical instruments, and which is now nothing more than the wake of the identity that man, at least what we baptize as 'Man-in-person' or 'ordinary Man', leaves behind in the World that the she traverses or the trembling that she introduces with her arrival. Obviously it remains to be shown that the generic of the sciences of the future has some relation with their human destination (without consequently being the 'human sciences' which only have man for their destination due to confusion and appearances).

The second source of the generic is societal and epistemological; it is a jumble of formulas and various language games which are said of a certain usage of the sciences on the one hand and manufactured products on the other. As a stranger to the primary approach to the first source, it apparently has nothing philosophical about it and instead bears witness to the most unbridled capitalistic economism. It is as conquering, turbulent, and confused as the philosophical seems worn out and 'tucked away' in its post-Hegelian museum. It is a deceptive appearance. Its usage corresponds with certain invariant traits and can give rise to a description. These traits indicate that a so-called 'generic' science (1) has no calling to posit itself as global or fundamental, as foundational for the other sciences as mathematics can claim to, or even as reductive of other sciences like physics in the case of 'physicalism;' (2) that it is valid for the domain of singular or specific objects for which it has been elaborated, while being able to support knowledges that remain local *in* another; (3) and that it no longer forms a new synthesis or 'hybrid' with another science, a combination to a superior degree. The generic sciences, the generic usage of the sciences and informatic programming, signifies that they neither found nor even envelop or derive from the others, but that they can intervene in other already constituted sciences without forming a new continuum together as epistemology envisions. Neither foundation nor auto-foundation, these sciences nevertheless have a 'suitability', one could almost say with Plato an 'agathon', with and for the others, yet a *non-reciprocal suitability* which must be investigated. Just like a so-called 'generic' medicine or product, it has lost its most specific, most original point and has become more common and been 'marked down'. A dress or vacation package gets 'downgraded' when it is no longer original, primary, and unique in its kind, is at a higher and less negotiable cost, is no longer the property of a label or a proper name but acquires a common value, and when it loses the sufficiency or pretention that could in turn make it 'philosophize' or give it 'unique' properties, not simply 'interesting' but originary and original.

The Marxist theory of fetishism can rediscover a new import if we distinguish that it does not create the generic usage of commodities and the theological and mystical, i.e. globally philosophical charge that they possess the moment they first appear on the market. They lose their natural or spontaneous drive to auto-affirm or reaffirm themselves as having a unique and absolute value, to posit themselves in a paradigmatic existence. Generic products and sciences cease to theologize and philosophize, at least seemingly. What Marx denounces as fetishism after a perhaps incomplete analysis of philosophy itself beyond the market, as we have already suggested, is no doubt the capacity of the commodity and the market to be bewitched: but all of this is quite relative. Fetishism is more widespread and more profound. There is a super-fetishism that is not specifically 'theological', for it is that of the philosophical All as power of auto-bewitching itself, re-enveloping itself, and auto-legitimating itself. This super-All is the God fluid in a million forms that *de jure* unites every philosopher in a mystical way, and not simply in any particular, always limited, doctrinal consciousness. The mystical and theological charge must not be understood simply as transcendence; in reality, it is also immanence fully deployed. The full and ultimate possibility of the philosophical, beyond what the philosopher lives through and thinks, is a system with double coordinates, immanence and transcendence variously balanced, no doubt, but reciprocally presupposing one another. But generic sciences and products seemingly stop aspiring to the All and the Absolute, or no longer recognize it except in their genre, *sui generis* called specificity. There is obviously a problem of commodity circulation of and in philosophy. But for the moment and as a symptom, the capitalist generic, if you will, is modest without being banal or everyday; it disposes of a simple and local force and gives rise, no doubt speaking broadly, to an incomplete or 'weak philosophy;' it is akin to the ordinary without falling, for example, into the conversational and demonetized linguistic exchange. It could be—this is a hypothesis—that the generic is the ordinary in a German mode. Measured against philosophy, it keeps a low profile. It is a position of knowledge or the commodity in terms of its usage, but it does not re-posit itself a second time; it has ceased to re-affirm itself and 'praise' itself. If it has its way of 'circulating' under this form, then is it still a commodity? And furthermore, isn't philosophy an organizer of circulation and the primary medium for the circulation of knowledges?

We could distinguish one generic by its apex and another by its nadir. In the algebraic model of knowledge, the generic is the acquisition of a supplement of universal properties (those of demonstration and manifestation) through a subtraction and an indetermination, a formalization of givens. In the commercial model of prescription medicine or clothes, generic universality is obtained through a mark down or downgrade and the loss of the proper or original name under which the product has been commercialized for the first time, a loss which is equivalent to an inferior form of formalization that plunges these products into the common circuit. There is, however, a difference between these two regimes of the generic. That which is scientific is already beyond-All or beyond-philosophy and only attains its generic regime through a subtraction that is a supplement of paradigmatic (extatico-vertical) properties, whereas the commercial or commodity sphere is philosophical from the start and only attains its generic value through the abasement of its philosophical and global quality.

Thus, in the philosophical context such as we are outlining in relation to super-fetishism and what we call the hallucination to which it gives rise, the generic is difficult to situate between banality, the median, and simply the milieu. For us, it will be a question of rediscovering *the identity of the generic in a new combination of its two symptoms-sources, man coming from philosophy and the subject or object coming from science, both transformed, something like the identity of the human middle, of 'ordinary man' and, in particular, the labours of the latter.*

FROM THE CONCEPT OF THE GENERIC TO GENERIC SCIENCE

Two tasks must be carried out.

It is therefore first a question of giving to the notion of 'generic science' its concept, which only appears in a fuzzy set, indeterminate and at the mercy of various discourses, objects, and disciplines. These include multiple discourses of extremely different origins (technical, scientific, medical, commercial, administrative), like an ambiguity or situation to be clarified, a set of 'phrases' that encroach upon one another and for a moment constitute a tangled web, but still not a formation of knowledge and statements. No doubt increasingly 'regular', these statements, allusions, references, or interdisciplinary invocations, for example relating to administration and the politics of research and which cross all the disciplines and old domains of research, still have not reached their epistemological threshold, neither as philosophical nor as objects of a science. In order to remove this indetermination as much as possible and elaborate a concept most aptly tailored to genericity, we shall reserve several surprises. It could be that the *generic power* of the so-called 'generic' sciences can form the object of an epistemology neither in a classical sense, nor in the sense of a philosophy in good and due form in terms which would still be those of Feuerbach. Even the transversality or diagonality of generic statements in relation to the classical divisions of the fields and domains of objects does not necessarily give rise to an 'archaeology' à la Foucault, nor does the 'epistemological plinth' rise to the genericity to which it nevertheless is so close.

The force of the generic seems to be the force of intervention of one knowledge in the other sciences to which it is foreign *(interdisciplinary force of intervention)*, or even a medicine, a force of marking down or 'downgrading', in general of subtraction through which any product whatsoever is forced to enter into a circuit to which it is foreign. But still, and this is more than another example for the generic because it is univocal for all phenomena, how can Strangers insert themselves 'by force' into a community? By force, yet, let us say, suddenly, without this forcing escalating to a reciprocal procedure of capture or war. The majority of the problems that set the Stranger, knowledges [*saviors*] or individuals, cognitions [*connaissances*] or subjects in play and which touch upon the problem of their entrance into an already determined community, are 'generic' problems *par excellence* and must, if possible, no longer be treated in this horrible style of 'omni-hybridization'. The generic is the real nucleus which is at the centre of the sexual, economic, and linguistic violence of the hybridization and worldly circulation of knowledges and individuals, thus transforming it through its extraction. Not that these phenomena do not exist; they form the transcendental yet objective appearance of the circulation of sciences and individuals, information and lives. But we only have some chance of transforming these consistent appearances in their materiality by grasping the problem by its root which is, as the generic wills, man. But which man? All that can be said at the moment is that the force of the generic is that of the Stranger who comes as a new type of universal.

Now, if—this is the second task—there is, upon the basis of these symptoms, a generic science-thought, a *universal genericity* to be illuminated as distinct from philosophical universality, something which resembles an epistemology without being one, it will probably in turn be called like all the other generic disciplines simpler or more positive for carrying out very precise functions now with disciplines more complex than the sciences from which we set off, with knowledges on the second level, those where philosophy is already explicitly judge and jury and no longer implicitly, namely the epistemologies and all the disciplines where philosophy makes its presence and even constitution known, as in aesthetics, ethics, technology, and theology.

This investment of the elaborated concept of genericity in the most complex disciplines is not to be understood in a violent or unitary way, through application or epistemological superposition stemming from a bad forcing, but as a double causality, 'occasional' on the one hand (the preceding symptoms of genericity) and on the other hand as determination by Man, which only results in the last instance, of these disciplines. Even if the generic is actually torn apart savagely by worldly economic forces, our endeavour in epistemology (we do not say 'in science') remains non-conquering and 'non-capitalist'. Its goal is to equip the existing disciplines with a new function of intervention or fecundity and with an unprecedented type of communication, something we call a 'circulation-sans-circle', neutral or sans-surplus-value, which is the veritable support of the generic in the sciences and elsewhere, i.e. generally, as we shall make clear, on behalf of an ecological thought. The generic no longer functions under the principle of the All [*le Tout*], redoubling itself, which still rules over the Foucauldian epistemological plinths, the Deleuzian machinic dispersions, and the Derridean textual disseminations one last time, which all fail to mention genericity while rushing to devote themselves to the All, even when this would only be to dismember it, above all to critique, deconstruct, and differentiate it.

Philosophers have not always noticed that the *apparently* middle level of the generic, which they take for mediocrity or sometimes for a simple materialist reversal like Feuerbach in relation to Hegel, has the greatest affinities in the heart of philosophy itself with science and allows, if it is manifested and radicalized, a delimitation of the epistemological grip upon the sciences. This grip testifies to a precipitation and 'spontaneism', or what could be called a certain savagery that throws everything, the All, into war. On the contrary, the generic 'democratically' equalizes the disciplines that it invests without completely destroying their specificity or their relative autonomy, but equalizes them only in-the-last-instance. It is univocally equal for them all; this is *its universality of service, its absence of foundational will*. It does not suffice to critique the foundational will of philosophy against the sciences, as is sometimes done, if this would not be to replace it with another function which would be that of fecundation, i.e. of the production and givenness of peace.

Moreover, since philosophy is hypergeneric and globalizing, an illusion or transcendental appearance, only the generic can manifest it to this extent that reaches or affects all epistemologies. Such a discipline has virtues and limits that can be called 'non-philosophical', no doubt in the sense of 'the' non-philosophy of which it is a by-product. It is pertinent for each of the mixtures or combinations of philosophy and science, and should at least allow us to vanquish these transcendental appearances that belong to any philosophy whatsoever. By all means it will not be, if we manage to set it on its feet, generic-contemplative or theoreticist, but will transform the disciplines as well as itself, which has been acquired with their aid.

Thus, the generic designates a *universality of unilateral intervention*, more exactly of interaction, but a weak interaction without reversibility; this is why the terms intervention and even interaction are imperfect and should be nuanced. This universality is distinct from other types, for example the universality of legality (by law), of domain (by field of objects), or of structure with models (by modelization). Effectuated as a specific discipline, this universal also requires its objects, procedures of deduction and induction, and axiomatic and experimental material, but each time under an original form. It does not constitute the epistemological transversal or the archaeological diagonal of the existing disciplines, but rather their *unilateral edge*, an edge of which it is impossible to say whether it is external or internal to the given formations of knowledge because it is what comes to the disciplines and attaches them through this arrival at their ground of positivity which gave rise to epistemology. We shall suggest that genericity, without destroying the market and capitalist structure of exchange and equivalence which is necessary to it as the element in which it intervenes and which is of another order, no longer simply reproduces it even with differe(a)nce, but contributes to transforming it through its operation which is of the order of idempotence, as we shall make clear later on. This is a transformation that takes place *according to* a subject of-the-last-instance and as its defence as Stranger against capitalist-and-epistemological sufficiency. It bears witness to a completely different 'program' of thought than the philosophies and thus the epistemologies. It no doubt stems from what we call a 'human messianism'. Since it is obviously an atheistic messianism, the generic science-thought is not the by-product of a 'shameful' creationism but rather always seeks to eradicate the constantly revived religious and metaphysical nostalgias concerning the scientific. We certainly do not imagine for an instant that we uphold the thesis that the intervention, for example, of tribology into ophthalmology would be a work of the Messiah! Universally equal or 'advening' *independently of their specificity of origin for* all sciences and all activities, the generic subject is a new theoretical subject. Generic power is not measured quantitatively in extension, qualitatively by frontiers and demarcation, or intensively through depth because it is operatory upon the All and upon the type of distinction that belongs to it. If the radicalized generic possesses a type of universal (non-)relation, it is unilaterality or, to speak more clearly, it is *being-Stranger rather than marginality* (which has produced the good days of philosophy). At this level, it is a question of elaborating a paradigm, both foreign and generic through its origin rather than being of a Platonizing nature, not necessarily a question of describing a phenomenon of the market, of supply and demand between positive sciences—this work has already been carried out *ad nauseam*. In the elaboration of our concept of human genericity, the sciences that practice generic interventions are simple *models* for us; they interpret the generic Idea and its non-philosophical employment. Its sphere of pertinence is tangentially equal for all totalizing-individual philosophies, just like epistemologies are in-the-last-instance.

IDEMPOTENT ADDITION. STERILE LIVED EXPERIENCE [*VÉCU*]. UNILATERALITY

Alongside the anti-Hegelian and naturalist path (Feuerbach) and the scientific path (with its two scientific models, Aristotle's anti-logical biological path and Badiou's set-theorism established on the basis of contemporary logical and mathematical works), there is a path in the phenomenological and symptomatological style, as we have suggested, for entering the generic. They are all ultimately philosophical (idealist or materialist), but we shall find use in the phenomenological path by collecting symptoms as material on behalf of establishing the concept of a generic science. At this level, the generic is still of the order of a predicate dispersed to the edge of the acts and objects of which it is said. Our problem is to progressively bring the predicate to the function of a scientifico-philosophical constant. Thus, there will be a problem related to the legibility of these symptoms.

Towards this goal, we shall assemble two or three guiding axioms. The first posits a new concept of the ultimate Real as a constant upon which these sciences can be edified, and this is necessarily Man. So as to distinguish Man from that of humanism and the problematic of the human Sciences, we shall not call Man 'generic' (this would be Feuerbachian man) but 'in-person' (or in a substitutive and more classically metaphysical way, lest we undo this initial sense, One-in-person). Man-in-person is defined *by immanence as a logical property of idempotent and thus sterile addition, not at all by a philosophical definition of the 'rational animal' type.* Nevertheless, even if this notion is important in the definition of the phenomenon of waves, we do not at all intend to again grasp it as a property of a physical phenomenon as such, still less to give the latter a philosophical interpretation (generally the 'transcendental' interpretation of quantum physics), but to isolate this property and make it account for the phenomenon of Lived Experience.

The second axiom simply posits this operation without substance under the form of a *lived operator of immanence*, sterile or neutralized lived experience in virtue of idempotence (*Erlebnis* in Husserl), non-egological or subjectless immanence.

The third axiom posits idempotent immanence as articulated *in a simply immanent way, without distance or mediation*, over the philosophical transcendence (symbol, term, position, concept) that it primarily transmits and transforms from the bifacial or transcendent object into a unifacial 'object' or a uni-jet; this is the universalizing action of lived idempotence. In other words, we have acquired the generic sought under the form of a duality, but as stranger, a duality with one term called 'unilateral', and whose other term, idempotence, is not a term or does not pass into the sphere of existence or representation. Idempotent lived experience does not exist or exists only on this side of being and manifestation. As for unilateral duality, it refuses to fall under the All which it transforms as a unilateral or unifacial term and attaches to itself. In sum, the generic is a *constant* of all knowledges which are determined in-the-last-instance by Man and not by philosophical authority.

There are three questions concerning the generic. (1) How is it individuated? It is individuated via a mode which is not that of totality, *not by the One-All*, but by the One-without-All or immanent One-in-One as non-cumulatively added or sterile lived experience entirely subtracted by itself from the philosophical One thus radically weakened. (2) What is its sphere of comprehension? It is a universal *a priori* without particular objects, precisely a grasping in immanence and, moreover, a unilateral content of transcendence, eventually of the philosophical without philosophies or without the philosophizable. Whereas calculability 'excludes' calculations, philosophizability excludes particular philosophies and fulfils the generic a priori. The auto-enveloping All has objects of knowledge in it, which are philosophical systems or doctrines, and, beyond, the matter of particular beings. Since the philosophizable lacks an object, it cannot fold back onto itself, reflect upon itself, or wind itself around a particular philosophy; it is a one-surface, a uni-face or unfolded. (3) What is the internal causality that articulates generic thought? On the reflected side of the philosophical One-All or bifacial transcendence, idempotent Lived Experience detaches or subtracts a single side, a uniface. If the philosophical One is divided and then reunified, if it is both a transcendental (either the divisible or relatively indivisible One) and real or absolutely indivisble One, the generic instead separates them, the universal sphere 'belonging' to the One-in-One alone; yet the latter never counts as a type of universal or one of its objects because it is foreclosed to the latter. The philosophizable no longer has philosophies; it is sans-object just as the immanent One-in-One itself is sans-philosophizable.

It should be noted that it is the prepossession of this constant that allows us to present philosophical complexity as duplicity, the excessively abstract complexity of the famous 'all', of 'totalization' and 'detotalization'. We have called 'super-All' the *system* of sub- and super-totalization, of de- and re-totalization, ultimately the surplus value to which philosophy and epistemology aspire. We shall call this 'all' a super-All for reasons given after the fact. As for the meaning of 'unilateral', we are forced to advance a new vocabulary little by little despite having to explain it later on to discover its unknowns.

THE DISTINCTIVE TRAITS OF THE GENERIC

Equipped with our three axioms, we can now locate several symptoms of the generic in philosophy and already present the principle of their transformation towards the acquisition of the non-philosophical generic we are seeking. If the preceding paragraph is clear in its technically difficult means and intents and can serve as our guiding thread, it is nevertheless more ambiguous because it designates a journey that journeys from the vagueness of doxa and philosophy towards the axioms of the generic.

1. Generic-being tends to present itself as a stranger. A product, technique, or knowledge can receive, alongside its specific importance (corresponding to an original domain, thus having universal value only for its domain), another universality which is not classically global and domineering [*de surplomb*],[2] a value or a function, a usage which is instead transversal in relation to the preceding. It fulfils tasks or services in domains which are not its own, but without a philosophical type of survey [*survol*] or foundation. Thus certain disciplines acquire a generic value, despite their specific character, through the usage made of their own means in other domains of objects. This term 'transversal' is nevertheless provisional for us because generic knowledge is not even supposed to fold itself onto the same general space that it would traverse and would serve as its reference. The unilateral generic changes the givens of reference. A 'uni-lateral' usage is an added function which in a sense has nothing in common with the knowledge ensuring the reception; it is not itself held in a face to face or in co-relation and 'interaction' if it is simply unilateral with another more classical knowledge; it thus does not come to annul or destroy this knowledge's legality, but guarantees its validity otherwise. A generic knowledge does not 'fold' itself to the laws of another domain of phenomena in which it intervenes. At the limit, every reciprocal action between the two knowledges, the specific and the generic that intervenes, is eliminated. The generic's essence is a non-acting that acts through a unilateral organon; this is why it is necessary to speak cautiously about intervention or inter-action. Later we shall speak of 'sub-vention' rather than 'intervention' and 'sub-action' or weak force rather than interaction.

2. Generic-being possesses an a priori function without being a philosophical a priori. Concentrated in a specific knowledge, it is valid for a series or a set of objects which it selects from all the givens. This is not the transcendental being of the particular object or being, ultimately of the philosophical All, but an a priori for the selected objects upon which it does not impose itself as a logico-philosophical form, as a universal and necessary knowledge, but as a unifacial or unilateral power of the immanent transformation of their objectivity. The distinction comes up against the philosophical confusions (the All in general) between the philosophical super-All and the simple all that produces the generic. Generic-being is not an All of the genre we call 'duplicitous' with which it would reciprocally affect itself, but it is valid also or in a supplementary

---

2. Literally 'overhanging', corresponding with the word 'survol', meaning 'flight-over'. [trans.]

way for every 'all' of the objects of this All or is a priori compatible with them through their transformation despite its Strangerhood [*Étrangeté*]. The 'all' therefore changes meaning and is no longer survey and torsion, but a simple and closed all, without the fold which is said of a multiple (the 'generic' of film). The philosophical super-All is certainly animated also by an intentionality *for* the particular, even singular, object and its multiplicity. But, on the one hand, here there is no reciprocal presupposition between the a priori of the simple all and its content, or if one still exists, it is simple or 'flat' without a redoubling. Their validity flows in a single or 'descending' direction, a 'for' without torsion or return, since they are, despite everything, within *the ultimate horizon of the philosophical act*, the intuitive forms of sensibility in relation to the materiality of the phenomenon (Kant for example). On the other hand, generic universality is relatively shut off in a sphere of objects ('alls'); it is an unlimited all, whatever it may be, simultaneously shut off in its own multiplicity and not indefinitely reopened like the super-All for maximum power. Ultimately, the generic is simply the sphere of anything whatsoever insofar as it is deprived not of such and such a predicate but of this predicate of all predicates which is the dimension of the super-All.

It is obvious that only science, prior to philosophy itself, can give us a somewhat rigorous concept of the generic and define a new type of knowledge that liberates itself from reversibility and duplicity. But which scientific property? Namely what we have posited as idempotent addition in tangential reference to quantum physics. For the generic also has a more restrained algebraic interpretation, but perhaps less of a non-philosophical scope because it is that of a 'positive' discipline. Any knowledge, object, or element whatsoever (in general a mathematical theory) is generic *for* ... a class or set of objects if every object of this class can be derived on the basis of this object by specializing or determining its unknowns. These are generally algebraic structures like the formulas of an equation. They are as universal as an invariant matrix or a function can be which must be determined in order to generate other objects. This object can represent whichever element of the class in the order of knowledge without ceasing to be one of its individuals. These generic objects have a weak but 'paradigmatic' value.

3. The generic represents the chance of a duality without a synthesis, for it is the attempt or matrix of every duality as such, of the Two that structures science or its subject. Whereas the philosophical commences through a duality and through its overcoming in the unity of an all or an auto-reflection that internalizes the individual in this machine for superior functions, and while the dialectic commences through a duality but induces the One from it which is rapidly devoted to the reigning uselessness or to the subaltern functions of the count, the generic is the point of view of any solitary individual whatsoever who knows herself to be taken from a human tissue beyond its subjectivity. The generic is the individual that has accepted being universal but limited, not being the point or expression of the absolute, and which therefore a priori resists its grip. The individual holds the universal in the order of her finitude itself, while conditioning and preventing it from developing itself in an uncontrolled way.

Philosophy sometimes throws itself into question in a contradictory way through generic man (Feuerbach), or even through the individual as extreme and pre-generic singularity. Hence a critique of this generic man to which one opposes individual or even pre-individual singularity or identity (Nietzsche, Deleuze, Henry) as opposed to the all, primary in relation to it. This is an insufficient critique, for it remains on the terrain of the all as philosophical super-All. It is necessary to radicalize the Two by first radicalizing the One, the concrete term or the individual which is idempotent rather than metaphysical. The generic will be the Two that has lost its totality or system. In Feuerbach, the Two is prevalent but certainly still philosophical; M. Henry has not noticed its interest and has erased it in the name of the radical individual.

4. The generic is an object or a knowledge that mounts a resistance to philosophical absolution, not simply because it reduces the super-All as a priori (while giving it again as appearance), but since it gives itself as a simple all without the double relation of torsion proper to the super-All. It is a 'material' constant because it possesses an a priori content, an intuition of the all or the Same given as simple or sans-fold, as 'unfolded/implified' [*implié*]. As Same in a radical sense, it lacks a verso, duplicitous depth, or an other-world; it does not even have a sur-face but a face-sans-surface, what we called a 'uniface'. This a priori constant is the true critique of philosophical other-worlds. It forms a plane without internal double torsion; it is a loop but simple or single, a uni-face of exposition or presentation.

Marx presents the material base as Productive Forces producing in Relations of Production. He retains in this material base something of Feuerbach's generic man but with a different concept of Man as immanent or organic productive force. This is not the abstraction of auto-affective life or the transcendental ego (M. Henry), but Productive Force insofar as it is still associated with the transcendent exteriority of the dialectic in Relations of Production. In other words, Marx's so-called material base is a veritable 'base' rather than a foundation, but it is not specifically generic and still remains somewhat transcendental. Now understood as generic Lived Experience in the sense of idempotence, it defines Man and is no longer added dialectically from the outside. Man as base, *these are the Productive Forces and Relations of Production together in their identity of idempotent or Productive Force.* This problem must neither be resolved according to Feuerbach, who confuses the individual and the genre under the name of man, nor according to Michel Henry who, when he should reintroduce Productive Force into Man under the form of labour power and surpass simple immanence (hence the concept of 'praxis'), separates Force and Relation too brutally in a quasi-dualist way, thus breaking their generic unity. Nor should it be resolved according to Althusser who makes of Man the simple support or empirical bearer of ideal structures. We resolve the problem in this way: it is Man as generic Real who, of herself or under the form of a subject, *subtracts* (we shall return to this concept) her own materiality of the a priori from the circular or philosophical doubling of content which is indeed a *mixture*, namely the mixture of Forces and Relations. Subtraction avoids the confusion between the individual and the genre as their absolute solitude, as well as their undetermined, secondary role of empirical support. Althusser is a sort of medium between Feuerbach and Michel Henry, but rather on the side of Feuerbach and thus the side of philosophy for which he substitutes structuralism, whereas the generic non-Marxism we propose is also the milieu (the mid-place) of the two, but more on the side of Michel Henry or the radical critique of philosophy.

5. The generic produces validity rather than authority, and truth rather than philosophical or epistemological knowledge (coupling of a singular science and a philosophical apparatus). Authority and validity must be distinguished. Validity is equivalent to a theoretical control over a domain, but, insofar as it is not sufficient and is inseparable from a certain power [*pouvoir*], validity does not have philosophy's political nature. But the generic always produces it under this apparent form of the 'Mid-place',

of half-validity or half-truth rather than under their unitary or duplicitous forms. The generic object determines a domain for which it has validity in accordance with Man-in-person, yet has little or no authority (it reduces knowledge as power and gives it back to the truth of human genericity). Truth and validity are completely secondarized or unilateralized in relation to Man-in-person as True-sans-truth or before-priority without hierarchy. Only the duplicitous or philosophical super-All claims to possess the full power and authority grafted onto knowledge; it turns validity back towards authority.

Generic validity is no longer a control and a completeness à la Husserl in his 'theory of multiplicities', i.e. a possibility of generation on the basis of the axioms of all true statements. It is a determination, but it is neither immediate or direct, like the scientific, nor oblique or in torsion like the philosophical. This is generally because in generic thought there is a restriction or subtraction that provides evidence for the Determination-in-the-last-instance. There are two things: on the one hand, the relative autonomy of the order of knowledge [*connaissance*] (or even, here, non-demonstrated truth decided by axioms), and, on the other hand, simultaneously the limitation of the eventual philosophical auto-foundation of knowledge [*savoir*]. Here we rediscover the generic, non-complete validity or non-total control (Gödel), the radical but not absolute non-sufficiency of axiomatics, and ultimately a certain effect of the deconstruction of the structure of auto-foundation. Auto-foundation will be prohibited for a stronger reason, which is not logical because positive science is not in question here, but *for an a priori reason, namely the a priori or immanent (non-Gödelian) defence against the assaults waged by philosophy and foundation (radicality against the absolute)*. Fully conceived, the generic or Man as uni-versal is a priori protected by itself from philosophy.

6. The generic requires the dissolution of the confusion between the subject and Man-sans-subject, which can exist through other means and amphibologies that accompany it. This dissolution allows us to posit the equality of humans at least in-the-last-instance. This is to autonomize Man and her labours which she nevertheless accomplishes through the subject, giving back to them a universality which is no longer global and of the objective order. For example, they are set *on the same plane of equality but in-the-last-instance*, philosophy by 'debasing' the level of its claims, and knowledges by recognizing if not elevating their own claims, yet by conserving the respective autonomy of one another. This is seemingly a weakening of philosophy. But it is rigorous, regulated, and rendered necessary; nothing, if not the founding prejudices of Greek thought, can prove that Man must be inscribed within the super-All or that the world suffices to define her. It is necessary to posit Man as sans-subject, as non-producer or non-creator of concepts, but by making use of the subject so as to transform the latter for philosophy. We are searching for the generic as a radically idempotent non-plane, in rigorous terms as a *unilateral or unifacial plane*, as Stranger of unique being. And since Man-in-person is sans-subject from the start, she is 'vanishing' or radically unpresented and thus not simultaneously localizable in or on a plane of existence. The generic is the dualysis of philosophical topology and the 'return' to the 'base'.

THE ACQUISITION OF THE GENERIC CONSTANT

Several moments are discernible in the operation of acquiring the generic constant.

1. Reduce the super-All or the One-of-the-One which is the true content of the metaphysical 'One;' impoverish it as a simple One or fold it out [*déplier*], unfold/implify [*implier*] it as idempotence of the 'One-in-One'. This is its first aspect. The Real

is neither ideal nor material; it avoids this disjunction but also this unity or synthesis of opposites. The other term for this Real is Lived Experience or 'Man-in-person;' this is our way of interpreting Feuerbach's generic man as being nothing but a symptom, yet Man-in-person will be more precisely the ensemble of the two aspects that form the generic constant, namely idempotent Lived Experience and the unilateral or a priori edge.

2. Empty it of all thought and knowledge [*connaissance*] to which it is foreclosed. Then what is its substance? Rather than as a transcendent 'knowledge' [*savoir*] of the Greek type like the *eidos* or the true Idea, we understand this unfolded/implified or added immanence as gnosis and the latter as Lived Experience which avoids the one-multiple of lived-experiences-of-consciousness still impregnated with transcendence (Husserl). We can no longer say of this immanent Lived Experience that it is subjective or objective; this is an opposition it avoids, along with that of the individual and the multiple, the ego [*moi*] and the self [*soi*], the ego and the world, which are all philosophical couplings. Man-in-person is defined by this idempotent 'gnosis', this indissolubly scientific-and-philosophical Lived Experience, which is not a being-in-the-world or a being-in-philosophy. The genericity of man is to be a knowledge that does not itself 'know', a Lived Experience which is thus not reflexive and cumulative.

3. Since it is not reciprocally determined by philosophy, it is indeed necessary to give a relative autonomy to the latter or to thought as Two, and not an absolute autonomy but a relative autonomy to the idempotent form of Lived Experience. Materialism makes of knowledge a dogmatic reflection of the Real (matter); we make of it a lived a priori both of … or for … philosophy—this is the unilateral or unifacial edge of Lived Experience.

4. In this unilateral knowledge, which is the generic a priori of science, we thus distinguish from the Real-in-person its a priori 'form' in its materiality, this single-faced border which deducts itself from the real through the reduction of the super-All. All these problems exist, for example in Kant's transcendental Aesthetics, but here they receive a simplification that attaches them to the super-All. Non-cumulatively added Lived Experience is itself foreclosed to the materiality of the a priori, but the latter, the simple All given a priori, is philosophy's form of reception. There is no gesture of attraction to the All by the Real; the All can also be immanent, not insofar as it is duplicitous, but insofar as this edge or face—this simple All—is also unfolded/implified.

What, then, is the effect of the Lived-in-person upon this entire complex, since there is no generic if Man, here as One-in-One or as 'sterile' immanence, does not intervene? *Unilaterality is subtracted by Man from the auto-enveloping All; it is subtracted by immanence.* It is a question of a de-duction, of a unilateral subtraction that removes philosophical transcendence or instead concentrates from it that which goes beyond the unilateral edge of immanence. One of the theses of non-philosophy is that immanence is not at all an interiority, fold, and folding (Deleuze), nor a pleating (Foucault); only the 'philosophies of immanence' sustain this confusion, but it is precisely what is radically unfolded and *precisely forever unfoldable*. Instead of shutting itself in and closing itself off like the super-All, the unfolded opens itself and can do nothing but open itself like an edge that never closes upon itself. Philosophy is founded among other things upon Heraclitus' maxim, 'nature (*physis*) seeks to hide itself;' non-philosophy is instead founded upon the maxim, 'because it is foreclosed to thought, the Real or Man loves to open itself'.

The generic constant de-duc(t)ed from philosophy by immanence is no longer a complete or partial object, a part which would express the whole. It is what should be called a *unilateral All* (in this case determined by Lived Experience alone—to which philosophy contributes without determining), *non-expressive* of itself (immanence as un-folder/implifier of transcendence), and *aprioritic without material* (insofar as it takes its materiality from the non-formal a priori of philosophy).

Generic activity is then distributed or distributable because of its being-separated in the various disciplines forming a complex level, such as epistemology, theology, aesthetics, etc., where it can intervene in their philosophical component and transform it. It stops being theoretico-experimental (the sciences) or contemplative-theoristic (philosophy) under the law of the refolded All. We can define it as a *Mid*-place, not a medium between two extremes or a half-measure, but literally as an '*unfolded between-two*'. It must be understood as a place whose simple identity has been subtracted from the philosophical place, which is always complex and folded back on itself. Since the latter always has two poles or faces and is at least definable by two coordinates (for example horizontal and vertical transcendences, or a foreground and background, or even internal and external horizons, etc.), *the generic will automatically be defined as an entity with one face or a single dimension*. To be sure, this *unifacial* being, which is *never in a face to face* or in mimetic rivalry with other knowledges, but assembles itself and sets itself up as a unilateral duality, is no longer the object or unity of counting (an arithemetic), but the unity of Man herself. Concretely, the generic constant, which can distribute itself in different knowledges, is foundationally estranged from the World or philosophy, the latter always being two-faced, a duality of de-doubling and redoubling.

The generic is thus not a double of what exists or has taken place, a new double of philosophy or the positive sciences; it comes as One, a Stranger in the world of sciences and philosophies; it does not repeat them but modifies or helps them transform their object and therefore transform themselves. We should also nuance the understanding of the formula that turns the generic into a force of inter-vention. Here, the inter- is not a way of occupying a between-two or of placing itself between two adversaries, as a neutral third or a referee. Similarly, the general formula of 'interdisciplinarity' could be corrected for the generic, and this is because it is that which forms the nucleus of reality of the objective appearance of the interdisciplinary. This is precisely why generic power always orients in a single direction or is unilateral, for it can do nothing but arrive at or come to the midst of the situation, or more exactly, to come as the only Mid-place of the situation which does not result from a fold. It has the being of a Stranger, at least insofar as one does not dissolve it in philosophical circulation. *Man is not in the midst of the All or the World, opened up to it by its two faces; she is the radical identity of the Mid-place.*

This is no longer a median solution of a milieu, of a side wretchedly torn between the extremes. It is instead the philosophical generic which has something of a middle as its phenomenology desires, which is thus a symptom to be treated. If we now posit the generic Identity of the two major types of philosophy (Idealism and Materialism) or any other division in the system of Idealism, this idempotent a priori will no longer be their middle or common element but their unilateral Identity in-the-last-instance, which is not suitable for all the total parts of philosophy, but for their transformation as all being symptoms. Here the generic Mid-place is instead the ordinary, i.e. the ordinary of the Logos or for it, but still not a supplementary mixture.

THE GENERIC A PRIORI: FROM THE SUBTRACTIVE TO THE SUBTRACTED-WITHOUT-SUBTRACTION

The a priori is generally a curious notion because in reality it is mixed, partially a posteriori if one relates it to the all of the philosophical act. From the point of view of the order of knowledge, it depends upon experience, here upon philosophy, or in Kant upon physical existence which gives it its materiality of 'formal intuition'. But in the order of the Real, it depends upon a real cause, either the transcendental in Kant, or more radically the idempotent Real in the generic. It implies the disjunction of the subtracted real and the operation of subtraction, which will be the basis for determination in-the-last-instance as a non-idealist combination of the real and knowledge. In short, this can be nothing but a simple vicious circle; it is already broken by a philosophical division in Kant on behalf of the transcendental One, or even by a unilateral duality in the generic (where the Lived real is foreclosed to knowledge). Thus we must seriously distinguish between, for example, the subtractive (Badiou) that still supposes an operation and is mixed—simultaneously a priori and a posteriori—and the lived subtractive which has nothing but the objective appearance of a subtraction and which reduces the a posteriori to a simple, non-constitutive, occasional cause of the Lived real. Measured by philosophical appearances, the generic obviously seems to be obtained by an operation of subtraction, but it presupposes a non-cumulative or real addition. As a materialist procedure, the Real and Being in their occurrence only subtract themselves from the Logos by also adding to it, which is nothing but a bilateral or double-edged procedure; Being thus winds up being less and more than the Logos: this is the philosophical but materialist subtractive, the Real as break/suture in the Logos. From our point of view, the subtractive is an objective appearance created by the addition that sub-venes indempotently and concentrates the transcendent term which presents itself, a term which is immediately or instantly transformed into unilaterality. As an effect of sterile addition, the material a priori is only seemingly subtracted from the Logos and has no effect of supplement, cumulative addition, or surplus value in relation to Lived Experience. The generic a priori, subtracted-sans-subtraction, is no longer an operation and rejects this object appearance of the operation upon the Logos. Thus, the latter is transformed in its essence and not divided for the greater glory of the philosophical Unity which would reconstitute it. This is the difference between transcendent and anonymous materialism and lived human materiality. We thus distinguish between the subtractive as an operation which conditions the Real as Being, namely by restraining or determining it (ultimately in materialism), and the subtracted-sans-subtraction as the idempotent transformation of merely philosophy or the world. The lesser-than [*en-moins*] deducted from philosophy is radical and does not balance a radical surplus which would subsist in Lived Experience, because the a priori adds nothing real to Lived Experience (it is not a new instance; it is thus 'transcendental' in an originary sense and announces the subject who precisely supposes a supplementary condition). Not being relative-absolute, the lesser-than is simply a transformation of philosophy, since knowledge has no effect upon the Real. It is not derived from a positive operation of re-partition, division, and recomposition, but from the immanent repetition of an addition which transforms the super-All without Man transforming herself. The generic does not augment knowledge (supplied by the existing positive disciplines), nor does it make the latter possible, but transforms it as truth or in-the-last-instance as True-sans-truth. The generic a priori is simply called 'subtractive' because it conserves its place with the occasional language that it does not leave behind.

PHILOSOPHICAL CIRCULATION AND GENERIC CIRCULATION. THEORY OF THE MID-PLACE

In order to clarify the preceding and the following, namely the radical distinction between the generic and the philosophical—their *unilateral duality* which we have hit upon—it must be remembered that we have substituted the philosophical and vicious auto-critique of the All for that of the super-All, and the critique of the Global for that of Duplicity (One and Two) and even double Duplicity (empirico-transcendental and transcendental-real doublets), which is the real ultimate content of philosophy as super-All. The concepts of global and partial, wholes and parts, dispersions, partial objects, disseminations, and fragments, which all nourish some of the contemporary attempts at the renewal of epistemology, are artefacts that produce philosophy itself; philosophy prolongs its sufficiency through them and continues to bewitch the subject by making it believe that any liberation is possible in this way. Philosophy is duplicity at the limit of the specular on each of its levels; the All is *de jure* the doublet of the transcendental or divisible All and of the real or indivisible All. We call this *de jure* ensemble by a single name: the super-All. The problem is that we are here, for lack of a better word, at the edge of philosophy as well as the edge of the void; although we are probably still fascinated, like the young Marx by Hegel, we are outlining a generic that would no longer go back to philosophy as these descriptions sufficiently show, although we still have not thematized it as such.

We can now clarify a Marxist equivocation: there must be a distinction between two circulations, namely the philosophical and the generic (which we shall begin to call 'non-Feuerbachian' without risking a return to the humanizing and naturalizing generic). Philosophy recognizes particular beings, systems, and the All of these alls, the absolute System, a perfect Circle, in the sense that it no longer circulates, almost cut off from circulation while circulating within itself. They are both unmoved movers [*mobiles fixes*], they only circulate in themselves in a rapid fashion and give rise to a stroboscopy of philosophical appearances. Plato lived through this contradiction more painfully than others, before Hegel took his place and obscured everything.

We shall distinguish a generic circulation of knowledges and products from the All-circulation of philosophy, which is perhaps the key to the capitalist economy deployed and grasped in its culmination. They do not simply enter into 'useful circuits' and hence into the vast circulation of philosophy within itself that comes to grip them once again, but into another more common and less intense 'circuit', above all into another logic than that of exchange. This is a universally local 'logic' whose universality does not form a synthesis or system with its locality. This is not a way of slightly intensifying the market or philosophical capital, which tends toward immobility, but a way of refusing its exclusivity. It is not to stop, inhibit, or reverse it in a revolutionary way. The generic is important because it is a disenchantment of every commercial type of circulation, though not its suppression; this is because the generic is a non-relation to the world and because it installs a sans-relation in the latter. The generic, for instance and for lack of better phrasing, circulates knowledges and products which do not have 'guarantors', unilateral merchandise, 'perspectives', or 'intentions' that give the All, but an All which has stopped re-affirming itself and has become modest, thus giving up philosophy and theology—a One which is sterile or inert in some way, atheistic if you will. This is still a circulation of demarcated products and hybrid sciences, but a circulation-sans-circle, a *semi*-circulation. Generic services or products are *semi*-markets;

they are interested in the Grand Circuit enveloping money, but do not for a moment obey its dialectical or even analytic logic, and therefore create another usage of the All which they attach to its auto-circulation. But what logic and for which circulation? What is it that most radically destroys the philosophical appearances of hybridization?

It should be noted that this *semi-* is not a half, the mid-place or the division between two borders of a place, *but the identity (of the) Mid-(place) or Unilaterality which is the major support of the generic 'logic' to the sciences* (and the determining concept of non-philosophy). The problem is that of knowing whether it is the *place* or the *mid-* of the milieu that is characteristic of idempotence, if not identity. For philosophy, it is the (mid-) place that reproduces itself according to its determining mid-(place). In the generic, things happen in a reverse fashion and necessarily more than reverse; the mid- is the idempotent before-first that determines the place 'in last place', i.e. 'in-the-last-instance'. The mid- of the milieu is not a half, but unlimited, infinite, and eternal idempotence which determines, i.e. transforms, the place—or, if one wishes, it is a half, but a half that is One.

This phenomenon of the Mid-place, which affects generic products and even unilateral services or tools, diminishes unity and its illusionary effects of conformism or social dignity without, however, being a middle between the total and the particular, the global and the specific, or the fundamental and the regional. The generic gives new media to the practice of the 'milieu' and perhaps to the practice of justice or democracy. It consigns the grand and aristocratic lord to oblivion as well as the moaning of the 'labourers of philosophy' (Nietzsche). Plato invents the Grand Genres, but Aristotle invents the 'genre'. The philosopher need not be so pure and divine to invent the generic. From this point of view, Materialism is useful. But will it perhaps be necessary to go a little further still and no longer to completely turn the generic into the milieu of philosophy? *Philosophy is already its own milieu, its mid-place through division*, which degrades itself to the state of banality and mediocrity, a sort of weakening of philosophy, if not its fall or ungrounding, at least its 'low profile'.

The generic makes possible a totally different type of circulation which could be called sans-circle or more exactly sans-redoubling; since simple circularity always finishes by having been there, the problem is how not to redouble it and fixate it in itself. It should be noted that philosophy only 'circulates' as a commodity to be captured in the conversations or debates of ideas because it truly only circulates in itself. Whatever sort of object, frontier, or division is inserted into it, the All passes over its obstacles because it is made to pass over itself, merely bordering on itself to envelop itself once again. Systems and doctrines are all simply particular and multiple warmongering entities; they mechanically strike upon closed or half-closed eyes, and at best simulate each other and capture one another in the element of a grand obscurity. Indeed there are flashes, but that's because philosophers flip the switch. This logic is well known; the Good consumes itself in the light of Reason and Reason in the luminescence of consciousness. No doubt we can speak superficially of 'circulation', but there is ultimately a *stroboscobic effect of immobility that fascinates philosophers and scientists*. The generic has other virtues which are no longer completely philosophical, related to utility, creativity, fecund circulation, and even less to compulsive repetition. The generic no doubt cuts across the contemporary operators of thought, like the transversality of Deleuze-Guattari, or Foucault's diagonality. These operators render the clear distinction between the philosophical style and what we could call the generic style more difficult, but not impossible. The first is tangential, through flashes and illuminations, and touches upon the All which it espouses, sometimes rather upon its internal face (the philosophical tradition, the external face being reserved for God), sometimes upon both faces at once (the philosophies of Difference and Wittgenstein in his own way) but of which it has no knowledge like God. Even the philosophies of Difference that mobilize themselves along its edge, sometimes more on one side than the other, acquire a certain divine knowledge of the All but have no theory of it. But would not God himself possess this theory of the all? No more than the philosophers. The generic-human point of view will precisely be necessary to perceive it, i.e. to annihilate the All as subject of its own knowledge, merely conserving it as material and symptom. This is because the generic abandons the contact of the edges to which philosophy devotes itself in order *to ultimately reduce the All to an edge, of whom? of Man*—the All as unilateral marginality of Man. It inverts the philosophical relation between Man and the All, and makes of the All disenchanted by itself the simple edge or margin of Man. But does Man have this power, or would we once again return to Feuerbach and his generic Man? One of our tasks is to defend Man against its philosophic-generic or mixed capture; this is the condition for elaborating a science of the generic. We must also guard against simply opposing Man as individual or ego to the generic as universal in a vague sense (Michel Henry).

TRUE-WITHOUT-TRUTH, WEAK FORCE, MINIMAL TORQUE

We distinguish between generic forcing and philosophical forcing in their transformative effect upon knowledge as well as in their respective mechanisms. Both are operations destined to assure the passage between two regimes of knowledge, from existing (scientific) knowledge to a form of universality of a different (philosophical) type, or indeed the reverse passage, the generic becoming-science of philosophy. The generic manifests itself as a weak force exerting itself upon knowledge rather than upon an operation of transcendental schematization.

The effect of sterile idempotent Lived Experience is to constrain philosophy to take note of its conditions of existence or validity which it spontaneously ignores because Lived Experience refuses itself to philosophy. The universal property that transmits the generic constant is inscribed by force in the existing knowledge as its transformation; it does not prolong the series of knowledge, for it does not inscribe itself in it without transforming the latter. As *universal-for* (*usage*) any object whatsoever, it contains a paradox which is a solution; it is the passage-in-force assured by idempotence, a passage or more exactly sub-vention to *unilaterality* without a schematism, i.e. without a synthetic unity of opposites or dualities. What, then, results from this? A new type of 'predicate' results, a priori but real, toward predicates or properties of the objective rank, toward a knowledge of any order whatsoever, and is reputed to be natural or empirically constituted *just like philosophy is*. Predicates of a different order can be attributed to philosophy without this final change of nature, as would be the case if they were reversible with the 'subject' that receives them. But it does not change nature or is not destroyed by the science that contains the generic, it is simply transformed. The generic is precisely this power of an instance—which is impossible for the All—of forcing and exceeding itself (*for*) towards the given or factual order of knowledge, all without *transforming itself in this operation*, without exchanging its nature with that of the given knowledge. Genericity is the property of being able to communicate truth or rather the True-without-truth to a thought that does not want it. Minimal torque is not simply a 'twist', a supplementary torsion; it is on the contrary an 'untwisting', a return to the Unfolded.

Against philosophy which is the continual forcing of and by the subject, a reversible torsion, the generic opposes itself as another forcing but a weak force, that which can be the non-acting of the idempotent, that of the generic a priori which forces philosophy or the super-All. It is not Man who is forced in her being; it is what happens to Man in the world as constituting the super-All. What Man-in-person, invisible to the world, uses against the latter is an a priori edge that produces the idempotent as a concentration of philosophical structure. This edge is the Other-than (not the Other-of) or better still the Stranger, unilateral or unifacial, the thrown-under-sans-throw [jeté-sans-jet][3]. The meaning of Kant's pure a priori conditions was already a forcing of philosophy by science which was still anthropological, a way of surpassing its limits in a non-metaphysical or non-'dialectical' way, of making an entirely new condition of truth recorded by philosophy. It is traditionally no longer a question of schematizing philosophy in Man, but of forcing the philosophical past through the True-without-truth of idempotence. Generic being-forced is not a reciprocal schematization with the imagination as its common root. It is weak forcing, the minimal torsion exacted upon philosophy that is ultimately no longer reversible but uni-directional, consequently a future. As if the most modest generic intervention in the existing state of things were that of the Future-in-person.

The generic thus forms a style of thought in two phases, like the philosophical, but transformed. The first is *constructing* this posture of Man as generic, non-transcendental, presupposed but invisible, a priori with the aid of the means supplied by philosophical representation. It is therefore the phase of naming or renaming it, not inscribing it in philosophical representation, but finding in it the language to treat it in the most adequate way in order to make this posture exist and leave behind its state as presupposition. The philosophical is then treated as a simple occasional and conjunctional moment of this operation. The real deduction of the a priori, its sub-vention, does not come without an induction, yet it determines its induction on the basis of the epistemological occasion.

The second phase is where a subject of an order which is generic, and thus not transcendental, comes into play, grasps the a priori and the return or uses its unilateral character against epistemological representation, forcing it by a minimal torque to receive it and transform itself. This is the inverse phase that prolongs the occasion or conjunctional epistemological event, the future of the True-without-truth which must create the vehicle or jet for the transformation of the statements of philosophy, in particular the specular structure of epistemology.

Truth is not determining for the Real or Man which, as generic or True-without-truth, is subtracted from philosophical knowledge and its subsets. Generic science sets to work 'axiomatic' decisions determined in-the-last-instance by the idempotent Real. They immediately exceed or subtract themselves from philosophical knowledge which they appeal to in order to find a language in which to forcibly incarnate themselves, even if it is a question of the weak force of a non-acting. Here the generic is the problematic that allows us to reformulate, on the one hand, the event as non-historical occasion or historical-without-history, and on the other hand the True-without-truth as transformation of the history-world.

---

3. Playing off the literal sense of the word 'subject', which means 'thrown under' [trans.].

The generic discipline has some affinity with a philo-fiction that forces the philosophical barrier, its norms, and its criteria of receptivity. It is forcefully heretical, it is an imperative for the most human future of passing-in-force the Greek image of thought and epistemological mytho-logy. It is more than a risk to take, it is the risk through which one must let oneself be taken: it is faithfulness to the ultimatum of the Future.

PHILOSOPHICAL STYLE AND GENERIC STYLE, AMPLIFICATION/ IMPLIFICATION

The first style is fold and overfold, the second is the outfold or even 'unfold' (unfolded, unfoldable), outfolding and even unfolding. The first is overload, overdetermination, redoubling, survey, hyperbolicity, duplicity, accumulation of an always more sufficient capital. The second is mid-place of the ordinary if not the median of unilateral distribution along a line of immanence. The first is the system as global element, while the second is the universal as simple element …, which does not reconstitute an auto-enveloping interiority but an a priori space internal and adjacent to Lived Experience. The first is auto-thesis, the second hypo-thesis which remains somewhat incomplete in relation to the imaginary super-All of philosophy. The first is absolute, the second radical and remains relatively autonomous without becoming absolute. We distinguish the topographical plane of rationalism, the infinite and topological plane, endorsed and idealized by certain contemporaries, from the unilateral edge which is neither topographical nor topological and which can be called a 'margin'. To sum up all these differences, the philosophical style is the capitalistic amplifier of fantastically inflated experience which has become bothersome, while the generic style is the unfolder/implifier not of experience but of philosophical capital.

The apparent weakness of the generic demonstrates itself in relation to philosophy's ambitions; yet this is not a weakness, it is the ordinary Mid-place that gathers together the scientist and the philosopher at the extremes (in the subject), and in other rivalries where philosophy is always judge and jury. The misunderstanding of the *real a priori, of the presupposed* and not of the presupposition of philosophy, is its idealist folly. Obviously we are tempted to ask what in turn is the presupposed of immanence; one then sees it as transcendent, it turns into a folded or pleated plane of immanence, *its radicalization becomes its absolution*. Only a sub-vention or a sterile addendum, rather than a subtraction which conserves its reality but nevertheless without sublating it, guards it from its philosophical capture and maintains its genericity or its ordinariness without letting it turn into the Logos. It is more valid to deconstruct idealism and its culmination than to immediately build upon materialism as a spontaneous philosophy, for then one forgets to deconstruct materialism itself. Materialism and non-philosophy are not equivalent.

Philosophy is a thought according to the All *which 'turns' in the All as in its prison*, which shakes its bars or tugs at its shackles, and in this sense is simply a thought of man. Man-in-person is not the subject that formulates axioms by envisioning a Platonic sky, but the immanent cause of the subject who formulates them and is thus the structure of which the axiom is the expression, the lived experience (of the) axiom or the axiom lived in an idempotent way rather than an anonymous object dragged along by the whole World.

NON-PHILOSOPHY AND THE GENERIC

Non-philosophy cannot be reduced to the theme of the generic, even if the unilateral Two is its a priori or constant. There will probably be a struggle between non-philosophy and materialism to find out who will best protect the generic without letting it return to Idealism. Both carry out the critique of the mixture that 'generic Man' is and dissolve it, materialism in order to return to philosophy and non-philosophy in order to guard Man from philosophical sufficiency. What are the stakes of this struggle?

In philosophy, the genre is a sub- or pre-philosophical concept; it forms the articulation between the individual and the duplicitous super-All which it singularizes as sub-totality, but which the duplicitous All prevents, thus as partial all or subordinated genre. It distinguishes itself in a weak way from the omni-philosophical or auto-enveloping All. Under this form we rediscover a continuity of the philosophical and the generic. It has a tendency to be effaced by the All itself which liberates itself from the individual or puts it back in its place through the pairing of a knowledge or a particular science (without practice) and Idealism/Materialism as positions of the All. The generic is the universal as concrete or human, the 'human genre', but it is then menaced by erasure on behalf of totality. One fundamental thesis is that the philosophical All is never simple, lest it return to the vulgar imagination of a circle (somewhat like the 'hermeneutic circle'). It is globally enveloping of itself, auto-enveloping, and not simply of the events of existence (Jaspers), but of every being. It is a de-doubled/redoubled circle, and it is both simultaneously while simply being single, first as auto-enveloping circle, thus as *transcendental-real doublet*, then as a circle enveloping the empirical, and thus as *empirico-transcendental doublet*. As we know and moreover as every philosopher does, Foucault only detects the second doublet through which he believes to have exhausted the modern philosophical act, but does not notice the first. This structure of duplicity is poorly perceived, it is complicated and extends to infinity, and by default does more than simply test the imagination. Yet it is in relation to this complete structure and not in relation to a vague and indeterminate notion of 'philosophy' that the generic must be situated if we wish to be able to determine its concept.

So how do we save the generic from its philosophical appropriation? In the name of the Real as radically immanent Lived Experience and not as thing-in-itself, we have reversed and transformed the Kantian structure of the transcendental Aesthetic: (1) the generic a priori is the object of a real or lived and not transcendental deduction, the generic begins with (philosophical) experience but does not completely derive from experience; (2) it is a form for...i.e. unilateral, the 'for' indicating the first access under its real form; (3) it is not exposed primarily as a supposedly empty and 'pure subjective form of intuition', but concretely as a 'formal intuition' to use Kantian terms, or, to use our terms, as a *material* a priori that possesses a specified content of knowledge.

The philosophical effacement of the generic is inevitable. More profoundly, from our point of view it is the effect of an ignorance of Man-in-person (which does not mean 'singular subject'); only it can determine a generic base or a universal Two of intervention which will no longer fall back under philosophical authority. Idealist by vocation, philosophy and what remains of it in materialism confuses Man-in-person with the subject and with a knowledge without practice; it confuses human substance with its operatory power. Here we radicalize it and fold it out to let it *defend* itself against philosophical harassment. In order to pass to what we could call the *genre-in-person* after philosophy, it suffices to leave the duality of the One and universal two as a unilateral being, without synthesis or reciprocity, without a third term or system, without the All returning once again to itself. From this angle, the generic is the dismemberment of the system, its 'dualysis'. Therefore it is not a simple term, being or thing abstracted from the system, it is always a duality but not a two-headed apparatus or a 'desiring machine'. As a philosopher, Deleuze also admits that man is a concretion abstracted or constituted from forces in a state of exteriority, a partial object cut out from a total flux, continuum or full body; machines are selections of flows. Similarly, Badiou ultimately cuts the generic out from the presupposed materialist position as other-plane.

Non-philosophy is instead a restraint for not exceeding the special duality of the generic towards the unity of the system, for not inscribing it in a universal horizon. Many philosophers identify the basic duality but raise it up into a superior universal. The phenomenological path is the simplest and extracts the essential traits that create the generic style on the basis of the *ordinary usages* of the term. It is on the basis of these *symptoms* that another properly non-philosophical path consists in 'surpassing', but in-the-last-instance', in 'forcing' the duality facing a One that we have now folded out as simplicity of the idempotent or non-cumulative addition. Deleuze's misinterpretation has been total when he confused the One-in-One, *the One added to the One without modifying itself, with the One-All which is the One multiplied by itself*, which is precisely the confusion between the radicalization and the absolution of duality. Leaving behind the philosophical generic at least as a tendency, we have dualyzed it and assigned it the trait of the being-forced of non-philosophical truth in epistemological knowledge.

It is a question of understanding the paradigmatic sense, which is here a non-Platonic concept, of the force of intervention of one science into the others. This is an intervention without capture or captivation (without what could be called by a biological metaphor of 'hybridization' or 'crossing' or even 'crossbreeding', in reality activities of capture where predator and prey cooperate and are at the threshold of exchanging their functions) and which can be formed upon the basis of the community of certain phenomena between the science which requests an intervention and can receive it and the science that offers it. Such phenomena are themselves called generic in relation to the domain of specific or global objects; they are characterized by their special identity, an *identity of unilateral distribution* which is an a priori constituted from the phenomena that they collect but without determining itself in its real essence with them reciprocally. Such an a priori assembles the diversity of the All without having the duplicity of the philosophical All and without being 'marginal' in the traditional sense of philosophy (this is another paradigm, that of 'marginality', that culminates in the twentieth century). How is 'unilateral' to be understood? In generic activity, only the offer is important because it is determining, rather than the request, the service rather than its reception. Although the request and reception truly exist, they cannot in turn determine the generic decision, nor can the offer determine itself reciprocally with the request. The generic no longer leaves certain phenomena to chance nor selects them in accordance with an Idea or a paradigm in the Platonic sense or even in Kuhn's epistemological sense. In short, contrary to the super-All, generic power is a priori (the All is transcendental and therefore claims to be real), selective (the All only selects itself or its own duplicity through the phenomena which are its expressive parts), and unilaterally determining (the duplicitous All has primacy over its parts which reciprocally determine themselves).

MATERIALISM AND THE GENERIC

Phenomena that obey generic logic are folded out or more precisely unfolded in the manner of the One-in-One or sterile addendum because they are non-totalizing and non-reflected universalities. The generic constant is opposed to idealist transcendental Unity but also to the materialist Two as transcendence. These two positions have nothing but a 'transcendental' unity in a new sense. They claim to be identical to the totality of Being, or to exhaust it, but it is precisely this superior or enveloping unity that wills two positions which is also transcendental in the Kantian sense of the 'Dialectic' well known by every philosophy. We will call transcendental appearance the claim to the real through the bias or under the guise of Being and the transcendental One (which correlates with a division or a duality). Fundamental ontology (Heidegger) is in this sense the meditation of an appearance. But the generic a priori is also opposed to 'regional' or specific categoriality, to the philosophical 'generic'. It invests the empirical or spontaneous genres of knowledge, science, religion, art, politics, erotics, and economics which are clusters of regulated phenomena and must be clearly distinguished from the specificity of the techniques of the positive sciences as well as the philosophical transcendental.

The a priori generic announces a quasi but 'transformed' materialism, as Marx would say. This problem becomes complicated because the generic, which fully involves the vastest relation to science and not simply to the philosophical tradition, is sometimes caught between a materialist position and a particular science. Materialism takes the generic for its object and risks confusing it with a supposedly fundamental specificity, thus with Being or its type of universality. It seems that the materialist also forgets with this problematic the problem *why the One*? *Why immanence*? Just as Heidegger chooses to privilege Being over the One, this is a philosophical spontaneism.

Instead, we posit the primacy of the Real as idempotent addition, as One-in-One, over Being or the transcendental and not simply the primacy of materialist Being over the transcendental. The Real must pass along the side of the One understood as immanence then as generic, Being thus being rejected towards the transcendental. This posture generically, i.e. in-the-last-instance, unifies two positions, the Platonic and the Aristotelian. Materialism itself posits the primacy of Being over presence, thus over being and the mixture of Being and being which is *the object*; its adversary is Being understood as transcendental or turned towards being. The before-first primacy of the One-in-person is allowed to be Platonic and Aristotelian in a unified way because this One-in-One is a stranger to both postures and allows for their non-synthetic unification. Man, precisely because of its universal but non-total being-One, is not the neo-Platonic One; Man is instead the passage through the material a priori that gives access to the Lived real towards the genre which has special, non-synthetic properties. The material a priori is simultaneously turned towards the empirical, here epistemology itself—this is the Aristotelian side—, and towards the universal and the ideal—this is its Platonic side. This is no longer a synthesis of philosophically mixed opposites in a hierarchy. It is a priori universal and empirical in a 'unilational', and not 'relational', way. Being is nothing more than a transcendental presence, an appearance overdetermining the invisible or non-appearing Real.

The generic thus changes context and frontier. Between it and the specific and/or the transcendental, there are no longer sutures of the materialism type but unilateral dualities or clones (the suture is not the break but the trace-scar of the subtraction of supposedly real Being). Thus sterile addition or the One-in-One is Other-than …, unilationally a priori, and immanentizes the *chorismos* which therefore ceases to be confused with transcendence. With radical immanence for its essence, the *chorismos* is reversed or turned back against philosophy; it is unilational or quasi-Aristotelian and in touch with the experience of the world. Instead of cutting the ontological base out of the all of philosophical origin, the Real has already subtracted the immanent generic instance *for* philosophy, without cutting it out, without a decision riddled with sutures, wounds, or traces, all while recognizing that it only belongs to it through its materiality.

Materialism interprets the generic as given with philosophy. It masks the nature of the latter's symptom and takes philosophical claims for 'spending money'. Moreover, it gives to the generic the basis of a particular science or model, it reduces it to its 'cause' of the 'operation' type and privileges subtraction rather than addition. It loses the sense of the symptom and 'non-total' universality proper to the generic by reifying it in an operation or a determined knowledge. This is to prevent Man-in-person as ultimate cause and to replace it through a philosophical position. It is to abstract knowledge or practice precisely from practice as human, to be given the knowledge constituted in its place and to derive the cause of practice under the form of a subjected subject. From this point of view, the axioms of set Theory are already products and givens, reified and dead from a knowledge which has already taken place; it is quite the contrary for generic science-thought which is a production of axioms as real radical lived experiences, not as axioms contemplated in a materialist way. As 'futural', thought-science creates itself and does not come readymade, whereas, positing a non-human generic, a knowledge already made, the materialist decision is conservative and annuls itself in knowledge already produced or annihilates itself in the contemplation of the past. Making the generic fall back on classes or sets is already to hand it over to the All, albeit backwards. If it's not a class, genre, or set, it is instead a provisionally unilateral duality, like 'desiring machines', that has organic and biological models through which the All succeeds in capturing it. The problem of protecting it is not of redoubling it but of emptying it as the (material) a priori of all content, at least all duplicitous content, just as the idempotent One-in-One is emptied of all content. A universal that does not totalize, it is not related to individuals or beings like the super-All that gathers everything together down to the last individuals.

Generic duality is no doubt re-appropriable by the objective appearance or philosophical hallucination. Being materialist is to assume the all of philosophical ambitions via the mode of a unilateral but transcendent duality, which is therefore somewhat reversible despite everything, a duality cut out from the interior of a philosophical All that continues to reign as sufficient and duplicitous. But the generic is not an ontological base, a position and a break, it is distinct from ontology and all philosophical splitting. It is not a base of consciousness, representation or ideology, but the last-instance-*for* ... philosophy. The radicalization of Feuerbach allows us to eliminate the philosophical super-All that would be constructed upon it and to extract it as human force *in order to transform* philosophy. When the latter is eliminated too quickly and too slowly, as is always the case for the materialist break, it then returns as reception and collection [*accueil et recueil*]. Liberating the generic from its scientifico-materialist inscription is carried out in two ways: 1. A specific science must, through its procedures and its objects and through withdrawal, stop *directly determining* the suture of the generic to the ontological or meta-ontological; 2. A science indirectly or in-the-last-instance determines the foreclosure and *suture* between the generic and philosophical or epistemological transcendence; 3. The reference to a particular science precisely subsists as support ('unilation') of an epistemological symptom. This science changes status: from the determining under philosophical conditions in materialism, it becomes determining in-the-last-instance. Materialism inscribes the generic in the relative-absolute and not in radical immanence; it subsumes it under the authority of the philosophical horizon. The axioms of the generic sciences are not without concrete reference, and non-philosophy is not without reference to an epistemological symptom. But they are no longer referred to an object or an objective void, not even a pulverizing object that tends to the void like Being, but instead a uni-jet, i.e. a uni-lational 'object'. Crafting a philosophy of the generic is possible and perhaps necessary, but then we would take it as *symptom* and *model* of a more universal science-thought, of a non-philosophy of the generic.

17

The Ontic Principle:
Outline of an Object-Oriented Ontology

Levi R. Bryant

> What follows is speculation, often far-fetched speculation, which the reader will consider or dismiss according to his individual predilection. It is further an attempt to follow out an idea consistently, out of curiosity to see where it will lead.
>
> —Sigmund Freud, *Beyond the Pleasure Principle*

> A book of philosophy should be in part a very particular species of detective novel, in part a kind of science fiction.
>
> —Gilles Deleuze, *Difference and Repetition*

> [I]f contemporary philosophers insist so adamantly that thought is entirely oriented towards the outside, this could be because of their failure to come to terms with a bereavement—the denial of a loss concomitant with the abandonment of dogmatism. For it could be that contemporary philosophers have lost the great outdoors, the absolute outside of pre-critical thinkers: that outside which was not relative to us, and which was given as indifferent to its own givenness to be what it is, existing in itself regardless of whether we are thinking of it or not; that outside which thought could explore with the legitimate feeling of being on foreign territory—of being entirely elsewhere.
>
> —Quentin Meillassoux, *After Finitude*

THE STERILITY OF THE CRITICAL PARADIGM

In the following paper I would like to attempt a philosophical experiment.[1] Traditionally, and especially since the seventeenth century, philosophy has been obsessed with questions of where to begin in thought. In particular, this question of beginnings has taken the form of questions about foundations. Since philosophy aims at a particular sort of knowledge, it has been natural since Descartes and Locke to begin philosophical investigation with an inquiry into the nature, conditions, and limits of knowledge.

1. I would like to express special thanks to Ian Bogost, Jon Cogburn, Melanie Doherty, John Protevi, Steven Shaviro, Nathan Gale, Nick Srnicek, and Pete Wolfendale. Without their helpful comments this paper would not have been possible.

The thesis here would be that *prior* to any claims about the nature of reality, *prior* to any speculation about objects or being, we must first secure a foundation for knowledge and our *access* to beings. Philosophy, the story goes, must begin with an analysis of ourselves. By way of analogy, what could be more obvious than first examining the fitness or suitability of our tools before building something? Where, for Aristotle, metaphysics was first philosophy, for us Moderns and Post-Moderns, epistemology has become first philosophy. Indeed, 'metaphysics' itself has become a dirty word. Philosophy thus becomes the project of *critique*, occupied primarily with questions of access[2] or the conditions under which knowledge is possible.

However, as promising as this point of entry appears, when we look about the battlefield of contemporary philosophy it very much appears that the project of critique today finds itself at a point of impasse in which it has largely exhausted its possibilities. Paraphrasing a title of a famous book by Paul Ricœur, we could say that everywhere we look in both Continental and Anglo-American thought we encounter a 'conflict of critiques', without the means of deciding the truth or priority of these various critiques and which constitutes the proper point of entry into philosophical thought. The Kantians tell us that we must first reflexively analyze the *a priori* structure of mind to determine how it conditions and structures phenomena. The phenomenologists tell us that we must first reflexively analyze the lived structure of intentionality and our being-in-the-world to determine the givenness of the given. The Foucauldians tell us that we must analyze the manner in which power and discursive constructions produce reality. The Derrideans and Lacanians tell us that we must analyze the manner in which language produces the objects of our world. The Marxists tell us that we must analyze history and social forces to determine the manner in which the world is produced. The Gadamerians tell us that we must analyze our historically informed understanding inherited through the wandering of the texts through which we are made. The Wittgensteinians tell us that we must analyze ordinary language to determine how it produces the various pseudo-problems of philosophy. The list could be multiplied indefinitely. And among all of these orientations we find disputes within each particular orientation of thought as to how the project of critique is to be properly completed. How is one to choose among all these competing orientations of critique? Each mode of critique appears equally plausible and equally implausible, such that any choice takes on the appearance of being an arbitrary decision based on temperament, political orientation, and interest without any necessitating ground of its own.[3]

Faced with such a bewildering philosophical situation, what if we were to imagine ourselves as proceeding naïvely and pre-critically as *first philosophers*, pretending that the last three hundred years of philosophy had not taken place or that the proper point of entry into philosophical speculation was not the question of access? In proceeding in this way we would not deny ourselves the right to refer to the history of philosophy; just as any plant refers to the soil from whence it came, philosophy too comes from its soil. Rather, this experiment would instead refuse the imperative to begin with the project

---

2. The term 'philosophies of access' was, to my knowledge, first introduced by Graham Harman. Philosophies of access begin by subordinating the questions of philosophy to questions of our access to the world. cf. Graham Harman, *Tool-Being: Heidegger and the Metaphysics of Objects*, Chicago, Open Court, 2002.

3. More than anyone else, François Laruelle has explored the role that decision, a decision prior to all philosophical argumentation and conceptualization, plays in philosophy. Unfortunately very little of his work has been translated. For an excellent and productive application of his thought in the context of realist thought, cf. ch. 5 of Ray Brassier, *Nihil Unbound: Enlightenment and Extinction*, New York, Palgrave Macmillan, 2007.

of critique. In short, what if we were to 'bracket' the project of critique and questions of access, and proceed in our speculations as the beginning student of philosophy might begin? This, of course, is impossible as the history of philosophy is, as Husserl might put it, sedimented in our consciousness. Nonetheless, we can still attempt such an experiment to see where it might lead. At the very least, such a naïve and pre-critical beginning might give us the resources to pose differently the philosophical questions we have inherited, thereby opening up new possibilities of thought and a line of flight from a framework that has largely exhausted itself and become rote.

THE QUESTION OF BEGINNINGS AND THE ONTIC PRINCIPLE

As first philosophers that refuse the project of critique and questions of access, we can begin by asking ourselves with what must we begin? What is the most fundamental and general claim we can make about the nature of *beings*? It will be noted that this question is already more basic than any question about our *knowledge* of beings for, as Heidegger made clear, questions of knowledge are already premised on a pre-ontological comprehension of being. In posing our question in this way, it is necessary to proceed in the spirit of Alfred North Whitehead with respect to his 'conceptual scheme' in *Process and Reality*. As Whitehead remarks,

> Philosophy will not regain its proper status until the gradual elaboration of categoreal schemes, definitely stated at each stage of progress, is recognized as its proper objective. There may be rival schemes, inconsistent among themselves; each with its own merits and its own failures. It will then be the purpose of research to conciliate the differences. Metaphysical categories are not dogmatic statements of the obvious; they are tentative formulations of the ultimate generalities.[4]

Consequently, in asking after the fundamental and the general, we are not making dogmatic statements predicated on claims of absolute certainty or 'apodicity', but rather are proposing tentative formulations subject to further clarification, revision, and even falsification. Where critical orientations of thought seek to secure knowledge in *advance*, we speculative, neo-pre-critical philosophers will see any secure foundation we might discover as an *outcome* of inquiry rather than as an αρχή governing our inquiry from the *outset*. In other words, we speculative, neo-pre-critical philosophers will not proceed like Hamlet, demanding that everything be clear before we act.

In this spirit, then, when we reflect on the basic questions of philosophy we note that in one way or another they all revolve around issues of difference. What are the relevant differences? How are differences to be ordered or hierarchized? How are differences related to one another? Let us therefore resolve straight away to begin with the premise that *there is no difference that does not make a difference*. Alternatively, let us begin with the premise that to be is to make or produce differences. How, in short, could difference be difference if it did not make a difference? I will call this hypothesis the 'Ontic Principle'. This principle should not be confused with a *normative* judgment or a statement of *value*. It is not being claimed that all differences are *important* to us. Rather, the claim that there is no difference that does not make a difference is an *ontological* claim. The claim is that 'to be' is to make or produce a difference.

In speaking of 'principles' we do not intend something apodictic or foundational with respect to questions of epistemology. Speaking of Leibniz's relationship to principles, Deleuze writes,

---

4. Alfred North Whitehead, *Process and Reality*, New York, The Free Press, 1978, p. 8.

'Everything has a reason …'. This vulgar formulation already suffices to suggest the exclamatory character of the principle, the identity of the principle and of the cry, the cry of Reason par excellence.[5]

Principles, according to Deleuze, are a sort of cry or exclamation, and in this respect they have a hypothetical status. While principles are ἀρχή, we must distinguish these ἀρχή as they function epistemologically and ontologically. Ontologically ἀρχή are that from whence things come and are. As Xavier Zubíri so nicely summarizes it,

> Aristotle saw clearly what is meant for anything to be a principle (ἀρχή): principle is always and only that from which anything comes in the ultimate instance (πρωτου). Principle is the *whence* itself (ὅθεν). I immediately introduced the tripartite division of principles, which had already become classical: principle whence something *is* (ἔστιν), whence something *becomes* (γίγνεται), whence anything is known (γίγνώσκεται).[6]

When Husserl evokes the famous 'principle of all principles'[7] or Descartes evokes 'clear and distinct ideas' and the *cogito*, or Hume impressions, they are all evoking principles in the sense of γίγνώσκεται or that from whence something is *known*. By contrast, when we evoke the Ontic Principle we are not evoking γίγνώσκεται, but rather principles in the sense of ἔστιν and γίγνεται, or that through which something *is* and that through which something *becomes*. Our hypothesis is thus that beings are and become through their differences. Epistemologically these principles have the status of *hypotheses*, not foundational certainties, and are therefore subject to further revision and even outright rejection as inquiry proceeds.

GROUNDS OF THE ONTIC PRINCIPLE

Leaving aside, for a moment, the question of what, precisely, difference *is*, or how this principle is to be understood, we can ask ourselves what consequences would follow were we to adopt this principle? However, prior to asking ourselves what philosophical consequences follow from the Ontic Principle, we can first ask ourselves whether there is any philosophical warrant in treating this principle as a fundamental principle.

A. First, it must be granted that difference has an *epistemic* priority in the order of knowledge. In its most naïve formulation, *prior* to any questions of access or the relation between mind and world, subjects and objects, knowledge is concerned above all with questions of difference. The naïve, incipient knower that has never yet heard of critique first wonders what differences characterize the object or event, what differences are abiding and what differences are changing, and what relations productive of differences there are between and among objects. In posing the question of knowledge in terms of the relation between subject and object, mind and world, or in terms of questions of access, epistemology *forgets* that it presupposes difference as the ground of all these distinctions. Paraphrasing Heidegger, it could be said that epistemology always and everywhere proceeds on the basis of a pre-epistemological comprehension of difference. This pre-epistemological comprehension of difference guides and directs both the manner in which the various epistemologies pose the question of knowledge and the sorts of epistemological theories they develop.

---

5. Gilles Deleuze, *The Fold: Leibniz and the Baroque*, trans. T. Conley, Minneapolis, University of Minnesota Press, 1993, p. 41.

6. Xavier Zubíri, *On Essence*, trans. A.R. Caponigri, Washington, The Catholic University of America Press, 1980, p. 451.

7. Edmund Husserl, *Ideas Pertaining to a Pure Phenomenology and to a Phenomenological Philosophy: First Book*, trans. F. Kersten, Boston, Martinus Nijhoff Publishers, 1983, pp. 44-45.

Consequently, prior to even posing questions of knowledge, of how we can know, whether we can know, and what we can know, the would-be knower is *already* situated among differences. Here we encounter one reason that the Ontic Principle is formulated as it is. Situated among differences, we must say that *there are* (*es gibt, il y a*) differences. However, this thereness is indifferent to human existence. It is not a thereness *for us*, but a thereness of being. The incipient knower would like to know something of these differences. She would like to know which differences in the object make a difference, what ordered relations there are between differences of differing objects, and so on. It is this 'thereness' of difference that first provokes wonder and inquiry into beings. Noting that differences come-to-be and pass-away, the incipient knower wishes to know something of this coming-to-be and passing-away and whether or not there are any enduring differences. Thus, far from difference having a status posterior to questions of knowledge, the thereness of difference is given and is what first provokes inquiry and questions of knowledge.

Paradoxically it therefore follows that epistemology cannot be first philosophy. Insofar as the question of knowledge presupposes a pre-epistemological comprehension of difference, the question of knowledge always comes *second* in relation to the *metaphysical* or ontological priority of difference. As such, there can be no question of securing the grounds of knowledge in *advance* or *prior to* an actual engagement with difference. Every epistemology or critical orientation favors its particular differences that it strives to guarantee, and these differences are always pre-epistemological or of a metaphysical sort. Thus, for example, Kant does not first engage in a critical reflection on the nature and limits of our faculties and then proceed to ground physics and mathematics, but rather first begins with the truth of physics and mathematics and then proceeds to determine how the structure of our faculties renders this knowledge possible. As I will attempt to show further on, difference requires no grounding from mind.

B. Second, difference has an *ontological* or metaphysical priority. Hegel famously argued that when we attempt to think 'being, pure being' we end up thinking nothing.[8] Being as such amounts to nothing precisely because it does not offer or donate any differences for thought. Hegel develops a similar critique of Kant's thing-in-itself in the *Phenomenology*.[9] We disagree with Hegel on two points, while nonetheless retaining the basic lesson of his argument that the concepts of pure being and the concept of things-in-themselves are incoherent. On the one hand, for Hegel the issue is what we are *able* to *think* when we attempt to think pure being or things-in-themselves, whereas for us the issue is not what is *thinkable* but rather what beings and things themselves *are* regardless of whether or not anyone thinks them. The question of ontology and metaphysics is not the question of what beings are *for-us*, nor of *our access* to beings, nor of how we relate to being. No. Ontology or metaphysics asks after the being of *beings simpliciter*, regardless of whether or not any humans relate to beings.

Second, for Hegel our attempt to think pure being leads us to the *negation* of being or the thought of nothingness. In attempting to think 'being pure being' we are led to think nothing. This observation leads Hegel to inscribe negativity in the heart of being. However, this inscription only arises when we begin one step removed from being, treating being in terms of *our* relation to being rather than in terms of being *sim-*

8. G.W.F. Hegel, *Science of Logic*, trans. A.V. Miller, Atlantic Highlands, Humanities Press, 1989, pp. 82-3.

9. G.W.F Hegel, *Phenomenology of Spirit*, trans. A.V. Miller, New York, Oxford University Press, 1977, pp. 88-9.

pliciter. For us this is an illicit move. Xavier Zubiri makes this point compellingly in his magnificent *On Essence.*[10] Zubiri asks,

> can it be said that to be, that reality itself, is constitutively affected by negativity? This is impossible. Reality is that which is, and, in that which is, there is distilled all its reality, no matter how limited, fragmentary and insufficient it might be. The negative, as such, has no physical reality whatsoever [...] Of two real things we say, and we see with truth, that the one 'is not' the other. This 'is not' does not, however, affect the physical reality of each of the two things, but it affects this physical reality only insofar as it is present to an intelligence, which, when it compares those things, sees that the one 'is not' the other.[11]

The plant does not 'negate' the soil or seed from whence it comes, and to speak in this way is to speak metaphorically and without precision. Therefore, we cannot share the thesis that *omni determinatio est negatio.* It is only from the standpoint of a consciousness regarding objects and comparing them to one another that the differences composing objects are taken by reference to what objects are *not.* Ontological, as opposed to epistemic difference is, by contrast, positive, affirmative, and differentiated without being negative. The temperature of boiling water is not the *negation* of other degrees. Philosophy perpetually conflates these epistemic and ontological registers, requiring us to untangle them with the greatest care if we are to understand anything of the real.

Where Hegel demands the inclusion of the subject in *every* relation—his famous identity of substance and subject—we are content to let difference belong to the things themselves with or without the inclusion of the subject in the relation to things. However, with regard to pure being and things-in-themselves, we have learned Hegel's lesson. There is no 'pure being', no 'being as such', for being and beings only are in and through their differences. Likewise, when we are told that the thing-in-itself is beyond all knowledge, that it has none of the properties presented to us in phenomena, this thesis is to be rejected on the grounds that it conceives the things-in-themselves as things making no differences. Yet there can be no coherence in the notion of an in-different being for 'to be' is to make a difference.

I have thus proposed that the Ontic Principle has both an epistemological and ontological priority in the order of philosophical questioning. Yet as principles go, the Ontic Principle is a strange and ironic principle. Just as Latour says that his Principle of Irreduction is a '... prince that does not govern ...',[12] we can say of the Ontic Principle that it is a 'principle without a prince'. In order to unpack this metaphor of princes and governance, I again make reference to Husserl. In articulating his Principle of All Principles, Husserl writes that,

> No conceivable theory can make us err with respect to the principle of all principles: that every originary presentative intuition is a legitimizing source of cognition, that everything originarily (so to speak, in its 'personal' actuality) offered to us in 'intuition' is to be accepted simply as what it is presented as being, but also only within the limits in which it is presented there.[13]

Although this principle might appear not to govern insofar as it takes things only in terms of how they are presented, difference here is nonetheless governed or ruled in

---

10. For an excellent discussion and productive critique of Xavier Zubiri's thought in the context of Speculative Realist thought, see Harman, *Tool-Being: Heidegger and the Metaphysics of Objects,* pp. 243-268.

11. Zubiri, *On Essence,* p. 81.

12. Bruno Latour, *The Pasteurization of France,* trans. A. Sheridan & J. Law, Cambridge, Harvard University Press, 1988, p. 158.

13. Husserl, *Ideas Pertaining to a Pure Phenomenology and to a Phenomenological Philosophy: First Book,* p. 44.

at least two senses. First, difference here is restricted to what is and can be *present-ed*. If difference does not present itself, then it is not, according to Husserl, legitimate. For Husserl, in order for a difference to be legitimate it must be presented or corre-lated with us.[14] Second, difference is therefore restricted to what relates to conscious-ness or intuition. If, then, the Principle of All Principles is a 'prince' that 'governs', then this is because it subordinates and governs all other beings in relation to conscious-ness and presentation. Husserl is led to this position by restricting ἀρχή to the domain of γίγνώσκεται or that from whence something is known, refusing ἀρχή as ἔστιν and γίγνεται. Indeed, ἔστιν and γίγνεται themselves come to be subordinated to γίγνώσκεται or the requirements of knowledge insofar as it is held that any reference to beings outside of the ἐποχή is illegitimate and dogmatically falls into the natural at-titude by virtue of referring to beings beyond the immediacies of presentation or given-ness. This point is, above all, confirmed when Husserl remarks, in the same text, that, 'the existence of a Nature *cannot* be the condition for the existence of consciousness, since Nature itself turns out to be a correlate of consciousness: Nature *is* only as being constituted in regular concatenations of consciousness'.[15] Husserl is led to this conclu-sion by requiring knowledge to have the characteristic of certainty. However, the key point here is that all beings, for Husserl, come to be governed in and through being subordinated to the requirements of consciousness and presentation.

THE PRINCIPLE OF THE INHUMAN: RADICAL ANTI-HUMANISM

If the Ontic Principle is a prince that does not govern, then this is precisely because difference *differs*. In other words, there can be no question here of tracing all other dif-ferences back to a single *type* of difference, prince, or ἀρχή. Being, as it were, is a *mul-tiplicity* or a pluralistic swarm of differences. It is for this reason that the Ontic Princi-ple is an *ironic* principle. As a consequence, two further related principles follow from the Ontic Principle. The first of these principles is a negative reminder and is what I refer to as the Principle of the Inhuman. Recalling that the Ontic Principle pertains to the orders of the ἔστιν and γίγνεται or that from whence something *is* and that from whence something *becomes*, the Principle of the Inhuman asserts that the differences that make a difference are not restricted to the domain of the human, the linguistic, the cultural, the sociological, or the semiotic. In short, the expression 'to make a differ-ence' is not restricted to the domain of γίγνώσκεται or that from whence knowledge comes, and is not a question of phenomenality, manifestation, givenness, experience or any of the other names we give to the ἀρχή of knowledge. Of course, within the order of γίγνώσκεται we are above all concerned with discovering those differences that make a difference. The point here, however, is that the *being* of difference is, in no way, dependent on knowledge or consciousness. The most insignificant quark on the other side of the universe makes its difference(s) without any relation to our conscious-ness or knowledge of that quark. Difference is thus a matter of the 'things themselves', not *our relationship* to things. In this regard, the Principle of the Inhuman is formulated not so as to *exclude* the human—humans and human artefacts, after all, make differ-ences too—but rather to underline the point that humans are beings *among* the swarm of differences and hold no special or privileged place with respect to these differences.

---

14. For a discussion of correlation, cf. ch. 1 of Quentin Meillassoux's brilliant *After Finitude: An Essay on the Necessity of Contingency*, trans. R. Brassier, New York, Continuum, 2008.

15. Husserl, *Ideas Pertaining to a Pure Phenomenology and to a Phenomenological Philosophy: First Book*, p. 116.

In this respect, the ontology suggested by the Ontic Principle is *flat* rather than *vertical*. Rather than tracing all beings back to an "ur-being" as in the case of the vertical ontologies of ontotheology or a humanism, the ontology that follows from the Ontic Principle is necessarily flat insofar as it does not trace back and relate all beings to either God, humans, language, culture or any of the other princes anti-realist thought and idealism has sought to ground being in. To be is a simple binary, insofar as something either is or it is not. If something makes a difference then it is, full stop. And there is no being to which all other beings are necessarily related. It is noteworthy here that most of the positions referred to as "anti-humanist" would still, from the standpoint of the Principle of the Inhuman, be counted as *humanisms* insofar as while they "split the subject" or demolish the Cartesian subject, they nonetheless shackle all beings to human related phenomena such as the signifier, language, culture, power, and so on.

PLATO'S FULL NELSON AND THE ALLEGED PRIMACY OF IDENTITY: MENO'S PARADOX

To this line of argument it will be objected, along Platonic lines as formulated in the *Meno* and the *Phaedo*, that in order to *speak* of difference we must have a *concept* of difference. Yet, the argument runs, a *concept* of difference entails a priority of *identity* over difference insofar as it localizes what is the same or identical in all instances of difference. As a result, two consequences would follow: first, difference cannot be a *fundamental* principle insofar as it requires a prior identity to be articulated. Second, the order of thought or the identity of thought must precede being insofar as any *talk* of being requires reference to a *concept*. This argument, in a nutshell, is the core argument of any and all correlationisms or anti-realisms. To this argument, I respond in two ways: First, this line of argument once again conflates two fundamentally different types of ἀρχή or principles: ἀρχή as γίγνώσκεται or that from whence *knowledge* comes and ἀρχή as ἔστιν and γίγνεται or the whence of what beings *are* and the whence of how beings *become*. The requirements pertaining to beings as beings and to the becoming of being need not, as we saw earlier in the case of our analysis of negation and negativity, be constrained by the requirements of our knowledge of being. The issues of how we know and of what beings *are* are two entirely distinct issues.

Second, from the standpoint of γίγνώσκεται or the principles governing knowledge, Alain Badiou has demonstrated how it is possible to work without a concept or without defined terms axiomatically as in the case of sets, without having to presuppose a prior delineated concept.[16] Within Zermelo-Fraenkel set theory, 'set' is left rigorously undefined so as to avoid falling into paradox. The element of a set—which is itself a set—is defined purely in terms of its membership. Set theory thus *operates* on sets without reference to a concept of set that would define what is common to any and all sets. Membership in a set thus becomes the result of a *stipulation* that does not govern or range over all sets. There is no reason a similar strategy cannot be adopted, in the order of γίγνώσκεται, with respect to differences. In the order of knowledge, differences can be stipulated without the requirement of a concept of difference *identifying* what is common to all differences. While I do not endorse Badiou's mathematical ontology, seeing his identification of being and thought as a variant of idealism, his point nonetheless holds where questions of knowledge are concerned: That identity in a concept is not necessary to operate on concepts.

---

16. cf. Alain Badiou, *Being and Event*, trans. O. Feltham, New York, Continuum, 2006.

THE ONTOLOGICAL PRINCIPLE: FLAT ONTOLOGY

This leads to a third principle that I refer to as the Ontological Principle. Following Deleuze, if it is the case that there is no difference that does not make a difference, it follows that being is said in a single and same sense for all that is. That is, being is univocal. As Deleuze puts it,

> [...] the essential in univocity is not that Being is said in a single and same sense, but that it is said, in a single and same sense, *of* all its individuating differences or intrinsic modalities. Being is the same for all these modalities, but these modalities are not the same. It is 'equal' for all, but they themselves are not themselves equal.[17]

If it is the case that there is no difference that does not make a difference, then it follows that the minimal criterion for being a being consists in making a difference. If a difference is made, then that being *is*. These differences can, of course, be of an inter- or intra-ontic sort. A difference is *inter*-ontic when it consists in making a difference with respect to another object. A difference is *intra*-ontic, by contrast, when it pertains to the processes belonging to the *internal* constitution or essence of the object as a system of ongoing differences. The key point here is that if a difference is made, then the being *is*.

If being is univocal, then it follows that being is not said in more than one way of those beings that are. For example, being is not divided between appearance and reality. Thus there is not a true reality consisting of Platonic forms, Badiouian multiples, the Deleuzian virtual, Bergsonian duration, the Nietzschean will to power, the materialists matter, etc., on the side of 'true reality', and appearance, consistent multiplicities, the actual, space, condensations of power, or mind on the side of appearances. Rather, wherever we have differences made we have beings. It will be noted that the minimal intension of being here yields a nearly infinite extension. Insofar as the minimal criteria for being a being consists in making a difference, the number and variety of beings is infinitely multiplied. Beings differ among themselves, but there is not one set of differences that consists of the 'true differences' or the 'true reality' and another set of differences that consists of only appearances. What we thus get is a realism, but it is a strange or weird sort of realism occasionally referred to by Graham Harman.[18] Because both quarks and the character of Half-Cock Jack in Neal Stephenson's *Quicksilver* both make differences, they both are, according to the Ontological Principle, *real*.

The ontology that follows from the Ontic Principle is thus, in addition to being a realist ontology, what Manuel DeLanda has aptly called a 'flat ontology'. As described by DeLanda,

> [...]while an ontology based on relations between general types and particular instances is *hierarchical*, each level representing a different ontological category (organism, species, genera), an approach in terms of interacting parts and emergent wholes leads to a *flat ontology*, one made exclusively of unique, singular individuals, differing in spatio-temporal scale but not ontological status.[19]

With DeLanda we affirm the thesis that being is composed of nothing but singular individuals, existing at different levels of scale but nonetheless *equally* having the status of being real. These entities differ among themselves, yet they do not have the character-

17. Gilles Deleuze, *Difference and Repetition*, trans. P. Patton, New York, Columbia University Press, 1994, p. 36.

18. Ray Brassier, Iain Hamilton Grant, Graham Harman, and Quentin Meillassoux, 'Speculative Realism', in *Collapse*, vol. 3, Falmouth, Urbanomic, 2007, p. 367.

19. Manuel DeLanda, *Intensive Science & Virtual Philosophy*, New York, Continuum, 2002, p. 41.

istic of being 'more' or 'less' beings in terms of criteria such as the distinction between reality and appearance. Nonetheless, while I have the greatest admiration for DeLanda's ontology, his individuals seem restricted to the world of *nature*. Insofar as the Ontic Principle dictates that whatever makes a difference *is*, it follows that the domain of being must be far broader than natural beings, including signs, fictions, armies, corporations, nations, etc.. Natural beings make up only a subset of being.

The Ontic Principle, the Principle of the Inhuman, and the Ontological Principle outline, roughly, the three legs of a general ontology. The Ontic Principle hypothesizes the general principle of what it means for an entity to be. The Principle of the Inhuman underlines that the questions of ontology are not questions of being *qua* subject, being *qua* consciousness, being *qua* Dasein, being *qua* body, being *qua* language, being *qua* human, or being *qua* power, but of beings *qua* being. Finally, the Ontological Principle hypothesizes that all beings are ontologically on equal footing or that they all *are* insofar as they make a difference. However, I have not, up to this point, said much pertaining to objects.

ONTICOLOGY: INTERNAL RELATIONS (ENDO-RELATIONS), EXTERNAL RELATIONS (EXO-RELATIONS), AND SUBSTANCE

In the past I have jokingly referred to the position I am outlining here as 'Onticology' to emphasize its orientation towards objects, or its status, as Graham Harman calls it, as an Object-Oriented Ontology. It would be a mistake, however, to suppose that difference, those differences that make a difference, consist of a pre-individual or transcendental field out of which objects emerge or are constituted as mere excrescences without any potency of their own. Were we to suggest this, the real would once again be divided between the true real and those condensations of the real constituting objects as epiphenomena. Rather, as Harman puts it, being comes in 'chunks', rather than out of a formless and chaotic ἄπειρον out of which beings are then constituted by mind or some other agency. In short, differences are always differences belonging *to* objects. While we readily acknowledge that all objects have their genesis, this genesis is a genesis *from* other objects or discrete individuals, and in many instances is productive *of* new individual entities. Consequently, we may retain terms like 'pre-individual' or 'transcendental' field if we like, so long as we understand that this field is not something *other* than objects, but consists of nothing but objects.

However, while differences always belong *to* objects, it would be a mistake to think, after the fashion of the first proposition of Spinoza's *Ethics*—'substance by nature is prior to its affections'—that objects or substances are one thing and that objects are substances in which differences inhere as predicates. Objects are nothing but their structured differences as, following Zubiri, a system of intra-ontic or intra-relational differences forming a system that persists through time. In short, in thinking objects and differences, we must simultaneously think their inter-ontic or exo-relational differences as they relate to other differences *and* their intra-ontic or endo-relational differences. Alternatively we could say that it is necessary to simultaneously think the relation between relations and relata without reducing one to the other. The latter are attained when an object gains totality and closure, constituting a system where certain differences are inter-dependent with one another and maintain only selective relations with other objects in the cosmos. Totality or closure does not mean that the object is immune to change, that it ceases to evolve or develop, or that it cannot be destroyed, but rather that the substances or objects persists through time as 'that' object. Here substance is not something other than its endo-relational differences, but rather is a particular state attained by difference. The caveat here is that the endurance of a substance need be no greater than the smallest possible unit of time.

Recently it has become fashionable to argue that an object is *nothing but* its relations. In part, this position has been inspired by Hegelian thought, and, in part, it has been inspired by French structuralism where it is argued that language consists of *nothing but* differential relations without *positive terms* related by these relations. In rejecting the existence of positive terms related by these relations, what is being rejected is the existence of *substances* in which predicates inhere. Depending on how substances are conceptualized, there are good philosophical reasons for rejecting the existence of substance. However, before proceeding to discuss these reasons it is first necessary to determine the problem to which the concept of substance responds. In my view, the concept of substance was developed to respond to the problem of the identity of objects as they change through time. As can be readily observed at the level of ordinary experience, objects persist through time while nonetheless undergoing change at the level of their qualities. How, then, are we to account for the persistence of an object as *this* object despite the fact that the object changes? The concept of substance is the solution to this problem. The thesis is that it is not the substance that changes, but rather the qualities *of* a substance that change. Qualities inhere in or belong to a substance, but do not *make* the substance what it is. Substance is therefore that which persists throughout time.

However, as Locke observed, problems begin to emerge when we ask ourselves precisely what substance is as distinct from qualities. We can grant that objects somehow remain the same while their qualities change, but when we attempt to specify what, precisely, it is that remains the same we seem to arrive at *nothing* at all. If this is so, then it is because when we subtract all qualities from a substance, there is nothing left to distinguish the substance. Substance itself is essentially nothing. As such, the argument runs, we would do well to simply banish the concept of substance altogether, treating objects as nothing but their qualities. This eventually leads to the position that objects are nothing but their relations.

While I do not share all of the claims of his ontology, Graham Harman has presented two compelling arguments against this relational view in his magnificent *Guerrilla Metaphysics*. On the one hand, Harman argues, the relational theory of objects is '[…]too reminiscent of a house of mirrors'.[20] In other words, in thinking objects as nothing but networks of relations, the object itself effectively *evaporates*. However, here evaporation is not simply a phase transition from a liquid state to a gaseous state, but is rather a complete annihilation of *all* objects. For if every object is its relation to other objects and if the other objects are, in their turn, their relations to other objects, there turns out to be *nothing* to relate. In an ironic twist, relational ontologies, motivated, in part, by the aim of avoiding the bare substratum problem formulated by Locke, end up in exactly the same place.

Second, argues Harman, '… no relational theory … is able to give a sufficient explanation of change'.[21] Where objects are nothing but networks of relations, relations without, as Harman aptly puts it, anything held in *reserve*, we seem to get a *frozen universe*

---

20. Graham Harman, *Guerrilla Metaphysics: Phenomenology and the Carpentry of Things*, Chicago, Open Court, 2005, p. 82.

21. Harman, *Guerrilla Metaphysics*, p. 82.

without any change. Here I think Harman puts his finger on the core assumption behind a problem of great importance in contemporary Continental philosophy. Within politically inflected French thought there has been a tremendous preoccupation with the question of how change is possible. Thus, in the case of thinkers such as Žižek, it is argued that change can only be thought if we theorize the existence of a subject that is in excess of any and all symbolic structuration, a subject that is a pure *void* irreducible to any and all of its predicates, and the act of which this subject is capable.[22] In the absence of such a subject and a completely undetermined act, it is held that any actions on the part of the agent would simply reproduce the existing system of relations. A similar line of thought can be discerned in Badiou's account of the void, events, subjects, and truth-procedures. In both cases, these conceptual innovations seem to emerge from anxieties of precisely the sort that Harman describes. However, it is difficult to see how either of these conceptualizations solves the problem of change. In the case of Žižek's subject as void, it is not clear how something that is *nothing* can act at all. Nor is it clear, in the case of Badiou, how an event can come from a void. Consequently, either these positions are only speaking metaphorically and are presupposing a prior *positivity* when they speak of subjects and voids, or they are conceptually incoherent.

The entire motivation of these concepts first arises from the presupposition of a *relational* concept of objects in which objects are neither substances nor hold anything in reserve. For, just as Harman points out, where objects are nothing but relations it is impossible to see how the universe could be anything but a frozen crystal. Consequently, while philosophers are quite right to reject the *traditional* concept of substance, the *problem* to which the concept of substance is designed to respond nonetheless persists. The appropriate response to the bare substratum problem is thus not to reject the concept of substance *tout court*, but to reformulate the concept of substance in a way that responds to this entirely justified critique. What is required is an ontology that is capable of explaining the relation of relation to relata in a way that does justice to both. With relational ontologists we agree that there are properties of objects that only emerge as a result of the manner in which the object relates to other objects. Daniel Dennett helps us to think about the nature of these inter-ontic relations in *Darwin's Dangerous Idea* with his valuable concept of 'design spaces'.[23] The concept of design space invites us to think of inter-ontic relations as posing a problem or setting constraints on the development of an entity. Thus, for example, one reason there are no insects the size of elephants on the planet Earth has to do with gravitational constraints on the development of exoskeletons. A design space can thus be thought as a sort of topological space of relations among objects that play a role in qualities an object comes to actualize. I speak of a topological space as opposed to a geometric space for topology allows us to think relations as undergoing continuous variations, whereas geometric relations are fixed. Thus, as a topological space, a design space admits of many variable solutions to the problem posed by the design space, while nonetheless possessing constraints. A point of crucial importance, in this connection, is that design spaces change with changes in relations among objects and in objects.[24] In short, design spaces are not fixed and immutable.

---

22. cf. Slavoj Žižek, *The Ticklish Subject: The Absent Center of Political Ontology*, New York, Verso Books, 1999.

23. Daniel C. Dennett, *Darwin's Dangerous Idea: Evolution and the Meanings of Life*, New York, Simon & Schuster, 1996, pp. 133-136.

24. For a fuller discussion of topology cf. ch. 6 of Levi R. Bryant, *Difference and Givenness: Deleuze's Transcendental Empiricism and the Ontology of Immanence*, Evanston, Northwestern University Press, 2008, and ch. 1 of DeLanda, *Intensive Science & Virtual Philosophy*.

However, as we have seen as a result of Harman's arguments, we run into insurmountable ontological problems if objects are reduced to exo-relations. With Harman and traditional substance ontology, we therefore grant that objects must also be thought in terms of their endo-relations or their intra-ontic structure as radically *independent* of their exo-relations or inter-ontic relations. In short, lest we fall into the vacuous hall of mirrors so colorfully described by Harman and thereby fall into the impossibility of explaining how change is possible, it must be granted that objects have some sort of substantiality independent of their exo-relations and that they hold something in reserve in relating to other objects. In short, it is necessary to account for the being of relata or objects independent of their relations.

A complete account of objects unfolding the intricacies of the relation of endo- and exo-relations pertaining to issues of ἀρχή as ἔστιν and γίγνεται or the whence through which an object *is* and the whence through which an object *becomes*, is a massive undertaking and therefore well beyond the scope of a single article. Nonetheless, I would like to outline some principles pertaining to objects that I believe follow from the Ontic Principle. As I have formulated it, the Ontic Principle states that there is no difference that does not *make* a difference. In claiming that there is no difference that does not make a difference, I am not making a normative judgment to the effect that all differences are *important*, but am instead making an *ontological* claim about the nature of difference. My hypothesis, in effect, is that difference is an *activity*. Under this hypothesis, existence is thought as a sort of doing or movement.

THE PRINCIPLE OF ACT-UALITY AND AFFECTS

This hypothesis, I believe, allows us to say something of the endo-relational structure of objects. If difference is an activity, and to exist is to make differences, then we can characterize the intra-ontic structure of objects with reference to the Principle of Act-uality which states that all objects are act-ual or acts. The intra-ontic characterization of objects as systems of activity requires a parsing of the structure of objects into affects, activity, and actuality. However, in distinguishing these three moments of the substantiality of an object or its endo-relations in this way, it is crucial to note that these three terms are not distinct *parts* of objects, but are *moments* of the molten core of objects belonging to objects *formally* in their independent existence. In attributing affects to objects I do not intend to signify *emotions*, but rather to the power of acting and being acted upon belonging to an object or individual. As articulated by Deleuze,

> An individual is first of all a singular essence, which is to say, a degree of power. A characteristic relation corresponds to this degree of power. Furthermore, this relation subsumes parts: this capacity for being affected is necessarily filled by affections. Thus, animals are defined less by the abstraction notions of genus and species than by a capacity for being affected, to which they react within the limits of their capability.[25]

In *A Thousand Plateaus*, Deleuze and Guattari give the example of a tick to illustrate this conception of affect. Ticks, they argue, possess three affects: the capacity to sense light, the capacity to sense the smell of mammals, and the capacity to move.[26] However, while Deleuze and Guattari attribute three determinate affects to the tick, it is worth noting that one of Deleuze's constant refrains is, following Spinoza, that we do not yet

25. Gilles Deleuze, *Spinoza: Practical Philosophy*, trans. R. Hurley, San Francisco, City Lights Books, 1988, p. 27.

26. Gilles Deleuze and Félix Guattari, *A Thousand Plateaus: Capitalism and Schizophrenia*, trans. B. Massumi, Minneapolis, University of Minnesota Press, 1987, p. 257.

know what a body can do.[27] In other words, as in the case of Harman's withdrawn objects, there is always something of the object held in reserve.

What Deleuze says here of animals holds equally, I believe, for all objects, whether animate or inanimate: all objects are defined by their affects or their capacity to act and be acted upon. Take a humble molecule of H_2O. It consists simply of two hydrogen atoms and one oxygen atom. In forming a new assemblage, new affects or capacities to act and be acted upon emerge. Combine a few H_2O molecules together and you get a liquid capable of flowing, wetting, and undergoing phase transitions such as entering into a gaseous or solid state. Remarkably, the objects out of which H_2O is composed themselves possess very different affects. For example, hydrogen and oxygen are both highly combustible, whereas water is not. Assemblages of objects thus generate new affects or new capacities for acting and being acted upon. Affects are thus the capacity for acting and being acted upon, activities are the exercise of affects as active (originating from the object) or passive (responding to the acts of other objects), and actuality consists in the states or qualities attained in the activity of an affect. The affects characterizing an object are a function of the structure of an object.

Returning to the question of the relation between relations and relata, the Principle of Act-uality allows us to make a crucial point with respect to relational ontologies. Where relational ontologies have it that objects are *nothing but* their relations, the Principle of Act-uality suggests that the condition for the possibility of any inter-ontic relation between two objects is dependent on the affects constituting those objects. In other words, in order for a relation to take place between two objects, it is necessary that the object being acted upon be *capable* of being acted upon. Most matter, for example, is incapable of being affected by neutrinos. Neutrinos slip right through matter in much the same way we glide through air. Consequently, far from objects being epiphenomena or effects of relational networks, objects are instead the *prior* condition of relations.

And this in two respects: first, relations are not simply 'there', but must be *made*. Insofar as relations must be made, it follows that objects must *act* to form these relations. In other words, in the active dimension of their affects, objects must be like solar flares bursting forth from the sun, forging relations with other objects. We seem to perpetually miss the active side of objects in the exercise of their affects. As Deleuze observes, '[…] we must note the immoderate taste of modern thought for this reactive aspect of forces. We always think that we have done enough when we understand an organism in terms of reactive forces. The nature of reactive forces and their quivering fascinates us'.[28] We can see that this reduction of objects to passivity is at the heart of the hall of mirrors described by Harman in his critique of relational ontologies. What we have is objects universally reduced to passivity such that they are only constituted by their relations. But where there is no activity to be found, where objects do not act in any way, where they lack any 'energetic principle' of their own, it is impossible to see how relations can be forged at all.

Second, in order for objects to be acted upon in a relation it is necessary that the object possess affects rendering it capable of being acted upon. I do not possess affects that allow infra-red light to act upon my eyes. The bat possesses affects that allow it to

---

27. Deleuze, *Spinoza: Practical Philosophy*, p. 17.

28. Gilles Deleuze, *Nietzsche and Philosophy*, trans. H. Tomlinson, New York, Columbia University Press, 2006, p. 41.

be acted upon by sound that far exceeds my own capacity to receive sounds. The rock possesses affects that make it susceptible to the gravitational force of other objects and through which it also exerts its own gravitational forces, yet it lacks affects that would render it capable of responding to psychoanalytic therapy. In each case, the affects that constitute the object are a *prior* condition of the relations the object is capable of entertaining with other objects. Far from the object being a product of its relations, relations are dependent on the powers of objects. All sorts of delicate ontological questions arise in this connection that I cannot develop here. How do affects come to be formed? What does it mean for an affect to be active or to act in a non-anthropomorphic or non-living fashion? What are the structures through which affects become open to being acted upon by other objects? At the epistemic level or the level of inquiry, what interests us is precisely the discovery of these sorts of relations or the ways in which objects can act and be acted upon.

THE PRINCIPLE OF TRANSLATION

At the level of inter-ontic relations, the Ontic Principle entails what I call the 'Principle of Translation' or 'Latour's Principle'. If we accept the hypothesis that there is no difference that does not make a difference, then it follows that there can be no object that is a mere *vehicle* for the acting differences of another object. As Latour puts it, there is no transportation without translation.[29] In evoking the terms 'vehicle', 'transportation', and 'translation', I have attempted to employ terms capable of covering a variety of very different types of ontological interactions. In short, 'translation' should not be understood as a hermeneutic concept, but as an ontological concept. 'Transportation' refers to the action of one object on another object. Not all transportations are of a causal variety, so it is important to employ terms capable of both capturing causality while allowing for other sorts of exercises of action. For example, the manner in which I am affected by a work of art differs from the manner in which a flower transports the differences of sunlight. And these manners of translating differences again differ from the manner in which the ocean transports the differences of the moon.

The concept of a 'vehicle' denotes the concept of one object being *reduced to* the carrier of the difference of another object without contributing any difference of its own. Thus, for example, when Lacan tells us that '[t]he universe is the flower of rhetoric'[30], he reduces the objects that populate the universe to mere vehicles of language. Although this characterization of Lacan's position is somewhat unfair, the point is that the differences contributed by language in his thought end up trumping any differences that might be contributed by objects independent of language. For example, the biological body is almost entirely absent in Lacan's account of subjectivization, instead being reduced to a topography written over by signifiers and the *a-objects* that are produced as indigestible remainders or excesses irreducible to language. The differences contributed by objects end up fading almost entirely from view, so much so that Žižek can write that

> [...] the Real cannot be inscribed, but we inscribe this impossibility itself, we can locate its place: a traumatic place which causes a series of failures. And Lacan's whole point is that the Real is *nothing but* this impossibility of its inscription: the Real is not a transcendent pos-

29. Bruno Latour, *Reassembling the Social: An Introduction to Actor-Network-Theory*, New York, Oxford University Press, 2005, pp. 106-109.

30. Jacques Lacan, *The Seminar of Jacques Lacan, Book XX, Encore: On Feminine Sexuality, the Limits of Love and Knowledge*, trans. Bruce Fink, New York, W.W. Norton & Company, 1998, p. 56.

itive entity, persisting somewhere beyond the symbolic order like a hard kernel inaccessible to it, some kind of Kantian 'Thing-in-itself'—in itself it is nothing at all, just a void, an emptiness in a symbolic structure marking some central impossibility.[31]

It will be objected that in this criticism I am conflating the Lacanian concept of the Real with reality. However, the point is that for Lacan reality is always an amalgam of the symbolic, the imaginary, *and* the real in the sense so nicely articulated by Žižek in this passage. There is no question here of an *independently* existing real object. Like Kafka's parable of the law in *The Trial* which Žižek himself references in this connection, the belief in objects independent of the triad of the symbolic, the imaginary, and the real is treated as a *transferential illusion.*[32]

The point here is not that Lacan is mistaken in holding that language plays an important role in how humans relate to the world, but that we must mark the differences. In light of the forgoing, the concept of translation becomes clearer. When a text is translated from one language to another, the source language must be *transformed* into the object language and the object language must be transformed into the source language. In this process, differences, something *new*, is always produced. Take the example of Heidegger. In translating the works of Heidegger into English, all sorts of neologisms needed to be created so that the differences of Heidegger's text could be transported into English. Indeed, in certain cases entirely new words had to be invented such as the notorious 'enowning'. In the translation, English does not function as a mere vehicle of the content of Heidegger's texts, but rather English contributes differences of its *own* to that content, creating surprising associations, resonances, and connections that were not there in the original text.

My thesis is that this phenomenon of transformation through transportation is not restricted to the translation of texts, but is true of *all* inter-ontic relations or all interactions between objects. Thus when Kant tells us that objects conform to the mind, not the mind to objects, that we can never know things as they are in-themselves, he is absolutely correct with this one qualification: what Kant says of mind-world relations is not unique to mind, but is true of *all* object-object relations. As Latour so nicely puts it, '[e]verything said of the signifier is right, but it must also be said of every other kind of [object]'.[33] To this we could add that everything said of iteration and *différance* is true, but must also be said of every other kind of object. Everything said of concepts and intuitions is true, but must also be said of every other kind of object. Everything said of power and social forces is true, but must also be said of every other kind of object. In this respect, Harman is absolutely correct to argue that objects withdraw from every relation in that in relating to other objects they are translated by these objects.

THE PRINCIPLE OF IRREDUCTION

If it is true that there is no transportation without translation, that all transportation of differences involves transformation, then another principle drawn from Latour follows: the Principle of Irreduction. The Principle of Irreduction states that 'nothing is, by itself, either reducible or irreducible to anything else'.[34] It is important that we understand what is *not* asserted in the Principle of Irreduction, lest we fall into confusion.

---

31. Slavoj Žižek, *The Sublime Object of Ideology*, New York, Verso Books, 1989, pp. 172-3.

32. Žižek, *The Sublime Object of Ideology*, pp. 36-47.

33. Latour, *The Pasteurization of France*, p. 184.

34. Latour, *The Pasteurization of France*, p. 158.

The Principle of Irreduction is not a *dualist* thesis to the effect that mind cannot be reduced to brain. Rather, the Principle of Irreduction is a *thermodynamic* principle or a
principle of *work*. In many respects, the Principle of Irreduction states nothing more
than the Principle of Translation, but simply approaches inter-ontic or exo-relations
from a different perspective. If the Principle of Irreduction is a thermodynamic principle or a principle of work, then this is because just as in the case of physics thermodynamics studies the conversion of energy into work and heat, Onticology, in one of its
ambitions, aims to investigate the translation of differences and their transformations
in inter-ontic relations. The transportation of difference never takes place in a smooth,
frictionless space, but always requires labour or work. Through the work of translation, objects can always *enlist* other objects for their own ongoing autopoiesis as in the
case of human cells enlisting mitochondrial DNA in the remote past, but this reduction always leaves a remainder and produces differences of its own. The Principle of
Irreduction therefore reminds us to track both work or the processes by which a reduction is effectuated, but also to track the differences contributed by the enlisted or reduced object, producing something that could not have been anticipated in the transported difference itself.

THE HEGEMONIC FALLACY

What, then, is the 'cash-value' of this proposed ontology? Earlier I evoked Latour's
observation that everything said of the signifier is true, so long as we recognize that
it is true of all other objects as well. When we paraphrase Latour saying that everything Kant says about mind-object relations is true with the qualification that all objects translate one another, it must be added that translation is not *unilateral*, but *bilateral*. The cardinal sin of anti-realisms, correlationisms, or philosophies of access is not
simply the claim that the human must be included in every relation, but also the *unilateralization* of all processes of translation. As Hegel might put it, correlationisms have
a marked tendency of thinking difference in a one-sided and abstract fashion. In processes of translation, there is a tendency to mark only one side of the process, ignoring
the other side. Thus, for example, in Kant, while it is indeed the case that things-in-
themselves are said to 'affect' mind, these affectations do little more than provide the
matter for reason, the pure concepts of the understanding, and the formal structure of
intuition to work over. Mind does all the translating but is not itself *translated* or transformed in any marked way by its encounter with these differences.

To mark this problem I draw a term from political theory, referring to this unilateralization of translation as the Hegemonic Fallacy. In political theory, hegemony refers to the predominant influence of one agency over all the others. In evoking the Hegemonic Fallacy, I take this term out of the exclusive domain of political theory, and
apply it to the broader domain of epistemo-ontological thought. The Hegemonic Fallacy thus consists in treating one difference as being the only difference that makes a
difference or as treating one difference as overdetermining all the other differences. If
it is the case that there is no transportation of differences without translation or transformation, then it follows that inter-object translation must be thought *bilaterally* in
such a way that one difference cannot function as the ground of all other differences.
In translating the differences of another object, the object is also translated by those
differences. This point can be illustrated by reference to my grandfather. My grandfather is a crusty old sailor who built many of the bridges of New Jersey. When you ob-

serve him walking you cannot fail to observe that he has a very unique gait, with his feet planting themselves on the ground like the trunks of trees, placed somewhat wide apart, his shoulders squared at a somewhat lower level of gravity.

How is this peculiar gait to be explained? The gait of my grandfather consists of petrified or embodied ocean waves inscribed in the fiber of his nerves and muscles of his body. This particular quality is not simply the way in which his *body* translated the moving waves of the ocean, but also the way in which his body *was translated* by the *waves*. We could say that my grandfather's gait is the result of a 'becoming-wave' in which neither wave nor body hold the hegemonic position in the process of translation. Onticology thus seeks a multilateral thought of difference that does justice to a variety of different differential processes without reducing all other differences to one hegemonic difference.

There can be no doubt that the work of theory and philosophy requires all sorts of simplifications, reductions, and processes of abstraction so that problems and questions might be properly posed. This is a work of translation that cannot be dispensed with. However, insoluble problems begin to emerge wherever we forget that these reductions and simplifications are selections, are the work of reduction, treating the real itself as being composed of simply these differences and no others. Such a forgetting or putting into abyss of the excess of objects that perpetually withdraw from their relations leads us to ask the wrong sorts of questions or to fall into fruitless lines of inquiry that emerge as a result of forgetting the role played by other differences. Throughout the foregoing I have attempted to form an ontology that does justice to the plural swarm of differences and their interactions, avoiding this sort of hegemony of a pet difference that we isolate for the sake of directed inquiry, yet forgetting the other differences.

18

The Actual Volcano: Whitehead, Harman, and the Problem of Relations

Steven Shaviro

Alfred North Whitehead writes that 'a new idea introduces a new alternative; and we are not less indebted to a thinker when we adopt the alternative which he discarded. Philosophy never reverts to its old position after the shock of a new philosopher'.[1] In the last several years, such a 'new alternative', and such a 'shock', have been provided by the group of philosophers—most notably, Graham Harman, Quentin Meillassoux, Ray Brassier, and Iain Hamilton Grant—who have come to be known as 'speculative realists'. These thinkers differ greatly among themselves; but they have all asked new questions, and forced us to look at the status of modern, or post-Kantian, philosophy in a new way. They have questioned some of the basic assumptions of both 'analytic' and 'continental' thought. And they have opened up prospects for a new era of bold metaphysical speculation. After years in which the 'end of metaphysics' was proclaimed by pretty much everyone—from Carnap to Heidegger and from Derrida to Rorty—these thinkers have dared to renew the enterprise of what Whitehead called Speculative Philosophy: 'the endeavour to frame a coherent, logical, necessary system of general ideas in terms of which every element of our experience can be interpreted'.[2] In what follows, I will compare and contrast Graham Harman's 'object-oriented philosophy'—one of the most impressive achievements of speculative realism to date—with Whitehead's own 'philosophy of organism'. My aim is to show both how Harman helps us to understand Whitehead in a new way, and conversely to develop a Whitehead-inspired reading of Harman.

The speculative realists all argue—albeit in vastly different ways—for a robust philosophical realism, one that cannot be dismissed (as realism so often is) as being merely 'naive'. They all seek to break away from the epistemological, and human-centred, focus of most post-Kantian thought. Nearly all contemporary philosophy is premised, as Lee Braver shows in detail, upon a fundamental antirealism; it assumes one version or another of the Kantian claim that 'phenomena depend upon the mind to exist'.[3]

---

1. Alfred North Whitehead, *Process and Reality*, New York, The Free Press, 1929/1978, p. 11.

2. Whitehead, *Process and Reality*, p. 3.

3. Lee Braver, *A Thing of This World: A History of Continental Anti-Realism*, Evanston, Northwestern Univer-

Such philosophy denies the meaningfulness, or even the possibility, of any discussion of 'things in themselves'. Modern thought remains in thrall to what Harman calls the idea of 'human access',[4] or to what Meillassoux calls correlationism.[5] It gives a privileged position to human subjectivity or to human understanding, as if the world's very existence somehow depended upon our ability to know it and represent it. Even at its best, such a philosophy subordinates ontology to epistemology; it can only discuss things, or objects, or processes, in terms of how a human subject relates to them. It does not have 'anything at all to tell us about the impact of inanimate objects upon one another, apart from any human awareness of this fact'.[6] It maintains the unquestioned assumption that 'we never grasp an object 'in itself', in isolation from its relation to the subject', and correspondingly that 'we can never grasp a subject that would not always-already be related to an object'.[7] In short, correlationism 'holds that we cannot think of humans without world, nor world without humans, but only of a primal correlation or rapport between the two'.[8] As a result, correlationist philosophy 'remain[s] restricted to self-reflexive remarks about human language and cognition'.[9] This is as much the case for recent thinkers like Derrida and Žižek, as it was before them for Kant, Husserl, and Heidegger. In contrast, the speculative realists explore what it means to think about reality, without placing worries about the ability of human beings to know the world at the centre of all discussion. They are realists, because they reject the necessity of a Kantian 'Copernican rift between things-in-themselves and phenomena', insisting instead that 'we are always in contact with reality' in one way or another.[10] And they are speculative, because they openly explore traditionally metaphysical questions, rather than limiting themselves to matters of logical form, on the one hand, and empirical inquiry, on the other. In this way, they reject both scientific positivism, and 'social constructionist' debunkings of science. Harman, in particular, cuts the Gordian Knot of epistemological reflexivity, in order to develop a philosophy that 'can range freely over the whole of the world', from 'a standpoint equally capable of treating human and inhuman entities on an equal footing'.[11] Harman proposes a non-correlationist, non-human-centred metaphysics, one in which 'humans have no privilege at all', so that 'we can speak in the same way of the relation between humans and what they see and that between hailstones and tar'.[12]

Harman gives Whitehead an important place in the genealogy of speculative realist thought. For Whitehead is one of the few twentieth-century thinkers who dares 'to venture beyond the human sphere',[13] and to place all entities upon the same footing. Whitehead rejects 'the [Kantian] notion that the gap between human and world is more philosophically important than the gaps between any other sorts of entities'.[14]

sity Press, 2007, p. 39 and passim.

4. Graham Harman, *Prince of Networks: Bruno Latour and Metaphysics*, Melbourne, re.press, 2009, pp. 102-103.

5. Quentin Meillassoux, *After Finitude: An Essay on the Necessity of Contingency*, trans. Ray Brassier, London, Continuum, 2008.

6. Graham Harman, *Guerrilla Metaphysics: Phenomenology and the Carpentry of Things*, Chicago, Open Court, 2005, p. 42.

7. Meillassoux, *After Finitude*, p. 5.

8. Harman, *Prince of Networks*, p. 122.

9. Harman, *Guerrilla Metaphysics*, p. 42.

10. Harman, *Prince of Networks*, p. 72.

11. Harman, *Guerrilla Metaphysics*, p. 42.

12. Harman, *Prince of Networks*, p. 124.

13. Harman, *Guerrilla Metaphysics*, p. 190.

14. Harman, *Prince of Networks*, p. 51.

Or, to restate this in Whitehead's own terms, Western philosophy since Descartes gives far too large a place to 'presentational immediacy', or the clear and distinct representation of sensations in the mind of a conscious, perceiving subject.[15] In fact, such perception is far less common, and far less important, than what Whitehead calls 'perception in the mode of causal efficacy', or the 'vague' (nonrepresentational) way that entities affect and are affected by one another through a process of vector transmission.[16] Presentational immediacy does not merit the transcendental or constitutive role that Kant attributes to it. For this mode of perception is confined to 'high-grade organisms' that are 'relatively few' in the universe as a whole. On the other hand, causal efficacy is universal; it plays a larger role in our own experience than we tend to realize, and it can be attributed 'even to organisms of the lowest grade'.[17]

From the viewpoint of causal efficacy, all actual entities in the universe stand on the same ontological footing. No special ontological privileges can distinguish God from 'the most trivial puff of existence in far-off empty space': in spite of all 'gradations of importance, and diversities of function, yet in the principles which actuality exemplifies all are on the same level'.[18] And what holds for God, holds all the more for human subjectivity. Whitehead refuses to privilege human access, and instead is willing to envision, as Harman puts it, 'a world in which the things really do perceive each other'.[19] Causal and perceptual interactions are no longer held hostage to human-centric categories. For Whitehead and Harman alike, there is therefore no hierarchy of being. No particular entity—not even the human subject—can claim metaphysical preeminence, or serve as a favoured mediator. All entities, of all sizes and scales, have the same degree of reality. They all interact with each other in the same ways, and they all exhibit the same sorts of properties. This is a crucial aspect of Whitehead's metaphysics, and it is one that Harman has allowed us to see more clearly than ever before.

It is in the context of this shared project that I want to discuss the crucial differences between Whitehead and Harman. Although both thinkers reject correlationism, they do so on entirely separate—and indeed incompatible—grounds. For Whitehead, human perception and cognition have no special or privileged status, because they simply take their place among the myriad ways in which all actual entities prehend other entities. Prehension includes both causal relations and perceptual ones—and makes no fundamental distinction between them. Ontological equality comes from contact and mutual implication. All actual entities are ontologically equal, because they all enter into the same sorts of relations. They all become what they are by prehending other entities. Whitehead's key term prehension can be defined as any process—causal, perceptual, or of another nature entirely—in which an entity grasps, registers the presence of, responds to, or is affected by, another entity. All actual entities constitute themselves by integrating multiple prehensions; they are all 'drops of experience, complex and interdependent'.[20] All sorts of entities, from God to the 'most trivial puff of existence', figure equally among the "really real' things whose interconnections and individual characters constitute the universe'.[21] When relations extend everywhere,

15. Whitehead, *Process and Reality*, pp. 61-70.

16. Whitehead, *Process and Reality*, pp. 120 ff.

17. Whitehead, *Process and Reality*, p. 172.

18. Whitehead, *Process and Reality*, p. 18.

19. Harman, *Guerrilla Metaphysics*, p. 52.

20. Whitehead, *Process and Reality*, p. 18.

21. Alfred North Whitehead, *Modes of Thought*, New York, The Free Press, 1938/1968, p. 150.

so that 'there is no possibility of a detached, self-contained local existence', and 'the environment enters into the nature of each thing',[22] then no single being—not the human subject, and not even God—can claim priority over any other.

For Harman, in contrast, all objects are ontologically equal, because they are all equally withdrawn from one another. Harman posits a strange world of autonomous, subterranean objects, 'receding from all relations, always having an existence that perception or sheer causation can never adequately measure ... a universe packed full of elusive substances stuffed into mutually exclusive vacuums'.[23] For Harman, there is a fundamental gap between objects as they exist in and for themselves, and the external relations into which these objects enter. 'The basic dualism in the world lies not between spirit and nature, or phenomenon and noumenon, but between things in their intimate reality and things as confronted by other things'.[24] Every object retains a hidden reserve of being, one that is never exhausted by, and never fully expressed in, its contacts with other objects. These objects can rightly be called substances, because 'none of them can be identified with any (or even all) of their relations with other entities'. So defined, 'substances are everywhere'.[25] And in their deepest essence, substances are 'withdrawn absolutely from all relation'.[26]

The contrast between these positions should be clear. Whitehead opposes correlationism by proposing a much broader—indeed universally promiscuous—sense of relations among entities. But Harman opposes correlationism by depriddeging relations in general. Instead, Harman remarkably revives the old and seemingly discredited metaphysical doctrine of substances: a doctrine that Whitehead, for his part, unequivocally rejects. Where Whitehead denounces 'the notion of vacuous actuality, which haunts realistic philosophy',[27] Harman cheerfully embraces 'the vacuous actuality of things'.[28] Whitehead refuses any philosophy in which 'the universe is shivered into a multitude of disconnected substantial things', so that 'each substantial thing is ... conceived as complete it itself, without any reference to any other substantial thing'. Such an approach, Whitehead says, 'leaves out of account the interconnections of things', and thereby 'renders an interconnected world of real individuals unintelligible'. The bottom line for Whitehead is that 'substantial thing cannot call unto substantial thing'. There is no way to bridge the ontological void separating independent substances from one another. An undetectable, unreachable inner essence might just as well not exist at all: 'a substantial thing can acquire a quality, a credit—but real landed estate, never'.[29] The universe would be entirely sterile and static, and nothing would be able to affect anything else, if entities were to be reduced to a 'vacuous material existence with passive endurance, with primary individual attributes, and with accidental adventures'.[30]

Harman, for his part, makes just the opposite criticism. He explicitly disputes the idea, championed by Whitehead (among so many others), that 'everything is related to everything else'. In the first place, Harman says, Whitehead's 'relational theory is too

22. Whitehead, *Modes of Thought*, p. 138.
23. Harman, *Guerrilla Metaphysics*, pp. 75-76.
24. Harman, *Guerrilla Metaphysics*, p. 74.
25. Harman, *Guerrilla Metaphysics*, p. 85.
26. Harman, *Guerrilla Metaphysics*, p. 76.
27. Whitehead, *Process and Reality*, pp. 28-29.
28. Harman, *Guerrilla Metaphysics*, p. 82.
29. Alfred North Whitehead, *Adventures of Ideas*, New York, The Free Press, 1933/1967, pp. 132-133.
30. Whitehead, *Process and Reality*, p. 309.

reminiscent of a house of mirrors'. When things are understood just in terms of their relations, an entity is 'nothing more than its perception of other entities. These entities, in turn, are made up of still other perceptions. The hot potato is passed on down the line, and we never reach any reality that would be able to anchor the various perceptions of it'. This infinite regress, Harman says, voids real things of their actuality. In the second place, Harman argues that 'no relational theory such as Whitehead's is able to give a sufficient explanation of change', because if a given entity 'holds nothing in reserve beyond its current relations to all entities in the universe, if it has no currently unexpressed properties, there is no reason to see how anything new can ever emerge'.[31] Harman thus turns Whitehead's central value of novelty against him, claiming that Whitehead cannot really account for it. If 'every actual entity is what it is, and is with its definite status in the universe, determined by its internal relations to other actual entities',[32] then we will be eternally stuck with nothing more than what we have already.

In this standoff between Whitehead and Harman, or between the idea of relations and the idea of substances, we would seem to have arrived at a basic antinomy of object-oriented thought. Whitehead and Harman, in their opposing ways, both speak to our basic intuitions about the world. Harman addresses our sense of the thingness of things: their solidity, their uniqueness, and their thereness. He insists, rightly, that every object is something, in and of itself; and therefore that an object is not reducible to its parts, or to its relations with other things, or to the sum of the ways in which other entities apprehend it. But Whitehead addresses an equally valid intuition: our sense that we are not alone in the world, that things matter to us and to one another, that life is filled with encounters and adventures. There's a deep sense in which I remain the same person, no matter what happens to me. But there's an equally deep sense in which I am changed irrevocably by my experiences, by 'the historic route of living occasions'[33] through which I pass. And this double intuition goes for all the entities in the universe: it applies to 'shale or cantaloupe'[34] and to 'rocks and milkweed'[35], as much as it does to sentient human subjects. Where does this leave us? As Whitehead suggests, we should always reflect that a metaphysical doctrine, even one that we reject, 'would never have held the belief of great men, unless it expressed some fundamental aspect of our experience'.[36] I would like to see this double intuition, therefore, as a 'contrast' that can be organized into a pattern, rather than as an irreducible 'incompatibility'.[37] Whitehead insists that the highest task of philosophy is to resolve antinomies non-reductively, by operating 'a shift of meaning which converts the opposition into a contrast'.[38]

Harman himself opens the way, in part, for such a shift of meaning, insofar as he focuses on the atomistic, or discrete, side of Whitehead's ontology. Whitehead always insists that 'the ultimate metaphysical truth is atomism. The creatures are atomic'.[39] And Harman takes the atomicity of Whitehead's entities as a guarantee of their concrete actuality: 'Consider the case of ten thousand different entities, each with a differ-

---

31. Harman, *Guerrilla Metaphysics*, p. 82.
32. Whitehead, *Process and Reality*, p. 59.
33. Whitehead, *Process and Reality*, p. 119.
34. Harman, *Guerrilla Metaphysics*, p. 83.
35. Harman, *Guerrilla Metaphysics*, p. 242.
36. Whitehead, *Modes of Thought*, p. 100.
37. Whitehead, *Process and Reality*, p. 95.
38. Whitehead, *Process and Reality*, p. 348.
39. Whitehead, *Process and Reality*, p. 35.

ent perspective on the same volcano. Whitehead is not one of those arch-nominalists who assert that there is no underlying volcano but only external family resemblances among the ten thousand different perceptions. No, for Whitehead there is definitely an actual entity 'volcano', a real force to be reckoned with and not just a number of similar sensations linked by an arbitrary name'.[40] For Harman, this is what sets Whitehead apart from the post-Kantian correlationists for whom we cannot speak of the actuality of the volcano itself, but only of the problem of access to the volcano, or of the way in which it is 'constructed' by and through our apprehension and identification of it. But at the same time, Harman also sets Whitehead's atomism against the way in which, for the speculative realist philosopher Iain Hamilton Grant, objects as such do not really exist, but only 'emerge as 'retardations' of a more primally unified force'.[41] For Grant, as presumably for Schelling, Deleuze, and Simondon before him, there would be no actual volcano, but only its violent, upsurging action, or its 'force to be reckoned with'.

The point is that, even as Whitehead's actualism links him to Harman, so his insistence on process and becoming—which is to say, on relations—links him to Deleuze and to Grant. Whitehead refers to the '"really real" things' that 'constitute the universe' both as 'actual entities' and as 'actual occasions'. They are alternatively things or happenings. These two modes of being are different, and yet they can be identified with one another, in much the same way that 'matter has been identified with energy' in modern physics.[42] (I am tempted to add a reference to the way that the quantum constituents of the universe behave alternatively as particles and as waves; but it is unclear to me how familiar Whitehead was with developments in quantum mechanics in the 1920s and 1930s). When Harman rejects Whitehead's claims about relations, he is not being sufficiently attentive to the dual-aspect nature of Whitehead's ontology.

This can also be expressed in another way. Harman skips over the dimension of privacy in Whitehead's account of objects. For Whitehead, 'in the analysis of actuality the antithesis between publicity and privacy obtrudes itself at every stage. There are elements only to be understood by reference to what is beyond the fact in question; and there are elements expressive of the immediate, private, personal, individuality of the fact in question. The former elements express the publicity of the world; the latter elements express the privacy of the individual'.[43] Most importantly, Whitehead defines concrescence, or the culminating 'satisfaction' of every actual entity, precisely as 'a unity of aesthetic appreciation' that is 'immediately felt as private'.[44] In this way, Whitehead is indeed sensitive to the hidden inner life of things that so preoccupies Harman. Privacy can never be abolished; the singularity of aesthetic self-enjoyment can never be dragged out, into the light.

But privacy is only one half of the story. The volcano has hidden depths, but it also explodes. It enters into the glare of publicity as it spends itself. Whitehead recognizes that, in the privacy of their self-enjoyment, 'actual entities ... do not change. They are what they are'.[45] But he also has a sense of the cosmic irony of transition and transience; and this is something that I do not find in Harman. Whitehead insists that every entity

40. Harman, *Guerrilla Metaphysics*, p. 82.

41. Graham Harman, 'OOO: a first try at some parameters', blog post found at http://doctorzamalek2. wordpress.com/2009/09/04/ooo-a-first-try-at-some-parameters/, 2009.

42. Whitehead, *Modes of Thought*, p. 137.

43. Whitehead, *Process and Reality*, p. 289.

44. Whitehead, *Process and Reality*, p. 212.

45. Whitehead, *Process and Reality*, p. 35.

must perish—and thereby give way to something new. Throughout Process and Reality, Whitehead keeps on reminding us that 'time is a "perpetual perishing"'. For 'objectification involves elimination. The present fact has not the past fact with it in any full immediacy'.[46] In this way, Whitehead entirely agrees with Harman that no entity can prehend another entity in its fullness. There is always something that doesn't get carried over, something that doesn't get translated or expressed. But the reason for this is not that the other entity somehow subsists, beyond relation, locked into its vacuum bubble. Rather, no entity can be recalled to full presence because, by the very fact of its 'publicity' or 'objectification', it does not subsist at all; indeed, it is already dead. The volcano explodes; and other entities are left to pick up the pieces. This reduction to the status of a mere 'datum' is what Whitehead calls, with his peculiar humour, 'objective immortality'.

All this follows from Whitehead's dual-aspect ontology: from the fact that his entities are also processes or events. But for Harman, actual entities only have one aspect. They are quite definitely, and exclusively, things or substances, no matter how brief or transient their existence.[47] This means that Harman tends to underestimate the importance of change over the course of time, just as he underestimates the vividness and the extent of relations among entities. Although he criticizes Whitehead for reducing existence to an infinite regress of relations, Harman himself gives us instead an infinite regress of substances: 'we never reach some final layer of tiny components that explains everything else, but enter instead into an infinite regress of parts and wholes'.[48] Having declared all relations to be 'vicarious' and inessential, he gets rid of the problem of explaining them by decreeing that 'any relation must count as a substance' in its own right (a stipulation which, as Harman admits, could just as easily be inverted). But this move doesn't really resolve any of the paradoxes of relationality; it simply shifts them elsewhere, to the equally obscure realm of hidden substances. Harman accounts for change by appealing to the emergence of qualities that were previously submerged in the depths of objects; but he does not explain how those objects came to be, or how their hidden properties got there in the first place.

This criticism can, again, be stated in another way. Harman fully approves of the 'actualism'[49] expressed in Whitehead's 'ontological principle': the doctrine that 'there is nothing which floats into the world from nowhere. Everything in the actual world is referable to some actual entity'.[50] From this point of view, Harman rejects all philosophies of 'the potential' or 'the virtual': 'the recourse to potentiality is a dodge that leaves actuality undetermined and finally uninteresting; it reduces what is currently actual to the transient costume of an emergent process across time, and makes the real work happen outside actuality itself …. Concrete actors themselves are deemed insufficient for the labour of the world and are indentured to hidden overlords: whether they be potential, virtual, veiled, topological, fluxional, or any adjective that tries to escape from what is actually here right now'.[51] All this is well and good, except that I fail to see why Harman's own doctrine of hidden properties should not be subject to the same critique. How can one make a claim for the actuality, here and now, of properties that are unmanifested, withdrawn from all relation, and irreducible to simple presence?

---

46. Whitehead, *Process and Reality*, p. 340.
47. Harman, *Guerrilla Metaphysics*, p. 85.
48. Harman, *Guerrilla Metaphysics*, p. 85.
49. Harman, *Prince of Networks*, pp. 127-129.
50. Whitehead, *Process and Reality*, p. 244.
51. Harman, *Prince of Networks*, p. 129.

Such properties are unquestionably real; but they are precisely not actual. But such a formulation—'real, without being actual'—is also how Whitehead defines the potentiality of the future,[52] and how Deleuze defines the virtual.[53] Once again, Harman has translated a problem about relations into a problem about substance. And such translation is, in itself, a brilliant creative act, since 'there is no such thing as transport without transformation'.[54] But relocating a difficulty, and forcing us to see it differently, is not the same as actually resolving it.

Because he insists upon enduring substances, as opposed to relations among 'perpetually perishing' occasions, Harman underestimates Whitehead's account of change. For Whitehead, an entity's 'perception of other entities' is not just the repetition and passing-along of pre-existing 'data'. It also involves 'an act of experience as a constructive functioning'.[55] Indeed, Whitehead uses the term 'prehension', rather than 'perception', precisely because the latter conventionally implies merely passive reception. For Whitehead, experience is never just 'the bare subjective entertainment of the datum'.[56] It always also involves what he calls the 'subjective aim' or 'subjective form' as well: this is the how, the manner in which, an entity grasps its data.[57] And this manner makes all the difference. An occasion may be caused by what precedes it; but, as Isabelle Stengers puts it, 'no cause, even God as a cause, has the power to define how it will cause. Nothing has the power to determine how it will matter for others'.[58] Prehension always involves some sort of revaluation: a new 'valuation up' or 'valuation down' of previously given elements.[59] Even more, prehension involves a whole series of deliberate exclusions and inclusions. 'By this term aim is meant the exclusion of the boundless wealth of alternative potentiality, and the inclusion of that definite factor of novelty which constitutes the selected way of entertaining those data in that process of unification .... "That way of enjoyment" is selected from the boundless wealth of alternatives'.[60] Every 'transmission' and 're-enaction'[61] of previously-existing 'data' is also a process of transformative reinvention.

To prehend a datum is therefore already to 'translate' it into a different form. Harman's worry is that, in a fully relational world, no such translation is possible. We are condemned to an endless repetition of the same. From Whitehead's point of view, however, this worry is misplaced. The problem is not how to get something new and different from an impoverished list of already-expressed properties; it is rather how to narrow down, and create a focus, from the 'boundless wealth' of possibilities that already exist. Harman seems to assume a primordial scarcity, which can only be remedied by appealing to substances, with their hidden reservoirs of 'currently unexpressed properties'.[62] Whitehead, in contrast, assumes a primary abundance of 'data': a plethora that

52. Whitehead, *Process and Reality*, p. 214.
53. Gilles Deleuze, *Difference and Repetition*, trans. Paul Patton, New York, Columbia University Press, 1994, p. 208.
54. Harman, *Prince of Networks*, p. 76.
55. Whitehead, *Process and Reality*, p. 156.
56. Whitehead, *Process and Reality*, p. 157.
57. Whitehead, *Process and Reality*, p. 23.
58. Isabelle Stengers, 'Thinking With Deleuze and Whitehead: A Double Test', in *Deleuze, Whitehead, Bergson: Rhizomatic Connections*, Keith Robinson (ed.), New York, Palgrave Macmillan, 2009, p. 40, my emphasis.
59. Whitehead, *Process and Reality*, p. 241.
60. Whitehead, *Modes of Thought*, p. 152.
61. Whitehead, *Process and Reality*, p. 238.
62. Harman, *Guerrilla Metaphysics*, p. 82.

needs to be bounded and made determinate. Where Harman sees 'countless tiny vacuums' separating objects from one another,[63] Whitehead sees the universe as a finely articulated plenum. There is no undifferentiated magma of being; even a volcano is a fully determinate entity. But there is also no gap to bridge between any one such entity and another. For 'an actual entity is present in other actual entities. In fact if we allow for degrees of relevance, and for negligible relevance, we must say that every actual entity is present in every other actual entity'.[64]

What keeps entities distinct from one another, despite their continual interpenetration, is precisely their disparate manners, or their singular modes of decision and selection. Novelty arises, not from some pre-existing reserve, but from an act of positive decision. Even the sheer 'givenness' of the world cannot be postulated apart from 'a "decision" whereby what is "given" is separated of from what for that occasion is "not given" ... every explanatory fact refers to the decision and to the efficacy of an actual thing'.[65] But the act of decision is spontaneous; it cannot be predicted, or determined in advance. All the materials of transformation are already at hand; there is no need to appeal to vast reserves of hidden qualities. What's needed is rather 'some activity procuring limitation'; Whitehead emphasizes that he uses the word decision 'in its root sense of a "cutting off"'.[66] A decision is thereby an act of selection, consisting in processes of choosing, adding, subtracting, relating, juxtaposing, tweaking, and recombining. This is the only way to account for novelty, without appealing to anything that 'floats into the world from nowhere'. Something new is created, each time that a decision is made to do things this way rather than that way; or to put this together with that, while leaving something else aside. Every such act is a new creation: something that has never happened before.

Whitehead envisions a dynamic world of entities that make decisions—or more precisely, of entities whose very being consists in the decisions they make. Harman's entities, in contrast, do not spontaneously act or decide; they simply are. For Harman, the qualities of an entity somehow already pre-exist; for Whitehead, these qualities are generated on the fly. Harman, as we have seen, discounts relations as inessential; his ontology is too static to make sense of them. In contrast, Whitehead's insistence on decision and selection allows him to answer William James' call for a philosophy that 'does full justice to conjunctive relations',[67] in all their 'great blooming, buzzing confusion'.[68] Only such a philosophy can be 'fair to both the unity and the disconnection' that we find among entities in the world.[69] Relations are too various, and come in too many 'different degrees of intimacy',[70] to be reducible to Harman's caricature of them as reductive, external determinations.

For Whitehead, echoing James, 'we find ourselves in a buzzing world, amid a democracy of fellow creatures'.[71] Such a world is no longer human-centred: this is what unites Whitehead with Harman and the other speculative realists. In addition, such

---

63. Harman, *Guerrilla Metaphysics*, p. 82.

64. Whitehead, *Process and Reality*, p. 50.

65. Whitehead, *Process and Reality*, pp. 42-43, 46.

66. Whitehead, *Process and Reality*, p. 43.

67. William James, *Essays in Radical Empiricism*, Lincoln, University of Nebraska Press, 1996, p. 44.

68. William James, *The Principles of Psychology*, Cambridge, Harvard University Press, 1983, p. 462.

69. James, *Essays in Radical Empiricism*, p. 47.

70. James, *Essays in Radical Empiricism*, p. 44.

71. Whitehead, *Process and Reality*, p. 50.

a world is one of discrete, individual entities, self-creating and self-subsisting to the extent that 'every component which is determinable is internally determined':[72] this unites Whitehead with Harman's 'object-oriented' approach, as opposed to other varieties of speculative realism. But the world envisioned by Whitehead is 'perpetually perishing'; thereby, it also promises a radically open future. And this is what divides Whitehead from Harman. Where Whitehead insists upon both internal decision and external relation, Harman has room for neither. And where Whitehead is concerned with both transience and futurity (which he calls 'creative advance'), Harman shows little interest in either of these. At his most Whiteheadian, Harman will concede that 'when two objects enter into genuine relation', then 'through their mere relation, they create something that has not existed before, and which is truly one'.[73] But Harman seems to backtrack from this concession, when he describes this new relation as yet another vacuum-sealed object, and when he therefore concludes that objects can only interact in the 'molten interiors'[74] of other objects. Harman strikingly asserts that 'the interior of an object, its molten core, becomes the sole subject matter for philosophy'.[75] But this is to affirm the actuality of the volcano only at the price of isolating it from the world, and reducing its dynamism to a sort of sterile display—which is all that it can be, in the absence of its direct effects upon other entities.

To sum up, I find Harman's critique of Whitehead unconvincing. This is because all the problems that Harman discovers in Whitehead's thought, and in relationalist thought more generally, also plague Harman's own substance-based philosophy. If Whitehead fails to account for the actual nature of objects, and for the ways that the world can change, then Harman also fails to account for these matters. But this can be put in positive terms, instead of negative ones. Harman's difference from Whitehead, and his creative contribution to Speculative Philosophy, consists in the 'translation' of the deep problems of essence and change from one realm (that of relations) to another (that of substances). These two realms, oddly enough, seem to be reversible into one another—at least in an overall anti-correlationist framework. Given that 'there is no such thing as transport without transformation', the only remaining question is what sort of difference Harman's transformation of ontology makes. I would suggest that the contrast between Harman and Whitehead is basically a difference of style, or of aesthetics. This means that my enjoyment of one of these thinkers' approaches over the other is finally a matter of taste, and is not subject to conceptual adjudication. And this is appropriate, given that both thinkers privilege aesthetics over both ethics and epistemology. Whitehead notoriously argues that 'Beauty is a wider, and more fundamental, notion than Truth', and even that 'the teleology of the Universe is directed to the production of Beauty'.[76] Harman, for his part, enigmatically suggests that, in a world of substances withdrawn from all relations, 'aesthetics becomes first philosophy'.[77]

The difference between Whitehead and Harman is best understood, I think, as a difference between the aesthetics of the beautiful and the aesthetics of the sublime. Whitehead defines beauty as a matter of differences that are conciliated, adapted to

---

72. Whitehead, *Process and Reality*, p. 47.

73. Harman, *Guerrilla Metaphysics*, p. 85.

74. Harman, *Guerrilla Metaphysics*, p. 189.

75. Harman, *Guerrilla Metaphysics*, p. 254.

76. Whitehead, *Adventures of Ideas*, p. 265.

77. Graham Harman, 'On Vicarious Causation', *Collapse*, no. 2, 2007, p. 205.

one another, and 'interwoven in patterned contrasts',[78] in order to make for 'intense experience'.[79] Harman, for his part, appeals to notions of the sublime: although he never uses this word, he refers instead to what he calls allure.[80] This is the attraction of something that has retreated into its own depths. An object is alluring when it does not just display particular qualities, but also insinuates the existence of something deeper, something hidden and inaccessible, something that cannot actually be displayed. Allure is properly a sublime experience, because it stretches the observer to the point where it reaches the limits of its power, or where its apprehensions break down. To be allured is to be beckoned into a realm that cannot ever be reached.

It should be evident that beauty is appropriate to a world of relations, in which entities continually affect and touch and interpenetrate one another; and that sublimity is appropriate to a world of substances, in which entities call to one another over immense distances, and can only interact vicariously. It should also be noted that the beautiful and the sublime, as I am conceiving them here, are alternative aesthetic stances that work universally, in relation to all entities and all encounters. They are not limited 'to the special metaphysics of animal perception', but apply to 'relations between all real objects, including mindless chunks of dirt'.[81] In addition, it is not the case that some objects are beautiful, while others are sublime. Whitehead's notion of beauty includes "Discord" as well as "Harmony", and gives a crucial role to what he calls 'aesthetic destruction'.[82] And Harman includes comedy as well as tragedy, and cuteness and charm as well as magnificence, within his notion of allure.[83]

It would seem that we are left with a definitive opposition or antinomy, between relations and an aesthetics of beauty on the one hand, and substances and an aesthetics of sublimity on the other. I have already made my own decision on this matter clear: by the very fact of seeking to turn the opposition into a contrast, by admitting Harman's metaphysics alongside Whitehead's, I have thereby already stacked the decks in Whitehead's favour. I have opted for relations and not substances, and for beauty and not sublimity. Evidently, any such gesture can and should be regarded with suspicion. As Kant says, we can quarrel about taste, but we cannot dispute about it. Speculative Philosophy has an irreducibly aesthetic dimension; it requires new, bold inventions, rather than pacifying resolutions.

I would like to end, however, with one final aesthetic consideration. Twentieth-century aesthetics tended overwhelmingly to favour the sublime, and to regard the beautiful as inconsequential and archaic at best, and positively odious in its conciliating conservatism at worst. Whitehead was working very much against the grain of his own time, in his peculiar celebration of beauty. Harman's aesthetics of allure, on the other hand, fits very well into what is now an extended modernist tradition. I wonder, however, whether today, in the twenty-first century, we might be at the beginning of a major aesthetic revaluation. We live in a world where all manners of cultural expression are digitally transcoded and electronically disseminated, where genetic material is freely recombined, and where matter is becoming open to direct manipulation on the atomic and subatomic scales. Nothing is hidden; there are no more concealed depths.

---

78. Whitehead, *Adventures of Ideas*, p. 252.
79. Whitehead, *Adventures of Ideas*, p. 263.
80. Harman, *Guerrilla Metaphysics*, pp. 141-144.
81. Harman, 'On Vicarious Causation', p. 205.
82. Whitehead, *Adventures of Ideas*, p. 256.
83. Harman, *Guerrilla Metaphysics*, pp. 142.

The 'universe of things' is not just available to us, but increasingly unavoidable. The volcano is actual, here and now; we cannot expect to escape its eruption. Our predominant aesthetic procedures involve sampling, synthesizing, remixing, and cutting-and-pasting. In such a world, the aesthetic problem we face is Whitehead's, rather than Harman's; its a question of beauty and 'patterned contrasts', rather than one of sublimity and allure. How can recycling issue in creativity, and familiarity be transformed into novelty? Through what process of selection and decision is it possible to make something new out of the massive accumulation of already-existing materials? Tomorrow, things may be different; but today, the future is Whiteheadian.

19

Response to Shaviro

Graham Harman

Steven Shaviro's article 'The Actual Volcano' draws several contrasts between my position and Alfred North Whitehead's. The results fall largely in Whitehead's favour, but not in a way that I could possibly find offensive. For all his criticisms, Shaviro ends by saying that 'the difference between Whitehead and Harman is best understood [...] as a difference between the aesthetics of the beautiful and the aesthetics of the sublime', hardly a withering dismissal of my position. But on his way to this conclusion, Shaviro does have some fairly critical things to say, and they need to be answered briefly. Before addressing some of Shaviro's specific complaints, it will be helpful to describe how I see Whitehead's position in contemporary philosophy, since this differs considerably from Shaviro's own view of the matter. We do agree that Whitehead is of towering significance. Our disagreement (more evident in his recent book *Without Criteria*[1] than in 'The Actual Volcano') is that he pairs Whitehead and Gilles Deleuze as philosophers of 'process and becoming'. My own position is presented by contrast as a philosophy of stasis that 'tends to underestimate the importance of change over time'. In fact, the true situation is different from what Shaviro imagines: Whitehead and Deleuze are no more joined through their interest in process and becoming than birds, bats, and hornets are joined through their capacity to fly. The similarity is certainly there, yet the supposed difference between process and stasis is insufficiently basic to power a valid taxonomy of philosophers.

Whitehead (like Bruno Latour) should be seen not as a philosopher of *becoming*, but of concrete, individual entities—a side of Whitehead that Shaviro also sees when remarking that 'Whitehead's actualism links him to Harman'. This turns out to be of greater importance than the current fashion that lumps together Whitehead, Henri Bergson, Deleuze, Latour, Iain Hamilton Grant, William James, and others as 'process philosophers'. My chief difference from Whitehead is not that he celebrates becoming (which is misleading) while I am the champion of stasis (which is outright false). The difference is that Whitehead turns entities into clusters of relations, while I hold that only a non-relational model of objects is capable of accounting for both the

1. Steven Shaviro, *Without Criteria: Kant, Whitehead, Deleuze, and Aesthetics*, Cambridge, MIT Press, 2009.

transient and enduring faces of reality. Shaviro denies this, mainly because he wrongly links relations with becoming, and objects with stasis. But in fact the only way to account for becoming is with a *non*-relational ontology. Contra Deleuze we must champion individual, actual things as the protagonists of philosophy, as Whitehead does in a very non-Deleuzian way. But contra Whitehead we cannot treat these individual things as bundles of relations.

Here I will begin with a brief sketch of how the various camps of the speculative turn are currently arrayed, and will then give a response to some of Shaviro's more detailed objections. His treatment of my work, in some respects quite flattering, goes roughly as follows: first, object-oriented philosophy has made important contributions to philosophy and to the revival of Whitehead. But second, I misread Whitehead and fall into a weaker position, or at least one that is equally weak despite my supposed tendency to blame Whitehead for faults that I also share in my own right. Yet third and finally, the difference between my position and Whitehead's is portrayed as mostly a difference of aesthetic preference—though even here Shaviro sees Whitehead as a timely patron of the cutting-edge vanguard, while I remain beholden to the sunset hour of aesthetic modernism. Before considering these claims, I would like to address the status of Whitehead in the school still known by the increasingly unloved name of 'continental philosophy'.

1. WHITEHEAD AND CONTINENTAL PHILOSOPHY

Heidegger's *Being and Time* and Whitehead's *Process and Reality* both rank among the masterpieces of twentieth-century philosophy; for my own part, I would rate them as the two greatest books in that category. When considering them as a pair, what is most remarkable is how little mutual influence the legacies of these two major works have had despite their near-perfect simultaneity. Heidegger's famous dedication to *Being and Time* is dated in 1926 and the work was published in 1927. Whitehead delivered *Process and Reality* as the Gifford Lectures during 1927-28 and published the book version in 1929. Yet not only did these two great philosophers apparently have no influence on each other: it is difficult even to imagine a conversation between them, whether in the late 1920's or indeed at any point in their lives. It is a wonderfully perverse confirmation of Whitehead's thesis (borrowed openly from Einstein) that contemporary realities do not affect one another.

Now, Heidegger is clearly the central figure in recent continental philosophy. But for many years Whitehead had no discernible influence on that tradition at all, except as the target of occasional passing sneers. And even when that influence did belatedly arrive, it arose from those quarters of continental thought where sympathy for Heidegger approaches the minimum. In Deleuze's *The Fold*[2] there are the famous positive references to Whitehead, but not in a way that links him with Heidegger. It was Isabelle Stengers in Belgium who did much of the legwork in bringing Whitehead into contact with Deleuze. Her allegiance to Whitehead was echoed (in a far less Deleuzian way) by Latour, who is a great heir of Whitehead despite preserving little of the terminology of *Process and Reality*. In 2009 Shaviro himself joined the ranks of significant continental readers of Whitehead, with the publication of his *Without Criteria*. Although Heidegger receives only five tangential references in Shaviro's book, he plays

---

2. Gilles Deleuze, *The Fold: Leibniz and the Baroque*, trans. T. Conley, Minneapolis, University of Minnesota Press, 1993.

a major role in the structure of that book, whose wonderful premise is the question: 'What if Whitehead, *instead of Heidegger*, had set the agenda for postmodern thought?'[3] But although this thought experiment is fresh and surprising, the disjunction it proposes between the two thinkers merely ratifies existing fact. For an even more surprising book might have asked the following question: 'What if *both Whitehead and Heidegger* had *simultaneously* set the agenda for postmodern thought?' There have been occasional efforts by scholars to link the two figures, if fewer such efforts than expected. But it is safe to say that my own object-oriented position is the first attempt at constructive systematic philosophy that might be called both Heideggerian and Whiteheadian à la fois. The withdrawal of objects from all presence is the 'Heidegger' side of my model, while the enforced breakup of the human-world monopoly is the 'Whitehead' side. The combination is obviously unusual. Philosophers inspired by Heidegger (such as Jacques Derrida) generally tell us much about the failures of presence, but nothing about those inanimate relations that occur in the absence of all sentient observers. And philosophers inspired by Whitehead (such as Latour) have much to say about relations, but are generally allergic to the notion of a hidden reality concealed from all presence. The combination of these two normally incompatible features is perhaps the most distinctive feature of my position.

Shaviro would presumably agree with this self-assessment. The Heideggerian aspects of my position are glaringly obvious, however dubious in the eyes of orthodox Heideggerians. And though Shaviro finds abundant fault with my interpretation of Whitehead, he also says that 'Harman helps us to understand Whitehead in a new way', and correctly notes that the shared focus on individual entities 'unites Whitehead with Harman's object-oriented approach, *as opposed* to other varieties of speculative realism'.[4] The point of saying this is that Shaviro's critique of my reading of Whitehead can largely be seen as a rejection of the Heideggerian flavour of that reading. My vacuum-sealed objects veiled from all relation do not impress Shaviro, who sees them as a ticket to ontological stasis: '[Whitehead] also has a sense of the cosmic irony of transition and transience; and this is something that I do not find in Harman'. On this basis Shaviro presents a different alliance that would leave me rather isolated: 'even as Whitehead's actualism links him to Harman, so his insistence on process and becoming—which is to say, on relations—links him to Deleuze and to Grant'. But here we find Shaviro's most unfortunate philosophical assumption: his view that relations must be associated with *change*.

Before addressing this point in the next section, I want to say briefly why Shaviro is wrong to make the increasingly typical link between Whitehead and Deleuze. The protagonist of Whitehead's philosophy is the 'actual entity' or concrete individual. As Whitehead puts it: '"Actual entities"—also termed "actual occasions"—are the final real things of which the world is made up. There is no going behind actual entities to find anything more real. They differ among themselves: God is an actual entity,

---

3. Shaviro, *Without Criteria*, p. ix, my emphasis.

4. Emphasis added. The latter point is most definitely true. Of the four original Speculative Realists, Grant's position is probably the most compatible with my own, but even Grant (whose starting point is not individual entities, to say the least) could hardly be called a Whiteheadian. And it would merely be ridiculous to call Brassier or Meillassoux an heir of Whitehead in any respect. It is the strong Whiteheadian flavor, no less than the phenomenological one, that differentiates my position from those of the other Speculative Realists.

and so is the most trivial puff of existence in far-off empty space'.[5] The reason they can be called 'occasions' is because 'the notion of an unchanging subject of change is completely abandoned'. An entity is not a durable substance undergoing accidental adventures in time and space: instead, 'actual entities "perpetually perish"'. They do not lie behind their accidents, qualities, and relations like dormant substrata, but are 'devoid of all indetermination'.[6] Actual entities are fully deployed in every instant and then instantly perish, attaining 'objective immortality' not by persisting over time (impossible for Whitehead) but by giving way to closely related yet *new* actual entities. In *Prince of Networks*[7] I showed that the same holds for Latour.

We can say that for both Whitehead and Latour the 'ontological principle' holds good: the reason for anything that happens or exists must be found in the constitution of some definite actual entity. In grammatically simplified terms, we could say that the ontological principle means that individual entities are the core of reality. The following is a true statement: 'For Whitehead, individual entities lie at the core of reality'. And so is this: 'For Latour, individual entities lie at the core of reality'. But if we plug in the names of other supposed allies of Whitehead in his supposed philosophy of process and becoming, we quickly arrive at falsehoods. Here is one example: 'For Deleuze, individual entities are the core of reality'. This can hardly be said with a straight face. The following example is perhaps even worse: 'For Bergson, individual entities are the core of reality'. Quite the contrary, since Whitehead's actual entity is always characterized by a definite 'satisfaction' or specific state of affairs, whereas Bergson forbids breaking reality into discrete, identifiable, momentary states. Here is another glaring falsehood: 'For Gilbert Simondon, individual entities lie at the core of reality'. While Whitehead and Latour see entities or actors as the root of everything that happens, Simondon finds it instead in the 'pre-individual', and severely criticizes those who focus on individuals for their 'hylemorphic' tendencies. We can bring this topic to a close with another falsehood, this time about a living thinker: 'For Manuel DeLanda, individual entities lie at the core of reality'. For in DeLanda's case there is always a topological invariant deeper than any actualized individual, and this is why the ontological principle is false in his case as well. A final falsehood would be this: 'For Iain Hamilton Grant, individual entities lie at the core of reality', whose falsity needs no proof for anyone who has read even a few pages of Grant.

What we are faced with here is not some vast alliance of philosophers of becoming, but rather with two groups of recent thinkers separated by a profound internal gulf: those who take individual entities as primary and those who view them as derivative. This is a more basic rift than that between the supposed philosophies of stasis and becoming—a false opposition used by Shaviro to pit both Whitehead and Deleuze against my position. You can say what you like about Whitehead and Latour being interested in process and history. But the real point for them is that all such process is produced by the work of individual entities—a claim that would merely be nonsense for Deleuze, Bergson, Simondon, DeLanda, and Grant. And whereas this latter group would also view it as nonsense to consider time as a series of discrete cinematic instants, such a concept is not at all ridiculous for the philosophy of *occasions* found in both Whitehead and Latour. Their shared commitment to the fully deployed and ut-

5. Alfred North Whitehead, *Process and Reality*, New York, Free Press, 1978, p. 18.

6. Whitehead, *Process and Reality*, p. 29.

7. Graham Harman, *Prince of Networks: Bruno Latour and Metaphysics*, Melbourne, re.press, 2009.

terly concrete state of specific entities even *requires* such a model of time. Time is a 'perpetual perishing' for Whitehead, but not really for Bergson, who recognizes nothing so highly determinate that its lifespan could be confined to a single instant. For Bergson, nothing is stable enough to perish in the first place. Having made this point, I will turn to some of Shaviro's more specific complaints.

2. RELATIONS, BECOMING, AND AESTHETICS

According to Shaviro, there are at least three weaknesses with my position when compared with Whitehead's: my philosophy denies relations, denies process, and remains trapped within a modernist aesthetics of the sublime. The first two points actually reduce to the same one in Shaviro's account, since he views relations and process as one and the same. True enough, Shaviro is correct to say that 'Whitehead's key term *prehension* [i.e. relation] can be defined as any process—causal, perceptual, or of another nature entirely—in which an entity grasps, registers the presence of, responds to, or is affected by, another entity'. But by unintentional sleight of hand, Shaviro then reverts to the everyday dictionary meaning of 'process' in English, which refers to a change elapsing over time, although Whitehead's 'process' as just defined entails nothing of the sort. The fact that Whitehead (or Latour) defines entities in terms of their relations in no way implies that their theories of time are incompatible with the existence of discrete cinematic instants. In fact, the exact opposite is the case.

The major difference between my position on the one hand and Whitehead's and Latour's on the other is that objects for me must be considered apart from all of their relations (and apart from their accidents, qualities, and moments as well—but let's keep things simple for now). This *does not* mean that I think objects never enter into relations; the whole purpose of my philosophy is to show how relations happen, despite their apparent impossibility. My point is simply that objects are somehow deeper than their relations, and cannot be dissolved into them. One of the reasons for my saying so is that if an object could be identified completely with its current relations, then there is no reason that anything would ever change. Every object would be exhausted by its current dealings with all other things; actuality would contain no surplus, and thus would be perfectly determinate in its relations. As I see it, this is the major price paid by the ontologies of Whitehead and Latour. If you deny that an object is something lurking beneath its current state of affairs, then you end up with a position that cannot adequately explain change; you will have an occasionalist theory of isolated, discrete instants. This is not to say that Whitehead and Latour say nothing about change: of course they do, since every philosopher must. But change for them is something produced after the fact, by the work of individual entities. The exact opposite is true for such thinkers as Bergson and Deleuze, for whom becoming is what is primarily real, and discrete individual entities are derivative of this more primal flux or flow. This position merely has the opposite problem, since it cannot explain how such a primary becoming could ever be broken up into independent zones or districts, let alone full-blown individuals. Hence it is by no means stupid to think of the world as made of isolated instants of time, since this is no worse a position than its opposite, and in many respects is even superior.

Shaviro cites me correctly as complaining that Whitehead's 'relational theory is too reminiscent of a house of mirrors'. When entities are made of nothing more than their perception of other entities, and these in turn made up of further entities, then 'the hot potato is passed on down the line, and we never each any reality that would be able to anchor the various perceptions of it'. Those words were published in 2007, and I would still endorse them today. Perspectives are perspectives on and by *something*, and if an actual entity has no reality over and above its perspectives, it will be nothing. My criticism is that Whitehead dissolves his actual entities into prehensions, with nothing left over. Shaviro counters that I am '[not] sufficiently attentive to the dual-aspect nature of Whitehead's ontology', meaning that 'Harman skips over the dimension of *privacy* in Whitehead's account of objects'. For Whitehead treats every entity as a 'concrescence' or culminating satisfaction that is felt by it alone, and hence 'Whitehead is indeed sensitive to the hidden inner life of things that so preoccupies Harman'. But though Whitehead certainly believes he is accounting sufficiently for privacy, this is not at all the case. At any given moment there are countless actual entities in the cosmos, and it is obvious that a dog, the moon, the sea, and a pencil will all have different relations to the other entities in the world. The question is not whether Whitehead sees and asserts this (he does both), but whether the principles of his ontology sufficiently support it. For if the privacy of the moon at this instant is to be distinguished from its 'public' prehension of other actual entities, we still need to know in what this privacy of the moon consists. And what we find is that the private reality of the moon is nothing more than a bundle of prehensions in its own right. There are no residual substances lying beneath prehensions, since Whitehead could only dismiss such substances as 'vacuous actualities'. As he puts it early in *Process and Reality*: 'The analysis of an actual entity into "prehensions" is that mode of analysis which exhibits the most concrete elements in the nature of actual entities'. In other words, to speak of actual entities in terms of anything but their prehensions is a mere abstraction; the entities themselves are concrescences, or systems of prehensions. The same goes for Shaviro's 'privacy' of the moon. It is true that the moon in this instant is something more than its current prehensions, but only as a concrescence of prehensions from the immediate past.[8] A thing must exist in order to prehend, but we find that for Whitehead this existence consists in nothing more than a previous set of prehensions. And this is a house of mirrors indeed, because there is no point or moment at which an actual entity is distinct from its relations with others. Recall that actual entities perpetually perish for Whitehead. Let's concede that the moon at Instant 5 is a 'private' reality distinct from its 'public' prehensions of other entities in that moment, and that this concrescence gives rise to the successor of the moon at Instant 6. But what exactly is this privacy of the moon at Instant 5? It is nothing but the concrescence of moon and prehensions in the previous moment, Instant 4. And so it goes backwards forever, and we never actually find a reality distinct from its relations. Shaviro's supposed difference between the private and public faces of the 'dual-aspect ontology' is really just a reflection of one set of relations passing to its successor.

At this point Shaviro claims that I fall into hypocrisy. For 'although he criticizes Whitehead for reducing existence to an infinite regress of relations, Harman himself gives us instead an infinite regress of substances'. Though I do not remember using the phrase 'infinite regress' when referring to Whitehead's house of mirrors, it is possible that I did so. But whether or not I used the same terms in both cases, the two sit-

---

8. An object as large as the moon is technically a 'society' for Whitehead rather than an 'actual entity'. But I generally find that this distinction fails in his works, and thus take the liberty of referring to the moon as an actual entity.

uations are completely different. The first is a very grave problem indeed: a 'pyramid scheme' of ontology. In financial pyramid schemes, no wealth exists independently of the scheme, but must always be provided by the next set of investors. In Whitehead's reverse-order version of the pyramid scheme, the supposed private reality of an entity apart from its prehensions turns out to be made only of a previous set of prehensions. In other words, reality never appears at any point in the chain. By contrast, in the second case my proposed infinite regress of objects is financially harmless, even if rather strange. If we say that a tree is made of certain pieces, that these are made of other pieces, and so on ad infinitum, there is actually no difficulty. For it is not a problem to say that the tree is real, that its pieces are real, that the pieces of those pieces are real, or any other such statement. Reality must not be confused with *ultimacy*. To say that the tree is made of pieces *is not* to pass the buck of reality to those pieces in the way that a relational house of mirrors passes the buck from one relation to the next to the next. If Whitehead argues impossibly for a hot potato of reality that can never be found anywhere, I argue for an infinitely descending chain of cold potatoes. If we use the phrase 'infinite regress' to describe both, then this is little more than an intellectual pun, since the two cases are completely different, even opposite.

Shaviro's next important critique is directed against my view that in a fully relational ontology nothing can ever change. As I present it, if a thing is fully exhausted or deployed in its current relations, with nothing held in reserve, then there is no reason that any current situation of the world would ever change. A thing would already be exactly and only what it is. No principle of movement could be found in the world. This is largely the same as Aristotle's critique of the Megarians in *Metaphysics* IX.[9] The Megarians believed only in actuality, not potentiality. There is no such thing as a house-builder who is not building a house: a person is a house-builder only when actually building. Among other difficulties, this theory would imply that there is no difference between an expert house-builder who now happens to be sleeping and a true ignoramus of construction projects, which seems puzzling. Even worse, it gives no explanation of how a person could ever pass from not building a house to building one. Each person, each entity, would be nothing more than what they are here and now. Latour embraces this situation by denying potentiality outright, and in *Prince of Networks* I argued that this leads him to the Megarian impasse of being unable to explain change at all. Whitehead by contrast recognizes the need for potentiality, but unlike Aristotle he removes potential from the individual entities and places them in the 'eternal objects' (more about these in a moment). And recently Latour has also seen that there is a problem with fully articulated *networks,* and thus has sometimes appealed to a vast and formless 'plasma' lying beneath all networks as the explanation for how they change.[10]

Shaviro is unimpressed by my basically Aristotelian critique of Whitehead. 'The problem [for Whitehead] is not how to get something new and different from an impoverished list of already-expressed properties; it is rather how to narrow down [...] the "boundless wealth" of possibilities that already exist'. And further: 'novelty arises, not from some pre-existing reserve, but from an act of positive decision [...]' and hence 'there is no need to appeal to vast reserves of hidden qualities'. He links this no-

9. Aristotle, *Metaphysics*, trans. J. Sachs, Santa Fe, Green Lion Press, 2002.

10. See especially Bruno Latour, *Reassembling the Social: An Introduction to Actor-Network Theory*, Oxford, Oxford University Press, 2005, p. 50, n. 48.

tion of the rich plenitude of possible properties to the idea of a continuum: 'Whitehead sees the universe as a finely articulated plenum. There is no undifferentiated magma of being; even a volcano is a fully determinate entity. But there is also no gap to bridge between one such entity and another'. But this all rests on Shaviro's conflation of two completely different aspects of Whitehead's philosophy: actual entities and eternal objects. Against Shaviro we could cite the following words of Whitehead: 'This mistake consists in the confusion of mere potentiality with actuality. Continuity concerns what is potential; whereas actuality is incurably atomic'. And further: 'this misapprehension is promoted by the neglect of the principle that, so far as physical relations are concerned, contemporary events happen in *causal* independence of each other'.[11] If it were really true as Shaviro holds that the world is 'a finely articulated plenum' then there would be no causal independence of contemporary events, since everything would in some sense already be in contact despite the ill-defined 'fine articulations' invoked by Shaviro (in the style of the 'heterogeneous yet continuous' reality adored by Bergson and DeLanda). If the world itself were a plenum, Whitehead could also never have said that 'actuality is incurably atomic'. The truth is that Whitehead sets up a dualistic ontology. On one side there is actuality, made up of fully articulated and exhaustively deployed actual entities, stripped of all residue of internal potential for change. But on the other side are the eternal objects, which Whitehead hesitates only slightly in linking with the Platonic forms,[12] much though this horrifies Deleuzians. These eternal objects are the qualities that need not ingress into any particular actual entity, but which might ingress into any. If I see two objects as being the exact same shade of blue, it is the same eternal object that ingresses into both. And it is the eternal objects, not the actual entities, that are a plenum of fine gradations without gaps, as well as being the source of all potentiality for change. In other words, the supposed 'boundless wealth of possibilities' invoked by Shaviro is not to be found in the actual entities. These have no potential. They simply are what they are; their story is already over, since they are always in the act of perishing as soon as they are born. In fact it is not I but Whitehead who appeals to 'vast reserves of hidden qualities'; he simply places those qualities outside any individual thing. As for actual entities themselves, they are incurably atomic and happen in causal independence of each other.

Shaviro then proceeds to the related false claims that 'for Harman, the qualities of an entity somehow already pre-exist; for Whitehead, these qualities are generated on the fly' and that 'relations are too various [...] to be reducible to Harman's characterizations of them as reductive, external determinations'. But it is actually *Whitehead* who thinks that qualities pre-exist: he calls them 'eternal', after all, and links them with the Platonic forms. No new *qualities* can ever be produced for Whitehead, for all his reputation as a philosopher of novelty: what is produced in his view is simply new constellations of actual entities, prehended according to pre-existing eternal objects. And as for Shaviro's beloved 'variety' of relations, they are admittedly quite various, but this point is not in dispute. The point is that if an entity is reduced to its relations (as Whitehead does) then that entity itself cannot be the home of any potentiality. This need to locate possibility outside all actual individuals is the reason that Whitehead must appeal to a continuum of eternal objects outside all entities, and why Latour toys now and then with a plasma stationed beneath or outside all networks of actors.

---

11. Whitehead, *Process and Reality*, p. 61.

12. Whitehead, *Process and Reality*, p. 44.

Shaviro adds that despite my dislike of such terms as 'potential' and 'virtual', my own preferred model is really no different:

> All this is well and good, except that I fail to see why Harman's own doctrine of hidden properties should not be subject to the same critique. How can one make a claim for the actuality, here and now, of properties that are unmanifested, withdrawn from all relation, and irreducible to simple presence? Such properties are unquestionably *real*; but they are precisely not *actual*. But such a formulation—real, without being actual—is also how Whitehead defines the potentiality of the future, and how Deleuze defines the virtual.

The problem arises when Shaviro says that 'such properties are unquestionably *real*; but they are precisely not *actual*'. What I would say instead is that they are both real and actual—they are simply not *relational*. The mistake of Shaviro and many others is to assume that the actual must be defined by its relations. This needs a brief explanation. Despite my debt to Aristotle, I agree with Latour that 'potentiality' is a bad concept. It allows us to borrow the future achievements of an entity in advance, without specifying where and how this potential is inscribed in the actual. (And notice further that the work of potentiality is so often ascribed to formless *matter*, as if that solved anything.) With Latour I hold that there is nothing but actuality, and with Whitehead I hold that actuality is incurably atomic, composed of discrete individual entities. Potentiality is merely 'potential for a future *relation*', when we really only ought to be talking about actuality. Thus I endorse the model of a non-relational actuality, devoid of potential, but containing reserves for change insofar as it is withheld from relations. So why then do I not drop the term 'actuality' and instead speak with Deleuze, DeLanda, and others of *virtuality*? For two reasons: First, theories of virtuality never seem to do justice to Whitehead's 'incurably atomic' character of reality (and this is why Whitehead is not a philosopher of the virtual). Virtual philosophers always attempt to say that the virtual is a sort of quasi-plenum that does not contain gaps, even while somehow magically avoiding fusion into a cosmic lump of molten slag. Second, insofar as singularities are admitted to exist in the virtual realm, they never bear any resemblance to my 'objects', which are genuine individuals and simply withdrawn from all relations. Consider DeLanda's virtual realm, for instance, which is made up of attractors, invariant topological structures, or genera such as 'vertebrate', not of anything resembling concrete individuals.

All of this leads to the broader problem of becoming vs. stasis, which Shaviro wrongly identifies with that of relation vs. non-relation. In the following passage he glimpses the heart of the issue but lets it slip away: 'even as Whitehead's actualism links him to Harman, so his insistence on process and becoming—which is to say, on relations—links him to Deleuze and Grant'. I have stated repeatedly that Whitehead's philosophy is guided by the ontological principle, which entails 'the description of the universe as a solidarity of many actual entities'.[13] For all the various merits of Deleuze and Grant, they obviously do not describe the universe as a solidarity of many actual entities. As I have argued elsewhere in this volume,[14] both Deleuze and Grant proceed by the method of *undermining* actual entities. An even more important problem is revealed in some of Shaviro's passing phrases, such as 'becoming—which is to say [...] relations'. I have already suggested that there is nothing inherently transient about relations. If we imagine an ontology of isolated, cinematic frames of time, we will find re-

---

13. Whitehead, *Process and Reality*, p. 40.
14. Graham Harman, 'On the Undermining of Objects: Bruno, Grant, and Radical Philosophy'.

lations even there. An instantaneous tree or butterfly already has relations; it is not the passage of becoming that first provides them. In fact, I contend that becoming happens only by way of some non-relational reality. An object needs to form a *new* connection in order to change, and this entails that an object must disengage from its current state and somehow make contact with something with which it was not previously in direct contact. My entire philosophical position, in fact, is designed to explain how such happenings are possible. Hence it is false when Shaviro claims that my rejection of Whitehead's 'perpetual perishing' of entities implies stasis. Quite the contrary. For Whitehead, after all, *nothing* can change. An entity can only be exactly what it is and then give way to other entities that are a bit different, which then perish in favour of further entities that quickly perish in turn. There is no change whatsoever in such a philosophy, but only an endless series of frozen statues, which give the illusion of continuous alteration as we flip through them as if through those novelty card decks that allow children to watch moving cartoons. In short, I do not see how my denial that entities last for only a moment strips me of 'a sense of cosmic irony of transition and transience [...] something that [Shaviro does] not find in Harman'. After all, my philosophy of objects allows perfectly well for the 'cosmic irony' of Rome crumbling beneath the gaze of Gibbon, and the 'transition and transience' of President Kennedy dying amidst the tears of a nation. Whitehead's model, by contrast, grants these incidents no more 'cosmic irony' than the act of combing my hair, moving a piece of paper from left to right, or even standing motionless, since here too a 'perpetual perishing' can already be found. In ontological terms, all major and minor changes are on the same footing for Whitehead, and it seems clear to me that in some ways this makes him less attuned to the irony and tragedy of change than any philosopher ever born. If all moments become any-moment-whatever, then no change is of more significance than any other.

Hence it is quite strange that Shaviro holds that 'Harman tends to underestimate the importance of change over the course of time', that my 'ontology is too static' to make sense of relations, or that I 'show little interest' in 'both transience and futurity'. Shaviro seems to think that either (a) entities last only for the flash of an instant, or (b) they persist in static, unchanging eternity. The truth between these two extremes appears nowhere in his critique, even though that is exactly where my position is located. Under my model of reality, objects can be melted in furnaces; they can be tightened in a vice and reduced to splinters; they can rust, grow old, or crumble with age; pets and grandparents can die before our eyes; Santorini can be destroyed by a volcano; Aquileia can be sacked and razed by the marauding Huns; Germanicus can be poisoned; rock stars can die of heroin overdoses; protons can be destroyed by cosmic rays; marriages can disintegrate; philosophical movements can break into recriminating factions; comets can be drawn to the sun and vaporized. All of these things can happen for Whitehead too, but they pose no greater tragic fascination for his ontology than the trivial motions of a grain of dust. *Everything* is a perpetual perishing for Whitehead—and when everything changes, nothing does. Whiteheads offers a series of statuesque instants, accompanied by vague supplementary phrases such as 'creative advance' to imply that somehow, in some way, one instant gives way to the next. By contrast, object-oriented ontology (OOO) is the true philosophy of becoming and events. By holding something in reserve from their current relations, my objects are prepared to enter new ones. By contrast it is Whitehead who is the true philosopher of stasis, despite the confusing distraction that he offers us trillions of static instants in a row instead of just one.

Shaviro's unjust suspicion of the object-oriented model is visible elsewhere as well. After praising my statement that two objects entering into relation create something that did not exist before, he claims that 'Harman seems to backtrack from this concession'. Why? For the following reason:

> [Harman] describes this new relation as yet another vacuum-sealed object, and [...] therefore concludes that objects can only enter in the 'molten interiors' of other objects. Harman strikingly asserts that 'the interior of an object, its molten core, becomes the sole subject matter for philosophy'. But this is to affirm the actuality of the volcano only at the price of isolating it from the world, and reducing its dynamism to a sort of sterile display— which is all that it can be, in the absence of its direct effects on other entities.

Shaviro seems to hold that if objects are withheld from other objects, they are stripped of all dynamism, though in fact such withholding is what makes all dynamism possible. My claim that any genuine relation between two objects forms a new vacuum-sealed object is quite harmless when viewed in terms of my ontology. To give an example, all it means is that if car-parts combine to form a new real entity called 'car', then this car is a new reality not exhausted by any possible uses of it. The parts remain in contact on the interior of that new object. True enough, this contact might indeed be called 'a sterile display', since nothing automatically results from it. But the point is that it need not always remain sterile. Things *can* and *sometimes do* happen in the midst of this sterile relation. The alternative to Whitehead's perpetual perishing is not permanent stasis, but something more like Stephen Jay Gould's 'punctuated equilibrium'. Experientially, this is quite clear to all of us. We return dozens of times to the same faculty gathering with nothing of note ever happening—but then one day we have a conversation or meet a person who changes our lives. Dangerous chemicals sit side by side in a warehouse with nothing happening—but then one day an interaction is triggered and they explode. This model of contiguous entities in 'sterile display', but punctuated once in awhile by dramatic events, strikes me as a more adequate account of change than the *truly* sterile proclamation that everything is constantly perishing all the time. Becoming does occur: but in sudden jumps and jolts, not through a meaningless accretion of any-instants-whatever that float away in the canal of fluxions.

'To sum up', Shaviro says, 'I find Harman's critique of Whitehead unconvincing'. Evidently so. But in fact his ultimate verdict is really rather mild. It is this: 'The difference between Whitehead and Harman is best understood, I think, as a difference between the aesthetics of the beautiful and the aesthetics of the sublime'. And while this final critique is not so painful, it does put me in a less appealing basket of figures than Whitehead himself:

> Twentieth century aesthetics tended overwhelmingly to favor the sublime, and to regard the beautiful as inconsequential and archaic at best, and positively odious at worst. Whitehead was working very much against the grain of his own time, in his peculiar celebration of beauty. Harman's aesthetics of allure, on the other hand, fits very well into what is now an extended modernist tradition.

It is a skilful piece of rhetoric, and I do not mean this dismissively. Nor will Shaviro take this badly, since he is already familiar with my view that rhetoric is not just devious ornamentation used to sex up good, honest argument. Instead, I see rhetoric as the art of the background—as already argued by both Aristotle (enthymemes) and Marshall McLuhan ('the medium is the message'). Over time the myth has taken root that only 'arguments' are of any cognitive value in philosophy, and that all else is nothing but fuzzy non sequitur, vile manipulation, cloudy emotion, or cloying poetry. But that is not the case: it is not true that we are presented with a rank of arguments, examine them carefully one by one, and then choose the best argument. Instead, we are receptive or resistant to specific arguments in advance because of a vague, general sense of what the truth *ought* to look like. No atheist will be as receptive to a proof for the existence of God as to a proof for his non-existence, even if both proofs are equally weak. More generally, we all have an unstated private vision of what good philosophical progress *looks like*, and what sounds retrograde by contrast. That does not mean that such gut hunches are beyond all critical feedback. It just means that they are extremely powerful, and often difficult to articulate in convincing argumentative terms.

It is in this sense that Shaviro's point on aesthetics can be called a skillful piece of rhetoric. For it suggests the following, in a manner powerful enough to convince some readers: 'In the end, there are mostly aesthetic differences between Whitehead and Harman. But Harman's is one of the sublime. And that's fine, but it's old hat. Kant was writing about that more than two centuries ago, and it is was followed by aesthetic modernism, which has now pretty much shot its wad. In a sense, then, Harman is living in the past, while Whitehead is better positioned to react to the emerging realities of contemporary life'. In closing I want to point to a few problems with this vision. First, it is by no means clear that aesthetic modernism hinges on the sublime. Shaviro is of course a fine scholar of literature, and must have a more detailed theory about this point than can be gathered from his brief concluding remarks in 'The Actual Volcano'. But I would have to ask him: in what sense is the whole of aesthetic modernism governed by the sublime? Is this true of Gertrude Stein? e.e. cummings? Jackson Pollock? Marcel Duchamp? Van Gogh? Anton Webern? Was James Joyce a novelist of the sublime? These examples are not remotely convincing to me; if anything, twentienth-century modernism seems *insufficiently* interested in the sublime. It would have made more sense if Shaviro had argued that the sublime links my position with the *Romantic* tradition, not with modernism as a whole.

But along with questioning the link between sublimity and modernism, I would also like to challenge Shaviro's identification of my concept of allure with the sublime. Thankfully, he is at least correct in his description of the concept:

> [Harman's 'allure'] is the attraction of something that has retreated into its own depths. An object is alluring when it does not just display particular qualities, but also insinuates the existence of something deeper, something hidden and inaccessible, something that cannot actually be displayed. Allure is properly a sublime experience, because it stretches the observer to the limits of its power, or where its apprehensions break down. To be allured is to be beckoned into a realm that cannot ever be reached.

This is well put. And true enough, there is some link here with the concept of the sublime. But a spirit of fair-minded comparison also requires that contrasts be mentioned no less than similarities, and Shaviro misses at least two major differences between allure and the sublime. First, the sublime is a theory about *human* experience of the world, while allure for me seeps down even into the heart of inanimate matter. Indeed, I have suggested at times that causation itself has the structure of allure (though this formulation is insufficiently precise, and will be refined in coming works). Shaviro has a tendency, especially in *Without Criteria*, to downplay the significance of Kant's imprisonment within the human-world coupling, and hence to link Kant somewhat implausibly with Whitehead (a thinker who takes great pleasure in appealing to the seventeenth century rather than to Kant). In the present context it is I rather than Whitehead who is forced by Shaviro into unwanted brotherhood with Kant, and precisely on the question of the sublime. For in no sense does Kant's theory apply the sublime to anything beyond the human-world relation. The sublime has nothing to do with cotton burning fire when no humans are watching, whereas allure does. Second, in the aesthetics of the sublime the sublime is generally treated as *one*. The roaring of the sea and a tornado are not said to give us two *different* sublimes. And here too allure is different, since for me the allure of each object is concretely different—shaped by the specific subterranean features of a priceless vase, courageous action, or cute little pony. The example of the pony, in particular, shows the difference between allure and the sublime, since even the wildest *aficionado* of horses would surely never call a pony sublime. Shaviro realizes this, since he notes that 'Harman includes comedy as well as tragedy, and cuteness and charm as well as magnificence, within his notion of allure'. But as far as I am aware, the sublime has never been given that sort of multiplicity or scope.

In today's world, Shaviro concludes, 'the aesthetic problem we face is Whitehead's, rather than Harman's. [...] Tomorrow, the future may be different; but today, the future is Whiteheadian'. And such a future looks fairly appealing to me. But if the object-oriented position is to be excluded from that future, then this exclusion needs to be for sounder reasons than its supposed link with passé aesthetic modernism or its non-existent 'philosophy of stasis'. Yet in all fairness, Shaviro does seem willing to let me and my confederates hang around a bit longer: 'Alfred North Whitehead writes that[...] "Philosophy never reverts to its old position after the shock of a new philosopher". In the past several years, such a "new alternative", and such a "shock", have been provided by the group of philosophers [...] known as "speculative realists"'. One can only be grateful for Shaviro's interest.

20

Reflections on Etienne Souriau's
Les différents modes d'existence[1]

Bruno Latour
translated by Stephen Muecke

'There is no ideal existence, the ideal is not a type of existence.'[2]
—Étienne Souriau

If we have never been modern, then what history are we supposed to inherit? For twenty years or so, I have been interested in the following question: if we have never been modern, then what has happened to us? This question is relevant to history and anthropology, as well as to the philosophy of the period that Whitehead describes with the phrase 'the bifurcation of nature'.[3] This bifurcation begins somewhere between Galileo and Locke and comes to an end, in Whitehead's opinion, with William James. This brief period, which I call 'the modernist parenthesis'—during which we thought we were modern—has three main characteristics: the conviction that the world can be divided into primary and secondary qualities (which can be called 'naturalism'[4]); the ever increased intermingling, in ever larger assemblages, of these same primary and secondary qualities (which can be called 'hybrids'); and lastly, a watertight division between the constantly repeated assertion that the division between primary and secondary qualities must be maintained, and the practical reality which is in fact the exact opposite of this theory (which one could call the 'obscurantism of the Enlightenment').[5]

This all revolves around the anthropological riddle that I think is captured by the phrase attributed to Indians in Western films: 'White man speaks with forked tongue …'. And, sure enough, 'white men' always do the opposite of what they say, because they have defined modernism with a feature that is the exact contrary of what they

---

1. I would like to thank Isabelle Stengers for having led me to Étienne Souriau (and to Whitehead, and to so many authors I would never have approached without her constant tutoring). The book under discussion is Souriau's *Les différents modes d'existence*, originally published by Presses Universitaires de France in 1943 (republished in 2009, also by PUF, with an introduction by Isabelle Stengers and Bruno Latour)..

2. Étienne Souriau, *Les différents modes d'existence*, Paris, Presses Universitaires de France, 1943, p. 157.

3. Alfred North Whitehead, *The Concept of Nature*, Cambridge, Cambridge University Press, 1920.

4. In the sense used by Philippe Descola, *Par delà nature et culture*, Paris, Gallimard, 2005.

5. Bruno Latour, *We Have Never Been Modern*, trans. Catherine Porter, Cambridge, Harvard, 1993.

do. While they insist on the strict separation of objectivity and subjectivity, science and politics, the real world and its representations, they have also worked in the other direction and mixed up humans and non-humans, natural laws and political ones, on such a massive scale that today we find ourselves, after four or five scientific or industrial revolutions, still sitting around discussing the politics of global warming or the ethics of stem-cell research. And yet this increasingly clear contradiction has done nothing to unsettle the certitude that the wave of modernization has swept or will sweep over the world. In the form of postmodernism we encountered only a slight doubt about this: a mere suspicion.

And yet this contradiction belongs not just to the present, since we already see it on one of Galileo's beautiful manuscript pages, dated 19 January 1610;[6] on the top left of this folio manuscript is one of the tinted sketches of the craters of the moon made visible by telescope for the first time, and on the bottom right Cosimo de Medici's horoscope, calculated by Galileo himself. Is Galileo 'still a bit irrational', then? Not at all. He is just like all the other moderns, doing the opposite of what he says: he insists on the importance of the distinction between primary and secondary qualities (which, incidentally, he was almost completely rethinking) while discovering in the very same breath a new way of linking the movement of the universe with universal mobility, and courtly flattery with the precise way to paint projected shadows in perspective,[7] thus producing the very monster that the idea of modernity was supposed to banish to the dark ages.

So, enough said by way of framing philosophical anthropology, to which I was led through many years of exploring the history of science and also what is called *science studies*. If we have never been modern, then what has happened to us? And more importantly, what can we derive from a history comprising the three features I have just described, instead of pretending to inherit just one of them? I want to inherit the *whole* of Galileo's page. I will not be bought off with part of this legacy, by being left just the top half, for instance—Enlightenment history or just the bottom half—the disappointment of noting that Galileo, too, was 'subject to the temptations of the irrational ...'.

So the initial question now becomes: is there an alternative philosophical tradition that allows us to take up European history in a different manner, by relocating the question of science and reason, even while forbidding the bifurcation of nature? If we follow Whitehead's suggestion we should be turning to James, and towards what the latter calls radical empiricism, but which I would rather call the second empiricism.[8] You will recall that as James saw it, the first empiricism would only take elementary sense-data into account. In order to create a synthesis, a human mind was supposed to enter at this point to create the relations that the initial experience could not initially provide. Here we find ourselves in such a 'bifurcated' nature that everything that comes out of experience has to make a choice, so to speak, and either line up on the side of the thing to be known, or on the side of the knowing consciousness, without having the right to lead somewhere or to come from somewhere.[9]

6. Owen Gingerich, *The Book Nobody Read: Chasing the Revolution of Nicolaus Copernicus*, Penguin, New York, 2004, p. 198.

7. Mario Biagioli, *Galileo's Instruments of Credit: Telescopes, Images, Secrecy*, Chicago, University of Chicago Press, 2006; Erwin Panofsky, *Galileo as a Critic of the Arts*, The Hague, Martinus Nijhoff, 1954.

8. Bruno Latour, *What is the Style of Matters of Concern. Two Lectures on Empirical Philosophy*, Van Gorcum, Amsterdam, 2008.

9. Isabelle Stengers, *Penser avec Whitehead: Une libre et sauvage création de concepts*, Paris, Gallimard, 2002.

Now the originality of James, which was clearly recognized by Whitehead, was to attack this situation—but not (as had been done for two centuries) in the name of subjective values, transcendence, or spiritual domains, but quite simply *in the name of experience itself.* It is undignified, says James, to call oneself an empiricist yet to deprive experience of what it makes most directly available: relations. For him it is scandalously inaccurate to limit experiential facts to sensory data, while waiting for a hypothetical mind to produce relations by some mysterious manoeuvre of which the world itself is entirely deprived. Here is the famous passage from the *Principles of Psychology*:

> But from our point of view both Intellectualists and Sensationalists are wrong. If there be such things as feelings at all, then so surely as relations between objects exist in rerum natura, and more surely, do feelings exist to which these relations are known. There is not a conjunction or a preposition, and hardly an adverbial phrase, syntactic form, or inflection of voice, in human speech, that does not express some shading or other of relation which we at some moment actually feel to exist between the larger objects of our thought. If we speak objectively, it is the real relations that appear revealed; if we speak subjectively, it is the stream of consciousness that matches each of them by an inward colouring of its own. In either case the relations are numberless, and no existing language is capable of doing justice to all their shades. We ought to say a feeling of and, a feeling of if, a feeling of but, and a feeling of by, quite as readily as we say a feeling of blue, a feeling of cold. Yet we do not, so inveterate has our habit become of recognizing the substantive parts alone that language almost refuses to lend itself to any other use.[10]

James explains this with typical humour: certainly, the radical empiricist wants *no more* what is given in experience, but he also wants *no less.* Thus, what the first empiricism thought it could impose on common sense is in fact a huge *reduction* of what is accessible to experience: 'You don't have the right', the philosophers seem to be saying, 'to keep the sensation of *red*, and to set aside the sentiment of *if*, or *and* ...'. And the really amazing thing, at which both James and Whitehead always marvelled, was that common sense *accepts* this incredible ruling. For three centuries it remained locked in the position of discerning nothing in experience other than red spots and the tingling of cold, while at the same time scratching its head and trying to understand where all the other stuff it needs in order to live is going to come from. All it can do then is turn towards its sad interiority, which it knows very well to be a total wasteland .... In the other direction, if prepositions are also a part of what we are experimenting with, it is perhaps superfluous to go looking for their place of origin in the solitary human mind—whether collective or individual—and especially in the types of domains towards which they seem to lead us. We know that Whitehead later draws an even more radical conclusion from James's lesson. In the *Concept of Nature* he states quite calmly: 'Natural philosophy should never ask, what is in the mind and what is in nature'. (30) It is 'fraudulent', he says, to drag in the question of knowledge to interfere with the passage of nature.

Radical empiricism wants to put experience (and not the severely amputated experience found among the first empiricists) at the centre of philosophy by posing a question that is both very ancient and very new: if relations (prepositions in particular) are given to us in experience, *where then* are they leading us? Could their deployment allow us a total rephrasing of the question of knowledge? Can the bifurcation of nature be brought to an end? We can put it even more simply: can philosophy be forced

---

10. William James, *Principles of Psychology*, 1. p. 245. This can be found, in a similar form, in numerous passages in William James' *Essays in Radical Empiricism*, Longman Green and Co. New York, 1912.

at long last to count beyond one or two (subject and object) or even three (subject, object, and going beyond subject and object through some dialectical sleight of hand)?

TWO LARGELY FORGOTTEN BOOKS ON DIFFERENT MODES OF EXISTENCE

Now, in the same neighbourhood as the pragmatism of James and the speculative philosophy of Whitehead, there is a tradition that seems to shine direct light on prepositions defined as modes of existence. The term is to be found in a fairly well-known book (though one with scarcely any successors) by Gilbert Simondon, a book that deals specifically with technology.[11] *Du Mode d'existence des objets techniques* is a philosophical work that obviously knows how to count beyond three. Simondon even goes as far as seven, linking his modes of existence in a kind of genealogy—he calls it 'genetic'—which is largely mythical, but which also has the great advantage of not reducing the number of possible solutions to only two or three. For Simondon there is no initial requirement to begin with the division of reality into subject and object positions. One quotation is enough to point to the trail he is trying to blaze:

> Let's assume that technicality is the result of a de-phasing of a unique, central and original mode of being in the world, the magical mode; the phase that balances technicality is the mode of being religious. At the neutral point between technique and religion, there appears a moment where primitive magical unity is doubled up: aesthetic thought. This is not a phase but a permanent reminder of the rupture of the unity of the magical mode and the striving for future unity.[12]

Clearly enough, Simondon has some interest in rehabilitating magic, in making the technical the counterpart of the religious, and later in extracting ethics from the technical, science from religion, and finally philosophy from aesthetics. But quite apart from all of this, it is the very notion of a plurality of modes of existence, each of which must be respected in its own right, that makes his strange intellectual adventure totally original. Although there was no real follow-up (the philosophy of technology continues to see Heidegger's likes and dislikes as profound thought)[13] Simondon grasped the idea that ontological questions could be removed from research on a particular material, a fascination for a particular knowledge, or the obsession with bifurcation, and could instead be put in terms of vectors. For him subject and object, far from being the beginning of thought like two hooks used to suspend a hammock destined for philosophical snoozing, are only the rather belated effects of a real history of modes of existence:

> This de-phasing of the mediation between figural characters and background characters translates the appearance of a distance between man and the world. And mediation itself, instead of being a simple structuration of the universe, takes on a certain density; it becomes objective in the technical and subjective in religion, making the technical object appear to be the primary object and divinity the primary subject, whereas before there was only the unity of the living thing and its milieu: objectivity and subjectivity appear between the living thing and its milieu, between man and the world, at a moment where the world does not yet have a full status as object, and man a complete status as subject.[14]

---

11. Gilbert Simondon, *Du Mode d'existence des objets techniques*, Paris, Aubier, [1958] 1989.

12. Simondon, *Du Mode d'existence des objets techniques*, p. 160.

13. Ustensility [*L'ustensilité*] is precisely the mode of existence the furthest from technicality. See Graham Harman, *Tool-Being: Heidegger and the Metaphysics of Objects*, Chicago, Open Court, 2002.

14. Simondon, *Du Mode d'existence des objets techniques*, p. 168.

Yet Simondon remains a classical thinker, obsessed as he is by original unity and future unity, deducing his modes from each other in a manner somewhat reminiscent of Hegel. Having reached a count of seven, in the end he returns to one .... Multirealism turns out to be nothing more, in the end, than a long detour that brings him back to a philosophy of being, the seventh of the modes he sketched. I would now like to turn to another book, this one completely forgotten, written by a philosopher who did not even enjoy the polite respect accorded to Simondon. With the assistance of this book, we will see if we can really take seriously this business of a prepositional philosophy as an alternative to the first empiricism.[15] When Étienne Souriau published his unique work Les différents modes d'existence in 1943, in the midst of war, he said nothing about geopolitics or the causes of the catastrophic defeat, nor did he attempt to boost the morale of the troops.[16] Instead, with amazing audacity, he tried to explore a metaphysics—one invented completely from scratch by means of a stupendous freedom of expression. His question was that of multirealism: in how many different ways can one say that a being exists? To make this quite ordinary phrase resonate further, one could suggest that Souriau is interested in manners of being, taking the verb 'to be' quite seriously of course, but also retaining the idea of manners, etiquette, protocol—as if following several centuries of bifurcation, the philosopher would finally get around to inventing the polite respectfulness of good manners in one's conduct with others.

PREPOSITIONS AND INSTAURATIONS

In order to understand Souriau's explicit definition of an empirical and systematic inquiry, we should keep two essential notions in mind.[17] The first we already know about, since Souriau explicitly links his project to the passage from James cited above, in which he defines empiricism as a respect for experience as given through prepositions:

> We know how much William James valued, in his description of the stream of consciousness, what he called 'a feeling for *or*, a feeling for *because*'. Here we would be in a world where the *or rather*, or the *because of*, the *for*, and above all the *and then, and thus*, would be true existences .... This would be a sort of grammar of existence, which we would thus decode piece by piece.[18]

The essential point is that the ontology of prepositions immediately takes us away from the all-too-familiar sorts of inquiry in the philosophies of being. Here, the preposition indicates neither an ontological domain, nor a region, territory, sphere, or

---

15. On Souriau I have only been able to find Luce de Vitry-Maubrey, *La pensée cosmologique d'Étienne Souriau*, Paris, Klinsieck, 1974, and in English from the same author, a lively introduction: 'Étienne Souriau's cosmic vision and the coming-into-its-own of the Platonic Other', *Man and World*, no. 18, 1985, pp. 325-345.

16. Étienne Souriau, *Les différents modes d'existence*, Paris, PUF, 1943 (to be republished by PUF with a foreword by Isabelle Stengers and Bruno Latour, followed by 'Le mode d'existence de l'oeuvre à faire' [1956].

17. I have to confess that the present reading of Souriau's book is quite different from the one we offered in the republication of his book. The reason is that here I used Souriau quite freely for my own inquiry on various modes of existence. But when we had to introduce the readers to what Souriau's own philosophy led to, it was a very different affair, and it is Isabelle Stengers's interpretation that should be followed. In this paper what interests me is how to define modes—a question of first degree says Souriau—while in reality, as we show in our introduction, it is really *instauration* that is the topic of the book.

18. Since the book is not available in English, I will quote at length, which will also give the reader an idea of his style. Unless otherwise stated, all the references are from Les différents *modes d'existence*. The italics are Souriau's.

material. The if or the and has no region. But as its name perfectly suggests, the preposition prepares the position that has to be given to what follows, giving the search for meaning a definite inflection that allows one to judge its direction or vector. This is why I quite often use, as a synonym for the mode of existence, the idea borrowed from semiotics of regimes of enunciation.[19] Just like prepositions, regimes of enunciation set up what comes next without impinging in the least on what is actually said. Like a musical score, the regime merely indicates the tonality, the key in which one must prepare to play the next part. So this is not about looking for what is underneath the statements, their condition of possibility, or their foundations, but a thing that is light but also decisive: their mode of existence. It tells us 'what to do next', as Austin would say; his idea of illocutionary force could quite easily be another useful synonym here.[20] Illocutionary force, one will recall, is not about the statement, but tells how one should entertain the felicity conditions so as to avoid category errors, such as mistaking a fictive narrative for a description, or a request for a prohibition. Whether we are concerned with a preposition, a regime of enunciation, a mode of existence, or an illocutionary force, the vector is the same: can one carry out serious research on relations, as one has for so long on sensations, without requiring them immediately to align themselves in one and only one direction leading either towards the object (and thus away from the subject) or towards the subject (and thus away from the object)?

And yet, by utilizing terms drawn from semiotics or linguistics as synonyms for modes of existence (metaphors which Souriau is also inclined to use) I run the risk of derailing the project before it ever gets on track. We are usually in the habit of asking questions either about language or about ontology, a habit that is obviously the consequence of the bifurcation we want to put to an end by learning to count on all fingers instead of just two or three. So we have to add a caveat: not only should we differentiate research on prepositions from research on substances or foundations, but we should also look for a term that allows us to link questions of language to the question of being, and this despite the demand that they be distinguished. This is Souriau's most important innovation in philosophy. He devoted his whole career to it, giving it the wonderful name of *instauration*.[21]

Those who have heard of Souriau tend to think of him an aesthetician. And he is one, true enough, being the main author (along with his daughter) of *Vocabulaire d'esthétique*.[22] Moreover, he did teach this branch of philosophy for quite a long time. But I think this is the wrong way to approach him. Souriau is a metaphysician who always operates on the privileged 'field' (if I may say so) of the reception of the artwork, all the better to grasp his key idea of instauration. How can we come to terms with the 'work to be made' (l'oeuvre à faire) if we avoid the necessary choice between what comes from the artist and what comes from the work? This is what really interests him, rather than aesthetics as such. The question is whether we can apply to this deeply bifurcated domain what Whitehead said about epistemology: 'No question can be clari-

19. Bruno Latour, in *Eloqui de senso. Dialoghi semiotici per Paulo Fabbri. Orizzonti, compiti e dialoghi della semiotica*, P. Basso and L. Corrain (eds.), Milano, Costa & Nolan, 1998, pp. 71-94.

20. J.L. Austin, *How to do Things with Words*, Oxford, Clarendon, 1962, citation in English in original, trans.

21. It is already in the title of Étienne Souriau, *L'instauration philosophique*, Paris, Félix Alcan, 1939, but the clearest version is in a much later paper by Souriau, *Bulletin de la société française de philosophie*, vol. 4, no. 44, 1956 (republished in the 2009 edition of *Les modes d'existence*).

22. Étienne Souriau, *Vocabulaire d'esthétique*, Paris, PUF, 1999.

fied by the fact of introducing a mind that knows', by saying equally, 'There is no aesthetic question that can be clarified by the fact of introducing a subject who will create it …'. In order to understand Souriau's obsession, let's consider one of his numerous descriptions of the creative act[23]:

> A pile of clay on the sculptor's base. An undeniable, total, accomplished, thingy [*réique*] existence.[24] But nothing of the aesthetic being exists. Each hand or thumb pressure, each stroke of the chisel accomplishes the work. Don't look at the chisel, look at the statue. With each act of the demiurge the statue little by little breaks out of its chains. It moves towards existence—towards the existence that will in the end blossom into an existence that is intense, accomplished, and actual. It is only insofar as the mass of earth is destined to be this work that it is a statue. At first only weakly existing via its distant relationship with the final object which gives it its soul, the statue slowly reveals itself, takes shape and comes into existence. First the sculptor is only pushing it into shape, then bit by bit he achieves it with each of the things he decides to do to the clay. When will it be finished? When the convergence is complete, when the physical reality of this material thing comes to correspond with the spiritual reality of the work to be made, and the two coincide perfectly. In its physical existence and its spiritual existence it then communes intimately with itself, each existence being the mirror of the other.[25]

Obviously we would misinterpret Souriau if we took this to be a description of the movement between form and matter, with the ideal of the form moving progressively into reality, a potentiality that would simply become real through the medium of a more-or-less inspired artist.[26] It is rather a case of instauration, a risk taken, a discovery, a total invention:

> But this growing existence is made, we can see, of a double modality that finally comes together, in the unity of a sole being progressively *invented* in the labouring process. Often there is no warning: up to a certain point the finished work is always a novelty, discovery, or surprise. So that's what I was looking for! That's what I was meant to make![27]

What fascinates Souriau about art (and what fascinates me about the laboratory), is the *doing of making* [le *faire faire*], the *making exist*, or in other words the replication and redundancy. It is the artist (or researcher) bouncing off the action and the reception of the work (or the autonomy of the fact). Souriau explains this again in a remarkable book, of which an entire chapter anticipates the one I am discussing here:

> Generally, one can say that to know what a being is, you have to instaure it, even construct it, either directly (happy are those, in this respect, who make things!) or indirectly through representation—up to the point where, lifted to the highest point of its real presence and entirely determined by what it thus becomes, it is manifested in its entire accomplishment, in its own truth.[28]

Instauration and construction are clearly synonyms. But instauration has the distinct advantage of not dragging along all the metaphorical baggage of constructivism—which would in any case be an easy and almost automatic association given that an

---

23. And incidentally, he is also not very interested in contemporary art. His examples come more from philosophical types than from art history.

24. '*Réique*' or 'thingy' is a neologism that we will later learn to call a phenomenon and which bears no relation with reification which is one of the favourite concepts of the 'bifurcators'.

25. Souriau, *Les différents modes d'existence*, p. 42.

26. This is Deleuze's classical distinction between the oppositions potential/real and virtual/actual. It is the latter that interests Souriau, which also explains why Deleuze was interested in him.

27. Souriau, *Les différents modes d'existence*, p. 44.

28. Étienne Souriau, *Avoir une âme*, Lyon, Annales de l'Université de Lyon, 1939.

artwork is so obviously 'constructed' by the artist.[29] To speak of 'instauration' is to pre-pare the mind to engage with the question of modality in quite the opposite way from constructivism. To say, for example, that a fact is 'constructed' is inevitably (and they paid me good money to know this) to designate the knowing subject as the origin of the vector, as in the image of God the potter. But the opposite move, of saying of a work of art that it results from an instauration, is to get oneself ready to see the potter as the one who welcomes, gathers, prepares, explores, and invents the form of the work, just as one discovers or 'invents' a treasure.[30]

But take careful note: despite the dated style, this is by no means a return to the Ideal of Beauty for which the work would be the crucible. In both cases Souriau does not hesitate at all: without activity, without worries, and without craftsmanship there would be no work, no being. Therefore, it is certainly an active modality. The em-phasis falls in a rather different place when it is a question of constructivism versus in-stauration. The constructivist can always sound a bit critical, because behind the des-ignation of 'constructor' one imagines some god capable of creating *ex nihilo*. There is always a certain nihilism in the Potter God: if facts are constructed, then the scien-tist constructs them out of nothing; all they are in themselves is so much mud perme-ated by the divine breath. But if there is an *instauration* by the scholar or artist, then facts as much as works come together, resist, oblige—and their authors, the humans, have to be devoted to them, which of course doesn't mean they act as simple cata-lysts for them.

Apply instauration to the sciences, and all of epistemology changes; apply instau-ration to God, all of theology changes; apply instauration to art, and all of aesthetics changes. What falls aside in all three cases is the idea, which is ultimately preposter-ous, of a spirit at the origin of the action whose consistency is then carried by rico-chet onto a material that has no other maintenance, no other ontological dignity, than what one condescends to give it. The alternative, which is incorrectly called 'realist', is in fact only the ricochet of that ricochet, or a boomerang effect. It favors the work, the fact, the divine, which impose themselves and offer their consistency to a human devoid of any invention.[31] Instauration allows exchanges and gifts that are interesting in other ways, transactions with rather different types of being, in science and religion as well as in art.[32] For Souriau all beings should be on the path of an instauration: the soul as well as God, the artwork as well as the physical thing. No being has substance. If it persists, it is because it is always restored (the two words restoration and instaura-tion have the same Latin etymology). Without a doubt, what is usually called 'reality' is still desperately short on realism.

---

29. We should note, by the way, that architects don't always speak in French of 'constructing' a build-ing, but of *obtaining* [*obtenir*] it ... which proves how much we are not using a vocabulary fine-tuned by late modernism.

30. The French legal term for someone who discovers a treasure is actually the 'inventor' .... French is constructivist by construction!

31. Bruno Latour, *Pandora's Hope. Essays on the Reality of Science Studies*, Cambridge, Harvard University Press, 1999.

32. It is not so distant from the delicate operation allowed for by 'factishes'. Bruno Latour *Petite réflex-ion sur la culte moderne des dieux Faitiches*, Paris, Les Empêcheurs de penser en rond, 1996, and La Décou-verte, 2010; *On the Cult of the Modern Factish Gods*, trans. Catherine Porter, Duke University Press, forth-coming. The whole difficulty with 'realism' comes from interferences between these three domains. Bruno Latour and Peter Weibel (eds.), *Iconoclash. Beyond the Image Wars in Science, Religion and Art*, Cambridge, MIT Press, 2002.

A SYSTEMATIC AND EMPIRICAL INQUIRY ON THE MODES OF EXISTENCE

With the two notions of preposition and instauration, we can now begin to look at what Souriau presents as a systematic inquiry into multi-realism. The key to this project is that he wants to be able to differentiate the modes of being themselves, not just the various different ways of saying something about a given being. The notion of modes is as old as philosophy itself, but up until now one's discursive orientation on the problem was that the modus was a modification of the dictum, which had the special status of remaining precisely the same as itself. In the series of phrases: 'he dances', 'he wants to dance', 'he would really like to be able to dance', 'he would so like to know how to dance', the 'dance' doesn't change despite the sometimes vertiginous encasing of the series of modalizations.[33] At first philosophers used this discursive model for the modalization of being by, for example, varying the degree of existence from potential to actual, but without ever going so far as to modalize whatever it was that went into the act. Predicates might be numerous and they might wander far afield, but they would always come back to nestle in their pigeonholes, in the same old dovecote of substance....

You can see the abyss that separates his project from the tried and true procedure of collecting categories, which goes all the way back to Aristotle: if in effect there are several ways of saying something about something, you cannot get around the fact that it is always a question of saying. So you remain in the same key, that of categories, which consist precisely of 'speaking publicly about or against something' according to the very etymology of the Greek word cata-agoureuo. In other words, the ancient Thomist expression 'quot modis praedicatio fit, tot modis ens dicitur' does not leave the narrow path of the several ways of saying something of something. Now, multirealism would like to explore rather different modes of existence than the sole action of saying several things about the same being. Its whole aim is that there be several ways of being.[34]

Once Souriau realized, not without considerable modesty, that philosophy has always been asking itself about this very issue of the plurality of modes—in Plotinus, for example—he saw that it was now obliged to confess that it has never really counted beyond one *single* mode. The point is simple: the tradition has been obsessed with the identity of substance ever since Parmenides's challenge. Of course non-being had to be added to being—this began with Plato, and philosophy has defined itself ever since with the addition of one form or another of non-being—but all these add-ons are more like epicycles that never contest the central privilege of substance. Hence Souriau's project of asking whether it is possible to ask the question about multiplicity not by beginning with being *qua* being (*l'être en tant qu'être*), but being *qua* another (*l'être en tant qu'autre*)? This formulation is my own, but it perfectly captures Souriau's intention: 'It is a matter (as the scholastics would say) of aseity or abaliety as if they were two modes of existence: being in and of oneself or being in and of something else'.[35]

So, one can see that research is no longer on the diverse ways that one and the

---

33. 'We have to then assume that the modality attributes another mode of existence to the predicate it modifies', Jacques Fontanille, *Sémiotique du discours*, Limoges, Presses Universitaires de Limoges, 1998, p. 169.

34. The same problem arises with Spinoza, according to Souriau: 'The *esse in alio* should mean not the fact of existing in another manner than that of substance, but the fact of being in its existence. In this proposition, the meaning of the word *in* is the key to all Spinozism, this attempt, not to go beyond, but to annul existential specificities, with an apparatus borrowed entirely from ontic order, is effective only in that order'.

35. Souriau, *Les différents modes d'existence*, p. 35.

same being can be modalized, but on the different ways the being has of altering itself (the verb 'alter' contains all the otherness we need). In a strange passage, in which Souriau wonders at how rarely philosophy has attempted to multiply the modes of existence, he makes an astonishing statement: 'Absolute or relative, this [philosophical] poverty is in any case sufficient reason for conceiving and testing the Other as a mode of existence'. Here everything is defined: can we perhaps try alteration as a mode of subsistence, instead of always going to look for the substance lying beneath the alterations? Souriau's formulation is not so distant from another thinker who has also been swallowed up by tradition. I speak of Gabriel Tarde. As he puts it: 'To exist is to differ; difference, to tell the truth, is in a certain way the substantial side of things, what they have that is both their very own and what they have in common'.[36] But Tarde did not ask himself the question: 'How many different ways are there to differ?', or 'How many distinct ways are there for a given being to alter itself? It was Souriau, and no one else before or since as far as I know, who took up this task in his book of 168 pages, printed on the low-quality paper of wartime. He sums up his project in one long citation:

> A key question we were discussing earlier, a crucial point where the biggest problems converge: what beings will we take on with our spirit? Should knowledge sacrifice entire populations of beings to Truth, striking out their existential positivity? Or in order to admit them, should it double or triple the world?
>
> And a practical question: there are such huge consequences for each of us to know if the beings one suggests or has suggested, dreams or desires—to know if they exist in the world of dreams or in reality. And if in reality, then in what reality? What kind of reality is being set up to receive them, is present to sustain them, or is absent to annihilate them? Or, if one mistakenly considers just one single genre, if one's thought lies fallow and one's life is left unable to inherit these vast and rich existential possibilities.
>
> On the other hand, there is a more significantly limited question. It is found, we can see, in whether the word 'exist' has the same meaning in all the different ways it is used; whether the different modes of existence that different philosophies have been able to highlight and distinguish deserve fully and equally the name of existence.
>
> And finally a positive question, and one of the most important as to its consequences into which philosophy can enter. It presents itself in the form of precise propositions that can be subjected to methodical critique. Let's make an inventory of the principles in these propositions, in the history of human thought. Let's draw up tables and find out what kind of critique they answer to. This is quite a task.[37]

It is now understandable why this has nothing to do with the questions put forth by those who cling to a bifurcated nature. They cannot even imagine that there are several modes, because everything one encounters is already caught in a pincer movement between subject and object, and then drawn and quartered into primary and secondary qualities. But we can also see that there might be good reasons not to embark on such a project. To gather up the multiplicity of categories was never going to get us very far as long as being *qua being* would be the guarantee of unity. But if you want to 'cash in' being *qua another*—well, then you have to be prepared for some rather different alterations, and without any guarantee of unification.

It's just that the world becomes so vast, if there is more than one type of existence. And if it is true that we have not exhausted it once we have covered everything within

---

36. Gabriel Tarde, *Monadologie et sociologie*, Paris, Les empêcheurs de penser en rond, 1999 [1895].

37. Souriau, *Les différents modes d'existence*, pp. 9-10.

just one of these modes (physical or psychical existence, for example); if it is true that to understand it one needs to encompass it with all that its meanings and values entails; if it is true that at each of its points, the intersection of a determinate network of constitutive relations (such as spatio-temporal ones), then like a portal opening onto anther world, we need to open up a very new grouping of determinations of being: atemporal, non-spatial, subjective perhaps, or qualitative, or virtual, or transcendental. And we must include those in which existence is only grasped as a fleeting and almost unutterable experience, or which demand an enormous intellectual effort to understand what it is they are not yet made of, and which only a more extensive thinking could embrace. If it is even true that it would be necessary to understand the universe in all its complexity, not only to make thought capable of all the multicoloured rays of existence, but of a new white light, a white light which unified them all in the brightness of a superexistence which surpasses all these modes without subverting their reality.[38]

We would find this vast world all the more astonishing if, in discovering it, we had to count an indefinite number of alterations. Giordano Bruno horrified the Holy Inquisition with his hypothesis of a plurality of inhabited worlds, but we are dealing here with an *infinity* of worlds within a sole mode. What would we do if we had to entertain the hypothesis of an infinity of modes?!

Yet Souriau is not just in favour of multiplicity for its own sake; this would run the risk of coming back to the same thing: the undifferentiated. This is the problem of atomists or Leibnizians who keep finding more and more atoms or monads, but end by considering them as the producers of assemblages that may be different, but which are composed of exactly the same ingredients.[39] Once again the multiple ends up in the one; the counting goes no further. Research into multirealism, into what James calls the 'multiverse', should therefore make sure to escape both unity and multiplicity. This is why Souriau has the good sense to announce that his inquiry has nothing systematic or a priori about it. Sure, he wants to 'sketch the outlines', but he also wants to avoid like the plague the mad idea of deducing modes of existence. 'A false lead', he calls it, or 'deceptive clarity'.

This is why we have to resist vigorously the temptation to explain or to deduce these ear-marked modes of existence. We should beware of the fascination for the dialectical. No doubt it would be easy, with a little ingeniousness, to improvise a dialectics of existence, painted in broad brushstrokes, in order to prove that there can only be just those modes of existence; and that they engender each other in a certain order. But by doing this we would subvert everything that might be important about the assertions being made here.[40]

We can see that Souriau would have been critical of Simondon's 'genetic' derivation of modes necessarily deriving from unity, found in the citations I made above. Even though the term may seem strange when applied to such a speculative philoso-

---

38. Souriau, *Les différents modes d'existence*, p. 5.

39. 'There are on the other hand philosophers who, far from proposing the unity of being, recognize a multitude of real and substantial beings. But the more these become a multitude, the more their existential status becomes similar and unique. Look at the atomists, whether Epicurus or Gassendi, or even in certain respects, Leibnitz. They divide a being to the limits of division. But these beings are similar, based for example on antitypicality or indivisibility, and, in spite of the apparent richness and complexity, the gathering of these innumerable beings is evidence in the end of only one kind of existence, for which the atom is presented as the prime and unique type'. Souriau, *Les différents modes d'existence*, p. 3.

40. Souriau, *Les différents modes d'existence*, p. 119.

pher as Souriau, the research he is proposing is certainly empirical, at least in the sense that it depends on 'fieldwork'.

It is not a matter of following the ontic beyond its attachments to phenomena and experience, all the way through to the void; this is the error of so many metaphysicians (and no doubt of phenomenology too). It is a matter of discovering or inventing (as in inventing a treasure) positive modes of existence, coming to meet us with their palm fronds, to greet our hopes and aspirations, or our problematic speculations, in order to gather them in and comfort them. All other research is a metaphysical famine.[41]

For someone like me who has always alternated between books of empirical field work and of speculation, there is some comfort in the idea (again so close to James) of following experience, but following it all the way to the end. The empiricists of the first order are like those who are so obsessed with the idea of building a bridge between two banks of a river, that no one considers perhaps *going down* the river to see what is there, or *following it upward* to discover its source. And yet, it is not ridiculous to entertain the idea that the *lateral* exploration of this river is just as integral a part of experiencing the river as the will to cross it. Above all else, Souriau's solution draws us away from all transcendental philosophies. In fact, the proof that the discovery of modes depends on experience is the very fact that such discovery remains fortuitous and contingent:

> They have to be taken as they are: as arbitrary. Consider it thus: a primitive painter might find coloured earths in his palette that give him his base and technical range: yellow ochre, red ochre, green clay, soot-black ....
>
> From an initial contingency, [the artist] perhaps necessarily draws out his modulations on the *other* in relation to this given, but the initial given is arbitrary. It is the same with modes. *The modes of being are contingent.* Each one taken as the original can call for such and such another in dialectical fashion. But each one taken in turn as original is arbitrary.[42]

To put this in my own words, let's say that these modes correspond to certain contrasts that European history has led us to believe we could settle on, and which we have turned into the most cherished values we hold, to the point that we would die if they were taken away from us: 'There where your treasure lies, there lies also your heart'. Here perhaps is a way of already defining the legacy I was speaking of at the beginning: inheriting a bit of modernism does not just mean that we inherit a little bit of Reason, but also what I call contrasts. Contingent? Yes. Arbitrary? Yes. But in any case these contrasts are historical, and they have made us into what we are now so attached to. Let me simply recall Souriau's quotation: 'positive modes of existence, coming to meet us with their palm fronds, to greet our hopes and aspirations or our problematic speculations in order to gather them in and comfort them'. One can understand why Souriau added: 'All other research is a metaphysical famine'. With Souriau ontology becomes historical, and the project of philosophical anthropology that I pursue entertains the idea, which one must admit is pretty crazy, of a 'European ontology'.[43] It is as if we said to other cultures (though we know they are no longer cultures), if we said to the 'former others': 'Here are the contrasts we thought we were able to figure out in the course of our history, which was supposed to be the history of modernization. Now it's your turn, you others, to define the contrasts that you have extracted, and the values to which you are so attached that without them you too would die'.

---

41. Souriau, *Les différents modes d'existence*, p. 92.

42. Souriau, *Les différents modes d'existence*, p. 120.

43. Thanks are due to Bruno Karsenti for this summation of my project.

At no point does Souriau speak of anthropology. He is not preparing us for a planetary diplomacy in which Europe is henceforth weakened (should one say ' henceforth *wiser*'?) after having closed the modernist parenthesis, and which is asking itself what history it has really inherited and how to make this heritage useful. But he has fixed our attention on the main point: the modes of existence are all of equal dignity. This pluralism and egalitarianism are enough to put him in the great anthropological tradition: 'Let us therefore reject any temptation to structure or hierarchize the modes by explaining them dialectically. You will always fail to know existence in itself if you deprive it of the arbitrariness that is one of its absolutes'.[44]

Before moving to the main part of Souriau's book—the description of the different modes—let me summarize the conditions of his inquiry. Philosophy has only ever generated differences by taking being *qua* being as a starting point (the Copernican revolution never happened: philosophy is still geocentric). It should be possible to adopt another position by 'trying out the Other'. This inquiry into the different ways of altering certainly has something empirical about it; in any case, it should stick as closely as possible to what is given in experience (in the full sense of the second empiricism, not the limited version of the first). The number of modes is greater than two, so we will ignore the subject/object dualism and call an end to the bifurcation of nature, not through going *beyond* it (that would only be counting to three) but through erasing it in a thousand different ways. The modes are of equal dignity; they are the product of a specific history—I would add of an historical anthropology—which does not aim to define a general ontology.

A FIRST MODE THAT HAS ALWAYS BEEN TREATED UNFAIRLY: THE PHENOMENON

The inquiry can now begin. Each mode will define itself through its own way of differing and obtaining being *by way of the other*. From mode to mode, therefore, the comparison should not be conducted by passing through the intermediary of a substance common to all, of which each would be a mere variation. Instead, each should be granted the capacity to produce, in its own way, the assemblage of ontological categories that are its very own. The situation is as if each mode possessed a specific *pattern* (in the sense that this word [*patron*] is used in the clothing trade), an ontological pattern that cannot be applied to other modes, or applied only by bringing about distortions, folds, discomforts, and innumerable category mistakes. To take an industrial metaphor borrowed from the procedure of 'putting out a tender', it is somewhat as if each mode of existence were following a specific set of terms of reference to which it had to conform.

The first mode taken up by Souriau may seem surprising. It is the *phenomenon*. Let us recall that Souriau (like James and Whitehead) is not operating within a bifurcated nature. What he calls the phenomenon has nothing to do with matter, with the plain empty object to be used as a picture hook for the sickly subjectivity of the modernists. No, he just wants to capture the phenomenon *independently* of the badly formulated notion of matter, and without immediately getting entangled in the eternal question of how much belongs to the object and how much to the subject. The experience offered by the phenomenon is quite different from what the first empiricists called sensation: 'In sensations the phenomenal character is very intense, but very mixed. Sen-

---

44. Souriau, *Les différents modes d'existence*, p. 121.

sations are in a sense the rowdy side of phenomena'.[45] What will define this mode is its 'obviousness'. (Souriau, who loves little-used words drawn from the mediaeval tradition, here says *patuité*).

> It is presence, flash, a given that can't be repelled. It is, and it announces itself for what it is. One can no doubt work to exorcize it of this irritating quality of presence by itself. One can denounce it as tenuous, labile, and fleeting. Would that not simply be admitting that one is unsettled by a rare existence in one sole mode?[46]

The phenomenon is unsettling! The phenomenon is 'rare' because it ultimately appears in one mode, one sole mode. Here as for Whitehead (and for the same reason) we find ourselves, for the first time since the first empiricism, in the presence of a *vector* (Souriau actually says 'vection'). We are finally delivered from the question of knowledge, and above all from the obligation of the phenomenon only being a respondent to intentionality. This phenomenon is the polar opposite of that found in phenomenology. With wicked humour, Souriau cites Kipling: 'In the end phenomenology is where one is least likely to find the phenomenon. *The darkest place is under the lamp,* as Kim says'.[47] As in Whitehead, Souriau's phenomenon is no longer caught in a pincer movement between what might be behind it (primary qualities) and what might be ahead of it (secondary ones).

> Let me insist that, in order to grasp phenomenal existence, one must above all avoid seeing the phenomenon as a phenomenon *of* something or *for* someone. That would be the aspect the phenomenon takes on when one has first begun to consider existence via some other modality, then meets up with it after the fact, such as in its role as manifestation. [...] One can really only conceive of it in its own existential tenor when one feels it to be supporting and presenting to itself alone what it is relying on and consolidating in, with and by it. And it is on this basis that it appears as a model and standard of existence.[48]

The phenomenon is not a phenomenon of anything else. What is attached to the phenomenon does not lead either to the stand holding it up, nor to the mind that has it in sight: it has better things to do; it is a grown-up; it is self-sufficient; it can quite simply lead to other phenomena, going all the way along a chain which gives itself permission to ignore absolutely any bifurcation into primary or secondary qualities. This is a kind of chain the first empiricism never told us anything about. Here then is the phenomenon well and truly freed of its Procrustean bed; it can reply to its own terms of reference, it can finally lead to relations one could call lateral as opposed to only transversal relations. One can see from this how misleading it would be to always take as an example some blunt object, like a pebble, in order to demonstrate in a somewhat macho fashion that one is a 'realist' (As we know, philosophers love talking about pebbles, yet without ever getting down and dirty among the geological multiplicities of stones and gem-stones.)[49]

> It is true that one clogs the mind right up by saying: the phenomenon implies ... it is called ... it presupposes .... So it doesn't exist independently of what surrounds it, teaches it, relates to it; and without which it would not exist. This is the effect of a mongrel kind of thinking, where one is looking for the phenomenon and the same time as inappropriately

45. Souriau, *Les différents modes d'existence*, p. 55.

46. Souriau, *Les différents modes d'existence*, p. 49.

47. Souriau, *Les différents modes d'existence*, p. 54. Citation in English in original.

48. Souriau, *Les différents modes d'existence*, p. 54.

49. See, *a contrario*, the last chapter of Ian Hacking, *The Social Construction of What?*, Cambridge, Harvard University Press, 1999.

moving away from it. It is presupposed that the phenomenon is dissected. Bloodless, surrounded by its organs. If you take it in its living form, you see that the phenomenon sets up in its phenomenal state its intentions and other real factors. Its vectors of appetition, its tendances towards the other, can be followed as they fan out, to the extent that they remain of the same material as the phenomenon.[50]

James would have loved these 'vectors of appetition', which direct our attention towards a phenomenal material no longer warped by the need to come to terms with the human mind, or to lean on the solid foundations of primary qualities. This is what von Uexküll tried to render in a different register with his distinction between the Umwelt (environment) and the surroundings of a living being. One might say that phenomena define an Umwelt where each establishes its own relations, whereas surroundings come from a rather different mode of existence.[51] But the 'natural philosophers' who since the nineteenth century have ceaselessly protested against the confusion of knowledge and phenomena never really succeeded in getting back to the original bifurcation, because they never had the power to deploy modes of existence that were sufficiently differentiated in quantity and quality. Above all, it is not clear by what sleight of hand two different modes of existence were confused in the notion of matter. From here Souriau does not appeal to a higher, organicist, vitalist knowledge. Like Whitehead, he quite simply asks that we respect the particular path that phenomena take. For him this is the best way to respect what is most particular about a second mode of existence: that of objective knowledge.

A SECOND MODE THAT WAS NEVER CLEARLY RECOGNIZED: THE THING

Souriau's second mode (this ordering is mine, not his own) goes by the name of *thing*. How, it might be asked, can we distinguish the patuity of the phenomenon from the thing? Does this not amount to designating the same object twice? But these objections have meaning only from the point of view of a bifurcated nature, a nature which under the name of matter has already confused two operations which are not linked by anything: the movement by which a phenomenon subsists, and another quite distinct movement by which we manage to remotely transport something which is not near us without losing it. Let us recall the celebrated phrase from Whitehead:

> Thus matter represents the refusal to think away spatial and temporal characteristics and to arrive at the bare concept of an individual entity. It is this refusal which has caused the muddle of importing the mere procedure of thought into the fact of nature. The entity, bared of all characteristics except those of space and time, has acquired a physical status as the ultimate texture of nature; so that the course of nature is conceived as being merely the fortunes of matter in its adventure through space.[52]

Although he knows Whitehead's work and mentions him a number of times in his book, Souriau never cites this particular phrase. But he introduces the same distinction, and follows with surgical precision the dotted line that finally allows the separation of the Siamese twins to which history gave birth in such monstrous form.[53] The

---

50. Souriau, *Les différents modes d'existence*, p. 54.

51. Jakob von Uexküll, *Mondes animaux et monde humain. Théorie de la signification*, Paris, Gonthier, 1965.

52. Whitehead, *The Concept of Nature*, p. 20.

53. And, just as with Whitehead, it is precisely through respect for the demands of reason that he does not allow himself to confuse the transport of knowledge and the movements of the known thing. It is probably their shared indifference towards politics which allows them to no longer confuse 'matters of fact' and

terms of reference for the two modes of existence are not therefore the same: what counts in the second is the possibility of maintaining continuity despite distance, a question that does not differentiate the first mode because distance has no meaning for it. In the second mode, it is as if two opposite conditions have to be held in opposition: to traverse the abyss that separates us from the object with continual transformations, but on the other pole to hold something constant—the future 'thing' in fact—via these transformations. Hence I call these 'immutable mobiles', corresponding to the invention of the 'thing' in Souriau:[54]

> The thing is defined and constituted through its identity as it passes through different apparitions. There is an agreement on the systematic character of the thing, and on the fact that what characterizes it specifically is that it remains numerically one through its appearances as noetic utilizations.[55]

Phenomena do not form systems, but things do. Phenomena are not the appearance of anything, but things are. The two can be linked, certainly, but they must not be confused:

> A technique of making-things-appear, as it dialectically informs both the experience of the physician and the mystic, is an art of branching any ontic onto the phenomenon. The manifest phenomenon thus becomes manifestation, the appearance apparition. But it is by sharing it with what supports it and in providing it with its unequivocal patuity. Such is the generosity of the phenomenon.[56]

A word of caution: we are engaged here in a project very different from that of 'being as being'; continuity of time or space—what semioticians call *anaphor*—is not surreptitiously guaranteed by the subterranean presence of a substance or self-identity. 'We try out the Other' and consequently, every continuity or subsistence that is gained must be *paid* for in genuine currency. If no alteration, then no being. This is what I designate as *being qua another*. For each mode of existence, we have to specify how many mediations are expended in order for it to gain its *isotopy*, its continuity in being. Now, if the phenomenon prolongs itself and shores itself up with its own type of 'fanning out', the 'thing' on the other hand can in no way take advantage of this type of vehicle. It must remain 'numerically one' through its 'multiple appearances'. So it needs a rather different type of go-between in order to remain similar to itself despite the succession of changes it must undergo to get from one point to another. We can think here of the cascade of operations necessary to do a brain scan, for instance, or of the number of steps gone through by a probe on Mars in order to send back signals as it sifts through the dust. Our brain is not maintained in existence in the same way as the successive passes of a scanner. Mars does not persist like a signal. Obvious, you might say? All right, then: let's draw out the consequences. Even though Souriau doesn't talk much about the sciences, he has the idea of treating knowledge as its own mode of existence.

> Let us take note that [thought] cannot be conceived as the product or result of the activity of a psychic being, itself conceived in a thingy fashion distinct from the assemblage of the thing, and which might be a subject or a carrier [*suppôt*] separated from thought. The

---

what I call 'matters of concern'.

54. This is an idea I have been working on ever since Bruno Latour 'Drawing Things Together', in Mike Lynch and Steve Woolgar *Representation in Scientific Practice*, Cambridge, MIT Press, 1990, right through Bruno Latour, *What is the Style of Matters of Concern. Two Lectures on Empirical Philosophy*, Amsterdam, Van Gorcum, 2008.

55. Souriau, *Les différents modes d'existence*, p. 60.

56. Souriau, *Les différents modes d'existence*, pp. 113-114.

latter has no other carrier that the thing itself which it assembles and probes. In some ways it is purely impersonal, and one has to prevent oneself from seeing it as it is working in its thingly status by putting everything we understand and know from elsewhere into thought. As this status implies, [this thought] is purely and simply liaison and communication. It is also a consciousness, but this is understood only as a phenomenal glow [*luisance phénoménale*][…]. In the final analysis, it is above all systematic cohesion, liaison, which is here essential and constitutive for the role of thought. One should even ask if it is not rather a *factor* more than an *effect* of thought.[57]

The passage is difficult, but the innovation is clear: the known object and the knowing subject do not *pre-exist* this mode of existence. There is not first a thought which then turns towards an object in order to draw out its form. There is first of all 'liaison and communication'. There is 'systematic cohesion', which he called in the previous citation the capacity to 'remain numerically one'. And only as a later consequence is there a particular capacity for thought, which he boldly designates as 'a phenomenal glow'…. Objective thought only glows when things pass by it!

In other words, there is no objective thought in the first place: there are objects, or rather things, whose circulation in the world will give objective thoughts to souls—another mode to be described shortly—which will find themselves amplified and deepened by this offer. To put it bluntly, a thinker begins to think objectively because s/he is traversed, bombarded by things, which are not in any way phenomena themselves, but an original mode of existence that adds itself to other modes without being able to reduce them to its own terms of reference. Thought 'has no other carrier than the thing itself which it assembles and feels'. This is why Souriau reverses the usual relationship by making objective thought the 'effect' and not the 'factor' in this mode of weird displacement of immutable mobiles invented in the seventeenth century. But instead of seeing a unique mode of existence here, philosophy of the modernist type thought it needed to split nature in two by inventing matter, that badly formed amalgamation of phenomena and things—and essentially for political reasons.[58]

Now we can understand why classical philosophy was never able to cash in on multiplicity except by attaching multiple predicates to one and the same substance: it never realized that it could grasp knowledge as a *separate* mode of existence. This is why Aristotle, for instance, can think that he is speaking of different categories of being, even though he never escapes from a single mode of interrogation: knowledge. It is also why Kant, when setting up his own table of categories centuries later, does not imagine for a moment that they are all in the same 'key', such that this multiplicity of approaches leads to the one never-ending *libido sciendi*. The epistemic mode of existence has always been exaggerated, always made out to be the one mode that asks of all beings nothing other than how they can be *known*. This does not take away from its dignity, originality, or truth, but does deny its right to take originality, dignity, or truth away from the other modes of existence.

Souriau fully and truly undoes the Kantian amalgam. We no longer have a knowing mind on one side and on the other side things-in-themselves, with a point of encounter in the middle where phenomena are generated (as in the First Critique). We have phenomena (as defined above) that finally circulate with their own 'patuity' with-

---

57. Souriau, *Les différents modes d'existence*, p. 69.

58. My little addition to the history of bifurcation, following Isabelle Stengers, *The Invention of Modern Science*, trans. Daniel W. Smith, Minneapolis, University of Minnesota Press, 2000, and more recently *La Vierge et le neutrino: les scientifiques dans la tourmente* , Paris, Les Empêcheurs de penser en rond, 2005.

out having to be accountable to a support behind them or an intentional subject in front of them. In addition, we also have things whose circulation, if I might say so, leaves (by way of traces) objective thoughts in the heads of those who are capable of allowing themselves to be towed along by them .... It is this fundamental innovation of Souriau—objective knowledge is a mode of existence, it does not reduce phenomena—that no doubt inspired Deleuze and Guattari in their definition of 'functives', probably picking up on Souriau's inversion of 'effect' and 'factor'.[59]

THE THIRD MODE OF EXISTENCE: THE SOUL, AND THE DANGER OF HAVING IT

It is meant euphemistically when I say that Souriau undoes Kantianism. In fact, he does not stop once he has liberated things-in-themselves—these are now *phenomena*—and obtained objective thought by allowing thought to circulate as a *bona fide* mode of existence. If we stopped at this point, we would have certainly unscrambled a badly trussed-up amalgamation of matter, but we would still only be counting as high as the number two .... But from here, Souriau will be able to profit from the opening created as the Kantian ship goes down, to encourage philosophy to add other modes of existence, by specifying other terms of reference and proposing other patterns, other 'envelopes' for many other types of beings.

At one time such a project would have been systematically forbidden. If something had to be added to matter, one would turn towards mind, since there was no other option. And if this mind could really attribute values, dimensions and qualities to the world, these would be cut off from any access to beings themselves—just as one says of a country that it might have, seek, or lack 'access to the sea'. Kant illustrates this deficiency perfectly: he stacks up his critiques one behind the other in order to add morality, religion, aesthetics, politics, but without in the end being able to accord them some kind of being. Being finds itself entirely monopolized by knowledge. And in any case knowledge is absolutely incapable of understanding how it can happen to understand the world objectively: a world which it is finally obliged to relinquish to the uninhabited desert of 'things-in-themselves'! What amazes those who know just how much we have never been modern is how this Kantian disaster was able to pass for good sense.... And indeed, Locke was already seen as the philosopher of common sense!

But Souriau does not have these kinds of limitations. All the modes of existence have an equal ontological dignity for him; none can monopolize being while referring to subjectivity as the one and only way out. And certainly not this one mode among others, which is capable of leaving objective knowledge in its slip-stream. With Souriau we will finally be able to count to three, and even higher: philosophical celebrations after centuries of forced abstinence! Unlike Whitehead whose speculative effort addressed itself essentially to cosmology, what really interests Souriau are the third and fourth modes. The particular pattern for the third is to produce what he is calling by the very old-fashioned name of 'souls'. A word of caution: this has so little to do with immortal substances that Souriau defines them pointedly 'as what can be lost, what can be instaured'. 'Having a soul' is no sinecure: it is a task to be accomplished, and it

59. Gilles Deleuze and Felix Guattari, *What is Philosophy?*, New York, Columbia University Press, 1996. Recall that 'fonctifs', are, along with 'concepts' and 'percepts' the three modes recognized by Deleuze and Guattari. For a less philosophical treatment of this idea, see Bruno Latour, 'A Textbook Case Revisited. Knowledge as a Mode of Existence', in E. Hackett, O. Amsterdamska, M. Lynch and J. Wacjman *The Handbook of Science and Technology Studies*, 3rd ed., Cambridge, MIT Press, 2007.

can be botched and most often is. But nor are these souls (which one might or might not have) the stuff that comes to inhabit the interiority of a subject. By the way, this is the subject that we just learnt does not have any knowledge either, since it is the effect rather than the cause of it!

The complete originality of the project now begins to unfold: souls too have their own existence, but one should not size up this mode by using the terms of reference belonging to others. Ontological politeness and etiquette now depend on a new respect for other modes of existence.

> If the phrase 'reified status' seems shocking, along with this 'thinginess' inapplicable to the soul, then let's keep the word thinginess [réité] for the special cosmos of physical and practical experience, and speak more generally of an ontic mode of existence which will be suitable for psychisms as well as for reisms.[60] All we can be sure about with regard to psychisms, in asserting here this same mode of existence, is that they have a sort of monumentality, which makes a law of permanence and identity from their organisation and their form. Far from compromising life in seeing it like this, it would be missed in other ways, for instance by not seeing the soul as architectonic, as an harmonious system which can be modified, enlarged, sometimes subverted or wounded … in a word, a being.[61]

It was previously impossible, under bifurcated nature, to ask the question about the monumentality or even objectivity proper to a soul. Even if Souriau acknowledges that the question is 'shocking', one can still not doubt that souls thus defined compel our recognition. Or rather, it was precisely in modernist times that one had such doubts, since any psychism that came on the scene took the form of a subject and not of a monument. It is now possible to define a type of requirement adapted for each mode: what defines psychisms is that they wound you; they can enlarge, diminish, or disappear…. What do we think we know about the world if we decide in advance, *a priori* and with no inquiry whatsoever, that this is 'quite obviously' a matter of unconscious fantasies? Once we are capable of letting phenomena run around the world as they please, could we not 'try out the Other' once more by letting psychisms off the leash? Where would they go if we detached them? Where would their infallible nose for things lead us? Surely not towards subjectivity, anyway.

> What is absurd and gross about thingness is the way it considers the soul as an analogue to something physical and material—especially in its conditions of subsistence. It is no longer permissible, or even adequate, to conceive it according to the ontic model of living things and their conditioning. But it is up to psychology, a psychology that would not fear the ontic (let it be called psychism if one is frightened of words), to spell out the specific conditioning. This would include the plurality of souls, their assemblages, their counterpoints, and all the interpsychics that put them together as a totality, or a cosmos.[62]

Oh dear, if epistemology is so profoundly bogged down in the question of objective knowledge, psychology is even further away from good ontological sense. What daring! To demand that the most modernized of the sciences 'not fear the ontic' … and as if one could speak of the 'cosmos' in relation to souls? Really, this Souriau has gone too far! Yes, far beyond the narrow bounds which require that there be only two modes of existence: one for pebbles and one for the unconscious (or to count to three, the real, the imaginary and the symbolic). So, just as stone-phenomena no

---

60. Actually, in the book Souriau counts what he calls 'psychisms' as another case of 'things' since they too obtain a continuity in space and time through some type of instauration.

61. Souriau, *Les différents modes d'existence*, p. 70.

62. Souriau, *Les différents modes d'existence*, p. 71.

longer resemble stone-things (or either of the two pebbles of the anti-realist polemicist), so too do souls no longer resemble subjectivities. If the soul is not a thing, it is in the first place because things in no way resemble matter, despite the absurd train of thought of those who want to 'solve the mind-body problem'.[63] No, souls have their own envelopes of thinghood, their own definition of anaphor, their own understanding of how to subsist.

> Let us not forget that the status of ontic existence in no way excludes the transitory nature of existence. Its basic ubiquity never presupposes a temporal subsistence that would be continuously guaranteed in a lazy, heavy, or mechanical manner. Rather we constantly observe, especially in the psychic domain, such rapid and flighty instaurations that we scarcely notice them. Thus we are sometimes presented with momentary souls (or they are presented in us), whose rapidity and kaleidoscopic succession contribute to the illusion of a lesser and weaker existence: even though these could have more grandeur and value than those which we instaure with the greatest of ease on a day-to-day basis.[64]

'Souls are presented in us'! I have no idea what experience Souriau is alluding to here—probably delicate scruples about marriage, as one finds in the deliciously quaint anecdotes of his book *Avoir une âme*! But for my part I was shaken to the core by the thinginess of the psychisms that were worked over, manipulated, redirected, deflected, and displaced by Tobie Nathan during the ethnopsychiatric sessions I was privileged to attend.[65] And I can attest to the fact that I was really worried about attributing a given ontology to these beings. For in fact they never stopped joining 'monumentality' with 'their transitory nature', not having any 'continuity', and not being present long enough ever to define a subjectivity or interiority, while at the same time being well and truly real, but in their own way. Yes, there is more than one dwelling place in the kingdom of realism. And each house is built of its own material. How have we been able to live for so long in this state of misery which forces us to construct all dwellings out of pebbles or out of interiority, the former freezingly sterile and the latter without any solidity or monumentality? We can understand that the moderns were only able to survive by doing the exact opposite of what they claimed: by multiplying the very modes they prohibited anyone from tabulating. Is it now possible to draw the map of what they were really capable of building, or rather to provide with an instauration? Has an anthropological philosophy of modernity finally become possible?

A FOURTH MODE: HOW DO FICTIONAL BEINGS EXIST?

For some unknown idiosyncratic reason, Souriau knows nothing about the narrow limits of modernism. He is not especially interested in negativity or consciousness; the question of the subject and the object leaves him cold. Apparently no one told him that philosophy should not count beyond three—and he is in magnificent ignorance of dialectics, in conformance with that French tradition (where does it come from?) running from Bergson to Deleuze.[66] This is why, very calmly and in all innocence, he gets ready to target a fourth mode of existence as different from souls as these were from things, and as those were from phenomena. What, then, are these fictional beings?

---

63. This relation is reworked by Souriau in the surprising form of 'a certain habit of being together' in a clearly plurimodal situation, Souriau, *Les différents modes d'existence*, p. 129.

64. Souriau, *Les différents modes d'existence*, p. 71.

65. Tobie Nathan, *L'influence qui guérit*, Paris, Editions Odile Jacob, 1994

66. Pierre Montebello, *L'autre métaphysique. Essai sur Ravaisson, Tarde, Nietzsche et Bergson*, Paris, Desclée de Brouwer, 2003.

On the other hand there are fragile and inconsistent entities, whose inconsistency makes them so different from bodies that one could hesitate to attribute any manner of existence to them at all. We are not thinking of souls here, but of all those phantoms, chimerae and spirits that are represented in the imagination: fictional beings. Do they have an existential status?[67]

At one time this question had no meaning, since fictions, just like souls, thoughts, and values, were all to be found 'in the subject' and all equally prohibited from opening out onto beings. But Souriau restores to this question all its meaning, from the moment that the aforementioned interiority is found to be dissolved and crossed out (and in no way 'gone beyond') as much as the abovementioned materiality. There is no doubt that fictional beings do not have the same density, continuity, or discontinuity as souls. And yet, can one assert that they do not exist?

> Wouldn't it be quite a nuisance to give them a specific existence, or even a mode of being, both because of their phantom character and their acosmic nature? Basically, fictions are beings from which all controlled and conditioned ontological cosmoses have been driven one after the other. They are united by one common complaint, which nevertheless does not make their whole company a pleromos[68] or a cosmos. Of course, one cannot characterize them essentially by the fact that, by way of representation, they do not correspond to objects or to bodies. This consideration relates to a second-degree problem, which in any case is purely negative. They exist in their own way only if they have a positive reason to exist. And they do.[69]

How could we define their terms of reference? We will see that the inquiry takes a systematic turn and that the picture that needs to be sketched will not be completed in a haphazard fashion. We now know that the continuity of constants is not a general property: on the contrary, it is the requirement of the anaphor that applies to 'things', to 'immutable mobiles', but which puts neither phenomena nor psychisms under any obligation. It would make no sense therefore to define fiction as 'true lies' or 'the suspension of disbelief',[70] which would come back to measuring them by the yardstick of the other modes—or, as would make even less sense, on the basis of the intentions of the receiving subject.[71] There is a thingness specific to fictional beings, an objective isotopy that Souriau defines by the pretty word syndoxic (that is, common doxa). In a certain way, we all share Don Juan, Lucien de Rubempré, Papageno, the Venus de Milo, Madonna, or Friends. This is certainly doxa, but a doxa held enough in common by us that we can recognize these beings as having a monumental form that is specific to them. Our tastes can vary, yet they are concentrated in elements that are shared sufficiently widely so as to sustain a common analysis. Psychisms may be aborted or bungled: fictional beings cannot. They possess more objectivity (if one is permitted to recycle this polysemic term).

> When Napoleon reread Richardson on St. Helena, he carefully constructed Lovelace's annual budget; Hugo, as he was researching Les Misérables, even ran the accounts for ten years of Jean Valjean's life when he was not in the novel. (Think about it: the remote

---

67. Souriau, *Les différents modes d'existence*, p. 74.

68. Pleromos [*plérôme*] is a Plotinian term that designated all the beings assembled in plenitude: another word beloved by Souriau, the philosopher of the architectonic.

69. Souriau, *Les différents modes d'existence*.

70. This phrase in English in the original—trans.

71. See Thomas Pavel's critique, *Fictional Worlds*, Cambridge, Harvard University Press, 1986.

presence[72] of a character in a novel, in relation to the novel. Now that is really an imagi-nation on fire!).[73]

Incidentally, it was in order to grasp this form of syndoxic continuity peculiar to fiction that Greimas (a friend of Souriau) borrowed the expression 'isotopy' from physics.[74] A story can only obtain continuity for its characters through redundancies that have to be extracted from alterity itself, because each page, instant, and situation are different from each other. In a fictional narrative, a fictional cosmos has to be rebuilt. 'In what way can one say that in Don Quixote the episode with the windmills precedes that of the galley-slaves?'[75] In a philosophy of being as other, continuity is never an acquired right, status, or effect of a substratum. Rather, it is always a result that causes one, ap-propriately, to wonder via which intermediary one managed to get there. Parmenides is the one who should draw the substance of isotopy from Heraclitus's river. Now for Souriau, this intermediary has the peculiarity of depending also on the way in which a work is received:

> Therefore, on the one hand this world tends to take on a quite positive syndoctic, social existence. There is, to paraphrase Lewis, 'a universe of literary discourse'. But on its oth-er frontier, this world dissipates and frays at the edges [...] it is precisely to this transito-ry and transitive character that imaginaries owe their particular dialectical situation.[76]

Today, one might say he is talking about '[reader] reception aesthetics'. Perhaps. But that would mean imagining social beings already in place, as it were: beings whose ex-istence could not be in doubt, who would then lend their subjectivity to something that had no solidity in itself. But, like all modes, they have to be welcomed by an instau-ration. And in Souriau's hands the notion of reception takes on a quite different onto-logical dimension:

> Their essential character is always that the size and intensity of our attention or sympathy is the basis of support of their monument, the bulwark on which we elevate them, with-out any other reality conditions than that. In this regard, the things that we would other-wise believe to be positive and substantial, are completely conditional and subordinate, and they have, when one looks closely, only a solicitudinary existence! These are by def-inition precarious existences; they disappear along with the basic phenomenon. So what is missing in them? Ubiquity, consistence, and an ontic and thingly bedding. These mock existences[77] or pseudo-realities are real; but false in that they formally imitate the status of things, without having the proper consistence, or, one could say, the matter.[78]

On the one hand, works of art have syndoxic objectivity. On the other hand, they depend on our *solicitude*. People do not necessarily produce works in the same way that they receive them. But they must guarantee that they do get a welcome, support them—yes, their reception!—because they constitute their 'basis of support'. It is as if works were leaning on us, or would fall over without us: like a Gallic chieftain standing on a shield that no one was carrying .... It is a strange metaphor to describe the con-tours of an envelope so peculiar that it has to include in its set of categories not only its

---

72. English in the original—trans.

73. Souriau, *Les différents modes d'existence*, p.77.

74. In Algirdas Greimas' *Sémantique Structurale*, Paris, PUF, 1968, a curious book of Souriau's is cited: *Les deux cent-mille situations dramatiques*, Paris: Flammarion, 1970.

75. Souriau, *Les différents modes d'existence*, p. 77.

76. Souriau, *Les différents modes d'existence*, pp. 77-78.

77. In English in Souriau—trans.

78. Souriau, *Les différents modes d'existence*, p. 79.

solidity—'it is always the same Don Juan'—but its lack of being—'without anyone to interpret him, Don Juan disappears'.

Psychisms, for their part, need neither this syndoxy nor our solicitude. On the contrary, they grab us, knock us about, destroy and obsess us, and no amount of effort will make them let go and stop attacking us. Yet if you turn off the radio, leave the cinema, or close the book, fictional beings disappear immediately. If they continue to obsess you, it is only because you really want them to. Do we have to assert that the one lot exists and the others not? Not at all, because it has to be said about all beings that they can vary in intensity: 'Before asking, does this exist and in what way, one has to know whether it can respond with a yes or a no, or whether it can exist a little, a lot, passionately, or not at all'.[79] You can see how unjust it would be to call Souriau a mere philosopher of aesthetics, when his fictional beings only occupy a few pages of the book. What is important for him is to compare them as exactly as possible with the *other* modes of existence.

But one can exist by way of the force of the other. There are certain things—poems, symphonies or homelands—that do not possess by their own means an access to existence. People have to devote themselves to their coming into being. And perhaps in this devotion people might, incidentally, find a real existence.[80]

A FIFTH MODE: SPEAK OF GOD IN HIS OWN LANGUAGE, IF YOU DARE

It would take several thick volumes to summarize this little book by Souriau …. But I don't want to let him go without making him sit through a couple of little tests that will allow us to grasp even more clearly the amazing originality of his project. The first test concerns the mode of existence most often associated with the idea of God; the second deals with those situations that blend together several different modes, and which he calls *synaptic*.

Let us recall the phrase cited above: the 'basic ubiquity' of a mode of existence 'never presupposes a temporal subsistence which is lazily, heavily, or mechanically guaranteed, not even in continuity'. If this is true for all modes, it is all the more so for beings 'seized' by the religious mode. Their subsistence, isotopy, or anaphor cannot be obtained 'lazily, heavily or mechanically'. So why talk about God?, someone might object. Either because He is simply there or, at the very least, because our tradition has developed the idea of Him. Let us recall that the modes are not deduced *a priori*; they are not necessary. We find them, as Souriau says, in our 'environs' in the same way that a Palaeolithic painter might grab some 'red ochre' or some charcoal that he finds in his cave where he has made camp. Discovery is arbitrary and contingent, but from that moment on it becomes a part of the contrasts that we will have to make use of in order to sort things out for their rest of our history.

No doubt. But to discern that God too is a mode of existence, isn't this suddenly revealing that Souriau is committing the 'spiritualist' crime? (An accusation that we know is sufficient to put an end to the conversation as well as to his reputation).[81] Yet this accusation cannot gain traction against someone who has just shown that his vis-à-vis, 'materialism', is itself but a more or less confused amalgam of two modes: the phe-

---

79. Souriau, *Les différents modes d'existence*, p. 13.

80. Souriau, *Les différents modes d'existence*, p. 46.

81. Especially because he wrote another book, in the opinion of Stengers his most accomplished: Étienne Souriau, *L'ombre de Dieu*, Paris, PUF, 1955.

nomenon and the thing, and that two types of movement are mixed there, that of the 'passage of nature' and that of the 'immutable mobiles', as we saw earlier. In any case materialism is a particularly hypocritical theology since, as Tarde put is so well, it presupposes a voice coming from Heaven which announces, without mouth or larynx, the (in)famous laws of nature to which phenomena are supposed to bend. How, no one knows. Souriau is no hypocrite, and if there is one thing he is not afraid of, it is doing metaphysics—and, let's not forget, 'trying out the Other'. So if we are to speak of God, let us do it clearly. Or better yet: let's 'speak God'.

We should get a good fix on his project. There is not on the one hand an immanent world down here, lacking souls, mind, and meaning, to which on the other hand any sort of transcendence would have to be added via some sort of bold leap. No, there are plenty of transcendences in Souriau, in any mode you choose, since it is always via the other that being is extracted. Let's leave the phantasm of immanence to those who believe in being *qua* being. As for identity with oneself, even a rock does not have it. Didn't Whitehead teach us that there is a transcendence of rocks also, since they form societies that persist?[82] What is impossible is persistence without change, and this applies to rocks as much as to God. But if everything is changing, it is nonetheless not all changing in the same fashion, extracting the same differences from the other, the same tone of otherness. If it is OK to talk about God, it is with dignity and politeness and therefore not giving him any extra concession than speaking in his language, but also without refusing him the right of pleading in his own name. As a matter of theology the expression might be a shock, but the best way of respecting 'talk of God' is by way of gathering his testimony and accepting that he is fulfilling his own 'set of categories', and not that of his neighbours. Phenomena, things, souls or fictions: none of these can be used to judge God exactly.

> God does not reveal himself in his essence; without which he would be incarnated in phenomena and in the world. He would be of the world. Yet he exceeds it, he distinguishes himself from it: his 'to exist' is developed beside it and outside it. Whether you want to or not, you define this mode of existence. In presupposing it, you set up this existence (albeit problematically) as a definite mode in itself. This is what is strong and ineluctable at the heart of the ontological argument. This is undeniable. It can be expressed in yet another way. One can say: By taking on board the ontic universe of representation, you have taken God on board, because he is part of it. He represents in it the mode of existence peculiar to him and his definite ontic status: a transcendent and even absolute mode. Now it is up to you to prove that he has to be done away with, that this existence is not one, or does not correspond to anything. The burden of proof lies with you.[83]

What? Is this the same old ontological proof coming back again? How can this apologetic invention possibly be of any use to us? How can the recourse to the notion of proof lead to anything but a very poor rationalization? But let's listen to how Souriau rehearses this traditional trope. You will remember the argument as put by the venerable St. Anselm. Either you are thinking about God, and he exists since existence is part of his essence, or you say, 'like a fool', that God doesn't exist, but that is because you are thinking about quite something else, whose idea does not imply its existence. Now, Souriau's clever move is to take up this argument once again: not to prove anything by way of a mode of existence defined elsewhere for 'things', but by way of a special, unique, mode, which in point of fact defines the peculiar mode of existence that

---

82. See Didier Debaise, *Un empirisme spéculatif. Lecture de Procès et Réalité*, Paris, Vrin, 2006.

83. Souriau, *Les différents modes d'existence*, pp. 93-94.

we call God. He is a being who is *sensitive to what one says about him*: a being who appears and disappears according to the way he is spoken of, proclaimed, pronounced, or uttered. So yes, he is one of these special beings who are dependent on the precise conditions of their utterance, including whether the tone that is made to resonate around them is true or false.

> So the ontological argument makes its way not from essence to existence, or from existence to essence, but from one mode of existence to the other [...] namely, to whatever mode of existence that one wishes to assert in the following conclusion: God exists. It is the passage from one mode of existence to another that *constitutes* the argument. In any case it presupposes that a positive answer, in the form of a real, concrete proposition, has been given to this question. What are we talking about when we ask what the divine is? And that some kind of model of it has been uttered, or some sort of glimpse, or conception, or example; that it has in some manner put in play, in movement, in action, in presence; that God has be summoned, has pleaded on his behalf, just as Job had requested him to appear in court. A terrible requirement. The only philosophers who would respond (the only ones to objectify the divine?) are those who dare to make the Word speak: St. Augustine, Malebranche, Pascal. In general, one could say that there is no divine testimony in the universe of human discourse, except in some twenty pages or so of all the Writings of all religions where one has the impression of hearing a God speak of God. And twenty is a lot. Perhaps there are really only five altogether.[84]

A hundred million pages of theology, but just five pages where God himself appears because he has been spoken to *in his language*! Even St. Anselm probably didn't realize that his argument could engender such terrible requirements. How negligible now is the feeble link between predicates and substances! We are talking here about the creation of a battleground, a judicial arena, more violent than the one where Jacob did battle with the angel, and in which the speaker and addressee find themselves convoked by the same absolutely specific mode of existence. 'One must be well aware, the problem [of ontological proof] does not arise except when the subject whose existence one claims has been compared to something. There are so many theological and metaphysical speculations where he makes absolutely no appearance!'[85] This is the Souriau one would accuse of spiritualism? Yet here he is stating that virtually no one has been able to carry the 'burden of proof' and that the majority of the remarks 'on God' or 'by God' are just lamentable category errors, applying to this precise mode of existence patterns cut from the cloth of others. Yes of course, we *lack* or *miss* God, but not because pathetic humans engulfed in the mire of immanence just need to follow believers and finally turn their eyes up to heaven. We miss God in the same way that we *miss* the phenomenon, *miss* knowledge, *miss* the soul, or even *miss* fiction: because we are incapable of recognizing that each mode of existence possesses its own tonality, a key to open its own speech, and that modernism has jumbled its own discoveries to such an extent that it can't even manage to make us inherit its treasures.

If there is one huge blunder in the way that we have inherited the contrasts discovered in the course of European history, theology is no doubt the place to find it. We have to wait for Whitehead and Souriau finally to begin to work out some new ways of speaking respectfully and politely of God.[86] Everything else, if one is to believe the

---

84. Souriau, *Les différents modes d'existence*, pp. 95-96.

85. Souriau, *Les différents modes d'existence*, p. 96.

86. On the originality of Whitehead's God, see the second section of Isabelle Stengers, *Penser avec Whitehead: Une libre et sauvage création de concepts*, Paris, Gallimard, 2002.

Decalogue, is ultimately just a kind of blasphemy: 'Do not take the name of the Lord in vain'. Oh dear, what else do we do, when we run at the mouth, spitting and spewing the unpronounceable? 'To live on God's terms is to bear witness for this God. But be careful also, about which God you bear witness for: he is judging you. You think you are responding for God; but this very God in responding for you, situates you within the scope of your action'.87 What is as rare in ethnography, no less than in theology is work that respects the exact ontological contours of religious beings.

This scarcity can be explained through the difficulty in exactly specifying the conditions of this mode of existence, even though this difficulty is not any greater than those pertaining to phenomena, to things known objectively, to the soul, or to fictions. In this sense God is not particularly irrational, he is simply pitched in another key (but so is a rock, and the same goes for any scientific instrument ...) But Souriau does add one feature: the religious being is sensitive to the word, and produces paradoxically the effect of 'an existence for the self'.88 This is obviously a paradox in a philosophy of 'otherness', and yet: 'Isn't this the way love thinks of them?' And in a note, Souriau adds: 'we are quite willing to believe that true faith is expressed not so much in "God for me", but in "me for God"'. The 'divine as it is objected' (in the sense of objection and not of objectivity), must also need instauration at the end of the day: God no less than an artwork, fiction, or objective knowledge. To say that people 'construct' or 'fabricate' gods therefore has none of the critical incisiveness imagined by those in whose bifurcated world one always has to choose between reality and mediation. The only worthwhile question (in theology as much as in art and science) concerns what it is *good* to fabricate, which then allows us to turn the initial relation on its head and allow the emergence of those beings that we knew we have to welcome in the first place:

> More than ever before, it is not a question of argumentation or speculation: it is the effective realization of certain acts or dialectical moments that would produce a transcendentalization (as it were) more than a transcendence of the divine as it is objected. This is situated entirely, as we can see, in an architectonic transformation of the system, which substitutes the pair in which God depends on man, with another pair made up of semantic elements—but one where, morphologically (to be precise about it) it is henceforth man who depends on God.89

We now see that Souriau's innovation is not one of adding spirituality to matter, as if that were the only opening available. His ideas are coming from somewhere else. On the one hand Souriau makes the modes of existence proliferate, but at the same time he *rarefies* the product in each of the modes. Let us recall: he said that the phenomenon itself is 'rare'. In theology there are only 'five pages' where He has been summoned to appear. The work of art? It can fail. The soul? You mostly run the risk of losing it.... The adherents of a philosophy of being-as-being really had it good! All they had to do was discover the foundation, the substance or the condition of possibility, and from that point on nothing could go wrong; continuity was assured by way of self-identity. When in doubt, just garnish with dialectics: even history, with as much sound and fury as you need, will inevitably lead you in any case to this 'for the self' of the 'in the self' which was already at the beginning and turns up again—heavens be praised!—at the end. But for the philosophers of being *qua* other (where are they? who are they?) histo-

---

87. Souriau, *Les différents modes d'existence*, p. 163.

88. Souriau, *Les différents modes d'existence*, p. 98.

89. Souriau, *Les différents modes d'existence*, pp. 99-100.

ry is not so gracious. It does not have these bolsters, these 'supports' [*suppôts*] as Souriau calls them. It can miss, it can fail, all can be lost. Being is there to be *made*, yes, to be the fragile and provisional result of an instauration.

FROM THE MODAL TO THE PLURI-MODAL

To sum up, we could say that the inquiry into different modes of existence comes down to constructing a type of spectrograph. With such a device the composition of a distant body is depicted via the particular distribution of those traces that make up its unique signature—something astronomers know how to do so well for stars. We cannot try to hide the fact that the 'signatures' obtained by Souriau's spectrometer are also characterized by missing bands.[90] He says nothing about technology that would indicate the presence of Simondon. Also absent is the law. There is nothing on economics, nor on politics, despite (or because of?) the tragic historical situation in which the book was written. A few traces are there, but they are scarcely discernible. And the same goes for morality.[91] And yet, in the last section of the work, Souriau in fact applies himself to the problem of how the modes are enchained. So far, in fact, we have only spoken of the modes of existence that he calls 'ontic' or monomodal, though any situation, any real body or entity is obviously multimodal. To move from the question of taking modes of existence one by one to modes of existence that are enchained with several modes—it is a bit like moving from a piano tuner who tries the notes one by one to the piano player who makes them all resonate in a melody. Now what really surprises Souriau is the way that philosophers continually exaggerate their preferred mode of existence. It is as if they wanted to make music by holding one note continually, or as if they were composing repetitive music. It seems that thinkers never have the necessary politeness for a true multirealism. Once they have sorted out the terms of reference for a particular mode, it will be through it and it alone that they imagine they can evaluate the quality of all the others: which will lead, or course, to a whole cascading series of distortions, category types and category errors. To remind us of the rules for philosophical politeness, Souriau includes an amazing sentence in another book that I have already mentioned:

> One does not have the right to speak philosophically of a being as real if, at the same time as one says that one has found in it a type of direct or intrinsic truth (I mean its way of being in its maximum state of present lucidity), one does not also say on what plane of existence one has, in a manner of speaking, sounded its death knell; in which domain one reached it and broke through.[92]

I will leave it up to the reader to take the trouble of figuring out if there is a single philosopher in existence who has been able to thus delineate his or her hunting ground....

---

90. With Souriau I could say, 'Even though we have not counted the genres of existence on [all] our fingers, we hope not to have left any essentials out', *Les différents modes d'existence*, p. 131. It is always possible that I have missed detecting certain spectra, either because my spectrogram is tuned to a different wavelength, or because the second half of Souriau's book is so elusive that I have to confess to finding it hellishly difficult. See our Introduction to the new edition for a more coherent treatment.

91. 'In truth, we believe we can reason otherwise for good, or for bad, just as for the beautiful or the ugly, the true and the false. In other words, in response to the question, how do they exist, one can say they exist in something else [*en autre chose*], they reside in certain treatments of reality, among which the idea of perfection can be a prime example. Without undertaking this huge problem, let us concede that we can say that they exist in themselves, which merely comes down to recognising that a *morally qualified existence* as a new pure mode of existence, to be added to those which we have already recognised'. *Les différents modes d'existence*, pp. 135-136.

92. Souriau, *Avoir une âme*, p. 22.

In order to avoid this continual exaggeration, to allow the modes to 'keep their distance', to mutually respect their different types of verification, we have to define yet another mode (one of the 'second degree' as he says) and which is defined this time by the movement and the variation or modulation of one mode into another: this is what he calls the *plurimodal*. Only they can make the superimposition of the 'traces' finally 'compossible', and give metaphysics the amplitude that it should have.

It order to completely achieve both the separation of the beings and the innovation of the existential status which is represented by the consideration of sole morphemes,[93] one would have to follow, for example, this imaginative enchainment:

> First imagine a picture where the being is detached from a determined ontic status, by being successively transposed into different modes, at different levels; for example a human personality successively transposed into a physical existence, by way of being a body present in the world of bodies, then into a psychic existence, by way of being a soul among other souls, then into a totally spiritual existence outside of time, etc. [...]. Finally, without worrying about the problem of the correspondence of these beings or their unity (which would happen at the second degree of existence), what if one took these very movements as sole realities. Let us evoke an existential universe where the only beings would be such dynamisms of transitions: deaths, sublimations, spiritualization, births and rebirths, fusions with the One or separations from him or individualization.[94]

As you can see, this is quite a step. Souriau already had the signal audacity of defining several modes of existence, each of which could circulate freely in the world without encroaching on its neighbour. But now it is *variation itself* that has to be considered equivalent to true beings. Alterity alters yet another degree. Difference differs even more differently. At the beginning of this presentation, I cited the sentences where Souriau was linking his project with that of James on prepositions as things we experience directly even though the first kind of empiricism has always denied it. 'Here we would be in a world where the *or rather*, or the *because of*, the *for*, and above all the *and then, and thus*, would be true existences'.[95] Listen now to how Souriau continues that passage:

> The modulations of existence *for*, existence *before*, existence *with*, are just so many types of the general mode of the synaptic. And by this route one can easily cure oneself of the over-importance given in certain philosophies to the famous man-in-the-world; because the man before the world, or even the man against the world (*adversus*: the against as conflict, which strikes and violently hits, which tries to gain the ascendancy in any offensive) are also real. And inversely, there is also the world in the man, the world before the man, the world against the man. The crucial thing is to get the sense that existence in all these modulations is invested neither in the man nor the world, not even in them together, but in this for, in this against where the fact of a genre of being resides, and from which, from this point of view, are suspended the man as much as the world.[96]

Heidegger is a typical case of a melody played on just one note, but the danger would be no less if one moved too quickly to define the unity of the melody by some collectivity greater or higher than the modes. This is why Souriau devotes the whole of his last chapter to guarding against the danger of returning too quickly to unity: 'So

---

93. In Souriau's philological metaphor, 'morphemes' are opposed to 'semantemes' just as verbs or relations are opposed to nouns or adjectives. *Les différents modes d'existence*, p. 101.

94. Souriau, *Les différents modes d'existence*, p. 104.

95. Souriau, *Les différents modes d'existence*, p. 108.

96. Souriau, *Les différents modes d'existence*, p. 111.

let us be careful, in wanting to cure ourselves of multimodality (which is the inherent condition of existence) of also curing ourselves of both existence and superexistence, in looking for the One to go towards the Nothing'.[97] Just like substance, unity is once again a nihilism. There is nothing surprising in that, since a being as being is by definition impossible: it is precisely lacking the other through which it alone it can arrive at subsistence. Here is a 'revaluation of values' as radical, in another way, as Nietzsche's. To search for any persistence of identity in itself—at the level of the parties involved as much as the overarching level—is evidence only of a will to head towards nothingness.

> A totalization does not have more reality at all because it assembles or unites. What interests us more about a totality like that is, beyond the plurality of genres of existence, is the way something appears that not only embraces them, but distinguishes itself from them and goes beyond them. So if superexistence has to be considered, it is not through any axiological consideration, not as if at a higher or more sublime degree of existence (even though it could have this sublime); it is though a strict and severe idea of a movement to second degree problems concerning existence, but stretching out of its plane.[98]

In the same way that each mode has the same dignity as all the others, one can say that each composition has the same dignity as all the others, without harmony or totality being able to predominate. Or rather, in the same way that each mode can fail its own existence, each totalization runs the risk of crushing 'this Tree of Jesse or Jacob's ladder: the surexistential order'.[99]

It would be tempting to multiply the possibilities. But Souriau is once again just as reluctant to proliferate as he is to unify, since this alternative is nothing more than the consequence of the incapacity to qualify the modes and their combinations starting from the position we are in at the moment. If the one is not privileged, then nor is the multiple. He indicates this with a very funny remark: who would go to a young man to advise him to be *both* a Don Juan and a saint on the pretext that there are two possibles there instead of one?![100] Father Charles de Foucault lived first the good life *before* being an ascetic, but he could never have been both at once ... compossibility works in a quite different way from simple accumulation. Here again, the difference lies in good and bad ways of protecting the multiplicity from the dangers of both unity and dispersal.

If the philosopher is the 'shepherd of being', the job of a Souriau-type shepherd would require more care, more attention, and more vigilance, as well as more politeness. First, because each being must be instaured according to its own special procedure which can also go wrong; and then, because each flock is made up of animals of different sorts that take off in different directions .... No doubt about it, the shepherd of beings *qua* others has more work than the shepherd of beings *qua* beings: 'Be careful which reality you are witness to, rich or poor, heading towards the more real or towards nothingness. Because if you are witness for this reality, it will judge you'.[101] And on the previous page, he had written the ultimate definition of the real Copernican revolution allowed by the notion of instauration: 'What made Michelangelo or

---

97. Souriau, *Les différents modes d'existence*, p. 140.

98. Souriau, *Les différents modes d'existence*, p. 140.

99. Souriau, *Les différents modes d'existence*, p. 151. A metaphor picked up later: 'Tree of Jesse and Jacob's ladder: there is an order and as? A genealogy of surexistence' *Les différents modes d'existence*, p. 155.

100. Souriau, *Les différents modes d'existence*, p. 150.

101. Souriau, *Les différents modes d'existence*, pp. 162-163.

Beethoven great, what turned them into geniuses, it was not their genius as such, it was their attention to the qualities of genius, not in themselves, but in the work'.[102]

CONCLUSION: WHAT PHILOSOPHY BEARS WITNESS FOR THE MODERNS?

We really do have an inheritance problem. How can we have confidence in an academic tradition capable of burying philosophies so profoundly and so forcefully? Does Souriau deserve to be forgotten like he has? And what can be said about Tarde, who was only recently disinterred? Or James, Dewey, and Whitehead, of whom we have almost completely deprived ourselves? But there is worse: when we inherit modernism, what and who do we inherit? Anthropology certainly knows the difficulties there are in other cultures in figuring out who is a reliable informant. Who should the anthropologist of the moderns confide in, in order to track down finally who they were, what they believed themselves to be, or what they might become? If he chooses John Searle or Étienne Souriau, will that not mean recreating completely different versions of his culture? I hope I have said enough to give a taste of Souriau, to show that it is not impossible to give an infinitely richer version of the ancient moderns than the usual miserable naturalism. Exoticism is always detestable, for Whites as well. If they 'speak with forked tongue', it is because they remain philosophically and anthropologically more interesting than they think they are, even if they pride themselves on having virtues they do not have, even if they despair about sins that they are really incapable of committing. I can't think of a better way of finishing this overly long presentation than with the final passage from Souriau's book. Here is the cosmos we would have to find a way to anthropologize:

> With Amphion's song the city walls began to rise. With Orpheus's lyre the Symplegades stopped and stared, letting the Argo sail by. Each inflection of our voice, which is the very accent of existence, is a support for higher realities. Within our few seconds of existence, between the abysses of nothingness, we can speak a song which rings beyond existence, with the power of magic speech, and which can make even the Gods, in their interworlds, feel a nostalgia for existence, and the desire to come down here to be by our sides, as our companions and our guides.[103]

---

102. Souriau, *Les différents modes d'existence*, p. 161.

103. Souriau, *Les différents modes d'existence*, p. 166.

21

Outland Empire:
Prolegomena to Speculative Absolutism[1]

Gabriel Catren
translated by Taylor Adkins

In what follows we shall outline a possible definition of speculative philosophy by re-activating, distorting and entangling four regulative concepts of German idealism, namely the *absolute*, the (philosophical) *system*, *phenomenology* (of 'spirit') and (absolute) *knowledge*. According to the speculative knot that we shall propose, knowledge will be locally inscribed in the philosophical system, the latter being a free falling *organon* for forcing the phenomenological mediation of the immanent and concrete self-experience of the absolute.

Far from simply rejecting the Kantian legacy and its contemporary avatars, the activation of such a post-critical conception of philosophy requires us to overcome the reactive pre-modern components of critical philosophy and to direct the resulting weapon of criticism towards a truly transcendental dehumanization of experience. Indeed, from a historical point of view, the critical motif inaugurated by Kant has been split by a crucial ambiguity. On the one hand, the Kantian project of exponentiating the Copernican revolution to an infinite series of transcendental powers constitutes an unavoidable regulative idea for the infinite tasks of (absolute) knowledge. The legitimate project of constructing an unconditional and universal rational knowledge of the real will remain intrinsically limited by a transcendental anthropocentrism if the subject of science does not perform a reflexive analysis on the different 'transcendental' conditions of research. However, instead of directing this necessary reflection on the transcendental localization of the subject of science towards a truly transcendental Copernican revolution, the critical motif has mainly triggered a 'Ptolemaic counter-revolution' (Meillassoux) that seeks to preserve the pre-modern landscape and stitch up the cosmological narcissistic wound. Rather than accepting that a genuine transcendental revolution is nothing but the angelic beginning of inhuman terror, even Kant used his critique to demonstrate that science would never be able to sublate the

1. I would like to thank Dorothée Legrand, Julien Page, Jérôme Rosanvallon, Nick Srnicek and François Wahl for their helpful comments on an earlier version of this text. I am also grateful to Taylor Adkins for translating it.

humanity of its subjective local supports. Whereas the Copernican 'critical' reflection on the contingent spatiotemporal localization of the earth was a 'determinate negation' that made the development of a rigorous astronomical science possible, the Kantian conservative revolution was an 'abstract negation' that did not produce what we could call a 'speculative cosmology', that is to say a conceptualisation of the real's global structure projectively absolved from the transcendental conditions presupposed by scientific cosmology. The persistent hegemony of a certain number of reactive premodern components of the critical motif implies that to a large extent modern philosophy is still yet to come. Philosophy will finally be modern only if it can sublate the critical moment, crush the Ptolemaic counter-revolution and deepen the narcissistic wounds inflicted by modern science.

THE FOURFOLD CRITICAL LANDSCAPE

First, we shall arrange the reactive pre-modern components of the critical motif in what we shall call the *fourfold critical landscape*. To do so, we can begin by remarking that the critical gesture tends to present itself as a healthy way of overcoming a supposed crisis. The pathetic announcement of a crisis seems to be the necessary prolegomenon to an articulated set of reactive 'critical' operations, such as a dogmatic limitation of theoretical reason, a reterritorialization on an unmoving last ground, and the concomitant theo-philosophical projection of a 'noumenal' transcendence. The canonical form of such a supposed disaster is the 'crisis of foundations', which is to say the loss of a firm ground, the occurrence of the fall and exile, the 'illness of uprootedness'[2]. In particular, if we forget that every veritable science must take root in the positive ground of experience, if we forget that the abstract constructions of the understanding are anchored in a *Lebenswelt* (lifeworld) that precedes all the scientific procedures of progressive idealization and convergence to the ideal limit-poles, and if we forget our finitude and the transcendental limits associated with it, then we fall into speculative waywardness, metaphysical folly, and transcendental illusion to the detriment of the patient construction of a well-founded theoretical edifice. Vis-à-vis such a crisis of foundations, the critique of reason must allow the judicious philosopher to travel upstream through the different forms of mediation—be they physiological, technical, imaginary, symbolic, linguistic, etc.—in order to reconquer the 'immediate' stratum that supports them (like, for example, sense-certainty, the *Lebenswelt*, the living present of the transcendental ego, the unveiling dehiscence of pre-objective *physis*, pre-symbolic duration, etc.). The critical overcoming of the crisis thus rests upon the pre-modern hypothesis according to which both human existence as well as any intellectual construction could be founded upon an immediate and unilateral last instance of experience. Hence, the authenticity of existence and the well-founded legitimacy of thought depend upon their distance in relation to such a privileged 'immediate' stratum. The first operation of critical redemption therefore corresponds with the reterritorialization upon a transcendental earth capable of establishing a legitimate orientation for thought, of healing its amnesiac waywardness and of supporting a new foundation. In this way, the mirage of a promised land necessarily follows exile and ungrounding. If the obscure disaster is to have lost the ground, it is necessary to conclude the Icarian odyssey of space by landing on an immobile earth, at home, here below, under the untouchable stars. As Husserl claimed, this rooting in an 'arche-originary Earth' (*Ur-Arche*

---

2. cf. Simone Weil, *The Need for Roots*, trans. A. Wills, London, Routledge & Kegan Paul, 1952.

Erde) that 'does not move' constitutes in the last instance a transcendental reduction of the Copernican revolution: the infinite spaces in which the decentred planet earth freely falls unfold in a phenomenological horizon constituted in the dreamlike immanence of the recentred transcendental ego. In this way, the conservative counter-revolution allows us to regain in a transcendental realm what has been lost in the empirical domain, namely an ultimate 'immediate' foundation for existence and a first 'Ur-axiom' for thought. By doing so, the critical motif substitutes the hapless rhetoric of crisis and the pre-modern myth of a transcendental 'immediate' ground for knowledge through the abysses of modern science.

An entire ensemble of operations and affects articulated around the master-signifiers *limits* and *finitude* follows the diagnosis of the crisis, the transcendental rescue and the Ptolemaic arche-foundation. The rooting of existence and thought upon an 'immediate' last instance necessarily conveys a sedentary fixity, a 'nationalist' attachment to the ground. The catastrophic declaration of a pestilent crisis and the concomitant construction of a protective wall of critical demarcation allows for the emplacement of a transcendental jurisprudence capable of sieving between the autochthonous and the foreigners, between 'true positivists' and intellectual imposters, between the thinkers of what merits being thought and calculative technocratic scientists of the uninteresting, and between those who hold onto a well-founded existence and the uprooted who have forgotten their at-homeness. However, this self-enclosure is lethal after all: if the critical delimitation restrains the range of possible movements, the projectively ideal accomplishment of this operation converges towards a stillness that coincides with terrestrial immobility. The immobile earth contains the black hole of the tomb: transcendental territorialization is always mortal, for it inexorably leads to the calm of interment. Here below, upon the *Ur-erde* (arche-earth), stands the calm monolith, there where the fall from an obscure disaster becomes a mortal crash.

In particular, the tracing of a demarcation line capable of defining theoretical reason's unsurpassable limits is the operation par excellence of this critical self-enclosure. We could thus say that *sedentary anchorage upon a transcendental earth* is necessarily coupled with the *theoretical inaccessibility of a 'noumenal' sky*. The horizon that defines the theatre of operations of worldly movements thus separates the immobile earth from the impossible sky. By reducing the Newtonian coalescence between the apple and the moon, the critical delimitation reestablishes a theoretically unsurpassable bifurcation of the real, namely that which divides the phenomena from the noumena, the knowable from the unknowable, the sayable from the showable, the physical from the metaphysical, being from 'beyond being', and totality from infinity. Once the Copernico-Newtonian revolution has been reduced, the blue of high noon can once again manifest the self-concealment of the unknown god. The homogeneity and isotropy of the real are therefore broken: the vertical gravitational field binds us to the immobile earth and prevents the light of reason from effectuating movements other than horizontal. Instead of spreading itself out in the indistinct homogeneity of the infinite spaces, the world of mortals henceforth extends itself—as long ago—between the hyper-transcendence of the most high and the earthly transcendental soil.

Even if it is impossible to access the noumenal sky via theoretical reason, there would be 'practical' means of crossing the horizon that separates the world of mortals from hyper-transcendence. We can thus say that the two principal problems of the critical motif are on the one hand the rootedness upon an immediate foundation and, on the other hand, the non-theoretical access to the hyper-transcendent sky. Inner experience, the mystical exhibition of the unsayable, acts capable of touching upon the non-symbolizable 'real', poetic infiltration through the limits of discursive language, the sovereign experience of the impossible, liturgy, laughter and ecstasy, are all non-theoretical protocols of transgression seeking to pierce the worldly-linguistic horizon and give access to a noumenal (non-)experience of that which remains prohibited to terrestrial phenomenality. In the framework of the critical motif, the *limitation of theoretical reason* and the *practical* 'thought of the outside' are two sides of the same critical demarcation: the limits of the scientist are the hope of the prophet, the apostle and the mystic. In this way, critical (theo-)philosophers can dispense with the patient work of the concept by instituting protocols of immediate access to a hyper-transcendent (pseudo-) absolute. If one accepts that 'the reason that has been extolled for centuries is the most stubborn adversary of thinking'[3], then it might seem legitimate to take the gun when we heard the word 'science': 'knowledge' of the 'absolute' will simply be 'shot out of a pistol'. By essentially being powerless to think the 'thing-in-itself', the authenticity of theoretical reason depends upon its capacity to recognize its own traits on the surface of the transcendental glass and to reflexively deconstruct its own metaphysical ingenuity through an endless work of rereading of its own textuality and history.

The anchorage in a fortified transcendental earth whose gravitational field prevents any possible uprooting spontaneously secretes the promise of a salutary grace. The transcendental bifurcation that separates the immobile earth from the noumenal sky therefore becomes an event horizon that can only be traversed by the unforeseeable advent of an appropriating grace, i.e. by a punctual and miraculous irruption of noumenal transcendence within the phenomenal world. By compactifying the continuity of angelic mediations, the discontinuity of the Christlike event hypostatizes the imaginary line that separates terrestrial existence from heavenly transcendence. The formal simplicity of the notion guarantees its secular perpetuation: as a singular point of junction capable of setting two 'regions' of the real in discontinuous relation (earth and sky, phenomena and noumena, finite and infinite, nature's nomological structure and hyper-chaotic multiplicity, etc.), it necessarily exceeds any production, causality, militancy, foresight and intelligibility immanent to the worldly stratum into which it bursts. Even when it is purified of every theo-philosophical transcendence, by reducing an effective process (be it politic, scientific, artistic, etc.) to an ideally punctual and gratuitously inflicted break, the pre-modern motif of the event renders any 'revolutionary' sequence illegibly opaque: a 'radical trembling' can neither be induced nor retrospectively understood, it 'can only come from the outside'.[4] Far from being the arduous result of the human labour of the negative, political revolutions, scientific discontinuities, and artistic subversions seem to fall haphazardly from heaven.

The subjective typologies that support these diverse types of correspondence between terrestrial finitude and the heavenly infinite take on three emblematic figures, namely the *prophet* who announces the unforeseeable advent of grace—always to come—through the opening of a messianic (non-)horizon, the *apostle* who declares and deploys his fidelity to the vanishing advent of a supernumerary event, and the *mystic* who forces an immediate and sovereign (non-)experience of the impossible and un-

---

3. Martin Heidegger, 'Nietzsche's Word: "God is Dead"', in *Off the Beaten Track*, trans. J. Young and K. Haynes, Cambridge, Cambridge University Press, 2002, p. 199.

4. Jacques Derrida, *Margins of Philosophy*, trans. A. Bass, Chicago, University of Chicago Press, 1985, p. 134.

sayable outside. All in all, it would not be—as Husserl believed—through a heroism of reason that we shall be able to overcome the crisis, but through prayer, ecstasy, or the expectancy of a grace to come. The critical fortress upon the immobile earth—the waiting room of interment—reveals itself to be a monastery whose only true aperture is directed towards the sky. Only a god, a grace, or a 'practical' act of transgression could save us from gravity, critical self-enclosure and red death. The fourfold critical landscape is henceforth complete: rooted upon the immobile earth under the inaccessible sky of immortals, those who exist for interment build, dwell, and think in the phenomenal world, between the downward pull of gravity and the promise—on the verge defined by the 'theo-critical' horizon—of appropriating grace.

ABSOLUTELY MODERN

In order to propel human thinking and dwelling out of the fourfold critical landscape, we shall claim that philosophy has to be *absolutely modern*, which is to say a modern philosophy of the absolute in the double sense of the genitive. More precisely, by *absolutely* modern philosophy we mean a philosophy capable of overcoming the Ptolemaic and narcissistic counter-revolution through which certain orientations of critical philosophy have attempted to reduce the consequences of the advent of modern science. Yet a philosophy capable of overcoming a critical moment and absolving itself of the transcendental limitations that follow must by definition be, as was the case for German idealism, an absolute philosophy of the absolute. By absolutely *modern* philosophy we mean a philosophy strictly 'synchronous'[5] with modern science, which is to say with *Galilean, Copernican, Newtonian, Einsteinian*, and *Heisenbergian* science. Following Badiou, we shall say that philosophy is *synchronous* with modern science if the former is both *conditioned by* and *desutured from* the latter. On the one hand, philosophy will be *conditioned by* modern science if it assumes the following theoretical and existential conditions provided by modern science. First, modern science is essentially Galilean, which means, in Husserl's terminology, that mathematics is a *formal ontology*, i.e. a theory of the generic categories of *being qua being*, like for instance the categories of *multiplicity* (set theory), *relation* (category theory), *quantity* (number theory), *localization* (geometry), *operativeness* (algebra), *symmetry* (group theory), *predication* (logic), *stability* (dynamical systems theory), and so on[6]. In other words, modern science is essentially determined by the *physical* entanglement of mathematical *logos* and natural *existence*, an entanglement which implies both the Galilean mathematization of nature and the Husserlian (and Badiousian) ontologization of mathematics. Second, modern science is essentially Copernican, Darwinian, and Freudian, which means that the narcissistically wounded subject of science can no longer be considered a (self)-centred fundamental first or last instance. Third, modern science is essentially Newtonian, which means that nature is *one*, i.e. that the pre-modern (transcendental) bifurcation between the (unmoving) *earth* and the (noumenal) *sky* has been definitively removed. Fourth, modern science is essentially Einsteinian, which means that nature suspends itself in its (cor)relational immanence by absorbing (or physicalizing) any sort of transcendental or metaphysical (back)ground. And finally, modern science is essentially *Heisenbergian*, which means that the phenomenological objective consistency of nature

5. cf. Jean-Claude Milner, *L'Œuvre claire. Lacan, la science, la philosophie*, Paris, Seuil, 1995, p. 38.

6. cf. Edmund Husserl, *Formal and Transcendental Logic*, trans. D. Cairns, The Hague, Martinus Nijhoff, 1969, § 24, pp. 77-78.

depends upon a certain number of quantum categories, which define the general conditions of logical predicability, (in)deterministic predictability, physical individuation, temporal reidentification, experimental observability, and intersubjective objectivity. Rather than supporting the anthropocentric critical reduction of the Copernican revolution, this (non-transcendental) quantum ontology implies that the count-as-one of the manifold of experimental intuition, far from being provided by a noetic synthesis performed by a transcendental ego, is the result of the immanent self-constitution carried out by the object in question itself.[7]

On the other hand, philosophy and science will be *desutured* if they manage to establish effective relations between themselves which preserve their respective sovereignties, i.e. if their relations assume neither the form of a subordination of philosophy to science ('only science thinks') nor the form of a philosophical domination of science ('science does not think'). On the basis of the birth of modern science, philosophy has had to confront a mode of thought which seems to be able to effectuate with rigor and virtuosity that which philosophy has always coveted, namely understanding the rational structure of the real. We can thus say that the existence of modern science has forced philosophy to reevaluate its theoretical prerogatives over the real. Faced with such a query of its theoretical authority, we can distinguish two principal kinds of philosophical reactions.

In the first place, we can say that philosophy has laid down its weapons and renounced its own sovereignty in order to proudly institute itself as the (non-requested) valet of science. Such a servile capitulation can take place in several ways. Philosophy can try to supply science with methodological, epistemological, hermeneutical, or metaphysical appendixes. It can pretend to provide a 'supplement of soul' capable of concealing the inhumanity of science under a 'human face'. It can attempt to orient the development of science through 'metaphysical research programs'. It can try to assure the conditions of mediation and translatability between different theoretical fields. It can endeavour to localise the 'epistemological obstacles' that impede the development of science and help science get over its 'foundational crises'. It can intervene in the 'spontaneous philosophy of the scientists' in order to trace a demarcation line between the 'ideological' and the 'scientific' components of science. It can furnish criteria so as to distinguish the legitimate sciences from pseudo-science. In the worst case, 'philosophy' becomes a sort of intellectual police apt to denounce the illegitimate uses of scientific knowledge and pursue intellectual imposters. But, we shall argue that there is no synchrony possible between science and a philosophy which sacrifices its sovereignty, resigns itself to leading a parasitic and secondary existence, and institutes itself as a self-proclaimed guardian of scientificity. We could affirm of this kind of relationship between philosophy and science what Friedrich Schlegel says of the philosophy of art, namely that 'one of two things is usually lacking', either philosophy or science.[8]

In the framework of the second kind of philosophical reaction to the emergence of modern science, philosophy has begun a struggle seeking to regain the theoretical prerogatives over the real usurped by science and to reduce the theoretical hegemony of the latter. In order to submit science to philosophical authority, establish its juridi-

---

7. cf. Gabriel Catren, 'A Throw of the Quantum Dice Will Never Abolish the Copernican Revolution', in *Collapse: Philosophical Research and Development*, vol. 5, Falmouth, Urbanomic, 2009 (and references therein).

8. Friedrich Schlegel, *Philosophical Fragments*, trans. P. Firchow, Minneapolis, University of Minnesota Press, 1991, p. 2.

cal limits, and occupy an overarching position in relation to it, philosophy has tried to define itself as a discourse with a wide range of capacities, including the ability to explain the conditions of possibility of science (be they transcendental, ontological, pragmatic, technological, discursive, institutional, etc.), subordinate *de jure* regional ontologies to a 'fundamental' ontology, ground science in a pre-scientific stratum (*Lebenswelt*, etc.), clarify its 'destinal' essence (be it technical, metaphysical, ontotheological, etc.), 'demonstrate' that science is nothing but an inductive stamp collection incapable of unveiling any rational necessity, or denounce science as a 'rationality of domination' and the ultimate cause of contemporary barbarism. In the first place, these attempts to trace the insurmountable limits of scientific thought permit philosophy to know what science does not know about itself. They therefore allow philosophy to formulate a *theory of science* by assuring a position of theoretical domination over the latter. The philosophical theory of science allows philosophy to think the relation between the immanence of scientific practice, on the one hand, and the transcendental, ontological, or metaphysical significance and consequences of science on the other. In this way, science becomes the object of a philosophical theory capable of founding and juridically circumscribing its field of validity. In the second place, this philosophical domination of science enables philosophy to know what scientific faculties cannot grasp concerning the real. Philosophy can thus establish itself as a *first*, *rigorous*, and *fundamental science* of the real. In order to trace the juridical limits of science and assure its submission to philosophy, philosophy proceeds to an operation that we can locate in almost all the arrangements that we have just enumerated, namely the bifurcation of the real in two. If science can construct a *knowledge of reality* (i.e. of phenomena, regional beings, structures, actual configurations, the 'contingent' laws of nature, etc.), only philosophical *thought* can with any legitimacy seek the *truth of the real* (i.e. of noumena, *being qua being*, pre-structural multiplicity, the virtual all-embracing 'apeiron', hyper-chaos, etc.). Thus philosophy justifies its existence by trying to localize a stratum of the real that would be subtracted *de jure* from scientific knowledge. Faced with the implacable progress of modern science, the philosopher—like the priest—is forced to constantly redefine his own tasks and pathetically crawl into niches each time more 'subtle', more 'profound', more 'transcendent', more 'generic', and more 'eminent' of the real. In the worst case, this pretension of philosophy to be the first science *par excellence* allows it to justify its *docta ignorantia* and abstain from the patient and arduous work of the genuine sciences (mathematics, physics, biology, etc.).

These different kinds of philosophical reactions to the emergence of modern science tacitly accept the postulate according to which philosophy will be theoretical knowledge or will not be at all, either a second and subordinate knowledge (namely 'epistemological' knowledge), or a knowledge alongside scientific knowledge (namely 'analytical' knowledge), or a first and fundamental knowledge (namely transcendental, ontological or metaphysical knowledge). Philosophy wants to be science, second science in the worst case, first science in the best. In this way, the philosophy of the modern times seems incapable of accepting the sovereignty of modern science as the canonical and eminent form of theoretical knowledge, and consequently it is incapable of definitively renouncing its theoretical prerogatives over the real. Following Badiou's terminology, we can say that philosophy remains *sutured* to (the idea of) science. Hence, philosophy does not manage to establish itself as a sovereign form of thought capable of involving relations with science which are not those of domination, submission, imitation, concurrence, juxtaposition, or identification. The theoretical domination of philosophy over science and the submission of philosophy to the idea of science are nothing but two sides of the same suture scenario. We shall say that a philosophy sutured to science remains in a state of pre-modern minority. The modernity of philosophy therefore depends upon its capacity to auto-determine itself in the suspension of every tutelary role exerted upon science and every mimetic submission to the tutelage of the latter.

In order to avoid any form of suture between philosophy and science and to put an end to their struggle for theoretical authority over the real and the corresponding conflict of the faculties, we shall follow the regulative imperative of forcing a hyperbolic divergence between them. In other words, instead of trying to weave any form of epistemological relation, ontico-ontological junction, empirico-transcendental division, or physico-metaphysical complementation whatsoever, instead of trying to relate philosophy and science either by means of a philosophy of science or by means of a non-philosophical 'science' of philosophy, instead of defining philosophy as a first, rigorous, or fundamental science, we shall attempt to heighten the divide between science and philosophy, deepen their difference, and break any form of identification between them. In particular, there will be no epistemological, analytic, transcendental, or ontological relation between science and philosophy. In order to guarantee the irreducible autonomy of science in relation to philosophy, we shall argue the necessity of expanding the definition of what we understand by science under the form of what we shall call *(absolute) knowledge*. By knowledge we mean a sovereign mode of thought that seeks to infinitely expand the theoretical experience of the real, i.e. to projectively construct a universal and unconditional rational knowledge of the real that does not recognize any form of aprioristic uncrossable limit to the development of its own infinite tasks. To achieve this, knowledge must expand what we understand by science in two senses. In the first place, far from limiting itself to studying the various ontic *regions* of the real (physics, chemistry, biology, etc.), knowledge must also examine its various *strata* (be they ontic, ontological, metaphysical, etc.). The philosophical assignation of science to a single stratum allows philosophy to proclaim science's constitutive incapacity to think the real, which necessarily exceeds the ontico-objective stratum. The infinite regulative idea of (absolute) knowledge contests this so-called essential limit of scientific thought by means of a stratified extension of science. This stratification permits knowledge to guarantee its self-sufficiency vis-à-vis other thought procedures. In order to characterize this stratified extended scientificity, we could adapt the following description: 'the stratified multiplicity of [knowledge, GC], which is inherent to the process of scientific production, is irreducible to any of its orders. [...] And this is a resistance (or limitation) only from the viewpoint of a [philosophical, GC] will. The will of [knowledge, GC] is the transformation-traversal of a stratified space, not its reduction'.[9] In the second place, knowledge must reactivate and generalize the Hegelian gesture through which *intentional* science and *transcendental* critique are subsumed in the self-reflection proper to *speculative* knowledge. The speculative movement *par excellence* is in effect the subsumption of extrinsic transcendental critique within an immanent speculative self-reflection. The reflexive passage from a *knowledge-in-itself* (i.e. a theoretical procedure

---

9. Alain Badiou, 'Mark and Lack: On Zero', trans. Z.L. Fraser and R. Brassier, in P. Hallward & K. Peden (eds.), *Concept and Form: The Cahiers pour l'analyse and Contemporary French Thought*, London, Verso, 2010 (forthcoming), http://www.web.mdx.ac.uk/crmep/varia/TR10.8Badiou15.2.2009RB.pdf. Badiou writes 'scientific signifier', 'metaphysical', and 'science' instead of 'knowledge', 'philosophical', and 'knowledge' respectively.

that does not reflect in its own transcendental conditions of possibility) to a *knowledge-for-itself* would thus constitute the immanent dialectic of speculative knowledge itself. Since we can neither exit the real in order to turn it into an intentional object nor project it into any form of 'noumenal' hyper-transcendence whatsoever, the ultimate gesturality of speculative knowledge can be neither objectifying intentionality nor the hyperbolic 'intentionality' of the 'practical' protocols of transgression, but instead reflexivity. Far from being an extrinsic philosophical operation capable of localizing the insurmountable limits of science, transcendental critique must allow the subject of science to identify and speculatively subsume the various transcendental conditions of scientific research. Among these conditions we can include: the (gravitational, thermodynamic, biologic, etc.) conditions that make the emergence of localized and temporalized cognitive entities possible; the conditions defined by the anthropic principle; the physiological conditions of sensible intuition; the technological conditions of instrumental observability and experimental verifiability; the associated limits to the possibility of gaining empirical access to the different regions, strata, scales, and dimensions of the real; the 'categories' of human understanding, the available 'imaginary' schemata that allow us to connect these categories with sensible intuition, the formal and linguistic structures that convey theoretical reason, and the technical and conceptual operations of analysis, synthesis, abstraction, selection, coarse-graining, decoherence, and renormalization through which we can constitute finite objects and define what is relevant at a given stage of research. One of the essential contributions of German idealism is the thesis according to which the transcendental critique, far from demonstrating the impossibility of absolute knowledge, constitutes its very condition of possibility. Indeed, the problem is not how to pierce a hole in the walls of the transcendental prison (built by philosophy itself), but rather to acknowledge that transcendental reflection is a necessary moment for absolving knowledge from the too human transcendental conditions of research. The infinite process of theoretical knowledge does not advance by attempting to grasp an 'uncorrelated absolute' through a philosophical 'ruse' capable of discontinuously leaping over the subject's shadow, but instead through a continual deepening of scientific labour seeking to locally absolve it from its conjunctural transcendental limitations, expand its categorical, critical, and methodological tools, and progressively subsume its unreflected conditions and presuppositions. Far from any 'humanist' or 'idealist' reduction of scientific rationality, this reflection upon the transcendental localization of the subject of science should allow the latter to radicalize the inhuman scope of knowledge by producing a differential surplus value of unconditionality and universality. In other words, such a reflexive torsion should permit the subject of science to continuously go through the transcendental glass and force its progressive escape from the transcendental anthropocentrism of pre-critical science: it is necessary to think the particular—empirical and transcendental—localization of the subject of science within the real in order for theoretical reason not to be too human.

According to this speculative sublation of transcendental critique, we must disclaim the dogmatic thesis according to which we cannot vary our transcendental 'position' vis-à-vis a given object. Indeed, transcendental reflection opens the possibility of generalizing Husserl's method of variation to transcendental variations, which is to say to modifications of the particular transcendental structure that makes our experience possible. In this way, transcendental critique must permit us to absolve our experience from its pre-modern attachment to a particular transcendental Arche-Earth.

Whereas each particular transcendental structure—like for instance the transcendental structures of a crystal, a baobab, an elephant, a human being, or a robot—defines a horizon of co-given profiles for every adumbrated object, the transcendental variations define a (non-)horizon of co-given horizons, which will be called *extended phenomenal plane*. Strictly speaking, the extended phenomenal plane is not itself a sort of 'cosmic' horizon, since it is not defined by any particular transcendental structure. In other terms, the extended phenomenal plane of impersonal experience is not Arche-Earth-centered. In this way we can oppose the infinite 'adumbrated' depths of the extended phenomenal plane—with its intrinsic structure of unveiling and concealment—to the unsurpassable critical bifurcation between phenomena and noumena. We can then define the *eidos* of an object as the germinal generator of its extended phenomenal sheaf of 'profiles'. This means that the *eidos* generates one set of orbits of profiles for each possible phenomenological horizon. Hence, the phenomenological dehiscence generated by the object's *eidos* extends far beyond the horizon defined by any particular transcendental structure. We could say that the suspension of the critical restriction of experience to a single phenomenological horizon opens experience to the extended phenomenal plane into which 'flowers endlessly open'.[10]

More generally, we shall maintain that not only transcendental reflection but also any other form of theoretical reflection upon science—be it epistemological, ontological, etc.—will by definition be included in the stratified extension of scientificity that we have called (absolute) knowledge. The self-reflexive immanence made possible by this heuristic expansion of the notion of science allows us to affirm the irreducible theoretical sovereignty of knowledge in relation to any other mode of thought. A theoretical procedure that legitimately wants to be absolute (i.e. universal and unconditional) cannot admit aprioristic extrinsic limits to its own immanent movement and to the process of mediation through which it reflexively enriches its (self-)critical weapons, assumes its presuppositions, and traverses its conjunctural limitations. This sovereignty of knowledge vis-a-vis any other mode of thought is the counterpart of its submission to the authority of the absolute real. The feigned modesty proper to the critical limitations of science constitutes an idealist ultra-dogmatism, the self-sufficient position of a supposedly irrevocable knowledge about the unsurpassable limits of theoretical reason. By using Adorno's terms, we could say that the critical tribunal overthrows 'the authority of the absolute' by 'absolutized authority'.[11] The only way of exerting a radical self-critique capable of preventing the degeneration of theoretical reason into dogmatic knowledge is to not give up on the desire to projectively construct an universal and unconditional knowledge of the real. In other terms, only the infinite idea of absolute knowledge can impede the dogmatic crystallization of knowledge. Far from tracing dogmatic delimitations between the knowable and the unknowable, the speculative appropriation of transcendental critique must assume the form of a determinate negativity on behalf of an effective production of knowledge. A determinate negation is a critique that works, i.e. a critique that supplies the means of effectively overcoming the limits it reveals. Far from legitimating a *practical* (namely poetic, aesthetic, ethical, liturgical, mystical, etc.) access to the absolute, the transcendental (self-)critique of science instead requires an expansion of the theoretical resources of the latter. Instead of impeding the necessary perfecting of the critical apparatus, this speculative *Aufhebung*

10. R.M. Rilke, *Duino Elegies*, trans. S. Cohn, Illinois, Northwestern University Press, 1989, p. 65.

11. Theodor Adorno, *The Jargon of Authenticity*, trans. K. Tarnowski & F. Will, New York, Routledge, 2003, p. 3.

of the transcendental critique must simply allow us to interrupt the unproductive, parasitic, and reactive redundancy of abstract negativity.

In short, we can say that the various forms of theoretical reflection upon the sciences (epistemology, transcendental critique, etc.) and every theoretical field seeking to rationally understand any stratum of the real whatsoever (be it ontic, ontological, metaphysical, etc.) will henceforth be a part of the stratified extension of scientificity that we have called knowledge. Thus a certain number of theoretical apparatuses historically introduced by philosophy will be transferred from philosophy to knowledge. We could say that philosophy will finally be desutured from modern science if it recognizes the unconditional autonomy of (the stratified extension of) science as a mode of thought that legitimately examines the real in its truth, and accepts delegating all its theoretical prerogatives over the real in order to affirm its own specificity as an autonomous form of thought disjoined from any form of scientificity (be it ontic, ontological, metaphysical or transcendental). This expropriation of philosophy in relation to any theoretical faculty generalizes and radicalizes Badiou's seminal thesis according to which (formal) ontology must be separated from philosophy. Far from being unfaithful to the philosophical tradition, 'this is a pattern spanning philosophy's entire history. Philosophy has been released from, or even relieved of, physics, cosmology, and politics, [...]. It is also important for it to be released from ontology',[12] epistemology, transcendental critique, metaphysics, and, in general, any theoretical field. Instead of simply being a terminological redefinition, the inclusion of these theoretical procedures in an expanded definition of science must enable their liberation from their reactive philosophical uses. In other words, such a scientific reappropriation of 'philosophical' theoretical faculties must allow us to differentiate what science can effectively recuperate from the theoretical contributions of inherited philosophy against the philosophical operations that merely seek to distort, limit, and dominate science (including, for instance, the philosophical utilization of transcendental critique in order to establish the juridical limits of science, or the various philosophical attempts of *founding*—an anti-Copernican gesture *par excellence*—science).

It is also important to emphasize that this stratified extension of science stems from a requirement posited by the regulative idea that opens and orients the infinite tasks of science, namely the idea of *truth*. Truth is an idea of reason deprived of any canonical conceptual representation. Being a regulative idea of reason, truth is nothing but the formal imperative to not give up on the desire to infinitely expand the rational comprehension of the real. However, the formal infinitude of the eidetic prescription can orient the effective local protocols of research by means of different conceptual representations of its local goals (adequacy, objectivity, experimental verifiability, formal demonstrability, nomological unification, etc.). We could say that the idea of truth is an eidetic operator that encompasses all the different local criteria of scientific selection. Hence, knowledge must be capable of absolving itself from the global canonization of any particular conceptual representation of truth, including, for instance, the 'truth of judgment' of representative understanding. Instead of being that which exposes itself to knowledge, truth is the regulative idea through which humanity opened at a particular moment of its history to a completely singular form of experience of the real, namely that of its rational comprehension. We can say that under the light of truth,

---

12. Alain Badiou, *Briefings on Existence: A Short Treatise on Transitory Ontology*, trans. N. Madarasz, Albany, State University of New York Press, 2006, p. 59.

the real exposes itself as that which is capable of being rationally understood. The fidelity of science to the idea of truth requires that it be able to expand all of its thematic regions, examined strata, conceptual, technical and methodological tools, and procedures of validation (hypothetical-deductive method, experimental protocols, formal and conceptual consistency, etc.). In particular, if the real cannot be reduced to the innerworldly beings or intentional objects studied by the natural sciences, then it is necessary to expand what we understand by science. If a theoretical problem posed by science cannot find a solution in the framework of the latter, then it is necessary to expand the scientific field by forcing the adjunction of the theoretical procedures that can generate the corresponding solutions. (Absolute) knowledge is by definition the projective compactification of the successive extensions of the scientific field required by its infinite regulative idea.

DAS GLASPERLENSYSTEM

The regulative extension of the idea of science deprives philosophy of a number of theoretical fields that traditionally define it (including, in particular, epistemology, transcendental critique, and ontology). It is thus necessary to evaluate what the specificity of philosophy could be if we unburden it from all its theoretical claims and faculties concerning the real. As we shall see, this ascesis will allow us to characterize the singular tasks and faculties of philosophy and resist the different attempts to overcome philosophy by means of a marginal, poeticizing, theological, deconstructive, or non-philosophical 'thought'.

Philosophy will be defined as a mode of thought that seeks to *systematically* mediate the experience of the real. The specificity of philosophy therefore depends on what Badiou calls its *systematicity*, i.e. its capacity of globally *compossibilizing* the different local procedures—such as science, art, or politics—in the horizon of a general economy of thought. Local thought procedures are by definition *virtuously* abstract, which is to say partial and unilateral. They mediate and expand the experience under the monochromatic light projected by the regulative ideas that orient their infinite tasks. On the contrary, philosophy can be defined as a non-local procedure whose aim is to unfold a *concrete* and *polychromatic* experience of the real. If each mode of thought forces the mediation of a certain dimension of *doxa* and labours inside a given *prismatic projection* of the real, philosophy is endowed with a systematic or global degree of variation. In more classical terms we could say that, instead of restricting itself to the tasks prescribed by a single eidetic 'transcendental', philosophy's mediation of the limits of experience orients itself by constellating the *Verum*, the *Bonum*, and the *Pulchrum*. A philosophical experience depends upon a *stereoscopic* co-deployment of the complementary intentional goals defined by the diverse local procedures. In other words, the philosophical disindoxication of experience exerts itself via a systematic *composition* and *concertation* of the mediating vectors that operate within the multiple spectral sections of the real. Even if a given local procedure can legitimately use operations and materials coming from other procedures (including, for instance, aesthetic criteria in scientific research or scientific operations in artistic compositions), its tasks continue to be regulated by its eidetic 'tonality'. On the contrary, the systematic variations performed by philosophical composition allow us to unfold an *atonal* experience of the real. The transversal 'atonal chords' produced in this way by definition exceed that of which the local modes of thought are capable. We could thus say that philosophy is an effective practice of the abolition of the division of labour among the different abstract modes of thought. This implies that *systematic ubiquity* does not impede its *specific productivity*. In other terms, philosophy forces the productive localization of a global systematic transversality. Far from being an abstract survey, an 'empty transcendence', an encyclopedic classification, or even a parasitic and stagnant exploitation of what is produced by these local procedures, the philosophical system opens up a polyphonic horizon of labour towards the effective production of *diagonal* or *non-local* forms of enacting and expanding experience. We could say that through the philosophical system, all the local modes of thought 'become one, and are increased by one' (Whitehead). In other words, each *concrete mediator* produced by the systematic composition is 'nothing more than a part alongside other parts, which it neither unifies nor totalizes, though it has an effect on these other parts simply because it establishes aberrant paths of communication between [them]'[13]. Analogously, the idea of producing a total work of art (*Gesamtkunstwerk*) capable of synthesizing all the existing arts brings forth nothing but a new artistic form among others, an operatic 'whole' which coexists with the local arts and is 'contiguous to them', a virtuous excrescence through which the set of artistic forms productively avoids its impossible totalization.[14] A given composition will be called philosophical only if it entangles a set of abstract mediating operations provided by the different local modes of thought in a non-trivial global section, i.e. in a concrete mediator that cannot be completely localized in the space of abstract procedures. In other words, the philosophical system is a delocalized concrete machine capable of connecting and articulating the various local abstract machines (be they artistic, political, scientific, etc.) in a non hierarchical way so as to set in place a generalized constructivism, a general *musaic* of thought. Paraphrasing Xenakis, we could say that such a 'symphilosophy' (F. Schlegel) *should be able to construct the most concrete musaical organon in which the disindoxicating vectors of Bach, Freud, Grothendieck, and Marx, for example, would be the singular components of a polyphonic mediator.*[15] Whereas the various local modes of thought are characterized by their subjective typologies (the scientist, the artist, the analyst, the militant, etc.), their regulative ideas (the True, the Good, the Beautiful, etc.), the typology of their productions (works, theories, effects, interventions, etc.), their modes of discourse (the university's discourse, the analytic discourse, etc.), and so on, philosophy's own task is that of diagonalizing these different local structures via operations of *translation/transduction, synthesis, transposition, crossbreeding, resonance, grafting, connection,* and *counterpoint*. It is only through this systematic transversality that it will become possible to produce mutant forms of 'spirit', inject new plugs into the (immanent) real, generate hybrid corporeal supports, project new infinite tasks, and evaluate, reactivate, and constellate the inherited regulative ideas. More importantly, such a philosophical diagonalization allows us to insert the sheaves of scientific, artistic, and political abstract perspectives into a concrete unfolding 'vision' of the real[16]. Due to the philosophical production of mutant

---

13. Gilles Deleuze and Felix Guattari, *Anti-Oedipus. Capitalism and Schizophrenia*, trans. R. Hurley, M. Seem and H.R. Lane, Minneapolis, University of Minnesota Press, 1983, p. 43.

14. It is worth stressing that, from a philosophical point of view, the Wagnerian project of a *Gesamtkunstwerk*, far from being too ambitious, lacks systematic generality, since it circumscribes itself to the restricted composition of artistic procedures and orients its tasks by means of a single regulative idea.

15. cf. Iannis Xenakis, *Formalized Music: Thought and Mathematics in Music*, Stuyvesant, Pendragon Press, 1992, p. 207.

16. cf. Alexander Grothendieck, *Promenade à travers une œuvre ou L'enfant et la Mère*, p. 16-17 (http://www.grothendieckcircle.org/).

forms of experience, the multiplicity of local forms of 'spirit' continuously avoids either any sort of totalizing closure or any form of innocuous cultural juxtaposition. Moreover, instead of sublating the different forms of 'spirit' in a linear and convergent series of potentializations, their systematic composition must hinder the serialization, totalization, or hierarchization of their egalitarian plurality. In this way, far from interrupting the immanent procession of 'spirit', the philosophical system is nothing but the beginning of an atonal and stereoscopic form of the mediation of its concrete self-experience.

The systematic composition of science, art, and politics has always been a hallmark of philosophical production. However, the latent systematic conception of philosophy has been hindered by the privilege of an eidetic 'transcendental' to the detriment of the others. In particular, the theoretical suture between philosophy and ontology allowed the former to justify its 'systematic' delocalization with respect to the different 'ontic' regions. The proposed break with the suture between philosophy and theoretical reason, and the concomitant inclusion of ontology in a stratified extension of science allows us to release philosophy from such an ontological validation of its systematicity. Thus the horizon of systematic concretion furnished by the philosophical plane of composition is a non-theoretical 'image of thought' deprived of any ontological foundation. Far from subordinating the different interests of reason to theoretical interest and effectuating a teleological closure of the philosophical system, the stratified extension of science is nothing but a local mode of thought. Knowledge is only one form of 'spirit' among others, an abstract mode of thought whose objective is to infinitely expand the *theoretical* experience of the real, a local form of experience *that only examines the real in its (rational) truth*. Since by definition philosophy no longer has any theoretical prerogative over the real, this local inscription of knowledge into the system does not risk disrupting the theoretical autonomy of knowledge. In other words, even if the system incorporates knowledge as a singular form of 'spirit', knowledge henceforth will have no theoretical need of philosophy at all, since it is by construction autonomous in its own form of virtuous abstraction.

THE WORLDLY ABSOLUTE

The critical conception of philosophy orients its own activity by means of the 'cardinal points' provided by the pre-modern fourfold critical landscape. In order to continue the characterization of an absolutely modern conception of post-critical philosophy, we shall use the conditions provided by modern science to posit a new provisional scenario for philosophical activity. It is worth stressing that the resulting *speculative landscape* is simply intended to sketch a provisional imaginary envelope of modern being-there whose only heuristic purpose is to propel the philosophical experience beyond the arche-terrestrial limits defined by the fourfold critical landscape.

In what follows we shall choose the term *absolute* as the name of (what we have previously called) the real. The thesis according to which speculative philosophy must be a philosophy of the absolute in the double sense of the genitive implies that philosophy will neither be an ontological first science of *being qua being*, nor a thought of an '*Other*' *beyond* (or otherwise than) *being* (the arche-difference, the infinite Other, the supernumerary event, the non-philosophical One, etc.), nor an 'analytic' localization of a 'real' ring that would be in a relation of noumenal excess or inconsistent subtraction with respect to the phantasmatic consistency of phenomenal reality or the structural properties defined by the symbolic order. As we shall show in what follows, the term 'absolute' has two important advantages, namely the impossibility of opposing the absolute to a separated non-absolute instance and the fact of conveying operations of absolution. By definition the absolute cannot be (hetero-)relative to something other than itself. Therefore the absolute cannot be found on this side of or beyond any line of demarcation whatsoever, including, for example, the line that separates the 'infinite' from the finite, the 'real' from the symbolic and the imaginary, the intelligible from the sensible, the noumena from the phenomena, *being qua being* from beings, the inconsistent multiple from structural consistency, the undifferentiated *apeiron* from differentiated structures, or the virtual from the actual. Instead of resulting from a theo-philosophical bifurcation, the absolute engulfs every 'wild blue yonder'. Since by definition the absolute cannot be a term of a duality, any form of difference, opposition, bifurcation, schism, transcendence, horizon, or polarization must unfold within its unitive neutrality. The absolute is thus the *one* that encompasses any division. In what follows we shall use the term *immanence* for denoting the impossibility of opposing the absolute to a separated (or *transcendent*) non-absolute instance.

If the absolute is one, if any form of horizon unfolds in its neutral immanence, then we cannot access it, there is no trajectory or operation capable of leading us there, for we are already within the absolute, *hic et nunc*. In Hegelian terms, we can say that the absolute, far from being a lost homeland or an eschatological kingdom, is always already with us, in and for itself: *das Absolute ist an und für sich schon bei uns*[17]. Philosophy therefore cannot have the objective of clearing a path towards the absolute, of setting in place, as if it were an absolutescope, a protocol of access capable of traversing the walls of the critical prison via a 'speculative' demonstration, an act of transgression, or an intellectual intuition. Every possible experience, be it doxic, illusory or ideological, is already an experience of the absolute: the 'falsehood' is nothing but a (partial and unilateral) moment of the 'truth'. Therefore, it is a question on the one hand of inserting the 'falsehood' in its proper place within the 'truth' and of understanding in this way the sources of its unilaterality, finitude, and abstract character. On the other hand, it is a question of deploying the concrete experience of the 'truth', i.e. of unsettling its conjunctural limitations and forcing its immanent unfolding. A philosophy of the absolute in the double sense of the genitive is a philosophy that seeks the absolute from the absolute itself, i.e. a philosophy that, far from attaining the absolute at the end of any process or operation whatsoever, expands the possible forms of the absolute's self-mediation. In order to do so, philosophy always acts upon a particular *environing world* (*Umwelt*) characterized by a certain restrained experience of the absolute: everything begins in our garden, sovereignly, in strict floral observance, narcotized in the midst of the worldly capsule. More precisely, we can identify the *Umwelt* with the Arche-Earth-centered phenomenological horizon of anticipations and possibilities defined by a particular transcendental structure. The doxic belief in the naturalness of the *Umwelt* as a unique and unsurpassable horizon of possibilities for the human experience of the absolute constitutes what we shall call—borrowing from Lacanian terminology—*reality*. We shall thus call *ideology* any theoretical and practical technology of legitimation and perpetuation of reality. The ideological prevention of any possibility of mediating the *Umwelt* and overcoming its limitations depends upon a certain set of narcotic operations seeking to hypostatize its partiality, unilaterality, and finitude. Due to ideology,

---

17. cf. G. W. F. Hegel, *Phänomenologie des Geistes*, Hamburg, Félix Meiner Verlag, 1988, p. 58 (G.W.F. Hegel, *Phenomenology of Spirit*, trans. A.V. Miller, Oxford, Oxford University Press, 1977, p. 47).

that which is nothing but a local fluctuation of the absolute's self-experience is fixated and endowed with an unshakeable necessity. Far from guaranteeing an access to the absolute as if it were an *instrument* or a *medium*, philosophical labour seeks to systematically mediate every form of doxic or ideological limitation of its self-experience. We could say that speculative philosophy depends upon the postulate according to which any form of finitude enfolds a renormalized infinity. As Whitehead writes: 'We are instinctively willing to believe that by due attention, more can be found in nature than that which is observed at first sight. But we will not be content with less'.[18] The dialectical blow-up of infinity within finitude requires a continuous mediation of any fundamental, archaic, elemental, unilateral, immediate, or eventual 'last' instance of experience. It is in this sense that philosophy can be defined as a systematic phenomenology of 'spirit', i.e. a work seeking to expand the absolute's 'self-consciousness' on the basis of a dialectical resolution of any given form of experience, a forcing of transcendental variations seeking to submerge the local subjects into the extended phenomenal plane, a production of new 'forms of spirit' (or formal subjective typologies), and a stereoscopic co-deployment of the mediating vectors that operate within the different spectral sections of the absolute. In the words of Novalis, we can say that philosophy must systematically 'romanticize' the absolute's experience, which is to say that philosophy must variously raise it to new powers and compose concrete mediators out of its different prismatic abstractions.

In the aftermath of Cartesian doubt and the Husserlian *epokhe*, the first operation of the protocol of philosophical production is the formal suspension of *doxa*, i.e. the bracketing of both the finitist naturalization of the conjunctural limits of experience and the ideological hypostasis of a given local configuration in a perennial *Weltanschauung* (worldview). We could say that a philosopher, being an inhabitant of a bracketed *Umwelt*, is an abducted subject '[...] who constantly experiences, sees, hears, suspects, hopes, and dreams extraordinary things [...]'.[19] Unlike for Descartes and Husserl, the *epokhe* as we understand it here does not grant access to an indubitable subjective foundation on the basis of which we could construct a first and rigorous science definitively subtracted from any critical mediation. Whereas the scope of Cartesian doubt and the Husserlian *epokhe* has been limited by a reterritorialization in the *ego cogito*, whereas the Heideggerian *Unheimlichkeit* (uncanniness) of the existential *Unzuhause* (not-at-home)[20] has been betrayed by the bucolic nostalgia of the Greek *Heimat* (homeland) and the substitutive military rootedness in the German *Lebensraum* (vital space), whereas the 'non-philosophical unilateralization' of worldly transcendence operates via a radical emplacement in a last subjective instance 'immediately' proven, the speculative suspension of the doxic capsule drops away every *Ur-Erde*, every ultimate enclave of an 'immediate' experience subtracted from mediation, and every salutary interruption of the Ur-fall. In other words, the speculative *epokhe* formally brackets the fundamental, radical, or immediate obstacles which impede the free fall down the rabbit-hole that winds through the transcendental earth. In turn, the launching of the *Ur-Erde* into orbit implies the suspension of the critical thesis according to which the unfolding of experience is restricted to the phenomenological horizon defined by a particular

---

18. Alfred North Whitehead, *The Concept of Nature*, New York, Dover Publications, 2004, p. 29.

19. Friedrich Nietzsche, *Beyond Good and Evil: Prelude to a Philosophy of the Future*, trans. J. Norman, New York, Cambridge University Press, 2002, §292, p. 174.

20. cf. Martin Heidegger, *Being and Time*, trans. J. Macquarrie & E. Robinson, Oxford, Blackwell Publishers, 1962, § 41, p. 234.

Umwelt. Such a suspension makes the teratological conception of new forms of 'spirit' possible. The resulting mutant transcendental structures span new phenomenological horizons for hosting the dehiscence of every germinal *eidos*. In this way, the *epokhe* opens the possibility of passing from the closed environing world to the infinite phenomenal plane. If the critical *epokhe* roots in an immobile earth, the speculative *epokhe* suspends worldly reality and opens experience to '[…] the immanence of the absolute to which [speculative, GC] philosophy lays claim'.[21] The *epokhe* can then be understood as a local subjective activation of the *Umwelt's* immersion into the groundless absolute. Faced with the pre-modern nostalgia of a rootedness in an original earthly ark, the fidelity to the Copernican revolution requires us to conceive the absolute as a phenomenal plane of abyssal immanence capable of receiving the successive launching into orbit of immobile earths. We could thus say that in the bracketed world, all that is the case freely falls. Far from any reterritorialization on an immediate apodictic experience or sacred Place, 'thinking consists in stretching a [phenomenal, GC] plane of immanence that absorbs the earth […]'.[22] The absolute thus constitutes the 'open' where the radical foundations and the last instances are suspended and towards which the successive transcendental potentializations of the Copernican revolution never cease to release experience. The plunging into the solaristic solution—and the concomitant ungrounding of any transcendental *Heimat*—blasts off the philosophical experience: twenty thousand leagues under the centre of the earth to the moon.

It is worth stressing that the *epokhe* does not entail an effective mediation of the doxic capsule. Simply being a formal bracketing of the naturalization of a given phenomenological horizon, the *epokhe* does not authorize dispensing with the labourious and patient work of mediation, resolution and fibration of reality. We could say that the *epokhe* just induces the *being-attuned* (*Stimmung*) to the absolute which is necessary for performing every effective mediation of the 'invisible and imperious circles that delimit'[23] the subject's *Umwelt*. Even if the effective experience of the abducted/attuned subject continues to be structured by the imaginary *Weltanschauung* that covers the inner surface of his *Umwelt*, 'the state in which he may be found' (*Befindlichkeit*) differs from that of those who assume the restriction of experience to the renormalized phenomenological horizon defined by their transcendental structures. This psychedelic coexistence between the suspension within the extended phenomenal plane of immanence activated by the *epokhe* and *being-there* in the worldly capsule will be called *coalescence*. Even if 'there is ever a World',[24] and never the uncapsulated absolute, worldly experience can be set in coalescence: through the *epokhe*, the philosopher can act upon the doxic capsule from the 'point of view' of the immanent absolute which is always already present. Paraphrasing Laruelle, we could say that the *epokhe* allows the philosopher to access a 'vision-in-absolute' of the world. The philosopher is a 'character who, believing in the existence of the sole Absolute, imagines he is everywhere in a dream (he acts from the Absolute point of view)'.[25] Instead of giving access to a transworldly outer space, the suspension of the renormalized world triggers the possibility of unfolding the 'world's inner space' (*Weltinnenraum*), i.e. of blowing-up the 'atoms'

---

21. Gilles Deleuze and Félix Guattari, *A Thousand Plateaus*, trans. B. Massumi, Minneapolis, University of Minnesota Press, 1988, p. 91.

22. Deleuze and Guattari, *A Thousand Plateaus*, p. 88.

23. 'Grothendieck, *Promenade à travers une œuvre ou L'enfant et la Mère*, p. 7.

24. Rilke, *Duino Elegies*, p. 64.

25. Stéphane Mallarmé, 'Igitur', in *Selected Poetry and Prose*, trans. M.A. Caws, New York, New Directions, 1982, p. 100.

of reality and releasing new dimensional ekstases and new immanent horizons of possibilities beyond the limits defined by the corresponding *Umwelt*. Rather than a 'cosmic' all-embracing *Umwelt*, the absolute is the immanent projective abyss continuously opened by the mediation of any hypothetical last instance of experience. As Žižek writes: 'transcendence is absolutely immanent, what is 'beyond' finite reality is nothing but the immanent process of its self-overcoming'.[26] In Heidegger's terms, the absolute can be surpassed '[...] only by itself [...] by expressly [falling, GC] into its own. Then [the absolute, GC] would be the unique which wholly surpasses itself [...] this transcending does not go up and over into something else; it comes up to its own self [...]. [The absolute, GC] itself traverses this going over and is itself its dimension'[27] Unlike the world renormalized by the natural attitude, the world submerged in coalescence within the solaristic solution is an interzone permeable to the floral resolution of experience. If we call *germ* every local instance of a dialectic flowering and *stalk* every systematic fibration of a germ, we can say that the philosopher is a *stalker* capable of systematically localizing, following, and intertwining the serpentine lines of mediation.

PRE-BREATH AND HYPER-CHAOS

The project of defining a post-critical philosophy of the absolute synchronous with modern science must demarcate itself from certain contemporary attempts seeking to reactivate what could be called a pre-modern synchrony between philosophy and theology. Such a theo-philosophical synchrony can be defined by the projection—and consequent relativization—of the absolute in a trans-worldly transcendence, which can be either external (i.e. trans-objective) or internal (i.e. pre-subjective). If we assume with Deleuze and Guattari the definition according to which 'there is religion every time there is transcendence',[28] then we can conclude that any attempt to localize the absolute in a trans-worldly outer space effectively submits philosophy to theology. In opposition to such a theo-philosophical relativization of the absolute, a properly speculative philosophy aims to systematically deploy an immanent experience of an 'absolute absolute' (F. Schlegel).

In order to characterize these theological deviations of the speculative turn, we can begin by remarking that the intentional correlation between a subject and an object (or, more generally, between two prehensive objects) prevents any attempt seeking to identify one of these terms with the absolute. Both the subject and the object are co-determined and co-constituted by the intentional correlations that unfold in the horizons of their phenomenal worlds. Hence, one possible strategy for overcoming the critical prohibition of an 'absolute knowledge' could be to try to attain an 'uncorrelated absolute' by going beyond intentional correlations. In order to do so, it is necessary to identify the absolute either with an outer superlative transcendence beyond the object or with an inner immediate experience on this side of the subject. According to theo-philosophy, the absoluteness of a hyper-transcendent 'relative absolute' relies upon its capacity to absolve itself from any worldly correlation.

---

26. Slavoj Žižek, 'Is it Still Possible to be a Hegelian Today?', in this volume.

27. Martin Heidegger, 'What are Poets for?', in *Poetry, Language, Thought*, trans. A. Hofstadter, New York, Harper & Row Publishers, 1975, p. 131. Heidegger writes 'entering' and 'Being' instead of 'falling' and 'Absolute'.

28. Gilles Deleuze and Felix Guattari, *What Is Philosophy?*, trans. G. Burchell and J. Tomlinson, Minneapolis, University of Minnesota Press, 1996, p. 46.

On the one hand, we could try to go beyond the intentional object with the hopes of attaining what we shall generically call a 'thing-in-itself'. The phenomenal transcendence opened by the transcendental faculties does not exhaust the outside. In order to access the supposed trans-objective 'great outdoors'—or non-transcendental transcendence—it would be necessary to suspend the transcendental sovereignty of the subject and go beyond the phenomenal horizon set in place by its constituting spontaneity. To do so, one should be able to force a (theoretical, ethical, or aesthetic) 'relationship' with a trans-objective instance absolved from any possible over-determination conveyed by such a worldly (cor)relation. Several alternatives have been proposed to accomplish this strategy. For instance, such a suspension of transcendental activity could be ethically brought about within the framework of a 'sublime' experience of the 'infinite' Other capable of deregulating the harmonic arrangement of distinct faculties and reducing every subjective effort seeking to impose the formal framework of objective recognition. We could alternatively try to construct a 'speculative demonstration' seeking to pierce a theoretical hole in the walls of the critical fortress and peep at an uncorrelated absolute subtracted from the laws of the phenomenal world. We could also attempt to 'show' *sub specie aeterni* the existence of the world as a limited whole—which by definition cannot be the object of a phenomenal experience—through a 'mystical feeling' capable of silently transcending linguistic objectification. In all these cases, 'how things are in the world is a matter of complete indifference for what is higher. God does not reveal himself in the world'.[29]

The second possibility of breaking the correlational circle is to move upstream to this side of the subject in order to attain what we shall call a 'human-in-itself', which is by definition subtracted from the objective transcendence of the world. If we accept that the conditions of possibility of objective phenomena are also the conditions of possibility of the subject's experience, then we have to conclude that the subject of the transcendental tradition is a subject mediated by the experience of the transcendent world, an interiority from the start alienated by the threads of intentionality, an ego essentially determined by its being-in-the-world. The transcendental ego is by definition open to a transcendent experience, even when—as it is the case in Husserl— the corresponding horizon of transcendence is constituted in its subjective immanence. It would therefore be necessary to radicalize the phenomenological return upstream towards the transcendental ego in order to attain a 'human-in-itself' which does not lapse into the transcendent world, a non-transcendental ego subtracted from any dependence and co-presence vis-à-vis the world. If the thing-in-itself is irreducible to any form of objectivity, the 'absolute' humanity of the human-in-itself is irreducible to any form of worldly subject. Whereas Henry understands this radical subjective 'immanence' in terms of a self-affective life subtracted from light, language, and worldly experience, Laruelle argues—even more radically—that every form of self-affection, self-manifestation, and self-position would open a distance of itself to itself, would dislocate subjective immanence, and would make the proof of itself into a mediate experience. Hence, whereas Henry radicalizes the Husserlian return upstream towards the transcendental ego by means of a radically 'immanent' pre-worldly subjectivity, Laruelle radicalizes Henry's project by ejecting every form of residual self-affective mediation outside the human-in-itself.

---

29. Ludwig Wittgenstein, *Tractatus Logico-Philosophicus*, trans. D.F. Pears & B.F. McGuinness, London, Routledge & Kegan Paul, 1974, § 6.432, p. 88.

In this way, the attempt of attaining a hyper-transcendent 'absolute' instance sub-tracted from intentional (or prehensive) correlations can assume either the form of a *thought of the outside* seeking 'an outside more distant than any external world', or the form of a *thought of the inside* turned towards 'an inside deeper than any internal world'. Whereas in Levinas the hyper-transcendence of the 'infinite' Other overturns the tran-scendental experience of the world (for the latter, not being sufficiently transcendent, cannot put the objectifying imperialism of the subject in question), in Henry and Laru-elle radical immanence 'unilateralizes' the transcendental experience of the world (for the latter, being too transcendent, puts the self-sufficiency of absolute humanity in ques-tion). In terms of the fourfold critical landscape, these strategies seek to transcend the phenomenal world either by leaping over the subject's shadow in order to attain a trans-constellational altitude, or by radicalizing Husserlian archaeology in order to rediscover an opaque, muted, and unworldly life in the immediacy of self-interment. This bifurca-tion of theo-philosophy between a pre-subjective 'human-in-itself' and a trans-objective 'thing-in-itself' has been clearly described by Laruelle in the following terms:

> The thinkers of extreme transcendence and radical immanence, the Jew and the non-philosopher, are thus opposed to the philosopher. Because the Real is the infinite of God or the Other or even the intrinsic radical finitude of Man-in-person, these are both fore-closed to representation, and hence a backwards transcending which is the effect or con-sequence of the leap into the Real [...]. The radical transcendence of the infinite, the rad-ical immanence of Man-in-person, this radical characteristic separates Transcendence and Immanence from the world.[30]

By means of this theo-philosophical bifurcation between a hyper-transcendent uncor-related 'absolute' (Good beyond Being, omnipotent hyper-chaos, immediate self-affec-tive Life, the non-philosophical 'One') and a relativized phenomenal world (Being, the nomological consistency of phenomenal nature, the alienated subject, the 'non-One'), theo-philosophers try to reject outside the absolute what seems to threaten its abso-luteness. The theo-philosophical projection of the absolute into a (trans-objective or pre-subjective) hyper-transcendence always depends upon a relativization of (every ra-tional thought of) the world. Instead of being the immanent draft that draws the abso-lutized world into its inner phenomenological depths, the absolute becomes 'a beyond whose shadow darkens the [world, GC]'.[31] This explains why the scientist will always remain the enemy *par excellence* of the theo-philosopher: the establishment of a first sci-ence of a hyper-transcendent 'Father'—or of his radically human Son—requires re-ducing and relativizing the 'second' science of phenomenal nature.

In sum, we can say that both the thinkers of the 'thing-in-itself' and the thinkers of the 'human-in-itself' agree in the attempt to identify the absolute with a hyper-tran-scendent uncorrelated instance to the detriment of mediated and alienated worldly ex-perience. As Novalis writes, whereas 'one still seeks a country behind these distant and bluish forms [...], another believes that a full future of life is hidden behind [himself]. Very few pause calmly amidst the beautiful forms that surround them and are content to grasp them in their integrity and their relations. Few do not forget the point when they are held fast by the details and sparkling chains that reconnect the parts with or-der [...]. Few feel their soul awaken to the contemplation of this living treasure that

30. François Laruelle, 'Les effets-Levinas. Lettre non-philosophique du 30 Mai 2006', 30 May 2006, <http://www.onphi.net/lettre-laruelle-les-effets-levinas-12.html>.

31. R.M. Rilke, 'Letter to W. von Hulewicz (November 13, 1925)', in *Letters of Rainer Maria Rilke—Vol. II: 1910-1926*, trans. J.B. Green, Leiserson Press, 2007, p. 374. Rilke writes 'earth' instead of 'world'.

floats on the abysses of the night'.[32] In order to grasp and unfold the correlational order which ties together the floating life that surrounds us, we shall assume the following 'Hegelian' inference. On the one hand, we have to be absolute beginners: the philosophical experience of the absolute must begin from an absolute which is already
present. The absolute cannot be identified with a trans-objective 'thing-in-itself' or a
pre-subjective 'human-in-itself' localized outside the phenomenal world, save to rela-
tivize it. A hyper-transcendent and relativized absolute, i.e. an absolute that coincides
with the term of a duality, is a squared circle. On the other hand, it is an existential
condition of the factice being-there that we are always already thrown into an alienated and mediated worldly experience. Therefore, we have to conclude that phenomenal experience is itself absolute and that any form of 'relative absolute' separated from
the world is, like Husserl's immobile *Ur-Erde*, nothing but a pre-modern theo-philosophical myth. Thus in the horizon of an absolutely modern philosophy, it is neither
a question of coveting a beyond more transcendent than any worldly exteriority, nor
of returning upstream towards a pre-subjective experience of a radical immediacy. It
is instead a question of remaining in the world by having activated its transfinite suspension, by means of the *epokhe*, in the absolute which is always already with us. Far
from transcending the phenomenal world, the speculative leap into the absolute brings
the absolutized world with it: we do not fall from the absolute into the world, it is the
worldly blossom that falls and opens endlessly in the immanent absolute.

MÜNCHHAUSEN'S BOOTSTRAPPING

In order to maintain that the transcendence of the world is a phenomenological distance opened within the immanence of the absolute, it is necessary to analyze to what
extent correlational mediation and worldly alienation are necessary conditions for the
effective realization of the absolute as absolute. In other words, it is necessary to evaluate the thesis according to which the immanent alienation of the absolute within itself
is one of the conditions of possibility of its ascent to absolute existence. Instead of trying to extract existence from the concept as in the ontological argument, we can begin to unfold a rational mediation between the *logos* and *existence* by attempting to identify the conceptual constraints imposed by the supposition of an absolute existence. In
other words, we can legitimately ask what an *existing* absolute must be like. The (supposed) impossibility of deducing existence from a mere concept does not entail the impossibility of deducing the 'concept' from existence. In other terms, we can legitimately
analyze the consequences of the regulating postulate according to which the rational structure of an existing absolute is not contingent. In particular, this programme
should allow us to evaluate the possible range of variability of this rational structure
and localize the hypothetical kernels of irreducible contingency. Such a strategy seeking to deduce the 'speculative categories' of the absolute and reactivate the problematic opened by the ontological argument from a certain angle, requires us to overcome one of the seminal theses of critical philosophy, namely the thesis according to
which there would be an uncrossable disjunction between being and beings. According to this thesis, if the 'how' of the world is the legitimate 'object' of the natural sciences, its very existence, juridically subtracted from any sort of analytical deduction,
could only be attested through a synthetic position of intra-worldly beings in percep-

---

32. Novalis, *The Novices of Sais*, trans. R. Manheim, Brooklyn, Archipelago, 2005.

tion. 'Kant's thesis about being' (and its Heideggerian variation[33]) only serves to obstruct the possibility of subtracting existence from its purely irrational contingency. The non-trivial Heideggerian thesis according to which being cannot be understood as a supreme being does not necessarily imply that it be impossible to construct a theoretical discourse—belonging by definition to the stratified extension of science that we have called knowledge—seeking to establish the aprioristic conditions of effective existence. It is worth remarking that, due to its very definition, (mathematical) formal ontology, which is a theoretical field seeking to unfold (the interrelations between) the generic categories of *being qua being* (multiplicity, localization, relation, and so on), does not address the effective givenness of beings. Formal ontology must therefore be supplemented by a new theoretical apparatus, which will be called *phenomenological ontology*, capable of speculatively spanning the gulf opened by ontological difference. By definition, phenomenological ontology is the science of the *being* of beings, insofar as 'being' names their effective givenness, which is to say their phenomenological *appearing*. It is perhaps time to advocate an active 'forgetting of being' and to reactivate the theoretical project of deploying conceptual mediations capable of continually rebinding being to (the effective givenness of) beings. Whereas formal ontology is an extension of mathematics capable of recognizing and unpacking its ontological scope, phenomenological ontology can be analogously considered an ontological extension of the natural sciences such as physics and biology. As we shall succinctly see in what follows, the concept of nature constructed by modern science furnishes a provisional model of a process of realization via an immanent specular procession and a continuous potentialization of nature's self-experience.

By definition, the existence of an 'absolute absolute'—i.e. of an absolute which is not relative to a separated non-absolute instance—must be an immanent property of the absolute, i.e. a property gauged against the standard of itself. As Kant argued in his refutation of the ontological argument, the effective existence of intra-worldly beings can only be established through a synthetic position in perception. As Hegel writes, 'this means simply that something, through its existence [...] is essentially in relationship with others, including also a percipient subject'.[34] We could thus say that a being exists insofar as it appears in a phenomenological plane, which is to say insofar as it is prehended by other beings (be them human or not). Indeed, 'if this content is considered as isolated, it is a matter of indifference whether it is, or is not; it contains no distinction of being or non-being [...]'[35] But the intentional (or prehensive) relationship between a perceived object and a perceiving subject (or between two prehensive objects) is, from the absolute point of view, a self-relationship of the absolute itself. Being both the subject and the object local concrescences of the absolute, their transcendent intentional prehension is a singular vector of the absolute's immanent reflexion. The speculative sublation of the critical refutation of the ontological argument amounts to the fact that the absolute exists if it is capable of positioning itself vis-à-vis itself, which is to say if it can become for itself through a self-differentiating and self-organizing process seeking to guarantee its self-manifestation, which is to say its self-interaction, self-perception, self-affection and, at the limit, self-comprehension. The categor-

---

33. 'Kant's thesis that being is not a real predicate cannot be impugned in its negative content. By it Kant basically wants to say that being is not a being', Martin Heidegger, *The Basic Problems of Phenomenology*, trans. A. Hofstadter, Bloomington, Indiana University Press, 1988, p. 55.

34. G.W. F. Hegel, *Science of Logic*, trans. A. V. Miller, London, Allen and Unwin, 1969, p. 88.

35. Hegel, *Science of Logic*, p. 87.

ical conditions of possibility of the absolute's existence are nothing but the conditions of possibility for its self-manifestation. The dawning process through which the absolute gradually awakens to itself therefore coincides with its effective *realization*, i.e. with the immanent deployment through which it takes out its being from itself. As Hegel writes, the absolute '[...] is in truth actual only in so far as it is the movement of positing itself [...]'.[36] Hence, the realization of the absolute depends upon its capacity to posit itself through an immanent correlational reflection and a phenomenological reflux. We could thus say that the absolute lifts itself to existence by means of a self-relational Münchhausen's bootstrapping.

If we assume (in the wake of Henry) that self-manifestation—which is the capacity to appear for itself within itself—is one of the defining properties of (not uniquely organic) *life*, we can say that absolute nature exists if it is a 'living substance' (Hegel). As Henry argues:

> The fact that life perseveres in its being is only possible because, given to itself in each point of its being and never ceasing in its self-affection of being, it does not at any moment fall into nothingness but, supported by itself in some way and taking out its being from the feeling that it has of itself, it in effect never stops being and being life.[37]

Nevertheless, unlike Henry, for whom the self-revelation of life springs up in an ego that precedes the intentional alienation of the subject in the transcendence of objective exteriority, the living self-manifestation of nature such as we understand it here can only take place within the phenomenological milieu of spatiotemporal transcendence, objectivity, and light.[38] Even before the emergence of local living organisms, nature phenomenalizes itself within worldly exteriority and bestows existence upon itself. The phenomenological dehiscence of '*physis*', far from being simply an ontic process causally unfolding in a pre-existent natural horizon, is the very condition of possibility of its continuous raising to existence. In this way, the speculative spanning of the ontological difference amounts to claim that self-appearing (or, in Hegelian terms, the 'reflection of itself within itself') constitutes the continuous mediation between being and beings. This immanent realization of nature through its phenomenological becoming for-itself is nothing but the process of its subjectification. A living substance is indeed a self-organizing substance capable of diversifying and progressively deepening its reflexive self-experience. We can thus conclude with Hegel that 'everything turns on grasping and expressing [absolute nature, GC], not only as [living, GC] *Substance*, but equally as *Subject*'.[39] We could say that Hegel elicited the properly speculative—i.e.

---

36. Hegel, *Phenomenology of Spirit*, p. 10.

37. Michel Henry, *La Barbarie*, Paris, Presses Universitaires de France, 2004, p. 169.

38. Concerning the differences between Henry's concept of revelation and Hegel's concept of manifestation, see the remarkable appendix titled 'The Bringing to Light of the Original Essence of Revelation in Opposition to the Hegelian Concept of Manifestation (*Erscheinung*)' in Michel Henry, *The Essence of Manifestation*, trans. G.J. Etzkorn, Springer, 1973. It is worth stressing that Henry's attempt to clarify these differences begins with a critique of the simplifying reduction of Hegel's thought to an anthropocentric idealism: 'The central affirmation of Hegelian philosophy is that the real is Spirit. What is proposed in such an affirmation is not an idealism [...]. Only a superficial interpretation aimed at degrading the thought of Hegel, from the ontological level on which it moves, to an ensemble of considerations of the ontic order can pretend to force philosophy, and that of Hegel in particular, to pose the question of knowing which is first the real and Being or Spirit. For example, the problem of an ontic deduction of the real beginning with the spirit does not arise. [...]. Now to say that the real is Spirit, is to say that it is essentially *the act of revealing itself and manifesting itself*, it is to say that the real is phenomenon'., Henry, *The Essence of Manifestation*, p. 689.

39. Hegel, *Phenomenology of Spirit*, p. 10.

neither anthropological nor transcendental—content of the Cartesian 'theorem' *cogito, ergo sum*. The becoming for-itself of nature through a process of self-differentiation, self-organization, and self-affection is a necessary and sufficient guarantee of its immanent realization as existing 'substance'. Nature exists because it is subject, which is to say because it is capable of positing itself through a process of self-manifestation. The existence of nature stems from the uninterrupted unveiling through which it actively absolves itself from its pre-subjective inexistence. We could thus say that even before the emergence of human beings, the existence of nature was strictly 'correlated' with its subjective self-experience. However, instead of positing itself in the pre-worldly immediacy of a radical Ego (like in Fichte and Henry), this speculative self-position can take place only through its worldly mediation. In this way, nature never ceases to engender itself through the specular deployment of its alienated, mutant, and mediated self-experience. Instead of being a last basis subtracted from restlessness and mediation, the absolute as subject constitutes itself in the phenomenological *Abgrund* opened by its immanent alienation. The absolute's subjectivity is alienated, abyssal, and barred: it 'only gains its truth insofar as [it] finds itself in absolute disarray'.[40] The absolute will thus have to stretch out upon its own couch and pass through the mediation of its self-analysis.

THE SPECULATIVE FALL

The natural realization of the absolute through its becoming for-itself is possible if the absolute opens within itself an immanent phenomenological distance. The immanent scission is thus one of the conditions of possibility of its self-manifestation. The self-splitting of the absolute under the form of an immanent horizon of transcendence defines what we shall call an *immanental plane*. As Deleuze writes in a sort of speculative extroversion of Husserlian idealism: '[…] all transcendence is constituted solely in the flow of [impersonal, GC] immanent consciousness that belongs to this plane. Transcendence is always a product of immanence'.[41] In particular, far from being transcendental obstructions to the knowledge of the 'absolute' thing-in-itself, the threefold pit and the unidimensional irreversible pendulum are necessary conditions of possibility of the absolute's self-experience.

But this immanent scission must itself be absolute, which means that it cannot be relativized in relation to a '*fundamental*' last instance subtracted from absolutory mediation. A philosophy of the *speculative absolute* only becomes possible on the basis of both a launching into orbit and an ungrounding of every *metaphysical foundation*. Hence, the immanent transcendence that the absolute opens within itself must be abyssal. The 'unconscious' abyss—i.e. the horizon of the absolute's immanent alienation—is one of the phenomenological conditions of possibility of its effective realization under the form of a 'self-consciousness'. The maintenance and potentialization of such a barred subjectivity require that the absolute be capable of detaching itself from the various local moments of its self-manifestation. Due to this immanent absolution, the bottom drops away: the anarchic absolute has no (back)ground, it is turtleless all the way down. Hence, any form of local 'last' instance descends everlastingly into the Maelstrom. Rather than any sort of crisis, the shipwreck is an 'eternal circumstance'

---

40. Hegel, *Phenomenology of Spirit*, p. 19 (trans. modified).

41. Gilles Deleuze, 'Immanence: A Life', in *Pure Immanence: Essays on a Life*, trans. A. Boyman, New York, Zone Books, 2005, p. 31.

of the absolute's life: the absolute is the immanent phenomenological 'draft [*Bezug*] to which all beings, as ventured beings, are given over', for absolute 'means something that does not block off. It does not block off because it does not set bounds. It does not set bounds because it is in itself' absolved from all bounds. The absolute 'is the great whole of all that is unbounded. It lets the beings ventured into the pure draft draw as they are drawn, so that they variously draw on one another and draw together without encountering any bounds. [...]. They do not dissolve into void nothingness [...]', but they endlessly fall into the open.[42] Due to this absolution in relation to every uncrossable transcendental bound, every finite product, every form of 'immediate' experience, every ideological hypostasis of a given horizon of possibilities, and every unilateral foundation capable of obstructing its self-mediation, the absolute never stops dissolving any reification of itself and reaffirming its turbulent absoluteness. The immobile transcendental earth, the supposed last instance capable of imposing an insurmountable limit to the restlessness of the negative, is nothing—from the absolute point of view—but 'a rock, a false manor right away evaporated in mists'.[43] We could thus say that the absolute lifts itself to existence by falling into itself. Due to this speculative fall, the absolute ungrounds and deepens its self-experience. To unground here means to penetrate the *Urgrund*, to mediate the 'impenetrable' basis in order to rediscover the opening in which every 'transcendental' earth is suspended. It is worth stressing that—unlike the theo-philosophical rejection of the 'relative' outside the 'absolute'—the speculative absolution with respect to any local ground does not flush the latter into an outer space. Since by definition nothing can fall outside the plane of absolute immanence, absolution can only be a free-falling immersion into the inner abyss. In this way, the eschatology of the absolute depends upon the scatological procession that provides the propulsion for the immanent unfolding of its self-experience. Through 'this pure universal movement, the absolute melting-away of everything stable',[44] the absolute absolves itself from its appropriating retention and fertilizes its self-manifestation.

If critical rootedness entails a transcendental bifurcation between a constituting last instance and a constituted world, absolution vis-à-vis any *Urgrund* turns absolute nature into a *suspended circle*. This means that, far from being a unidirectional and irreversible procession stemming from an 'axiomatic' infrastructure (transcendental ego, physical matter, primordial chaos, etc.), constitution is a circular and non-founded self-positing process. In particular, any intentional transcendence from a local subject towards a finite object is, from the absolute point of view, a reflexive immanent loop. The only means of suspending every metaphysical foundation, the only means of assuring that no instance is either first or last, is to accept the speculative circle of correlation, the circle through which nature can be called *causa sui*. There is no privileged instance or stratum: all local concrescences mutually involve themselves with one another due to the specular play of suspended correlation, for it is a 'daydream prohibited by Science [...] to find out if such an element is the supreme'.[45] Hence, we shall respectively substitute *correlational suspension* and *reflexive circularity* for the *transcendental foundation* upon an 'immediate' last instance and the corresponding *unidirectional constitution*. The absoluteness of the absolute entails in this way its immanent self-relativity.

42. Heidegger, 'What are Poets for?', p. 106.

43. Mallarmé, 'Dice Thrown Never Will Annul Chance', in *Selected Poetry and Prose*, p.121 (trans. modified).

44. Hegel, *Phenomenology of Spirit*, p. 117.

45. Stéphane Mallarmé, 'Les mots anglais', in *Œuvres Complètes*, Paris, Editions Gallimard, Bibliothèque de la Pléiade, 1945, p. 1048.

As Novalis writes:

> [Speculative, GC] philosophy *detaches* everything—relativizes the universe—. And like the Copernican system, eliminates the *fixed* points—creating a floating system out of one at rest. Philosophy teaches the relativity of all foundations and all qualities [...].[46]

The critical foundation constitutes a philosophical motif completely foreign to modern science. There is an irreversible divergence between modern rationality on the one hand and the pre-modern nostalgia for a foundation upon an archaic, infrastructural, or axiomatic ground on the other: 'earthly alienation is and has remained the hallmark of modern science'.[47] The regulative idea that orients the infinite tasks of the stratified extension of science does not call for establishing an ultimate foundation, a transcendental 'axiom' (*Grundstaz*), a 'material' infrastructure (be it corpuscular, economical, libidinal, etc.), or a last point of genesis for any logical deduction or ontic causality. The advance of modern science shows that the height of rationality comes hand in hand with the progressive implementation of the regulative principle of *(cor)relational suspension* or *self-consistent bootstrapping*. For instance, in the framework of the geometric theories of space-time, this principle requires substituting new interactive degrees of freedom immanent to nature itself for the aprioristic conditions or transcendental foundations of experience. The provisional recourse to a pre-natural transcendental condition is nothing but a local impasse of theoretical reason, a symptom of the fact that the prevailing concept of nature is still too restrained, for it does not suffice to hold its occurrence within its own immanental plane. More generally, the necessity of adding a transcendent 'agent' to the natural 'substance' (like, for instance, an organizing transcendental subject to the inconsistent multiplicity of hyletic data, a vital force to mechanistic inanimate matter, a supernumerary event to the inertial repetition of an unhistorical structure, mental states to material bodies, or a God-given existence to the purely ideal concept of nature) shows that the corresponding concept of substance is still too poor. Rather than adding a transcendent agent to the substance—and thus accepting the irreducibility of the corresponding dualism—the faithfulness to the absolute immanence of nature requires us to enrich the very concept of natural substance. In the case of Newtonian mechanics, the stakes were not that of philosophically founding its validity by considering 'absolute' space-time as a transcendental condition of possibility of every sensible intuition of natural phenomena. Instead, as Leibniz already understood, it was a question of performing an effective critique of Newtonian physics by considering the necessity of an 'absolute' spatiotemporal framework as a conceptual impasse to be overcome by means immanent to physics itself. It was thus necessary to traverse the bifurcation between the pre-natural spatiotemporal container and contained physical phenomena by *suspending* nature. Indeed, in the aftermath of Leibniz, Einstein's general theory of relativity replaces Newtonian space-time with new dynamic degrees of freedom (modulo the residual background dependence of Einstein's theory[48]). These degrees of freedom describe the inertio-gravitational field, which is nothing but the geodesic texture of relativist space-time itself. Weight can thus be understood as a symptom of

---

46. Novalis, *Notes for a Romantic Encyclopaedia (Das Allgemeine Brouillon)*, trans. D.W. Wood, New York, State University of New York Press, 2007, p. 111 (trans. modified).

47. Hannah Arendt, *The Human Condition*, Chicago, The University of Chicago Press, 1998, p. 264.

48. The residual background dependence of general relativity depends on the fact that the *dimension*, the *topology* and the *differential structure* of the spatiotemporal manifold constitute a fixed non-dynamical geometric structure.

the very opening of the immanent phenomenological horizon. In order to guarantee nature's absoluteness, it was necessary to extend the concept of nature: far from being a transcendental pre-natural framework of experience, space-time is henceforth a physical component of nature universally coupled with any physical field (including itself). In this way, the different physical components of the ungrounded natural circle that results from this relational suspension hold each other through their reciprocal interactions. We can thus maintain with Mallarmé that 'Nature takes place, we shall not add to it […]. Every available [theoretical, GC] act simply […] remains to grasp the rare or multiple relations […] according to some internal state'.[49] The amphibology between the gravitational spacing of the absolute within itself and its self-affective occurrence guarantees its suspended existence. Phenomenological ontology must unfold a conceptual interpolation—without adding any pre-natural transcendental condition—between the spanning of its (temporalized) place and the taking place of its self-awakening. Every available act will be to grasp the internal correlational states, i.e. the immanent relations through which absolute nature extracts its being from itself at each stage of the specular exponentiation of its self-experience. If we perform an angelic diagonalization of the pre-modern quadripartition between the earth and sky, the divines and the mortals, absolute nature remains as *the ring that encircles itself while it plays the game of reflections*.[50] Every local instance *exists* insofar as it is grasped in correlational transpropriation and specular potentialization. In the absence of every extrinsic foundation, reflection is the mirror-play of powers through which nature bestows existence upon itself: the game of nature 'cannot be explained by anything else […] causes and grounds remain unsuitable'[51] for fathoming its immanent dehiscence.

THE AIR IS ON FIRE

Yet, as Hegel affirms, the immanental plane that nature opens within itself is nothing but 'the abstract universality' and 'mediationless indifference' of 'Nature's self-externality […] the possibility and not the actual positedness of being-outside-of-one-another'.[52] In particular, the space-time manifold is nothing—modulo its dynamical affine and metric structures—but a '*principium individuations*' which allows for the introduction of a non-qualitative difference between indiscernible terms, which is to say a primitive *thisness* irreducible to *suchness*. In order to become an externality-for-itself, nature radiates *interactions* capable of connecting what will then be localized in spatiotemporal extension. The paradigmatic example of a connective interaction is light.[53] Due

49. S. Mallarmé, 'La Musique et les Lettres', in *Igitur, Divagations, Un coup de dés*, Paris, Editions Gallimard, 2003, p. 376.

50. cf. Martin Heidegger, 'The Thing', in *Poetry, Language, Thought*, p. 180.

51. Heidegger, 'The Thing', pp. 179-180.

52. Georg Wilhelm Friedrich Hegel, *Hegel's Philosophy of Nature: Encyclopaedia of the Philosophical Sciences Part II*, trans. A.V. Miller, Oxford, Oxford University Press, 2004, §254, p. 28-29.

53. This 'speculative' utilization of scientific concepts needs some clarifications. As we claimed above, modern philosophy must by definition be conditioned by modern science, which is to say that it must submit itself to the provisional theoretical representations of the real provided by the latter. The theoretical characterization of the speculative landscape for philosophical activity in terms of concepts coming from modern physics (including, for instance, the characterization of the immanent phenomenological distance and the internal correlations in terms of space-time and physical interactions respectively) is just a provisional description subjected to the progress of physics. In particular, the construction of a satisfactory quantum theory of gravity capable of harmonizing general relativity and quantum mechanics will probably entail a radical modification of the speculative landscape. However, we claim that modern philosophy must always prefer

to the iridescent fields that traverse the open, nature escapes from darkness. Its night-like abyss thus becomes a *clearing (Lichtung)*, i.e. an *illuminated space*. The gravity's rain-bow that entwines spatiotemporal geodesics and the free falling radiance defines the causal conification of the open. In order to concretely occupy the clearing and reveal light, nature distils chromatic matter fields, i.e. continuous extensions of local quali-ties. The connective interactions mediate these qualitative fields by providing them with a *cohesion*, which is to say by connecting local qualities situated in different spa-tiotemporal positions.[54] It is remarkable that the inertio-gravitational field that opens and weaves together the spatiotemporal extension simultaneously supplies the contrac-tion principle for the stellar concrescences which will fall into it. Indeed, the flexibili-ty of the gravitational tissue induces an attractive 'force' that concentrates matter and locally breaks the homogeneity of space-time. Thus the dialectics of nature becomes a galactics. The thermodynamic conditions of non-equilibrium induced by the gravita-tional inhomogeneities of space-time make the emergence of local morphogenetic self-organizing processes possible. Hence, the stellar self-positioning of nature in its local positions supplies the entropic conditions necessary for the embodiment of local points of view, which is to say for the localization of its global and impersonal subjectivity. In this way, the immanental structure that enables nature's self-experience brings forth the emergence of local organisms (vegetal, animal, human, etc.) endowed with partic-ular transcendental faculties. In turn, these transcendental structures allow these local subjects to navigate through the transcendent experience of the immanent nature in which they are immersed. Nature exponentiates its immanent self-experience by pro-ducing and multiplying 'transcendent' perspectives on itself carried out by local sub-jects endowed with transcendental structures. In this way, every intentional (or pre-hensive) experience—enabled by the local subject's transcendental structure—must be understood, from the Absolute point of view, as a reflexive relation of nature to itself, which is enabled by the immanental structure of the latter. The resulting local subjects effectuate perspectival prehensions of nature and radiate phenomenological sheaves for other prehensions. We could say that the opening of a gravitational clearing criss-crossed by connective light rays requires the germination of floral mirrors and *vitraux* capable of locally effectuating reflection and diffraction: '[…] the silent and noctur-nal growing of vegetation prepares an oval and crystalline identity, where an isolated group achieves a communication similar to a universal mirror'.[55] In this way, the self-manifestation of nature in its abyss nourishes on its own light. Vegetal photosynthesis is nothing but an exponentiation to a superior power of such a phenomenological prin-ciple. Whereas the inertio-gravitational field splits nature under the form of an abyss-al opening, electromagnetic radiance slides into the scission by making possible its im-manent dehiscence. The speculative role of these various perceptive and expressive

---

the possibility of being 'wrong' by being conditioned by modern science than to disdainfully avoid any com-merce with it with the hopes of being preserved from the perishable character of every scientific world-view. Indeed, the 'falsifiability' of scientific theories is just an index of the extent to which scientific labor does grasp the rational structure of the real. A (partially) successful theory (like for instance classical mechanics) which comes to be superseded by a more satisfactory one (like quantum mechanics), far from being simply false, is just a partial and unilateral moment of the truth. Paraphrasing Lacan, we could say that science *al-ways speaks the truth. Not the whole truth* […]. *Yet it's through this very partiality that science holds onto the real* (cf. Jacques Lacan, *Television*, trans. D. Hollier, R. Krauss, and A. Michelson, MIT Press, 1987, p. 6).

54. cf. Gabriel Catren, 'Geometric Foundations of Classical Yang-Mills Theory', in *Studies in History and Philosophy of Modern Physics*, 39, 2008, p. 511-531.

55. José Lezama Lima, *Paradiso*, Madrid, Ediciones Cátedra, 1997, p. 298.

subjects is thus to locally support, unfold, and potentialize the specular self-affection of this cosmos in bloom: 'only from the chalice of this realm of spirits foams forth for [it its] own infinitude'.[56]

A local subject is not simply a mirror capable of prehending and reflecting phenomenological sheaves, but also a germ of an internal fibration of the abyss. Far from being the enclave of an immediate and apodictic arche-experience, nature's local subjectification opens up new forms of abyssality, namely inner voids. The potentialization of nature's self-manifestation requires both a deepening of the spatiotemporal chasm and the fibrated opening of new spaces towards which to descend. The irruption of these private vortices will thus enable the diffraction of the shipwreck into several gulfs: through the local foldings of its impersonal subjectivity, nature can intensify its disarray by multiplying the ways of falling into itself. Far from opposing itself to a non-conscious nature that would be seamless, unbarred, unreflected, gapless, unhistorical, and entirely exteriorized, the (vegetal, animal, human, etc.) contraction of 'spirit' is nothing but a local instantiation of nature's abyssal subjectivity, of its intrinsic castration and constitutive being for-itself. We can thus say that nature potentializes its inherent reflexivity by means of a local subjective fibration of its unconscious chasm. This local subjectification in turn entails a 'spherical' umweltification of experience: every local subjective germ is surrounded by a worldly capsule, which partially extends throughout spatiotemporal extension and its private unconscious abyss. The intentional polarizations of the subject-object type are nothing but a particular sort of specular correlation among the infinite local diversifications of nature's reflexivity. Nevertheless, 'we risk more' than plants or animals because we also fall into internal spaces. And the angel will risk even more than us, because he will fall into the projective gulf $n \rightarrow \infty$ opened by the n-Copernican revolutions.

GRAVITY'S ANGEL

The speculative sublation of transcendental philosophy implies that the phenomenological potentialization of the 'experience of consciousness', far from being constrained to unfold within the horizon defined by a fixed transcendental aprioristic structure, can submit the very conditions of possibility of experience to the dialectic restlessness of natural, historical, and technical genesis. Hence, the aprioristic structure of human experience can be the object of a reflexive labour of mediation and transcendental variation explicitly assumed. In particular, the effective subjective embodiment of the advocated speculative absolutism requires us to subsume the pre-modern components of the critical philosopher's formal subjective typology.

It must first be emphasized that strictly speaking the modern subject—i.e. a subjective typology synchronous with modern science—is yet to come. Through the most various forms of narcissistic reterritorialization, human building, dwelling, and thinking continue to take place in a Ptolemaic pre-modern landscape. Strictly speaking, the subject of modern times constitutes a transitory subjective typology which is no longer that of pre-modern subject, but is still not that of the subject of science. In order to indicate the gap between the subject of enunciation of scientific discourse and a subject capable of assuming the very consequences of this discourse regarding its existence within the absolute, we shall characterize a new subjective typology, namely what we shall designate by means of the acronym *angel*, which means *Absolunaut Navigating in*

---

56. Hegel, *Phenomenology of Spirit*, p. 493.

Gravitational Extraterrestrial Levitation. Paraphrasing Heidegger, we could say that we are too late for the gods and too early for angels.[57]

By definition, the angel results from the mediation of the pre-modern subject's existentialia (*Existenzialien*). First, this means that the angel is a human who irreversibly fell from transcendental earth. In other words, the angel is a subjective form that assumes the lack of a transcendental anchorage. The longing for an immediate and unilateral *Urgrund* subtracted from orbital revolution is a reactive passion elicited by the abysses opened up by modern science. In opposition to this pre-modern nostalgia, the angel's desire is not homesickness, but the desire to be at home nowhere: being-angel [*être-ange*] means nothing more than being-there as stranger [*étranger*]. In this way, if Narcissus is the subject of the Ptolemaic counter-revolution, the angel is the subject of the Copernican revolution, i.e. a subject capable of assuming the passage from earth as a transcendental dwelling of an authentic existence to 'spaceship earth' (Buckminster Fuller) as a decentred and contingent support of an epiphytic mankind. Far from being an accident brought about by his egotism, Narcissus' fall into the spherical liquid sky that surrounds him is nothing but a speculative passage to the act seeking to sublate his transcendental solipsism. If Narcissus sees in the objective world nothing but the harmonious ensemble of his properties reflected upon the surface of the transcendental glass (namely the reflection of his physiological structures, his measuring devices, his categories, his imaginary schemata, his linguistic structures, and so on), the modern angel——by overcoming the mirror stage—becomes a stranger to himself: 'Some sort of angel was sitting on the edge of a fountain. He stared there… His own figure and the pain that plagued him seemed foreign to him'.[58]

Whereas the landing on a transcendental earth necessarily projects a sheltering sky, modern deterritorialization triggers the gravitational venture. Without a transcendental support capable of compensating for the force of gravity and unilaterally founding existence, gravity acts freely. However, the resulting state of free-fall takes place in complete immobility. As we know from Galileo and Einstein, without a fixed geometric background endowed with an 'absolute' reference frame capable of breaking the physical indiscernibility between different locations, free fall in the groundless abyss is indistinguishable from rest. The geodesic 'lines of beauty and grace' interweaving space-time trace the paths of the still fall. The incorrectly labelled 'state of weightlessness' (or 'zero gravity') is nothing but a state upon which gravity freely acts. In particular, the orbital revolution is nothing but a closed instantiation of the gravitational subversion: 'Subversion, if it has existed somewhere and at some time, is not to change the point of that which circles—it is to replace *it turns* with *it falls*'.[59] Hence, modern being-there is not a rooting upon, but a suspended falling through. In order to be there, it is no longer possible—nor even necessary—to find an immobile earth capable of preventing the fall and supplying a last instance upon which to build and dwell. Whereas the critical fall is a crisis that must be overcome by a transcendental interment, the speculative fall is a groundless levitation, an immobile sliding—*mobilis in mobili*—along geodesic tracks. If 'the place, before being a geometric space […] is a base',[60] the prop-

---

57. Heidegger's original text reads: 'We are too late for the gods and too early for Being'. Martin Heidegger, 'The Thinker as Poet', in *Poetry, Language, Thought*, p. 4.

58. Paul Valery, 'L'Ange', in *La Jeune Parque et poèmes en prose*, Paris, Editions Gallimard, 1974, p. 39.

59. Jacques Lacan, *On Feminine Sexuality: The Limits of Love and Knowledge: The Seminar of Jacques Lacan, Book XX*, trans. Bruce Fink, New York, Norton, 1998.

60. Emmanuel Levinas, *Existence and Existents*, trans. A. Lingis, Plattsburgh, Duquesne University Press, 2001.

erly modern experience of geometric space takes place by means of a covariant absolution in relation to every transcendental base. Whereas the transcendental earthly base is the pre-modern Place of mortals, modern 'geometry expressly concerns angels'.[61] The speculative utilization of transcendental reflection aims to recognize the aprioristic stages that made a given form of experience possible in order to let these conditions of possibility fall away into the unconscious abyss when they start to impede phenomenological unfolding. Like a multistage rocket, the launch of the 'experience of consciousness' out of the *Lebenswelt*'s atmosphere requires unburdening itself from its propulsive stages. We could thus say that the absolution into the unconscious is the condition of possibility of the progressive sublation of the 'experience of consciousness'. In particular, whereas the Husserlian variation of transcendental critique seeks to ground geometry in the ante-predicative *Lebenswelt*, the speculative sublation of the 'origin of geometry' intends to use the more 'concrete' branches of geometry (including, for instance, algebraic geometry or quantum geometry) to absolve being-there from the abstract unilaterality of the 'immediate' experience of lived space. The angel floats far above the transcendental earth: he 'left the Place. [He exists] beyond any horizon—everything around [him is] sky or, more exactly, everything [is] geometrical space'. The angel exists 'in the absolute of homogeneous space'.[62] If, by launching the earth into orbit, the Copernican revolution brings forth the terror of the uprooting fall, the Galilean-Einsteinian subversion shows that, strictly speaking, existence can dispense with every transcendental reterritorialization: a fall from no disaster, gravity is grace [*la pesanteur est la grace*]. If the angel goes 'where there is danger', if he goes deeper into the 'distress of modern times', it is not so that he might sense the trace of fugitive gods, but to establish itself in groundless flotation.

The relativist indiscernibility between the immobile suspension and the free fall allows the angelic subject of science to relieve himself of the orni-theological mystification according to which angels would have wings. Instead of having wings that would allow them to avoid the fall, angels absolved themselves from any metaphysical foundation capable of preventing it. Far from imitating the flight of birds, the angels 'fly' because they have learned 'again to fall and go with gravity's law'[63]. Instead of attempting to critically overcome any crisis whatsoever—*crisis? what crisis?*—, a philosophy synchronous with modern science must be able to shy away from the reactive litanies that diagnose crises and promise transcendental lands. For the falling angels, the only veritable 'crisis' would be the presence of an ultimate earth capable of turning their fall into a flattening, transforming that which falls [*ce qui tombe*] into a tomb. As Poe has definitively informed us, the angel of the odd has no wings, his flight is his fall:

> And I ventured to reply 'but I was always under the impression that an angel had wings'. 'Te wing!' [the angel of the odd] cried, highly incensed, 'vat I pe do mitt e wing? Mein Gott!! Do you take me vor a shicken?'[64]

In the framework of the fourfold critical landscape, the revolutionary abolition of the transcendental ownership of land unleashes dread vis-à-vis the inhumanity of the in-

61. Jacques Lacan, *Séminaire XXIV, L'insu que sait de l'une-bévue s'aile à mourre*, session of 15 March 1977 (unpublished).

62. Emmanuel Levinas, 'Heidegger, Gagarin and Us', in *Difficult Freedom: Essays on Judaism*, trans. S. Hand Baltimore, Johns Hopkins University, 1997, p. 223.

63. R.M. Rilke, *The Book of Hours*, trans. A.S. Kidder, Illinois, Northwestern University Press, 2001, p. 127.

64. Edgar Allen Poe, 'The Angel of the Odd', in *Poetry and Tales*, New York, Library of America, 1984, p. 758.

finite spaces and the loss of an *Urgrund* capable of stopping the fall. In particular, the philosopher of the sacred Place is authentically frightened by the lunatic uprooting and technical devastation of the *Heimat*:

> [...] technology tears men loose from the earth and uproots them. [...] I was certainly scared when I recently saw the photographs of the earth taken from the moon. We don't need any atom bomb. The uprooting of man has already taken place. [...] This is no longer the earth on which man lives. [...] According to our human experience and history, [...] I know that everything essential and everything great originated from the fact that man had a home and was rooted in a tradition.[65]

Faced with this diagnosis, the duty of speculative absolutism is to save us from a theo-philosophical salvation: if only a god can save us from the worst [*pire*], only absolute immanence can save us from the hyper-transcendent Father [*père*]. Instead of leading back towards the hominess of a transcendental land, the mediating tasks prescribed by the infinite regulative ideas (the Beautiful, the True, the Good) are—*Worstward Ho!*— 'the beginning of the terrible'.[66] In particular, it is necessary to become transcendental vandals and, as Levinas writes in his call to waste the land, 'destroy the sacred groves' and 'disenchant Nature', relieve ourselves of the superstitious nostalgia of the Place and the idolatry of the (arche-)earth, uproot existence and launch the transcendental diaspora[67]. In this way, the concrete universality of the high-tech angel crushes the metaphysical hypostases of tribal and national particularisms, and abolishes the abstract difference between autochthonous and foreigners. The angel's self-expropriation vis-à-vis his reifying properties—i.e. the release of a generic subjective essence capable of perduring, without attempting to stitch up the narcissistic wounds inflicted by modern science, through the continuous forcing of his alienation—does nothing but bet from the turning-away from the hyper-transcendent Father to the worstward life in the unshielded absolute: '*De ce qui perdure de perte pure à ce qui ne parie que du père au pire*'.[68]

In the wake of the Newtonian homogenization of nature, the characterization of the angel as a *messenger* capable of crossing the pre-modern bifurcation between the earth and the sky follows from the fact that for the angel the absolute is *one*. As Heidegger notes, Rilke's angel is 'the being who brings out the radiant appearance of the way in which that oneness unifies'.[69] Strictly speaking, the angel is not a *messenger*, but rather a local *mediator* of the absolute's self-experience. Without a transcendental earth there is no longer an event horizon capable of establishing an uncrossable limit to the mediation of experience. Without a hypostatized horizon, there is no longer an inaccessible transcendence. The Copernican launch to orbit of the 'Earth who was the Mother of all living creatures under the sky' and the 'turning-away [...] from a god who was the father of men in heaven'[70] are the two faces of the same secular absolution. In this way, the angel overcomes the 'objectifying turning away from the open',[71] i.e. the theo-philosophical projection of the absolute into any form of trans-objective or

---

65. Martin Heidegger, 'Only a God Can Save Us: Der Spiegel's Interview with Martin Heidegger', trans. M.P. Alter & J.D. Caputo, in *Philosophical and Political Writings*, New York, Continuum, 2006, p. 37.

66. R.M. Rilke, *Duino Elegies*, p. 20 (trans. modified).

67. cf. Levinas, 'Heidegger, Gagarin and Us'.

68. 'From that which perdures through pure dross to that which does nothing but bet from the father to the worst', Lacan, *Television*, p. 50 (trans. modified).

69. Heidegger, 'What are Poets for?', p. 136.

70. Arendt, *The Human Condition*, p. 2.

71. Heidegger, 'What are Poets for?', p. 120.

pre-subjective hyper-transcendence whatsoever. Without theological transcendence, the deepening of experience neither depends upon the promise of an evental grace nor upon a liturgical protocol of transgression. We could say that the absolute is the (ab)solvent solution that dissolves the narcotics division and makes the mediation of the transcendental boundaries of *Geviert* possible: 'Angels, it's said, are often unsure whether they pass among living or dead'[72], mortals or immortals. The angel is thus a subjective diagonalizer of the *Geviert*, i.e. a subjective typology capable of locally supporting and effectuating the unbounding oneness of the absolute. As Rilke writes:

> The true figure of life extends through *both* spheres [life and death], the blood of the mightiest circulation flows through *both: there is neither a here nor a beyond, but the great unity* in which the beings that surpass us, the 'angels', are at home.[73]

In Rilke, the angelic sublation of the theo-philosophical relativization of the absolute—i.e. the Newtonian conversion of the transcendental bifurcation between the immobile earth and the noumenal sky 'into an arriving into the widest [gravitational, GC] orbit of the Open'[74]—is symbolized by 'the passing over of the balance from the merchant to the Angel'.[75] Whereas 'the customary life of contemporary man is the common life of the imposition of self on the unprotected market of the exchangers',[76] the life of a properly modern subject depends on the abolition of every identification between its generic subjective essence and its particular (private) properties. More generally, the holy family, the national *Heimat*, the division of labour, monolingualism, and private property all prevent the speculative fall into the 'identical neutrality of the abyss'. From this point of view, Marx did nothing but bring the vast process of expropriation that begins with Copernicus even further: if humanity is no longer at the centre of the universe, if humanity is nothing but a local link in an evolutionary chain which, far from any metaphysical eschatology, results from a blind play between chance and necessity, if 'the ego is not master in its own house',[77] Marx calls to reactivate the 'good infinite' of generic human subjectivity via the abolition of private property. As Deleuze and Guattari argue, the generic '[…] subjective essence is discovered by capitalism only to be put in chains all over again, to be subjugated […] in the element, itself subjective, of private property […]. It is the form of private property that constitutes the centre of the factitious reterritorializations of capitalism'.[78] Only the activation and deepening of Marx's fourth narcissistic wound would enable the angelic sublation of the 'merchant'. The angel has nothing but his pure subjective capacity of going beyond himself, dissolving any appropriating retention, and mediating any essentialization of his existence: having no country, the angel is a stranger without nostalgia; having no profession, he can systematically abolish the division of labour; always speaking in a sort of foreign language, he can practice a generalized translatability between the local modes of thought and aspire to 'pure language' (Benjamin); in short, being nothing but a local germ of subjectification, he can be everything. In particular, the angel opposes the expropriating di-

72. Rilke, *Duino Elegies*, p. 24.

73. Rilke, 'Letter to W. von Hulewicz (November 13, 1925)', p. 373.

74. Heidegger, 'What are Poets for?', p. 131.

75. Heidegger, 'What are Poets for?', p. 137.

76. Heidegger, 'What are Poets for?', p. 136.

77. Sigmund Freud, 'A Difficulty in the Path of Psycho-Analysis', in *The Standard Edition of the Complete Psychological Works of Sigmund Freud, Volume XVII (1917-1919)*, trans. J. Strachey and A. Freud, London, The Hogarth Press and the Institute of Psycho-Analysis, 1955, p. 143.

78. Deleuze and Guattari, *Anti-Oedipus*, p. 303.

alectic to the appropriating event, the alienating self-sublation to the self-affirmation in vital space, and the orbital land revolution to the 'inner truth and greatness' of National Socialism. All in all, we could say that Hegelian speculative absolutism (and its Marxist outcome) is the most powerful weapon against the Heideggerian critical fundamentalism and the concomitant pre-modern theo-philosophical landscape.

Hence, in the properly modern stage of the potentialization of its self-experience, the immersion of the absolute in its phenomenological depths coagulates into falling angels. We could thus say with Artaud that 'an Angel is born from this Manifestation [of the Absolute in its, GC] Abysses'.[79] The angel is a subjective typology synchronous with modern science, which is to say a barred, errant, (trans)finite, mutant, and outcast human being; an unidentified flying subject lacking any transcendental at-homeness; an alien whose transcendental structure, far from being the enclave of an immediate and apodictic experience, is the condition of possibility of its irreversible alienation in an uncanny immanental plane. The grace of angelic descent and the unconditional confidence in gravitational fall, the indifference vis-à-vis any pathetic announcement of a crisis and any promise of critical salvation, the mediation of any event horizon whose opacity could impede the whole phenomenological draft through the immanent 'open', the dialectical blow-up of any appropriating event, the resolution of any supposed last instance of experience, the scatological absolution from every retentive identification with its properties, and the willingness to deepen and multiply the narcissistic wounds inflicted by modern science are some of the modern existentialia that turn the angel into a formal subjective figure capable of dropping away the *Ur-Erde*, navigating the system and 'storming heaven'.

1807: A SPIRIT ODYSSEY

It would be misleading to establish a break between the 'terrorist' Hegel on the one hand—i.e. the Hegel of absolute unrest, the melting-away of every substance, and dialectic negativity—and, on the other, the 'bureaucratic' Hegel of the system, absolute knowledge, and the state. By extolling the young incendiary to the detriment of the old Berliner fireman (or vice versa), we would lose what constitutes the core of his *anarchic constructivism*, namely the ultramodern bond between *speculative ungrounding* on the one hand and *systematic construction* on the other. Far from having 'worked out the system in order to escape [...] the extreme limit' that it touched upon and to attain salvation as Bataille maintains,[80] the system is a perforating concrete machine seeking to wriggle through the *Urgrund* and regain the abyss. The speculative operation that makes the system possible is not the *foundation* upon an immobile earth, but instead the *absolution* vis-à-vis any fundamental last instance. Hence, the architectonic of systematic reason can no longer be that of a cathedral enrooted in the arche-earth and raised towards the inaccessible sky, but rather that of a spatial station, i.e. a Laputian outland empire freefalling into the absolute. The philosopher, that is the local subjective support of this speculative absolunautics, glides in coalescence upon the surfaces of the extended phenomenal plane, composing concrete mediators out of the prismatic vectors of scientific, artistic, and political disindoxication, potentializing the phenomenological unfolding of the self-experience of the absolute which is always already with us.

---

79. Antonin Artaud, 'Lettre à Jean Paulhan (Kabhar Enis—Kathar Esti) du 7 octobre 1943', in *Œuvres*, Paris, Éditions Gallimard, 2004, p. 901.

80. Georges Bataille, *Inner Experience*, trans. L.A. Boldt, Albany, SUNY Press, 1988, p. 43.

22

Wondering about Materialism

Isabelle Stengers

Thirty years ago, when writing *La Nouvelle Alliance* (translated as *Order out of Chaos*) with Ilya Prigogine[1], I proposed a definition of materialism from the scientific point of view—not 'matter as defined by sciences but materialism as a challenge to the sciences'. Materialism, I wrote, demands 'that we understand nature in such a way that there would be no absurdity in affirming that it produced us'. At that time, this sentence was meant only to emphasize that the far-from-equilibrium physics which was presented in that book was a step in this direction, because the possibility of matter spontaneously adopting, far from equilibrium, a collective self-organized form of activity was somehow diminishing the gap between life and non-life.

Today the situation has changed. On the one hand, what I took for granted thirty years ago—that understanding nature is at stake in natural sciences—would now be hotly contested by those who are busy deconstructing and eliminating any connection between the sciences and the claims associated with understanding. But on the other hand, happily equating our understanding with an active elimination of everything about 'us' that cannot be aligned with a so-called 'scientific' conception of matter, is now widely endorsed in the name of scientific rationality. Eliminativists do not refer to the 'materialist' tradition, rather to a so-called naturalist one, which in fact confers full authority to the physics and the array of 'molecular sciences'—what I will later characterize as 'physicalism'. This is why—and it will be the theme of this paper—I now propose that the demands of materialism cannot be identified in terms of knowledge alone, scientific or other. Rather, just like the Marxist concept of class, materialism loses its meaning when it is separated from its relations with struggle.

Struggle must obviously be distinguished from the academic war games conducted around so many versions of what can be called 'eliminativism'. I would disagree with Alain Badiou critically associating the post-modern (academic) claim that there are only bodies and languages with what he calls a 'democratic materialism'[2]. I would

1. Ilya Prigogine and Isabelle Stengers, *La Nouvelle Alliance: Metamorphose de la Science*, Paris, Gallimard, 1980; translated as *Order out of Chaos: Man's New Dialogue With Nature*, Shambala, 1984.

2. Alain Badiou, 'Democratic Materialism and the Materialist Dialectic', *Radical Philosophy*, no. 130, 2005.

emphasize that the eliminative claim expressed by 'only' may well sound democratic, in the sad sense of erasing all differences that oppose general equivalence, but it is first and foremost part of such an academic (that is very non-democratic) war game. Indeed the ones who make this claim take the classic academic high ground: they know while others just believe.

Against such a 'democratic' materialism, it is tempting to invoke Spinoza: 'We do not even know what a body can do'. But we also have to invoke other, more compromising voices. To accept being endangered is part of the struggle. It is academically fashionable to quote Spinoza today, but less so to recall that both religion and the craft of magic implied some knowledge of what language can do—of the power of words crafted to bless or kill, or save, or curse—of ritual or ancestral words. Only languages indeed!

However, my point here is not about what we know, and what we do not know, or refuse to know. My point is to radically distinguish between the link between materialism and struggle on the one hand, and the proud opposition between those who believe and those who know on the other. Academic bickering is usually reducible to a matter of mere rivalry for a very disputed title: who is the thinking brain of humanity? Such a rivalry was sadly exhibited some years ago, in the famous 'science wars', with scientists aggressively reacting against the thesis that science was a practice like any other. Whatever the dogmatic rigidity of this reaction, it would be a mistake to identify it with a mere defence of their privileges. It may well be that some of the angry protesters would have accepted, as would any heir to Marx, that sciences are practices, and that whatever claims to truth, objectivity or validity they produce, these have to be actively related to those practices. But what scientists heard, and what made them angry, was an attack by academic rivals and judges, claiming that science was 'only' a practice, as 'any' other, implying that those rivals and judges possessed the general definition of a practice.

It is important in this connection to refer to the struggle of radical scientists such as Hilary and Stephen Rose against what they defined as bad science. As Hilary Rose forcefully testified, this struggle was made difficult because their radical allies were not ready to recognize that there are 'bad sciences', as this would imply that there is something like a 'good' science. As if the only opposite of bad is good. Rose's point was not to 'defend a good science', but it implied to characterize the practices of science in order to resist those who betray the specific constraints of such practices and to identify those who encourage or take advantage of this betrayal.

Today, the relevance of such resistance has become a matter of public and political concern. Together with the wide protest and struggle against GMOs, it is the conception of living beings, which dominates contemporary biology that has been turned into a stake in the dispute. Here we do not deal with academic rivalry but with a struggle, which, like all struggles, produced novel connections between many issues. It has connected the risks of biotechnology, the industrial (unsustainable) redefinition of agriculture, the role of patents in industrial strategies, and the mode of production of scientific knowledge, with the certainties of lab biologists silencing those colleagues who work outside of the lab and ask different and perplexing questions. The great voice of Vandana Shiva is raised not only against biopiracy and the privatization of life forms but also against the abstract definition of those life forms that is exhibited in the project of modifying them at will.

It would be a catastrophic mistake, I believe, to recognize the importance of Vandana Shiva's struggle against capitalism while associating her protest against the paradigm of contemporary biology with words like holistic, traditional or romantic. Hers is a call not for 'an other science', but for a relevant science, a science that would actively take into account the knowledge associated with those agricultural practices that are in the process of being destroyed in the name of progress.

The thesis I am defending—that materialism should be divorced from (academic) eliminativism in order to connect with struggle—does not deny that elimination may have been utterly relevant, when it entailed struggling against the allied powers of state and church, for instance. Today, however, the situation has changed. Elimination has become the very tool of power. It is not only a tool for capitalism, but also for what I would call, together with Hilary Rose, 'bad science'.

PHYSICALISM

The connection between the science called physics and eliminativism is vague at best. Physicalism is a rather a war machine for the conquest of new territories. Inside the academic world it is clear that humanities are the target. This is exemplified by Daniel Dennett denouncing what he derisively calls 'skyhooks', miraculous lifters that he defines as transcending the working of evolutionary processes. In order for those processes to be compatible with physics, Dennett claims, they must be understood in terms of replicators and the competition among replicators, producing what he calls 'cranes'. In order not to confuse academic polemic and operations of conquest with a materialist struggle, it is important to be concrete. Such operations, undertaken in the name of progress and reason, are about power. Take two recent books, Daniel Dennett's *Breaking the Spell: Religion as a Natural Phenomenon* and Richard Dawkins' *The God Delusion*. What is characteristic about such books, and the flourishing industry of evolutionary psychology more generally, is the complete ignorance and contempt their authors entertain about the work of their colleagues: historians of religion or anthropologists, for instance. As if this work, the controversies and learning it has produced, the slow and difficult resistance it entails against the easy temptation of projecting the ideas of the West onto other people (that is, of judging them in terms of this standard) was of no interest at all. Dennett would say that all this work is saturated with skyhooks as are all cultural studies because they try and take seriously what should be eliminated, reduced to the working of evolutionary cranes. Further he would argue that it is now irrelevant since the 'cranes' science is a truly objective science, the universality of which has nothing to do with the ideas of the West. This science will not be stopped by scholarly niceties. Its object is the 'real' human behind cultural appearances, the human defined as the result of the working of evolutionary cranes. 'Alas, poor Darwin' ....

Anthropologists, historians of religion and others will protest that this leads us back to the imperialist 19th century, but if their protest remains in the academic world, if the situation does not become a matter of political concern and struggle, it will be of no great avail. They will be left to dry away in their libraries, with all the research money and new students going to the new evolutionary anthropologists who travel everywhere in order to submit people to questions the aim of which is to identify universal human affective and cognitive features.

This may be only an academic war, but like the conception of life-forms dominating contemporary biology, as denounced by Vandana Shiva, such wars may also be breaking the ground for other kind of operations. I am thinking of the future great techno-scientific revolution that is now heralded, the great NBIC convergence—the convergence between Nanotechnology, Biotechnology, Information Technology and Cognitive Science. Such a convergence, which is not about understanding but about transforming, requires from knowledge a definition of what is to be conquered in the perspective of the legitimacy of this conquest. That is, it requires an elimination of all obstacles as not really mattering, just like the Indian peasants' knowledge must not matter if GMOs are to prevail. And this is precisely what skyhook-hunting and slaying is doing. The universal acid of the so-called dangerous idea of Darwin is just what is needed. It brings no effective understanding of evolutionary processes but is eliminating, dissolving away, all reasons to resist the redefinition of humans as a piece of engineering that can be understood in terms of algorithms, and modified at will. And those who struggle against this operative redefinition of our worlds will have against them the authority of reason and science.

Now a radical theorist may claim that cultural anthropology or history of religion were of interest in the colonial epoch, but that in the present epoch of global, delocalized capitalism, dematerialization, substrate independent algorithms and universal flexibility are what matters. The changes in contemporary science, the destruction of those fields, would then just be the expression of this transformation. This is a very smart proposition indeed, but it may be a bit too smart, as it first warrants that the one who produces such an analysis is not a dupe, does not entertain any illusion. Nobody will be able to say to him or her 'What! You still believe that…'. This is a good position in the academic game, but a position that is not connected with any possibility of struggle. It rather emphasizes the power of capitalism to do and undo, and all the theorist can tell to besieged, angry or protesting scientists is: despair, lose your illusions that what you were doing was worth doing, was mattering. Eliminative materialism indeed.

Like Donna Haraway, who has chosen now to dare writing no longer about fashionable cyborgs, but about her dogs, about the creation of a relation that matters between her and the dog Cayenne with whom she practices agility sports, I am convinced that we need other kinds of narratives, narratives that populate our worlds and imaginations in a different way. When writing about Cayenne and about what she has learned with her, Haraway is exposing herself to her colleagues' derision, and knowingly so, but she is making present, vivid and mattering, the imbroglio, perplexity and messiness of a worldly world, a world where we, our ideas and power relations, are not alone, were never alone, will never be alone. As she recalls with joy and wonder, human genomes can be found in only about 10% of the cells that live in what we call our body, the rest of the cells being filled with the genomes of bacteria, fungi, protists, and such. Her last book, *When Species Meet*[3], is a radically materialist one, but it is a materialism of another kind, a kind that may be connected with the many struggles that are necessary against what simplifies away our worlds in terms of idealist judgments about what would ultimately matter and what does not.

It is in the same spirit that I wish to associate the question of materialism today with the active memory of Denis Diderot, and more particularly with the well-known exclamation that marks his *Conversation* with D'Alembert: 'Do you see this egg? With this you can overthrow all the schools of theology, all the churches of the earth'.

---

3. Donna Haraway, *When Species Meet*, Minneapolis, University of Minnesota Press, 2008.

WIT, FLESH, BLOOD, ELOQUENCE—AND POLEMICS

As we know, Diderot is traditionally classified among French materialists who are heirs to Baconian empiricism. It is important, however, not to confuse Diderot's 'Do you see this egg?' with the expression of a Baconian trust in the power of empirical knowledge against theology or metaphysics. D'Alembert, the one he addresses in his *Conversation*, the one who is asked to 'see the egg', was not a metaphysician. He was what we would call now a physicist, but at that time a physicist was interested in natural phenomena, in chemistry, medicine, magnetism or electricity. D'Alembert was a mathematician and a mechanist, one who contributed to ending the speculative quarrels between Newtonian, Cartesian and Leibnizian interpretations of motion, of conservation and of force, and to turning the science that started with Galileo into a definitive set of functional, self-contained equations, what was to be called 'rational mechanics'. In other words, Diderot's *Conversation* with D'Alembert may be read as witnessing a struggle that is foreign to the historical Bacon because it concerns the very scope and meaning of modern science, a kind of science that Bacon ignored for obvious historical reasons. What Diderot challenges is the benign indifference and scepticism of D'Alembert, the mathematician but also the Academician: D'Alembert who promotes a closed definition of rational science, and ignores—considering it a matter of arbitrary opinion that must be kept outside science—everything that exceeds such a definition.

This is why, when Diderot tells about the egg as what enables the overthrow of all schools of theology and all temples on the earth, it is not only the theology of a Creator God, he alludes to, featuring the One who, through some Intelligent Design, organized common matter into a being able to get out of the egg, to move and be moved, to feel, suffer and rejoice. It is also that other temple, the Academic science of his time, that the egg should overthrow. Diderot is fighting a double fight: against a theology with God as the author of the world, and against the authority of a science which refuses the challenge of the egg, in the name of its own restricted definitions. For him the question 'What is matter?' does not have its answer in a particular science. If there must be a materialist understanding of how, with matter, we get sensitivity, life, memory, consciousness, passions, and thought, such an understanding demands an interpretative adventure that must be defended against the authority of whoever claims to stop it in the name of reason.

Diderot did not only add 'wit, flesh, blood, and eloquence' to English materialism, as Karl Marx wrote in *The Holy Family*, he also added polemics, polemics against what was considered as the epitome of human reason, the mathematical science of matter and motion. At the end of the *Conversation* D'Alembert just wants to sleep, but Diderot warns him 'you will dream on your pillow about this conversation'; and indeed what follows is the famous *Dream of D'Alembert*, with a delirious D'Alembert haunted by Diderot's proposition that the egg requires matter to be gifted with sensation, imagining the famous cluster of bees, with a bee pinching a neighbour, and the neighbour another one, and suddenly the whole swarm gets animated as one unique being ....

Let me be clear. I am not proposing a revival of Diderot's materialism as a good definition of a sensitive matter against the bad physicalist one. If I am an heir to Diderot, if I wish to situate myself as such, it is because of the demanding, not the eliminativist, nature of his materialism. Diderot's materialism is not demanding that we *respect* challenging facts. Few facts are challenging by themselves. The egg offers no challenge—it is an egg. Diderot's empiricism is not about the facts and only the facts. He does not ask D'Alembert to observe the egg, but to accept *seeing* the egg, seeing the developing embryo, the small chicken who breaks the shell and comes out. What Diderot asks D'Alembert is that he *give* to the egg *the power to challenge* his well-defined categories.

Recalling that what a temple, any temple, signifies, is separateness, the stake for Diderot is that science does not become a new temple, marked by a cut, or, to follow Louis Althusser, by an epistemological rupture, between scientific, rational definition and everything else that may be ignored, eliminated, silenced as only a matter of opinion. Accept 'seeing' the egg, Diderot asked. Accept grappling with the messiness of the world, Haraway now asks. This does not mean produce a theory, but pay attention to the idealist temptation, which is inside science as it is inside any claimed separation giving to ideas the power to separate, silence and disqualify. I must admit I feel this temptation at work when Alain Badiou proposes a general definition of science on the model of set theory. Whatever his will to affirm the event and the procedures of truth against rational calculation and reason, the separation is too clean, and makes too many victims. A temple is needed in order for the truth-event to punch a hole in its roof, and the kind of knowledge Haraway gained in agility sport will probably not be admitted in this frame.

My proposition should not be confused with a free-for-all position claiming that all opinions are to be equally admitted. This would be only the reverse of the same coin, a very Dostoyevskian coin by the way. If God does not exist, everything is permitted. If we have no criteria to oppose reason against opinion, we will have to admit everything and illusion will rule. I am not a judge, thinking in terms of what to admit and what not to admit. Opinion as such does not interest me. It functions indeed as an abstract Dostoyevskian term fabricated in order to trap us and have us recognize that we need science, or theory, or whatever. It transforms us into a thinking brain having to direct an opinionated body. What I am interested in is *practice*, the *plurality* and *diverging* character of practices. If Haraway is able to become a witness for her dog Cayenne, it is because of the practice they entered together, of agility sport. And if D'Alembert was able to participate in the definition of what are called the laws of motion, it is because he was an heir to the very strange practice Galileo initiated: the experimental practice that succeeded in turning heavy falling bodies into reliable witnesses of the way their gain of speed should be described.

I propose as a materialist motto: we never get a relevant answer if our practices have not enabled us to produce a relevant question. How could D'Alembert's physico-mathematical categories be relevant for the egg when they were not the result of practices that address, as mattering, the development of the chicken in the egg? The point is not that the egg has the secret of what matter is. The challenge of the egg points to what is required from matter in order for the development of the chicken not to be a miracle, or the expression of some intelligent design. And the tentative answers to that challenge depend on the practices for which such a development matters.

THE POWER OF WONDER

One of the many beauties of the English language is the double 't' in the spelling of 'matter'. It moves us away from substance, or any kind of stuff with which a general reason or cause for what we observe can be associated, and it connects us with the verb 'to matter'. But here many philosophers will immediately react. They will object that I am confusing epistemology and ontology, the problem of knowledge and the problem of the way things exist for themselves and by themselves. And some will even add that this confusion is the sign that what I am proposing is just another version of an instrumentalist conception of knowledge, reducing it to the answers we get to the questions that matter for us. This is a replay, again and again, of the same powerful tune that also poisoned the history of orthodox Marxism since Lenin.

I must admit it took me some time to overcome the surprise I experienced when I first encountered this kind of objection. It was some time before I realized how swiftly one proposition had been transformed into another one. My proposition had emphasized that a problem must matter in order to get a possibly relevant answer. The proposition that came back against me was that we impose on what we claim to understand the kind of questions that matter for us, so that all our answers can be explained away, reduced to our own human, too-human interests. The same ambiguity characterizes the use of the term 'interest'. Either we use it as what explains our questions, or we affirm that to be interested by something has the character of an event, since it gives to that something a power it does not generally possess: the power to cause us to think, feel and wonder, the power to have us wondering how practically to relate to it, how to pose relevant questions about it.

In order to make this point more forcefully, let us call what Diderot tried to mobilize against D'Alembert scepticism: 'the power of wonder'. This is a dangerous term, obviously, because of its association with mysticism, bowing down in front of what cannot be understood. But Diderot was not asking that D'Alembert bow down in front of the wonderful miracle of the egg. He was just asking D'Alembert not to explain it away with his conception of matter. To wonder is a word for which, as a French speaker, I envy English speakers. It means both to be surprised and to entertain questions. It thus may refer to the double operation Diderot wanted to achieve on D'Alembert: to have him accept being affected, troubled, surprised, but also being forced to think and question his own knowledge, not in terms of its sad limitations, but in terms of the restricted set of practical situations in which it is positively relevant. The point was not to have the wondering D'Alembert enter into the demanding practice upon which depends the eventual production of relevant questions about the egg, but to have him renounce any claim that would imply a privileged link between his knowledge and general overbearing adjectives like 'rational', 'objective' and 'scientific'.

Wonder, as I understand it, is not a general attitude in front of a wonderful world. What is general—the idealist attitude—is the explaining away of what would complicate our judgments, or worse, what we see as dangerous, encouraging irrationality. This is why silencing the power of wonder is not to be identified with a scientific attitude. Rather, it designates science as it has been mobilized in defence of public order.

Together with the historian Robert Darnton,[4] I would situate the end of Enlightenment in France when scientists officially accepted this role. It was at a time when French authorities decided to react against the popularity of Mesmerism, which spread across France like an epidemic, and was not devoid of political dimensions. Indeed, Franz Mesmer's magnetic fluid was taken as a concrete affirmation of human equality, because it put into relation any human, whatever his or her social class. The scientific commission named by the King included renowned scientists such as Lavoisier and Benjamin Franklin. Confronted with the surprising effects and affects attributed to

---

4. Robert Darnton, *Mesmerism and the End of the Enlightenment in France*, Cambridge, Harvard University Press, 1968.

Mesmer's fluid, they put into action a procedure that turns experimentation into a true judicial trial, imposing on the fluid the question *they* decided was crucial. And, rather unsurprisingly, the magnetic fluid was found guilty of not existing, its effects proving to have imagination as a necessary condition. Imagination, a natural animal feature, was thus defined as a sufficient explanation, Mesmer was only a quack and there was no need at all to wonder about magnetic healing. Circulate! There is nothing to see.

The commissioners' argument may appear strong, and it is still in use today, but it manifests its authors' complete ignorance or contempt for the practice they were condemning. Already Paracelsus, the father of magnetism, had proclaimed that this force was impotent without will and imagination. This, however, was not the commissioners' problem—their problem was to bring reason to a population that was no longer defined, in the Enlightenment mode, as a potential ally in the process of emancipation, but as gullible, ready to follow any quack or swindler. Modern science as a blind destroyer of traditional practices did not begin with colonization but in Europe, when scientists accepted the role of guardians of an infantile public.

We cannot affirm the constraining relation between intelligibility—as it must be produced and as the Commissioners did not produce it—and practice, as its mode of production, without also defending the power of wonder against the alliance of science with public order. But this means learning how to address scientists, how to activate their disentanglement from the role of guardians of rationality that has captivated them and put them at the service of power, both state and capitalist power. In the so-called 'Science Wars', if scientists had been asked 'What is your practice? What matters for you as practitioners?', it may well be that the resulting situation would have been much more interesting from the point of view of political struggle. It may even be that some scientists would have been confident enough to tell about the so-called knowledge economy as it threatens to destroy their practice.

How should we listen to such anxious scientists? The temptation is to explain away their disarray in terms of resistance to renouncing their pretence to disinterested knowledge and autonomy. The knowledge economy is nothing new: the first value of scientific knowledge is, and has always been, its potential consequences for interested economic and industrial partners. This looks like a materialist interpretation, explaining away the eventual disarray of scientists to a matter of ideology. The problem is that this is also the interpretation proposed by promoters of the knowledge economy, except for the fact that they do not speak about ideology but about psychological resistance, a refusal by scientists to change their habits, to become more flexible. The two interpretations thus converge on the fact that the scientists' disarray is not worth taking into account. They will still have the resources, the equipment and the facilities they need. The only point being that they will have to propose research programmes that are in explicit agreement with the interests of their partners.

I think that the anxious scientists know better, and that the convergence in not seeing the point of their protest and disarray marks the shortcoming of what merely *looks like* a materialist interpretation. What is at stake in a practice, in any practice, cannot be reduced to the generality of a human socially organized activity. When you address a practitioner, you do not address only a human with a specialized activity. Practices are always collective, and you address somebody who belongs to a collective, the gathering of which cannot be reduced to a question of mere ideology; the gathering of which, furthermore, *can well be destroyed*, for instance if it is effectively dealt with as mere ideology.[5] Scientists know better because they know their practice may be destroyed even if they go on working.

CELEBRATING THE EXCEPTION

This is why I claimed that the statement 'science is only a practice like any other' was bound to provoke war, independently of the scientists' exceptionalist claims about rationality and objectivity. What was denied or eliminated is the importance of the question of what matters for each practice and of how what matters effectively connects practitioners. For instance, if we take the science of motion initiated by Galileo, Heidegger was quite right to emphasize that the scientists involved did not really think about questions like matter, space or time. But he was quite wrong to conclude that those scientists do not think. What matters for them, what causes them to think, imagine and object positively diverges from what may matter for philosophers. What matters for them—and because of which they may quite happily subvert any settled conception of space, time and matter, including the settled ones in their discipline—is the very specific achievement of an experimental science. In *The Invention of Modern Science*, I characterized this achievement as 'the invention of the power to confer on things the power of conferring on the experimenter the power to speak in their name'.[6] Galileo's inclined plane proving able to turn falling bodies into reliable witnesses of the way their accelerated motion should be interpreted marks an event, something new in human history, and what matters for experimental practitioners, what they celebrate when announcing that 'nature has spoken', is the eventual repetition of such events. Again, an experimental device has achieved the practical high feat of having the phenomenon make a difference such that it forces any competent, interested person to bow down and agree.

I know that many critics of science have found it necessary to deconstruct this high feat, and affirm that phenomena are unable to make such a difference, that scientists always talk in the name of a reality that remains decidedly mute. This, for experimenters, indeed means war, because it is a direct attack against what first matters for them, the verification of which gathers them as practitioners and causes them to imagine and object. And I would add that this war is completely beside the usual point, namely that it is needed in order to demystify the exceptionalism claimed by scientists. What is needed instead, and drastically so, is that experimental achievement not be abstracted from the practice that produced it; that experimental objectivity be not transformed into the normal reward for a general rational or scientific method, a method that would silence the power of wonder and explain away the egg in terms of belief statements about the possibility of reducing it to the terms of physicalist working cranes. What is needed against scientists' exceptionalism is that the experimental achievement be indeed celebrated as an event, as the exception, not the rule. Diderot's egg has not become an experimental reliable witness.

Celebrating the exceptional character of the experimental achievement very effectively limits the claims made in the name of science. For instance, the way Lavoisier and his colleagues invented a scientific judiciary process against Mesmerism is best described not as an objective demonstration, but as a case of instrumentalization, uni-

---

5. For practices and their eventual destruction, see Isabelle Stengers, *La Vierge et le neutrino*, Paris, Les Empêcheurs de penser en rond/Le Seuil, 2006.

6. Isabelle Stengers, *The Invention of Modern Science*, trans. D. W. Smith, Minneapolis, University of Minnesota Press, 2000, p. 88.

laterally imposing a binary alternative on what they dealt with. Theirs was no achievement at all since the situation they created is unable to produce a reliable witness for the way magnetic cures should be interpreted. It only authorizes a verdict against one possible and unnecessary interpretation, a verdict the only interest of which was to serve public order, to silence the irrationality of the public.

Taking seriously the singularity of experimental practices also leads us to understand the strong possibility of their destruction by the coming knowledge economy. The point is not that the scientific enterprise would lose a neutrality it never had. From the beginning, experimental scientists have taken an active, and even entrepreneurial, part in industrial and commercial development. What is at risk is rather the very social fabric of scientific reliability, that is, the constitutive relation between an experimental achievement and the gathering of what can be called 'competent colleagues', colleagues assembled by the question of verifying, objecting, of putting to the test the eventual power of an experimental fact to force agreement by silencing other possible interpretations. Such a social fabric emphatically does not ensure anything about propositions that have failed, for whatever reason, to become a matter of collective practical concern. But it relates the reliability of the consensus about an experimental scientific proposition to such a collective concern, to the critical attention of colleagues who will use their imagination to test and criticize a claim, whatever its interest and promises.

This quite specific social fabric will be destroyed when scientists as practitioners do not depend upon each other any longer, but are tied instead to competing industrial interests. It becomes then a matter of survival to confirm the kind of promises that attracted the appetites of investors, and to produce patentable results. As the future of those results is independent of concerned colleagues, what will prevail is the general wisdom that you do not saw off the branch on which you are sitting together with everybody else. Nobody will then object too much, if objecting against a scientific argument may lead to a general weakening of the promises of a field. This amounts to saying that, with the knowledge economy, we may have scientists at work everywhere, producing facts with the speed that new sophisticated instruments make possible, but that the way those facts are interpreted will now mostly follow the landscape of settled interests. In other words, the deconstructivist-eliminativist view will then be fully verified. We will more and more deal with instrumental knowledge. But the verification will not result from the deconstructivist's daring perceptiveness, but from the fact that capitalism will have destroyed yet another practice, just as it is an ongoing process of destruction of the commons.

Here is probably my greatest divergence from the orthodox Marxist tradition, and this divergence is directly connected with my materialist standpoint, linking knowledge-production with practices. We live in a cemetery of already destroyed practices, as capitalism, together with state's regulations and ongoing pressure to conform to the demands of public order, are Great Destroyers of practices. But it may also be claimed that radical materialist thinkers have turned a blind, or even a blessing, eye on the ongoing destruction of practices and the attachments those practices cultivate. And it is still the case: when confronting the disarray of scientists who understand that the knowledge economy means the destruction of their practice, many are tempted to answer: 'Well, for a long time you have believed that you could be a partner of capitalism, that you would be respected because you were useful. You have just learned that capitalism respects nothing. Do not come and complain about the destruction of your practice. Rather, come and join those who struggle, as ones among the multitude'.

My proposition is that we do not accept at face value the scientists' complaint that rationality is under attack, that the economy should stop and respect the temple of disinterested science, but that we take seriously the fact that rejecting scientists' complaints on those grounds itself leaves the field free for their destruction. Indeed, it justifies it, even if regretfully. My point is that there is no practice the destruction of which cannot be justified, either by the privileges they benefited, or by their alienating archaism, or by their closure and resistance to change, but all those reasons, if they amount to justifying why destruction is not a cause for struggle, also amount to giving free elbowroom to capitalism in its ongoing destructive redefinition of the world.

My proposition is not restricted to scientific practices. Those practices are privileged only because they force us to make a crucial transition from materialism as a theory of knowledge to materialism as concerned by production, and also destruction, of what exists. What I am confronting here is the fact that the orthodox Marxist vision, whatever its conceptual beauty, left practices undefended. It even defined practitioners as 'not to be trusted' because they would always cultivate their own way of having situations and questions matter, or, in brief, because they have something else to lose than their chains. And we get the same perspective again when Michael Hardt and Toni Negri celebrate the general intellect, and propose that we consider the multitude not in terms of identities that are in danger of contradicting each other, but in terms of singularities that have no identity to lose and may thus act together in the production of the common.

The dilemma 'either identities or singularities' is a binary choice that primordially expresses, as do all such choices, the transcendent power attributed to abstract discursive reasoning. The point is not to choose, but to escape. Here, this means emphasizing that practices do not contradict each other. Rather, they have diverging ways of having things and situations matter. They produce their own lines of divergence as they produce themselves.

The difference between a contradiction and a divergence is not a matter of fact, of empirical or logical definition, but a matter of struggle: it is something that must be produced and maintained against the idealist oblivion of practice. Indeed, we get contradiction as soon as practice is forgotten and the answers obtained by practitioners present themselves as free from practical constraints; that is, free to be compared with each other and to contradict each other.

However, divergence does not permit the conceptual derivation and warranting of the production of the common, as Hardt and Negri envisage it. We could say that practices are commons, but that the addition of the commons does not logically lead to the common. I am not at all sure that I can imagine physicists and practitioners of such crafts as tarot-card reading or of the art of healing, affirming together anything else than a rather empty common goodwill tolerance. As I remarked about Diderot's egg, the power of wonder with which Diderot tried to infect D'Alembert was not intended to inspire a common conception of matter, but to have D'Alembert accept that his conception of matter was not *the* 'rational' one, but the one his practice produced as relevant.

What may happen among diverging practitioners is the creation of what Deleuze and Guattari describe as 'rhizomatic connections': that is, connections as events, the event of an articulation without a common ground to justify it, or an ideal from which to deduce it. We may recall the famous example given by Deleuze of the '*noce contre nature*', between the wasp and the orchid. Their connection is an event that matters in diverging ways for the wasp and for the orchid. Its achievement is not to lead the wasp and the orchid to accept a common aim or definition, but having the wasp and the orchid presuppose the existence of each other in order to produce themselves.

CHALLENGE AND DIAGNOSIS

How can such events be correlated to the need and concern for unity in struggle or the production of the common? This problem should be addressed in materialist terms, as a practical one, not as a problem the solution of which must be conceptually grounded and warranted, as is the case with the nice image of the multitude as the fountainhead of human creativity. Such an image suggests that if the price of a concept of the common related to free singularities is the destruction of divergent practices, this destruction is no great loss anyway. The fountainhead will produce whatever we may need. The plausibility of this idea may be related to the past polemical use of the concept of practice, when it was mainly in charge of the elimination of any transcendent source of authority, but was not a matter of interest or concern as such. This allows us not to 'see' the systematic destruction of practices, or of commons, as part and parcel of the power of capitalist expansion, that both conditions it and feeds it. From a materialist, non-eliminativist standpoint, a standpoint that does not accept the nude abstraction of the 'creative human', it may well be that this destruction is the destruction of what enables humans to think, imagine and resist.

Starting from that standpoint, in *La Sorcellerie Capitaliste*[7] I have, together with Philippe Pignarre, addressed the problem of the kind of unity in struggle that may be produced without smoothing away the diverging plurality of practices. We have not produced a general answer but some practical suggestions that may arouse an appetite to counter the nostalgia of a conceptual solution. I will limit myself here to the presentation of a challenge and a diagnosis.

The challenge, which I deem a materialist challenge, is that whatever the mess and perplexity that may result, we should resist the temptation to pick and choose among practices—keeping those which appear rational and judging away the others, tarot-card reading, for instance. The need for such a resistance is something naturalists have learned, when learning to avoid judging animal species as either useful or pests. This does not mean that some animal species cannot be considered as destructive or dangerous. In the same way, some practices may well be considered intolerable or disgusting. In both cases, the point is to refrain from using general judgmental criteria to legitimate their elimination, and to refrain from dreaming about a clean world with no cause to wonder and alarm.

This challenge is not for the future. I come now to the diagnosis. If we have chosen the term 'sorcery' in order to characterize capitalism, it was not as a metaphor, but as an active proposition. It was meant to produce wonder, the kind of wonder the present-day situation may well provoke, when capitalism is utterly divorced from all the usual pretence relating it to human progress, but has nevertheless lost nothing of its power. Such a situation, which nobody would have anticipated thirty years ago, may certain-

---

7. Philippe Pignarre et Isabelle Stengers, *La Sorcellerie capitaliste. Pratiques de désenvoûtement*, Paris, La Découverte, 2005.

ly be explained, but the many clever interpretations provided may also appear as so many versions of the famous Bergsonian retroactive move, when, after an event, the past is understood in its light, and is given the power to explain it. Retroactively there is no wonder. Associating capitalism with sorcery aims first at thwarting this move, that is, at dramatizing the event, at giving to it the power to have us wonder. But it aims also at asking the questions that all sorcery traditions in the world would ask, that is, the question of the vulnerability that the sorcerer's attack is exploiting and the correlative question of the necessary protection against such attacks.

Becoming able to take these questions seriously is connected to the challenge I have just presented. Issues like vulnerability and protection were part of practices the destruction of which has consensually signified the coming into adulthood of humankind, leaving behind superstitions and what was described as belief in supernatural powers. From this point of view, explaining capitalist power through alienation is much more convenient—a bit too convenient, since it both confirms the West's self-assigned mission of demystifying the world, and ratifies what philosophers have not stopped diagnosing, namely, that humans usually resist the truth they are indicating—whatever this truth. This criticism is rather well known in post-colonial studies. But the point here is not to criticize but to accept—against the conceptual convenience of concepts such as alienation—to have practices and their destruction mattering. It may well be that their convenient dismissal as causes for thinking, feeling and struggling is part of our vulnerability to capitalist attacks. Is it not the case, indeed, that capitalism is exploiting to its own advantage any trust we may have in a conveniently settled perspective, turning it into an opportunity for new operations? Is it not the case also that conveniently escaping a confrontation with the messy world of practices through clean conceptual dilemma or eliminativist judgments has left us with a theatre of concepts the power of which, to understand retroactively, is matched only by their powerlessness to transform? Naming sorcery the power of what has been able to profit from any assurance our convenient simplifications entailed, means that it may well be we have something to learn from those practices we have eliminated as superstitious, the practices of those for whom sorcery and protection against sorcery, is a matter of serious practical concern. I do not claim we should mimic those practices, but maybe we should accept to 'seeing' them, and wonder.

23

Emergence, Causality and Realism

Manuel DeLanda

If a body is propelled in two directions by two forces, one tend-
ing to drive it to the north and the other to the east, it is caused
to move in a given time exactly as far in both directions as the
two forces would separately have carried it; and it is left precisely where it would have arrived if it had been acted upon
first by one of the two forces, and afterwards by the other. [...]
I shall give the name of the Composition of Causes to the principle which is exemplified in all cases in which the joint effect
of several causes is identical with the sum of their separate effects. [...] This principle, however, by no means prevails in all
departments of the field of nature. The chemical combination
of two substances produces, as is well known, a third substance
with properties different from those of either of the two substances separately, or both of them taken together. Not a trace
of the properties of hydrogen or of oxygen is observable in
those of their compound, water.[1]

—John Stuart Mill, *A System of Logic*

With these words John Stuart Mill began the modern debate on the question of emergence. While he himself did not use the term, one of its definitions, that of a property of a whole that is more than the sum of its parts, is clearly stated in this quote. Mill
goes on to qualify this statement because two joint causes may interfere with each other and subtract rather than add their effects: a reservoir may be fed by a stream of
water on one side while a drain empties it on the other side, the joint product being
no change in the amount of water stored. Yet, for Mill, this is just another version of
the Composition of Causes. So the real distinction between physical and chemical interactions is not so much that a joint effect is a mere sum but that it is entirely different or novel, 'as in the experiment of two liquids which, when mixed in certain pro-
portions, instantly become, not a larger amount of liquid, but a solid mass'.[2] The term

1. John Stuart Mill, *A System of Logic. Ratiocinative and Inductive*, London, Longmans, Green, and Co., 1906, p. 243.
2. Mill, *A System of Logic*, p. 244.

'emergent' was introduced in 1875 by another philosopher, George Henry Lewes, also in the context of a discussion of joint causes and their effects. When two separate causes simply add or mix themselves in their joint effect, so that we can see their agency in action in that effect, the result is a mere 'resultant' but if there is novelty or heterogeneity in the effect then we may speak of an 'emergent'.[3]

Both authors viewed the difference between physics and chemistry as pivoting on the possibility of explanation: while in physics to explain an effect is to deduce it from a law, in chemistry deduction is not possible because of the existence of novelty in the effect. To know what effect the combination of two causes will have, what molecule will be synthesized from the interaction of two different atoms, for example, one needs to actually carry out an experiment. Mill did not think that this was a cause for despair: in due time chemical laws could be discovered that made the properties of water, for instance, deducible from those of oxygen and hydrogen. But to Lewes this possibility implied that water would cease to be an emergent and would become a resultant. As he wrote: 'Some day, perhaps, we shall be able to express the unseen process in a mathematical formula; till then we must regard the water as an emergent'.[4] In other words, something is an emergent only to the extent that we cannot deduce it from a law, and it ceases to be so the moment a law becomes available. This is an unfortunate conclusion, one that involves a serious misunderstanding of the nature of explanation in general and of causal explanation in particular.

Before attempting to correct the misunderstanding let's give a few examples of the kind of philosophical thinking to which it gave rise in the early decades of the twentieth century, a line of thought that helped discredit the notion of emergence for several generations. The basic attitude informing this philosophy is captured in the following quote from C. Lloyd Morgan's 'Emergent Evolution':

> The essential feature of a mechanical—or, if it be preferred, a mechanistic—interpretation is that it is in terms of resultant effects only, calculable by algebraical summation. It ignores the something more that must be accepted as emergent. It regards a chemical compound as only a more complex mechanical mixture, without any new kind of relatedness of its constituents. [...] Against such a mechanical interpretation—such a mechanistic dogma—emergent evolution rises in protest. The gist of its contention is that such an interpretation is quite inadequate. Resultants there are; but there is emergence also. Under naturalistic treatment, however, the emergence, in all its ascending grades, is loyally accepted, on the evidence, with natural piety.[5]

The expression 'natural piety' belongs to the philosopher Samuel Alexander who coined it to stress his belief that the existence of emergents must be accepted under the compulsion of brute fact, that is, in a way that admits of no explanation.[6] Despite some mystical overtones in the work of Alexander, such as his arrangement of emergent levels of ascending grade into the sequence space-time, life, mind, deity, neither he nor Morgan accepted the existence of entities like a 'life force', 'vital energy', or 'entelechy'. In fact, the notion of emergence was for them a way of get rid of those suspect notions.[7] The real problem with their position, what made the concept of emergence suspect of mysticism, was their rejection of explanation. Contemporary realist philoso-

---

3. George Henry Lewes, *Problems of Life and Mind. Volume Two*, London, Trübner & Co., 1875, p. 412.

4. Lewes, *Problems of Life and Mind.*, p. 415.

5. C. Lloyd Morgan, *Emergent Evolution*, New York, Henry Holt, 1931, p. 8.

6. Samuel Alexander, *Space, Time, and Deity*, vol. 2, London, MacMillan, 1920, pp. 46-47.

7. Alexander, *Space, Time and Deity*, pp. 64-65; and Morgan, *Emergent Evolution*, pp. 9-12.

phers, on the other hand, have embraced the concept of 'emergent property' precisely because they do not see any problem in accounting for irreducible properties through some mechanism. As the philosopher Mario Bunge puts it, the 'possibility of analysis does not entail reduction, and explanation of the mechanisms of emergence does not explain emergence away'.[8] The rehabilitation of causal explanations in recent decades is partly due to the work of philosophers like Bunge who have rid the concept of causality of its connotations of linearity and homogeneity.

The kind of causal mechanism that emergentist philosophers like Morgan and Alexander rejected is based on linear causality. The formula for linear causal relations is 'Same Cause, Same Effect, Always'. Different forms of nonlinear causality can be derived by challenging the different assumptions built into this formula. The word 'same' can be challenged in two ways because it may be interpreted as referring both to the intensity of the cause ('same intensity of cause, same intensity of effect') as well as to the very identity of the cause. Let's begin with the simplest departure from linear causality, the one challenging sameness of intensity. As an example we can use Hooke's Law capturing a regularity in the way solid bodies respond to loads, like a metal spring on which a given weight is attached. In this case the event 'changing the amount of weight supported by the spring' is the cause, while the event 'becoming deformed'—stretching if pulled or shrinking if pushed—is the effect. Hooke's law may be presented in graphic form as a plot of load versus deformation, a plot that has the form of a straight line (explaining one source of the meaning of the term 'linear'). This linear pattern captures the fact that if we double the amount of weight supported by the spring its deformation will also double, or more generally, that a material under a given load will stretch or contract by a given amount which is always proportional to the load.

While some materials like mild steel and other industrially homogenized metals do indeed exhibit this kind of proportional effect many others do not. Organic tissue, for example, displays a J-shaped curve when load is plotted against deformation. 'A gentle tug produces considerable extension whereas a stronger tug results in relatively little additional extension', as one materials scientists puts it, a fact that can be easily verified by pulling on one's own lip.[9] In other words, a cause of low intensity produces a relatively high intensity effect up to a point after which increasing the intensity of the cause produces only a low intensity effect. Other materials, like the rubber in a balloon, display a S-shaped curve representing a more complex relation between intensities: at first increasing the intensity of the cause produces almost no effect at all, as when one begins to inflate a balloon and the latter refuses to bulge; as the intensity increases, however, a point is reached at which the rubber balloon suddenly yields to the pressure of the air rapidly increasing in size but only up to a second point at which it again stops responding to the load. The fact that the J-shaped and S-shaped curves are only two of several possible departures from strict proportionality implies that the terms 'linear' and 'nonlinear' are not a dichotomy. Rather than being a unique opposite, nonlinear patterns represent a variety of possibilities of which the linear case is but a limiting case.

A stronger form of nonlinear causality is exemplified by cases that challenge the very identity of causes and effects in the formula 'Same Cause, Same Effect, Always'. When an external stimulus acts on an organism, even a very simple bacterium, the stimulus acts in many cases as a mere trigger for a response by the organism. A bio-

---

8. Mario Bunge, *Causality and Modern Science*, New York, Dover, 1979, p.156.

9. James E. Gordon, *The Science of Structures and Materials*, New York, Scientific American Books, 1988, p. 20.

logical creature is defined internally by many complex series of events, some of which close in on themselves forming a causal loop (like a metabolic cycle) exhibiting its own internal states of equilibrium as a whole. A switch from one stable state to another, the effect, can in this case be triggered by a variety of stimuli. That is, in such a system different causes can lead to the same effect. For similar reasons, two different components of a biological entity, each with a different set of internal states, may react completely differently to external stimulation. That is, the same cause can lead to different effects depending on the part of the organism it acts upon. Bunge uses the example of auxin, a vegetable hormone, that applied to the tips of a plant stimulates growth but applied to the roots inhibits growth.[10]

While organic materials (tissue, rubber) and organic creatures serve as good illustrations of weak and strong nonlinear causality, biology does not have a monopoly on nonlinearity. Even purely physical processes can behave in ways that demands a departure from the old formula. As Bunge writes:

> The act of releasing the bow is usually regarded as the cause of the arrow's motion, or, better, of its acceleration; but the arrow will not start moving unless a certain amount of (potential elastic) energy has been previously stored in the bow by bending it; the cause (releasing the bow) triggers the process but does not determine it entirely. In general, efficient causes are effective solely to the extent to which they trigger, enhance, or dampen inner processes; in short, extrinsic (efficient) causes act, so to say, by riding on inner processes.[11]

Another way of expressing this thought is to say that explanations must take into account not only an entity's capacity to affect but also its capacity to be affected. And the latter is not just the passive side of the active capacity to affect but equally active on its own, although depending on activity at another level of organization, that of the components parts. In the case of organic tissue or rubber, for example, their nonlinear response curves are explained by facts about the microstructure of the materials determining their capacity to be affected by a load. And by the time we consider cases like a bacterium and its internal stable states their capacity to be affected dominates their response to external causes, the latter having been reduced to mere triggers.

The third and final departure from linearity, the one that challenges the 'always' part of the linear formula, also depends on this distinction. As soon as we stop considering a single entity and move on to think of populations of such entities causality becomes statistical. Even if a population is composed of entities of the same type each of its members may be in slightly different internal states and hence be capable of being affected differently by one and the same cause. The explanation given by the proposition 'Smoking cigarettes causes cancer', for example, is not that a cause (smoking) always produces the same effect (the onset of cancer). Rather, given that the capacity of smokers to be affected depends in part on their genetic predispositions, the claim is that a cause increases the probability of the occurrence of the effect in a given population.[12]

These remarks on the nature of causality are important because the ontological commitments of a philosophy can be accurately predicted from its conception of the causal link. If the relation between a cause and its effect is viewed as reducible to conceptual or linguistic categories then the philosophy in question is most likely idealist;

---

10. Bunge, *Causality and Modern Science*, p. 49.

11. Bunge, *Causality and Modern Science*, p. 195.

12. Wesley C. Salmon, *Scientific Explanation and the Causal Structure of the World*, Princeton, Princeton University Press, 1984, p. 30-34.

if causality is reduced to the observed constant conjunction of a cause and its effect then the philosophy is typically empiricist or positivist; and if causality is considered to be an objective relation of production between events, that is, a relation in which one event produces another event, then the philosophy will tend to be realist or materialist.

Realist philosophers, on the other hand, must be careful when asserting the mind-independence of causal relations because capacities to affect and be affected have a complex ontological status. Let's illustrate this point with a simple example. A knife considered as an autonomous entity is defined by its properties, such as having a certain shape or weight, as well as being in certain states, like the state of being sharp. Sharpness is an objective property of knives, a property that is always actual: at any given point in time the knife is either sharp or it is not. But the causal capacity of the knife to cut is not necessarily actual if the knife is not currently being used. In fact, the capacity to cut may never be actual if the knife is never used. And when that capacity is actualized it is always as a double event: to cut-to be cut. In other words, when a knife exercises its capacity to cut it is by interacting with a different entity that has the capacity to be cut. This implies a realist commitment not only to the mind-independence of actual properties but also of causal capacities that are real but not necessarily actual.[13]

Let's return to the question of emergence to finally give a definition: a property of a whole is said to be emergent if it is produced by causal interactions among its component parts. Those interactions, in which the parts exercise their capacities to affect and be affected, constitute the mechanism of emergence behind the properties of the whole. Once we adopt a more complex view of causality there is no reason to conceive of mechanisms of emergence as clockworks or other simple devices. Some component parts, for example, may be part of feedback loops in which one part that is affected by another may in turn react back and affect the first; other components may remain unaffected until the level of activity around them reaches a critical threshold at which point they may spring into action; yet other components may be produced or destroyed during an interaction. This level of complexity is typical of many chemical mechanisms. In other cases a mechanism of emergence may involve interacting parts operating at different scales and exhibiting different degrees of organization: some parts may be relatively large and have internal structure so their interactions with another part may simply trigger an effect that is part of their internal repertoire of behaviors, while others may be small, simple, and exist as parts of populations contributing to the emergence of the whole through effects that are statistical. This complex coexistence of components can be usually found in the mechanisms responsible for the properties of organs like the kidney.

There is, therefore, nothing in the definition of 'mechanisms of emergence' that limits their complexity. The only conceptual limitation implied by the definition is that the component parts must not fuse together into a seamless totality. In other conceptions of irreducible wholes it is assumed that the properties of the parts are determined by their role in the whole, so that detaching them from it would change their very identity. But for parts to play a role in a mechanism they must have their own properties, removing them from the whole preventing them only from exercising their capacities, and must remain separate to be able to interact. This can be summarized by saying that irreducibility must go hand in hand with decomposability. A different way of expressing this limitation is to require that the relations between the parts not be relations of interiority in which the very identity of the terms is determined by their rela-

---

13. Roy Bhaskar, *A Realist Theory of Science*, London, Verso, 1997, p. 51.

tions. The rejection of explanation of holistic properties by mechanisms is often root-ed on an assumption of the interiority of relations. As Hegel puts it:

> This is what constitutes the character of mechanism, namely, that whatever relation ob-tains between the things combined, this relation is extraneous to them that does not con-cern their nature at all, and even if its accompanied by a semblance of unity it remains nothing more than composition, mixture, aggregation, and the like.[14]

Instead, as the realist philosopher Gilles Deleuze has emphasized, we need to con-ceive of the parts of a mechanism in terms of relations of exteriority, so that 'a rela-tion may change without the terms changing'.[15] The terms 'interiority' and 'exteriori-ty' should not be confused with spatial terms like 'internal' and 'external': organs like the kidney, the heart, or the liver, may be internal to the body but they interact with each other through their own external surfaces or membranes, by excreting biochem-ical substances or sensing them through embedded receptors. And their intimate re-lations are not explained by their necessary mutual constitution, but by their contin-gent coevolution.

I mentioned above that an attitude of agnostic resignation or natural piety towards emergence was based on a serious misunderstanding of the nature of explanation. A linear conception of mechanisms, a conception that includes clockworks but not steam engines, transistors, or thermostats, is only one aspect of that misunderstanding. The other aspect has to do with the concept of general law and the idea that explaining an effect is deducing it from a general law. The two aspects are related because if we take the linear formula 'Same Cause, Same Effect, Always' as the typical case then it is easy to confuse it with a logical formula like 'If C then necessarily E'. Even Mill, who was the most lucid of the earlier emergentists, thought that the case in which two linear causes have an additive effect was the more general one, chemical or biological effects being a special case, and that explanation implied deduction.[16] But as we have seen, nonline-arity is the norm while linearity is the exception. On the other hand, the second aspect constitutes an additional problem, one that would still be an obstacle to a correct con-ception of explanation even if we accepted nonlinearity. This other problem is related to the ontological commitments entailed by the concept of 'law'. To a positivist, that is, to someone who believes in the mind-independent existence of only that which can be directly observed, the term 'law' refers to the equations capturing a causal regularity, equations being directly observable when written on a piece of paper. To a realist, on the other hand, the term refers to the immanent patterns of being and becoming man-ifested in objective causal interactions, whether or not these are directly observable.[17] The question then is whether the very concept of 'law', a concept that, it may be argued, constitutes a kind of theological fossil embedded in modern science, is adequate to think about these immanent patterns. Let's take a closer look at this problematic concept.

In his analysis of the character of physical law, the late physicist Richard Feyn-man, argued that the law of gravity has three completely different versions. There is the familiar one in terms of forces and accelerations, the more recent one referring to fields, and the least well known version cast in terms of singularities, such as the min-

14. G. W. F. Hegel, *The Science of Logic*, trans. A. V. Miller, Amherst, New York, Humanity Books, 1999, p. 711 (emphasis in the original).

15. Gilles Deleuze and Claire Parnet, *Dialogues II*, trans. Hugh Tomlinson, Barbara Habberjam, and Eliot Ross Albert, New York, Columbia University Press, 2002, p. 55.

16. Mill, *A System of Logic*, pp. 430-432.

17. Bunge, *Causality and Modern Science*, pp. 22-23.

imum or maximum values of some parameter. As a positivist, Feynman believed that the task of physics was not to explain the inner workings of the world but only to produce compact descriptions that are useful to make predictions and that increase the degree of control we have over processes in the laboratory. But since the three versions of the law of gravity make the same predictions it is useless to speculate which one of the three 'really' explains gravitational processes. Are there really forces which act as causes to change the velocity of celestial bodies? Or does reality really contain gravitational fields? Or, even more strangely, is it all a matter of singularities? For Feynman there is no answer to these questions.[18] Realist philosophers, on the other hand, do not have to abide by positivist proscriptions, so when it comes to laws they can take the reality of immanent patterns seriously even if it means confronting the embarrassment of riches offered by the multiplicity of versions of one and the same law. The first two versions offer no problem if we think that many physical entities behave both like discrete particles (the kinds of entities to which forces can be applied) as well as continuous fields. In other words, the divergence in our models tracks an objective divergence in reality. But what to make of the third version, that is, what are singularities supposed to be? The simple answer is that singularities define the objective structure of a space of possibilities. To see what this definition implies we need to explore, however briefly, the history of this version of classical mechanics, the so-called 'variational' version.

In one of its forms the variational version is, indeed, well known. In 1662 Pierre de Fermat proposed that light propagates between two points so as to minimize travel time. His basic insight can be explained this way: if we knew the start and end points of a light ray, and if we could form the set of all possible paths joining these two points (straight paths, crooked paths, wavy paths) we could find out which of these possibilities is the one that light actualizes by selecting the one that takes the least amount of time. In the centuries that followed other 'least principles' were added to Fermat's (least action, least effort, least resistance, least potential energy). But the real breakthrough was the development in the eighteenth century of a way to extend this insight into the world of differential functions, the basic mathematical technology underlying most models in classical physics. This was the calculus of variations created by the mathematician Leonard Euler. Before Euler the main problem was to find a way to specify the set of possible paths so that it was maximally inclusive, that is, so that it contained all possibilities. This was done by 'parametrizing' the paths, that is, by generating the paths through the variation of a single parameter.[19] But there are many physical problems in which the possibilities cannot be parametrized by a discrete set of variables. Euler's method solved this problem by tapping into the resources of the differential calculus. Without going into technical details, these resources allowed him to rigorously specify the space of possibilities and to locate the minimum, maximum, and inflection points (that is, all the singularities) of the functions that join the start and end points.[20]

By the mid-nineteenth century all the different processes studied by classical physics (optical, gravitational, mechanical, electrostatic) had been given a variational form and were therefore unified under a single least principle: the tendency to minimize the difference between kinetic and potential energy. In other words, it was discovered that

---

18. Richard Feynman, *The Character of Physical Law*, Cambridge, MIT Press, 1997, pp. 50-53.

19. Don. S. Lemons, *Perfect Form. Variational Principles, Methods and Applications in Elementary Physics*, Princeton, Princeton University Press, 1997, p. 7.

20. Lemons, *Perfect Form*, pp. 17-27.

a simple singularity structured the space of possibilities of all classical processes. The unification of all known fields of physics under a single equation from which effects could be derived deductively led in some philosophical circles to doubt the very usefulness of the notion of a causal mechanism: if we can predict the outcome of a process using variational methods then what is the point of giving a causal explanation? But as Euler himself had argued a century earlier explanations in terms of singularities and causes (or of final and effective causes) are not mutually exclusive but complementary. As he wrote:

> Since the fabric of the universe is most perfect, and is the work of a most wise Creator, nothing whatsoever takes place in the universe in which some relation of maximum and minimum does not appear. Wherefore there is absolutely no doubt that every effect in the universe can be explained as satisfactorily from final causes, by the aid of the method of maxima and minima, as it can from the effective causes themselves. [...] Therefore, two methods for studying effects in nature are open to us, one by means of effective causes, which is commonly called the direct method, the other by means of final causes. [...] One ought to make a special effort to see that both ways of approach to the solution of the problem be laid open; for thus is not only one solution greatly strengthened by the other, but, more than that, from the agreement of the two solutions we secure the highest satisfaction.[21]

In the late nineteenth century singularities began to appear in other branches of mathematics like the study of topological spaces, abstract spaces where the familiar notions of length, area, and volume are meaningless. The mathematician Henri Poincare, for example, explored the relations between the maxima and minima of the variational calculus and the newly discovered topological singularities. More specifically, he used topology to investigate the structure of the space of possible solutions to specific mathematical models. Since these models are used to predict the future states of a particular physical process, each solution to the equation representing one state, the space of all solutions is known as state space (or 'phase space'). The structure of state space, Poincare found, is defined by different types of singularities. Some have the topological form of a point, much like the maxima and minima of the variational calculus. The existence of a point singularity in the state space of a process defines a tendency to be in a steady-state, that is, either a state of no change or one in which change takes place uniformly (as in the steady flow of a liquid). Singularities with the topological shape of a closed loop (limit cycles) define stable oscillations, that is, the tendency of a process to have a precise rhythm and to return to this very rhythm when disturbed by external shocks.[22] Poincare even got a glimpse of the more exotic singularities that today are referred to as 'strange' or 'chaotic'.[23]

The tendencies towards different types of stability (steady, periodic, turbulent) predicted to exist by mathematical singularities have indeed been confirmed in laboratory experiments. These tendencies play an important role in explaining emergent properties in purely physical processes. This is important because the early emergentists, from Mill to Morgan, thought chemistry marked a threshold of complexity below which there were no emergent effects. Soap bubbles and crystals, for example, acquire their stable shapes by the fact that the process that produces them has a ten-

---

21. Leonard Euler, quoted in Stephen P. Timoshenko, *History of Strength of Materials*, New York, Dover, 1983, p. 31.

22. June Barrow-Green, *Poincare and the Three Body Problem*, Providence, American Mathematical Society, 1997, pp. 32-33.

23. Ian Stewart, *Does God Play Dice: The Mathematics of Chaos*, Oxford, Basil Blackwell, 1989, pp. 70-71.

dency towards a steady-state, the state that minimizes surface energy or bonding energy respectively. Similarly, the periodic circulatory patterns that characterize certain wind currents (like the trade winds or the monsoon) and the underground lava flows that drive plate tectonics are explained by the existence of a tendency towards a stable periodic state in the process that gives rise to them. The fact that the same tendency appears in physical processes that are so different in detail shows that the explanatory role of singularities is different from that of causes. When a classical physical process is taking place one can discern specific causal mechanisms producing specific effects, and these mechanisms vary from one type of process to another: optical mechanisms are different from gravitational ones and these from electrostatic ones. But the fact that underneath these mechanisms there is the same tendency to minimize some quantity shows that the singularity itself is mechanism-independent.

It follows from this that explaining a given emergent effect involves describing not only a concrete mechanism but also the singularities structuring the possibility space behind the stabilizing tendencies manifested in those mechanisms. In the case of mechanisms it was important to distinguish linear from nonlinear causality to counteract the criticism that the homogenous effects of the former made causal explanation of emergence impossible. In the case of mechanism-independent structure a similar distinction must be made to counteract the idea that explanation is deduction from a general law, and that emergence implies the absence of such a law. The state space of linear differential equations is structured by a single point singularity while that of nonlinear equations can have many singularities of different type. Given that the tendency to approach a singularity is entirely deterministic, knowing the structure of a linear state space is sufficient to deduce what the final state of a process will be. But with multiple singularities, each with its own sphere of influence or 'basin of attraction', that knowledge is not enough. There are several possible tendencies and several possible outcomes, so the one currently actualized is in large part a product of the history of the process. In other words, the current state cannot be deduced from the equation alone because it depends on the historical path that the process followed.

Like capacities to affect and be affected tendencies can be real even if they are not actual: a tendency may be prevented from manifesting itself by some constraint acting on a process but that does not make it any less real since it will become actual the moment the constraint is removed. The fact that both tendencies and capacities can be only potential, on the other hand, makes them similar in status as modal concepts, like the concepts of 'possibility' or 'necessity', and this can cause difficulties for realist philosophers. In addition, as the first sentence of Leonard Euler's quote above shows, realists must deal with the mystical feelings produced by the concept of singularity, a feeling not unlike that created by the concept of emergence. Maupertuis, a contemporary of Euler, went as far as thinking that singularities provided a mathematical proof for the existence of a rational god. So special care must be exercised not to make singularities into something transcendent and to rigorously maintain their immanent ontological status. Thus, while much of the work on causal mechanisms and mechanism-independent singularities is performed by scientists and mathematicians, the elucidation of the modal status of capacities and tendencies and the enforcement of immanence must be performed by philosophers.

In the case of tendencies, thinking about modal questions can be based either on the study of physical tendencies as performed in laboratories or on the study of the tendencies of the solutions to equations as performed by mathematicians. State space, for example, is populated by different entities with different modal status. The space itself is made out of points each one of which represents a possible state for the process being modeled. At any instant in the history of the process its current state will be one of these possible points, and as the process changes states this point will draw a curve or trajectory in state space. This trajectory represents an actual series of states of the process, that is, a chunk of the actual history of the process. Finally, in addition to possible points and actual trajectories there are the singularities themselves. Albert Lautman, a follower of Poincare, was the first one to emphasize the difference in ontological status between the singularities, depending for their mathematical reality only on the field of vectors or directions defined by the differential equation, and the trajectories that are generated by the use of integration to find specific solutions. In his words:

> The geometrical interpretation of the theory of differential equations clearly places in evidence two absolutely distinct realities: there is the field of directions and the topological accidents which may suddenly crop up in it, as for example the existence of [...]. singular points to which no direction has been attached; and there are the integral curves with the form they take on in the vicinity of the singularities of the field of directions. [...] The existence and distribution of singularities are notions relative to the field of vectors defined by the differential equation. The form of the integral curves is relative to the solution of this equation. The two problems are assuredly complementary, since the nature of the singularities of the field is defined by the form of the curves in their vicinity. But it is no less true that the field of vectors on one hand and the integral curves on the other are two essentially distinct mathematical realities.[24]

What this distinction implies is that the ontological status of singularities cannot be the same as that of trajectories. That is, singularities cannot be actual. Does that mean that singularities should simply be given the modal status of possibilities, like all the other points constituting state space? No, because when we observe the behaviour of trajectories as they approach a singularity we notice that they get closer and closer but never reach it. In Poincare's terms, the trajectories approach the singularity asymptotically. This implies that unlike all the other non-singular points the singularity itself never becomes actual.

Influenced by Lautman, as well as by the work of that other early emergentist Henri Bergson, Gilles Deleuze introduced a new modal category to define the peculiar ontological status of singularities, the category of the virtual. As he writes:

> The virtual is not opposed to the real but to the actual. The virtual is fully real in so far as it is virtual. [...] Indeed, the virtual must be defined as strictly a part of the real object—as though the object had one part of itself in the virtual into which it is plunged as though into an objective dimension. [...] The reality of the virtual consists of the differential elements and relations along with the singular points which correspond to them. The reality of the virtual is structure. We must avoid giving the elements and relations that form a structure an actuality which they do not have, and withdrawing from them a reality which they have.[25]

These ideas provide us with the beginning of an account of the structure of the possibility spaces involved in tendencies. But this still leaves unexplained the singular struc-

---

24. Albert Lautman, quoted in Gilles Deleuze, *Logic of Sense*, trans. Paul Lester and Charles Stivale, New York, Columbia University Press, 1990, p. 345.

25. Gilles Deleuze, *Difference and Repetition*, trans. Paul Patton, New York, Columbia University Press, 1994, pp. 208-209 (emphasis in the original).

ture of the spaces associated with capacities, a structure that is hardly known at all. Unlike tendencies, which are typically limited in number even in the nonlinear case, capacities are potentially infinite in number because they depend not only on the power of an entity to affect but also on that of innumerable other entities to be affected by it. To return to an earlier example, a knife has the actual property of being sharp and the virtual capacity to cut. If we imagined instead of a manufactured object a sharp obsidian stone existing before life, we could ascribe to it that same capacity to cut, a capacity it occasionally exercised on softer rocks that fell on it. But when living creatures large enough to be pierced by the stone appeared on this planet the stone suddenly acquired the capacity to kill. This implies that without changing any of its properties the possibility space associated with the capacities of stone became larger. This sudden enlargement of a space of possibilities is even more striking when we consider interactions not between a stone and a living creature but those between different species of living creatures, or of living creatures like ourselves and an ever increasing number of technological objects.

One way of approaching the study of the structure of these more complex possibility spaces is by going beyond mathematical models into computer simulations. Even when the latter use equations they typically deploy an entire population of them and, more importantly, stage interactions between their solutions. In other cases equations are replaced with more flexible formal rules but always in populations and always with a view on what emerges from their interactions. Perhaps one day the imaginative use of these technologies of virtual reality will help us map the structure of the real virtuality associated with capacities.[26]

Let's conclude this essay with some remarks about the epistemological implications of both emergent properties and singularities. When a particular property emerges from the interactions between the components of a whole, and when the property is endowed with asymptotic stability, it becomes enduring enough to be used as a factor in an explanation. In other words, a stable property is typically indifferent to changes in the details of the interactions that gave rise to it, the latter being capable of changing within limits without affecting the emergent property itself. In turn, this ontological indifference translates into epistemological irrelevance: when giving an explanation of the outcome of the interaction between two different wholes we do not have to provide any details about their component parts. Or what amounts to the same thing, including details about their components becomes causally redundant because the emergent properties of the two interacting wholes would be the same regardless of those details.[27] Thus, when explaining the emergence of a complex meteorological entity like a thunderstorm, we have to describe the emergent wholes that interact to give rise to it—wholes like periodic flows of air, gradients of temperature or pressure—but not any details about the molecular populations that are the component parts of air flows or intensity gradients. Many different combinations of collisions between those molecules would lead to the same temperature gradient or the same air current, so any description of those collisions is redundant in an explanation of the mechanism of emergence of a thunderstorm.

Because many material entities display several levels of the part-to-whole relation—atoms compose molecules that in turn compose macromolecules like proteins;

26. Manuel DeLanda, *Philosophy, Emergence, and Simulation*, (forthcoming)
27. Alan Garfinkel, *Forms of Explanation*, New Haven, Yale University Press, 1981, pp. 58-62.

cells compose tissues that in turn compose organs and organisms—the relative indifference of stable wholes to changes in the details of their interacting parts explains why partial models of reality can work at all. We can illustrate this with models from two fields of physics operating at different scales. In the nineteenth century the field of thermodynamics was able to create successful models of wholes like steam engines using as causal factors entities like temperature and pressure gradients. In these models the emergent tendency of a gradient to cancel itself, and its capacity to drive a process as it cancels itself, could both be taken for granted. The assumption was that some other field at some other time would explain these emergent tendencies and capacities. And indeed this is what happened: towards the end of that century the field of statistical mechanics was born and explained why gradients behave as they do in terms of the interactions between the members of molecular populations. This illustrates the interplay between ontology and epistemology. On the one hand, emergent properties give reality a means to enter into an open-ended becoming, with new wholes coming into existence as tendencies and capacities proliferate. On the other hand, this objective divergence explains the divergence of scientific fields, that is, it accounts for the fact that rather than converging into a single field to which all the rest have been reduced the number of new fields is constantly increasing.

Singularities also exhibit this interplay. Their existence has the ontological consequence that many different mechanisms, such as the mechanisms studied by classical mechanics, can share a single explanation for their asymptotic stability. But it also has the epistemological consequence of explaining why the solutions to mathematical equations can exhibit behaviour that is isomorphic with that of those mechanisms. Positivists, of course, can argue that singularities are simply theoretical constructs that are useful to give classical physics a unified form but this is equivalent to adopting an attitude of natural piety towards the explanatory power of mathematical models. If we, on the other hand, think of the structure of a possibility space as a virtual entity that is every bit as real as any actual one, then the behavioral isomorphism between models and the processes they model can be explained as the product of a co-actualization of that structure. To put this differently, the mechanism-independence of singularities implies not only that they can become divergently actualized in many different material mechanisms but also in the formal mechanisms characterizing differential equations. When the explanatory capacity of mathematical models is accounted for this way we become committed to assert the autonomous existence not of eternal and immutable laws but of an immanent real virtuality that changes and grows as new tendencies and capacities arise.[28]

The view of the material world that emerges from these considerations is not one of matter as an inert receptacle for forms that come from the outside, a matter so limited in its causal powers that we must view the plurality of forms that it sustains as an unexplainable miracle. It is not either an obedient matter that follows general laws and that owes all its powers to those laws. It is rather an active matter endowed with its own tendencies and capacities, engaged in its own divergent, open-ended evolution, animated from within by immanent patterns of being and becoming. This other material world can certainly inspire awe in us but does not demand from us to be accepted with pious resignation. This is the kind of reality worthwhile being a realist about.

---

28. Manuel DeLanda, *Intensive Science and Virtual Philosophy*, London, Continuum Press, 2002, ch. 4.

24

Ontology, Biology, and History of Affect

John Protevi

ONTOLOGY OF AFFECT.

For Deleuze and Guattari (hereafter 'DG') 'affect' comprises the active capacities of a body to act and the passive capacities of a body to be affected or to be acted upon. In other words, affect is what a body can do and what it can undergo. The use of this term derives from Deleuze's reading of Spinoza, in which Deleuze carefully distinguishes 'affect', (*affectus*) as the experience of an increase or decrease in the body's power to act, from 'affection' (*affectio*) as the composition or mixture of bodies, or more precisely the change produced in the affected body by the action of the affecting body in an encounter. *Affectus* or what we could call 'experiential affect' is not representational, Deleuze remarks, 'since it is experienced in a living duration that involves the difference between two states'. As such, an experience of difference, *affectus* is 'purely transitive'.[1] In the main discussion of affect in *A Thousand Plateaus*[2], DG do not maintain the Spinozist term 'affection', but they do distinguish the relations of the extensive parts of a body (including the 'modification' of those relations resulting from an encounter), which they call 'longitude', from the intensities or bodily states that augment or diminish the body's 'power to act [*puissance d'agir*]', which they call 'latitude'. In other words, the 'latitude' of a body comprises the affects, or the capacities to act and to be acted upon, of which a body is capable at any one time in an assemblage. What are these 'acts' of which a body is capable? Using one of the key terms of ATP, DG define affects as 'becomings' or capacities to produce emergent effects in entering assemblages.[3] These emergent effects will either mesh productively with the affects of the body, or clash with them. Meshing emergent effects will augment the power of that body to form other connections within or across assemblages, resulting in joyous affects, while clashing emergent effects will diminish the power of the body to act producing sad affects.

---

1. Gilles Deleuze, *Spinoza: Practical Philosophy*, trans. Robert Hurley, San Francisco, City Lights, 1988, p. 49.

2. Gilles Deleuze and Félix Guattari, *A Thousand Plateaus*, trans. Brian Massumi, Minneapolis, University of Minnesota Press, 1987, pp. 256-7. Hereafter ATP.

3. John Protevi, 'Deleuze, Guattari, and Emergence', *Paragraph: A Journal of Modern Critical Theory*, vol. 29, no. 2, 2006, pp. 19-39.

For DG, knowledge of the affects of a body is all-important: 'We know nothing about a body until we know what it can do [*ce qu'il peut*], in other words, what its affects are' (ATP, 257). Affect is part of DG's dynamic interactional ontology, so that defining bodies in terms of affects or power to act and to undergo is different from reading them in terms of properties of substantive bodies by which they are arranged in species and genera (ATP, 257). At this point in their text, DG illustrate the way affect is part of the process of assembling by reference to the relation between Little Hans and the horse in Freud's eponymous case study . While we will not do a thematic study of the horse in ATP, we should recall the prevalence of horses (alongside wolves and rats) in the discussions of affect in ATP: besides the Little Hans case, we also find the becoming-horse of the masochist being submitted to dressage (ATP, 155), and of course the repeated analyses of man-horse assemblages in the Nomadology chapter (the stirrup, the chariot, etc.).

The horse allows one to illustrate affect as the capacity to become, to undergo the stresses inherent in forming a particular assemblage; note that in a grouping based on affect, a racehorse (carries a rider in a race; i.e., enters the racing assemblage) has more in common with a motorcycle than with a plow horse (pulls a tool that gouges the earth; i.e., enters the agricultural assemblage), which has more in common with a tractor. This is not to say that what is usually named a 'plow horse' or 'tractor' cannot be made to race, just as 'race horses' and 'motorcycles' can be made to pull plows. These affects as changes in the triggers and patterns of their behaviour would, however, constitute another becoming or line of flight counter to their usual, statistically normal ('molar') usages; it would constitute their enlistment in assemblages that tap different 'machinic phyla' (bio-techno-social fields for the construction of assemblages [(ATP, 404-11)] and 'diagrams' (the patterns that direct the construction of assemblages [(ATP, 141)] than the ones into which they are usually recruited. Whether or not the bodies involved could withstand the stresses they undergo is a matter of (one would hope careful) experimentation. Such experimentation establishing the affects of assemblages, the potentials for emergent functionality, is the very process of transcendental empiricism.

To recap, then, DG follow Spinoza, defining affect as a body's ability to act and to be acted upon, what it can do and what it can undergo. DG operationalize the notion of affect as the ability of bodies to form 'assemblages' with other bodies, that is, to form emergent functional structures that conserve the heterogeneity of their components. For DG, then, 'affect' is physiological, psychological, and machinic: it imbricates the social and the somatic in forming a 'body politic' which feels its power or potential to act increasing or decreasing as it encounters other bodies politic and forms assemblages with them (or indeed fails to do so). In this notion of assemblage as emergent functional structure, that is, a dispersed system that enables focused behaviour at the system level as it constrains component action, we find parallels with novel positions in contemporary cognitive science (the 'embodied' or 'extended' mind schools), which maintain that cognition operates in loops among brain, body, and environment.[4] In noting this parallel, we should note that DG emphasizes the affective dimension of assemblages, while the embodied-embedded school focuses on cognition. While we follow DG's lead and focus on the affective, we should remember that both affect and

---

4. cf. Andy Clark, *Natural-Born Cyborgs: Minds, Technologies, and the Future of Human Intelligence*, New York, Oxford University Press, 2003, and Evan Thompson, *Mind in Life: Biology, Phenomenology, and the Sciences of Mind*, Cambridge, Harvard University Press, 2007.

cognition are aspects of a single process, affective cognition, as the directed action of a living being in its world.[5]

In discussing affect, we should note that DG place feeling as the subjective appropriation of affect. An example would be the way pleasure is for them the subjective appropriation of de-subjectizing joyous affect: 'pleasure is an affection of a person or a subject; it is the only way for persons to 'find themselves' in the process of desire that exceeds them; pleasures, even the most artificial, are reterritorializations' (ATP, 156). In the same way, our lead passage implies that 'feeling' (*sentiment*) is the subject's appropriation of physiological-emotional changes of the body, the recognition that 'this is me feeling this way'. DG's point about affect's extension beyond subjective feeling dovetails with the analysis we will develop of extreme cases of rage and panic as triggering an evacuation of the subject as automatic responses take over; as we will put it, drastic episodes of rage and fear are de-subjectivizing. The agent of an action undertaken in a rage or panic state can be said to be the embodied 'affect program'[6] acting independently of the subject. Here we see affect freed from subjective feeling. There can be no complaints about eliminating the 'first person' perspective in studying these episodes, because there is no 'first person' operative in these cases. Agency and subjectivity are split; affect extends beyond feeling; the body does something, is the agent for an action, in the absence of a subject.[7]

Let me give a brief example of research in social psychology that recognizes the ontology of affect in bodies politic, bodies that are socially constructed in 'dialogue' with our shared genetic heritage. Nisbett and Cohen[8] go below the conscious subject to examine physiological response, demonstrating that white males of the southern United States have markedly greater outputs of cortisol and testosterone in response to insults than a control group of northern white males.[9] They go above the individual subject to examine social policy forms, showing that southern states have looser gun control laws, more lenient laws regarding the use of violence in defence of self and property, and more lenient practices regarding use of violence for social control (domestic violence, corporal punishment in schools, and capital punishment)[10]. They also offer in passing some speculation as to the role played by slavery in the South in constructing these bodies politic in which social institutions and somatic affect are intertwined in diachronically developing and intensifying mutual reinforcement. No one should think that these Southern males have a significantly different genetic makeup from other groups (or better, that any genetic variation is larger within the group than is present between this group and others); the difference in reaction comes from the differences in bodies politic formed by different subjectification practices, that is, the differences in the way social practices have installed triggers and thresholds that activate the anger patterns we all share due to our common genetic heritage.

---

5. cf. John Protevi, *Political Affect: Connecting the Social and the Somatic*, Minneapolis, University of Minnesota Press, 2009.

6. cf. Paul Griffiths, *What Emotions Really Are: The Problem of Psychological Categories*, Chicago, University of Chicago Press, 1997.

7. cf. John Protevi, 'Affect, Agency, and Responsibility: The Act of Killing in the Age of Cyborgs', *Phenomenology and the Cognitive Sciences*, vol. 7, no. 3, 2008, pp. 405-13.

8. cf. Richard E. Nisbett and Dov Cohen, *Culture of Honor: The Psychology of Violence in the South*, Boulder, Westview Press, 1996.

9. Nisbett and Cohen, *Culture of Honor*, pp. 44-45.

10. Nisbett and Cohen, *Culture of Honor*, pp. 57-73.

Thus, as we have seen, affect is inherently political: bodies are part of an eco-social matrix of other bodies, affecting them and being affected by them. As we will now see, important schools of biological thought accord with this notion of affect as bio-cultural.

BIOLOGY OF AFFECT

Let's first consider the neuroscience of affect. We'll focus on rage, as the triggering of this de-subjectizing affect was the target of constructions in the geo-bio-techno-affective assemblages of ancient warfare. Rage is a basic emotion, which is not to be confused with aggression, though it sometimes is at the root of aggressive behaviour. A leading neuroscientist investigating rage is Jaak Panksepp, whose *Affective Neuroscience*[11] is a standard textbook in the field. He argues that aggression is wider than anger[12], distinguishing at least two forms of 'aggressive circuits' in mammalian brains: predation and rage.[13] Predation is based on what Panksepp calls the 'seeking' system, which is activated by physiological imbalances, those that can be experienced as hunger, thirst, or sexual need. In predatory hunting, based in seeking, the subject is still operative; there is an experience to hunting, we can experience 'what it is like' to hunt. Now we must be careful about too strictly distinguishing predation and rage in the act of killing. Concrete episodes are most often blends of anger and predation; as one expert puts it: 'Real-life encounters tend to yield eclectic admixtures, composites of goal and rage, purpose and hate, reason and feeling, rationality and irrationality. Instrumental and hostile violence are not only *kinds* of violence, but also violence qualities or *components*'.[14]

Although in many cases we find composites of brute rage and purposeful predation, we can isolate, at least theoretically, the pure state or 'blind rage' in which the subject drops out. We take the Viking 'berserker rage' as a prototype, a particularly intense expression of the underlying neurological rage circuits that evacuates subjectivity and results in a sort of killing frenzy without conscious control. The notion of a blind de-subjectified rage is confirmed by Panksepp's analysis of the 'hierarchical' architecture of the neural circuits involved: 'the core of the RAGE system runs from the medial amygdaloid areas downward, largely via the stria terminalis to the medial hypothalamus, and from there to specific locations with the PAG [periaqueductal gray] of the midbrain. This system is organized hierarchically, meaning that aggression evoked from the amygdala is critically dependent on the lower regions, while aggression from lower sites does not depend critically on the integrity of the higher areas'.[15] We must admit that there are huge issues here with the relation of Panksepp's anatomical focus on specific circuits and neurodynamical approaches which stress that the activity of multiple brain regions are involved in the activation of any one brain function; this anatomy versus dynamics relation must itself be seen in the historical context of the perennial localist versus globalist debate. We are in no position to intervene in these most complex issues, but we should note that Panksepp's notion of hierarchical circuits does allow for the possibility that 'higher areas provide subtle refinements to the orchestration that is elaborated in the PAG of the mesencephalon [midbrain]. For instance, various

---

11. Jaak Panksepp, *Affective Neuroscience*, New York, Oxford University Press, 1998.

12. Panksepp, *Affective Neuroscience*, p. 187.

13. Panksepp, *Affective Neuroscience*, p. 188.

14. Hans Toch, *Violent Men: An Inquiry Into the Psychology of Violence*, Washington, American Psychological Association, 1992, pp. 1-2 (emphasis in original).

15. Panksepp, *Affective Neuroscience*, p. 196.

irritating perceptions probably get transmitted into the system via thalamic and cortical inputs to the medial amygdala'.[16] While these 'irritating perceptions' may simply stoke the system to ever-greater heights of rage, we do need to allow that in some cases conscious control can reassert itself. Nonetheless, Panksepp's basic approach, as well as the volumes of warrior testimony about the berserker rage[17], licenses our description of the 'pure' berserker rage as 'blind' and de-subjectified.

Now it is not that the Viking culture somehow presented simply a stage for the playing out of these neurological circuits. To provoke the berserker rage, the Vikings, through a variety of training practices embedded in their customs, distributed traits for triggering the berserker process throughout their population. Presumably, they underwent an evolutionary process in which success in raiding undertaken in the berserker frenzy provided a selection pressure for isolating and improving these practices. (We will return to the question of cultural evolution below; for the moment, please note that I am not implying that genes were the target of that selection pressure.) In other words, the Vikings explored the bio-social machinic phylum for rage triggering in their military assemblages. While one researcher cites possible mushroom ingestion as a contributing factor[18], we will later focus on the role of dance and song in triggering the berserker state. In his important work, *Keeping Together in Time: Dance and Drill in Human History*, the noted historian William McNeill notes that 'war dances' produced a 'heightened excitement' that contributed to the 'reckless attacks' of the 'Viking berserkers'.[19]

There is no denying that the social meaning of blind rages differs across cultures—how they are interpreted by others and by self after waking up—as do their triggers and thresholds.[20] However, I think it is important to rescue a minimal notion of human nature from extreme social constructivism and hold that the rage pattern is the same in some important sense across cultures, given variation in genetic inheritances, environmental input, and developmental plasticity. Even with all that variation, there is remarkable similarity in what a full rage looks like, though how much it takes to get there, and what the intermediate anger episodes look like ('emotion scripts'[21]) can differ widely. Even James Averill, a leading social constructivist when it comes to emotion, relates 'running amok' in Southeast Asian societies to Viking berserker rages. Averill writes: 'Aggressive frenzies are, of course, found in many different cultures (e.g., the *'berserk'* reaction attributed to old Norse warriors), but amok is probably the most studied of these syndromes'.[22] It is the very *commonality* of 'aggressive frenzies' that we are after in our notion of 'rage pattern'.

---

16. Panksepp, *Affective Neuroscience*, pp. 196-7.

17. cf. Jonathon Shay, *Achilles in Vietnam*, New York, Scribner, 1995 for the tip of the iceberg in these discussions.

18. cf. Howard Fabing, 'On Going Berserk: A Neurochemical Inquiry', *American Journal of Psychiatry*, no. 113, pp. 409-415.

19. cf. William McNeill, *Keeping Together in Time, Dance and Drill in Human History*, Cambridge, Harvard University Press, p. 102 and Michael Speidel, 'Berserks: A History of Indo-European "Mad Warriors"', *Journal of World History*, vol. 13, no. 2, pp. 253-90, p. 276.

20. cf. Ron Mallon and Stephen Stich, 'The Odd Couple: The compatibility of social construction and evolutionary psychology', *Philosophy of Science*, no. 67, pp. 133-154.

21. cf. Brian Parkinson, Agneta Fischer and Athony Manstead, *Emotions in Social Relations: Cultural, Group and Interpersonal Processes*, New York, Psychology Press, 2005.

22. James R. Averill, *Anger and Aggression: An Essay on Emotion*, New York, Springer, 1982, p. 59 (emphasis in original).

I propose that in extreme cases of rage a modular agent replaces the subject with what is called an 'affect program', that is, an emotional response that is 'complex, co-ordinated, and automated ... unfold[ing] in this coordinated fashion without the need for conscious direction'.[23] Affect programs (panic is another example) are more than re-flexes, but they are triggered well before any cortical processing can take place (though later cortical appraisals can dampen or accelerate the affect program). Griffiths makes the case that affect programs should be seen in light of Fodor's notion of modularity, which calls for a module to be 'mandatory ... opaque [we are aware of outputs but not the processes producing them] ... and informationally encapsulated [the information in a module cannot access that in other modules]'.[24] Perhaps second only to the ques-tion of adaptationism for the amount of controversy it has evoked, the use of the con-cept of modularity in evolutionary psychology is bitterly contested. I feel relatively safe proposing a rage module or rage agent, since its adaptive value is widely attested to by its presence in other mammals, and since Panksepp is able to cite studies of direct elec-trical stimulation of the brain (ESB) and neurochemical manipulation as identifying homologous rage circuits in humans and other mammalian species.[25] Panksepp pro-poses as adaptive reasons for rage agents their utility in predator-prey relations, fur-ther sharpening the difference between rage and predator aggression. While a hunting attack is by definition an instance of predatory aggression, rage reactions are a prey phenomenon, a vigorous reaction when pinned down by a predator. Initially a reflex, Panksepp claims, it developed into a full-fledged neural phenomenon with its own cir-cuits.[26] The evolutionary inheritance of rage patterns is confirmed by the well-attest-ed fact that infants can become enraged by having their arms pinned to their sides.[27]

Now that we have seen how neuroscientists discuss rage, and broached the is-sues of the unit of selection in cultural evolution and those of modularity and adapta-tionism in evolutionary psychology, we have to insist right now that we cannot think bodies politic as mere input/output machines passively patterned by their environ-ment (that way lies a discredited social constructivism) or passively programmed by their genes (an equally discredited genetic determinism). We thus turn to an important school of thought in contemporary critical biology, 'developmental systems theory' (DST), which is taken from the writings of Richard Lewontin[28], Susan Oyama[29], Paul Griffiths and Russell Gray[30] and others.[31] With the help of this new critical biology we

23. Paul Griffiths, *What Emotions Really Are*, p. 77.

24. Griffiths, *What Emotions Really Are*, p. 93, my comments in brackets.

25. Jaak Panksepp, *Affective Neuroscience*, p. 190.

26. Panksepp, *Affective Neuroscience*, p. 190

27. Panksepp, *Affective Neuroscience*, p. 189.

28. cf. Richard Lewontin, *The Triple Helix: Gene, Organism, and Environment*, Cambridge, Harvard Univer-sity Press, 2002.

29. cf. Susan Oyama, *The Ontogeny of Information: Developmental Systems and Evolution*, 2nd ed., Durham, Duke University Press, 2000

30. cf. Paul Griffiths and Russell Gray, 'Replicator II—Judgement Day', *Biology and Philosophy*, vol. 12, 2001, pp. 471-492; Paul Griffiths and Russell Gray, 'Darwinism and Developmental Systems', in Susan Oya-ma, Paul Griffiths and Russell Gray (eds.), *Cycles of Contingency: Developmental Systems and Evolution*, Cambridge, MIT Press, 2004, pp. 195-218; Paul Griffiths and Russell Gray, 'The Developmental Systems Perspective: Organism-environment systems as units of development and evolution', in Massimo Pigliucci and Katherine Preston (eds.), *Phenotypic Integration: Studying the Ecology and Evolution of Complex Phenotypes*, New York, Oxford University Press, 2005, pp. 409-430; and 'Discussion: Three ways to misunderstand developmental systems theory', *Biology and Philosophy*, no. 20, 417-425.

31. cf. Susan Oyama, Paul Griffiths and Russell Gray, *Cycles of Contingency*, Cambridge, MIT Press, 2001.

can see the body politic as neither a simple blank slate nor a determined mechanism, but as biologically open to the subjectification practices it undergoes in its cultural embedding, practices that work with the broad contours provided by the genetic contribution to development to install culturally variant triggers and thresholds to the basic patterns that are our common heritage. Griffiths uses the example of fear to make this point, but the same holds for the basic emotion of rage we discussed above. 'The empirical evidence suggests that in humans the actual fear response—the output side of fear—is an outcome of very coarse-grained selection, since it responds to danger of all kinds. The emotional appraisal mechanism for fear—the input side—seems to have been shaped by a combination of very fine-grained selection, since it is primed to respond to crude snake-like gestalts, and selection for developmental plasticity, since very few stimuli elicit fear without relevant experience'.[32]

DST is primarily a reaction to genetic determinism or reductionism. Genetic determinism is an ontological thesis proposing that genes are the sole source of order of (that is, that genes determine) physiological and developmental processes, beginning with protein synthesis and extending upward to organic, systemic, and organismic processes. No one has ever upheld such an absolute position if by that one means epigenetic conditions have no influence whatsoever, that developmental and physiological processes are determined the way a stone is determined to fall by gravity. The real target of critique by DST thinkers is the idea that there are two classes of developmental resources, genetic and epigenetic, and that genes provide the information, blue-print, plan or program, such that the epigenetic resources are the materials or background upon which and / or in which genes act.[33] The real question of so-called genetic determinism, then, is the locus of control rather than absolute determination.

Genetic reductionism is an epistemological issue. It's my impression that many practising biologists think of reductionism as asking the question: can the portion of physiology and development due to genetic control be considered separately from the portion due to epigenetic influences? The DST response to this question is known as the 'parity thesis'[34], which rests upon the idea that there is a distributed system with both genetic and epigenetic factors (e.g., at least cell conditions and relative cell position) that controls gene expression and protein synthesis. It's a mistake however to attribute portions of control to components of that system, such that one could isolate the portion of genetic control. That would be analogous to saying that prisoners are partially under the control of the guards, when it would be better to say they are under the control of the prison system in which guards play a role (alongside architectural, technological, and administrative components). In the view of Griffiths and Gray, the undeniable empirical differences in the roles played by DNA and by non-DNA factors does not support the metaphysical decision to create two classes of developmental resources, nor the additional move to posit genes as the locus of control and epigenetic factors as background, as matter to be molded by the 'information' supposedly carried in genes.[35]

---

32. Paul Griffiths, 'Evo-devo meets the mind: Toward a developmental evolutionary psychology', in Robert Brandon and Roger Sansom (eds.), *Integrating Evolution and Development: From Theory to Practice*, Cambridge, MIT Press, 2007, p. 204.

33. cf. Oyama, *The Ontogeny of Information*; Griffiths and Gray 'Replicator II—Judgement Day'; and Paul Griffiths and Russell Gray, 'The Developmental Systems Perspective'.

34. cf. Oyama, *The Ontogeny of Information*; Griffiths and Gray 'Replicator II—Judgement Day'; and Griffiths and Gray, 'The Developmental Systems Perspective'.

35. cf. Griffiths and Gray 'Replicator II—Judgement Day'; and Griffiths and Gray, 'The Developmen-

A second key notion for DST thinkers is 'niche-construction'. Rather than seeing evolution as the adaptation of organisms to independently changing environments (the organism thus being reactive), DST follows Richard Lewontin[36] and others in focusing on the way organisms actively shape the environment they live in and in which their offspring will live. They thus play a role in selecting which environmental factors are most important for them and their offspring. Therefore, evolution should be seen not simply as the change in gene frequency (a mere 'bookkeeping' perspective) but as the change in organism-environment systems, that is, the organism in its constructed niche.[37] Allied with niche-construction, a third key notion of DST is that the 'life cycle' should be considered the unit of development and evolution. For DST adherents, the developmental system considered in an evolutionary perspective is the widest possible extension of developmental resources that are reliably present (or better, re-created) across generations. The 'life cycle' considered in an evolutionary perspective is the series of events caused by this developmental matrix that recurs in each generation.[38] The evolutionary perspective on the developmental system and life cycle is thus different from the individual perspective, where events need not recur: a singular event might play a crucial role in the development of any one individual, but unless it reliably recurs, it will not have a role in evolution; DST thus avoids the spectre of Lamarckism. In their evolutionary thinking, DST thinkers extend the notion of epigenetic inheritance from the intra-nuclear factors of chromatin markings to the cytoplasmic environment of the egg (an extension many mainstream biologists have come to accept) and beyond to intra-organismic and even (most controversially) to extra-somatic factors, that is, to the relevant, constructed, features of the physical and social environments (for example, normal [i.e., species-typical] brain development in humans needs language exposure in critical sensitive windows).[39]

Such a maximal extension of the developmental system raises the methodological hackles of many biologists, as it seems suspiciously holistic. These methodological reflections remain among the most controversial in contemporary philosophy of science. It would take us too far afield to explore fully all the implications of these debates, but we can see them as well in the background of the notions of developmental plasticity and environmental co-constitution found in West-Eberhard.[40] That the development of organisms is 'plastic' and 'co-constituted' with its environment means that it is not the simple working out of a genetic program. Rather, development involves a range of response capacities depending on the developing system's exposure to different environmental factors, just as those responses feed back to change the environment in niche-construction. Thus the notion of developmental plasticity displaces gene-centric notions of programmed development just as organism-environment co-constitution displaces notions of gene-centric natural selection in favour of a notion of multiple levels of selection.

---

tal Systems Perspective'.

36. cf. Lewontin, *The Triple Helix*.

37. cf. Griffiths and Gray, 'Discussion: Three ways to misunderstand developmental systems theory'.

38. cf. Griffiths and Gray, 'Replicator II—Judgement Day'; Griffiths and Gray, 'Darwinism and Developmental Systems'; Griffiths and Gray, 'The Developmental Systems Perspective'.

39. cf. Griffiths and Gray, 'Replicator II—Judgement Day'; Griffiths and Gray, 'Darwinism and Developmental Systems'; Griffiths and Gray, 'The Developmental Systems Perspective'; and Eva Jablonka and Marion J. Lamb, *Evolution in Four Dimensions: Genetic, Epigenetic, Behavioral, and Symbolic Variation in the History of Life*, Cambridge, MIT Press, 2005.

40. cf. Mary Jan West-Eberhard, *Developmental Plasticity and Evolution*, New York, Oxford University Press, 2003.

We cannot enter the details of the controversy surrounding the notion of multiple levels of selection here, but we can at least sketch the main issues surrounding the notion of group selection, which plays a key role in any notion of bio-cultural evolution.[41] In considering the notion of group selection we find two main issues: emergence and altruism. If groups can have functional organization in the same way individuals do, that is, if groups can be emergent individuals, then groups can also be vehicles for selection. For example, groups that cooperate better may have out-reproduced those which did not. The crucial question is the replicator, the ultimate target of the selection pressures: again, for our purposes, the unit of selection is not the gene or the meme (a discrete unit of cultural 'information'), but the set of practices for forming bodies politic. With the co-operation necessary for group selection, we must discuss the notion of 'altruism' or more precisely, the seeming paradox of 'fitness-sacrificing behaviour'. It would seem that natural selection would weed out dispositions leading to behaviors that sacrifice individual fitness (defined as always as the frequency of reproduction). The famous answer that seemed to put paid to the notion of group selection came in the concept of 'kin selection'. The idea here is that if you sacrifice yourself for a kin, at least part of your genotype, the 'altruistic' part that determines or at least influences self-sacrifice and that is [probably] shared with that kin, is passed on. But again, all the preceding discussion operates at the genetic level. We will claim that the ultimate target of selection pressure in group selection is the set of social practices reliably producing a certain trait by working with our genetic heritage. This need not have any implications for genetic fitness-sacrificing in group selection, if we restrict ourselves to bodies politic and the social practices for promoting behaviour leading to increased group fitness. In other words, we are concerned with the variable cultural setting of triggers and thresholds for minimally genetically guided basic patterns.

The important thing for our purposes here is the emphasis DST places on the life cycle, developmental plasticity and environmental co-constitution. In following these thinkers, we can replace the controversial term 'innate' with (the admittedly equally controversial) 'reliably produced given certain environmental factors'. In so doing, we have room to analyze differential patterns in societies that bring forth important differences from common endowments. In other words, we don't genetically inherit a subject, but we do inherit the potential to develop a subject when it is called forth by cultural practices. It is precisely the various types of subject called forth (the distribution of cognitive and affective patterns, thresholds, and triggers in a given population) that is to be analyzed in the study of the history of affect.

HISTORY OF AFFECT

We have seen how DST enables us to explore the bio-cultural dimension of bodies politic by thematizing extrasomatic inheritance as whatever is reliably reproduced in the next life cycle. Thus, with humans we're into the realm of bio-cultural evolution, with all its complexity and debates. We have to remember that the unit of selection here is not purely and simply genetic (indeed, for the most part genes are unaffected by cultural evolution, the classical instances of lactose tolerance and sickle-cell anemia notwith-

---

41. cf. Elliott Sober and David Sloan Wilson, *Unto Others: The Evolution and Psychology of Unselfish Behaviour*, Cambridge, Harvard University Press, 1999; Kim Sterelny and Paul Griffiths, *Sex and Death: An Introduction to the Philosophy of Biology*, Chicago, University of Chicago Press, 1999; Eva Jablonka and Marion J. Lamb, *Evolution in Four Dimensions: Genetic, Epigenetic, Behavioral, and Symbolic Variation in the History of Life*, Cambridge, MIT Press, 2005; and Richard Joyce, *The Evolution of Morality*, Cambridge, MIT Press, 2006.

standing), but should be seen as sets of cultural practices, thought in terms of their ability to produce affective cognitive structures (tendencies to react to categories of events) by tinkering with broadly genetically guided neuro-endocrine developmental processes.

Regarding historically formed and culturally variable affective cognition, I work with Damasio's framework for the most part.[42] Brain and body communicate neurologically and chemically in forming 'somatic markers', which correlate or tag changes in the characteristic profile of body changes with the encounters, that is, changes in the characteristic profile of body-world interactions, which provoke them. Somatic markers are formed via a complex process involving brain-body-environment interaction, in which the brain receives signals from the body, from brain maps of body sectors, and from its own internal self-monitoring sectors. Thus the brain synthesizes how the world is changing (sensory input, which is only a modulation on ongoing processes), how the body is being affected by the world's changing (proprioception or 'somatic mapping', again, a modulation of ongoing processes), and how the brain's endogenous dynamics are changing (modulation of ongoing internal neurological traffic or 'meta-representations'). This synthesis sets up the capacity to experience a feeling of how the body would be affected were it to perform a certain action and hence be affected in turn by the world (off-line imaging, that is, modulation of the ongoing stream of 'somatic markers'). I cannot detail the argument here, but a neurodynamical reading of Damasio's framework is broadly consonant with the Deleuzean emphasis on differential relations, that is, the linkage of rates of change of neural firing patterns, and on their integration at certain critical thresholds, resulting in 'resonant cell assemblies'[43] or their equivalent.[44] The key is that the history of bodily experience is what sets up a somatic marker profile; in other words, the affective cognition profile of bodies politic is embodied and historical.

With this background, we see that the limitations of much of the controversy around 'cultural evolution' are due to the assumption that 'information transfer' is the target for investigation.[45] But the notions of 'meme' and 'information transfer' founders on DST's critique—it's not a formed unit of information that we're after, but a process of guiding the production of dispositions to form somatic markers in particularly culturally informed ways. We have to think of ourselves as bio-cultural, with minimal genetically guided psychological modularity (reliably reproduced across cultures) and with a great deal of plasticity allowing for bio-cultural variance in forming our intuitions.[46] In other words, we have to study political physiology, defined as the study of the production of the variance in affective cognitive triggers and thresholds in bodies politic, based on some minimally shared basic patterns.

All this means we can't assume an abstract affective cognitive subject but have to investigate the history of affect. However, the objection might go, don't we thereby risk

---

42. cf. Antonio Damasio, *Descartes' Error*, New York, Avon, 1994; Antonio Damasio, *The Feeling of What Happens*, New York, Harcourt, 1999; Antonio Damasio, *Looking for Spinoza*, New York, Harcourt, 2003.

43. cf. Francisco Varela, 'Resonant Cell Assemblies: A new approach to cognitive functions and neuronal synchrony', *Biological Research*, no. 28, 2005, pp. 81-95.

44. cf. J. Scott Kelso, *Dynamic Patterns: The Self-Organization of Brain and Behaviour*, Cambridge, MIT Press, 1995; and Gerald Edelman and Giulio Tononi, *A Universe of Consciousness: How Matter Becomes Imagination*, New York, Basic Books, 2000.

45. WG Runciman, 'Culture Does Evolve', *History and Theory*, vol. 44, no. 1, 2005, p. 13.

46. cf. Jonathan Haidt, ' The emotional dog and its rational tail: A social intuitionist approach to moral judgment', *Psychological Review*, no. 108, 2001; and Bruce Wexler, *Brain and Culture: Neurobiology, Ideology, and Social Change*, Cambridge, MIT Press, 2006.

leaving philosophy and entering historical anthropology? Answer: we only 'leave' philosophy to enter history if we've surreptitiously defined philosophy ahead of time as ahistorical. Well, then, don't we leave philosophy and enter psychology? Answer: only if we've defined philosophy as concerned solely with universal structures of affective cognition. But that's the nub of the argument: the abstraction needed to reach the universally 'human' (as opposed to the historically variant) is at heart anti-biological. Our biology makes humans essentially open to our cultural imprinting; our nature is to be so open to our nurture that it becomes second nature. However, just saying that is typological thinking, concerned with 'the' (universal) human realm; we need to bring concrete biological thought into philosophy. It's the variations in and across populations which are real; the type is an abstraction.

Having said all that, we must be clear that we are targeting variation in the subjectification practices producing variable triggers and thresholds of shared basic patterns. Now almost all of us reliably develop a set of basic emotions (rage, sadness, joy, fear, distaste) we share with a good number of reasonably complex mammals.[47] Many of us also have robust and reliable prosocial emotions, (fairness, gratitude, punishment—shame and guilt are controversial cases) which we share with primates, given certain basic and very wide-spread socializing inputs.[48] Although some cultural practices can try to expand the reach of prosocial emotions to all humans or even all sentient creatures (with all sorts of stops in between), in many sets of cultural practices, these prosocial emotions are partial and local (Hume's starting point in talking about the 'moral sentiments'). Why is the partiality of prosocial emotions a 'default setting' for sets of bio-cultural practices? One hypothesis is that war has been a selection pressure in bio-cultural evolution, operating at the level of group selection and producing very strong in-group versus out-group distinctions and very strong rewards / punishments for in-group conformity.[49]

There are difficult issues here concerning group selection and the unit of selection[50], but even if we can avoid the genetic level and focus on group selection for sets of social practices producing prosocial behaviors, we must still take into account a bitter controversy in anthropology about the alleged universality of warfare in human evolution and history.[51] There are three elements to consider here: the biological, the archaeological, and the ethnographic. (1) Regarding the biological, an important first step is to distinguish human war from chimpanzee male coalition and aggressive hierarchy, in short, the humans as 'killer ape' hypothesis.[52] Several researchers point out that we are just as genetically related to bonobos, who are behaviorally very different from chimpanzees.[53] (2)

---

47. Panskepp, *Affective Neuroscience*.

48. cf. Frans DeWaal, *Primates and Philosophers: How Morality Evolved*, Princeton, Princeton University Press, 2006; and Richard Joyce, *The Evolution of Morality*.

49. e.g., Samuel Bowles and Herbert Gintis, 'The Origins of Human Cooperation', in Peter Hammerstein (ed.), *The Genetic and Cultural Origins of Cooperation*, Cambridge, MIT Press, 2003.

50. cf. Doyne Dawson, 'Evolutionary Theory and Group Selection: The Question of Warfare', *History and Theory*, vol. 38, no. 4, 1999.

51. For a brief review of the literature from the anti-universalist position, see Leslie Sponsel, 'Response to Otterbein', *American Anthropologist*, vol. 102, no. 4, 2000; for a book-length statement of the universalist position, see Keith Otterbein, *How War Began*, College Station, Texas A&M Press, 2004.

52. cf. Dale Peterson and Richard Wrangham, *Demonic Males: Apes and the Origins of Human Violence*, New York, Houghton Mifflin, 1997.

53. DeWaal, *Primates and Philosophers*, p. 73; see also Douglas Fry, *Beyond War: The Human Potential for Peace*, New York, Oxford University Press, 2007; and Brian Ferguson, 'Ten Points on War', *Social Analysis*, vol. 52, no. 2, 2008.

Proponents of universal war often point to the archaeological record.[54] Critics reply that claims of war damaged skulls are more plausibly accounted for by animal attacks.[55] (3) Finally, we must couple the archaeological record with the current ethnographic record. In order to do that we must distinguish simple hunter-gather (forager) bands from more complex hunter-gatherer tribes (with chiefs). The former have murder and revenge killing and/or group 'executions' (sometimes by kin of the killer—weeding out the mad dogs), but not feuding or the 'logic of social substitutability' which enables warfare.[56] We also have to look to current tribal warfare in the context of Western contact and territorial constriction and/or rivalry over trading rights.[57]

The question would be how much war was needed to form an effective selection pressure for strong in-group identification and hence partiality of pro-social emotions? Richerson and Boyd argue that between group imitation can also be a factor in spreading cultural variants.[58] Richerson and Boyd cite the example of early Christianity, where the selection pressure for subjectificaiton practices of 'brotherhood' and hence care for the poor and sick was the high rate of epidemics in the Roman Empire. So war need not be the only selection pressure, nor does group destruction and assimilation of losers have to be the only means of transmitting cultural variants. We will assume in the following section that we haven't had time for selection pressures on genes with regard to warfare.[59] But we have had time for selection pressures on bio-cultural subjectification practices relative to warfare, that is, for example, how to entrain a marching phalanx versus how to trigger berserker rage.

If war was a selection pressure on group subjectification practices for forming different bodies politic, we have to consider the history of warfare. With complex tribal warfare, you get loose groups of warriors with charismatic leaders.[60] Virtually all the males of the tribe take part in this type of warfare; in other words, there is no professional warrior class/caste, except in certain rare cases. The argument of Fry[61] is that the Chagnon/Clastres school, which focuses on the Yanomami as prototypical 'primitive' warriors, picked complex horticultural hunter-gatherers and missed the even more basic simple foragers, who represented the vast majority of human history. But that's okay, because we're not talking about genes, but about bio-cultural evolution, about group selection of affective practices. So we don't have to claim warfare is in our genes; we need only investigate the geo-bio-affective group subjectification practices, once warfare is widespread. And I accept that this spread is post-agricultural, even for complex tribal 'primitive' societies, who have always had States on their horizon (both immanently as that which is warded off, and externally, as that which is fought against; again.[62]

---

54. cf. Lawrence Keeley,. *War Before Civilization: The Myth of the Peaceful Savage*, New York, Oxford University Press, 1997.

55. Fry, *Beyond War*, p. 43.

56. cf. Raymond Kelly, *Warless Societies and the Origin of War*, Ann Arbor, University of Michigan Press, 2000; and Fry, *Beyond War*.

57. cf. Sponsel, 'Response to Otterbein'; and Ferguson, 'Ten Points on War'.

58. Peter Richerson and Robert Boyd, *Not by Genes Alone: How Culture Transformed Human Evolution*, Chicago, University of Chicago Press, 2005, pp. 209-10.

59. cf. Doyne Dawson, 'Evolutionary Theory and Group Selection'.

60. cf. Pierre Clastres, *Society Against the State: Essays in Political Anthropology*, trans. by Robert Hurley in collaboration with Abe Stein, New York, Zone Books, 1989.

61. Fry, *Beyond War*.

62. See Brian Ferguson, *Yanomami Warfare: A Political History*, Santa Fe, School for American Research

This tribal egalitarianism changes with agriculture and class society. We need not enter DG's 'anti-evolution' argument and the notion of the Urstaat, though we can note some fascinating new research which broadly supports their claim, derived from Jane Jacobs,[63] of the urban origins of agriculture.[64] Consider thus the situation in Homer: we see vast differences between the affective structures of the warriors (bravery), the peasants (docility) who support them, the artisans who supply the arms (diligence), and the bards who sing their praises and who thus reinforce the affective structures of the warriors: the feeling that your name will live on if you perform bravely is very important. Thus here the selection pressure is for sets of bio-cultural practices producing specialized affective structures relative to position in society, that is, relative to their contribution to the effectiveness of wars fought by that society. Once again, our concern is with the bio-cultural production of bodies politic, which tries to reliably produce bio-affective states. The triumph of hoplite warfare marks a shift in bio-cultural production. Compare Aristotle's golden mean of courage with what the Homeric warriors meant by courage. For Aristotle, courage means staying in the phalanx with your mates: charging ahead rashly is as much a fault as cowardly retreat.[65] But for the Homeric heroes, charging ahead rashly is all there is.

Press, 1995, for a political history of Yanomami warfare.

63. cf. Jane Jacobs, *The Economy of Cities*, New York, Vintage Books, 1970.

64. cf. Michael Balter, 'Why Settle Down? The Mystery of Communities', *Science*, vol. 282, no. 5393, 20 November 1998; but see the nuanced multiple-origins account in Heather Pringle, 'The Slow Birth of Agriculture', *Science*, vol. 282, no. 5393, 1998.

65. Aristotle, *Nicomachean Ethics*, 3.7.1115a30; b25-30; cf. Victor Davis Hanson, *The Western Way of War*, Berkeley, University of California Pres, 1989, p. 168.

25

Interview

Slavoj Žižek and Ben Woodard

Slavoj Žižek: There are two ways to answer the questions. I can offer a brief clarification of the precise point a question is raising, or engage with the difficult background of basic philosophical issues. I'll try to combine the two.

Ben Woodard: Speculative Realism can be seen as a response not only to the inadequacies of deconstruction and phenomenology but also to the increasingly loose deployment of the term 'materialism' itself. How does your own formulation of materialism avoid being a covert idealism? How do you see the term realism beyond its positivist limitations?

SZ: Who is a materialist today? Many orientations claim to be materialist: scientific materialism (Darwinism, brain sciences), 'discursive' materialism (ideology as the result of material discursive practices), what Alain Badiou calls 'democratic materialism' (the spontaneous egalitarian hedonism)... Some of these materialisms are mutually exclusive: for 'discursive' materialists, it is scientific materialism which, in its allegedly 'naïve' direct assertion of external reality, is 'idealist' in the sense that it does not take into account the role of 'material' symbolic practice in constituting what appears to us as reality; for scientific materialism, 'discursive' materialism is an obscurantist muddle not to be taken seriously. I am tempted to claim that discursive materialism and scientific materialism are, in their very antagonism, the front and the obverse of the same coin, one standing for radical culturalization (everything, inclusive our notions of nature, is a contingent discursive formation), and the other for radical naturalization (everything, inclusive our culture, can be accounted for in the terms of natural biological evolution).

My starting point here is Lenin's thesis that every great scientific breakthrough changes the very definition of materialism. The last great breakthrough was quantum physics, and it compels us to turn against Lenin himself and drop the assertion of 'fully existing external reality' as the basic premise of materialism—on the contrary, its premise is the 'non-All' of reality, its ontological incompleteness. (Recall Lenin's deadlock when, in *Materialism and Empiriocriticism*, he proposes as a minimal philosophical definition of materialism the assertion of an objective reality which exists independently of human mind, without any further qualifications: in this sense, Plato himself is a materialist!) It has also nothing to do with any positive determination of content, like 'matter' versus 'spirit', i.e., with the substantialization of Matter into the only Absolute (Hegel's critique is here fully justified: 'matter' in its abstraction is a pure *Gedankending*). One should thus not be afraid of the much-decried 'dissolution of matter in a field of energies' in modern physics: a true materialist should fully embrace it. Materialism has nothing to do with the assertion of the inert density of matter; it is, on the contrary, a position which accepts the ultimate Void of reality—the consequence of its central thesis on the primordial multiplicity is that there is no 'substantial reality', that the only 'substance' of the multiplicity is Void. This is why the opposite of true materialism is not so much a consequent idealism but, rather, the vulgar-idealist 'materialism' of someone like David Chalmers who proposes to account for the 'hard problem of consciousness' by postulating 'self-awareness' as an additional fundamental force of nature, together with gravity, magnetism, etc.—as, literally, its 'quintessence' (the fifth essence). The temptation to 'see' thought as an additional component of natural/material reality itself is the ultimate vulgarity.

It is here that, in order to specify the meaning of materialism, one should apply Lacan's formulas of sexuation: there is a fundamental difference between the assertion 'everything is matter' (which relies on its constitutive exception—in the case of Lenin who, in his *Materialism and Empiriocriticism*, falls into this trap, the very position of enunciation of the subject whose mind 'reflects' matter) and the assertion 'there is nothing which is not matter' (which, with its other side, 'not-All is matter', opens up the space for the account of immaterial phenomena). What this means is that a truly radical materialism is by definition non-reductionist: far from claiming that 'everything is matter', it confers upon the 'immaterial' phenomena a specific positive non-being.

When, in his argument against the reductive explanation of consciousness, Chalmers writes that 'even if we knew every last detail about the physics of the universe—the configuration, causation, and evolution among all the fields and particles in the spatiotemporal manifold—*that* information would not lead us to postulate the existence of conscious experience',[1] he commits the standard Kantian mistake: such a total knowledge is strictly nonsensical, epistemologically *and* ontologically. It is the obverse of the vulgar determinist notion, articulated, in Marxism, by Nikolai Bukharin, when he wrote that, if we were to know the entire physical reality, we would also be able to predict precisely the emergence of a revolution. This line of reasoning—consciousness as an excess, surplus, over the physical totality—is misleading, since it has to evoke a meaningless hyperbole: when we imagine the Whole of reality, there is no longer any place for consciousness (and subjectivity). There are two options here: either subjectivity is an illusion, or reality is *in itself* (not only epistemologically) not-All.

One should thus, from the radically materialist standpoint, fearlessly think through the consequences of *rejecting* 'objective reality': reality dissolves in 'subjective' fragments, *but these fragments themselves fall back into anonymous Being, losing their subjective consistency.* Fred Jameson drew attention to the paradox of the postmodern rejection of consistent Self—its ultimate result is that we lose its opposite, objective reality itself, which gets transformed into a set of contingent subjective constructions. A true materialist should

---

1. David Chalmers, *The Conscious Mind*, Oxford, Oxford University Press, 1996, p. 101.

do the opposite: refuse to accept 'objective reality' in order to undermine consistent subjectivity. This ontological openness of the one-less multiplicity also allows us to approach in a new way Kant's second antinomy of pure reason whose thesis is: 'Every composite substance in the world consists of simple parts; and there exists nothing that is not either itself simple, or composed of simple parts'.[2] Here is Kant's proof:

> For, grant that composite substances do not consist of simple parts; in this case, if all combination or composition were annihilated in thought, no composite part, and (as, by the supposition, there do not exist simple parts) no simple part would exist. Consequently, no substance; consequently, nothing would exist. Either, then, it is impossible to annihilate composition in thought; or, after such annihilation, there must remain something that subsists without composition, that is, something that is simple. But in the former case the composite could not itself consist of substances, because with substances composition is merely a contingent relation, apart from which they must still exist as self-subsistent beings. Now, as this case contradicts the supposition, the second must contain the truth—that the substantial composite in the world consists of simple parts.

> It follows, as an immediate inference, that the things in the world are all, without exception, simple beings—that composition is merely an external condition pertaining to them—and that, although we never can separate and isolate the elementary substances from the state of composition, reason must cogitate these as the primary subjects of all composition, and consequently, as prior thereto—and as simple substances.[3]

What, however, if we accept the conclusion that, ultimately, 'nothing exists' (a conclusion which, incidentally, is exactly the same as the conclusion of Plato's *Parmenides*: 'Then may we not sum up the argument in a word and say truly: If one is not, then nothing is?')? Such a move, although rejected by Kant as obvious nonsense, is not as un-Kantian as it may appear: it is here that one should apply yet again the Kantian distinction between negative and infinite judgment. The statement 'material reality is all there is' can be negated in two ways, in the form of 'material reality *isn't all there is*' and 'material reality *is non-all*'. The first negation (of a predicate) leads to the standard metaphysics: material reality isn't everything; there is another, higher, spiritual reality.... As such, this negation is, in accordance with Lacan's formulas of sexuation, inherent to the positive statement 'material reality is all there is': as its constitutive exception, it grounds its universality. If, however, we assert a non-predicate and say 'material reality *is non-all*', this merely asserts the non-All of reality without implying any exception—paradoxically, one should thus claim that 'material reality *is non-all*', not 'material reality is all there is', is the true formula of materialism.

So, to recapitulate: since materialism *is* the hegemonic ideology today, the struggle is *within* materialism, between what Badiou calls 'democratic materialism' and... what? I think Meillassoux's assertion of radical contingency as the only necessity is not enough—one has to supplement it with the ontological incompleteness of reality. It is Meillassoux who is not 'materialist' enough here, proposing a materialism in which there is again a place for virtual God and the resuscitation of the dead—this is what happens when contingency is not supplemented by the incompleteness of reality.

BW: In *Nihil Unbound* Ray Brassier extends the death drive to the realm of the cosmological, as an extension of 'the originary purposelessness of life'.[4] How would you re-

---

2. Immanuel Kant, *Critique of Pure Reason*, London, Everyman's Library, 1988, p. 264.

3. Kant, *Critique of Pure Reason*, pp. 264-5.

4. Ray Brassier, *Nihil Unbound: Enlightenment and Extinction*, New York, Palgrave Macmillan, 2007, p. 236.

spond to this more Freudian (and less Lacanian) reading of the death drive, one possibly more based in scientific discourse?

SZ: Let me just recapitulate my position: I think the cosmological notion of the 'purposelessness of life' is a useless metaphor with no cognitive value. Furthermore, I agree with Jean Laplanche that Freud's 'cosmologization' of life- and death-drive (Eros and Thanatos) was an ideological regression, an index of his inability to think through the consequences of his own discovery. I think that Lacan's re-conceptualization of the death drive as the 'immortal' compulsion-to-repeat simply does a better job, introducing a concept that allows us to think the most basic level of how humans break with the animal domain.

I especially want to avoid any too fast cosmological speculations—when Meillassoux writes about the contingent emergence *ex nihilo* of Life out of matter and of Thought out of Life, he comes dangerously close to a new version of old 'regional ontologies' in the style of Nicolai Hartmann, where the universe is conceived as the superposition of more and more narrow levels of reality: physical reality, life, mind. I think such an ontology is inadmissible from the standpoint of radical contingency—to put it in somewhat naïve terms, what if we discover that this hierarchy is false? That the dolphins' thinking process is more complex than ours? And, incidentally, in *what* science is the Freudian death drive based?

BW: Concerning the Real—one of Brassier's significant touchstones is François Laruelle's non-philosophy. Laruelle defines the real as 'Instance defined by its radical immanence under all possible conditions of thought: thus by its being-given (of) itself, yet called Vision-in-One or One-in-One, and by its being-foreclosed to thought. The Real is neither capable of being known or even 'thought', but can be described in axioms. On the other hand, it determines-in-the-last-instance thought as non-philosophical'. How would you respond to the concept of a real which is supra-discursive yet ultimately undecidable?

SZ: Since I've written quite a lot about the Real, I will again just recapitulate my position: Lacan's Real does a better job. What—as far as I can see—is missing in Laruelle is the Real as a purely formal parallax gap or impossibility: it is supra-discursive, but nonetheless totally immanent to the order of discourses—there is nothing positive about it, it is ultimately just the rupture or gap which makes the order of discourses always and constitutively inconsistent and non-totalizable.

BW: In Saas-Fee [the location of the European Graduate School], you mentioned that you disagreed with Quentin Meillassoux's use of non-totalizable infinity to negate certainty (or non-contingency). Several similar critiques have been made (you yourself mentioned Adrian Johnston's)—how would yours differ?

SZ: I disagreed with Meillassoux's use of the Cantorian non-totalizable multiple infinity to undermine the probabilist argument against contingency (if nature is thoroughly contingent, why does it behave in such a regular way?): I agree with Johnston that the fact of non-totalizable infinity is not enough to disqualify the probabilist argument. The only thing I have to add here is that, in a Hegelian-speculative way, the regularities of nature are precisely the highest assertion of contingency: the more nature behaves regularly, following its 'necessary laws', the more contingent is this necessity.

BW: Furthermore, how would you respond to Brassier's critique of your articulation of subjectivity following from Meillassoux's necessary contingency? Consider the following quote:

> Unlike Hegel, Meillassoux does not claim that contingency is necessary in the sense of being incorporated within the absolute, but that contingency and contingency alone is absolutely necessary. Where the speculative idealist affirms that 'contingency is necessary in the absolute'—as in Žižek's favoured example, where a contingent material determinant is retroactively posited by the subject as necessary for the realization of its own autonomy[15]—the speculative materialist affirms that 'contingency alone is absolute and hence necessary'. As we now know, this 'principle of un-reason', far from allowing anything and everything, actually imposes a hugely significant constraint on the chaos of absolute time: the latter can do anything, except bring forth a contradictory entity.[5]

And the connected footnote:

> Freedom is not simply the opposite of deterministic causal necessity: as Kant knew, it means a specific mode of causality; the agent's self-determination. There is in fact a kind of Kantian antinomy of freedom: if an act is fully determined by preceding causes, it is, of course, not free; if, however, it depends on the pure contingency which momentarily severs the full causal chain, it is also not free. The only way to resolve this antinomy is to introduce a second-order reflexive causality: I am determined by causes (be it direct brute natural causes or motivations), and the space of freedom is not a magic gap in this first-level causal chain but my ability retroactively to choose/determine which causes will determine me' (Žižek 2006, p. 203). In Žižek's Hegelianism, the subject achieves its autonomy by retroactively positing/reintegrating its own contingent material determinants: freedom is the subjective necessity of objective contingency. But by dissolving the idea of a necessary connection between cause and effect, Meillassoux's absolutization of contingency not only destroys materialist 'determinism' understood as the exceptionless continuity of the causal nexus, but also the idealist conception of subjective 'freedom' understood in terms of the second-order reflexive causality described by Žižek. The subject cannot 'choose' or determine its own objective determination when the contingency of all determination implies the equal arbitrariness of every choice, effectively erasing the distinction between forced and un-forced choice. Thus it becomes impossible to distinguish between objective compulsion and subjective reflexion, phenomenal heteronomy and noumenal autonomy. The principle of factuality collapses the distinction between first and second order levels of determination, thereby undermining any attempt to distinguish between objective heteronomy and subjective autonomy.[6]

SZ: I think that when Brassier attributes to me the assertion of the *necessity of contingency* and of the free act as a gesture in which 'a contingent material determinant is retroactively posited by the subject as necessary', he is distorting my position, depriving it of its crucial aspect: the *contingency of necessity*. The act of retroactively positing a contingent determination as necessary *is itself contingent*.

To fully clarify this point, we have to go back to Meillassoux. He is right in opposing contradiction and the movement of evolution, and to reject the standard notion of movement as the deployment of a contradiction. According to this standard notion, non-contradiction equates immovable self-identity, while, for Meillassoux, the universe which would to assert fully the reality of contradiction would be an immovable self-identical universe in which contradictory features would immediately coincide.

5. Brassier, *Nihil Unbound*, p. 72.

6. Brassier, *Nihil Unbound*, p. 247n15.

Things move, change in time, precisely because they *cannot* be directly A and non-A—they can only gradually *change* from A to non-A. There is time because the principle of identity, of non-contradiction, resists the direct assertion of contradiction. This is why, for Meillassoux, Hegel is not a philosopher of evolution, of movement and development: Hegel's system is 'static', every evolution is contained in the atemporal self-identity of a Notion.

Again, I agree with this, but I opt against evolution: Hegel's dialectical movement is not evolutionary. Meillassoux fails to grasp how, for Hegel, 'contradiction' is not opposed to (self-)identity, but its very core. 'Contradiction' is not only the real-impossible on account of which no entity can be fully self-identical; 'contradiction' is pure self-identity as such, the tautological coincidence of form and content, of genus and species—in the assertion of (self-)identity, genus encounters itself as its own 'empty' species. What this means is that the Hegelian contradiction is not a direct motionless 'coincidence of the opposites' (A is non-A): it is identity itself, its assertion, which 'destabilizes' a thing, introducing the crack of an impossibility into its texture. Therein resides already the lesson of the very beginning of Hegel's logic: how do we pass from the first identity of the opposites, of Being and Nothing, to Becoming (which then stabilizes itself in Something(s))? If Being and Nothing are identical, if they overlap, why move forward at all? Precisely because Being and Nothing are not directly identical: Being is a form, the first formal-notional determination, whose only content is Nothing; the couple Being/Nothing forms the highest contradiction, and to resolve this impossibility, this deadlock, one passes into Becoming, into oscillation between the two poles.

What makes Meillassoux's endeavour so interesting is that it is nonetheless much closer to Hegel than it may appear. With regard to the experience of facticity and/or absolute contingency, Meillassoux transposes what appears to transcendental partisans of finitude as the limitation of our knowledge (the insight that we can be totally wrong about our knowledge, that reality in itself can be totally different from our notion of it) into the most basic positive ontological property of reality itself—the absolute '*is simply the capacity-to-be-other as such, as theorized by the agnostic*. The absolute is the *possible transition*, devoid of reason, of my state towards any other state whatsoever. But this possibility is no longer a 'possibility of ignorance', viz., a possibility that is merely the result of my inability to know [...]—rather, it is the *knowledge* of the very real possibility'[7] in the heart of the In-itself:

> We must show why thought, far from experiencing its intrinsic *limits* through facticity, experiences rather its *knowledge* of the absolute through facticity. We must grasp in fact not the inaccessibility of the absolute but the unveiling of the in-itself and the eternal property of what is, as opposed to the perennial deficiency in the thought of what is.[8]

In this way, 'facticity will be revealed to be a knowledge of the absolute *because we are going to put back into the thing itself what we mistakenly mistook to be an incapacity in thought*. In other words, instead of construing the absence of reason inherent in everything as a limit that thought encounters in its search for the ultimate reason, we must understand that this absence of reason *is*, and can *only* be the *ultimate* property of the entity'.[9] The para-

---

7. Quentin Meillassoux, *After Finitude: An Essay on the Necessity of Contingency*, trans. Ray Brassier, London, Continuum, 2008, p. 56.

8. Meillassoux, *After Finitude*, p. 52.

9. Meillassoux, *After Finitude*, p. 53.

dox of this quasi-magical reversal of epistemological obstacle into ontological premise
is that 'it is through facticity, and through facticity alone, that we are able to make our
way towards the absolute'[10]: the radical contingency of reality, this 'open possibility, this
'everything is equally possible', is an absolute that cannot be de-absolutized without being thought as absolute once more'.[11]

How, then, can this access to the absolute be reconciled with the obvious limitation of our knowledge of reality? A reference to Brecht can be of some use here: in one
of his reflections about the stage, Brecht ferociously opposed the idea that the background of the stage should render the impenetrable depth of the All of Reality as the
obscure Origin of Things out of which all things we see and know appear as fragments.
For Brecht, the background of a stage should ideally be empty, white, signalling that,
behind what we see and experience, there is no secret Origin or Ground. This in no
way implies that reality is transparent to us, that we 'know all'; of course there are infinite blanks, but the point is that these blanks *are just that, blanks*, things we simply do
not know, not a substantial 'deeper' reality.

Now we come to the properly *speculative* crux of Meillassoux's argumentation: how
does Meillassoux justify this passage from (or reversal of) epistemological limitation to
(or into) positive ontological feature? As we have seen, the transcendental criticist conceives facticity as the mark of our finitude, of our cognitive limitation, of our inability to access the absolute In-itself: to us, to our finite reason, reality appears contingent,
ohne Warum, but considered in itself, it may well be true that reality is non-contingent
(regulated by a deep spiritual or natural necessity), so that we are mere puppets of a
transcendent mechanism, or that our Self is itself generating the reality it perceives,
etc. In other words, for the transcendentalist, there is always the radical '*possibility of ignorance*'[12]: we are ignorant of how reality really is, there is always the possibility that reality is radically other than what it appears to us. How, then, does Meillassoux make
the step from this epistemological limitation to the unique access to the absolute? In a
deeply Hegelian way, he locates in this very point the paradoxical overlapping of possibility and actuality:

> How are you able to *think* this 'possibility of ignorance' [...]? The truth is that you are only
> able to think this possibility of ignorance because you have *actually* thought the *absoluteness*
> of this possibility, which is to say, its non-correlational character.[13]

The ontological proof of God is here turned around in a materialist way: it is not that
the very fact that we can think the possibility of a Supreme Being entails its actuality;
it is, on the contrary, that the very fact that we can think the possibility of the absolute contingency of reality, the possibility of its being-other, of the radical gap between
the way reality appears to us and the way it is in itself, entails its actuality, i.e., it entails
that reality in itself is radically contingent. In both cases, we are dealing with the direct
passage of the notion to existence, with existence which is part of the notion; however,
in the case of the ontological proof of God, the term that mediates between possibility
(of thinking) and actuality is perfection (the very notion of a perfect being includes its
existence), while in the case of Meillassoux's passage from notion to existence, *the mediating term is imperfection*. If we can *think* our knowledge of reality (i.e., the way reality ap-

---

10. Meillassoux, *After Finitude*, p. 63.
11. Meillassoux, *After Finitude*, p. 58.
12. Meillassoux, *After Finitude*, p. 58.
13. Meillassoux, *After Finitude*, p. 58.

pears to us) as radically failed, as radically different from the Absolute, *then this gap (between for-us and in-itself) must be part of the Absolute itself*, so that *the very feature that seemed forever to keep us away from the Absolute is the* only *feature which* directly *unites us with the Absolute.* And is exactly the same shift not at the very core of the Christian experience? It is the very radical separation of man from God which unites us with God, since, in the figure of Christ, God is thoroughly separated *from itself*—the point is thus not to 'overcome' the gap which separates us from God, but to take note of how *this gap is internal to God himself* (Christianity as the ultimate version of the Rabinovitch joke)—only when I experience the infinite pain of separation from God, do I share an experience with God himself (Christ on the Cross).

Two things are to be noted here. First, Meillassoux's frequent and systematic use of Hegelian terms, even (and especially) in his critique of Hegel. Say, he repeatedly characterizes his own position as 'speculative' (in the sense of the post-Kantian assertion of the accessibility to our knowledge of the absolute) in contrast to 'metaphysical' pre-critical dogmaticism (which claims access to transcendent absolute necessity). Paradoxically, Hegel counts for him as 'metaphysical', although it was precisely Hegel who deployed the 'metaphysical', the 'critical' (in the sense of Kantian criticism), and the 'speculative' as the three basic stances of thought towards reality, making it clear that his own 'speculative' stance can only arise when one fully accepts the lesson of criticism. No wonder that Meillassoux, following Hegel, designates his own position as that of 'absolute knowledge', characterized in a thoroughly Hegelian way as 'the principle of an *auto-limitation* or *auto-normalization of the omnipotence of chaos*'[14]—in short, as the rise of necessity out of contingency:

> We can only hope to develop an absolute knowledge—a knowledge of chaos which would not simply keep repeating that everything is possible—on condition that we produce necessary propositions about it besides that of its omnipotence. But this requires that we discover norms or laws to which chaos itself is subject. Yet there is nothing over and above the power of chaos that could constrain it to submit to a norm. If chaos is subject to constraints, then this can only be a constraint which comes from the nature of chaos itself, from its own omnipotence. [...] [I]n order for an entity to be contingent and un-necessary in this way, *it cannot be anything whatsoever.* This is to say that in order to be contingent and un-necessary, the entity must conform to *certain determinate conditions*, which can then be construed as *so many absolute properties of what is.*[15]

Is this not exactly Hegel's program? At the beginning of his *Logic*, we have the process of Becoming (the unity of Being and Nothingness), which is the thoroughly contingent process of generating the multiplicity of Somethings. The 'spurious infinity' of Somethings and Something-Others is chaos at its purest, with no necessity whatsoever underlying or regulating it, and the entire development of Hegel's *Logic* is the deployment of the immanent process of '*auto-limitation* or *auto-normalization of the omnipotence of chaos*': 'We then begin to understand what the rational discourse about unreason—an unreason which is not irrational—would consist in: it would be discourse that aims to establish the constraints to which the entity must submit in order to exercise its capacity-not-to-be and its capacity-to-be-other'.[16]

This 'capacity-to-be-other', as expressed in the gap that separates for-us and In-itself (i.e., in the possibility that reality-in-itself is totally different from the way it appears to

---

14. Meillassoux, *After Finitude*, p. 66.

15. Meillassoux, *After Finitude*, p. 66.

16. Meillassoux, *After Finitude*, p. 66.

us), is the self-distance of the In-itself, i.e., *the* negativity *in the very heart of Being*—this is what Meillassoux signals in his wonderfully dense proposition that 'the thing-in-itself is nothing other than the facticity of the transcendental forms of representation',[17] i.e., nothing other than the radically contingent character of our frame of reality. To see reality the way it 'really is' is not to see another 'deeper' reality beneath it, but to see this same reality in its thorough contingency.—So why does Meillassoux not openly admit the Hegelian nature of his breakthrough? The first answer, at least, is a simple one: he endorses the standard reading of Hegelian dialectics as the description of the necessary self-deployment of the Notion:

> Hegelian metaphysics maintains the necessity of a moment of irremediable contingency in the unfolding of the absolute; a moment which occurs in the midst of nature as the pure contingency, the reality devoid of actuality, the sheer finitude whose chaos and gratuitousness are recalcitrant to the labour of the Notion [...]. But this contingency is deduced from the unfolding of the absolute, which in itself, *qua* rational totality, is devoid of contingency. Thus, in Hegel, the necessity of contingency is not derived from contingency as such and contingency alone, but from a Whole that is ontologically superior to the latter.[18]

As I have already mentioned, Meillassoux here crucially simplifies the properly Hegelian relationship between necessity and contingency. In a first approach, it appears that their encompassing unity is necessity, i.e., that necessity itself posits and mediates contingency as the external field in which it expresses-actualizes itself—contingency itself is necessary, the result of the self-externalization and self-mediation of the notional necessity. However, it is crucial to supplement this unity with the opposite one, with contingency as the encompassing unity of itself and necessity: the very elevation of a necessity into the structuring principle of the contingent field of multiplicity is a contingent act, one can almost say: the outcome of a contingent ('open') struggle for hegemony. This shift corresponds to the shift from S to \$, from substance to subject. The starting point is a contingent multitude; through its self-mediation ('spontaneous self-organization'), contingency engenders-posits its immanent necessity, in the same way that Essence is the result of the self-mediation of Being. Once Essence emerges, it retroactively 'posits its own presuppositions', i.e., it sublates its presuppositions into subordinated moments of its self-reproduction (Being is transubstantiated into Appearance); however, this positing is retroactive.

Consequently, not only does Hegel (quite consistently with his premises) deduce the *necessity of contingency*, i.e. how the Idea necessarily externalizes itself (acquires reality) in phenomena which are genuinely contingent. Furthermore (and this aspect is often neglected by many of his commentators), he also develops the opposite—and theoretically much more interesting—aspect, that of the *contingency of necessity*. That is to say, when Hegel describes the progress from 'external' contingent appearance to its 'inner' necessary essence, the appearance's 'self-internalization' through self-reflection, he is thereby not describing the discovery of some pre-existing inner Essence, the penetration towards something that was already there (this, exactly, would have been a 'reification' of the Essence), but a 'performative' process of constructing (forming) that which is 'discovered'. Or, as Hegel puts it in his *Logic*, in the process of reflection, the very 'return' to the lost or hidden Ground produces what it returns to. What this means is that it is not only the inner necessity that is the unity of itself and contingency as its

---

17. Meillassoux, *After Finitude*, p. 76.
18. Meillassoux, *After Finitude*, p. 80.

opposite, necessarily positing contingency as its moment. It is also contingency which is the encompassing unity of itself and its opposite, necessity; that is to say, *the very process through which necessity arises out of necessity is a contingent process.*

The way one usually reads the Hegelian relationship between necessity and freedom is that they ultimately coincide: for Hegel, true freedom has nothing to do with capricious choices; it means the priority of self-relating to relating-to-other, i.e., an entity is free when it can deploy its immanent potentials without being impeded by any external obstacle. From here, it is easy to develop the standard argument against Hegel: his system is a fully 'saturated' set of categories, with no place for contingency and indeterminacy, i.e., in Hegel's logic, each category follows with inexorable immanent-logical necessity from the preceding one, and the entire series of categories forms a self-enclosed Whole... We can see now what this argument misses: the Hegelian dialectical process is not such a 'saturated' self-contained necessary Whole, but the open-contingent process through which such a Whole forms itself. In other words, the reproach confuses being with becoming: it perceives as a fixed order of Being (the network of categories) what is for Hegel the process of Becoming which, retroactively, engenders its necessity.

The same point can also be made in the terms of the distinction between potentiality and virtuality elaborated by Meillassoux.[19] In a first approach, there is massive evidence that Hegel is *the* philosopher of potentiality: is not the whole point of the dialectical development as the development from In-itself to For-itself that, in the process of becoming, things merely 'become what they already are' (or, rather, were from all eternity)? Is the dialectical process not the temporal deployment of an eternal set of potentialities, which is why the Hegelian System is a self-enclosed set of necessary passages? However, this mirage of overwhelming evidence dissipates the moment we fully take into account the radical *retroactivity* of the dialectical process: the process of becoming is not in itself necessary, but the *becoming* (the gradual contingent emergence) *of necessity itself.* This is (also, among other things) what 'to conceive substance as subject' means: subject as the Void, the Nothingness of self-relating negativity, is the very *nihil* out of which every new figure emerges, i.e., every dialectical reversal is a passage in which the new figure emerges *ex nihilo* and retroactively posits/creates its necessity.

And this brings me to the great underlying problem: the status of the subject. I think that, in its very anti-transcendentalism, Meillassoux remains caught in the Kantian topic of the accessibility of the thing-in-itself: is what we experience as reality fully determined by our subjective-transcendental horizon, or can we get to know something about the way reality is independently of our subjectivity. Meillassoux's claim is to achieve the breakthrough into independent 'objective' reality. For me as a Hegelian, there is a third option: the true problem that arises after we perform the basic speculative gesture of Meillassoux (transposing the contingency of our notion of reality into the thing itself) is not so much what more can we say about reality-in-itself, but how does our subjective standpoint, and subjectivity itself, fit into reality. The problem is not 'can we penetrate through the veil of subjectively-constituted phenomena to things-in-themselves', but 'how do phenomena themselves arise within the flat stupidity of reality which just is, how does reality redouble itself and start to appear to itself'. For this, we need a theory of subject which is neither that of transcendental subjectivity nor that of reducing the subject to a part of objective reality. This theory is, as far as I can see, still lacking in speculative realism.

---

19. See Quentin Meillassoux, 'Potentiality and Virtuality', in this volume.

Bibliography

Adorno, Theodor, *The Jargon of Authenticity*, New York, Routledge, 2003.

Alexander, Samuel, *Space, Time, and Deity. Volume Two*, London, MacMillan, 1920.

Althusser, Louis, *For Marx*, trans. Ben Brewster, London, Allen Lane, 1969.

Althusser, Louis, *The Humanist Controversy*, trans. G. M. Goshgarian, London, Verso, 2003.

Althusser, Louis, 'Lenin and Philosophy', trans. Ben Brewster, in *Philosophy and the Spontaneous Ideology of the Scientists*, London, Verso, 1990, pp. 167-202.

Althusser, Louis, 'Overdetermination and Contradiction', in *For Marx*, trans. by Ben Brewster, New York, Verso, 2005, pp. 87-128.

Althusser, Louis,'Philosophy and the Spontaneous Philosophy of the Scientists', trans. Warren Montag, in *Philosophy and the Spontaneous Ideology of the Scientists*, London, Verso, 1990, pp. 102-105.

Althusser, Louis, 'Theory, Theoretical Practice and Theoretical Formation: Ideology and Ideological Struggle', trans. James H. Kavanagh, in *Philosophy and the Spontaneous Philosophy of the Scientists*, London, Verso, 1990.

Arendt, Hannah, *The Human Condition*, Chicago, The University of Chicago Press, 1998.

Aristotle, *Metaphysics*, trans. Hugh Tredennick, Cambridge, Harvard University Press, 1961-62.

Aristotle, *Metaphysics*, trans. J. Sachs, Santa Fe, Green Lion Press, 2002.

Artaud, Antonin, 'Lettre à Jean Paulhan (Kabhar Enis – Kathar Esti) du 7 octobre 1943', in *Œuvres*, Paris, Éditions Gallimard, 2004.

Arthur, Christopher, *The New Dialectic and Marx's* Capital, Boston, Brill Publishing, 2004.

Atran, Scott, *Cognitive Foundations of Natural History: Towards an Anthropology Science*, Cambridge, Cambridge University Press, 1993.

Augustine, *Confessions*, trans. Henry Chadwick, Oxford, Oxford University Press, 1998.

Austin J.L., *How to do Things with Words*, Oxford, Clarendon, 1962.

Averill, James R., *Anger and Aggression: An Essay on Emotion*, New York, Springer, 1982.

Bachelard, Gaston, *The Philosophy of No*, trans. G.C. Waterston, New York, Orion Press, 1968.

Bachelard, Gaston, *The Formation of the Scientific Mind*, Manchester, Clinamen, 2002.

Badiou, Alain, *Being and Event*, trans. Oliver Feltham, New York, Continuum, 2005/2006/2007.

Badiou, Alain, *Briefings on Existence: A Short Treatise on Transitory Ontology*, trans. N. Madarasz, Albany, State University of New York Press, 2006.

Badiou, Alain, *Deleuze: The Clamor of Being*, trans. Louise Burchill, Minneapolis, University of Minnesota Press, 2000.

Badiou, Alain, 'Democratic Materialism and the Materialist Dialectic', *Radical Philosophy* no. 130, March/April 2005.

Badiou, Alain, *L'être et l'événement*, Paris, Seuil, 1988.

Badiou, Alain, *Logics of Worlds*, trans. Alberto Toscano, London: Continuum, 2009.

Badiou, Alain, *Logiques des mondes: L'être et l'événement, 2*, Paris, Éditions du Seuil, 2006.

Badiou, Alain, 'Mark and Lack: On Zero', trans. Z.L. Fraser and R. Brassier, in P. Hallward & K. Peden (eds.), *Concept and Form: The Cahiers pour l'analyse and Contemporary French Thought*, London, Verso, 2010. (forthcoming)

Badiou, Alain, 'Politics and Philosophy: An Interview with Alain Badiou [with Peter Hallward]", in *Ethics: An Essay on the Understanding of Evil*, trans. Peter Hallward, London, Verso, 2001.

Badiou, Alain, 'Preface', in Quentin Meillassoux, *After Finitude: An Essay on the Necessity of Contingency*, trans. R. Brassier, London, Continuum, 2008.

Badiou, Alain, *Saint Paul: The Foundation of Universalism*, trans. Ray Brassier, Stanford, Stanford University Press, 2003.

Badiou, Alain, *Théorie du sujet*, Paris: Éditions du Seuil, 1982.

Balter, Michael, 'Why Settle Down? The Mystery of Communities', *Science*, vol. 282, no. 5393, 20 November 1998, pp. 1442-45.

Barberousse, A., P. Ludwig, and M. Kistler, *La Philosophie des sciences au XXè siècle*, Paris, Flammarion, 2000.

Barbour, Julian, *The End of Time: The Next Revolution in Physics*, New York, Oxford University Press, 1999.

Barrow, J.D. and F.J. Tipler, *The Anthropic Cosmological Principle*, Oxford, Oxford University Press, 1986.

Barrow-Green, June, *Poincaré and the Three Body Problem*, Providence, American Mathematical Society, 1997.

Bataille, Georges. *Inner Experience*, trans. L.A. Boldt, Albany, State University of New York Press, 1988.

Beierwaltes, Werner, *Identität und Differenz*, Frankfurt am Main, Klostermann, 1980.

Bhaskar, Roy. *A Realist Theory of Science*, London, Verso, 1997.

Biagioli Mario, *Galileo's Instruments of Credit: Telescopes, Images, Secrecy*, Chicago, University of Chicago Press, 2006.

Boghossian, Paul, *Fear of Knowledge: Against Relativism and Constructivism*, Oxford, Oxford University Press, 2007.

Bosanquet, Bernard, *Logic, or the Morphology of Knowledge*, 2nd ed., Oxford, Oxford University Press, 1911.

Bowles, Samuel and Herbert Gintis, 'The Origins of Human Cooperation', in Peter Hammerstein (ed.), *The Genetic and Cultural Origins of Cooperation*, Cambridge, MIT Press, 2003.

Boyer, Pascal, 'Natural Epistemology or Evolved Metaphysics? Developmental Evidence for Early-Developed, Intuitive, Category-Specific, Incomplete and Stubborn Metaphysical Presumptions', in *Philosophical Psychology*, no. 13, 2000, 277 -297.

Boyer, Patrick and H. Clark Barrett, 'Evolved Intuitive Ontology: Integrating Neural, Behavioral and Developmental Aspects of Domain-Specificity', in David Buss (ed.), *Handbook of Evolutionary Psychology*, New York, Wiley, 2005.

Brandom, Robert, *Making it Explicit: Reasoning Representing and Discursive Commitment*, Cambridge, Harvard University Press, 1994.

Brandom, Robert, *Articulating Reasons: An Introduction to Inferentialism*, Cambridge, Harvard University Press, 2000.

Brassier, Ray, Iain Hamilton Grant, Graham Harman, and Quentin Meillassoux, 'Speculative Realism', *Collapse: Philosophical Research and Development*, vol. 3, 2007, pp. 307-449.

Brassier, Ray, 'Alien Theory: The Decline of Materialism in the Name of Matter', unpublished doctoral thesis, University of Warwick, 2001, <http://www. cinestatic.com/trans-mat/>.

Brassier, Ray, 'Axiomatic Heresy: The Non-Philosophy of François Laruelle', *Radical Philosophy*, no. 121, 2003, pp. 24-35.

Brassier, Ray, *Nihil Unbound: Enlightenment and Extinction*, New York, Palgrave Macmillan, 2007.

Brassier, Ray, Personal communication with Nick Srnicek, 1/26/09.

Brassier, Ray, 'Speculative Realism: Presentation by Ray Brassier', *Collapse: Philosophical Research and Development*, vol. 3, 2007, pp. 308-333.

Brassier, Ray, 'The Expression of Meaning in Deleuze's Ontological Proposition', *Pli: The Warwick Journal of Philosophy*, no. 19, 2008, pp. 1-36.

Braver, Lee, *A Thing of This World: A History of Continental Anti-Realism*, Evanston, Northwestern University Press, 2007.

Brown, James Robert, 'Critique of Social Constructivism', in *Scientific Enquiry: Readings in the Philosophy of Science*, R. Klee (ed.), Oxford, Oxford University Press, 1999, pp. 260-64.

Brown, Nathan, 'On *After Finitude*: A Response to Peter Hallward', in *The Speculative Turn: Continental Materialism and Realism*, Levi Bryant, Graham Harman, and Nick Srnicek (eds.), Melbourne, re.press, 2010.

Brown, Nathan, 'To Live Without an Idea', *Radical Philosophy*, no. 154, March/April 2009.

Bruno, Giordano, *Cause, Principle and Unity*, trans. R. de Lucca, Cambridge, Cambridge University Press, 1998.

Bryant, Levi R., *Difference and Givenness: Deleuze's Transcendental Empiricism and the Ontology of Immanence*, Evanston, Northwestern University Press, 2008.

Bunge, Mario, *Causality and Modern Science*, New York, Dover, 1979.

Catren, Gabriel, 'A Throw of the Quantum Dice Will Never Abolish the Copernican Revolution', *Collapse: Philosophical Research and Development*, vol 5, 2009.

Catren, Gabriel, 'Geometric Foundations of Classical Yang-Mills Theory', *Studies in History and Philosophy of Modern Physics*, vol. 39, 2008, pp. 511-531.

Chalmers, David, *The Conscious Mind*, Oxford, Oxford University Press, 1996.

Changeaux, Jean-Pierre, *The Physiology of Truth: Neuroscience and Human Knowledge*, Cambridge, Harvard University Press, 2009.

Churchland, Paul, *A Neurocomputational Perspective: The Nature of Mind and the Structure of Science*, Cambridge, MIT, 1989.

Clark, Andy, *Natural-Born Cyborgs: Minds, Technologies, and the Future of Human Intelligence*, New York, Oxford University Press, 2003.

Clastres, Pierre, *Society Against the State: Essays in Political Anthropology*, trans. Robert Hurley in collaboration with Abe Stein , New York, Zone Books, 1989.

Colletti, Lucio, 'Marxism and the Dialectic', *New Left Review*, col. 1, no. 93, 1975.

Colletti, Lucio, *Marxism and Hegel*, trans. Lawrence Garner, London, New Left Books, 1973.

Damasio, Antonio, *Descartes' Error*, New York, Avon, 1994.

Damasio, Antonio, *The Feeling of What Happens*, New York, Harcourt, 1999.

Damasio, Antonio, *Looking for Spinoza*, New York, Harcourt, 2003.

Darnton, Robert, *Mesmerism and the End of the Enlightenment in France*, Cambridge, Harvard University Press, 1968.

Dawson, Doyne, 'Evolutionary Theory and Group Selection: The Question of Warfare', *History and Theory*, vol. 38, no. 4, 1999, pp. 79-100.

Debaise, Didier, *Un empirisme spéculatif. Lecture de Procès et Réalité*, Paris, Vrin, 2006.

De Caro, Mario and David Macarthur (eds.), *Naturalism in Question*, Cambridge, Harvard University Press, 2004.

d'Espagnat, Bernard, *Physics and Philosophy*, Princeton, Princeton University Press, 2006.

DeLanda, Manuel, *Intensive Science and Virtual Philosophy*, London, Continuum, 2002.

DeLanda, Manuel. *Philosophy, Emergence, and Simulation*, Forthcoming.

Deleuze, Gilles, and Félix Guattari, *Mille Plateaux*, Paris, Minuit, 1980.

Deleuze, Gilles, and Felix Guattari, *Anti-Oedipus*, Minneapolis, University of Minnesota Press, 1983.

Deleuze, Gilles and Félix Guattari, *A Thousand Plateaus: Capitalism and Schizophrenia*, trans. B. Massumi, Minneapolis, University of Minnesota Press, 1987.

Deleuze, Gilles, *Logic of Sense*. Trans. Paul Lester and Charles Stivale, New York, Columbia University Press, 1990.

Deleuze, Gilles, *The Fold: Leibniz and the Baroque*, trans. T. Conley, Minneapolis, University of Minnesota Press, 1993.

Deleuze, Gilles, *Difference and Repetition*, trans. P. Patton, New York, Columbia University Press, 1994.

Deleuze Gilles, and Félix Guattari, *What is Philosophy?*, trans. Hugh Tomlinson and Graham Burchell, New York, Columbia University Press, 1994/1996.

Deleuze, Gilles and Claire Parnet, *Dialogues II*, trans. Hugh Tomlinson, Barbara Habberjam, and Eliot Ross Albert, New York, Columbia University Press, 2002.

Deleuze, Gilles, *Difference and Repetition*, trans. Paul Patton, New York, Columbia University Press, 2004.

Deleuze, Gilles, 'Immanence: A Life', in *Pure Immanence: Essays on a Life*, trans. A. Boyman, New York, Zone Books, 2005.

Deleuze, Gilles, *Nietzsche and Philosophy*, trans. H. Tomlinson, New York, Columbia University Press, 2006.

Dennett, Daniel, *Consciousness Explained*, Boston, Little and Brown, 1991.

Dennett, Daniel, *Darwin's Dangerous Idea: Evolution and the Meaning of Life*, New York, Simon and Schuster, 1995/1996.

Derrida, Jacques, 'Ousia and Grammè', in *Margins of Philosophy*, trans. A. Bass, Chicago, University of Chicago Press, 1984.

Derrida, Jacques, *Margins of Philosophy*, trans. A. Bass, Chicago, University of Chicago Press, 1985.

Derrida, Jacques, *Spectres of Marx: The State of the Debt, the Work of Mourning, and the New International*, trans. P. Kamuf, London, Routledge, 1994.

Descola, Philippe, *Par delà nature et culture*, Paris, Gallimard, 2005.

DeWaal, Frans. *Primates and Philosophers: How Morality Evolved*. Princeton: Princeton University Press, 2006.

Edelman, Gerald and Giulio, Tononi, *A Universe of Consciousness: How Matter Becomes Imagination*. New York: Basic Books, 2000.

Edelman, Gerald, *Second Nature: Brain Science and Human Knowledge*, New Haven, Yale University Press, 2006.

Egginton, William, 'On Radical Atheism, Chronolibidinal Reading, and Impossible Desires', *CR: The New Centennial Review*, vol. 9.1, 2009, pp. 191-208.

Engels, Frederick, *Ludwig Feuerbach and the Outcome of Classical German Philosophy*, C.P. Dutt (ed.), New York, International Publishers Co., 1941.

Fabing, Howard, 'On Going Berserk: A Neurochemical Inquiry', *American Journal of Psychiatry*, no. 113 November 1956, pp. 409-415.

Faraday, Michael, *Experimental researches in Electricity*, 3 vols., Vol. 1, London: Taylor, 1839.

Feinmann, J.P., *La filosofía y el barro de la historia*, Buenos Aires, Grupo Editorial Planeta, 2008.

Ferguson, Brian, *Yanomami Warfare: A Political History*, Santa Fe, School for American Research Press, 1995.

Ferguson, Brian, 'Ten Points on War', *Social Analysis*, vol. 52, no.2, 2008, pp. 32-49.

Feynman, Richard, *The Character of Physical Law*, Cambridge, MIT Press, 1997.

Fichte J.G., *Fichtes sämmtliche Werke*, I.H. Fichte (ed.), XI vols., Berlin, de Gruyter, 1971.

Fichte J.G., *Some Lectures concerning the Scholar's Vocation (1794)*, in *Fichtes sämmtliche Werke*, I.H. Fichte (ed.), vol. VI, XI vols., Berlin, de Gruyter, 1971, 291-346.

Fichte, J.G., *The Science of Knowledge*, trans. John Lachs and Peter Heath, Cambridge, UK: Cambridge University Press, 1982.

Fichte, J.G., *Some Lectures concerning the Scholar's Vocation (1794)*, in *Early Philosophical Writings*, trans. Daniel Breazeale, Ithaca, Cornell University Press, 1988, pp. 137-184.

Fichte, J.G., *Foundations of Natural Right*, trans. Frederick Neuhouser, Cambridge, Cambridge University Press, 2000.

Fontanille Jacques, *Sémiotique du discours*, Limoges, Presses Universitaires de Limoges, 1998.

Fox, Robin, *The Search for Society: Quest for a Biosocial Science and Morality*, New Brunswick, Rutgers University Press, 1989.

Fracchia, Joseph and Richard Lewontin, 'Does Culture Evolve?', *History and Theory*, vol. 38, no. 4, 1999, pp. 52-78.

Fracchia, Joseph and Richard Lewontin, 'The Price of Metaphor', *History and Theory*, vol. 44, no. 1, 2005, pp. 14-29.

Franklin, James, 'Stove's Discovery of the Worst Argument in the World', *Philosophy*, no. 77, 2002, pp. 615-24.

Freud, Sigmund, 'A Difficulty in the Path of Psycho-Analysis', in *The Standard Edition of the Complete Psychological Works of Sigmund Freud, Volume XVII (1917-1919)*, trans. J. Strachey and A. Freud, London, The Hogarth Press and the Institute of Psycho-Analysis, 1955.

Freud, Sigmund, *Beyond the Pleasure Principle*, New York, W. W. Norton, 1961.

Freud, Sigmund, *Introductory Lectures on Psychoanalysis*, New York, W. W. Norton, 1977.

Fry, Douglas, *Beyond War: The Human Potential for Peace*, New York, Oxford University Press, 2007.

Galileo Galilei, 'The Assayer', *Discoveries and Opinions of Galileo*, trans. Stillman Drake, New York: Anchor Books, 1957.

Garfinkel, Alan, *Forms of Explanation*, New Haven, Yale University Press, 1981.

Geoffroy Saint-Hilaire, Etienne, 'Divers mémoires sur des grands sauriens', *Mémoires de l'Academie Royale des Sciences de l'Institut de France*, no. 12, 1833, pp. 63-92.

Ghiselin, Michael T., 'Folk Metaphysics and the Anthropology of Science', in *Behavioural and Brain Sciences*, no. 21, 1998, pp. 573-574.

Gingerich Owen, *The Book Nobody Read: Chasing the Revolution of Nicolaus Copernicus*, Penguin, New York, 2004, p.198.

Goodman, Nelson, *Fact, Fiction and Forecast*, 4th ed., Cambridge, Harvard University Press, 1983.

Gordon, James E., *The Science of Structures and Materials*, New York, Scientific American Books, 1988.

Gould, Stephen Jay, *Ontogeny and Phylogeny*, Cambridge, Harvard University Press, 1977.

Grant, Iain Hamilton, *Philosophies of Nature After Schelling*, London, Continuum, 2006.

Greimas, Algirdas, *Sémantique Structurale*, Paris, PUF, 1968.

Hacking, Ian, *The Social Construction of What?*, Cambridge, Harvard University Press, 1999.

Griffiths, Paul, *What Emotions Really Are: The Problem of Psychological Categories*, Chicago, University of Chicago Press, 1997.

Griffiths, Paul, 'Evolutionary Psychology', in Sahotra Sarkar (ed.), *The Philosophy of Science: An Encyclopedia*, New York, Routledge, 2006.

Griffiths, Pau, 'Evo-devo meets the mind: Toward a developmental evolutionary psychology', in Robert Brandon and Roger Sansom (eds.), *Integrating Evolution and Development: From Theory to Practice*, Cambridge, MIT Press, 2007, pp. 195-226.

Griffiths, Paul and Russell Gray, 'Replicator II – Judgement Day', *Biology and Philosophy*, vol. 12, 1997, pp. 471-492.

Griffiths, Paul and Russell Gray, 'Darwinism and Developmental Systems', in Susan Oyama, Paul Griffiths, and Russell Gray (eds.), *Cycles of Contingency: Developmental Systems and Evolution*, Cambridge, MIT Press, 2001, pp. 195-218.

Griffiths, and Russell Gray, 'The Developmental Systems Perspective: Organism-environment systems as units of development and evolution', in Massimo Pigliucci and Katherine Preston (eds.), *Phenotypic Integration: Studying the Ecology and Evolution of Complex, Phenotypes*, New York, Oxford University Press, 2004, pp. 409-430.

Griffiths, and Russell Gray, 'Discussion: Three ways to misunderstand developmental systems theory', *Biology and Philosophy*, vol. 20, 2005, pp. 417-425.

Grothendieck, A., *Promenade à travers une œuvre ou L'enfant et la Mère*, <http://www.grothendieckcircle.org>.

Haddad, Samir, 'Language Remains', *CR: The New Centennial Review*, vol. 9, no. 1, 2009, pp. 127-146.

Hägglund, Martin, *Radical Atheism: Derrida and the Time of Life*, Stanford, Stanford University Press, 2008.

Hägglund, Martin, 'The Challenge of Radical Atheism: A Response', *CR: The New Centennial Review*, vol. 9, no. 1, 2009, pp. 227-252.

Haidt, Jonathan, 'The emotional dog and its rational tail: A social intuitionist approach to moral judgment', *Psychological Review*, vol. 108, 2001, pp. 814-834.

Hallward, Peter, 'The Singular and the Specific: Recent French Philosophy', *Radical Philosophy*, no. 99, 2000 pp., 6-18.

Hallward, Peter, *Absolutely Postcolonial: Writing Between the Singular and the Specific*, Manchester, Manchester University Press, 2001.

Hallward, Peter, 'The One or the Other? French Philosophy Today', *Angelaki*, vol. 8, no. 2, 2003, pp. 1-32.

Hallward, Peter, *Badiou: A Subject to Truth*, Minneapolis, University of Minnesota Press, 2003.

Hallward, Peter (ed.), *The One or the Other: French Philosophy Today*, Special Issue of *Angelaki*, vol. 8, no. 2, 2003.

Hallward, Peter, 'The Politics of Prescription', *South Atlantic Quarterly*, vol. 104, no. 4, 2005, pp. 769-789.

Hallward, Peter, 'Staging Equality: On Rancière's Theotrocracy', *New Left Review*, no. 37, 2006, pp. 109-129.

Hallward, Peter, *Out of This World: Deleuze and the Philosophy of Creation*, London, Verso, 2006.

Hallward, Peter, *Damming the Flood: Haiti, Aristide, and the Politics of Containment*, London, Verso, 2007.

Hallward, Peter, 'Anything is possible', *Radical Philosophy*, no. 152, 2008, pp. 51-57.

Hallward, Peter, 'Order and Event', *New Left Review*, no. 58, 2008, pp. 97-122.

Hallward, Peter, 'The Will of the People: Notes Towards a Dialectical Voluntarism', *Radical Philosophy*, no. 155, 2009, pp. 17-29.

Hallward, Peter, 'Anything is Possible', in Levi Bryant, Nick Srnicek, and Graham Harman (eds.), *The Speculative Turn: Continental Materialism and Realism*, Melbourne, re.press, 2010, pp. 130-141.

Hanson, Victor Davis, *The Western Way of War*, Berkeley, University of California Press, 1989.

Haraway, Donna, *When Species Meet*, Minneapolis, University of Minnesota Press, 2008.

Harman, Graham, 'Object-Oriented Philosophy' blog, http://doctorzamalek2.wordpress.com/

Harman, Graham, *Tool-Being: Heidegger and the Metaphysics of Objects*, Chicago, Open Court, 2002.

Harman, Graham, *Guerilla Metaphysics: Phenomenology and the Carpentry of Things*, Chicago, Open Court, 2005.

Harman, Graham, 'On Vicarious Causation', *Collapse*, vol. 2, 2007.

Harman, Graham, 'Quentin Meillassoux: A New French Philosopher', *Philosophy Today*, vol. 51, no. 1, Spring 2007.

Harman, Graham, 'Speculative Realism: Presentation by Graham Harman', *Collapse*, vol. 3, pp. 367-407.

Harman, Graham, 'OOO: a first try at some parameters', URL: http://doctorzamalek2.wordpress.com/2009/09/04/ooo-a-first-try-at-some-parameters/, 2009.

Harman, Graham, *Prince of Networks: Bruno Latour and Metaphysics*, Melbourne, re.press, 2009.

Harman, Graham, 'On the Undermining of Objects', in Levi Bryant, Nick Srnicek and Graham Harman (eds.), *The Speculative Turn: Continental Materialism and Realism*, re.press, Melbourne, 2010, pp. 21-40.

Hegel, G.W.F., *Science of Logic*, trans. A. V. Miller, London, Allen and Unwin, 1969.

Hegel, G.W.F., *Jenaer Realphilosophie*, Hamburg, Felix Meiner Verlag, 1969.

Hegel, G.W.F., *Philosophie der Geschichte*, in *Werke*, vol. XI, Frankfurt, Suhrkamp Verlag, 1970.

Hegel, G.W.F., *Philosophie der Religion*, in *Werke*, vol. XVI, Frankfurt, Suhrkamp Verlag 1970.

Hegel, G.W.F., *Philosophy of Nature: Part Two of the Encyclopaedia of the Philosophical Sciences*, trans. A.V. Miller, Oxford, Oxford University Press, 1970/2004.

Hegel, G.W.F., *The Difference Between Fichte's and Schelling's System of Philosophy*, trans. Walter Cerf and H.S. Harris, New York, State University New York Press, 1977.

Hegel, G.W.F, *Phenomenology of Spirit*, trans. A.V. Miller, Oxford, Oxford University Press, 1977.

Hegel, G.W.F., *Philosophie des subjektiven Geistes*, Dordrecht, Riedel 1978.

Hegel, G.W.F., *Phänomenologie des Geistes*, Hamburg, Felix Meiner Verlag, 1988.

Hegel, G.W.F., *Science of Logic*, trans. AV Miller, Atlantic Highlands, Humanities Press International, 1989/1999.

Hegel, G.W.F., *Philosophy of Mind*, Oxford, Clarendon Press, 1992.

Heidegger, Martin, *Being and Time*, trans. J. Macquarrie and E. Robinson, Oxford, Blackwell, 1962.

Heidegger, Martin, 'The Thing', in *Poetry, Language, Thought*, trans. A. Hofstadter, New York, Harper & Row Publishers, 1975.

Heidegger, Martin, 'The Thinker as Poet', in *Poetry, Language, Thought*, trans. A. Hofstadter, New York, Harper & Row Publishers, 1975.

Heidegger, Martin, 'What are Poets for?', in *Poetry, Language, Thought*, trans. A. Hofstadter, New York, Harper & Row Publishers, 1975.

Heidegger, Martin, *The Basic Problems of Phenomenology*, trans. A. Hofstadter, Bloomington, Indiana University Press, 1988.

Heidegger, Martin, *The Principle of Reason*, trans. Reginald Lilly, Bloomington, Indiana University Press, 1991.

Heidegger, Martin, 'Nietzsche's Word: 'God is Dead', in *Off the Beaten Track*, trans. J. Young and K. Haynes, Cambridge, Cambridge University Press, 2002.

Heidegger, Martin, 'Only a God Can Save Us: Der Spiegel's Interview with Martin Heidegger (September 23, 1966)', trans. M.P. Alter and J.D. Caputo, in *Philosophical and Political Writings*, New York, The Continuum International Publishing Group Inc, 2006.

Henry, Michel,. *The Essence of Manifestation*, trans. G.J. Etzkorn, Springer, 1973.

Henry, Michel, *La Barbarie*, Paris, Presses Universitaires de France, 2004.

Hindrichs, Gunnar, *Das Absolute und das Subjekt: Untersuchungen zum Verhältnis von Metaphysik und Nachmetaphysik*, Frankfurt, Vittorio Klostermann, 2008.

Hodges, Aaron F., 'Martin Hägglund's Speculative Materialism', *CR: The New Centennial Review*, vol. 9, no. 1, 2009, pp. 87-106.

Hülsen, August Ludwig, 'Über den Bildungstrieb', in *Philosophisches Journal einer Gesellschaft Teutscher Gelehrten*, vol.7 (1798). Cited from Martin Oesch, *Aus den Frühzeit des deutschen Idealismus. Texte zur Wissenschaftslehre Fichtes 1794-1804.*

Hume, David, *Enquiry Concerning Human Understanding*, C. W. Hendel (ed.), New York, The Liberal Arts Press, 1957.

Hume, David, *An Enquiry Concerning Human Understanding*, 2nd ed., Eric Steinberg (ed.), Indianapolis: Hackett, 1993.

Husserl, Edmund, *Formal and Transcendental Logic*, trans. D. Cairns, The Hague, Martinus Nijhoff, 1969.

Husserl, Edmund, *Ideas Pertaining to a Pure Phenomenology and to a Phenomenological Philosophy: First Book*, trans. F. Kersten, Boston, Martinus Nijhoff Publishers, 1983.

Hutton, James, 'Theory of the Earth; or an Investigation of the Laws Observable in the Composition, Dissolution and Restoration of Land upon the Globe', *Transactions of the Royal Society of Edinburgh*, no. 1, 1788, pp. 209-305.

Jablonka, Eva and Marion J. Lamb *Evolution in Four Dimensions: Genetic, Epigenetic, Behavioral, and Symbolic Variation in the History of Life*, Cambridge, MIT Press, 2005.

Jacobi, Friedrich Heinrich, *Über die Lehre des Spinoza*, Hamburg, Felix Meiner Verlag, 2000.

Jacobs, Jane, *The Economy of Cities*. New York, Vintage Books, 1970.

James, William, *Essays in Radical Empiricism*, New York, Longman Green and Co., 1912.

James, William, *The Principles of Psychology*, Cambridge, Harvard University Press, 1983.

James, William, *Essays in Radical Empiricism*, Lincoln, University of Nebraska Press, 1996.

Janicaud, Dominique, et al., *Phenomenology and The 'Theological Turn': The French Debate*, trans. Bernard Prusak, New York, Fordham University Press, 2000.

Johnston, Adrian, *Badiou, Žižek, and Political Transformations: The Cadence of Change*, Evanston, Northwestern University Press, 2009.

Johnston, Adrian, 'Conflicted Matter: Jacques Lacan and the Challenge of Secularizing Materialism', *Pli: The Warwick Journal of Philosophy*, vol. 19, Spring 2008, pp. 166-188.

Johnston, Adrian, 'Phantom of Consistency: Alain Badiou and Kantian Transcendental Idealism', *Continental Philosophy Review*, vol. 41, no. 3, September 2008, pp. 345-366.

Johnston, Adrian, 'Slavoj Žižek's Hegelian Reformation: Giving a Hearing to *The Parallax View*', *Diacritics*, vol. 37, no. 1, Spring 2007.

Johnston, Adrian, 'What Matter(s) in Ontology: Alain Badiou, the Hebb-Event, and Materialism Split From Within', *Angelaki: Journal of the Theoretical Humanities*, vol. 13, no. 1, April 2008, pp. 27-49.

Johnston, Adrian , 'The World Before Worlds: Quentin Meillassoux and Alain Badiou's Anti-Kantian Transcendentalism', *Contemporary French Civilization*, vol. 33, no. 1, 2008, pp. 73-99.

Johnston, Adrian, *Žižek's Ontology: A Transcendental Materialist Theory of Subjectivity*, Evanston, Northwestern University Press, 2008.

Jonas, Hans, *The Imperative of Responsibility*, Chicago, University of Chicago, 1985.

Joyce, Richard, *The Evolution of Morality*, Cambridge, MIT Press, 2006.

Kant, Immanuel, *Kants gesammelte Schriften*, Königlich Preussische Akademie der Wissenschaften, XXIX vols, Berlin, Walter de Gruyter, 1902.

Kant, Immanuel, *Critique of Judgment*, trans. W. Pluhar, Indianapolis, Hackett, 1987.

Kant, Immanuel, *Critique of Pure Reason*, trans. Paul Guyer and Allen W. Wood, Cambridge, Cambridge University Press, 1998.

Kant, Immanuel, *Critique of Pure Reason*, London, Everyman's Library, 1988.

Keeley, Lawrence, *War Before Civilization: The Myth of the Peaceful Savage*, New York, Oxford University Press, 1997.

Kelly, Raymond, *Warless Societies and the Origin of War*, Ann Arbor, University of Michigan Press, 2000.

Kelso, J. Scott, *Dynamic Patterns: The Self-Organization of Brain and Behavior*, Cambridge, MIT Press, 1995.

Kitcher, Philip, *The Advancement of Science: Science without Legend, Objectivity without Illusions*, Oxford, Oxford University Press, 1993.

Kolozova, Katerina, *The Real and 'I': On the Limit and the Self*, Skopje, Euro-Balkan Press, 2006.

Lacan, Jacques, *Séminaire XXIV, L'insu que sait de l'une-bévue s'aile à mourre*, session of 15 March 1977, unpublished.

Lacan, Jacques, *Television*, trans. Denis Hollier, Rosalind Krauss, and Annette Michelson, MIT Press, 1987.

Lacan, Jacques, *Le seminaire, livre IV: La relation d'objet*, Paris, Editions du Seuil, 1994.

Lacan, Jacques, *The Seminar of Jacques Lacan, Book XX, Encore: On Feminine Sexuality, the Limits of Love and Knowledge*, trans. Bruce Fink, New York, W.W. Norton, 1998.

Laland, Kevin, and Gillian Brown, *Sense and Nonsense*, Oxford, Oxford, 2002.

Land, Nick, *The Thirst for Annihilation: Georges Bataille and Virulent Nihilism*, London, Routledge, 1992.

Land, Nick, 'Making It with Death: Remarks on Thanatos and Desiring Production', *British Journal of Phenomenology*, vol. 24, no. 1, 1993.

Land, Nick, 'Machinic Desire', *Textual Practice*, vol. 7, no. 3, 1993.

Laruelle, François, *Le déclin de l'écriture*, Paris, Aubier-Flammarion, 1977.

Laruelle, François, 'Les effets-Levinas. Lettre non-philosophique du 30 Mai 2006', 30 May 2006, trans. T. Adkins, <http://www.onphi.net/lettre-laruelle-les-effets-levinas-12.html>.

Laruelle, François, 'Identity and Event', *Pli: The Warwick Journal of Philosophy*, no. 9, 2000, pp. 174-189.

Laruelle, François, *Introduction au non-Marxism*, Paris, PUF, 2000.

Laruelle, François, *En tant qu'un: la non-philosophie expliqué au philosophes*, Paris, Aubier, 1991.

Laruelle, François, *Principes de la Non-Philosophie*, Paris, Presse Universitaires de France, 1996.

Laruelle, François, 'A Summary of Non-Philosophy', *Pli: The Warwick Journal of Philosophy*, no. 8, 1999, pp. 138-148.

Laruelle, François, 'What Can Non-Philosophy Do?', *Angelaki*, vol. 8, no. 2, 2003, pp. 169-189.

Laruelle, François, 'A New Presentation of Non-Philosophy' <http://www.onphi.net/texte-a-new-presentation-of-non-philosophy-32.html> [accessed 15 July 2008].

Latour, Bruno, *Science in Action: How to Follow Scientists and Engineers Through Society*, Cambridge, Harvard University Press, 1987.

Latour, Bruno, 'Irreductions'', trans. John Law, in *The Pasteurization of France*, trans. Alan Sheridan and John Law, Cambridge, Harvard University Press, 1988.

Latour, Bruno, *The Pasteurization of France*, trans. Alan Sheridan & John Law, Cambridge, Harvard University Press, 1988/1993.

Latour, Bruno 'Drawing Things Together', in Mike Lynch and Steve Woolgar (eds.), *Representation in Scientific Practice*, Cambridge, MIT Press, 1990.

Latour, Bruno, *We Have Never Been Modern*, trans. Catherine Porter, Cambridge, Harvard University Press, 1993.

Latour, Bruno, in *Eloqui de senso. Dialoghi semiotici per Paulo Fabbri. Orizzonti, compiti e dialoghi della semiotica*, P. Basso and L. Corrain (eds.), Milano, Costa & Nolan, 1998.

Latour, Bruno, *Pandora's Hope: Essays on the Reality of Science Studies*, trans. Catherine Porter, Cambridge, Harvard University Press, 1999.

Latour, Bruno and Peter Weibel (eds.), *Iconoclash: Beyond the Image Wars in Science, Religion and Art*, Cambridge, MIT Press, 2002.

Latour, Bruno, *Reassembling the Social: An Introduction to Actor-Network-Theory*, New York, Oxford University Press, 2005, pp. 106-109.

Latour, Bruno, 'A Textbook Case Revisited. Knowledge as a Mode of Existence', in E. Hackett, O. Amsterdamska, M. Lynch and J. Wacjman (eds.), *The Handbook of Science and Technology Studies*, 3ʳᵈ ed., Cambridge, MIT Press, 2007.

Latour, Bruno, *What is the Style of Matters of Concern. Two Lectures on Empirical Philosophy*, Van Gorcum, Amsterdam, 2008.

Latour, Bruno *Petite réflexion sur la culte moderne des dieux Faitiches*, Paris, Les Empêcheurs de penser en rond, 1996, and La Découverte, 2010. (English version: *On the Cult of the Modern Factish Gods*, trans. Catherine Porter, Duke University Press, In press).

Lebrun, Gerard, *La patience du concept*, Paris, Gallimard, 1973.

Lebrun, Gerard, *L'envers de la dialectique. Hegel a la lumiere de Nietzsche*, Paris, Editions du Seuil, 2004.

Leibniz, G.W., *Philosophical Writings*, R. Ariew & D. Garber (eds.), Indianapolis, Hackett, 1989.

Lemons, Don S. *Perfect Form, Variational Principles, Methods and Applications in Elementary Physics*, Princeton, Princeton University Press, 1997.

Lenin, V.I. *Materialism and Empirio-Criticism*, in *Collected Works of V.I. Lenin*, vol. XIII, New York, International Publishers, 1927.

Lenin, V.I., *Materialism and Empirio-Criticism*, Peking, Foreign Languages Press, 1972.

Lenin, V.I., *Revolution at the Gates: Selected Writings of Lenin from 1917*, Slavoj Žižek (ed.), London, Verso, 2002.

Levinas, Emmanuel, 'Heidegger, Gagarin and Us', in *Difficult Freedom: Essays on Judaism*, trans. S. Hand Baltimore, Johns Hopkins University, 1997.

Levinas, Emmanuel, *Existence and Existents*, trans. Alphonso Lingis, The Hague, Martinus Nijhoff, 1988.

Levinas, Emmanuel, *Existence and Existents*, trans. Alphonso Lingis, Plattsburgh, Duquesne University Press, 2001.

Lewes, George Henry. *Problems of Life and Mind*, vo;. 2, London, Trübner, 1875.

Lewontin, Richard. *The Triple Helix: Gene, Organism, and Environment*, Cambridge, Harvard University Press, 2002.

Lewontin, Richard, 'The Wars Over Evolution', New York Review of Books, 20 October 2005, http://www.nybooks.com/articles/18363, retrieved 5 December 2008.

Lima, José Lezama, *Paradiso*, Madrid, Ediciones Cátedra, 1997.

Lyell, Charles, *Principles of Geology*, James Secord (ed.), Harmondsworth, Penguin, [1830-33] 1997.

Mackay, Robin, 'Editorial Introduction', *Collapse: Philosophical Research and Development*, vol. 1, pp. 3-10.

Mallarme, Stephane, 'Les mots anglais', in Œuvres Complètes, Paris, Editions Gallimard, Bibliothèque de la Pléiade, 1945.

Mallarmé, Stephane, 'Igitur', in *Selected Poetry and Prose*, trans. M.A. Caws, New York, New Directions, 1982.

Mallarme, Stephane, 'Dice Thrown Never Will Annul Chance', in *Selected Poetry and Prose*, trans. M.A. Caws, New York, New Directions, 1982.

Mallarme, Stephane, 'La Musique et les Lettres', in *Igitur, Divagations, Un coup de dés*, Paris, Editions Gallimard, 2003.

Mallon, Ron and Stephen Stich, 'The Odd Couple: The compatibility of social construction and evolutionary psychology', *Philosophy of Science*, no. 67, pp. 133-154, 2000.

Mao Tse-Tung, *Selected Readings from the Works of Mao Tse-Tung*, Peking, Foreign Languages Press, 1971.

Mareschal, Denis, Mark H Johnson, Sylvain Sirois, Michael W Spratling, Michael S C Thomas, and Gert Westermann, *Neuroconstructivism: How the Brain Constructs Cognition*, vol. 1, New York, Oxford University Press, 2007.

McNeill, William, *Keeping Together in Time: Dance and Drill in Human Histor*, Cambridge, Harvard University Press, 1995.

Meillassoux, Quentin, *L'inexistence divine*, unpublished manuscript.

Meillassoux, Quentin, 'Temps et surgissement ex nihilo', <http://www.diffusion.ens.fr/index.php?res=conf &idconf=701>

Meillassoux, Quentin, '*Nouveauté et événement*', Alain Badiou: Penser le multiple—*Actes du Colloque de Bordeaux, 21-23 octobre 1999*, Charles Ramond (ed.), Paris, L'Harmattan, 2002.

Meillassoux, Quentin, *Après la finitude: Essai sur la nécessité de la contingence*, Paris, Seuil, 2006.

Meillassoux, Quentin, 'Temps et surgissement ex nihilo', presentation in the seminar series *Positions et arguments* at the École Normale Supérieure, April 2006.

Meillassoux, Quentin, '*Deuil à venir, dieu à venir*', *Critique*, no. 704/705, January/February 2006, pp. 105-115.

Meillassoux, Quentin, 'Spéculation et contingence', in Emmanuel Cattin et Franck Fischbach, (eds.), *L'Héritage de la raison: Hommage à Bernard Bourgeois*, Paris, Ellipses, 2007.

Meillassoux, Quentin, 'Speculative Realism: Presentation by Quentin Meillassoux', *Collapse*, vol. 3, 2007, pp. 408-449.

Meillassoux, Quentin, 'Matérialisme et surgissement ex nihilo', *MIR: Revue d'anticipation*, no. 1, June 2007.

Meillassoux, Quentin, 'Potentiality and Virtuality', trans. Robin Mackay, *Collapse*, vol. 2, 2007, pp. 55-81.

Meillassoux, Quentin, *After Finitude: An Essay on the Necessity of Contingency*, trans. Ray Brassier, New York, Continuum, 2008.

Meillassoux, Quentin, 'Spectral Dilemma', *Collapse: Philosophical Research and Development*, no. 4, 2008, pp. 261-276.

Meillassoux, Quentin, 'Time without Becoming', talk presented at Middlesex University, 8 May 2008.

Meillassoux, Quentin, '*Histoire et événement chez Alain Badiou: Intervention au séminaire «Marx au XXI* siècle: l'esprit et la letter*—Paris: 2 février 2008»*', http://semimarx.free.fr/ IMG/pdf/Meillassoux_Paris-fev08.pdf

Meillassoux, Quentin, 'Potentiality and Virtuality', in Levi Bryant, Nick Srnicek, and Graham Harman (eds.), *The Speculative Turn: Continental Materialism and Realism*, re.press, Melbourne, 2010, pp. 224-236.

Metzinger, Thomas, *Being No One: The Self-Model Theory of Subjectivity*, Cambridge, The MIT Press, 2004.

Mill, John Stuart, *A System of Logic. Ratiocinative and Inductive*, London, Longmans, Green & Co., 1906.

Milner, J.C., *L'Œuvre claire. Lacan, la science, la philosophie*, Paris, Seuil, 1995.

Molnar, George, *Powers: A Study in Metaphysics*, Oxford, Oxford University Press, 2003.

Montebello, Pierre, *L'autre métaphysique. Essai sur Ravaisson, Tarde, Nietzsche et Bergson*, Paris, Desclée de Brouwer, 2003.

Morgan, C. Lloyd, *Emergent Evolution*, New York, Henry Holt, 1931.

Mullarkey, John, *Post-Continental Philosophy: An Outline*, New York, Continuum, 2006/2007.

Musgrave, Alan, 'Realism and Antirealism' in *Scientific Enquiry: Readings in the Philosophy of Science*, R. Klee (ed.), Oxford, Oxford University Press, 1999, pp. 344-352.

Nancy, Jean-Luc, 'Corpus', trans. C. Sartiliot, in Jean-Luc Nancy, *The Birth to Presence*, trans. B. Holmes & Others, Stanford, Stanford University Press, 1993.

Nathan, Tobie, *L'influence qui guérit*, Paris, Editions Odile Jacob, 1994.

Negarestani, Reza, 'The Corpse Bride: Thinking with Nigredo', *Collapse*, vol. 4, 2008, pp. 129-160.

Negri, Antonio, 'Towards an Ontological Definition of Multitude', trans. Arriana Bove, <http://multitudes.samizdat.net/spip.php?article269> [accessed 15 July 2008].

Nietzsche, Friedrich, *Beyond Good and Evil: Prelude to a Philosophy of the Future*, trans. J. Norman, New York, Cambridge University Press, 2002.

Nisbett, Richard E. and Dov Cohen, *Culture of Honor: The Psychology of Violence in the South*, Boulder CO, Westview Press, 1996.

Novalis, *The Novices of Sais*, trans. R. Manheim, Brooklyn, Archipelago, 2005.

Novalis, *Notes for a romantic encyclopaedia (Das Allgemeine Brouillon)*, trans. D.W. Wood, New York, State University of New York Press, 2007.

Oersted, Hans Christian, *Materialen zu einer Chemie des Neunzehnten Jahrhunderts*, Regensburg, Montag- und Weißische Buchhandlung, 1803.

Oesch, Martin, *Aus den Frühzeit des deutschen Idealismus. Texte zur Wissenschaftslehre Fichtes 1794-1804*, Würzburg, Königshausen und Neumann, 1987.

O'Shea, James, *Wilfrid Sellars: Naturalism with a Normative Turn*, Cambridge, Polity, 2007.

Otterbein, Keith. *How War Began*, College Station, Texas A&M Press, 2004.

Oyama, Susan. *The Ontogeny of Information: Developmental Systems and Evolution*, 2nd ed., Durham, Duke University Presso, 2000.

Oyama, Susan, Paul Griffiths and Russell Gray. *Cycles of Contingency*, Cambridge, MIT Press, 2001.

Panksepp, Jaak, *Affective Neuroscience*. New York, Oxford University Press, 1998.

Panksepp, Jaak, 'Damasio's Error?', *Consciousness & Emotion*, vol. 4, no. 1, pp. 111-134, 2003.

Pannekoek, Anton, *Lenin as Philosopher*, ed. Lance Byron Richey, Milwaukee, Marquette University Press, 2003

Panofsky, Erwin, *Galileo as a Critic of the Arts*, The Hague, Martinus Nijhoff, 1954.

Parkinson, Brian, Agneta Fischer and Athony Manstead. *Emotions in Social Relations: Cultural, Group and Interpersonal Processes*, New York, Psychology Press, 2005.

Pascal, Blaise, *Pensées*, trans. A.J. Krailsheimer, London, Penguin Books, 1966.

Pavel, Thomas, *Fictional Worlds*, Cambridge, Harvard University Press, 1986.

Peterson, Dale and Richard Wrangham, *Demonic Males: Apes and the Origins of Human Violence*, New York, Houghton Mifflin, 1997.

Pignarre, Philippe et Isabelle Stengers, *La Sorcellerie capitaliste. Pratiques de désenvoûtement*, Paris, La Découverte, 2005.

Plotinus, *The Enneads*, trans. Stephen MacKenna, New York, Larson Publications, 1992.

Poe, Edgar Allen, 'The Angel of the Odd', in *Poetry and Tales*, New York, Library of America, 1984.

Popper, Karl, *The Logic of Scientific Discovery*, London, Routledge, 2002.

Prigogine, Ilya and Isabelle Stengers, *Order out of Chaos: Man's New Dialogue With Nature*, Shambala, 1984.

Pringle, Heather, 'The Slow Birth of Agriculture', *Science*, vol. 282, no. 5393, pp. 1446-50, 1998.

Protevi, John, 'Deleuze, Guattari, and Emergence', *Paragraph: A Journal of Modern Critical Theory*, vol. 29, no. 2, pp. 19-39, 2006.

Protevi, John, 'Affect, Agency, and Responsibility: The Act of Killing in the Age of Cyborgs', *Phenomenology and the Cognitive Sciences*, vol. 7, no. 3, pp. 405-13, 2008.

Protevi, John, *Political Affect: Connecting the Social and the Somatic*, Minneapolis, University of Minnesota Press, 2008.

Read, Jason, *The Micro-Politics of Capital: Marx and the Prehistory of the Present*, Albany, State University of New York Press, 2003.

Richerson, Peter and Robert Boyd, *Not by Genes Alone: How Culture Transformed Human Evolution*, Chicago, University of Chicago Press, 2005.

Rilke, R.M. *Duino Elegies*, trans. S. Cohn, Illinois, Northwestern University Press, 1989.

Rilke, R.M., *The Book of Hours*, trans. A.S. Kidder, Illinois, Northwestern University Press, 2001.

Rilke, R.M., 'Letter to W. von Hulewicz (November 13, 1925)', in *Letters of Rainer Maria Rilke – Vol. II: 1910-1926*, trans. J.B. Green, Leiserson Press, 2007.

Rosch, Eleanor, 'Principles of categorization', in Eleanor Rosch and Barbara Lloyd (eds.), *Cognition and Categorization*, Hillsdale, Lawrence Erlbaum, 1978.

Runciman, W.G., 'Culture Does Evolve', *History and Theory*, vol. 44, no. 1, pp. 1-13, 2005.

Runciman, W.G., 'Rejoinder to Fracchia and Lewontin', *History and Theory*, vol. 44, no. 1, pp. 30-41, 2005.

Salmon, Wesley C., *Scientific Explanation and the Causal Structure of the World*, Princeton, Princeton University Press, 1984.

Shay, Jonathon, *Achilles in Vietnam*, New York, Scribner, 1995.

Schelling, Friedrich, *Schellings sämmtliche Werke*, XIV vols, Stuttgart and Augsburg, J.G. Cotta, 1856-61.

Schelling, Friedrich, *Ideas for a Philosophy of Nature*, trans. Errol E. Harris and Peter Heath, Cambridge, Cambridge University Press, 1988.

Schlegel, Friedrich, *Philosophical Fragments*, trans. P. Firchow, Minneapolis, University of Minnesota Press, 1991.

Schwarz, Laurent, *Analyse I*, Paris, Hermann, 1991

Sellars, Wilfrid, *Science and Metaphysics: Variations on Kantian Themes*, London, Routledge & Kegan Paul, 1968.

Sellars, Wilfrid, *Empiricism and the Philosophy of Mind*, Cambridge, Harvard University Press, 1997.

Shaviro, Steven, 'The Body of Capital', *The Pinocchio Theory (Blog)*, 2008 <http://www.shaviro.com/ Blog/?p=641> [accessed 26 June 2008].

Shaviro, Steven, 'Monstrous Flesh', *The Pinocchio Theory (Blog)*, 2008 <http://www.shaviro.com/Blog/?p=639> [accessed 26 June 2008].

Shaviro, Steven, *Without Criteria: Kant, Whitehead, Deleuze, and Aesthetics*, Cambridge, MIT Press, 2009.

Shaviro, Steven, 'On the Undermining of Objects: Bruno, Grant, and Radical Philosophy', in Bryant, Levi, Nick Srnicek, and Graham Harman (eds.), *The Speculative Turn: Continental Materialism and Realism*, Melbourne, re.press, 2010. pp. 279-290.

Simondon, Gilbert, *Du Mode d'existence des objets techniques*, Paris, Aubier, [1958] 1989.

Simondon, Gilbert, *L'indivduation à la lumière des notions de forme et d'information*, Grenoble, Millon, 2005.

Sober, Elliott and David Sloan Wilson, *Unto Others: The Evolution and Psychology of Unselfish Behavior*. Cambridge, Harvard University Press, 1998.

Souriau, Étienne, *Avoir une âme*, Lyon, Annales de l'Université de Lyon, 1939.

Souriau, Étienne, *L'instauration philosophique*, Paris, Félix Alcan, 1939.

Souriau, Étienne, *Les différents modes d'existence*, Paris, Presses Universitaires de France, 1943. (Reprinted in 2009, also by PUF, with an introduction by Isabelle Stengers and Bruno Latour.)

Souriau, Étienne, *Bulletin de la société française de philosophie*, 4-44, 1956. (Reprinted in the 2009 PUF edition of Souriau, *Les différents modes d'existence*).

Souriau, Étienne, *Vocabulaire d'esthétique*, Paris, PUF, 1999.

Speidel, Michael, 'Berserks: A History of Indo-European "Mad Warriors"', *Journal of World History*, vol. 13, no. 2, pp. 253-90, 2002.

Spinoza, Baruch, *Ethics, Treatise on the Emendation of the Intellect and Selected Letters*, trans. Samuel Shirley, Indianapolis, Hackett, 1992.

Sponsel, Leslie, 'Response to Otterbein', *American Anthropologist*, vol. 102, no. 4, pp. 837-41, 2000.

Staten, Henry, 'Derrida, Dennett, and the Ethico-Political Project of Naturalism', *Derrida Today*, no. 1, 2008, pp. 19-41.

Stauffer, Robert, 'Speculation and experiment in the background of Oersted's discovery of electromagnetism', *Isis*, no. 48, 1957, pp. 33-50.

Stengers, Isabelle, *Cosmopolitiques*, 2 vols., Paris, La Découverte, 2003.

Stengers, Isabelle, *The Invention of Modern Science*, trans. D. W. Smith, Minneapolis, University of Minnesota Press, 2000.

Stengers, Isabelle, *Penser avec Whitehead: Une libre et sauvage création de concepts*, Paris, Gallimard, 2002.

Stengers, Isabelle, *Power and Invention: Situating Science*, trans. Paul Bains, Minneapolis, University of Minnesota Press, 1997.

Stengers, Isabelle, 'Thinking With Deleuze and Whitehead: A Double Test' in *Deleuze, Whitehead, Bergson: Rhizomatic Connections*, Keith Robinson (ed.), New York, Palgrave Macmillan, 2009, pp. 28-44.

Stengers, Isabelle, *La Vierge et le neutrino: les scientifiques dans la tourmente* , Paris, Les Empêcheurs de penser en rond, 2005.

Sterelyny, Kim and Paul Griffiths, *Sex and Death: An Introduction to the Philosophy of* Biology, Chicago, University of Chicago Press, 1999.

Stewart, Ian, *Does God Play Dice: The Mathematics of Chaos*. Oxford, Basil Blackwell, 1989.

Stove, David, 'Idealism: A Victorian Horror Story (Part Two)', in *The Plato Cult and Other Philosophical Follies*, Oxford, Blackwell, 1991, pp. 135-178.

Strawson, Galen, *Real Materialism and Other Essays*, Oxford, Oxford University Press, 2008.

Suárez, Francisco, *On Efficient Causality: Metaphysical Disputations 17, 18, and 19*, trans. A. Freddoso, New Haven, Yale University Press, 1994.

Tarde, Gabriel, *Monadologie et sociologie*, Paris, Les empêcheurs de penser en rond, [1895] 1999.

Thompson, Evan, *Mind in Life: Biology, Phenomenology, and the Sciences of Mind*, Cambridge, Harvard University Press, 2007.

Timoshenko, Stephen P., *History of Strength of Materials*, New York, Dover, 1983.

Toch, Hans, *Violent Men: An Inquiry Into the Psychology of Violence*, Washington, American Psychological Association, 1992.

Tsouyopolis, Nelly, 'Die neue Auffassung der klinischen Medizin als Wissenschaft unter dem Einfluß der Philosophie im frühen 19. Jahrhundert', *Berichte zur Wissenschaftsgeschichte*, no. 1, 1978, pp. 87-100.

Turner, William, 'Giordano Bruno', in *The Catholic Encyclopedia*, online version, http://www.newadvent.org/cathen/03016a.htm

Uexküll, Jakob von, *Mondes animaux et monde humain, Théorie de la signification*, Paris, Gonthier, 1965.

Varela, Francisco, 'Resonant Cell Assemblies: A new approach to cognitive functions and neuronal synchrony', *Biological Research*, no. 28, 1995, pp. 81-95.

Valery, Paul, 'L'Ange', in *La Jeune Parque et poèmes en prose*, Paris, Gallimard, 1974.

Vernes, Jean-René, *Critique de la raison aléatoire*, Paris, Aubier, 1981.

Virno, Paolo, *A Grammar of the Multitude*, Los Angeles, Semiotext(e), 2004.

Vitry-Maubrey, Luce de, 'Étienne Souriau's cosmic vision and the coming-into-its-own of the Platonic Other', *Man and World*, no. 18, 1985, pp. 325-345.

Vitry-Maubrey, Luce de, *La pensée cosmologique d'Étienne Souriau*, Paris, Klinsieck, 1974.

Watt, Douglas, 'Emotion and Consciousness: Part II: A Review of Antonio Damasio's *The Feeling of What Happens*', *Journal of Consciousness Studies*, vol. 7, no. 3, 2000, pp. 72-84.

Weil, Simone, *The Need for Roots*, trans. A. Wills, London, Routledge & Kegan Paul, 1952.

West-Eberhard, Mary Jane, *Developmental Plasticity and Evolution*, New York, Oxford University Press, 2003.

Wexler, Bruce, *Brain and Culture: Neurobiology, Ideology, and Social Change*, Cambridge, MIT Press, 2006.

Whitehead, Alfred North, *The Concept of Nature*, Cambridge, Cambridge University Press, 1920/2004.

Whitehead, Alfred North, *Process and Reality*, New York, The Free Press, 1929/1978.

Whitehead, Alfred North, *Adventures of Ideas*, New York, The Free Press, 1933/1967.

Whitehead, Alfred, *Modes of Thought*, New York, The Free Press, 1938/1968.

Wittgenstein, Ludwig. *Tractatus Logico-Philosophicus*, trans. D.F. Pears & B.F. McGuinness, London, Routledge & Kegan Paul, 1974.

Xenakis, I. *Formalized Music: Thought and Mathematics in Music*, Stuyvesant, Pendragon Press, 1992.

Zambrana, Rocío, 'Hegel's Hyperbolic Formalism', *Bulletin of the Hegel Society of Great Britain*, nos. 60/61, 2010.

Žižek, Slavoj, 'An Answer to Two Questions', in Johnston, *Badiou, Žižek, and Political Transformations*, pp. 174-230.

Žižek, Slavoj, 'The Fear of Four Words: A Modest Plea for the Hegelian Reading of Christianity', in Slavoj Žižek and John Milbank, *The Monstrosity of Christ: Paradox or Dialectic?*, Creston Davis (ed.), Cambridge, MIT Press, 2009.

Žižek, Slavoj, 'Foreword to the Second Edition: Enjoyment within the Limits of Reason Alone', in *For they know not what they do: Enjoyment as a political factor*, 2nd ed., London, Verso, 2002.

Žižek, Slavoj, 'Is it Still Possible to be a Hegelian Today?', in Levi Bryant, Nick Srnicek and Graham Harman (eds.), *The Speculative Turn: Continental Materialism and Realism*, Melbourne, re.press pp. 202-223.

Žižek, Slavoj, *The Parallax View*, Cambridge, The MIT Press, 2006.

Žižek, Slavoj, 'Postface: Georg Lukács as the Philosopher of Leninism', in Georg Lukács, *A Defense of History and Class Consciousness: Tailism and the Dialectic*, trans. Esther Leslie, London, Verso, 2000.

Žižek, Slavoj, *The Sublime Object of Ideology*, New York, Verso Books, 1989.

Žižek, Slavoj, *The Ticklish Subject: The Absent Center of Political Ontology*, New York, Verso Books, 1999.

Žižek, Slavoj and Glyn Daly, *Conversations with Žižek*, Cambridge, Polity Press, 2004.

Zubíri, Xavier, *On Essence*, trans. A.R. Caponigri, Washington, Catholic University Press, 1980.

Lightning Source UK Ltd.
Milton Keynes UK
UKOW021155101111

181828UK00001B/9/P